Successful Dispute Resolution

edited by

Professor Burkhard Hess,
Max-Planck-Institute Luxembourg for International, European and Regulatory Procedural Law, Luxembourg

Professor Rüdiger Wolfrum,
Max Planck Institute for Comparative Public Law and International Law, Heidelberg

Professor Thomas Pfeiffer, Institute of Foreign and International Private and Economic Law, University of Heidelberg

Volume 1

Dominik Zimmermann

The Independence of International Courts

The Adherence of the International Judiciary to a Fundamental Value of the Administration of Justice

HART PUBLISHING

Nomos

Die **Deutsche Nationalbibliothek** lists this publication in the Deutsche Nationalbibliografie; detailed bibliographic data is available in the Internet at http://dnb.d-nb.de

a.t.: Ruprecht-Karls Universität Heidelberg, Diss., 2013

ISBN: HB (Nomos) 978-3-8487-1248-9

British Library Cataloguing-in-Publication Data
A catalogue record for this book is available from the British Library.

ISBN: HB (Hart): 978-1-84986-741-4

Library of Congress Cataloging-in-Publication Data
Zimmermann, Dominik
The Independence of International Courts
The Adherence of the International Judiciary to a Fundamental Value of the Administration of Justice
Dominik Zimmermann
597 p.
Includes bibliographic references and index.

ISBN 978-1-84946-741-4 (hardcover Hart)

1. Edition 2014

For Çağla

Foreword

The adjudication of international disputes by permanent judicial bodies has over the course of the 20th century grown to become an indispensable pillar of modern international law. From modest beginnings with the signing of the Convention for the Pacific Settlement of International Disputes in 1899, establishing a permanent mechanism for judicial dispute settlement, to a remarkable diversification of new judicial institutions in recent decades, the emerging international judiciary has been a much discussed topic among both academics and practitioners of international law. History has taught us, however, that the utilization of international courts has a tendency to be shaped by geopolitical considerations and competition from more flexible international arbitration. The fate of the Permanent Court of International Justice, the activities of its successor, the International Court of Justice, as well as other global and regional courts, bear witness of this interplay. It is therefore of the essence that more efforts are dedicated towards modelling these international adjudicatory bodies in a way conducive to an evolving international community and an evolving legal order, which is shaped not only by the need to co-ordinate and co-operate between various actors but increasingly also the demand for solidarity among States based on shared values.

Aware of the sometimes challenging relationship between standing judicial bodies and various other actors of international law, the *Institut de Droit International* adopted a resolution during its 1959 session of Neuchâtel, under the guidance of its Rapporteur, C. Wilfred Jenks, recommending increased use of international courts and arbitral tribunals while at the same time "[r]ecognizing the importance of confidence as a factor in the wider acceptance of international jurisdiction". Certainly, still today, the significance of international courts relies profoundly on their ability to realize the idea of peaceful dispute settlement in a particularly objective and reliable fashion. However, even more than at the time when the *Institut de Droit International* drew our attention to the subject, the future of international adjudication is challenged not only by the political environment and policy issues but also by its own success. The increasing number of international courts has therefore triggered academia and practice to engage in a much needed discussion addressing the appropriate substantive and procedural law to accompany the work of the institutions. The present book by Dr. Dominik Zimmermann makes an important contribution in this field by drawing attention to an important aspect of the international adjudication before standing bodies, namely their independence.

The book, which was accepted as a Ph.D. thesis at the Faculty of Law, Ruprecht-Karls-Universität Heidelberg, Germany, in the summer term of 2013, analyses, on the basis of a comparative approach, the contents and scope of the principle of judicial independence as currently applied to and by the international judiciary. Rooted in a functional understanding of judicial independence, the study begins by examining the theoretical foundation for the principle's application and by developing a working definition of judicial independence in an international law context. Taking some of the most influential international courts of our time as examples (the International Court of Justice, the International Tribunal for the Law of the Sea, the International Criminal Court, the *Ad Hoc* International Criminal Tribunals for the Former Yugoslavia and Rwanda, and the European Court of Human Rights), the study presents a comprehensive analysis of the extent to which these courts, while taking into account their particularities, can be claimed to follow and codify parameters which bolster the assertion that they are indeed independent. For this purpose, the study presents a thorough examination of relevant treaties, statutes, secondary rules and practices from two distinct viewpoints: Whereas Dr. Zimmermann applies a collective perspective to identify the protection of the independence of the court as a judicial institution, focusing on parameters such as administration, financing, composition, and the procedural control, the individual perspective is used to highlight the protection of the individual legal position of the judges by examining *inter alia* the personal requirements of judges, tenure, remuneration and immunities.

Dr. Zimmermann reaches valuable conclusions on the extent to which the normative requirements for judicial independence in the evaluated courts show a general consensus and he is able to point to special requirements, beyond the common core, that are applicable to different kinds of jurisdictions (e.g. human rights courts). The study, thus, not only fills a gap in the scholarly evaluation of the organizational setup of current international courts but also functions as a manual for reviewing potential future permanent judicial bodies.

The quality of the analysis in particular and the topicality of the subject in general were the justification for having acceded to Dr. Zimmermann's request to write this Foreword. And it is for the same reasons that I warmly recommend this firstling of my former student as a valuable guide for both academics and practitioners involved in the work of current and future international courts.

em. Professor Dr. Dr. h.c. Rüdiger Wolfrum
Judge of the International Tribunal for the Law of the Sea
Managing Director, Max Planck Foundation for International Peace and the Rule of Law

Preface and Acknowledgments

> "For there is nothing that tends so much to produce greatness of mind as a methodical and conscientious investigation of the objects that fall under our notice in life."
> **Marcus Aurelius, *Meditations*, III, 11**

The present study was accepted as a Ph.D. thesis at the Faculty of Law, Ruprecht-Karls-Universität Heidelberg, Germany, in the summer term of 2013. Legal developments, judicature and literature up to July 2013 have in essential parts been taken into account.

The role and functioning of international courts first attracted my attention as an undergraduate at Uppsala University, and it turned into a passion whilst I was conducting research at the Max Planck Institute for Comparative Public Law and International Law. The idea behind this thesis, analysing the protection of the independence of international judges, was conceived in early 2008. At that time, the independence of international courts was made one of the pillars of the Minerva Research Group on Judicial Independence, the overall aim of which was to develop theoretical principles and parameters of judicial independence in the context of globalization and internationalization. As could be observed especially in the last two decades, the rapid development of international law in general and of the international judiciary in particular has given rise to a wide array of legal and procedural issues. Among them is the question to what extent the proper administration of justice in the international sphere ought to and in fact does adhere to certain fundamental values that already constitute the foundation of most national judicial systems. The subject of this thesis therefore also fitted into the wider discourse on the evolution of international courts.

No scientific treatise is ever the result of the author's efforts alone. I therefore wish to express my gratitude to those who supported, encouraged and assisted me throughout the process of conducting the research and reducing it to writing. I am particularly grateful to my supervisor, Professor Dr. Dr. h.c. Rüdiger Wolfrum, for his academic supervision and guidance and for continuously sharing his knowledge and experience. I also thank my second supervisor, Professor Dr. Anja Seibert-Fohr, who was a constant source of encouragement, information and insight. To both I owe genuine thankfulness for promoting my career at the Max Planck Institute and for sustainably influencing my way of thinking of and about international law. I also extend my appreciation to Professor Dr. Thomas Pfeiffer, for the rapid preparation of the second opinion and the valuable suggestions contained therein.

I would also like to thank Professor Dr. Burkhard Hess, Professor Dr. Dr. h.c. Rüdiger Wolfrum and Professor Dr. Thomas Pfeiffer, editors of the Successful Dispute Resolution series, for agreeing to publish the thesis and Nomos Verlagsgesellschaft for turning the manuscript into book form. Generous financial support for the publication was provided by Professor Dr. Burkhard Hess, Professor Dr. Dr. h.c. Rüdiger Wolfrum and the International Max Planck Research School (IMPRS) Successful Dispute Resolution in International Law. I am also grateful to the German Federal Foreign Office for supporting the publication with a grant.

The thesis was made possible against the background of the excellent working conditions at the Max Planck Institute. I particularly wish to highlight the direct, or indirect, support I received from John Dingfelder Stone and Dr. Johann Woltag. Representative of the staff of the library of the Institute, I extend a warm thank you to Ali Zakouri for continuous support in finding even the most inaccessible documents.

The fact that this thesis could be written in today's *lingua franca* of public international law and still be adopted as a Ph.D. thesis at the Ruprecht-Karls-Universität in Heidelberg, is essentially thanks to the persistent and untiring support of my supervisor, Professor Dr. Dr. h.c. Rüdiger Wolfrum. Right from the outset he shared my conviction not only that the choice of language ought to be guided by the aspiration to contribute to a globalized scholarly discourse, but also that the thesis should strive to carry the seal of one of the most esteemed academic institutions in Europe.

More than any professional support, however, this work has been made possible thanks to the support of my family. I feel particularly indebted to my parents for their unquestioning belief in me, their continuous support and the necessary stimulation they have constantly provided, and to my brother for being the best friend I could possibly ask for. Finally I would especially like to thank my wife Çağla for being a constant source of love, inspiration and support. You complete me.

Dominik Zimmermann Vienna, March, 2014

Overview

Table of Contents

List of Abbreviations

1899 Hague Convention I	International Convention for the Pacific Settlement of International Disputes
1907 Hague Convention I	1907 Hague Convention for the Pacific Settlement of International Disputes
AC	Appeals Chamber
AChHPR	African Charter on Human and Peoples' Rights
ACHR	American Convention on Human Rights "Pact of San José, Costa Rica"
ACommHR	African Commission on Human and Peoples' Rights
Add.	Addendum
Art./Arts.	Article/Articles
ASEAN	Association of Southeast Asian Nations
ASP	Assembly of States Parties
BGH	Bundesgerichtshof
BVerfG	Bundesverfassungsgericht
BVerfGE	Entscheidungen des Bundesverfassungsgerichts
BSP	British Foreign and State Papers
CETS	European Treaty Series (Council of Europe)
cf.	confer (compare)
CoE	Council of Europe
CoM	Committee of Ministers of the Council of Europe
Conf.	Conference
Corr.	Correspondence
CSCE	Conference for Security and Cooperation in Europe
CTS	Consolidated Treaty Series
Doc.	Document
EC	European Community
ECHR	Convention for the Protection of Human Rights and Fundamental Freedoms
ECJ	European Court of Justice
ECtHR	European Court of Human Rights
ECommHR	European Commission on Human Rights
ECR	Reports of the Court of Justice of the European Communities (European Court Reports)
ECT	Consolidated Version of the Treaty establishing the European Community
ed./eds.	Editor/Editors
edn.	Edition

EFTA	European Free Trade Association
e.g.	exempli gratia (for example)
EMRK	Europäische Mentschenrechtskonvention (Convention for the Protection of Human Rights and Fundamental Freedoms)
et al.	et alii (and others)
et seq.	et sequentes (and the following)
etc.	et cetera
EU	European Union
fn.	Footnote
GRULAC	Latin American and Caribbean Group
HRC	Human Rights Committee
HRLJ	Human Rights Law Journal
IACommHR	Inter-American Commission on Human Rights
IACtHR	Inter-American Court on Human Rights
ICC	International Criminal Court
ICCPR	International Covenant on Civil and Political Rights
ICESCR	International Covenant on Economic, Social and Cultural Rights
ICJ	International Court of Justice
ICJ Rep.	International Court of Justice, Reports of Judgments, Advisory Opinions and Orders
ICJ Statute	Statute of the International Court of Justice
ICSID	International Centre for Settlement of Investment Disputes
ICTY	International Criminal Tribunal for the Former Yugoslavia
ICTY-S	Statute of the International Criminal Tribunal for the Former Yugoslavia
ICTR	International Criminal Tribunal for Rwanda
ICTR-S	Statute of the International Criminal Tribunal for Rwanda
i.e.	id est (that is)
IHRR	International Human Rights Reports
ILC	International Law Commission
ILM	International Legal Materials
ILO	International Labour Organization
IMT	International Military Tribunal in Nuremberg
IRMCT	International Residual Mechanism for Criminal Tribunals
ISA	International Seabed Authority
ITLOS	International Tribunal for the Law of the Sea
K.B.	King's Bench
LAWASIA	Law Association for Asia and the Pacific
lit.	Literal
LNTS	League of Nations Treaty Series
LoN	League of Nations

MERCOSUR	Mercado Común del Sur (Common Southern Market)
NAFTA	North American Free Trade Agreement
N.E.	North Eastern Reporter
NGO	Non-Governmental Organization
No./Nos.	Number/Numbers
OAS	Organization of American States
OJ	Official Journal of the European Union
OSCE	Organization for Security and Co-operation in Europe
OTP	Office of the Prosecutor
PACE	Parliamentary Assembly of the Council of Europe
Para./Paras.	Paragraph/Paragraphs
PC	Preparatory Commission
PCA	Permanent Court of Arbitration
PCIJ	Permanent Court of International Justice
pp.	pages
PrepCom	Preparatory Committee on the Establishment of an International Criminal Court
PRST	Presidential Statement
Rep.	Reporter
Res.	Resolution
Rev.	Revised
RIAA	Reports of International Arbitral Awards
Rome Statute	Rome Statute of the International Criminal Court
SCR	Supreme Court Reports (Canada)
SCSL	Special Court for Sierra Leone
Ser.	Series
SPLOS	Documents of the Meeting of States Parties to the United Nations Convention on the Law of the Sea
SSRN	Social Science Research Network
Supp.	Supplement
transl.	translator
UDHR	Universal Declaration of Human Rights
UN	United Nations
UNC	Charter of the United Nations
UNCHR	United Nations Commission on Human Rights
UNCITRAL	United Nations Commission on International Trade Law
UNCLOS	United Nations Convention on the Law of the Sea
UNCSW	United Nations Commission on the Status of Women
UNESCO	United Nations Educational, Scientific and Cultural Organization
UNGA	United Nations General Assembly
UNICEF	United Nations Children's Emergency Fund

UNKRA	United Nations Korean Reconstruction Agency
UNRWA	United Nations Relief and Works Agency for Palestine Refugees in the Near East
UNSC	United Nations Security Council
UNSG	United Nations Secretary General
UNTS	United Nations Treaty Series
v.	versus (against)
VCDR	Vienna Convention on Diplomatic Relations
VCLT	Vienna Convention on the Law of Treaties
Vol.	Volume
WEOG	Western European and Others Group
WHO	World Health Organization
WTO	World Trade Organization
ZaöRV	Zeitschrift für ausländisches öffentliches Recht und Völkerrecht

Chapter A: Introduction

I. Introduction to the Research Theme

Essentially, all legal systems serve two elemental functions: the regulation of conduct and the peaceful settlement of disputes between those subject to the law.[1] This is reflected in the organizational structure of western-style States in the shape of a legislative branch, establishing the norms governing the behavioural framework of a society; the executive, entrusted with ensuring the enforcement of these norms; and a variety of adjudicatory organs, such as courts and other judicial and quasi-judicial bodies,[2] responsible for the settlement of disputes arising between legal subjects.[3] The international legal order,[4] although providing for a variety of special conditions mandating its distinct character, is no exception.[5] Here, as at the national level, a growing number of norms, in the form of treaties, custom or soft law,[6] regu-

---

1 Raz, Joseph, *The Concept of a Legal System: An Introduction to the Theory of Legal System* (Clarendon Press Oxford 2nd edn. 1980), 229. "For men to live together successfully they need rules that keep peace among them, make them deal justly with one another, and enable them to collaborate effectively." Fuller, Lon L., *Anatomy of the Law* (Praeger New York 1968), 6-7. See also Russell, Peter H., 'Toward a General Theory of Judicial Independence', in: Russell, Peter H. *et al.* (eds) *Judicial Independence in the Age of Democracy – Critical Perspectives from around the World* (University Press of Virginia Charlottesville 2001), 9.

2 For a definition of the term *court* see *infra* Chapter C.IV(1).

3 Regarding the range of entities that may be qualified as *subjects of public international law* see Walter, Christian, 'Subjects of International Law', in: Wolfrum, Rüdiger (ed) *The Max Planck Encyclopedia of Public International Law* (Oxford University Press Online Edition 2012).

4 Hereinafter, the term *international law* is used in the narrower sense of *public international law*.

5 Malanczuk, Peter, *Akehurst's Modern Introduction to International Law* (Routledge London 7th edn. 1997), 3; Allott, Philip, 'The Concept of International Law' (1999) 10 European Journal of International Law 1, 31; Perkins, John A., 'The Changing Foundations of International Law: From State Consent to State Responsibility' (1997) 15 Boston University International Law Journal 2, 506.

6 Whereas the number of treaties registered with the UN pursuant to Art. 102 UNC was around 2,554 in 1954, today the UNTS contains around 200,000 treaties and related subsequent actions (see 'United Nations Treaty Collection' available at <http://treatie

late the interaction between the various, and increasing number of, actors, and different dispute settlement mechanisms provide for controlled and peaceful settlement of the disputes arising between them.[7] This development is still in an early phase and has yet to materialize fully. However, mandated by technological and cultural progress, States, international organizations, natural and legal persons and other actors have irrevocably pierced the limitations previously posed by geographical, political and legal borders and have thus begun to intensify their interaction across and despite the limits previously posed by the different national legal orders. The importance of international law as a reliable regulating and pacifying force in these transnational relations has steadily increased. As a consequence, the *legalization* of international relations,[8] i.e. the increased density of norms governing international relations,[9] can be observed as well as an accompanying expansion of international law to new areas (*fragmentation*).[10] Consequentially and much like what happens in municipal legal orders committed to the rule of law, this development requires "correspondingly sophisticated dispute-

---

s.un.org/> (last visited: 21 March 2014)). Generally on the growing number and types of sources in international law see Abi-Saab, Georges, 'Sources of International Law', in: Wolfrum, Rüdiger (ed) *The Max Planck Encyclopedia of Public International Law* (Oxford University Press Online Edition 2012).

7 Besides judicial settlement of international disputes, this includes negotiation, good offices, mediation, establishment of an international commission of inquiry, conciliation, and arbitration. See Pellet, Alain, 'Peaceful Settlement of International Disputes', in: Wolfrum, Rüdiger (ed) *The Max Planck Encyclopedia of Public International Law* (Oxford University Press Online Edition 2012), paras. 31-40.

8 *Legalization* is used here to circumscribe the inclusion of legal norms, principles and arguments into a language of political conditions. Generally on the legalization of transnational relations see Brütsch, Christian (ed) *Law and Legalization in Transnational Relations* (Routledge London 2007); Kreide, Regina & Brunkhorst, Hauke (eds), *Transnationale Verrechtlichung: nationale Demokratien im Kontext globaler Politik: Hauke Brunkhorst zum 60. Geburtstag* (Campus-Verlag Frankfurt 2008).

9 Terris, Daniel, et al., *The International Judge – An Introduction to the Men and Women who Decide the World's Cases* (Oxford University Press Oxford 2007), 6.

10 On the phenomenon of fragmentation in international law see Pauwelyn, Joost, 'Fragmentation of International Law', in: Wolfrum, Rüdiger (ed) *The Max Planck Encyclopedia of Public International Law* (Oxford University Press Online Edition 2012); Report of the Study Group of the International Law Commission, *Fragmentation of International Law: Difficulties Arising from the Diversification and Expansion of International Law: Finalized by Martti Koskenniemi* (13 April 2006) UN Doc. A/CN.4/L.682.

settlement institutions to guarantee the smooth operation of the new legal arrangements and the continued clarification and development of their norms."[11] Hence alongside and necessitated by the fragmentation of international law and legalization of international relations a structural consequence can be witnessed in the multiplication of institutions enforcing the law thus created (a process usually referred to as *judicialization/institutionalization*).[12] In this regard, the appearance of other subjects of international law, in particular international organizations,[13] is a significant incentive for the ensuing phenomenon of the creation of international courts and tribunals. Since such courts and tribunals apply a system of law which either is or has the potential of being applicable to more than one State, the institutional backing of an international organization usually proves indispensable.[14]

From a historical perspective, the proliferation of international courts and tribunals is commonly considered to have commenced with the three mixed claims commissions established under the Jay Treaty in 1794.[15] Following the extraordinary political events of the early to mid-twentieth century, there arose important opportunities for institution-building, both represented and furthered by the creation of the League of Nations (LoN) and its successor, the United Nations (UN). Since this has inevitably taken place at the expense of power- and State-oriented diplomacy, it has left its mark on the relationship between States and the various kinds of international courts and tribunals that have been set up. The development accelerated dramatically with the

---

11 Shany, Yuval, *The Competing Jurisdictions of International Courts and Tribunals* (Oxford University Press Oxford 2003), 3.

12 Although it ought to be emphasized that the international judiciary is but one of a number of mechanisms that may be resorted to as a method of enforcing the law; others are diplomacy, negotiation and sanctions. Another noteworthy structural consequence is the increased exercise of public authority by different international organs; on this see von Bogdandy, Armin, et al. (eds), *The Exercise of Public Authority by International Institutions: Advancing International Institutional Law* (Springer Heidelberg 2010).

13 Tomuschat, Christian, 'International Courts and Tribunals', in: Wolfrum, Rüdiger (ed) *The Max Planck Encyclopedia of Public International Law* (Oxford University Press Online Edition 2012), paras. 7-10.

14 The relationship between international courts and possible parent organizations will be one essential object of investigation in this thesis.

15 Nussbaum, Arthur, *A Concise History of the Law of Nations* (Macmillan New York 1954), 129. See also Ziegler, Katja S., 'Jay Treaty (1794)', in: Wolfrum, Rüdiger (ed) *The Max Planck Encyclopedia of Public International Law* (Oxford University Press Online Edition 2012). See further *infra* Chapter C.II(1).

transformation of the global political framework after the 1990s. Today, there are around 120 different international dispute settlement organs,[16] including high-profile institutions such as the two *ad hoc* Tribunals for the former Yugoslavia (ICTY) and Rwanda (ICTR), established respectively in 1993 and 1994, the International Tribunal for the Law of the Sea (ITLOS), inaugurated in 1996, and the International Criminal Court (ICC), which came into being in 2002.

In accordance with the expansion of the system of international norms and exploration of new areas to be governed by the international legal order, the functions of these bodies have gradually expanded to include variations between (traditional) optional adjudication of mere inter-State disputes to compulsory jurisdictions addressing complaints initiated by individuals, independent prosecutors and international organizations. Essentially, it can be said that their activities have become intrusive upon areas previously thought to lie exclusively within national sovereignty.[17] It should come as no surprise that this development, which can be summarized as an assimilation of the international adjudicatory system to that of national legal systems, has not and is not taking place without encountering complications. In particular, it raises profound questions concerning the relationship between different, yet parallel existing levels of public authority, including the management of the risk of diverging jurisprudence and competing jurisdictions.[18] Further, a number of issues relating to the proper administration of international justice

---

16 The Project on International Courts and Tribunals, 'The International Judiciary in Context' available at <http://www.pict-pcti.org/publications/synoptic_chart/synop_c4.pdf> (last visited: 21 March 2014).

17 Mackenzie, Ruth, et al. (eds), *The Manual on International Courts and Tribunals* (Oxford University Press Oxford 2nd edn. 2009), x; Shany, *The Competing Jurisdictions of International Courts and Tribunals*, 7. See also Kokott, Juliane, 'States, Sovereign Equality', in: Wolfrum, Rüdiger (ed) *The Max Planck Encyclopedia of Public International Law* (Oxford University Press Online Edition 2012), paras. 6-14.

18 These central concerns have *inter alia* been addressed in the following scholarly works: Charney, Jonathan I., 'The Impact on the International Legal System of the Growth of International Courts and Tribunals' (1999) 31 New York University Journal of International Law & Politics 4; Brown, Chester, *A Common Law of International Adjudication* (Oxford University Press Oxford 2007); Brown, Chester, 'The Proliferation of International Courts and Tribunals: Finding Your Way Through the Maze' (2002) 3 Melbourne Journal of International Law 2; Spelliscy, Shane, 'The Proliferation of International Tribunals – A Chink in the Armor' (2001) 40 Columbia Journal of Transnational Law 1.

as such call for feasible and well-structured responses from both practice and academia. As stated by Y. Shany, "one of the key challenges in the 21st century for the international judiciary (and the international community on behalf of which it operates) will be to develop legal doctrines, best-practices, and institutional safeguards to address" issues of the efficacy and legitimacy of international adjudication.[19] One such aspect, which has received only modest scholarly attention so far, is the subject of the present study: the adherence of the international judiciary[20] to the standard of judicial independence.

In the wake of the establishment of new international courts, their independence has become a recurrent contentious issue in practice.[21] One *prima facie* explanation which imposes itself is that with the gradual opening up of international law, both towards new subjects and new areas of social interaction, it has become intolerable in practice and difficult to justify the fact that reliable, robust and, most importantly, fair procedures in law enforcement and adjudication are maintained on one level of the law but not on another.[22] In a more profound sense, the greater willingness and ability of different actors, especially individuals, to resort to international courts results in an increasing demand addressed to them to provide for a fair trial; a standard known from national legal systems to have developed to such a degree that it can be claimed to have acquired the status of "one of the fundamental pillars of international law to protect individuals against arbitrary treatment".[23] The main problem that thus has to be faced when this line of argument is pursued further is that the different aspects of the fair trial principle have for long received only fragmentary treatment in organizational or procedural rules

19 Shany, Yuval, 'No Longer a Weak Department of Power? Reflections on the Emergence of a New International Judiciary' (2009) 20 European Journal of International Law 1, 91.

20 The notion of *international judiciary* is here understood as a collective term for what is generally referred to as international courts and tribunals.

21 Examples of this will be presented in the course of the study.

22 It is not a coincidence that the principle of judicial independence is considered to be the core element of the human right to a fair trial, which is laid down in numerous human rights treaties (e.g., Art. 6 Convention for the Protection of Human Rights and Fundamental Freedoms [ECHR]); see Boston, Ana D., 'The Right to a Fair Trial: Balancing Safety and Civil Liberties' (2004) 12 Cardozo Journal of International and Comparative Law 1, 4.

23 Doswald-Beck, Louise, 'Fair Trial, Right to, International Protection ', in: Wolfrum, Rüdiger (ed) *The Max Planck Encyclopedia of Public International Law* (Oxford University Press Online Edition 2012), para. 1.

governing international courts. However, although the right to a fair trial may transpose the principle of judicial independence so that it applies to proceedings before certain international courts, especially human rights courts, its focus on protecting *individuals* against arbitrary treatment suggests that it does not serve as a sufficient (or even germane) explanation for why international courts in general ought to adhere to this principle. In particular, the application of the fair trial principle does not seem appropriate in proceedings that build on the equality of parties, i.e. where such proceedings are usually non-compulsory. This hypothesis is supported by empirical evidence: a swift glance at the founding documents of the early examples of standing international courts which were also confined to managing inter-State disputes, such as the Permanent Court of International Justice (PCIJ), certainly indicates that the institution's independence was valued.[24] But this independence was based on an adherence to a basic fairness in the treatment of the parties appearing before it, i.e. ultimately the equality of States. This relationship between fairness in procedures and State sovereignty shines through in a statement made by the successor organ to the PCIJ in *Military and Paramilitary Activities in and against Nicaragua (Nicaragua v United States of America)*:

> "The provisions of the Statute and Rules of Court concerning the presentation of pleadings and evidence are designed to secure a proper administration of justice, and a fair and equal opportunity for each party to comment on its opponent's contentions."[25]

Although this quotation at first glance refers only to the procedural rules regarding pleadings and evidence presented before the International Court of Justice (ICJ), it allows for the careful deduction of a hypothesis regarding proceedings before international courts as a whole, at least when such proceedings involve parties operating roughly on a formally equal level: Demanding the proper administration of justice, i.e. performance of the judicial task of a court based on sound procedural principles, as well as fairness and an equal opportunity to be the basis for judicial decisions,[26] emphasizes that

---

24 Cf. e.g. on the PCIJ Hudson, Manley O., *International Tribunals: Past and Future* (Carnegie Endowment for International Peace Washington 1944), 236-237.

25 *Military and Paramilitary Activities in and against Nicaragua (Nicaragua v United States of America) (Merits)* ICJ Rep. 14 (1986), para. 31.

26 Wolfrum, Rüdiger, 'International Courts and Tribunals, Evidence', in: Wolfrum, Rüdiger (ed) *The Max Planck Encyclopedia of Public International Law* (Oxford University Press Online Edition 2012), para. 7.

the litigating body stands above the parties and proves itself to be inaccessible to any kind of extra-legal/political parameters. Whether this is indeed the case and, if so, how it relates to a general principle of judicial independence will form one of the chains of analysis of this thesis.

II. Motivation for the Research

The need to engage in this research topic arises from the perspective of both practice and academia. A superficial evaluation of the concrete situations where the independence of international judges, and thus of the institutions for which they work, has been discussed by international courts themselves already indicates the need for a more systematic and coherent approach. An example is the number of applications before international criminal jurisdictions to exclude individual judges from proceedings due to their (perceived) bias. Similarly, a brief glance at the practice from different international courts indicates that even in seemingly identical circumstances the question of judicial independence has been assessed diametrically differently by the courts themselves.[27] This can mainly be attributed to the fact that the content of the principle of judicial independence has been neither substantially and holistically concretized in both scholarly writing and binding instruments, nor consistently defined for the purpose of practical implementation in the international legal order. Although the willingness of international courts seriously to address these matters must be welcomed, the lack of a common

27 This is, e.g., the case regarding statements made by a judge before assuming office at an international court and in which conditions are addressed that are later dealt with in proceedings before that court. The Appeals Chamber of the ICTY in the *Furundžija* Case of 2000 dismissed allegations of bias against one of the judges due to her previous work and statements, stating that "it must be assumed that the Judges of the International Tribunal can disabuse their minds of any irrelevant personal beliefs or predispositions." (*Prosecutor v. Furundžija, Appeals Chamber, Judgement* (ICTY) Case No. IT-95-17/1-A (21 July 2000), para. 197.) The Special Tribunal for Sierra Leone, however, reached a different conclusion in a seemingly similar case in 2004 (*Prosecutor v. Sesay, Decision on Defence Motion Seeking the Disqualification of Justice Robertson from the Appeals Chamber* (ICTR) Case No. SCSL-2004-15-AR15, A.Ch. (12 March 2004)): The Appeals Chamber held that the impression of bias could arise with regard to a judge due to critical remarks he had made earlier on the crimes for which the accused was standing trial, without having referred to particular actions which the accused had allegedly committed or mentioning any names.

standard in this regard risks the coherence of international law being questioned, thereby endangering its predictability and legal security.[28]

It comes as no surprise that from the perspective of legal scholarship, the issue of judicial independence has so far primarily been seen and explored in the context of national legal orders.[29] Those research initiatives that did not merely confine themselves to the context of a particular national legal system frequently choose a comparative approach.[30] Whereas some guidance can be obtained from these sources for addressing the same issue in a purely international context, the special nature of the international legal order merits fresh and autonomous approaches. The desire to identify common standards for national judiciaries is, for example, vividly illustrated by the numerous projects to draft transnational standards for the independence of national judges.[31] It is only in the past decade, however, that judicial independence

28 Coherence, despite the pluralistic nature of international law, is (here) valued positively; as an aim towards which the international legal order ought to strive, since only a coherent legal system treats legal subjects equally. Cf. Report of the Study Group of the International Law Commission, *Fragmentation of International Law: Difficulties Arising from the Diversification and Expansion of International Law: Finalized by Martti Koskenniemi*, para. 491.

29 "The discourses on judicial independence and accountability are primarily national." Andenas, Mads, 'A European Perspective on Judicial Independence and Accountability ' (2007) 41 International Lawyer 1, 7. In this particular discourse the constitutional dimension, e.g. judicial independence as part of the separation of powers doctrine or the positioning as an autonomous rule-of-law principle, has been the main focus. For the German-speaking context see, e.g., Eichenberger, Kurt, *Die richterliche Unabhängigkeit als staatsrechtliches Problem* (Stämpfli Bern 1960); for the United Kingdom see, e.g., Shetreet, Shimon, *Judges on Trial – A Study of the Appointment and Accountability of the English Judiciary* (North-Holland Publishers Amsterdam 1976).

30 See, e.g., Shetreet, Shimon (ed) *Judicial Independence the Contemporary Debate* (Nijhoff Dordrecht 1985); Oberto, Giacomo, 'Richterliche Unabhängigkeit: Rechtsvergleichende Betrachtung ihrer Institutionellen Ausgestaltung in den Ländern Europas' (2004) 37 Zeitschrift für Rechtspolitik 6; Bell, John, 'Judicial Cultures and Judicial Independence' (2001) 4 Cambridge Yearbook of European Legal Studies; Seibert-Fohr, Anja (ed) *Judicial Independence in Transition: Strengthening the Rule of Law in the OSCE Region* (Springer Heidelberg 2012).

31 Some of the more important such codification efforts are: the Committee of Experts, *Draft Principles on the Independence of the Judiciary ("Siracusa Principles")* (1981) available at <http://www.mpil.de/shared/data/pdf/pdfjudind/syracusa_principles.pdf> (last visited: 21 March 2014); the International Bar Association, *Minimum Standards of Judicial Independence* (1982) available at <http://www.ibanet.org/Document/Default.aspx?DocumentUid=BB019013-52B1-427C-AD25-A6409B49FE29> (last

has also been examined in the context of the multiplication of international courts, and thus as an issue of public international law.[32] It is also clear that the hitherto existing scholarly literature does not go beyond the identification of the issues involved. What is lacking is thus a study that goes past the *if* question, and instead embraces the current status of an existing international judiciary in order to analyse *how* – especially on the basis of already existing case law of international courts, agreements establishing courts and court rules and statutes – judicial independence is understood on the level of public international law and whether common standards for the international judiciary can already be identified.[33] To quote the words of C. Amerasinghe:

---

visited: 21 March 2014); the First World Conference on the Independence of Justice, *Universal Declaration on the Independence of Justice* (1983) available at <http://www.mpil.de/shared/data/pdf/pdfjudind/montreal_declaration.pdf> (last visited: 21 March 2014); the Seventh United Nations Congress on the Prevention of Crime and the Treatment of Offenders, *United Nations Basic Principles on the Independence of the Judiciary* (1985) available at <http://www.ohchr.org/EN/ProfessionalInterest/Pages/IndependenceJudiciary.aspx> (last visited: 21 March 2014) or regional agreements such as the Conference of the Chief Justices of Asia and the Pacific, *Beijing Statement of Principles of the Independence of the Judiciary in the LAWASIA Region* (19 August 1995) available at <http://lawasia.asn.au/beijing-statement.htm> (last visited: 21 March 2014) and the Multilateral Meeting on the Statute for Judges in Europe, *European Charter on the Statute for Judges* (10 July 1998) available at <http://www.coe.int/t/dghl/monitoring/greco/evaluations/round 4/European-Charter-on-Statute-of-Judges_EN.pdf> (last visited: 21 March 2014).

32 A seminal work in this regard was an article by D. Shelton in which international standards for the independence of the national judge are elevated to the level of international judges: Shelton, Dinah, 'The Independence of International Tribunals', in: Trindade, Antônio Augusto Cançado (ed) *The Modern World of Human Rights: Essays in Honour of Thomas Buergenthal* (Instituto Interamericano de Derechos Humanos San José 1996). See also the work by C. Brown, who recognized the development and illuminated it from a historical perspective: Brown, Chester, 'The Evolution and Application of Rules Concerning Independence of the "International Judiciary"' (2003) 2 The Law and Practice of International Courts and Tribunals 1. See also the Burgh House Principles on the Independence of the International Judiciary (Study Group of the International Law Association on the Practice and Procedure of International Courts and Tribunals & Project on International Courts and Tribunals, *Burgh House Principles on the Independence of the International Judiciary* (2004) available at <http://www.ucl.ac.uk/laws/cict/docs/burgh_final_21204.pdf> (last visited: 21 March 2014).

33 According to C. Brown it is timely that attention is devoted to the question of overarching principles on independence and impartiality and that a "uniform approach to standards for the international judiciary may be an idea whose time has come."

> "The work which has already been done or begun is only a starting point. It would seem that the recognition that the judicial independence of international courts and tribunals must be protected and secured has come to be established. What is required is in-depth study of how the protection of independence and of the qualities which flow from independence may be ensured."[34]

It is in this context and spirit that this study seeks to make a contribution.

III. Outline of the Research and Methodology

The study has its starting point in the assertion that international courts ought to be independent. Uncontested as this statement is in the context of national legal systems of western complexion, it is not self-evidently equally essential or even applicable in the context of international judicial institutions, as has already been indicated above. The common derivation of the concept from the trisection of governmental powers,[35] a concept that cannot be applied to the international setting,[36] demands that the theoretical foundation for its application *vis-à-vis* international courts be separately analysed. Thus although international law scholarship almost intuitively and unanimously ascribes to the principle of judicial independence real importance for international courts in some shape or form,[37] it has yet to be shown not only what

---

Brown, 'The Evolution and Application of Rules Concerning Independence of the "International Judiciary"', 96.

34 Amerasinghe, Chittharanjan Felix, 'Reflections on the Judicial Function in International Law', in: Ndiaye, Tafsir Malick *et al.* (eds) *Law of the Sea, Environmental Law and Settlement of Disputes: Liber Amicorum Judge Thomas A. Mensah* (Nijhoff Leiden 2007), 125.

35 See *infra* Chapter B.IV(3).

36 Cf. e.g. *Prosecutor v. Duško Tadić, Appeals Chamber, Decision on the defence motion for interlocutory appeal on jurisdiction* (ICTY) Case No. IT-94-1-AR72 (2 October 1995), para. 43.

37 See, e.g., C. Tomuschat: "[N]o adjudicatory body can qualify as a tribunal unless its members enjoy an independent status which shields them in particular against instructions from their national Governments." Tomuschat, Christian, 'International Courts and Tribunals with Regionally Restricted and/or Specialized Jurisdiction', in: Mosler, Hermann *et al.* (eds) *Judicial Settlement of International Disputes, International Court of Justice, Other Courts and Tribunals, Arbitration and Conciliation; An International Symposium* (Springer Berlin 1974), 294; P. Sands & R. Mackenzie: "Judges in every international court and tribunal must be 'independent' and 'impartial'." Mackenzie, Ruth & Sands, Philippe J., 'International Courts and Tribunals and the Independence of the International Judge' (2003) 44 Harvard International Law

is meant by the principle in an international context but also what the theoretical foundation is for its application. For this reason, *Chapter B: The Notion of Judicial Independence – The Analytical Framework* will provide an introduction to the topic of judicial independence and make available for the study a conceptual basis from which to conduct further analysis.

The underlying thesis of this work, that any international court ought to be independent, builds on two indispensable premises: First, it assumes that the organ for which the claim of independence is made is classified as an *international court*. As mentioned above, there are numerous international judicial dispute settlement organs which could potentially be subsumed under this terminology, and not all could reasonably be addressed in this thesis. Instead, to provide for clarity in the arguments building on this premise but also to keep the research undertaking within reasonable limits, it is necessary to elaborate an operational definition of this term. This will be provided in *Chapter C: The International Judiciary – Defining the Object of Investigation,*[38] which begins with a brief historical overview of the role played by the principle of judicial independence in international law. Appropriately, this account is provided against the background of the proliferation of international judiciaries, which is thus suggested to be the catalyst for the concept. Furthermore, the objects of investigation *in concreto* of this study, the international courts which shall subsequently be analysed as regards their adherence to the principle of judicial independence will be specified. In this context, a narrow selection of courts that meet the definition of an *international court* is called for.

Verification of the second fundamental premise, the assertion that all international courts thus defined in principle ought to adhere to a standard of independence, constitutes the main body of the present study. Building on the basic understanding, developed in *Chapter B*, of what can be encompassed

---

Journal 1, 275; F. Pocar: "What is more important than unity of jurisdiction is that all tribunals that are established, in whatever form, meet the criteria of independence and impartiality set forth in international norms, including human rights legal instruments, and receive the support of the international community as a whole." Pocar, Fausto, 'The Proliferation of International Criminal Courts and Tribunals – A Necessity in the Current International Community' (2004) 2 Journal of International Criminal Justice 2, 308.

38 It must be stated, first, that the selection of international courts analysed in this study is necessarily limited. This study cannot and does not seek to achieve a holistic overview of the protection of judicial independence in all international courts and tribunals.

by the attributed characteristic *independent*, the study will analyse the selected courts and scrutinize to what extent they can be claimed to follow and codify parameters which bolster the assertion that the court in question is indeed independent (*Chapters D-H*). The vantage point of this central part of the study is the contention that an international court's independence "depends … upon its constitution, its judges and the way in which they function".[39] What this means is that the notion of judicial independence, perhaps unlike intuition, can never be an entirely standardized notion. This was suggested already above, with the thought-provoking suggestion that judicial independence might be called for both in an attempt to protect individuals against arbitrary treatment and to ensure that fairness and equal opportunity are the basis for judicial decisions. Thus the study proceeds from the idea that judicial independence must be understood as a flexible concept which has different balance points and priorities according to the operational features and function of the particular court under investigation. This understanding is not entirely different from what can be observed in national court systems. As an example: even an instinctively essential parameter of a court's independence, such as judges' non-reliance for their (re-) election on individuals or political organs which may both appear before a court and have an interest in the outcome of court proceedings, is not always observed. Yet this condition in and of itself can hardly justify an assessment to the effect that the court/judges concerned would not be independent. This means that a holistic, although by no means exhaustive, study of the normative framework, including statutes, rules of courts, treaties establishing courts, case law of the courts themselves and other norms influencing their functioning, is required.[40] It is not *a priori* possible to determine which parameters need to be in place in order for a court to qualify as an independent judicial dispute settling institution, but instead safeguards for judicial independence must be in place wherever they are also conducive to the fulfilment of a court's function. However, focusing on a court's function to assess its independence has to go beyond the core of any international court's purpose, which lies in deciding issues presented to it by the parties to a dispute,[41] and which is but the

39 *Prosecutor v. Duško Tadić, Decision on Defence Motion of Jurisdiction* (ICTY) Case No. IT-94-1 (10 August 1995), para. 32.

40 Wittreck, Fabian, *Die Verwaltung der Dritten Gewalt* (Mohr Siebeck Tübingen 2006), 231.

41 Hudson, *International Tribunals: Past and Future*, 236; Caron, David D., 'Towards a Political Theory of International Courts and Tribunals' (2006) 24 Berkeley Journal

smallest common denominator. Following only a function this narrowly defined would prevent us from identifying a number of safeguards that may be mandated by a more diverse judicial function, for example due to courts' different jurisdictions. Hence it will be necessary briefly to analyse the functions of the courts under investigation. In order better to structure the analysis, judicial independence will be examined from a collective and individual perspective. The collective (or structural) perspective aims at identifying the protection of the judicial independence of the court as a judicial institution. Here, the establishment of courts, their administration, financing, composition, and the procedural control are examples of parameters that demand scrutiny. The individual (or personal) perspective instead highlights the protection of the individual legal position of the judges. Questions that require investigation here are e.g. the personal requirements of judges, tenure, remuneration and immunities.

In the final chapter (*Chapter I: Summary of Conclusions and Outlook*), the results of the study will be summarized and assessed. As throughout earlier parts of the thesis, the aim here is to build on the flexibility of the notion of judicial independence and to demonstrate to what extent the normative requirements for judicial independence in the evaluated courts show a consensus, which could be used as a basis for the contention that any new court that may be established and that aspires to be classified as an *international court*, in the definition here adopted,[42] ought to provide for a certain set of requirements for its independence. Furthermore, assertions will be made regarding special requirements for different kinds of jurisdiction, which go beyond the common core.

IV. Focal Questions

The present study is guided by three different yet closely interlinked questions relating to the independence of the international judiciary:

(I) *What is the content of the principle of judicial independence applied in international law?*

---

of International Law 2, 408; Anand, 'Role of International Adjudication', in: Gross, Leo (ed) *The Future of the International Court of Justice* (Oceana Publishers Dobbs Ferry, New York 1976), 5; Higgins, Rosalyn, *Problems and Process: International Law and How we Use it* (Clarendon Press Oxford 1994), 202-204.

42 See *infra* Chapter C.

Underlying the entire research agenda is the analysis of which requirements potentially ensure the independence of international courts. The range of conceivable requirements is nearly infinite and is primarily limited by the functions served by courts and normative parameters provided by the sources chosen for this study, such as court statutes, rules of court, treaties establishing courts, and courts' own judicial practice.

(II) *Is there a common (minimum) core of requirements that has to be met by an international court for it to be independent?*
If the number of normative elements that impact on the assessment of a court's independence is extensive, what (if any) is the common core of elements that remains the same irrespective of the court's jurisdictional nature? Bearing this question in mind throughout the study will not only deliver readily accessible conclusions which help grasp the international judiciary, and thus incidentally to the international legal order as a whole. It will moreover help to provide guidance for the establishment of future courts, which by their creators are designed to meet the same high standards in the administration of justice as their predecessors and sister organs.

(III) *Are there necessarily special requirements applicable and linked to certain special jurisdictions?*
Parallel to the previous question is the query whether there are certain elements of judicial independence that separate particular groups of international courts from others, but nonetheless appear to be coherent within that same group.

Chapter B: The Notion of Judicial Independence – The Analytical Framework

I. Introduction

As is the case with all legal research that revolves around a particular terminology, the determination of a comprehensible definition of that terminology is a necessary precondition for ensuing substantive legal enquiry. Especially when this terminology is given the role of a gatekeeper to a legal discourse, in the sense that it forms the central structure of the discussion, the value of the legal arguments being made and its persuasive quality depend on the clarity of the terminological characterization. Only when the language used is sufficiently precise can a particular point be made convincingly. Definitions therefore are often not only desirable but indeed necessary "in the sense that premises are indispensable for a logical or systematic investigation of a matter".[43] This holds true also with regard to a study on the notion of *judicial independence*, which is a term diligently used in various legal and political contexts. Relying on these considerations, this chapter seeks to clarify what can be subsumed under this notion and what the meaning of the concept and its fundamental facets might be.[44]

II. The Usefulness of Legal Definitions

The search for terminological definitions has always provided important jurisprudential battlefields, and although the aim of this work is not to open up yet another arena for the balancing of theoretical concepts, it is nevertheless a precondition for engagement in terminological discussion. Why? First and foremost, ordinary language possesses an inbuilt vagueness which must

43 Cairns, Huntington, 'A Note on Legal Definitions' (1936) 36 Columbia Law Review 7, 1100.

44 "Any analysis of judicial independence must begin with some idea of its core meaning"; Larkins, Christopher M., 'Judicial Independence and Democratization. A Theoretical and Conceptual Analysis' (1996) 44 The American Journal of Comparative Law 4, 608.

be overcome in order to meet the requirement inherent in legal research, namely to provide detailed and precise propositions. In addition, all legal research has to struggle with the inevitability of borrowing language without also wishing necessarily to assume the substantive concretization it may have received in other contexts. Thus when this thesis utilizes a certain interpretation of the notion of judicial independence, this has to be disclosed to the reader in order not to cloud his[45] perception of the terminology by other content, which could impede access to the ensuing reasoning of the thesis. The definition thus serves the need to prevent the *contamination* of legal arguments through off-topic or irrelevant content. Furthermore, and perhaps most importantly, the necessity of defining crucial terminology derives from the demand for premises for undertaking logical and systematic investigation. Applied to the research agenda of this thesis, this implies that only a comprehensive understanding of the meaning of judicial independence, for example, allows for an assessment of *if* and *how* the concept can be safeguarded in international law. In sum, drafting a definition is not an end in itself, but rather serves to overcome the vagueness of ordinary language and to create a viable environment for legal argument.

Irrespective of this apparent advantage of providing a legal definition, due consideration should nevertheless be given to the risk of focusing on language instead of content.[46] Within the framework of this thesis, this danger is met with the unassuming acknowledgement that the following exposition on the notion of judicial independence will result in little more than a working definition. The intention is not to provide a general definition, or

45 Throughout the thesis it is understood that all references to the masculine include the feminine and *vice-versa*.

46 Certainly, a potential for academic discourse arises from the contention that all definition in law is dangerous, for one can rarely be found that cannot be overturned ("Omnis definitio in jure periculosa est; parum est enim ut non subverti posset." Scott, Samuel P. (transl.), *Codex Iustinianus: The Civil Law: Including: The Twelve Tables, The Institutes of Gaius, The Rules of Ulpian, The Opinions of Paulus, The Enactments of Justinian, and The Constitutions of Leo* (Central Trust Company Cincinnati 1932), Dig. 50, 17, 202). According to R. Bernhardt, "Jede Arbeit über Fragen der juristischen Hermeneutik muß Fragment bleiben, denn sie versucht sich an rational nur begrenzt Erfassbarem." (Bernhardt, Rudolf, *Die Auslegung völkerrechtlicher Verträge – Insbesondere in der Rechtsprechung internationaler Gerichte* (Karl Heymanns Verlag KG Köln 1963), 1.) Thus there is an obvious danger in allowing an excessive emphasis to be put on terminological issues, as this threatens to dilute the quality of the substance of this research.

even to present a general theory on judicial independence,[47] but one that facilitates the further study of how judicial independence is safeguarded in the international judiciary. Elaboration of the definition will assist in several ways to identify the build-up of the concept of judicial independence, and thus more thoroughly to disclose what may threaten and what may help to safeguard judicial independence. Hence the intellectual fruitfulness of the legal discourse generated by the scrutiny of a definition is embraced and taken advantage of.

III. Textual Approach – What do We Mean by Judicial Independence?

1. The Protected Apparatus – The Subject of Independence

As was indicated in the previous chapter, the notion of judicial independence is used in many contexts, sometimes with a substantive connotation but usually not so.[48] In recognition of the influence language has on judicial discourse,[49] a linguistic approach therefore may provide some much needed opening clarity in a discourse otherwise characterized by a diverse realm of concepts and meanings. A purely linguistic approach also enables one to close in on a notion without the burden of legal argument because language itself is freed from every body of legal thought.

The term *judicial* refers to "pertaining to the administration of justice"[50] or, more generally, "involving a court of law".[51] In other words, the term *judicial* determines the identity of the subject we are dealing with and establishes that the subject must be a judicial organ in the wider sense. This term

---

47 For such attempts see, e.g., Russell, 'Toward a General Theory of Judicial Independence'; Pasquino, Pasquale, 'Prolegomena to a Theory of Judicial Power: The Concept of Judicial Independence in Theory and History' (2003) 2 The Law and Practice of International Courts and Tribunals 1.

48 See, e.g., S. Burbank who suggests that "[j]udicial independence exists primarily as a rhetorical notion rather than as a subject of sustained, organized study." Burbank, Stephen B., 'What do we Mean by "Judicial Independence"?' (2003) 64 Ohio State Law Journal 1, 324.

49 Koskenniemi, Martti, *From Apology to Utopia: The Structure of International Legal Argument* (Lakimiesliiton Kustannus Helsinki 1989), XXII-XXIII.

50 'Oxford English Dictionary' available at <http://www.oed.com/> (last visited: 21 March 2014): "judicial".

51 'Cambridge Advanced Learner's Dictionary' available at <http://dictionary.cambridge.org/> (last visited: 21 March 2014): "judicial".

alone, however, does not with any degree of certainty establish whether the court as an institution or *merely* the individual judge is at the centre of attention. Both possibilities open up and both may thus be used as the focal point for further scientific analysis.[52] A determination in this regard appears to lie at the discretion of the author and to rely on the context in which the term *judicial*, and indeed the complete notion of *judicial independence*, is eventually used. For the purpose of this thesis, which seeks to study judicial power with all its components, a commitment in this regard does not seem to be necessary or even useful. Interestingly enough, this linguistic uncertainty with regard to the subject is, at least *prima facie*, not mirrored in e.g. the German expression *richterliche Unabhängigkeit*.[53] Here the term *richterliche*, meaning *of the judge*,[54] indicates that the independence is attributed to the individual judge. To stay for a while with the example of how judicial independence is incorporated and understood in the German legal order, the German Constitution mentions the independence of the judicial power explicitly only in connection with judge(s): according to Article 97(1) Basic Law, "[j]udges shall be independent and subject only to the law."[55] But a suggestion derived from a textual interpretation of the law, to the effect that the focus lies on the individual judge, does not correspond to the actual usage and material content of the principle of judicial independence; indeed such a purely linguistic approach is deceiving. *Richterliche* is in fact understood to mean *the judicial power*, i.e. it is used as a collective (encompassing a

---

52 Cf. Eichenberger, *Die richterliche Unabhängigkeit als staatsrechtliches Problem*, 26-27.

53 The French translation, *l'indépendance judiciaire*, appears to follow the same diction as the English. For a more detailed overview of the French perspective on the terminology see Heuschling, Luc, 'Why Should Judges Be Independent?', in: Ziegler, Katja S. (ed) *Constitutionalism and the Role of Parliaments* (Hart Publishers Oxford 2007).

54 The German word for judge is *Richter*, whereas the word for court is *Gericht*.

55 Judicial independence is furthermore implicitly protected in Articles 20 (section 3 provides that "Die Gesetzgebung ist an die verfassungsmäßige Ordnung, die vollziehende Gewalt und die Rechtsprechung sind an Gesetz und Recht gebunden." ["The legislature shall be bound by the constitutional order, the executive and the judiciary by law and justice."]) and 92 Basic Law ("Die rechtsprechende Gewalt ist den Richtern anvertraut; sie wird durch das Bundesverfassungsgericht, durch die in diesem Grundgesetze vorgesehenen Bundesgerichte und durch die Gerichte der Länder ausgeübt." ["The judicial power shall be vested in the judges; it shall be exercised by the Federal Constitutional Court, by the federal courts provided for in this Basic Law, and by the courts of the Länder."]).

group of judges) and institutional (referring to the court as a body) term,[56] and, therefore, judicial independence is regarded as an institutional safeguard for the judiciary rather than a right or privilege of the individual judge.[57]

The conclusion that can be drawn from this is that judicial independence, seen from a purely linguistic analysis of the first part of the notion, is not determined with regard to the subject that is circumscribed. For the purpose of this thesis, that is in the context of international law, both the international judge as an individual and the institutions in which judges gather as a collective (i.e. courts) may be covered. From a purely linguistic viewpoint, either (or both) may be intended to be protected by the idea of judicial independence in any given context. A differentiation will be possible, and then even necessary, only when the linguistic analysis includes substantive criteria.[58]

2. The Attribute of Independence

The more complex part of the notion of judicial independence is its second component, namely the term *independence*. From a purely linguistic perspective, the term may be described as the "exemption from external control or support; freedom from subjection, or from the influence of others; individual

56 See, e.g., Eichenberger, *Die richterliche Unabhängigkeit als staatsrechtliches Problem*, 26.

57 Regarding the German legal system see, e.g., the decisions of the German Constitutional Court *Bundesverfassungsgericht* (BVerfG) BVerfGE 27, 211 (14 November 1969), at 217, and of the German Federal Court of Justice *Bundesgerichtshof* (BGH) RiZ(R) 5/09 (21 October 2010), at para. 24. See further Reinhardt, Michael, *Konsistente Jurisdiktion* (Mohr Siebeck Tübingen 1997), 102 and Seibert-Fohr, Anja, 'Constitutional Guarantees of Judicial Independence in Germany', in: Riedel, Eibe *et al.* (eds) *Recent Trends in German and European Constitutional Law* (Springer Heidelberg 2006), with further references.

58 See on this *infra* Chapter B.IV.

liberty of thought or action".[59] It is a rather strong notion[60] which, depending on the context in which it is used, can be substituted by terms such as *sovereignty, autonomy, non-alignment, separation, individualism, boldness, liberation, unconstraint*, or *unrestraint*.[61] None of these circumscriptions is entirely congruent, yet most have in common that they implement terms with a vigorously positive connotation (e.g. *exemption, freedom, liberty*), to describe a notion that appears to negate influence of some sort (*in-dependent*). It must be kept in mind, however, that with this observation no verdict has yet been passed on the nature of the influence; this may be objectively good or bad.[62] From this follow two central assumptions; one relating to the relational validity of the concept and one amounting to a value judgment.

Initially, it is evident that the term *independence* describes a relationship between two (or more) entities where the one entity, which for exemplary purposes may be labelled A, does not dependent upon the other, here labelled B.[63] However, the statement that entity A is in a state of dependence in relation to entity B does not necessarily have to rely upon reciprocity: it is fully conceivable and does not narrow the claim of independence made in relation to entity A that entity B is either dependent on or independent from entity A. Indeed no specification concerning entity B has been made with the original claim. It is further proper to state that entity A's independence from entity B must not imply *total* independence, in the sense of a freedom from

---

59 'Oxford English Dictionary' available at <http://www.oed.com/> (last visited: 21 March 2014): "independence". Similar definitions in Soanes, Catherine & Stevenson, Angus (eds), *Oxford Dictionary of English* (Oxford University Press Oxford 2nd edn. 2007), "independent"; Fowler, Henry W. & Thompson, Della (eds), *The Concise Oxford Dictionary of Current English* (Clarendon Press Oxford 9th edn. 1995), "independent"; Dudenredaktion, *Duden: das große Wörterbuch der deutschen Sprache in sechs Bänden: Band 6: Sp-Z* (Bibliographisches Institut Mannheim 1981), "unabhängig"; Rey-Debove, Josette, et al., *Le nouveau Petit Robert: dictionnaire alphabétique et analogique de la langue française* (Dictionnaires Le Robert Paris Nouv. éd. du Petit Robert de Paul Robert, 40. éd. 2007), "indépendant".

60 This impression derives not only from common language but also from legal language: see for example the notion of an independent state.

61 Kirkpatrick, Elizabeth M., *The Oxford Paperback Thesaurus* (Oxford University Press Oxford 1994): "independence".

62 See on this further *infra* Chapter B.IV(5).

63 This relatedness aspect of the term is, e.g., expressed in the definition of the adjective "independent" in Kirkpatrick, *The Oxford Paperback Thesaurus*: "... 3. *the two firms are quite independent of each other* separate, unconnected, unrelated, unattached, distinct, individual."

all dependencies, or even the absence of all interaction.[64] Although an ill-considered claim of independence might have this meaning, it is usually not suggested that entity A entirely and only depends on itself, either on its own will and desires defined *ad hoc* (i.e. a free subsistence) or only on its own rules (i.e. autonomous). It is instead at least thinkable that entity A is independent of entity B with relation to one particular type of conduct, but dependent regarding a different set of behaviour(s) (or *vis-à-vis* a potential entity C). This becomes evident when we revert from the hitherto abstract level and revisit the concept of judicial independence. It would witness a monistic and totalitarian ethos, inherently alien to a fair judiciary of western complexion, to demand the judiciary's *absolute* lack of dependence, i.e. in *every* regard and from *any* influence. To illustrate this, the unpretentious yet practically relevant example of the judiciary's financing may be drawn from. Were courts not able to rely on the larger state apparatus to gather funds for their activities, they would have to establish their own executive functions which would create unbearable tensions with the remaining organizational structure. Moreover, it seems to be a rather uncontroversial claim that judicial independence cannot translate into independence from the law, whether statutory or customary (even irrespective of whether the law "pre-exists" the judiciary because it has been drafted by a legislature or because it is claimed to exist objectively[65]).[66] Instead, a proper judiciary will by most standards be considered such only if in a particular case it faithfully applies the applicable law that has been established by other state organs, which in democratic States are those that are far more suited to expressing a people's majority opinion than the judiciary could possibly be.

Closely linked to these relational assertions is the value judgment that is insinuated by, and thus can be derived from the notion of, independence. As was indicated above, the term independence is rarely used in an absolute manner, but instead commonly refers to autonomy, freedom or liberty from

64 Cf. *infra* Chapter B.IV(5)(a).

65 I.e. subject to civil law or common law approaches.

66 Eichenberger, *Die richterliche Unabhängigkeit als staatsrechtliches Problem*, 28-29. This idea has also been proposed by C. Schmitt: "*Die Unabhängigkeit der Richter von dienstlichen Befehlen hat ihr wesentliches Korrelat in der Abhängigkeit der Richter vom Gesetz.*": see Schmitt, Carl, *Verfassungslehre* (Duncker & Humblot Berlin 1993), 155. See also Heuschling, 'Why Should Judges Be Independent?', 244-245.

a particular parameter.[67] The linguistic approach suggests that this parameter is valued negatively; although this is by no means a necessary conclusion.[68] But, at least from the perspective of a subject that seeks to be independent, this independence relates to influences that would generally, if allowed to flourish, be considered to be negative. The definition of what is meant by the circumscription *negative* thus depends on the subject that we seek to describe, in the present context the judiciary, the courts, and the judge(s).[69] Following the reasoning of K. Eichenberger, independence understood in this way would include influences resulting in falsifications, a turn to the artificial and improper.[70] What is real and proper, on the other hand, goes far beyond a linguistic approach and necessitates the substantial evaluation of what is the judiciary's central task, i.e. from what the judiciary could diverge if exposed to this negative influence. Yet, when read together with the word judicial, as defined above, we can nonetheless conclude that independence must at the very least mean isolation from extra-legal[71] political parameters and actors; an independent judiciary is thus characterized by providing conflict resolution by a neutral third who is allowed, able and compelled to consider only the facts of a particular case and the relevant laws.[72] The judiciary must be able to exercise its judicial function(s), however defined. Turning yet further to the concrete subject of this thesis, the *international* judiciary, the core function is to decide issues presented to it by parties to a dispute.[73] Were international courts to hold functions that reach beyond this (basic) definition, which will be clarified in later parts of the thesis, they too would have to be protected from extra-legal parameters and actors.

---

67 It is fully conceivable that although item A is independent of item B, there remain other kinds of influence having an effect on item A and which may be tolerated or even desirable.

68 Item A can well be independent of an influence caused by item B which could, if allowed to affect item A, have objectively positive outcomes.

69 See *supra* Chapter B.III(1).

70 Eichenberger, *Die richterliche Unabhängigkeit als staatsrechtliches Problem*, 24.

71 As stated above, independence cannot be interpreted as isolation from law.

72 Cf. Shapiro, Martin M., *Courts: A Comparative and Political Analysis* (University of Chicago Press Chicago 1986), 1-2.

73 Hudson, *International Tribunals: Past and Future*, 236; Caron, 'Towards a Political Theory of International Courts and Tribunals', 408; Anand, 'Role of International Adjudication', 5; Higgins, *Problems and Process: International Law and How we Use it*, 202-204.

Before turning to the substantive approach, one further point, which has already been touched upon, deserves to be addressed, namely the (in)determinacy concerning the source of influence. As will be shown below, it is of some importance not only for the historical development of the concept of judicial independence but also for its contemporary understanding who the potential antagonist of the judiciary's good functioning is.[74] Yet the term *independence* does not reveal from whom the dependence that countervails judicial independence originates. However, an initial reply may be structured to encompass both external and internal influences. Whereas the former refers to pressure being exerted by an entity different from the judiciary (the executive or legislative branch of government, in the context of national legal orders; other States, legal entities, including governmental and non-governmental organizations (NGOs), or natural persons, including the parties to a particular conflict, in international law), the latter covers isolation between judges and courts and, perhaps most far-reaching, judges' isolation from their own personality, opinions and individually held preferences.

IV. Substantive Approach – Theoretical Justification and Concretization

1. Preliminary Reflections

In the context of municipal legal orders the principle of judicial independence is usually linked to the concept of the rule of law[75] and to the doctrine of the separation of powers.[76] It was first evolved in the ambit of constitutional developments of national legal systems and has there developed into an "essential feature of liberal democracy"[77] and a "common value".[78] This

74 Heuschling, 'Why Should Judges Be Independent?', 243.

75 As an example, according to the group of eminent jurists which in 2003 reviewed the law and practice of judicial appointments to the ECtHR, "[t]he independence of the judiciary is one of the cornerstones of the rule of law." Limbach, Jutta, et al., *Judicial Independence: Law and Practice of Appointments to the European Court of Human Rights* (Interights London 2003), 15. It should, however, be emphasized that such statements always ought to be seen in the context of the legal system for which they were made.

76 See e.g. Heuschling, 'Why Should Judges Be Independent?', 245-250; Seibert-Fohr, 'Constitutional Guarantees of Judicial Independence in Germany', 269.

77 Russell, 'Toward a General Theory of Judicial Independence', 1.

78 Bell, 'Judicial Cultures and Judicial Independence', 47.

eminent position is derived from its central functions of shielding the judicial process from external and off-topic influence or legally unwarranted reasons for decision,[79] in order to facilitate objective judgments, especially in situations where the State itself has an interest in the outcome of a particular case. Without enjoying independence, the judiciary is in danger of being manipulated to prevent it from questioning illegal or arbitrary acts potentially committed by public authorities.[80] Judicial independence can thus never just be an end in itself or a privilege of judges.[81] Instead it amounts to an institutional safeguard: by protecting the neutrality of judges and the objectivity of the judicature, judicial independence by necessity mandates a separation of the judicial branch not only from the various parties to a conflict but more importantly from entities acquiring both the executive and legislative functions in a particular legal order. Better to identify the logic and dynamics of judicial independence in the international legal order, the following will attempt to bring these preliminary thoughts into their respective historical and theoretical contexts.

2. Origin of the Concept of Judicial Independence – A Practical Example

A historical approach to the development of judicial independence unfolds the picture of the increasing freedom of the judiciary from political and executive control; the emancipation of the judiciary as an autonomous branch of government. Its origin is closely linked to the question why any judiciary should be independent in the first place or, rather, what purpose an *independent* judiciary might serve. Until the early 13th century, judges were often considered the King's judges, and by no means autonomous arbitrators. In fact, for long periods of human history and in many different cultures, the function of adjudication was not even attributed to a distinct judicial body but was instead reserved for the same authority that already exercised exec-

---

79 See remarks by S. J. Burton in American Society of International Law, 'The Independence and Impartiality of International Judges', American Society of International Law: proceedings of the 83rd Annual Meeting, Chicago, Illinois, April 5-8, 1989, Conference in Chicago, Illinois (1989), 514.

80 Larkins, 'Judicial Independence and Democratization. A Theoretical and Conceptual Analysis', 606.

81 Agmon-Gonnen, Michal, 'Judicial Independence: The Threat from Within' (2005) 38 Israel Law Review 3, 122.

utive functions.[82] Thus although some scholars tend to place the historical origin of the concept of judicial independence at a much earlier point in history,[83] the actual elevation of the idea to a fundamental principle of practical value has to be reserved for a time when state branches developed and began to diverge from each other. How this development came about can be lucidly illustrated by the example of the evolution of the judiciary in England and Wales.

In 1178, King Henry II, who at the time was eager to maintain good order in his land and to strengthen the central authority through judicial reforms,[84] chose five members of his household, two clerks and three laymen, "to hear all the complaints of the realm and to do right".[85] This step was an innovation in that it meant the founding of a distinct judicial council for the settlement of disputes, which until then had been the sole responsibility of the King with the support of his officials.[86] Despite the fact that this council did not initially emerge as a body separate from the king's court (the so-called *curia regis*),[87] it nevertheless represented a moderation of the King's judicial

82 See Pasquino, 'Prolegomena to a Theory of Judicial Power: The Concept of Judicial Independence in Theory and History', 13, who highlights that in many early societies the function of adjudication was not attributed to a distinct judicial body.

83 For example, D. Flatto suggests that the "etiology of an independent judiciary lies in antiquity" (see Flatto, David C, 'The Historical Origins of Judicial Independence and Their Modern Resonances' (2007) 117 Yale Law Journal Pocket Part 8).

84 See on this Hosler, John D., *Henry II: A Medieval Soldier at War* (Brill Leiden 2007), 76-82.

85 The five members were to hear civil disputes between individuals, as opposed to litigation in which the crown was involved as a party. Pollock, Frederick & Maitland, Frederic William, *The History of English Law Before the Time of Edward I* (The Lawbook Exchange New Jersey 2008), 198; Hosler, *Henry II: A Medieval Soldier at War*, 78.

86 Lord Justice Brooke, 'Judicial Independence – Its History in England and Wales', in: Cunningham, Helen (ed) *Fragile Bastion: Judicial independence in the nineties and beyond* (Judicial Commission of New South Wales Sydney 2000), 90. To provide an accurate picture of the judicial system and power balance especially in England of the High Middle Ages, the existence of local courts controlled by local barons, who in many aspects challenged the crown's power, should not be overlooked. These courts, which in theory still operated under the crown but often applied only local customary law, were under the direct influence of landholders, barons and local magnates and were thus at the centre of the struggle between local barons and the king. See further on this Shapiro, *Courts: A Comparative and Political Analysis*, 70-76.

87 Effectively, it remained a part of that court.

monopoly and a pre-stage to the Court of Common Pleas, a court that heard actions between two subjects, which did not concern the King. This common law court developed in the late 12th to early 13th century and it was a distinct formalization of judicial dispute settlement, although still under the administration and strong influence of the King.[88] One practical reason for this was that judges were for long commonly chosen from the group of royal clerks, i.e. from those who had knowledge of the law and who were close to the King. In addition, the administration of English courts of the High Middle Ages and beyond was characterized by a strong collegial character,[89] which for example manifested itself in the fluctuating separation of personnel between judges deciding on common pleas and those deciding disputes touching directly on the interests of the crown. Taken together, these factors prohibited a real, objective autonomy *vis-à-vis* the executive from materializing, the way common in most western-style States of today.

Whereas the King usually had the authority to appoint judges and could thus also remove them from office,[90] suspend them or transfer them from one position to another, Parliament had its own influence over the developing judiciary. Examples are impeachment procedures or the demand that individual judges defend and explain their adjudication in individual cases.[91] It was in the wake of these mounting tensions between the King and Parliament, which were part of a broader political conflict, that the judiciary seriously began to evolve its distinct identity, separate from both the crown and Parliament. One hurdle that had to be overcome in this process was that many judges were not paid enough for their duties on the bench and thus had to depend on other sources of income. This in turn led to the widespread taking

88 Adams, George Burton, 'The Origin of the English Courts of Common Law' (1920) 30 Yale Law Journal 8, 803-808. Cf. also Baker, John H., *An Introduction to English Legal History* (Butterworths London 4th edn. 2002), 166-169.

89 Shapiro, *Courts: A Comparative and Political Analysis*, 76.

90 One of the most famous of such removals from office resulted from the conflict between King James I and Chief Justice Edward Coke. In the *Case of Commendams* (*Colt and Glover v. Bishop of Coventry ("Case of Commendams")* (King's Bench) Hobart's Reports 140:6 (1616)), Coke and other judges refused to follow an order by the King to stop or delay proceedings. As a consequence, they were summoned before the King and his Council. All the judges except for Coke submitted. Coke, who attempted to defend his position, was dismissed from office. See Holdsworth, William Searle & Goodhart, Arthur L., *A History of English Law: Vol. 5* (Sweet and Maxwell London 1945), 439-440.

91 Shetreet, *Judges on Trial – A Study of the Appointment and Accountability of the English Judiciary*, 2-8.

of bribes, making judges' salaries a crucial element in the development of an autonomous judiciary.[92]

Early support for the idea of judicial independence was provided by Sir Edward Coke (1552-1634), first a Chief Justice of the Common Pleas and later Chief Justice of the King's Bench, whose loyalty proved to lie with the common law rather than the crown. He defended the position that common law courts ought to be subject to the law alone, and not to the King, a position that for obvious reasons provoked a conflict with the King. In the case of *Prohibitions del Rey*, Coke when questioned by the King declared "that the law was the golden met-wand and measure to try the causes of the subjects."[93] In his opinion, "the King in his own person cannot adjudge any case" and he instead advised that "this ought to be determined and adjudged in some court of justice, according to the law and custom of England; and always judgments are given, *ideo consideratum est per curiam*, so that Court gives the judgment".[94] These statements reveal two features that seem to be characteristic of most concepts of judicial independence: On the one hand, the prerogative of the courts to adjudicate on cases without interference from the crown, i.e. independence from political influence. And on the other hand, the sole dependence of the courts, in the exercise of this function, on the law.

A further important step towards an independent judiciary was the enactment in 1701 of the Act of Settlement, which, together with the Bill of Rights of 1689, ended the Glorious Revolution and rang in modern English parliamentary democracy.[95] In the Act essential features such as the principle of

92 Cf. Rule 6.1 Multilateral Meeting on the Statute for Judges in Europe, *European Charter on the Statute for Judges*; Principle 11 Seventh United Nations Congress on the Prevention of Crime and the Treatment of Offenders, *United Nations Basic Principles on the Independence of the Judiciary*, demanding sufficient remuneration so as to shield judges from outside pressure.

93 *Prohibitions Del Roy* (King's Bench Division) 77 E.R. 1342 (1616). Coke, Sir Edward, *The reports of Sir Edward Coke, Knt. in Thirteen Parts – A new Edition, with Additional Notes and References, and with Abstracts of the Principal Points, Volume VI, Parts XI-XII-XIII* (Joseph Butterworth and Son London 1826), 282.

94 Coke, *The reports of Sir Edward Coke, Knt. in Thirteen Parts – A new Edition, with Additional Notes and References, and with Abstracts of the Principal Points, Volume VI, Parts XI-XII-XIII*, 281. Similar statements questioning the King's influence over the courts later led to an abrupt end to Sir Edward Coke's career in the judiciary.

95 See Browning, Andrew (ed), *English Historical Documents: Vol. 8: 1660-1714* (Eyre & Spottiswoode London 1953), 129-134; Plucknett, Theodore Frank Thomas, *A Concise History of the Common Law* (Butterworth London 5th edn. 1956), 59.

security of judicial tenure (judges hold their office *quamdiu se bene gesserint*, i.e. during good behaviour) combined with a set framework for removal from office (namely upon the address of both Houses of Parliament) were formally recognized.[96] With the enactment of these characteristics, the separation of the three powers was codified and put on comparatively solid ground. Nevertheless, from today's perspective, the Act of Settlement "did not create an independent judiciary at the stroke of a pen".[97] The entanglement of the judiciary with the executive branch was far from unravelled, and the King and his ministers still had ample opportunities to exert pressure on judges in individual cases.[98] Moreover, threats to an independent judiciary often lay in the details, such as that the tenure during good behaviour ceased on the death of the reigning King;[99] this was altered by an Act of Parliament in 1760. Moreover, throughout the 18th century it was not uncommon for judges to serve as members of the cabinet, i.e. in executive positions.[100] This by most modern standards of the independence of the judiciary amounts to an unacceptable entanglement and is not in accord with the most basic understanding of judicial independence.[101]

---

96 "That after the said Limitation shall take Effect as aforesaid Judges Commissions be made Quam diu se bene Gesserint and their Salaries ascertained and established but upon the Address of both Houses of Parliament it may be lawful to remove them." An Act for the further Limitation of the Crown and better securing the Rights and Liberties of the Subject (1700 & 1701) Statutes of the Realm: Volume 7: 1695-1701 (1820), 636-638, Chapter II. Rot. Parl. 12 & 13 Gul. III. p. 1. n. 2. According to T. Plucknett, this permanently established "the complete independence of the bench", Plucknett, *A Concise History of the Common Law*, 61.

97 Shetreet, *Judges on Trial – A Study of the Appointment and Accountability of the English Judiciary*, 12.

98 For references see ibid, 13-15.

99 Ibid, 10-11.

100 One example is the complex role of the Lord Chancellor, who is a member of the Cabinet and, by law, is responsible for the efficient functioning and independence of the courts. Until the enactment of the Constitutional Reform Act of 2005, he was also the presiding officer of the House of Lords and the head of the judiciary in England and Wales. See Woodhouse, Diana, 'Judges and the Lord Chancellor in the Changing United Kingdom Constitution: Independence and Accountability' (2005) 16 Public Law Review 3; Smith, Roger, 'Constitutional Reform, the Lord Chancellor, and Human Rights: The Battle of Form and Substance' (2005) 32 Journal of Law and Society 1.

101 Cf. e.g. Standards 35-39 International Bar Association, *Minimum Standards of Judicial Independence*; Arts. 2.26-2.31 First World Conference on the Independence of Justice, *Universal Declaration on the Independence of Justice*.

The above cursory view of the evolution of the judiciary in England suggests that the role and functioning of courts, as we perceive them today, originated in demands voiced by enlightened individuals and, more importantly, in the struggle between the executive and the legislative arms of government. It may thus be assumed that the independence of judges becomes a relevant feature when the executive and the legislative branches, to use a terminology that already anticipates the following reasoning with regard to the idea of separation of powers, engage in a struggle for power, and in doing so seek to exploit the judiciary for their own political purposes. It is furthermore noticeable that the concretization of judicial independence begins when it is recognized that the judiciary has real power, when influence over judges and courts translates into a greater likelihood of reaching political goals. In other words, it is in the shadow of the struggle for power that judicial independence is born.[102] These fundamental reflections form the vantage point for the theoretical grounding of today's conception of judicial independence, and thus possibly also for a theoretical basis for the concept's application *vis-à-vis* the international judiciary. The following chapter will analyse these questions in more detail.

3. Separation of Powers and Independence of the Judiciary

a) Historical and Philosophical Context

Judicial independence is often understood to be a corollary of the division of powers, and as such considered to share the rationale underlying that principle.[103] To understand why that is so it is advisable to refer to the his-

---

102 Denham, Susan, 'The Diamond in a Democracy: An Iindependent, Accountable Judiciary – Keynote Address to: The Annual Conference of the Australian Institute of Judicial Administration, Darwin, Northern Territory, Australia, 14-16 July 2000' available at <http://www.aija.org.au/2000ac/Papers/Denham.pdf> (last visited: 21 March 2014), 9.

103 See, e.g., Eichenberger, *Die richterliche Unabhängigkeit als staatsrechtliches Problem*, 64; cf. Explanatory Memorandum of the Recommendation No. R(94)12 of the CoM: "The independence of judges is first and foremost linked to the maintenance of the separation of powers", Committee of Ministers of the CoE, *Recommendation No. R (94) 12 of the Committee of Ministers to Member States on Independence, Efficiency and Role of Judges* (adopted 13 October 1994) available at

torical context, especially the history of the development of ideas. The notion of separation of powers has its modern roots in the writings of the French social commentator and enlightened political thinker Charles de Secondat, Baron de Montesquieu (1689-1755). Based on what he had learned during his study of political systems throughout Europe, but in particular that of the constitutional monarchy developing in the early 18th century in the Kingdom of Great Britain, he described the division of the legislative, executive and judicial powers in his treatise on *The Spirit of the Laws* (*De l'Esprit des Lois*) as a cornerstone of political liberty:[104] "[t]here is no liberty, if the judiciary power be not separated from the legislative and the executive."[105] By making this division between the three branches of government, Montesquieu expanded the theory of John Locke, who in his *Second Treatise on Government* made the distinction between the legislative, executive and federative powers.[106] According to Montesquieu, the idea of a unity of political power ought to be rejected, as every human being tends to abuse the power he has been vested with and thus is inclined to infringe the individual liberty of others.[107] Therefore, the proposition is that all political power ought not only

---

<https://wcd.coe.int/ViewDoc.jsp?id=524871&Site=CM> (last visited: 21 March 2014), para. 15.

104 The notion of "political liberty", as used by Montesquieu, can today best be understood as personal security, i.e. living under laws that protect us from harm while at the same time granting us the freedom to do what we wish, and that provide a sense of confidence that if we obey those laws, the governmental powers will not be directed against us. According to Montesquieu, political liberty is that "tranquillity of spirit which comes from the opinion each has of his security, and in order for him to have this liberty the government must be such that one citizen cannot fear another citizen": Montesquieu, Charles de Secondat, *The Spirit of the Laws* (Cambridge University Press Cambridge 1989), Book 11 Chapter 6, 157 and Book 11 Chapter 3, 155.

105 "Nor is there liberty if the power of judging is not separate from legislative power and from executive power. If it were joined to legislative power, the power over the life and liberty of the citizens would be arbitrary, for the judge would be the legislator. If it were joined to executive power, the judge could have the force of an oppressor." Ibid, Book 11 Chapter 6, 157. Yet Montesquieu himself never uses either the term *judicial independence*, or *separation of powers*. Cf. also Hamilton, Alexander, *The Federalist Papers* (Independent Journal 1788), 270.

106 Locke, John, *The Second Treatise of Government* (Barnes & Noble Publishing New York 2004), paras. 143-148. J. Locke did not entirely omit the judiciary from his political construct, but instead considered the judicial power to be comprehended within the (his) executive power.

107 Montesquieu, *The Spirit of the Laws*, Book 11 Chapter 4, 155.

to be divided between independent branches of government but the different branches must also control each other so as to prevent abuse that otherwise might result from total independence. In other words, a balance must be struck between independence and interdependence (checks and balances). It is interesting to note that in Montesquieu's opinion independence is a desirable attribute not only of the judiciary but indeed of all three branches of government. This suggests that Montesquieu's understanding of independence is a broad one and different from that utilized in this thesis. However, Montesquieu exempts the judiciary from the need to interdepend with the other branches as, in his view, compared to the legislative and executive branches the judiciary "is in some measure next to nothing."[108] According to Montesquieu, judges "are no more than the mouth of the law, mere passive beings, incapable of moderating either its force or rigour",[109] simply the *pouvoir nul*. The reason Montesquieu makes this rather harsh assessment is that the judicial power for him ought to be attached "neither to a certain state nor to a certain profession", but should instead be exercised by persons drawn from the body of the people, thereby making the power of judging invisible and null.[110] In other words, it is an ideal composition of the judiciary that Montesquieu has in mind, and one based on particular concepts of power and the role and function of the judiciary. The idea most important for this thesis that may be derived from this is the notion that the judge produces a sentence through application of the exact letter of the law, without expressing a personal will. Since no proper will is expressed, judges are unable to misuse their position, which in consequence makes control of the judiciary superfluous.[111] This conception of the judiciary, as merely the mouth that speaks the words of the law, must be appraised as a syllogism inapplicable in practice.[112]

---

108 Ibid, Book 11 Chapter 6.

109 Id. Cf. ibid, Book 6 Chapter 3, where Montesquieu observes that in various political systems the judge is but the *bouche de la loi*.

110 See Montesquieu, *The Spirit of the Laws*, Book 11 Chapter 6, 158.

111 Indeed, building further on this ideal representation, the only way the legislative and executive branches are to influence the judiciary is by enacting legislation. See further, Heuschling, 'Why Should Judges Be Independent?', 248-249.

112 Immanuel Kant described this syllogism accurately in § 45 of his treatise *Science of Right*: "Ein jeder Staat enthält drey Gewalten in sich, d.i. den allgemein vereinigten Willen in dreyfacher Person (trias politica): die Herrschaftsgewalt (Souveränität), in der des Gesetzgebers, die vollziehende Gewalt, in der des Regierers (zu Folge dem Gesetz) und die rechtsprechende Gewalt, (als Zuerkennung des Seinen eines jeden nach dem Gesetz) in der Person des Richters (potestas legislatoria, rectoria et iudiciaria) gleich den drey Sätzen in einem praktischen Vernunftschluss:

Nevertheless, the theoretical construct proposed by Montesquieu as such underlines two essential hypotheses: firstly, that the judiciary, unlike the other two branches of government, should be accorded a higher degree of independence, and that this status is generally desirable in a society that follows the rule of law. In particular it should not be exposed to political and extra-legal pressure. Secondly, a logical consequence of Montesquieu's model is that if the judiciary does not merely read and apply the clear provisions of the (statute) law, i.e. if it does have some real power, then its independence must be flanked by some degree of interdependence in order to prevent an abuse of isolated independence.[113] In other words, if independence is combined with the exercise of real power, it ought to have a counterweight in interdependence to prevent it from developing into a potential abuse of power in itself.

Energized by the events of the French Revolution, the idea of the separation of powers became an important model for governance in democratic States, and the detachment of the judiciary from the other branches and the accentuation of the judiciary have remained an essential part of it. Separating the judiciary from the legislator and the executive enables this branch to exercise adjudication; separation means the absence of entanglement with and the prohibition of both the executive and legislative on resuming adjudicative functions.[114] At the same time, and to come back to a point that was made earlier in a different context,[115] separation of powers thus defined rarely entails absolute separation of the different branches. The doctrine is first and foremost to be seen as a concept that seeks to establish a balance

---

dem Obersatz, der das Gesetz jenes Willens, dem Untersatz, der das Gebot des Verfahrens nach dem Gesetz, d.i. das Princip der Subsumtion unter denselben, und dem Schlußsatz, der den Rechtsspruch (die Sentenz) enthält, was im vorkommenden Falle Rechtens ist." Kant, Immanuel, *Metaphysische Anfangsgründe der Rechtslehre* (Friedrich Nicolovius Königsberg 1797), 165.

113 Cf. *supra* at fn. 107.

114 Cf. *Board of Com'rs of White County v Gwin* 36 N.E. 237 (1894): "What is meant by the 'independence of the judicial department' is that it may exercise its functions of expounding and enforcing law in the administration of justice, and that no part of its functions can be exercised, either directly or indirectly, by either the legislative or the executive; indeed, that those in authority in the other departments cannot even so much as cross the line dividing the domain of the judicial and other departments to make a suggestion as to how the judicial department shall perform its functions".

115 See *supra* at fn. 66.

between the forces involved so as to enable each one of them to fulfil the task with which it is entrusted.

b) The International Judiciary and the Trisection of Powers

Applying the notion of separation of powers to the international sphere in an attempt to find a rational basis for analysing the functioning of judicial independence in the international judiciary is not without its problems. As the Appeals Chamber of the ICTY famously held in its decision on the defence motion for interlocutory appeal on jurisdiction in *Prosecutor v. Duško Tadić*, "[i]t is clear that the legislative, executive and judicial division of powers which is largely followed in most municipal systems does not apply to the international setting".[116] The Appeals Chamber reached this conclusion while answering the question whether the requirement that a court be "established by law", when applied to the international level, implies that the administration of justice is not a matter of executive discretion, but is regulated by laws made by the legislature.[117] Whereas the Court's conclusion is worth supporting, it does not, however, negate that even on the international level there are different organs that perform functions which can be classified as executive, legislative and judicative. The obstacle is, however, that, in particular with regard to the UN, which was the main subject of investigation for the Appeals Chamber in the above-mentioned decision, "the divisions between judicial, executive and legislative functions are *not clear cut*" (emphasis added). The ambiguity of the trisection of powers in international law

---

116 *Prosecutor v. Duško Tadić, Appeals Chamber, Decision on the defence motion for interlocutory appeal on jurisdiction*, para. 43. A similar statement was made by the ICJ when it found in the *Nicaragua* case that the argument of the US, that the UNSC held the exclusive power on the determination of the legitimacy of armed actions allegedly taken in self-defence was "an attempt to transfer municipal-law concepts of separation of powers to the international plane, whereas these concepts are not applicable to the relations among international institutions for the settlement of disputes." *Military and Paramilitary Activities in and against Nicaragua (Nicaragua v. United States of America) (Jurisdiction and Admissibility) (Judgment)* ICJ Rep. 392 (1984), para. 92. See also Chesterman, Simon, 'Rule of Law', in: Wolfrum, Rüdiger (ed) *The Max Planck Encyclopedia of Public International Law* (Oxford University Press Online Edition 2012), para. 44.

117 This is the common interpretation given to the requirement, according to e.g. *Zand v. Austria* (ECommHR) Application No. 7360/76 (12 October 1978), 80; *Piersack v. Belgium* (ECtHR) Application No. 8692/79 (1 October 1982), 12.

is but a sign of the infancy and the primitive nature of international law as a legal system[118] and mélange of different interests coming together in the international legal order. Therefore, the rationale of the need to separate institutions vested with powers from each other so as to avoid abuse of these powers deserves to be thought through in analogy.

A principal conclusion from this, which also leans on the findings of the previous sub-chapter on the historical and philosophical context, is that international courts, if vested with powers,[119] are to be separated from any other subject similarly vested with (different) powers to prevent these powers being bundled. This on its part poses the question whether international courts are exercising power in the first place. The anticipated objection, raised in Montesquieu's spirit, that the international judiciary is but the *bouche de la loi*[120] cannot be claimed to mirror today's conditions on the international level. Although international courts for long either did not appear on the international stage at all or were equipped with very limited powers, today they can by no standards be labelled "weak department[s] of power".[121] As was indicated earlier, from an empirical viewpoint, the number of international courts has increased considerably in recent decades alone.[122] These institutions are often equipped with compulsory jurisdiction within a particular treaty regime in the sense that they can be invoked unilaterally.[123] Already existing international courts have been strengthened through in-

118 Cf. Chesterman, 'Rule of Law', para. 40.

119 See *infra* Chapter C.III, on the question why international courts ought to be independent.

120 It shall not be analysed further in this context to what extent international law can at all be claimed to be law, as presupposed by the maxim.

121 See Hamilton, *The Federalist Papers*, Federalist No. 78: "It proves incontestably, that the judiciary is beyond comparison the weakest of the three departments of power".

122 R. Alford even characterizes the time between 1980 and 2000 as an "explosion of new international courts and tribunals." Alford, Roger P., 'The Proliferation of International Courts and Tribunals: International Adjudication in Ascendance', in: Hargrove, John Lawrence (ed) *On violence, money, power and culture: reviewing the internationalist legacy, March 24-27, 1999 Washington, D.C.: Proceedings of the Annual Meeting / American Society of International Law* (American Society of International Law Washington D.C. 2000), 160.

123 On this topic see Romano, Cesare P. R., 'The Shift from the Consensual to the Compulsory Paradigm in International Adjudication: Elements for a Theory of Consent' (2007) 39 New York University Journal of International Law & Politics 4.

creased membership of their constitutive instruments (e.g. the European Court of Justice (ECJ), European Court of Human Rights (ECtHR)) or by way of reforms of these instruments (e.g. the ECtHR).[124] The decisions issued by international courts can help to solve multi billion euro trade disputes, protect fundamental human rights of individuals against their own governments, bring to justice alleged war criminals or enforce the laws of the sea. Furthermore, the increased usage of international courts[125] and the increased relevance for national courts of issues raised by decisions of international courts[126] have further strengthened the *real* influence exercised by the international judiciary. A consequence of this acknowledgment that international courts not only are *vested* with power, like their municipal counterparts, but that they indeed exercise *real power*, suggests, if we are to continue to apply Montesquieu's rationale, that not only ought international courts to be independent, but that this independence be complemented by interdependence with the other subjects that are vested with and exercise powers in this same legal order. In other words, independence in the international legal order is a necessity but ought not to be perceived as total independence.

---

124 See, e.g., on the reform of the ECtHR through Protocol No. 11 to the Convention for the Protection of Human Rights and Fundamental Freedoms Restructuring the Control Machinery Established Thereby (adopted 11 May 1994, entered into force 1 November 1998) 2061 UNTS 12. See further *infra* Chapter H.

125 Sands, Philippe J., 'Enhancing Participation in International Litigation' (1998) 24 Commonwealth Law Bulletin 1, 548-550.

126 Mackenzie, et al. (eds), *The Manual on International Courts and Tribunals*, x. See also on the same issue Jennings, Robert Y., 'The Proliferation of Adjudicatory Bodies: Dangers and Possible Answers', in: Boisson de Chazournes, Laurence (ed) *ASIL Bulletin No. 9: Implications of the Proliferation of International Adjuidatory Bodies for Dispute Resolution: Proceedings of a Forum Co-Sponsored by the American Society of International Law and the Graduate Institute of International Studies, Geneva, Switzerland, May 13, 1995* (American Society of International Law Washington 1995), 2, who speaks of a "quiet revolution in international law" that has taken place over the decades before the mid-1990s, characterized by the breaking down of borders between municipal law and international law.

4. The Rule of Law and the Independence of the International Judiciary

The interweaving of the principle of the rule of law (often also referred to using the German term *Rechtsstaat*, or the French notion of *État de Droit*)[127] with the principle of judicial independence is regularly highlighted by different voices raised in international law discourse, and especially in scholarly literature.[128] The reason for this rather reflexive derivation is, however, blurred by the difficulties inherent in the definition of the notion of the rule of law and its transmission onto the international legal order. In the context of domestic law it is, in a formal sense, usually understood as prescribing that no one is above the law, i.e. that the law applies to all people equally.[129] This necessarily entails, in its consequence, that all branches of government must be constrained by law.[130] Furthermore, if all government actions are governed by the law, then no power of the State is exercised arbitrarily,[131]

127 Although e.g. the term *Rechtsstaat* is wider than the rule of law principle. See, e.g., Chesterman, 'Rule of Law', paras. 7-8.

128 "Unter allen Institutionen unseres Rechtslebens feiert die Idee des Rechtsstaates ihren höchsten Triumph in der Unabhängigkeit der richterlichen Entscheidung." Grünhut, Max, 'Die unabhängigkeit der richterlichen Entscheidung' (1930) 1930 Monatszeitschrift für Kriminalpsychologie und Strafrechtsreform 3, 1. According to the Rule of Law Resolution of the International Bar Association, "[a]n independent, impartial judiciary … [is a] fundamental principle of the Rule of Law." International Bar Association, *Rule of Law Resolution* (September 2005) available at <http://www.ibanet.org/> (last visited: 21 March 2014).

129 Garner, Bryan A. (ed) *Black's Law Dictionary* (Thomson Reuters St. Paul 9th edn. 2009), 1448. The notion of the rule of law is sometimes ascribed to early writers such as Aristotle ("… for this is law, for order is law; and it is more proper that *law should govern* than any one of the citizens" (emphasis added) Aristotle, *Politics* (Dover Publications Inc. Ontario 2000), Book III, Chapter XVI). Its popularization can substantially be attributed to A. V. Dicey, who wrote extensively on the notion (in particular, see Part II in Dicey, Albert Venn, *Introduction to the Study of the Law of the Constitution* (Macmillan 1885)).

130 In the Anglo-American understanding of the concept the vantage point is, again, the struggle to subject the King to the law which began in the 17th century. The continental European, and in particular German, viewpoint is more closely linked to a demand for a constitution as the basis for the exercise of governmental powers: "Rechtsstaatlichkeit bedeutet, daß die Ausübung staatlicher Macht nur auf der Grundlage der Verfassung und von formell und materiell verfassungsmäßig erlassenen Gesetzen mit dem Ziel der Gewährleistung von Menschenwürde, Freiheit, Gerechtigkeit und Rechtssicherheit zulässig ist." (Stern, Klaus, *Das Staatsrecht der Bundesrepublik Deutschland, Band 1* (C.H. Beck München 2nd edn. 1984), 781.)

131 Chesterman, 'Rule of Law', para. 2.

which typically is linked to claims that laws be prospective, accessible and clear.[132] In a further consequence, this presupposes that an independent institution, such as a judiciary, applies the law to specific cases, and that this judiciary is not aligned with the other governmental organs which equally exercise powers.[133]

Primarily, and ideally, the rule of law and judicial independence intersect when serving combined to ensure that justice is being done. If possible, judges (the *neutral third*) should not have any interest in the cases before them and ought to be free from any bias toward any of the parties to a conflict. Neither the social or political standing of the disputants, nor potential personal benefits of the judge himself should guide the decision-making, but merely the commitment toward the applicable law. In a further step, judicial independence takes on a special significance in achieving the rule of law when the government itself is one of the parties to a dispute. Only in the absence of any bias in favour of the government can the rule of law be secured. It is thus essential to prevent the government's direct or indirect control over the judiciary, so as to shield the latter against threats and manipulations.[134]

---

132 Cf. the very early codification of restraints for the arbitrary power of the various arms of government in the Magna Carta of 1215: "No freeman shall be captured or imprisoned or disseised or outlawed or exiled or in any way destroyed, nor will we go against him or send against him, except by the lawful judgment of his peers or by the law of the land." Magna Carta, para. 39; reprinted in Holt, James Clark, *Magna Carta* (Cambridge University Press Cambridge 2nd edn. 1992), 448-473.

133 It should thus not come as a surprise that the independence of the judiciary is regularly mentioned when the attempt is made to define the rule of law. For example, the Declaration of Delhi, which was the final document of the group of 185 judges, lawyers and academics, assembled in New Delhi in January 1959 under the aegis of the International Commission of Jurists, dealt with the concept of rule of law and reaffirmed "that independent judiciary and legal profession are essential to the maintenance of the Rule of Law and to the proper administration of justice and the administration of justice throughout the world". International Commission of Jurists, *Executive action and the rule of law: a report on the proceedings of the International Congress of Jurists, Rio de Janeiro, Brazil, December 11-15, 1962* (International Commission of Jurists Geneva 1962), 4.

134 "Da nun im perfekten Rechtsstaat jedes nicht rechtsprechende Organ in die Rolle der Prozeßpartei greaten kann und da außerdem alle öffentlichen Gewalten und Organe – außer der richterlichen – miteinander verflochten sind, so müssen die Rechtsprechungsorgane von allen übrigen Staatsorganen unabhängig sein, damit die Neutralität der rechtsprechenden Staatsgewalt gewährleistet wird." Bettermann, Karl August, et al. (eds), *Rechtspflege und Grundrechtsschutz – Die Grundrechte,*

This formal understanding of the rule of law is of very limited assistance in our quest to comprehend the notion's role in justifying the application of judicial independence and understanding its concretization in the international sphere. The apparent problem is the structural difference between international and domestic law, rendering the former unsuitable to be seen through the lens of a municipal understanding of the rule of law. Hence, direct application of the rule of law to the international sphere is not being proposed here. Instead, the argument is advanced that it ought, like the municipal discourse, to serve as a catalyst: it helps to understand the necessity of judicial independence while it remains unabsorbed, its application in itself therefore not acknowledged.[135] Accordingly, I submit that a functionalist understanding of the rule of law, namely as a tool to protect core values of the international legal order such as human rights, the promotion of development and the protection of peace, provides us with a consistent and coherent framework that allows valuable conclusions to be drawn regarding the role of judicial independence.

To use a trisection suggested by S. Chesterman, the rule of law thus defined demands (I) non-arbitrariness in the exercise of power, (II) supremacy of the law, and (III) equality before the law. Moving towards non-arbitrariness in the exercise of power materializes, for example, in the efforts to protect human rights through the increased use of international institutions[136] which follow processes and standards acknowledged by the world community as a whole.[137] Whereas non-arbitrariness mandates on the one hand a further codification of international law to provide a framework for systematic interaction, it can only be achieved if, on the other hand, institutions are available that are able to enforce the law thus created in an unbiased manner. Supremacy of the law, although international law is not always a hierarchical structure where questions arise between the subjects and sovereign, demands an (increased) usage of *independent* arbiters to confirm that it is actually the law that governs and not the interests of those who make the law. The inter-

---

Handbuch der Theorie und Praxis der Grundrechte (Duncker & Humblot Berlin 1959), 528.

135 'Oxford English Dictionary' available at <http://www.oed.com/> (last visited: 21 March 2014), "catalyst".

136 See on this Seibert-Fohr, Anja, *Prosecuting Serious Human Rights Violations* (Oxford University Press Oxford 2009).

137 See generally Watts QC, Sir Arthur, 'Codification and Progressive Development of International Law', in: Wolfrum, Rüdiger (ed) *The Max Planck Encyclopedia of Public International Law* (Oxford University Press Online Edition 2012).

national judiciary here takes on a function as a guarantor for the intended application of the law, a function that would be seriously undermined if the judiciary itself were subject to undue influence. Equality in international law, understood at least as sovereign equality between States,[138] is little more than a "myth",[139] and the adherence to this principle should not be overemphasized. However, the functionalist understanding of why the rule of law is applied in the international sphere, namely to promote certain common values, demands "more general and consistent application of international law to States and other entities."[140] It is submitted that this can best be achieved, or secured, through the use of international courts that are independent of any influence from primarily States but also other (ascending) subjects of international law.

5. Judicial Independence: Meaning and Elements

a) The Rejection of the Notion's Absoluteness

The above abstract theoretical considerations have at times already touched upon practical implications, namely the translation of the notion of judicial independence into a workable concept. This concretization will be intensified and specified in what follows. As already indicated, judicial independence cannot be understood as *absolute* independence, in the sense of the absence of every form of interaction between the judiciary and other actors.[141] In Western-style democracies the judiciary can, in the broadest sense, be "defined as the organ of government not forming part of the executive and legislature, which is not subject to personal, substantive and collective controls, and which performs the primary function of adjudication."[142] In other words, how the judiciary is defined, how it is structured and functions is fundamentally shaped by its main function, adjudication, i.e. peaceful settlement of disputes by way of judgments based on the relevant facts and the applicable law. It is this function and its specification that judicial independence must serve and which ultimately limit the requirements posed by it.

---

138 Cf. Kokott, 'States, Sovereign Equality'.
139 Chesterman, 'Rule of Law', para. 40.
140 Ibid, para. 45.
141 Cf. *supra* Chapter B.III(2).
142 Shetreet (ed) *Judicial Independence the Contemporary Debate*, 597-598.

On an institutional level,[143] judgments usually go hand in hand with an expectation of being backed by the executive arm of government, if they are not already voluntarily complied with by the parties to the relevant dispute. Consequently, the judiciary, by necessity, relies on other branches in order to fulfil its own vocation. In international law, with its horizontal organization of sovereign and quasi-sovereign entities and with its lack of a legislature and executive or governing entity,[144] this relationship is complicated since courts may have to rely on different entities, often States, for the enforcement of their judgments. Moreover, courts often rely on branches of public authority for their establishment and administration. Since courts have no (substantial) income of their own they must, for example, rely on outside financing. Furthermore, on the individual level, every judge is a personality subject to various influences, external and internal. Many of these influences could be potentially dangerous in the sense that they may distort the objective result of adjudication solely based on the applicable law and the facts of a given case (e.g. threats, manipulation, prejudices, and bigotry). Others are not only harmless but may even be desired stimuli for adjudication (e.g. critical writings of legal scholars, wisdom, and experience). Judicial independence requires not that one of the two extremes be followed, but instead that a balance be struck between them.[145]

The above considerations appeal to a realistic approach and should influence our fundamental understanding of the principle of judicial independence to the effect that it is not to be understood as an absolute notion. Judicial independence, at least when seen as a practical concept and not merely as a theoretical, even utopian optimal construction of ideas, is not an invariable concept because it is linked to organs that are part of a political and social reality where everything is connected and where nothing is entirely without bias. That said it should nevertheless not lead us to discard idealism and prevent the development of bold proposals of what judicial independence could and should entail. Unattainability due to the grandeur of an ideal does

143 On the distinction between *institutional* and *individual* independence see *infra* Chapter B.IV(5)(c).

144 Shaw, Malcolm N., *International Law* (Cambridge University Press Cambridge 6th edn. 2009), 3.

145 See also S. Burbank who also rejects what he calls "complete decisional independence", namely "freedom to decide a case as the court sees fit without any constraint, exogenous or endogenous, actual or prospective." Burbank, 'What do we Mean by "Judicial Independence"?', 326.

not negate its attracting effect as an ennobling aspiration, especially since forces are in play which constantly attempt to work against the independence of the judiciary. If the standard were not kept high, the courtroom would run the risk of being degraded to little more than another arena for the display of power; the cluttered world of politics would threaten to give the upper hand to political prejudices and pressures. Therefore, a study of the principle of judicial independence must be about focusing on the negative margins – on menaces to independence which threaten to hamper the fulfilment of the judiciary's function. Judicial independence is at risk only when a particular influence undermines the judge's/court's ability to adjudicate.[146] Bearing this in mind, in what follows a more practical perspective will be adopted to identify a number of elements the awareness of which will better facilitate the later assessment of how judicial independence can be safeguarded at various international courts.

b) Modes of Exercising Influence

Defining judicial independence as the freedom of the judiciary to exercise judicial powers without interference or influence implies that the notion and principle are directed against dependencies.[147] To describe these dependencies in all their details, or even to provide a complete taxonomy, is not the aim of this thesis. Such an undertaking would, for the reason of the diversity of the sources of such dependencies, be a herculean task. Nevertheless, if the attempt is made to show how and by what means judicial independence is safeguarded in the international judiciary it becomes essential to understand how dependencies may unfold and may be exercised. Therefore, in what follows some characteristics which help to explain and fathom the phenomenon of the establishment of dependencies, which are less relevant for the conceptual definition but more so for the practical compilation of the notion, will be highlighted.

(I) Influence can be exerted with the aim of regulating the entire spectrum of decisions taken by a court or, more circumspectly, to give directions in a specific case regarding a particular action undertaken by a court.

146 K. Eichenberger speaks of "wertwidrige Faktoren" (value incompatible factors), where the values are defined by the aim of the judicial function. Eichenberger, *Die richterliche Unabhängigkeit als staatsrechtliches Problem*, 27.

147 Ibid, 36.

Whereas the former is most obvious in a legal and political system where the judiciary's general dependence does not stand out as unlawful or at least precarious, the latter may occur even in constitutional cultures which follow the rule of law but which nevertheless *ad hoc* allow, passively or actively, for the exertion of such influence. Its scope can similarly be wide so as to affect the court as an institution, i.e. as a whole, or limited to an individual judge.[148]

(II) Dependencies can have their basis either in a positive action by the entity trying to impose pressure, such as a statement demanding certain action/inaction of the judiciary, or an omission to act, e.g. not to disburse necessary funding. Although a positive act more easily reveals the aim for which it was created, the absence of an act where such would have meant a (necessary) manifestation of the judiciary's independence can be equally, if not more, effective in unduly influencing judicial decision-making.

(III) Pressure may be exerted temporarily (e.g. disciplinary measures) or for a longer period of time (e.g. the shaping of modalities regarding supervision of the activities of a court and/or the judges).

(IV) Whereas some exertion of influence is easily recognizable as such (e.g. directives or orders from a different branch of government), in other situations the intent to limit the judiciary's autonomy may appear less obvious. Examples of the latter are regulations concerning the permitted outside activities of judges, the determination and alteration of salaries, and procedures for the assignment of cases. Although measures of this type do not necessarily limit a court's or a judge's scope of action, they may very well have this effect in reality. Similarly, the exertion of influence may appear in the form of actual dependencies or mere threats of exertion of influence.

(V) Some actions that constitute a dependency for the judiciary are based on applicable law, whereas others do not have the coverage of any legal framework. The example mentioned above of withholding financial assets required for the exercise of the activities of the judiciary may be interpreted as a way of substantially limiting the freedom of action of the courts for a particular purpose, although the act itself does form part of the lawful and obligatory process of balancing a

---

148 On the distinction between *institutional* and *individual* independence see *infra* Chapter B.IV(5)(c).

(state) budget. In contrast, threats of sanctions or even violence to a judge and/or his family in order to prompt him to take a particular action clearly violate the law.

(VI) In close relation to the aforementioned, dependencies may manifest their effect in observable practices (e.g. procedures for the nomination and selection of judges) or rather relate to the internal aptness of a judge (e.g. distance from parties, exclusion of bias, conflicts of interest).

Perhaps the most obvious conclusion that can be drawn from these different aspects of exerting influence on the judiciary, which by no means constitute an exhaustive list of indicators, is that judicial independence may be threatened not just by activities that apparently aim to distort the autonomous and objective functioning of the courts. Instead, dependencies which have such a negative effect on the judiciary as to render the judiciary dependent may take a variety of different and often inconspicuous shapes and forms.

c) Institutional v. Individual Independence

In the analysis so far, the notion of judicial independence has presented itself as most comprehensible if approached dynamically in terms of relationships and interdependencies. In the same way as the notion of judicial independence does not refer to a single kind of dependency, as shown above, the relationships which the notion expresses are equally multifaceted. To approach this topic systematically, a first distinction may be made by directing attention either at the source of dependencies,[149] or at the target of the influence or control. In the latter case, a further distinction may be made between the independence of the individual judge (for the purposes of the present study called *personal* or *individual independence*) and that of the collective of the judges of a particular court (here called either *collective* or *institutional independence*).[150] A similar distinction is made by C. Larkins who provides and uses the following definition of judicial independence:

---

149 The sources of intervention will be analysed in greater detail below: see *infra* Chapter B.IV(5)(d).

150 See, e.g., Agmon-Gonnen, 'Judicial Independence: The Threat from Within', 122; Larkins, 'Judicial Independence and Democratization. A Theoretical and Conceptual Analysis', 608-611; Akkas, Sarkar Ali, *Judicial Independence and Accountability: A Comparative Study of Contemporary Bangladesh Experience* (University of

> "Judicial independence refers to the existence of judges who are not manipulated for political gain, who are impartial toward the parties of a dispute, and who form a judicial branch which has the power as an institution to regulate the legality of government behaviour, enact 'neutral' justice, and determine significant constitutional and legal values."[151]

The organizational detachment of the executive and legislative branches of government from the judiciary which, due to the relationship to the principle of separation of powers described above is often brought to the forefront, primarily draws attention to the perceived independence of the courts as institutions. The same applies to e.g. practically relevant concerns such as how a court is financed, who is competent to adopt rules of procedure or rules of evidence of a court, how the adjudicative function is detached from e.g. executive functions, the competences relating to the employment and dismissal of personnel such as Registrars and Registry staff, or the internal structure of the court (in particular the competence to assign cases). Whereas these questions reveal a relevance pertaining to the independence of the institution, they are not directly linked to the individual judge, who nonetheless may or may not still be able to exercise his adjudicatory function independently.

Instead, judges' independence can be challenged by assaults on aspects of their decision-making process and their personal status (working and living conditions) such as instructions pertaining to particular cases, potential disciplinary measures, their tenure, the regulation of possible outside activities, and personal convictions, beliefs and integrity. Building on this, as an example, German law adheres to the further division of individual independence between the judge's *substantive independence*, declaring that in the exercise of his judicial functions he is bound only by the law, and *personal independ-*

Wollongong Thesis Collections Online 2002), 14-15; Russell, 'Toward a General Theory of Judicial Independence', 11; Burbank, Stephen B., 'The Architecture of Judicial Independence' (1999) 72 Southern California Law Review 2, 317; Ferejohn, John, 'Independent Judges, Dependent Judiciary: Explaining Judicial Independence' (1999) 72 Southern California Law Review 2, 355; Masterman, Roger, *The Separation of Powers in the Contemporary Constitution: Judicial Competence and Independence in the United Kingdom* (Cambridge University Press Cambridge 2011), 208-212.

151 Larkins, 'Judicial Independence and Democratization. A Theoretical and Conceptual Analysis', 611. The differentiation between "an independent and impartial judicial branch, [and] independent and impartial judges" is also used as a tool with which to examine judicial independence systematically by M. Agmon-Gonnen, see Agmon-Gonnen, 'Judicial Independence: The Threat from Within', 120.

ence, meaning that his position must be protected from any interference.[152] In this thesis, no such further terminological division of individual independence will be made.

What is said about the independence of the individual judge cannot be interpreted as meaning that the independence serves the individual judge, in the sense that it is an end in itself, a class privilege, or protection of the personal display of the judge. Instead personal independence, just like the institutional one, has to be understood as an official safeguard which seeks to ensure a factually and legally accurate judgment, submitted in the exercise of the judiciary's duty towards the parties to a conflict.[153] This fundamental truth also applies to the international judiciary. Moreover, and from a more theoretical perspective, individual independence is considered a significant element of the rule of law doctrine, and thus serves to protect the individual citizen who seeks justice before the courts.[154]

d) The Source of Intervention – (In-)Dependence from Whom?

The second facet of the relational term of judicial independence is the question for the potential intervenor, the entity that exerts the influence and which thus is the focus of the defensive side of the notion of judicial independence.[155] The identity of the intervenor is another parameter that enables one better to identify to what extent judicial independence is (or is not) protected in the various instruments that govern the activities of a court. The following entities that may exert influence on the international judge and/or judiciary and thus trigger a violation of the notion of judicial independence, will be portrayed:[156] (I) the parties to a conflict; (II) States and other political actors;

152 Seibert-Fohr, 'Constitutional Guarantees of Judicial Independence in Germany', 270-275; Haberland, Stephan, 'Problemfelder für die richterliche Unabhängigkeit' (2002) 80 Deutsche Richterzeitung 8.

153 See, e.g., Haberland, 'Problemfelder für die richterliche Unabhängigkeit', 301.

154 Creifelds, Carl & Weber, Klaus, *Rechtswörterbuch* (Beck München 19th edn. 2007), 1186.

155 Eichenberger, *Die richterliche Unabhängigkeit als staatsrechtliches Problem*, 31-32; Pasquino, 'Prolegomena to a Theory of Judicial Power: The Concept of Judicial Independence in Theory and History', 14.

156 On this categorization using the source of intervention see Bettermann, et al. (eds), *Rechtspflege und Grundrechtsschutz – Die Grundrechte, Handbuch der Theorie*

(III) other courts and judges; (IV) the general public; and (V) the persona of the individual judge himself. Initially, however, judicial independence will be defined in relation to the term of judicial impartiality, which is not bound to a particular intervenor but rather functions as a generic term for all kinds of bias resulting from a close connection to a particular subject.

(1) The Ideal Judge is Impartial

If judicial independence is defined as the freedom of the judiciary to exercise judicial functions without extra-legal or political interference or influence, as has been done so far, the judiciary is essentially understood as a neutral third element[157] that makes decisions only on the basis of facts and their subsumption under the law. At the core of the concept of judicial independence is thus also the idea that judges make their decisions without any preferences or discrimination towards any of the parties: the idea that decisions are made impartially.[158] The relationship between this impartiality and the notion of judicial independence is in need of some clarification, as these terms are often used side by side, occasionally with little substantive differentiation and sometimes, unfortunately, interchangeably.

Some scholars perceive independence as a precondition for impartiality;[159] others identify impartiality as being part of the broader notion of independ-

---

und Praxis der Grundrechte, 523 et seq.; Eichenberger, *Die richterliche Unabhängigkeit als staatsrechtliches Problem*, 43-53.

157 On the change from a dyadic to a triadic structure of dispute settlement through the introduction of a neutral third see Aubert, Vilhelm, *In Search of Law: Sociological Approaches to Law* (Robertson Oxford 1983), 58-76.

158 Cf. 'Oxford English Dictionary' available at <http://www.oed.com/> (last visited: 21 March 2014): “impartial”: “Not partial; not favouring one party or side more than another; unprejudiced, unbiased, fair, just, equitable. (Of persons, their conduct, etc.).”

159 Cf. e.g. Van-Hoa, To, *Judicial Independence: A Legal Research on its Theoretical Aspects, Practices from Germany, the United States of America, France, Vietnam, and Recommendations for Vietnam* (Juristförlaget Lund 2006), 85-86; Rädler, Peter, 'Independence and Impartiality of Judges', in: Weissbrodt, David *et al.* (eds) *The Right to a Fair Trial* (Springer Berlin 1998), 727-730; Trechsel, Stefan, 'Gericht und Richter nach der EMRK', in: Hauser, Peter (ed) *Gedächtnisschrift für Peter Noll* (Schulthess Polygraphischer Verlag Zürich 1984), 393.

ence.[160] The view taken in practice is equally divided: The Canadian Supreme Court holds the two notions to be in "a close relationship", yet "separate and distinct values or requirements". It defines impartiality as "a state of mind or attitude of the tribunal in relation to the issues and the parties in a particular case", whereas independence means "not merely a state of mind or attitude in the actual exercise of judicial functions, but a status or relationship to others, particularly to the executive branch of government that rests on objective conditions or guarantees".[161] The ECtHR has been called upon to set out its conception of the relationship between the two notions in its case law pertaining to Art. 6 Convention for the Protection of Human Rights and Fundamental Freedoms (ECHR). A decision to which the ECtHR still refers is that of the European Commission on Human Rights (ECommHR) dating back to 1983 in *Bramelid and Malmström v. Sweden*. Here the Commission asserted, without providing clear justification, that independence is essentially a precondition for impartiality.[162] This interpretation, which may surprise one in light of the definitions that have been used so far, builds on a broad understanding of the notion of independence, as the ECommHR defines it in relation not only to the executive but also to the parties to a case.[163] In a number of decisions, the ECtHR interprets independence pursuant to Art. 6 ECHR more clearly as independence from the executive and the parties to the case,[164] i.e. in relation to other actors, including in the sense of the doctrine of the separation of powers. Impartiality on the other hand is more often determined following a dual test, firstly on the basis of the personal conviction of a particular judge in a given case (the so-called subjective test), and secondly by ascertaining whether the judge offered guarantees sufficient to exclude any legitimate doubt in this respect (the so-called objective test).[165]

---

160 E.g. Larkins, 'Judicial Independence and Democratization. A Theoretical and Conceptual Analysis', 609.

161 *Valente v. The Queen* 2 SCR 673 (1985), para. 15.

162 The ECommHR referred to the wording of Art. 6(1) ECHR ("... everyone is entitled to a fair and public hearing within a reasonable time by an independent and impartial tribunal established by law.") and observes that there is a "functional relationship between independence and impartiality" and that "the former being essentially a precondition for the latter". See *Bramelid and Malmström v. Sweden* (ECommHR) Applications No. 8588/79; 8589/79 (12 December 1983), para. 33.

163 Ibid, para. 36.

164 See in particular *Ringeisen v. Austria* (ECtHR) Application No. 2614/65 (16 July 1971), para. 95.

165 See, e.g., *Pétur Thór Sigurðsson v. Iceland* (ECtHR) Application No. 39731/98 (10 July 2003), para. 37.

But the Strasbourg case law is neither always clear nor consistent in its differentiation of the two notions. As an example, in *Demicoli v. Malta* the ECtHR analysed as a question of impartiality issues that the ECommHR in its report in the same case treated as questions of independence.[166] The description of independence in terms of autonomy from other branches of government and the parties, and impartiality defined as a judge's subjective convictions and their objective manifestation[167] is also shared by the Inter-American Court on Human Rights (IACtHR).[168] Furthermore, and similarly to the finding of the ECommHR in *Bramelid and Malmström v. Sweden*, the United Nations Commission on Human Rights (UNCHR) has in a final report on the right to a fair trial assumed that "independence is a prerequisite and essential precondition for the impartiality of a trial".[169]

---

166 *Demicoli v. Malta* (ECtHR) Application No. 13057/87 (27 August 1991), paras. 40-41; *Demicoli v. Malta* (ECommHR) Application No. 13057/87 (15 March 1990), paras. 40-41.

167 See, e.g., *De Cubber v. Belgium* (ECtHR) Application No. 9186/80 (26 October 1984), para. 24; *Langborger v. Sweden* (ECtHR) Application No. 11179/84 (22 June 1989), para. 32. For a similar interpretation see Udombana, Nsongurua J., 'The African Commission on Human and Peoples' Rights and the Development of Fair Trial Norms in Africa' (2006) 6 African Human Rights Law Journal 1, 326.

168 In an advisory opinion of 6 October 1987 the IACtHR elaborated on the effectiveness of a remedy, and in this context found that effectiveness did not exist "when the Judicial Power lacks the necessary independence to render impartial decisions" (*Judicial Guarantees in States of Emergency (Arts. 27(2), 25 and 8 of the American Convention on Human Rights), Advisory Opinion* (IACtHR) OC-9/87 (6 October 1987), para. 24). The ACommHR has not yet expressed an opinion on the relationship between the two notions of independence and impartiality. This may depend on the fact that the AChHPR deals with those terms in two different provisions. Whereas Art. 7(1)(d) AChHPR attributes "the right to be tried within a reasonable time by an impartial court or tribunal" to the notion of a fair trial, Art. 26 AChHPR refers to the guarantee of the independence of the Courts as a duty for States Parties "the establishment and improvement of appropriate national institutions entrusted with the promotion and protection of the rights and freedoms guaranteed by the present Charter."

169 See, e.g., *UN Sub-Commission on Prevention of Discrimination and Protection of Minorities, Report of the Sub-Commission on Prevention of Discrimination and Protections of Minorities on its 46th Session, The Administration of Justice and the Human Rights of Detainees* (UNCHR) UN Doc. E/CN.4/Sub.2/1994/24 (3 June 1994), para. 67. Art. 8 ACHR, as Art. 6 ECHR, mentions both independence and impartiality as prerequisites for a fair trial ("Every person has the right to a hearing, with due guarantees and within a reasonable time, by a competent, independent, and impartial tribunal, previously established by law, in the substantiation of any

The position that is ultimately taken on this issue of terminological delimitation depends in part on how the two notions are defined in substance and in what relational terms. As stated above, impartiality is in the context of this thesis applied to refer to non-involvement with the parties to a case. This is based on the consideration that partiality, fundamentally, is the unequal treatment of the like, and equal treatment of the unlike.[170] A judge is thus partial if he privileges or disadvantages a party towards whom he instead, pursuant to the law, should act as a neutral third. As a consequence, impartiality is understood to encompass the "state of mind or attitude of the tribunal in relation to the issues and the parties in a particular case"; since this desired state of mind can be influenced by more than the parties themselves, the notion is broader and also encompasses opposition towards sources of influence other than those stemming from the parties. Being impartial is thus a quality, a characteristic of the behaviour of judges. This quality may be, and in most cases is, a consequence of dependencies, but this is not a logical or practical necessity. Nor is the quality identical with judicial independence, which, if defined as the freedom of the judiciary to exercise judicial functions without extra-legal or political interference or influence, as it has been defined so far, is best described as a status, a characteristic of a function, rather than a quality of its actors. Thus although for the purposes of this study we uphold that there is "a close relationship" between the two notions, they are nevertheless "separate and distinct values or requirements" which describe two different things. The focus of this thesis is judicial independence, and impartiality will be the subject of discussion where it is deemed relevant.

(2) Non-Involvement – Independence from the Parties

One potential threat to the independence of the judiciary stems from the parties to a particular conflict. The reason is that the parties have an inherent and justified interest in leading the pertinent court in a certain direction, namely one that supports their own agenda, and parties thus *per definitionem* are expected to represent a certain cause and to do anything within the realm of the law to further that cause. The independent judge is one who has no

---

accusation of a criminal nature made against him or for the determination of his rights and obligations of a civil, labor, fiscal, or any other nature.").

170 Cf. 'Oxford English Dictionary' available at <http://www.oed.com/> (last visited: 21 March 2014): "Partiality".

relation to, is autonomous *vis-à-vis* the litigants – irrespective of their identity – is neither identical to nor unduly entangled (formally or actually) with the parties. The non-involvement[171] of the judiciary, or the idea that judges will base their decisions not on any association with one of the litigants but only on the law and the facts of a case, is at the core of its independence. The basis for involvement with the parties to a dispute can often be the status of a judge, e.g. a judge's family relationship with, or economical, ethnic, or cultural nearness to one of the parties, which can transform into a coercive affiliation. Since such dependencies, such as family status, memberships and social and political activities, are often easily verifiable, non-involvement may often be effectively ensured with the help of procedural rules. For example, the regulation of a judge's permitted outside activities and associations, the procedure for selection of candidates, recusal and consequences of (the appearance of) bias. It may be added that with the definition of non-involvement as the absence of dependencies towards a particular source of intervention, namely the parties to a case before a court, no limitation has been imposed on the identity of such sources. Therefore, in the context of international law, the involvement of courts and judges with States, governmental or non-governmental organizations or even individuals may be considered detrimental for the international judiciary's independence.

(3) Political Insularity – Influence Exerted by States and Other Political Actors

Due to the theoretical foundation of the principle of judicial independence as closely linked to the idea of a separation of powers,[172] one significant component remains independence from the executive and legislative arms of government. This relationship is particularly delicate as the judiciary is irrevocably dependent on these other branches, for instance for administrative

171 K. Eichenberger makes the further differentiation between non-involvement (*Unbeteiligtheit*) and impartiality (*Unparteilichkeit*). Whereas the earlier in his classification circumscribes autonomy *vis-à-vis* influences that have their origin in the parties, the latter refers to the individual judge's behaviour. In the classification adopted here, the two notions may overlap where judges' behaviour privileges one of the parties. See Eichenberger, *Die richterliche Unabhängigkeit als staatsrechtliches Problem*, 44.

172 See *supra* Chapter B.IV(3).

arrangements or for necessary legislative acts.[173] For the international judiciary, where there is neither a definite executive nor a distinct legislative, this translates into the courts' independence from entities that ensure compliance with international norms and those entities creating such norms. These include primarily States,[174] in their function as the main lawmakers and enforcers of international law, and international organizations, due to their pivotal role in the establishment of international courts. Particularly in international law, political insularity may overlap with the earlier mentioned detachment from parties since the litigants appearing before international courts are usually also those who created the applicable norms or those who are responsible for ensuring compliance with them. Furthermore, the separate consideration of this source of influence reveals a limited picture of the potential sources of influence for another reason, namely due to the fact that international law develops in the direction of directly addressing subjects that do not simultaneously take on a political role in the international sphere, e.g. individuals.

Seen from this perspective, an independent judiciary is one that shields itself against being used as a tool to further political aims and against being punished for preventing the realization of such aims.[175] Political insularity,[176] however, does not imply complete independence from every political entity;[177] the reliance of the judiciary on other actors e.g. to ensure its proper functioning by the provision of financial resources exemplifies this. Insularity may be achieved primarily through the prohibition of the removal of judges for reaching particular decisions, external influence on the composition of

173 Ideally, the judiciary is dependent only on the legislative act, not the legislative organ. The latter may have the ability, channelled through the power to enact law, to subjugate the judiciary and/or the individual judge. But this ability will remain unrealized if the legislative function is exercised only to achieve the necessary normative framework within which the judiciary can operate.

174 According to N. Miller, "[t]he independence of judges from States is an endemic question in international law" and it will be considered as the core of the meaning of judicial independence here; Miller, Nathan J., 'Independence in the International Judiciary: General Overview of the Issues', Meeting of the Study Group of the International Law Association, Conference in Burgh House, Hampstead, London (2002), 10.

175 Larkins, 'Judicial Independence and Democratization. A Theoretical and Conceptual Analysis', 609.

176 The term political insularity was first introduced by Fiss, Owen M., 'The Limits of Judicial Independence' (1993) 25 Inter-American Law Review 1, 59-60.

177 Cf. *supra* Chapter B.IV(5)(a).

a court (i.e. nomination and selection procedures), and factors affecting the position of individual judges such as the scope of the privileges and immunities of judges, security of tenure, disciplinary measures, and terms and conditions of service (especially protection against the lowering of salaries while judges are in office).

(4) Judicial Insularity – Independence Within the Judiciary

Modelled on the previous terminology of political insularity, in addition to the subjugation of the judiciary to a political branch, certain modalities of the organizational structure within the judiciary may equally pose a threat to judicial independence.[178] These include what could be circumscribed with direct instructions exchanged between courts, but also more subtle directions flowing from the authority of one court which are perceived as binding by another. The individual court must remain free from such off-topic influences for the reason that they are likely to constitute a diversion from what is relevant in a particular case and what constitutes the only legitimate guideline for judicial decision-making, namely the applicable law and the facts of a case. Interestingly, the international legal order, due to its distinct character, provides for certain means which may enable courts better to thwart this sort of exertion of influence. Decisions of international courts are generally not considered to be legally binding either on themselves or on other courts, although they may nevertheless have varying persuasive force as models of how to solve a particular legal issue or how to interpret a certain norm.[179] Thus there is in principle no reason for any international court to feel bound by the decisions of any other, unless legal reasoning happens to apply equally between two cases. On the other hand, no court can hold a reasonable expect-

---

178 Cf. the notion of "richterliche Eigenständigkeit" (judicial autonomy) used by K. Eichenberger, by which is meant the independence *vis-à-vis* organs of the judiciary; Eichenberger, *Die richterliche Unabhängigkeit als staatsrechtliches Problem*, 48-49.

179 See, e.g., Doehring, Karl, *Völkerrecht – Ein Lehrbuch* (Müller Heidelberg 2nd edn. 2004), 123; Shaw, *International Law*, 109-112; Oellers-Frahm, Karin, 'International Courts and Tribunals, Judges and Arbitrators', in: Wolfrum, Rüdiger (ed) *The Max Planck Encyclopedia of Public International Law* (Oxford University Press Online Edition 2012), para. 27. See also Art. 38(1)(d) ICJ Statute; Pellet, Alain, 'Article 38 ICJ Statute', in: Zimmermann, Andreas *et al.* (eds) *The Statute of the International Court of Justice – A Commentary* (Oxford University Press Oxford 2006), 784-790.

ation that its decisions have a direct or in any sense binding effect on another court.[180] In particular, the persuasive force of the legal arguments of any court may not influence other international courts to the degree that they are stripped of their own prerogative to apply the applicable law or to assess the facts in an individual case. Beyond this argument a second reason is the less formalized organizational development of the judiciary in the international sphere which does not provide for any clear hierarchy.[181] Where no hierarchical structure between different stages of appeal exists, an important precondition for the exertion of influence, based on a sense of superiority and correspondingly the obligation to submit to superior verdict, is eliminated.

Moreover, individual judges may establish negative and off-topic influence over their colleagues in the same court which can curtail their independence. To grasp this, O. Fiss coined the notion of "individual autonomy" circumscribing "collegial relationships or the power of one judge over another".[182] Such influence may e.g. be felt in the form of pressure from a senior judge or court president to reach a particular decision. O. Fiss illustrates this with the example of judicial councils in the 1980s in the US which were given the power to investigate complaints against trial judges and to take disciplinary action that the judicial council deemed appropriate. Through this procedure, "one group of judges, acting through an organization rather than the traditional appellate procedures" was given the opportunity "to review the work of an individual judge and discipline him or her".[183] Certainly, not every such form of interaction between judges in a court and not even every form of collegial control threatens the independence of judges. Instead the focus ought to be on mechanisms that prevent the individual judge from exercising his judicial duties autonomously. For this reason, the appeal and possible quashing of a judgment cannot be considered a real threat to judicial insularity, and thus judicial independence. The setting aside of a judgment by a higher level of jurisdiction, in fact, has positive effects in that it amounts to a unifying element between the different instances which are all orientated by the legal system which they serve. To overcome the above-mentioned

---

180 In which case it can be argued that the court is in actual fact bound by the rational reasoning as such, independent of the organ that happened to pronounce it and that may be referred to.

181 See on the problems that arise from this Shany, *The Competing Jurisdictions of International Courts and Tribunals*.

182 See Fiss, 'The Limits of Judicial Independence', 58.

183 Ibid.

threats to independence it is necessary to look at how the relationship between individual judges, and in particular between court presidents and ordinary judges, is tailored. An insight into such issues may be gained through a study of the assignment of cases, and the preconditions and procedures laid down for the court to prevent a judge from sitting on a case or to remove him from the bench altogether.

(5) Social Liberty – Independence Vis-À-Vis Social Actors

The term *social liberty* accommodates the observation that the individual judge, besides being a representative of a professional group, is always also a member of a social community. As such he is continuously exposed to the different influences stemming from other social actors. The various forms of such influence are diverse and include habits, customs and traditions. The particular problem raised by these types of influences stems from the fact that the relationships cannot always be captured in legal terms, and thus it is fairly difficult to shield individual judges from all such currents. In contrast, it may even be desirable that the international judge is a person who is shaped by social interactions and is aware of the occurrences in his surroundings, in order to reach his own and contemporary understanding of what the law ought to be.[184] As indicated, it is the borderline case that is of interest; the case where influence threatens to distort the eventual decision because it threatens to deter the judge from an objective application of the law to the facts. These cases become obvious, for example, when looking at the relationship between courts and the public (insight into procedures, transparency), and restrictions on the outside activities of individual judges.

(6) Inner Sovereignty – Personal Suitability for Judicial Office

One of the most hidden and difficult sources of extra-legal parameters that may influence a judge is the individual judge himself. The term *inner sover-*

184 Representative of the considerable body of literature addressing the subject in the context of national law, see Jackson, Vicky, 'Judicial Independence: Structure, Context, Attitude', in: Seibert-Fohr, Anja (ed) *Judicial Independence in Transition: Strengthening the Rule of Law in the OSCE Region* (Springer Heidelberg 2012), 21-22.

eignty circumscribes the freedom from influences of the persona, the beliefs, convictions and the ideas of the individual judge. This distinction is important because many of the influences already mentioned stem from sources other than the judge himself and they become a threat to the independence of the judiciary only if the individual judge permits them to have an effect in a particular case, although he is not the source of that influence. Inner sovereignty excludes bias, prejudice and off-topic narrowing of the spirit. Judges' internal freedom gains particular significance as it has a bearing on the realization of negative influences stemming from any of the other sources mentioned above. All subtle external attempts to influence the decision-making of an individual judge in particular may materialize only if the judge allows them to do so. This central role is coupled with a near unfeasibility to ensure inner sovereignty, as it is impossible to look into the mind of a judge or candidate for judicial office. It may best be controlled by establishing clear preconditions for nomination/election to office, selection procedures that ensure their observance, and the regulation of outside activities and rules on recusal and removal from office; all of which have an influence on allowing only the most honourable individuals to sit on a bench.

V. Summary

What has so far emerged in the analysis of the notion of judicial independence is that it is a multi-facetted term, which at its core circumscribes the protection of the judiciary, on the collective as well as individual level, against external, extra-legal or political influences. Using analogies of the notions of separation of powers and the rule of law, both of which concepts in the municipal context reveal the significance of judicial independence, demonstrates the role of judicial independence as serving the balance of powers and the peaceful settlement of disputes in societies. The concept is thus best described functionally: the judiciary must be isolated from influence which prevents it from exercising its judicial functions, which may be defined differently, depending on the broader context of a judiciary, but in essence amounts to the peaceful settlement of disputes between different actors of a given legal system. Judicial independence is furthermore never absolute; it does not translate into total isolation of courts or judges, but must be understood as the counterbalance to the judiciary's necessary dependence on the applicable law.[185] The realization of the notion in practice is best assessed if it is analysed on the level of the individual representatives of the court and on the level of the institutional context in which the decision-maker operates, the judge's court. Judicial independence addresses courts but does not isolate courts from interacting with other organs operating on the international plane. Furthermore, judicial independence addresses the individual judge but it is not his individual privilege. A helpful tool in this analysis is to bear in mind that dependencies may not only influence different levels of the judiciary, but may also stem from a variety of different actors, for which different safeguards may be necessary to avert any potentially negative influence.

185 Cf. Schmitt, *Verfassungslehre*, 155: "Die Unabhängigkeit der Richter von dienstlichen Befehlen hat ihr wesentliches Korrelat in der Abhängigkeit der Richter vom Gesetz." See also Eichenberger, *Die richterliche Unabhängigkeit als staatsrechtliches Problem*, 48-49.

Chapter C: The International Judiciary – Defining the Object of Investigation

I. Introduction

The central assertion of this thesis, that international courts must be independent, presupposes that the notion of *international courts* has a certain definable contour, so as to provide an ascertainable object onto which the notion of judicial independence can be applied. Due to the multifaceted, decentralized and fragmented nature of international law and the adolescence of its institutionalization this contour cannot be taken for granted. Indeed in the organizational structure of international law these occurrences appear to suggest that "there is no clear-cut, universally accepted definition of an international court",[186] a difficulty this thesis has to face. What follows will therefore establish, on the basis of substantive criteria usually applied in scholarly literature, what is meant when the term *international court* is used. To keep the subsequent analysis within manageable proportions a selection of the institutions that meet the definition thus reached will then form the basis for the ensuing study. Before this delimitation, the historical development of the international judiciary will be outlined briefly to set the stage for the elaboration of provisions concerning the independence of international courts.

II. Judicial Independence in its Historical Context – From Ad Hoc Arbitration to Compulsory Jurisdiction

1. Early Development of Third Party Adjudication

Usually referred to as the starting point of modern adjudication of international disputes[187] is the 1794 treaty concluded between the United States and Great Britain to settle legal issues arising from the American Revolution. The Treaty of Amity, Commerce, and Navigation between the United States

---

186 Terris, et al., *The International Judge – An Introduction to the Men and Women who Decide the World's Cases*, 4.

187 See, e.g., Hudson, *International Tribunals: Past and Future*, 3.

and Great Britain, the so-called Jay Treaty,[188] provided for the creation of commissions which were to deal with issues that could not be solved during the negotiation of the treaty itself. Among those were the establishment of a US-Canadian boundary, numerous private claims based upon maritime seizures, and compensation by the US for pre-war debts.[189] Due to the success of these arbitration commissions[190] they are commonly considered to stand for a revival of the judicial process of arbitration and for the beginning of modern international arbitration.[191] But the Jay Treaty primarily resembled a diplomatic, rather than a judicial exercise, which is underlined by the fact that none of the commissioners was expressly required to be neutral.[192] This example was continued by numerous other arbitrations such as those set up under the Treaty of Ghent of 1814 between the United Kingdom and the United States[193] and the Alabama Arbitrations under the Washington Treaty of 1871[194].[195] During the 19th century, not only did mixed arbitration commissions develop into a widespread means of judicial third party adjudication but sole arbitrators were also frequently used to settle disputes between States.[196] The all too political character of certain of these arbitrations does

188 Treaty of Amity, Commerce and Navigation, between His Britannick Majesty; and The United States of America, by Their President, with the advice and consent of Their Senate (adopted 19 November 1794, entered into force 28 October 1795) 1 BSP 784.

189 Hudson, *International Tribunals: Past and Future*, 3.

190 Two of the three were able to settle the disputes put before them. See Ziegler, 'Jay Treaty (1794)', paras. 6-9.

191 Brower II, Charles H, 'Arbitration', in: Wolfrum, Rüdiger (ed) *The Max Planck Encyclopedia of Public International Law* (Oxford University Press Online Edition 2012), paras. 9-11.

192 Although the members of the commissions were not required to be neutral, the Jay Treaty nevertheless demands that "Commissioners ... shall be Sworn impartially to examine and decide the said question ..." See Art. 5 Jay Treaty.

193 Treaty of Peace and Amity, between His Britannic Majesty and The United States of America (adopted 24 December 1814) 2 BSP 357.

194 Treaty between Her Majesty and the United States of America, for the Amicable Settlement of all Causes of Differences between the two Countries (adopted 8 May 1871, entered into force 17 June 1871) 61 BSP 40.

195 Others were the Portendick Case between the United Kingdom and France in 1842, mixed arbitration commissions set up under a treaty between the United Kingdom and the US in 1853, arbitrations before the Senate of Hamburg, and the Commission of Caracas of 1869 dealing with British claims relating to the civil war in Venezuela.

196 Seminal examples in this regard are the 1814 arbitration on the interpretation of Art. 1 of the Treaty of Ghent between the US and the United Kingdom submitted

not contradict the overall trend towards the law-based settlement of disputes between States. Illustrative examples are the cases where heads of State were asked to function as arbitrators, but in effect merely signed awards that were drafted by experts, often jurists, such as the award submitted to the French President by an expert commission in a dispute between the United Kingdom and Portugal concerning Delagoa Bay in 1872.

Altogether, in the relatively short period between 1794 and 1900, roughly 177 international arbitrations took place, more than 75 per cent of them in the last 40 years and more than 50 per cent in the last 20 years.[197] These numbers indicate the rise of judicial arbitration to form a real alternative to purely political or military dispute settlement. The reason the development in dispute settlement went from political or military means to arbitration before a fully developed international court could begin to take shape is most likely to be seen in the relative cost-effectiveness and the benefit that arbitration panels provide States in not having to consent to the jurisdiction and not being obliged to comply with their judgments. However, the advantages provided by a consensual procedure for the final settlement of disputes between States based on law[198] quickly turned into disadvantages due to the changing attributes of the broader political and legal context in which States and other international actors began to find themselves. The fact that arbitration took place only on an *ad hoc* basis[199] and involved arbiters who could by no means be considered independent judges of autonomous courts, was

---

to the Tsar Alexander I of Russia; the Portendick Case, the Bulama Island Case or the San Juan de Fuca Case in 1872 where the German Emperor was called upon to decide on a frontier question between the US and the United Kingdom; the arbitration by the French President in the dispute between the United Kingdom and Portugal over the islands in the Delagoa Bay; the San Juan Boundary dispute between the United Kingdom and the US, in which the German Emperor functioned as arbiter in 1872; and the 1885 arbitration by the Pope in the dispute between Germany and Spain regarding the Caroline and Pelew Islands.

197 La Fontaine, Henri, *Pasicrisie Internationale 1794 – 1900: Histoire documentaire des arbitrages internationaux* (Nijhoff The Hague 1997). Indeed, judicial arbitration during this time (end of 19th century) was so frequently used that it has been called "the handmaiden of international legislation", Hudson, *International Tribunals: Past and Future*, 6.

198 See Merrills, John G., *International Dispute Settlement* (Cambridge University Press Cambridge 5th edn. 2011), 83-86.

199 On the separation between three different kinds of *ad hoc* arbitral bodies (single arbitrator, joint commission, and mixed commission) see Bowett, Derek W., *The Law of International Institutions* (Stevens Sons London 4th edn. 1982), 258.

forced to turn into a burden once international law began to create stability and predictability in international affairs.

2. From the Permanent Court of Arbitration to the End of the World Wars

Driven by the aspiration to escape an international arms race, the increasing influence of peace movements, alarm over the growing alliance system and a general desire to codify international law, delegates from twenty-six States met in The Hague in 1899 to conclude agreements on warfare, the avoidance of war and the limitations of arms.[200] Although the Conference could not, as expected, agree upon the limitation of arms, all participating States did sign the Convention for the Pacific Settlement of International Disputes (1899 Hague Convention I),[201] which provided not only for the limitation of recourse to the use of force, by obliging States in the event of differences between two or more of the Signatory Powers to have recourse to "the *good offices* or *mediation* of one or more friendly Powers" (Art. 2; emphasis added). The Convention also, in Chapter II of its Part IV, laid the foundation for a Permanent Court of Arbitration (PCA) competent for all arbitration cases.[202] The 1899 Hague Convention I thus contained an important acknowledgment of the role international arbitration was envisaged to play in the broader system of dispute settlement.

According to Art. 15 of the Convention, the Signatory Powers maintain that "[i]nternational arbitration has for its object the settlement of differences between States by judges of their own choice, and on the basis of respect for law." Furthermore, in Art. 16 the Convention recognizes arbitration to be "the most effective, and at the same time the most equitable, means of settling disputes". Although this was a strong statement in favour of the judicial process, as the quoted passage of Art. 15 indicates, arbitration remained under the direct and strong influence of the parties to a particular conflict. The PCA was (and still is) to be "accessible at all times and operating, unless

200 According to D. Caron, "the raison d'être of the 1899 Peace Conference was not dispute settlement but, rather, the avoidance of war." Caron, David D., 'War and International Adjudication: Reflections on the 1899 Peace Conference' (1999) 94 American Journal of International Law 4, 5.

201 International Convention for the Pacific Settlement of International Disputes (adopted 29 July 1899, entered into force 4 September 1900) 187 CTS 410.

202 See generally, 'Permanent Court of Arbitration' available at <http://www.pca-cpa.org/> (last visited: 21 March 2014).

otherwise stipulated by the parties, in accordance with the Rules of Procedure inserted in the … Convention".[203] Despite its name, the only permanent feature of the Court is its Bureau situated in The Hague.[204] In substance though, the PCA is merely a list of names from which arbitrators can be selected as soon as the occasion arises.[205] The list of potential arbitrators of the PCA is made up of four people selected by each Signatory Power. Art. 23 1899 Hague Convention I demands that every such chosen individual must be "of known competency in questions of international law [and] of the highest moral reputation". The 1899 Hague Convention I did not contain an express requirement that the members of the list of arbitrators be either *independent* or *impartial*, although it can be and has been claimed that this can be read from the demand for the highest moral reputation.[206] Generally, however, it must be accepted that the codification of any standards protecting the members' independence was weak, as is for example shown by the lack of any provision prohibiting them from exercising certain incompatible functions, which would seem appropriate for a dispute settlement mechanism that has committed itself to international law alone.[207] The approach to judges' selection for a particular dispute settlement is especially difficult to defend against the allegation of attempting to influence the outcome before adjudication has even begun. The default procedure provides that whenever a dispute is brought before the PCA the parties appoint two arbitrators from the panel and the four arbitrators thus chosen, or a third party, select an umpire.[208] The judges of the PCA are hence selected by the parties *ad hoc*.[209]

---

203 Art. 20 1899 Hague Convention I.

204 Art. 22 1899 Hague Convention I.

205 "It is difficult to call a court 'permanent', which does not exist, and which only comes into being when it is created for the trial of a particular case, and goes out of existence as soon as the case is tried." Scott, James Brown (ed) *The Hague Court Reports: Vol. 1* (Oxford University Press New York 1916), xvii-xviii.

206 Cf. Brown, 'The Evolution and Application of Rules Concerning Independence of the "International Judiciary"', 68.

207 It must be recognized, however, that a requirement that chosen potential arbitrators limit their other activities, or even abstain from any other occupation to avoid a conflict of interest, is hardly realistic or enforceable. This argument will be dealt with in greater detail in subsequent chapters.

208 Art. 32 1899 Hague Convention I.

209 On this feature of influence by the parties see *infra* Chapter C on the definition of *international courts*.

Despite the boost the creation of the PCA gave to arbitration in general,[210] the Signatory Powers were unable, even at the Second Conference in The Hague in 1907, to transform the PCA into a more substantial institution.[211] Interestingly, although proposals were made by several Signatory Powers to the Convention for the creation of a truly permanent tribunal,[212] these at-

210 The first panel that was set up under the PCA in 1902 dealt with the so-called Pious Fund Case between the US and Mexico (*Pious Fund (United States of America v Mexico)* 9 RIAA 11 (1902)). Between 1902 and 1920 fourteen other arbitration tribunals were established.

211 The need to do so was especially promoted by the then US Secretary of State Elihu Root. According to Root, it should be the US American delegation's "effort to bring about in the Second [Hague] Conference a development of the [Permanent Court of Arbitration] into a permanent tribunal composed of judges who are judicial officers and nothing else, who are paid adequate salaries, who have no other occupation, and will devote their entire time to the trial and decision of international causes by judicial methods and under a sense of judicial responsibility." Elihu Root, 'Instructions to the American Delegates to the Hague Conference of 1907', in Scott, James Brown (ed) *Instructions to the American Delegates to the Hague Peace Conferences and their Official Reports* (Oxford University Press New York 1916), 79.

212 At the Conference a Draft Convention Relative to the Creation of a Court of Arbitral Justice was recommended; see Scott, James Brown, *The Reports to the Hague Conferences of 1899 and 1907* (Clarendon Press Michigan 1917), 226-231. In this draft convention, some provisions related to the independence of the court's judges. For example, Art. 2 required that judges must have "the highest moral reputation", a requirement that was mirrored in both the 1899 Hague Convention I (Art. 23) and the 1907 Hague Convention I (Art. 44; cf. Hudson, Manley O., *The Permanent Court of International Justice 1920-1942 – A Treatise* (MacMillan New York 1943), 125). As to the judges' substantive qualification, the draft convention demanded that they either "be jurists of recognized competence in matters of international law" or – and this was not contained in the two Hague Conventions – fulfil "conditions qualifying them, in their respective countries, to occupy high legal posts". The tenure of judges was, compared to today's international courts, relatively long (twelve years). Art. 5 equipped judges with diplomatic privileges and immunities as a further protection of the independent exercise of their functions, and they were called upon to swear or make a solemn affirmation to exercise their functions impartially and conscientiously. Moreover, in Art. 7 the draft convention establishes an important demand on the incompatible activities of judges: "A judge may not exercise his judicial functions in any case in which he has, in any way whatever, taken part in the decision of a national tribunal, of a tribunal of arbitration, or of a commission of inquiry, or has figured in the suit as counsel or advocate for one of the parties. A judge cannot act as agent or advocate before the Court of Arbitral Justice or the Permanent Court of Arbitration, before a special tribunal of arbitration or a commission of inquiry, nor act for one of the parties in any capacity whatsoever

tempts eventually failed mainly due to disagreement over the selection process for judges to such a new forum:[213] the dispute boiled down to the Great Powers demanding permanent representation while other States insisted upon equal rights.[214] This tension, which cannot be explained away by reference to the infancy of international law at the time, clearly illustrates that States were by no means willing to allow the judges to be appointed independently of their political interests. The same pessimistic fate awaited the goal of the 1907 Conference to establish obligatory arbitration. The disappointment over the latter point is vividly expressed in the addition to Art. 16 of the Convention for the Pacific Settlement of International Disputes reached in The Hague (1907 Hague Convention I),[215] which in effect weakened the entire provision considerably: "it would be *desirable* that, in disputes ..., the Contracting Powers *should*, if the case arose, have recourse to arbitration, *in so far as circumstances permit*" (emphasis added). The 1907 Convention with respect to the independence of members of PCA tribunals presented two changes to the 1899 Convention, which can be considered as moderate improvements: Firstly, whereas the 1899 Convention in the default composition of a PCA tribunal permitted that both members selected by a party could be its own nationals, the 1907 Convention stated that "one only can be its national or chosen from among the persons selected by it as Members of the Permanent Court".[216] The new convention thus for the first time contained a restriction on the participation of national judges. Secondly, following some negative experiences in early PCA tribunals, where members of the PCA acted as counsel, the 1907 Convention prescribed in Art. 62 that "[t]he Members of the Permanent Court may not act as agents, counsel, or advocates except on behalf of the Power which appointed them Members of the Court."

so long as his appointment lasts." According to J. B. Scott, the draft convention in this part looks to the impartial administration of justice and the provision was of such undisputed character that it was adopted without observation (Scott, *The Reports to the Hague Conferences of 1899 and 1907*, 253).

213 Mackenzie, Ruth, et al., *Selecting International Judges: Principle, Process, and Politics* (Oxford University Press Oxford 2010), 10-12.

214 Fachiri, Alexander P., *The Permanent Court of International Justice – Its Constitution, Procedure and Work* (Oxford University Press Oxford 2nd edn. 1932), 3.

215 Convention for the Pacific Settlement of International Disputes (adopted 18 October 1907, entered into force 26 January 1910) 205 CTS 233.

216 Cf. Art. 32 1899 Hague Convention I and Art. 45 1907 Hague Convention I.

Such a basic protection of judicial independence was, as mentioned, lacking under the 1899 Convention.[217]

Yet another permanent court of the early 20th century was the Central American Court of Justice (*Corte de Justicia Centroamericana*), which was established in 1907 but after deciding only ten cases was dissolved again in 1918 due to a lack of support and poorly developed procedures.[218] What is noticeable here is that the Court was criticised for less than ideal procedures regarding the selection of judges, and for allowing judges' salaries to be paid directly by the appointing States.[219]

Due to the unprecedented magnitude of human suffering caused by the First World War, the creation of a permanent court for the settlement of international disputes was brought back to the political agenda again after 1918. One of the provisions of the Covenant of the League of Nations envisaged the creation of the PCIJ.[220] It was ultimately established in 1921 through the signature and ratification of its Statute. Although the PCIJ Statute did not provide for obligatory jurisdiction, the Court delivered numerous judgments and advisory opinions at the request of the LoN's Council. Many of the provisions relating to the independence of judges built on experiences from the PCA and the preparatory work that was provided by the Draft Convention Relative to the Creation of a Court of Arbitral Justice, which had been annexed to the Final Act of the Second Hague Peace Conference

217 See *supra* at fn. 207.

218 Cortado, Rosa Riquelme, 'Central American Court of Justice (1907–18)', in: Wolfrum, Rüdiger (ed) *The Max Planck Encyclopedia of Public International Law* (Oxford University Press Online Edition 2012).

219 According to M. Hudson, "the justices of the court seem to have been looked upon not as international officials of all five States, but as officials of their respective States ... as there was no method for a cooperative election of the justices." Hudson, *The Permanent Court of International Justice 1920-1942 – A Treatise*, 44. As further reasons, Hudson refers to the salaries of the judges. The Central American Court of Justice was to be revived in 1962 under the new Organization of Central American States; see Hudson, *International Tribunals: Past and Future*, 172-173; Nussbaum, *A Concise History of the Law of Nations*, 222-223.

220 Art. 14 of the Covenant of the League of Nations (adopted 28 June 1919, entered into force 10 January 1920) (1919) 225 CTS 195 provides: "The Council shall formulate and submit to the Members of the League for adoption plans for the establishment of a Permanent Court of International Justice. The Court shall be competent to hear and determine any dispute of an international character which the parties thereto submit to it. The Court may also give an advisory opinion upon any dispute or question referred to it by the Council or by the Assembly."

in 1907.[221] The procedure for electing judges was hence linked to the LoN in an attempt to circumnavigate the tensions that had blocked the Draft Convention fourteen years earlier. The nomination of judges was to be undertaken by the national groups of the PCA in order to prevent "political intrigues in the elections, because of the 'moral weakness of all political bodies'";[222] in other words, to ensure an independent selection. Yet it could be observed that even the national groups' role did not guard against candidates being nominated for political conformity with their government's will.[223] In an attempt to gather support for the PCIJ the ability to appoint an *ad hoc* judge if a State in a dispute did not have a judge of its own nationality on the court was also introduced.[224] In sum, it has to be kept in mind that the above-mentioned examples of international adjudication, although there are indications that judicial independence has been taken increasingly seriously since the early 20th century, merely concern dispute settlement between States. This fact should induce us not to have too high expectations or to assess critically the achievements with respect to judicial independence. It was not until the end of the Second World War that the international legal order opened up to the inclusion of other legal subjects and thereby created the necessary precondition for the broader and more meticulous evolution of international judicial institutions and with it of their legal framework.

3. The Post-World War and Cold War Period

The experience of the Second World War could well have led politicians to believe that the tools of international judicial arbitration developed before

221 Cf. Art. 2 of the Draft Convention requiring that judges must fulfil "conditions qualifying them, in their respective countries, to occupy high legal posts, or be jurists of recognized competence in matters of international law." This provision is mirrored in Art. 2 Statute of the PCIJ. The text of the Draft Convention is reprinted in Rosenne, Shabtai (ed) *The Hague Peace Conferences of 1899 and 1907 and International Arbitration: Reports and Documents* (T.M.C. Asser The Hague 2001), 216-221.

222 Hudson, *The Permanent Court of International Justice 1920-1942 – A Treatise*, para. 140.

223 Reut-Nicolussi, Eduard, 'The Reform of the Permanent Court of International Justice', in: Grotius Society (ed) *Transactions of the Grotius Society* (Longmans, Green & Co. London 1939); Hudson, *The Permanent Court of International Justice 1920-1942 – A Treatise*, para. 252.

224 Art. 31 Statute of the PCIJ.

1939 had not delivered on their promise to promote peace[225] and thus would not be worth developing further. However, the view taken by leading politicians after 1945 was, fortunately, a different one. Not only was the tool of an international criminal tribunal used for the first time to prosecute those responsible for heinous acts and violations of international law during war. But apart from the International Military Tribunal in Nuremburg (IMT) and the International Military Tribunal for the Far East in Tokyo being created, it was agreed to continue the legacy of the PCIJ. Under Arts. 7(1) and 92 of the Charter of the newly established UN, the new ICJ was to be its principal judicial organ.[226] Unlike the PCIJ, the ICJ is now an integral part of its parent organization. One of the consequences of the establishment of the Court under the Charter of the United Nations (UNC) – its Statute being annexed to the Charter – is that the ICJ identifies more closely with the aims and methods of and is bound to co-operate with the other organs of the UN.[227] Many of the provisions relating to the independence, impartiality and accountability of its judges were taken from the Statute of the PCIJ and applied unchanged, bearing witness to at least an apparent satisfaction with the earlier system in this regard.[228]

Following the end of the Second World War, the concept of judicial arbitration was also incorporated into international co-operation at the regional level, contributing to diversity in the way questions of judicial independence and impartiality could be approached. In Europe the ECJ was established in 1952 under the Treaty of Paris for the European Coal and Steel Community. This brought a further component to the development of an international judicial sector, namely the regional development of courts with a close rela-

---

225 See, e.g., von Bogdandy, Armin & Venzke, Ingo, 'Zur Herrschaft internationaler Gerichte: Eine Untersuchung internationaler öffentlicher Gewalt und ihrer demokratischen Rechtfertigung' (2010) 70 Zeitschrift für ausländisches öffentliches Recht und Völkerrecht 1, 6-11.

226 Cf. Art. 92 of the UNC: "The International Court of Justice shall be the principal judicial organ of the United Nations. It shall function in accordance with the annexed Statute which is based upon the Statute of the Permanent Court of International Justice and forms an integral part of the present Charter."

227 Simpson, John Liddle & Fox, Hazel, *International Arbitration: Law and Practice* (Stevens London 1959), 25.

228 For more on the details and the relationship between the PCIJ and ICJ see *infra* Chapter D.II.

tionship to local legal systems *sui generis*.[229] In the Americas, too, the Central American Court of Justice was revived in 1962.[230] The Benelux Court of Justice[231] and the Court of Justice of the Andean Community[232] followed in 1974 and 1979 respectively. The establishment of the International Centre for the Settlement of Investment Disputes (ICSID)[233] extended the judicial organs to investment disputes between States and non-State actors. In this context, the arbitration mechanisms in the framework of the International Chamber of Commerce and further *ad hoc* arbitrations also deserve to be mentioned.[234] In the broader field of international economic relations the General Agreement on Tariffs and Trade of 1947 provided for the setting up of panels; a system that was developed further with the adoption of the Understanding on Rules and Procedures Governing the Settlement of Disputes adopted in 1994 and annexed to the Agreement Establishing the World Trade Organization. The Dispute Settlement Understanding envisaged a quasi-judicial system of dispute settlement,[235] which included the possibility to appeal panel reports to an Appellate Body. For several reasons this system more closely resembles arbitral tribunals than courts in the narrower sense,[236] a fact which shines through in particular in the way judicial independence is valued.[237] A further crucial development is the establishment of numerous regional human rights courts. With the doctrinal development of human rights and the related openness of international law to *inter alia* the individual

229 Romano, Cesare P. R., 'The Proliferation of International Judicial Bodies: the Pieces of the Puzzle' (1999) 31 New York University Journal of International Law & Politics 4, 710.

230 Statute of the Central American Court of Justice (1995) 34 ILM 921.

231 Treaty concerning the establishment and the statute of a Benelux Court of Justice (adopted 31 March 1965, entered into force 1 January 1974) 924 UNTS 41.

232 Treaty Creating the Court of Justice of the Cartagena Agreement (adopted 28 May 1979, entered into force 19 May 1983) 18 ILM 1203.

233 Convention on the Settlement of Investment Disputes between States and Nationals of Other States (adopted 18 March 1965, entered into force 14 October 1966) 575 UNTS 159.

234 Sands, Philippe J. (ed) *Manual on International Courts and Tribunals* (Butterworths London 1999), xxvii.

235 Hobe, Stephan & Kimminich, Otto, *Einführung in das Völkerrecht* (Francke Tübingen Basel 8th edn. 2004), 378.

236 See below on the definition of *international courts*.

237 For an assessment of judicial independence in the WTO see Charnovitz, Steve, 'Judicial Independence in the World Trade Organization', in: Boisson de Chazournes, Laurence *et al.* (eds) *International Organizations and International Dispute Settlement: Trends and Prospects* (Transnational Publishers Ardsley New York 2002).

as a (partial) subject of international law, the creation of judicial organs at the (regional) international level, able to adjudicate on alleged violations of human rights was a natural but nevertheless bold step. The ECtHR, created under the ECHR in 1950, was the first of its kind and has to date proven to be rather influential through its case law, which sometimes severely criticizes the national legal orders which have accepted its jurisdiction and authorities exercising public power. The IACtHR, with its seat in San José, Costa Rica, was established in 1979, and in 2004 the African Court of Human and Peoples' Rights followed.

4. The Trend Towards Compulsory Jurisdiction

The most important recent development affecting the relevance of judicial independence in international courts is the rise of courts with compulsory jurisdiction in specific areas of international law, which helps to detach the judicial dispute settlement still further from the subjects that may appear as parties before it. In 1982, the United Nations Convention on the Law of the Sea (UNCLOS) envisaged the creation of an ITLOS, which became operative in 1996 once the UNCLOS entered into force. The creation of the ITLOS marked the beginning of a phase of institutional additions to the international judiciary that we are still witnessing today and which includes a number of bodies that to a greater extend resemble what within national legal frameworks would be considered to be courts of law.[238] As indicated, the establishment of new judicial organs went hand in hand with the extension of international adjudication to previously untouched areas of substantive international law. Hence this phase of the history of the multiplication of international judicial bodies is tangent to and even functions as an indicator of the development of the diversification and fragmentation of international law. One vivid example is the ICTY and the ICTR established by the UN Security Council (UNSC) in 1993 and 1994 respectively. Those courts were equipped with a comparatively strong mandate, being created by UNSC resolutions, and established concurrent jurisdiction with primacy over proceedings before national courts. This significantly contributed to the ultimate success of the work of these institutions and to promoting the enforcement of international criminal law in general. A momentary climax was reached in 2002 when the

238 On the definition of international courts see *infra* Chapter C.IV.

long expected ICC, established in 1998, became operative and opened its doors to its first cases. Although the Rome Statute of the International Criminal Court (Rome Statute) has experienced far from universal ratification,[239] the Court's inception and its initial activities have nevertheless contributed to the strengthening of the status of international criminal law.

International criminal law also provided the forum in which a new form of court could be established: the so-called mixed or hybrid courts, which are based on close interdependence between national and international law by applying both national and international substantive and procedural law and by providing for the participation of both national and international judges. Examples of this category of courts, which is rather diverse in itself, include the Crimes Panels of the District Court of Dili in East Timor, the 'Regulation 64' Panels in the Courts of Kosovo, the Extraordinary Chambers in the Courts of Cambodia, the Special Court for Sierra Leone (SCSL), and the War Crimes Chamber of the State Court of Bosnia and Herzegovina.[240]

A number of other international courts were established in the late 1990s and first decade of the new millennium. In Africa, the Court of Justice for the Common Market of Eastern and Southern Africa began its work in 1994; in Europe the European Free Trade Association (EFTA) created its own judicial body, the Court of Justice of the EFTA States, which took up its duties in 1994.

This brief overview of the development of the international judiciary provides a basic awareness of the complexity of the judicial system and the uneven and ill- coordinated manner of its progression, which are factors that necessarily influence the way in which the notion of judicial independence is accommodated.

---

239 As of 21st March 2014, 122 countries had signed and ratified the Rome Statute of the International Criminal Court. See 'ICC – The States Parties to the Rome Statute' available at <http://www.icc-cpi.int/en_menus/asp/states%20parties/Pages/the%20states%20parties%20to%20the%20rome%20statute.aspx> (last visited: 21 March 2014).

240 For a recent study of the independence of mixed courts see Bertelman, Hanna, 'International Standards and National Ownership? Judicial Independence in Hybrid Courts: The Extraordinary Chambers in the Courts of Cambodia' (2010) 79 Nordic Journal of International Law 3.

III. Why does Independence Matter?

A brief glance at the treaties establishing international courts and the complementing statutes of implementation proves, on an empirical level, that judicial independence has been increasingly considered a matter of real concern for the international judiciary and for the system's principal designers.[241] In addition, a number of both binding and non-binding but nevertheless notable international instruments list judicial independence as a human right. These include the International Covenant on Civil and Political Rights (ICCPR),[242] the American Convention on Human Rights (ACHR),[243] the Banjul

241 That judicial independence has not always been considered one of the primary values of international judges as opposed to rather conservative values is for example expressed in the statement made by Lord Phillimore that a judge "must have loyalty, probity, a certain breadth of vision, patience and courage." Permanent Court of International Justice & Advisory Committee of Jurists, *Procès-Verbaux of the Proceedings of the Committee, June 16th-July 24th 1920 with Annexes* (Van Langenhuysen Brothers The Hague 1920), 105. Express requirements that judges be independent can e.g. be found in Art. 2 Statute of the International Court of Justice (adopted 26 June 1945, entered into force 24 October 1945) 145 BSP 832; Art. 2 Statute of the International Tribunal for the Law of the Sea (Annex VI of the United Nations Convention on the Law of the Sea) (adopted 10 December 1982, entered into force 16 November 1994) 1833 UNTS 561; Art. 40 Rome Statute of the International Criminal Court (adopted 17 July 1998, entered into force 1 July 2002) 2187 UNTS 90; Art. 11 Statute of the Inter-American Court of Human Rights (adopted October 1979, entered into force 1 January 1980) OAS Official Records OEA/Ser.P/IX.0.2/80, Vol 1, 98; Art. 11 UNSC, *Statute of the International Tribunal for Rwanda* (8 November 1994) UN Doc. S/RES/955 (1994); Art. 12 UNSC, *Statute of the International Tribunal for the Former Yugoslavia* (25 May 1993) UN Doc. S/RES/827 (1993); Art. 253(1) Consolidated Version of the Treaty on the Functioning of the European Union (signed 13 December 2007, entered into force 1 December 2009) OJ C83/47. See also Art. 2 Statute of the Permanent Court of International Justice (adopted 16 December 1920, entered into force 20 August 1921) 6 LNTS 389.

242 Art. 14(1) International Covenant on Civil and Political Rights (adopted 19 December 1966, entered into force 23 March 1976) 999 UNTS 171.

243 Art. 27(2) American Convention on Human Rights (Pact of San José, Costa Rica) (adopted 22 November 1969, entered into force 18 July 1978) 1144 UNTS 123.

Charter,[244] the Arab Charter on Human Rights,[245] the ECHR[246] and the Geneva Conventions.[247] These observations necessarily raise the question where this significant interest of international law in the concept of judicial independence originates. In other words, why does independence matter for the international judiciary?

As we saw in the historic review in Chapter C.II but also in the short overview provided in the introduction (Chapter A.I), the rise of judicial independence in the international sphere has progressed hand in hand with more international courts, wider jurisdiction and more cases, in other words with the evolution of real powers exercised by international courts. Without claiming that international courts are the most influential or, empirically, the most important method of peaceful dispute settlement, it without doubt appears to be a continuing story of success and of progression. The conclusion that could be drawn from this is that respect for the notion of judicial independence either directly serves, i.e. is beneficial for, the international judiciary and hence for the main actors operating in the background, or, at least, does not conflict substantially with the international judiciary and its interests and therefore does not hamper its development. This view, however, is not as unquestionable as it may initially seem. To scrutinize this rationale, it is useful to look at some of the counter-arguments that have been summarized by E. Posner and J. Yoo. One of the central contentions of their much celebrated 2005 article entitled "Judicial Independence in International Tribunals", in which the relationship between judicial independence and the allure of international courts is examined, is that independent international courts "pose a danger to international co-operation because they can render decisions that conflict with the interests of state parties."[248] They furthermore assert that States will not decide to make use of international courts unless they have control over judges, and that therefore judicial independence prevents international courts from being effective. As a consequence, the only effective courts are dependent ones, which, according to Posner and Yoo, are courts

244 Arts. 7 and 26 African Charter on Human and Peoples' Rights (Banjul Charter) (adopted 27 June1981, entered into force 21 October 1986) 1520 UNTS 217.

245 Art. 13 Arab Charter on Human Rights (revised) (adopted 22 May 2004, entered into force 15 March 2008) (2005) 12 IHRR 893.

246 Art. 6 Convention for the Protection of Human Rights and Fundamental Freedoms (adopted 4 November 1950, entered into force 3 September 1953) 213 UNTS 221.

247 Common Art. 3.

248 Posner, Eric A. & Yoo, John C., 'Judicial Independence in International Tribunals' (2005) 93 California Law Review 1, 7.

staffed with members who have a strong incentive to serve the interests of the disputing States. At the outset, the argument that Posner and Yoo present appears plausible only if the point of departure for the analysis is the assumption that States are likely to refrain from international adjudication unless the judicial exercise itself is at the very least susceptible to direct influence: in other words, that the effectiveness of international courts is directly and essentially influenced by their independence. However, associating these two features of the international judiciary in an almost exclusive relationship to one another should counsel caution due to the manifold additional aspects that may have an influence on how both effectiveness and independence can be measured and assessed. For example, to evaluate the relative effectiveness of an international court it is paramount to consider what can be circumscribed with judicial access rules, i.e. the rules determining who has access to a court and under what circumstances.[249] Whereas the ECtHR, which is open to individuals under particular circumstances, delivered an impressive 1,157 judgments in 2011,[250] the ICJ, which hears only inter-State disputes, issued four judgments and roughly six orders in the same time (between 1 August 2010 and 31 July 2011).[251],[252] There is no doubt that the relative effectiveness of these courts differs significantly. But is it not equally certain that this difference is primarily attributable to the different jurisdictions of these courts rather than to their independence? Furthermore, it should be cautioned against the assumption that (independent) international courts pose a danger to international co-operation, since the judicial access rules of international courts often demand that international co-operation has taken place but failed to yield a satisfying result. In other words, the adjudication of a dispute by international courts can hardly be in conflict with international co-operation since the two methods are non-overlapping. This point also touches upon a further loophole in the argument presented by Posner and Yoo, namely its suffering from being state-centred and disregarding the role played by other international actors appearing before international courts. Assuming that a

---

249 In addition to that certain courts, due to their regional character or because a particular State has not agreed to its jurisdiction, may further be barred from exercising their adjudicatory power.

250 European Court of Human Rights, *Annual Report 2011* (Registry of the European Court of Human Rights Strasbourg 2012), 83.

251 International Court of Justice, *Report of the International Court of Justice, 1 August 2010-31 July 2011* (1 August 2011) UN Doc. A/66/4(SUPP), 5.

252 The jurisdiction of international courts will therefore be highlighted in the different chapters below.

"tribunal is independent when its members are institutionally separated from the *state parties*"[253] (emphasis added) and the argument that independent international courts pose a danger to international co-operation since their decisions may conflict with the interests of States,[254] is indicative of this. Whereas it is true that international courts must be based on and apply international law,[255] which is still governed by States to a significant degree, "[i]nternational adjudication is no longer a matter over which states have a monopoly".[256] The increased accessibility of international adjudicatory fora to non-State actors and the increased use of *amicus curiae* interventions and individual complaint mechanisms under the Convention on the Elimination of All Forms of Discrimination against Women[257] and International Covenant on Economic, Social and Cultural Rights (ICESCR)[258] show that other actors, whose interests are substantially different from those of States, are increasingly relevant. Whereas, for example, State interests are undeniably involved when an individual stands trial before the ICC for actions committed in an armed conflict, the eventual judgment of the court first and foremost has an effect on the rights of the accused and the victims. Moreover, it appears that as regards these other actors, the adherence of States to their commitments under international law can be supervised adequately only by international courts that are independent precisely in the sense that they are unconstrained by State control. Finally, in the view of Posner and Yoo, international courts are "simple, problem-solving devices"[259] which are unable either to transform the interests of States or to "cause States to ignore their own interests for the sake of a transnational ideal."[260] This assertion on the one hand fails to paint an accurate picture of the landscape of international courts today.[261] On the other hand, it reveals a very narrow interpretation of the interests of States, namely one where States opt for judicial dispute settlement only where the exercise is unable to generate a loss for them. What is more, the concept of

---

253 Posner & Yoo, 'Judicial Independence in International Tribunals', 7.
254 Ibid.
255 See *infra* Chapter C.IV(2)(c).
256 Mackenzie, et al. (eds), *The Manual on International Courts and Tribunals*, xiv.
257 Convention on the Elimination of All Forms of Discrimination against Women (adopted 18 December 1979, entered into force 3 September 1981) 1249 UNTS 13.
258 International Covenant on Economic, Social and Cultural Rights (adopted 16 December 1966, entered into force 3 January 1976) 993 UNTS 3.
259 Posner & Yoo, 'Judicial Independence in International Tribunals', 6.
260 Ibid, 7.
261 See further *infra* Chapter C.IV.

politics as a utility-maximising strategic action which reduces States to rational egoists, seeking only the most effective means to realize individual and collective interests,[262] cannot account for the way in which international law and international institutions have developed into fora for "discursive struggles over legitimate political agency and action".[263] In failing to see how States, let alone other international actors, might more broadly see their interests as being protected and even promoted by international courts, the connection between the progressive development of the international judiciary and judicial independence as one of several interlinked and positive factors of the process is never made.

But the above examination still leaves unanswered the question whether it is possible to formulate reasons why States and other international actors support and turn to international courts, reasons which could at the same time suggest that judicial independence is a valuable or even indispensable feature in the formation of an international judiciary. As stated earlier, one of the main reasons for the increase in the number of international courts is the greatly increasing number of international norms especially in the last two decades, which is closely linked to the increasingly complex relationships between States and other actors since the end of the Cold War.[264] The current standing of international courts is thus linked to the increased relevance of international law in general.[265] An understanding of why international actors

262 Byers, Michael, 'International Law', in: Reus-Smit, Christian *et al.* (eds) *The Oxford Handbook of International Relations* (Oxford University Press Oxford 2008), 619.

263 Reus-Smit, Christian, 'The Politics of International Law', in: Reus-Smit, Christian (ed) *The Politics of International Law* (Cambridge University Press Cambridge 2004), 20.

264 Guillaume, Gilbert, 'Editorial Comments on the Proliferation of International Courts – Advantages and Risks of Proliferation: a Blueprint for Action' (2004) 2 Journal of International Criminal Justice 2, 300-301; Romano, 'The Proliferation of International Judicial Bodies: the Pieces of the Puzzle', 728-729; Pinto, Moragodage Christopher Walter, 'The Court and other International Tribunals', in: Peck, Connie (ed) *Increasing the effectiveness of the International Court of Justice – Proceedings of the ICJ/UNITAR Colloquium to celebrate the 50th anniversary of the Court* (Nijhoff The Hague 1997), 282-284; Brownlie, Ian, 'Blaine Sloan Lecture: The Peaceful Settlement of International Disputes in Practice' (1995) 7 Pace International Law Review 2, 276; Hafner, Gerhard, 'Should one Fear the Proliferation of Mechanisms for the Peaceful Settlement of Disputes?', in: Caflisch, Lucius (ed) *The Peaceful Settlement of Disputes between States: Universal and European Perspectives* (Kluwer Law International The Hague 1998), 34.

265 Cf. Buergenthal, Thomas, 'Proliferation of International Courts and Tribunals – Is it Good or Bad?' (2001) 14 Leiden Journal of International Law 2, 271-272.

follow international rules in general might therefore also provide valuable suggestions as to why independent international courts are increasingly successful. What explanations are thinkable?

According to a classical coercion model, international law is followed because the different international actors are compelled to follow it.[266] While this approach might serve as an explanation for some of the behaviour of certain States, it is difficult to reconcile with the voluntary nature of obligations created in international treaty law, i.e. the idea that States are not bound by international treaty law unless they wish to accede to it.[267] In particular, it can hardly serve as an explanation of why a growing number of international courts are being established since this process occurs voluntarily, and the argument furthermore fails to explain why States recognize the jurisdiction of international courts and tribunals where this decision is optional.[268] A rationalist approach, which is less dismissive of international law than its realist counterpart,[269] suggests that international rules are followed because the benefits generally outweigh the costs and because States therefore have

266 See, e.g., Goldsmith, Jack L. & Posner, Eric A., *The Limits of International Law* (Oxford University Press Oxford 2005). Downs, George W., et al., 'Is the Good News About Compliance Good News About Cooperation?' (1996) 50 International Organization 3, 380, asserting that further international regulatory cooperation depends on a higher level of enforcement.

267 See, e.g., Art. 19 Vienna Convention on the Law of Treaties (adopted 23 May 1969, entered into force 27 January 1980) 1155 UNTS 331, according to which "[a] treaty does not create either obligations or rights for a third State without its consent." For a typical statement to this effect, see American Law Institute, *Restatement of the Law (Third), Foreign Relations Law of the United States* (American Law Institute Philadelphia 1987), part 1, chapter 1, introductory note at 18: "Modern international law is rooted in acceptance by states which constitute the system."

268 Cf. Helfer, Laurence R. & Slaughter, Anne-Marie, 'Why States Create International Tribunals – A Response to Professors Posner and Yoo' (2005) 93 California Law Review 3, 914.

269 The realist approach to international law shall not be dealt with separately here. In essence, realist legal scholars contend that States adopt and obey only international legal rules which enhance their own power, that international law is determined by dominant States and that it will not be followed if it is considered to conflict with their political interests. International law therefore is not enforceable unless supported by the will of powerful States, and can thus also not be considered binding. According to C. Reus-Smit, at least three inherent problems can be identified in the realist view of international law: "it does not adequately address the existence of a growing body of law; it does not offer an account of how law comes to constrain strong states; and it has no account of how weak states and other actors use law to shape outcomes." Reus-Smit, 'The Politics of International Law', 17.

consented to these rules. Whereas this school of thought may account for some behaviour of States, it does so only based on the centrality of the State as an analytical unit. The increase in how public international law addresses not only States but also other actors and how the understanding of "interests" has gone beyond concepts of e.g. national security and State economic prosperity, is difficult to fathom using this approach. The success of regional human rights tribunals, for example, shows that States are apparently not discouraged by the prospect of being found in violation of human rights provisions and, as a consequence, having to pay compensation for such violation. In other words, even if States have consented to the jurisdiction of these courts, it remains to be explained for the rationalist why this consent is considered binding, why legal rules *per se* are considered binding.[270] Moreover, as was mentioned above, a static and rational-choice driven approach does not serve as a sufficient explanation for the proliferation of international courts as fora for "discursive struggles over legitimate political agency and action". However, the cost-benefit perspective indicates another conclusive and more weighted theory, namely that international rules are followed, despite the considerable costs that may be attached to them because international actors fear the loss of reputation if they do not follow them. L. Helfer and A.-M. Slaughter take up this idea when suggesting that States choose to establish (formally) independent international courts "to enhance the credibility of their commitments".[271] The underlying assertion is that impartial information about compliance allows States in particular to pursue cooperative strategies and helps them to make credible commitments.[272] This theory encapsulates the realities of increased global interaction and interdependence which have made States as well as other international actors depend more on the perception of their compliance with or possible violations of international commitments.[273] Put more frankly: in a world of increased global interdependence characterized by international institutions and norms,

---

270 See on this, Hart, Herbert Lionel Adolphus, *The Concept of Law* (Oxford University Press Oxford 2nd edn. 1994), 224.

271 Helfer & Slaughter, 'Why States Create International Tribunals – A Response to Professors Posner and Yoo', 902.

272 See on this e.g. Keohane, Robert Owen, et al., 'Legalized Dispute Resolution: Interstate and Transnational' (2000) 54 International Organization 3; Majone, Giandomenico, 'Two Logics of Delegation: Agency and Fiduciary Relations in EU Governance' (2001) 2 European Union Politics 1.

273 Helfer & Slaughter, 'Why States Create International Tribunals – A Response to Professors Posner and Yoo', 934-935.

violating international law is a grave step due to the loss of reputation and influence in the global society it entails or the increased difficulty of entering into new agreements.[274] In this context, only independent international courts can, from the perspective of other States or other actors, assist in credibly ensuring that commitments are obeyed. In particular, if States were only to subject themselves to the jurisdiction of dependent courts, in the sense that those courts' decisions following the exertion of influence would be easily made to conform with States' interests, the anticipated dependence and submission to pressure would make the circumvention of international obligations all too simple, indeed arbitrary. Lastly, the perhaps most idealistic but nevertheless reputable position is that obedience is generated because actors consider the rules to be fair and legitimate.[275] According to T. Franck, a legal obligation that is perceived to be "fair" exerts a "compliance pull" that leads States to conform with it.[276] The role of judicial independence in achieving fairness and legitimacy of the international judiciary has not yet been fully revealed by international law scholarship, and here is not the place to engage in that undertaking. However, it deserves to be noted that in an attempt to describe the scholarly landscape in this regard, E. Benvenisti and G. W. Downs go so far as to assert that in recent years there has developed "a growing acceptance among international legal scholars that the future legitimacy and credibility of international tribunals will be critically tied to

274 On the question of reputation costs of non-compliance see Guzman, Andrew, 'The Cost of Credibility: Explaining Resistance to Interstate Dispute Resolution Mechanisms' (2002) 31 Journal of Legal Studies 2 (Part 2), 304-305. A more diverse theory is presented by Downs, George W. & Jones, Michael A., 'Reputation, Compliance, and International Law' (2002) 31 Journal of Legal Studies 1, suggesting a more diverse theory of the reputation-treaty compliance interaction.

275 According to T. Franck, compliance with international obligations is "secured at least in part by perception of a rule as legitimate by those to whom it is addressed." Franck, Thomas M., 'Legitimacy in the International System' (1988) 82 American Journal of International Law 4, 706. H. Koh proposes a theory according to which "a transnational actor's moral obligation to obey an international norm becomes an internally binding domestic legal obligation when that norm has been interpreted and internalized into its domestic legal system." Koh, Harold Hongju, 'Why Do Nations Obey International Law?' (1997) 106 Yale Law Journal 8. See also C. Jenks, according to whom the basis of States' obligations in international law is the will of "the world community", Jenks, Clarence Wilfred, *Law, Freedom, and Welfare* (Stevens & Sons London 1963), 83-100.

276 Franck, Thomas M., *Fairness in International Law and Institutions* (Clarendon Press Oxford 1995), 7-9.

the extent to which they are viewed as independent."[277] Yet more tangibly, Benvenisti and Downs find that growing competition between powerful States and developing powers might be a catalyst for a more independent international court system, the rulings of which less closely reflect the preferences of powerful States.[278] At least as far as politicians and the public of those States, are concerned, it indeed appears plausible that increased legitimacy may be achieved in this way. Overall a case can certainly be made for the argument that the search for legitimacy and fairness in a world where the number of entanglements and the necessity for reliability as regards commitments increases can be adequately answered only with a set of independent courts that apply the rules and the facts irrespective of any particular interests. Without providing a deeper analysis or even a definite answer to whether compliance with judgments of international courts is increased by their independence, it shall suffice to conclude that the independence of courts is a significant factor in the perception of those courts as fairer and more legitimate.

In conclusion, it does not appear reasonable to claim that any one of the prevailing theories on the relationship between international relations and international law is sufficient to explain either the behaviour of States and other actors, or, consequently, the appeal of independence as a feature of the ever-growing international judiciary. But this is far from necessary in the present context. The only aim was to show that a case can be made for linking the support of States and other international actors for international courts to the feature of those courts' judicial independence. This can be considered to have been accomplished. Although judicial independence is often at odds with the interests of States, international courts are not competing with international co-operation and both the changing relevance of the concept of "interests" in international relations and the shifting role played by States in international law suggest that the independence of international courts is a notion that is here to stay for the international judiciary. Be it as a catalyst of enhanced credibility of commitments, or as a pulling factor due to the

277 Benvenisti, Eyal & Downs, George W., 'Prospects for the Increased Independence of International Tribunals' (2011) 12 German Law Journal 5, 1057. See also von Bogdandy, Armin & Venzke, Ingo, 'In Whose Name? An Investigation of International Courts' Public Authority and its Democratic Justification' (2012) 23 European Journal of International Law 1, 32-36.

278 Benvenisti & Downs, 'Prospects for the Increased Independence of International Tribunals'.

fairness and legitimacy of the insulation from politically entrenched interests, judicial independence fits in the current system of international relations and international law, both of which are inextricably linked to each other.

IV. The Basis for a Systematic Approach – Defining International Courts and Tribunals

1. Court or Tribunal?

Having shed light on the historical development of the notion of independence in the context of the evolving international judiciary and following a review of possible explanations of why judicial independence in general is of relevance in the international realm, we must pay attention to a more precise definition of the object of this study. The term used so far to circumscribe international judicial dispute settlement bodies is *international courts and tribunals*. A large part of pertinent scholarly literature uses this broader circumscription,[279] while not always distinguishing between a *court* and a *tribunal*.[280] The question whether there is any substantive differentiation

279 Other terms which further add to the terminological diversity are *international judicial bodies* (see, e.g., Romano, 'The Proliferation of International Judicial Bodies: the Pieces of the Puzzle', 711), *international judicial organs* (Art. 92 UNC: "The International Court of Justice shall be the principal judicial organ of the United Nations." [Emphasis added.]), *international dispute settlement bodies* (see, e.g., Boisson de Chazournes, Laurence, et al. (eds), *International Organizations and International Dispute Settlement – Trends and Prospects* (Transnational Publishers Ardsley New York 2002), xxi.), or *international judicial machinery* (see, e.g., Lauterpacht, Elihu, *Aspects of the Administration of International Justice* (Grotius Cambridge 1991), 9).

280 See, e.g., Cheng, Bin, *General Principles of Law as Applied by International Courts and Tribunals* (Stevens London 1953); Haesler, Thomas, *The Exhaustion of Local Remedies in the Case Law of International Courts and Tribunals* (Sijthoff Leyden and Bonn 1968). The expression *International Courts and Tribunals* is also used by the Max Planck Encyclopedia for Public International Law for all entries that deal with international judicial dispute settlement, see, e.g., Tomuschat, 'International Courts and Tribunals'. According to S. Rosenne, "[t]he expression 'court or tribunal' is in common use but without any formal implications and any hint that it implies any sort of hierarchical, systemic, or other relationship between or among the different international courts and tribunals that are functioning at any given moment." Rosenne, Shabtai, 'International Courts and Tribunals, Jurisdiction and Admissibility of Inter-State Applications', in: Wolfrum, Rüdiger (ed) *The Max Planck Encyclopedia*

embedded in this terminology and whether such differentiation should have an influence on the determination of the object of investigation here shall be shortly addressed in what follows.

Both terms are used in international legal literature and, when used separately, preference for one over the other appears not always to be a conscious choice.[281] The frequent use of the collective term of *international courts and tribunals*, on the other hand, firstly reveals that the two terms do not circumscribe the same thing, or it would not be necessary to mention them both, and secondly demonstrates that they nevertheless have certain similarities which make it useful to mention them together. A substantive distinction could be based on the jurisdiction of the body; whereas court refers to organs of a broader jurisdiction, such as the ICJ which can deal with virtually any legal dispute referred to it by States, tribunals are only those bodies that exercise special jurisdiction, such as *ad hoc* criminal tribunals or arbitral tribunals. A second approach suggests that whereas court is used to refer to a body which is of permanent jurisdiction, tribunals may be considered to be only transient institutions. But both of these observations are only imperfectly suitable for elevation to a general rule. For example, whereas the ITLOS has a specialized jurisdiction *ratione materiae*, dealing with disputes under the UNCLOS,[282] it is not of limited jurisdiction *ratione temporis*. The situation is similar with the ICC which, although being a permanent institution,[283] tries only those accused of having committed "the most serious crimes of concern to the international community as a whole".[284] As a consequence, although there are parameters along which one could differentiate between international courts and tribunals, these cannot be followed consistently and thus are weak focal points for a more general distinction.[285] For this reason,

---

of Public International Law (Oxford University Press Online Edition 2012), para. 1.

281 Cf. e.g. Hudson, *International Tribunals: Past and Future*; Boczek, Boleslaw Adam, *Historical Dictionary of International Tribunals* (Scarecrow Press Metuchen, New Jersey 1994); E. Lauterpacht favours the notion *tribunal* (Lauterpacht, *Aspects of the Administration of International Justice*), whereas e.g. M. Janis prefers the use of *court* to describe the various international judicial bodies (Janis, Mark Weston (ed) *International Courts for the Twenty-First Century* (Nijhoff Dordrecht 1992)).

282 See Art. 1 UNCLOS.

283 See Art. 1 Rome Statute.

284 Art. 5 Rome Statute.

285 See also H. Mosler, according to whom there is no general rule prescribing a certain distinction between the two terms; Mosler, Hermann, 'The International Judiciary from the Point of View of an International Judge' *Thesaurus Acroasium of the Insti-*

this thesis will use the terms *court* and *tribunal* interchangeably, however, preferably reverting to the term *international court* when a particular body is referred to.

2. Elements of a Substantive Definition

What is of greater importance for this study is the substantive characterization of these courts. International legal scholarship contains a number of attempts to discern criteria for what constitutes an international court,[286] although the anticipated problems linked to any attempt to define the notion of international courts sometimes lead scholars to avoid it altogether.[287] A common definition of international courts usually lists the following five elements as cumulative fundamentals:[288] (I) courts are permanent judicial bodies that (II) adjudicate on international disputes (III) on the basis of international law and following a (IV) pre-determined set of rules of procedure in order to (V) reach decisions which are binding on the parties. In what follows, each of these common characteristics will be analysed in order more closely to determine the subject of investigation.

---

tute of Public International Law and International Relations of Thessaloniki (Institute of Public International Law and International Relations of Thessaloniki 1998), 151.

286 See, e.g., Tomuschat, 'International Courts and Tribunals with Regionally Restricted and/or Specialized Jurisdiction'; Terris, et al., *The International Judge – An Introduction to the Men and Women who Decide the World's Cases*; Romano, 'The Proliferation of International Judicial Bodies: the Pieces of the Puzzle'; Schlochauer, Hans-Jürgen, 'Internationale Gerichtsbarkeit', in: Strupp, Karl *et al.* (eds) *Wörterbuch des Völkerrechts: Zweiter Band* (de Gruyter Berlin 1961), 56; Mosler, 'The International Judiciary from the Point of View of an International Judge', 150.

287 For example, the "Manual on International Courts and Tribunals" wholly steers clear of defining the central terminology of international courts and tribunals. Instead the Manual focuses on "the principal bodies – both global and regional", thus using utilization as a limiting factor, but leaving open the question of substantive criteria that may identify the object of investigation.

288 See Romano, 'The Proliferation of International Judicial Bodies: the Pieces of the Puzzle'; Tomuschat, 'International Courts and Tribunals with Regionally Restricted and/or Specialized Jurisdiction'; Terris, et al., *The International Judge – An Introduction to the Men and Women who Decide the World's Cases*.

a) The Permanence Criterion

The wish to create permanent courts is a development that began in the early 20th century.[289] Today, as a requirement for institutional design, permanence is expressly laid down in many statutes of international courts; e.g. Art. 23 ICJ Statute states that "the Court shall remain permanently in session", and according to Art. 1 Rome Statute the ICC "shall be a permanent institution". The criterion is sometimes weakened in the sense that at least detachment from a given case[290] but not necessarily from a given situation[291] is required. The permanence requirement is based mainly on functional considerations. Courts must be organs that operate independently of a particular case in order to ensure a certain degree of continuity.[292] Neither the parties nor a particular case before the organ should be decisive for or even have an influence on the existence of that organ. For the purpose of this study the less rigid understanding of permanence is employed, perceived as delimitation between organs that are depending on potentially rapidly changing variables and those that have a set and constant – yet sometimes final – existence.[293] This understanding is in line with the functional considerations mentioned above and also allows for the inclusion of such high-profile and standing institutions as the *ad hoc* criminal tribunals for the former Yugoslavia and Rwanda.[294]

289 See Brown, 'The Evolution and Application of Rules Concerning Independence of the "International Judiciary"', 69; *supra* Chapter C.II(1)-(2).
290 Tomuschat, 'International Courts and Tribunals with Regionally Restricted and/or Specialized Jurisdiction', 307-311.
291 Terris, et al., *The International Judge – An Introduction to the Men and Women who Decide the World's Cases*, 4 fn. 8.
292 Tomuschat, 'International Courts and Tribunals', para. 2.
293 See on the adoption of this wider definition Spelliscy, 'The Proliferation of International Tribunals – A Chink in the Armor', 146-147 and Romano, 'The Proliferation of International Judicial Bodies: the Pieces of the Puzzle', 718.
294 Another challenge for the permanence criterion is the recently established International Residual Mechanism for Criminal Tribunals (IRMCT). Although it has been claimed that the IRMCT is a *court* (see Frolich, Ruth, 'Introductory Note to the United Nations Security Council Resolution 1966: International Residual Mechanism for ICTY and ICTR' (2011) 50 ILM 1), and even if the IRMCT has the mandate over "essential functions" of the *ad hoc* Tribunals (para. 4 of the preamble of UNSC, (22 December 2010) UN Doc. S/RES/1966 (2010)), the very specialized and *ad hoc* character of the Mechanism's work (e.g. trials before the IRMCT can be conducted before a single judge (Art. 12(1) of the Statute of the IRMCT), the bench shall consist only of a roster of judges (Art. 8) which may exercise their functions

Organs that can be excluded from the notion of international courts on the basis of a lack of permanence in the sense used here are *ad hoc* arbitral tribunals such as those based on the United Nations Commission on International Trade Law (UNCITRAL) Model Law on International Commercial Arbitration,[295] or ICSID arbitrations[296],[297] which are often convened by the parties to a particular case only to be dissolved once a judicial decision (award) has been delivered. Moreover, the Permanent Court of Arbitration,[298] being little more than a list of experts who may function on an *ad hoc* basis as arbitrators, cannot be considered to be a court due to the lack of permanence of a standing body.[299] However, since the members of the PCA play an important role in the nomination of judicial candidates to the ICJ, there will be reason to revert to this institution.[300]

---

remotely, away from the seats of the Mechanism) does raise questions similar to those of the *ad hoc* Tribunals as to the permanence of the IRMCT.

295 UNCITRAL (ed) *UNCITRAL Model Law on International Commercial Arbitration 1985: With Amendments as Adopted in 2006* (United Nations Vienna 2008).

296 Chapter IV Convention on the Settlement of Investment Disputes between States and Nationals of Other States.

297 It deserves to be mentioned that the term *arbitration* in the 19th century was more broadly used than *adjudication*. It was only in the early 20th century that a distinction between the two terms was followed; cf. Hudson, *International Tribunals: Past and Future*, 99-100.

298 The same applies e.g. to the Court of Conciliation and Arbitration of the OSCE, which is composed of a number of recognized experts in the field of international law who are appointed by the States Parties to the Convention on Conciliation and Arbitration within the CSCE (adopted 15 December 1992, entered into force 5 December 1994) 32 ILM 557and who make up arbitral tribunals on an *ad hoc* basis. Consequently, the Court's own website provides that it "is not a permanent body." 'Court of Conciliation and Arbitration' available at <http://www.osce.org/cca/43 295> (last visited: 21 March 2014).

299 N. Ando describes the PCA as "an institutional mechanism to facilitate the formation of an arbitration tribunal when Contracting States choose to organize one for settling their differences." Ando, Nisuke, 'Permanent Court of Arbitration (PCA)', in: Wolfrum, Rüdiger (ed) *The Max Planck Encyclopedia of Public International Law* (Oxford University Press Online Edition 2012), para. 3. The PCA, despite the name that suggests otherwise, was unable to develop into a standing, permanent institution; merely the Bureau, but not the organ in charge of dispute settlement, is a feature which exists irrespective of the occurrence of any dispute. According to Art. 43 Convention for the Pacific Settlement of International Disputes, the "International Bureau serves as registry for the Court [functions as] the channel for communications relative to the meetings of the Court [and] has charge of the archives and conducts all the administrative business."

300 See *infra* Chapter C.

b) Adjudication of International Disputes

The requirement that courts must be made to adjudicate on international disputes is not meant to reserve this terminology only for organs dealing with inter-State disputes.[301] Although dispute settlement between States remains at the core of international dispute settlement in general, and judicial dispute settlement in particular,[302] the development in international law compels this criterion to be read in conjunction with the nature and current state of international law. Hence it also includes disputes where international organizations and individuals are parties, as long as their international status is affected.[303] The requirement of an international dispute further demands that at least one of the parties to a particular dispute is either a sovereign State or an international organization. If this is not the case, as e.g. in the International Chamber of Commerce, which facilitates commercial arbitration merely between private parties, the dispute ought to be classified as a civil law legal dispute and thus falls outside the scope of this study.[304] Furthermore, the fact that international courts are primarily devoted to an adjudicatory function does not exclude the fact that they may also provide advisory opinions, the purpose of which "is not to settle—at least directly—disputes between States, but to offer legal advice to the organs and institutions requesting the opinion."[305] Whereas advisory opinions may be and often have been used as a method of settlement of international disputes,[306] they are usually

301 As was the case under the traditional understanding of international law: see, e.g., the definition provided by H.-J. Schlochauer, which explicitly demands that international courts adjudicate inter-State disputes, Schlochauer, 'Internationale Gerichtsbarkeit', 56.

302 Pellet, 'Peaceful Settlement of International Disputes', para. 65.

303 Tomuschat, Christian, 'International Courts and Tribunals', in: Bernhardt, Rudolf (ed) *Encyclopedia of Public International Law: Instalment 1 Settlement of Disputes* (North-Holland Publishing Company Amsterdam 1981), 93.

304 Romano, 'The Proliferation of International Judicial Bodies: the Pieces of the Puzzle', 715.

305 *Legality of the Threat or Use of Nuclear Weapons (Advisory Opinion)* ICJ Rep. 226 (1996), para. 15.

306 For example, a State and an international organization which are involved in a dispute may choose to request an advisory opinion of the ICJ with the aim of considering themselves bound by this opinion as if it were a judgment purely because international organizations do not have standing to appear before the court in contentious proceedings pursuant to Art. 34 of the Statute of the ICJ ("1. Only states may be parties in cases before the Court …").

non-binding advice on a legal question.[307] Since the power to give advisory opinions is not inherent in the judicial status of international tribunals,[308] it is not a constitutive but nevertheless important element of international courts' functions.

c) Application of International Law

Already M. Hudson stated that "[a]ny international tribunal meriting characterization as such must function within established judicial limitations and must apply international law."[309] The central component of this requirement is the demand for the application of law, i.e. of legal rules.[310] This prerequisite in itself provides a strong argument for the idea that international courts in their decision-making are to be protected against extra-legal and political influence from the parties appearing before them, in particular States.[311] It adds to the robustness, in the sense of consistency and predictability, of judicial dispute settlement, a purpose already served by the above-mentioned requirement of the permanence of international courts. Particularly and despite the lack of a codification or even compilation of the applicable rules in international law, by envisaging international law, the applicable rules are not at the disposal of the parties. Numerous organic instruments of international judicial bodies therefore unambiguously provide for the application of international law, sometimes combined with certain limitations. The UNCLOS

---

307 Cf. *Interpretation of Peace Treaties with Bulgaria, Hungary and Romania (Advisory Opinion)* ICJ Rep. 65 (1950), 71.

308 The right to give advisory opinions must be conferred on international courts by their constituent instruments (see Thirlway, Hugh, 'Advisory Opinions', in: Wolfrum, Rüdiger (ed) *The Max Planck Encyclopedia of Public International Law* (Oxford University Press Online Edition 2012), para. 4). See, e.g., for the PCIJ, Art. 14 Covenant of the League of Nations; for the ICJ, see Art. 96 UNC; Art. 65 ICJ Statute; for the ECtHR, Protocol No 2 to the ECHR.

309 Hudson, *International Tribunals: Past and Future*, 99.

310 According to the ILC international arbitration is characterized as the "procedure for the settlement of disputes between States by a binding reward *on the basis of law* and as the result of an undertaking voluntarily accepted." (Emphasis added.) See ILC, *Report of the International Law Commission Covering the Work of its Fifth Session* (1 June-14 August 1953) UN Doc. A/CN.4/76, 202.

311 On this conclusion see Tomuschat, 'International Courts and Tribunals with Regionally Restricted and/or Specialized Jurisdiction', 294.

in its Art. 293 demands that the ITLOS apply only "this Convention and other rules of international law not incompatible with this Convention".

Requiring permanent judicial bodies to adjudicate on international disputes on the basis of international law does not rule out the fact that other sources may equally be resorted to; the organic instruments of a court can for example allow (or require) it to use municipal law as well as international law.[312] Furthermore, international law is neither to be limited to the written law, such as treaties, conventions, and agreements, nor can it be understood to comprise only the rules applying to the whole international community. In particular, regional international law, such as the European legal order, which is often qualified as a legal order *sui generis*,[313] must equally be understood as international law in this sense as it is law that applies beyond national borders. This requirement especially excludes dispute settlement by political institutions, such as international organizations, from the scope of this thesis.

d) Pre-Determined Rules of Procedure

International courts can be considered such only if they decide a contentious case following rules of procedure which pre-exist the case and which are not at the disposal of the parties. Thereby international courts are set apart from mere arbitration where the conduct of the judicial exercise either follows a procedure that is in its entirety decided *ad hoc* by the parties to the dispute or, where the parties have opted for applying a set of already existing procedural rules, is at least subject to such changes as the parties agree to during the course of the proceedings.[314] As an example, the PCA provides a number of rules for arbitrating disputes, such as the Permanent Court of Arbitration

---

312 According to Art. 5 Statute of the Special Court for Sierra Leone (adopted 16 January 2002) 2178 UNTS 145 "[the court] shall have the power to prosecute persons who have committed … crimes under Sierra Leonean law."

313 "The European Economic Community constitutes a new legal order of international law for the benefit of which the states have limited their sovereign rights, albeit within limited fields, and the subjects of which comprise not only the member states but also their nationals." *Case 26/62 NV Algemene Transport- en Expeditie Onderneming van Gend & Loos v Netherlands Inland Revenue Administration* ECR 1 (1963).

314 Cf. Brower II, 'Arbitration', paras. 55 and 59.

Optional Rules for Arbitrating Disputes between Two States.[315] However, these rules are, as the title indicates, optional, and even if two States opt to apply these Rules they are nevertheless not barred from making "such modification as [they] may agree in writing" (see Article 1(1) of the Rules).

Fundamental rules on the procedure before an international court are usually laid down in the treaties establishing the court in question, including a statute of implementation. Furthermore, general principles of law may provide for certain procedural rules if the written sources are silent on a particular issue. International courts are usually also vested with the power to frame additional rules which add to the instruments provided by the drafters.[316] Indeed, the fact that the various instruments with which the court was equipped by its founders can hardly provide an exhaustive assembly of relevant legal rules, the codification of its rules of procedure is one of "the first obligations which an international tribunal has to discharge after taking up its functions."[317] This self-regulation of international courts as regards their procedural rules adds considerably to their independence from the organ and/or actors responsible for their creation.[318]

e) The Binding Character of Judicial Decisions

As international courts seek to settle disputes by their adjudication, a significant characteristic is that their decisions are binding. They are not merely recommendations or opinions which the parties to a dispute may or may not obey.[319] Once a decision has been given, the dispute is settled at least from the legal perspective, and the decision has to be followed by the losing party

---

315 See 'Permanent Court of Arbitration – Rules of Procedure' available at <http://www.pca-cpa.org/showpage.asp?pag id=1188> (last visited: 21 March 2014).

316 See, e.g., Art. 60 American Convention on Human Rights (Pact of San José, Costa Rica); Art. 25(d) ECHR; Art. 30 Statute of the International Court of Justice; Art. 52 Rome Statute of the International Criminal Court; Art. 253(6) Consolidated Version of the Treaty on the Functioning of the European Union.

317 Tomuschat, 'International Courts and Tribunals with Regionally Restricted and/or Specialized Jurisdiction', 312.

318 Sorel, Jean-Marc, 'International Courts and Tribunals, Procedure', in: Wolfrum, Rüdiger (ed) *The Max Planck Encyclopedia of Public International Law* (Oxford University Press Online Edition 2012), para. 1.

319 The binding character of judicial decisions of international courts is usually established in the treaties establishing the courts. See, e.g., Art. 59 ICJ Statute, Art. 33 ITLOS Statute. See also Art. 105 Rome Statute.

regardless of any further objections or disapproval of the outcome. As a consequence, this criterion is on the one hand the foundation for real power that international courts exercise, and on the other a central reason why adherence to the jurisdiction of some international courts is far from universal, and why instead compliance with judgments of international courts is such a sensitive issue in practice. Every State that is prepared to subject itself to judicial adjudication has to accept the real possibility that it will be faced with an unfavourable outcome, and therefore has to weigh carefully its decision to submit. According to C. Tomuschat, any party to such dispute settlement "cannot ignore the fact that by agreeing to judicial settlement it is automatically allowing dicey incalculable elements to exercise a decisive influence."[320] It is no surprise then that international courts and judges can find themselves potentially exposed to the exertion of influence from outside the courtroom to direct decision-making to favour one party's cause.[321] The bodies this criterion excludes from the scope of this thesis are primarily organs which are "only" equipped with the ability to deliver non-binding determinations or communications for the solution of a dispute. The UN Human Rights Committee (HRC), for example, is such an organ which has no power to issue decisions binding on States.[322] Nevertheless, although the HRC lacks the power to make decisions characteristic of international courts, the ICCPR

---

320 Tomuschat, 'International Courts and Tribunals with Regionally Restricted and/or Specialized Jurisdiction', 301.

321 It deserves to be mentioned that the fact that many international judicial bodies are *also* equipped with the competence to give advisory opinions does not mean that their character as international courts is thereby questioned. Cf. the advisory jurisdictions of the ICJ, the ITLOS and ECtHR; see the respective chapters below.

322 With regard to its main activity, the review of State reports, the HRC is confined to studying such reports and submitting its own report together with "such general comments as it may consider appropriate" to the States Parties to the ICCPR (Art. 40(4) ICCPR). As regards inter-State disputes, the HRC is allowed only to formulate a report containing a brief statement of the facts (Art. 41(h)(ii) ICCPR) and, if an *ad hoc* Conciliation Commission is unable to bring about an amicable solution, the Conciliation Commission shall formulate a report containing "its findings on all questions of fact relevant to the issues between the States Parties concerned, and its views on the possibilities of an amicable solution of the matter." (Art. 42(7)(c) ICCPR). The examination of individual complaints, pursuant to the First Optional Protocol to the ICCPR, may result in the delivery of "final views" by the HRC (Art. 5 (4) Optional Protocol), which equally lack legally binding force; although States Parties are obliged to consider them in good faith.

does provide for the members of the HRC to have a status that in some respects reminds of features seeking to ensure the independence of a judge.[323]

It finally ought to be mentioned that requiring judicial decisions to be of binding character is not the same as requiring that they be enforced. In other words, a distinction must be made between the binding character of decisions and the effectiveness of the body issuing such decisions. In order to ensure that judgments of international courts are followed, courts rely on organs which have been vested with executive powers. In the case of the ICJ, for example, the enforcement of decisions is entrusted to the UNSC;[324] for the ECtHR the execution of judgments is supervised by the Committee of Ministers of the Council of Europe (CoM).[325] Thus international courts follow the divide between different branches of governance. This reliance for the court's efficiency on other actors is not necessarily but indeed potentially a threat to their independent functioning.

V. Summary

In this chapter, the historical development of institutionalized judicial adjudication seen through the lens of the development of provisions relating to independence has shown that increasing importance has been accorded to these issues, starting from the first Hague Conventions and leading to modern day international courts such as the ITLOS and the ICC. Virtually each of the principal international courts in its founding document(s) demands independence (and often impartiality) from its judges, and such instruments often include myriad provisions that can be interpreted as relating to this. The historical origin of this is to be found in the Hague Conventions establishing the PCA, the 1907 Draft Convention Relative to the Creation of a Court of Arbitral Justice, and the PCIJ. The question why judicial independence matters at all has been answered by the development of the international legal order as such. In an increasingly intertwined and globalized world, international courts serve in many and an increasing number of fields as serious

323 For example, Art. 28(2) ICCPR provides that the members of the HRC "shall be persons *of high moral character* and recognized competence in the field of human rights" and that they "shall be elected and shall *serve in their personal capacity*." (Emphasis added.).

324 Cf. Art. 94 UNC.

325 Cf. Art. 46(2) ECHR.

conflict solvers. But recourse to them will be made only if the actors are confident that the decision-making process is not dependent on the interests of other actors; only recourse taken to an independent court is suited to ensure predictability which in turn increases the credibility of the relevant actor's commitments.

In a last step, this chapter has provided a clarification of what is meant by the term *international court*, which serves as the subject of investigation of this study. In adopting a definition that follows the most common characteristics, international courts must be distinguished in particular from organs that in both their structure and functioning follow the free discretion of the parties. Their temporal existence does not depend on a particular conflict; the disputes that come before them are to be settled by the application of (international) law, without influence from political bias; the procedure that is followed may not be altered by the parties (although the parties may be allowed to have an influence on certain parts of it); and the findings of the courts are binding (at least) on the parties to the dispute. These characteristics already suggest that courts are, at least in some sense, independent institutions operating in the international sphere. Some authors have gone one step further by considering independence to be an integral part of the very definition of international courts.[326] Although drawing this conclusion on the sole basis

326 See, e.g., Shelton, Dinah, 'Form, Function, and the Powers of International Courts' (2009) 9 Chicago Journal of International Law 2, 540; Tomuschat, 'International Courts and Tribunals', para. 1; Tomuschat, 'International Courts and Tribunals with Regionally Restricted and/or Specialized Jurisdiction', 294. Other authors rather consider *impartiality* to be the common characteristic. According to K. Doehring "[e]very judicial jurisdiction, whether national or international, presupposes – per definitionem – that its judges exercises their function impartial." (Translation by the author.) Doehring, Karl, 'Zur Befangenheit internationaler Richter', in: Ando, Nisuke *et al.* (eds) *Liber Amicorum Judge Shigeru Oda* (Kluwer Law International The Hague 2002), 23. Judge T. Buergenthal considers in his dissenting opinion to the ICJ's order on Legal Consequences of the Construction of a Wall in the Occupied Palestinian Territory: "A court of law must be free and … is required to consider whether one of its judges has expressed views or taken positions that create the impression that he will not be able to consider the issues raised in a case or advisory opinion in a fair and impartial manner … In my view, all courts of law must be guided by this principle, whether or not their statutes or other constitutive documents expressly require them to do so. That power and obligation is implicit in the very concept of a court of law charged with the fair and impartial administration of justice." *Legal Consequences of the Construction of a Wall in the Occupied Palestinian Territory (Order) (Dissenting Opinion of Judge Buergenthal)* ICJ Rep. 7 (2004), para. 11.

of intuition is tempting even at this stage of the thesis, the study will in the following chapters proceed to analyse to what degree this is reflected in the governing instruments of courts that meet the above definition. The institutions chosen for this purpose represent a diverse set of international courts, but are all linked together by the shared common characteristics outlined above. The ICJ (Chapter D) and the ITLOS (Chapter E) represent a category of courts appropriately circumscribed as global courts. They live up to this circumscription either by being available to all States (ICJ) or by having a potentially unlimited jurisdiction *ratione materiae* (ICJ, ITLOS). The second category, that of international criminal courts, represents the most recent family of international courts which is distinguished from the others by not having as its main function the settlement of disputes, but rather the issuing of decisions on the perpetration of international crimes as regards individuals as defendants. They are represented here by the ICC as a permanent institution (Chapter F) and the two *ad hoc* Tribunals for Yugoslavia and Rwanda (Chapter G). The third category is that of human rights courts, which for reasons of limitation are exemplified in this study by the ECtHR (Chapter H).

Chapter D: Judicial Independence in the International Court of Justice

I. Introduction

The ICJ[327] was established in 1945 as the "principal judicial organ"[328] of the UN and accepted at that time the inheritance of the PCIJ. The latter had been the first genuine international experiment in a permanent judicial system,[329] and during its lifespan had established a significant jurisprudence contributing to the interpretation and development of substantive international law.[330] Although the ICJ is not, in a strictly legal sense, the successor to the PCIJ,[331] the modelling of the Court's main statutory instruments on those

---

327 Hereinafter also referred to as "the Court".

328 Art. 92 UNC.

329 Amr, Mohamed Sameh M., *The Role of the International Court of Justice as the Principal Judicial Organ of the United Nations* (Kluwer Law International The Hague 2003), 13.

330 In 1933 the expectations vested in the PCIJ were still rather high. According to H. Lauterpacht, "[t]he Permanent Court is the solid rock upon which statesmen will set their feet in time of trouble when all other means have failed." Lauterpacht, Hersch, *The Function of Law in the International Community* (Clarendon Press Oxford 1933), 241.

331 Oppenheim characterized the ICJ not as the legal successor to the PCIJ but as a factual continuation of it. Oppenheim, Lassa F. & Lauterpacht, Hersch, *International Law, A Treatise – Disputes, War and Neutrality* (Longmans Green London 7th edn. 1952), 47. See, however, the comments by the Rapporteur of the First Committee of the Fourth Commission: "In a sense ... the new Court may be looked upon as the successor to the old Court which is replaced." United Nations Information Organizations, *Volume XIII – Commission IV – Judicial Organization* (United Nations Information Organizations London New York 1945), 384. Schwarzenberger speaks of an "institutional break between the two Courts and [a] limited character of continuity of jurisdiction." Schwarzenberger, Georg, *International Law as Applied by International Courts and Tribunals – Vol. 4 – International Judicial Law* (Stevens & Sons Limited London 1986), 265. The ICJ itself in the *Aerial Incident* case (1959) acknowledged that it was not identical to the PCIJ, speaking of "the dissolution of the old Court and the institution of a new Court", and later in the Barcelona Traction case (1964) interpreted the outcome of the San Francisco conference to be "the decision to create an international court of justice which would in law be a new entity, and not a continuation of the existing Permanent Court" (*Case concerning*

of the PCIJ still merits an occasional glance at the practices and characteristics of the earlier institution. The new Court, established under the umbrella of a new organization of collective security, was given a prominent position by being made one of the six principal organs of the UN[332] and, more specifically, its principal *judicial* organ, its Statute being an integral part of the UNC. This makes the question of the independence of the Court a delicate one as it is called upon to fulfil its functions in close conformity with the remaining activities of the UN. The disputes brought before it are often such that they can easily deteriorate into situations that pose a threat to international peace and security, pushing the activities of the Court into the centre of high politics. In addition, the analysis of the ICJ's independence, and in particular the strength of the normative framework which the Court itself may invoke, is influenced by the irrevocable perception of the ICJ as the prototype of an international court.

II. Genesis and Organizational Setting of the ICJ

1. The Prototype of the PCIJ's Organizational Ties

The PCIJ was already closely linked to a parent organization, namely the LoN, and the various facets of this link have been interpreted differently. Whereas they are sometimes seen to establish an organic relationship between the PCIJ and the LoN,[333] which would not allow the PCIJ to be effectively independent of the LoN, other scholars have opted to consider the PCIJ rather as a separate and independent organization.[334] More important than the label, however, is the actual arrangement of this organizational contextualization, which has been instructive also for the conceptualization of the ICJ.[335]

---

the Aerial Incident of July 27th, 1955 (Israel v. Bulgaria) (Preliminary Objections) ICJ Rep. 127 (1959); United Nations Information Organizations, *UNCIO XIII*, 137; *Barcelona Traction, Light and Power Company, Limited (Belgium v. Spain) (Preliminary Objections)* ICJ Rep. 6 (1964), 31).

332 Art. 7(1) UNC.

333 Amr, *The Role of the International Court of Justice as the Principal Judicial Organ of the United Nations*, 14 fn. 34.

334 Ibid, 14 fn. 33.

335 Rosenne, Shabtai, 'Permanent Court of International Justice (PCIJ)', in: Wolfrum, Rüdiger (ed) *The Max Planck Encyclopedia of Public International Law* (Oxford University Press Online Edition 2012), para. 38.

Art. 1 PCIJ Statute establishes the PCIJ "*in addition* to the Court of Arbitration organized by the Conventions of The Hague of 1899 and 1907, and to the special Tribunals of Arbitration to which States are always at liberty to submit their disputes for settlement" (emphasis added). Hence the drafters of the statute were eager to emphasize that neither was the PCIJ the only international judicial dispute settlement mechanism available to States, nor did it assume a formally higher rank or even priority as a judicial dispute settlement mechanism compared to existing or future courts or tribunals. Nevertheless, numerous sources support the ascription of a special status to the PCIJ within the League system. Art. 415 of the Versailles Treaty referred to the Court as "the Permanent Court of International Justice of the League of Nations".[336] Furthermore, during the preparations for setting up the Court it was called "a most essential part of the organization of the League of Nations"[337] by the Council of the League. The Committee of Jurists, which was to draft a statute for the PCIJ, declared that

> "[t]he new Court, being the *judicial organ of the League of Nations*, can only be created within this League. As it is to be *a component part of the League*, it must originate from an organization within the League, and not from a body outside it." (Emphasis added.)[338]

To use the words of one of the distinguished judges of the PCIJ, Judge M. Hudson, reading the various drafts for the League Covenant makes it "inescapable [to conclude] that the League was conceived to include a court and that [this] court … was not to be independent of the organs of the League".[339]

336 "Each of these Governments shall within one month inform the Secretary-General of the League of Nations whether or not it accepts the recommendations contained in the report of the Commission- and if not, whether it proposes to refer the complaint to the Permanent Court of International Justice of the League of Nations." Art. 415 Treaty of Peace between the Allied and Associated Powers and Germany (Versailles Peace Treaty) (signed 28 June 1919, entered into force 10 January 1920) 225 CTS 188.

337 League of Nations, *Official Journal – Number 1, February 1920* (Imprimerie 'Sonor', S.A. Genève 1920), 37.

338 Permanent Court of International Justice & Advisory Committee of Jurists, *Procès-Verbaux of the Proceedings of the Committee, June 16th-July 24th 1920 with Annexes*, 704. In the report on the organization of a Permanent Court of International Justice submitted by M. Léon Bourgeois the future PCIJ was called the "instrument of the League of Nations"; League of Nations, *Official Journal – Number 1, February 1920*, 36.

339 Hudson, *The Permanent Court of International Justice 1920-1942 – A Treatise*, 111.

Although it is debatable what he meant by independence, and especially because it is likely that he did not intend to deny the Court an independence that would encroach upon the Court's judicial function, the PCIJ itself, once established, preferred to describe its role as slightly more autonomous: while considering itself to be "one of the principal organs of the League", it saw itself occupying within the League "a place similar to that occupied in many States by the Judiciary".[340]

Beyond these statements a glance at the constitutive instruments of the PCIJ reveals that a relatively close relationship between the court and the League characterized the administrative and financial aspects of the Court. Although neither the Covenant nor the PCIJ Statute contained any specific provision constituting an institutional bond,[341] the integral relationship was nevertheless emphasized by numerous provisions contained in both instruments. The League was entrusted with the election of the Court's judges,[342] the Court's budget was part of the League's budget,[343] the Court closely co-

---

340 See the inaugural speech of the first president of the PCIJ: "The Court is one of the principal organs of the League, and at the same time exercises its powers in full and sovereign independence. It occupies within the League of Nations a place similar to that occupied within in many States by the Judicature, which is an integral part of the State, and depends upon the national legislature as regards all that concerns its constitution, its organization, its powers, its maintenance, – but which recognises no master in the exercise of its duties, in regard to which it enjoys absolute liberty and is bound only by the law which it is its task to apply." PCIJ, *Acts and Documents concerning the Organisation of the Court: No. 2 Preparation of the Rules of Court* (30 January-24 March 1922) Ser. D, No. 2, 326.

341 Art. 14 of the Covenant is the only provision that refers to the PCIJ and it does not provide any basis for a special, elevated organizational relationship between the League and the Court. Art. 2 of the Covenant, which lists the organs of the League, envisages merely the creation of an Assembly and of a Council (with a permanent Secretariat) but makes no mentioning of a court. Nevertheless, Art. 1 of the Statute underlines the close link between the two founding documents by providing that the Court is established in accordance with Art. 14 Covenant.

342 The Assembly and the Council of the League were jointly to conduct the elections: see Art. 4 PCIJ Statute. This feature led A. Fachiri to classify the relationship between the PCIJ and the League as merely "momentary" Fachiri, *The Permanent Court of International Justice – Its Constitution, Procedure and Work*, 300.

343 Judges' salaries were to be fixed by the Assembly on the proposal of the Council (Art. 32(1)); the Assembly decided on the conditions for pensions (Art. 32(2)); the budget of the court was paid for by the League and decided by the Assembly upon the proposal of the Council (Art. 33). The financial ties are emphasized by Bustamante y Sirven, Antonio Sánchez de, *La Cour Permanente de Justice Internationale* (Recueil Sirey Paris 1925), 174.

operated with the Council and the Assembly of the League by providing advisory opinions,[344] and – perhaps most importantly – the Court was part of the overall effort of the League to promote the peaceful settlement of international disputes.[345, 346] One forceful contention in opposition to the close relationship is the autonomous character of the founding document of the PCIJ, its Statute. It was drafted by the Advisory Committee of Jurists, set up in accordance with the wording of Art. 14 Covenant.[347] On 24 July 1920 the Committee adopted a "draft scheme" for the establishment of the PCIJ, which was submitted for consideration by the Council between 30 July and 5 August 1920 and by the Assembly of the League beginning in November 1920.[348] The Assembly declared its unanimous approval of the Statute in a resolution on 13 December 1920[349] which envisaged a separate protocol

344 Art. 14 Covenant of the League of Nations and Art. 65 PCIJ Statute.

345 Art. 12 Covenant lists judicial settlement as one of the methods which the members of the League agree to use as soon as any dispute arises which is "likely to lead to a rupture". Art. 13 furthermore commits the members of the League to submitting any justiciable dispute which cannot be solved by diplomatic means to either arbitration or judicial settlement. Art. 13(3) Covenant explicitly lists the PCIJ, besides any other tribunal agreed on by the parties, as the appropriate forum. Art. 14 contains the so-called "assignment-clause" on the establishment of the PCIJ: "The Court shall be competent to hear and determine any dispute of an international character which the parties thereto submit to it. The Court may also give an advisory opinion upon any dispute or question referred to it by the Council or by the Assembly."

346 Another link between the Statute and the Covenant is the provision determining the jurisdiction *ratione personae* of the PCIJ: according to Art. 34 PCIJ Statute both States and "members of the League of Nations" may appear as parties before the PCIJ.

347 Art. 14 Covenant: "The Council shall formulate and submit to the Members of the League for adoption plans for the establishment of a Permanent Court of International Justice. The Court shall be competent to hear and determine any dispute of an international character which the parties thereto submit to it. The Court may also give an advisory opinion upon any dispute or question referred to it by the Council or by the Assembly." See further on the drafting background Scott, James Brown, *The Project of a Permanent Court of International Justice and Resolutions of the Advisory Committee of Jurists – Report and Commentary* (Carnegie Endowment for International Peace Washington 1920.).

348 Among the changes that were made by both the Council and the Assembly was the rejection of compulsory jurisdiction by the Council.

349 The Assembly referred consideration of the draft scheme to its Third Committee, which, on 22 November 1920, appointed a sub-committee entrusted with the task of considering the question in detail. After holding ten meetings between 11 November and 7 December 1920, the sub-committee submitted its results to the

containing the Statute and which was to be submitted to the members of the League for adoption. The Resolution furthermore provided that the Statute of the court should enter into force as soon as the protocol of signature, which was later prepared by the secretariat,[350] had been ratified by a majority of the League's members.[351] Hence the court was established neither by the Covenant of the League, nor by some action of the League's organs. Instead it was based on a separate international treaty. One of the consequences of this solution is that the Statute was open even for non-members of the League to sign and ratify.[352] Paradoxically, however, it speaks out in favour of States' presumption of a close link between the court and the League that no State ever became a party to the Statute of the court without at the same time being a member of the League.[353] It furthermore deserves mentioning that the protocol of signature does provide for some ambiguity when it comes to determining the court's link to the League, as the French official text describes the court as "la Cour permanente de Justice internationale *de la Sociéte des Nations*" (emphasis added). Although the – equally official – English text merely speaks of "the Permanent Court of International Justice", considering that the work in drafting the Statute had mainly been conducted in French[354] this wording at the very least reflects the drafters' considerations. On the other hand, the protocol was not drafted by the committee but by the Secretariat of the League, and in combination with the other examples of

---

Third Committee in a report which was considered, and on 11 December the statute was unanimously adopted by the Third Committee.

350 The protocol was adopted by the council on 14 December 1920 and announced to the assembly on 17 December 1920, yet it is dated 16 December 1920, and was made available for signature on 17 and 18 December 1920. See Hudson, *The Permanent Court of International Justice 1920-1942 – A Treatise*, 124-125.

351 This took place on 1 September 1921. The protocol of signature, however, was not registered pursuant to Art. 18 Covenant until 8 October 1921: see 6 LNTS 379.

352 Riedel, Eibe, 'Article 55 (c) UNC', in: Simma, Bruno (ed) *The Charter of the United Nations: A Commentary – Volume II* (Oxford University Press Oxford 2nd edn. 2002), 929.

353 Hudson, *International Tribunals: Past and Future*, 234-235. At the same time, some members of the League never became members of the Court, which may well be explained by the pioneering connotation that the establishment of the PCIJ had at the time, which still raised some doubts about the threats to member States' sovereignty from such an institution.

354 Spiermann, Ole, 'Historical Introduction (ICJ Statute)', in: Zimmermann, Andreas *et al.* (eds) *The Statute of the International Court of Justice – A Commentary* (Oxford University Press Oxford 2006), 44.

ambiguous drafting noticeable in this document[355] it cannot be assumed that this wording reflected the actual position of the committee on the court's relationship with the League.

In view of these observations the question arises why the covenant did not contain a provision expressly proclaiming an organic connection between the League and the court. Explanations may be found in the tentative character of the League itself, the lack of experience in the operation of any permanent international tribunal with general jurisdiction, and thus the desire to wait and see how these institutions, simultaneously but separately, operated in practice.[356] Linking the court too explicitly to the League would have meant putting all those States which were considering joining the new organization into a position of either adopting a package deal or being left outside multilateral co-operation. As both the model of a global organization of collective security and the institution of a permanent global court had thus far not been tested, such integration would have put both on rather shaky foundations from the beginning. In sum, considering the wide array of considerations mentioned above, it is appropriate to classify the court "as an independent international judicial organ formally separate from the League but available to the League for certain purposes".[357] At the same time, due to the strength of the arguments outlined above, emphasis should be placed on the word "formally".

2. The Organizational Contextualization of the ICJ

The relationship between a global organization of collective security and a permanent international court was retained and advanced with the creation of the UN replacing the LoN. The founders of the new international organization were initially faced with the decision either to retain the PCIJ as the new organization's main judicial organ or to establish an entirely new

---

355 See Hudson, *The Permanent Court of International Justice 1920-1942 – A Treatise*, 125-126.

356 Cf. Amr, *The Role of the International Court of Justice as the Principal Judicial Organ of the United Nations*, 16. See also the same assessment by the Informal Inter-Allied Committee on the Future of the Permanent Court of International Justice, United Nations, 'Report of the Inter-Allied Committee on the Future of the Permanent Court of International Justice, February 10, 1944' (1945) 39 American Journal of International Law 1, Supplement: Official Documents, 5.

357 Rosenne, 'Permanent Court of International Justice (PCIJ)', para. 8.

court.[358] At the San Francisco conference convened in 1945, the First Committee of the Fourth Commission, entrusted with the task of drafting the provisions in the Charter of the UN pertaining to an international court of justice (now Chapter XIV UNC) and a statute for that court, opted for the creation of a new court. This was based on both practical (e.g. the impossibility of including necessary amendments in the PCIJ Statute or electing new judges following the discontinuance of the League of Nations) and political considerations (e.g. neither the US nor the Soviet Union was a member of the PCIJ at the time).[359]

The new court established under the umbrella of the UN was made one of the six main organs of the UN[360] and its principal judicial organ. With this contextualization, which is the central dividing line in comparison with the status of the PCIJ, the drafters clearly went against the proposals of the Informal Inter-Allied Committee on the Future of the Permanent Court of International Justice, which in February 1944 had suggested that the new court ought to have no organic relationship with the new system of collective security.[361] The reason the potential shared fortune of the court and the organization was not brushed aside was that through its inclusion in the organization of the UN the ICJ was expected automatically to receive the much needed support of the members of that organization.[362] Moreover, this solution was considered well suited to emphasize the importance ascribed to the judicial process within the new international organization, which had grown over the first half of the 20th century.[363] A greater willingness to acknowledge

358 For an overview of the views of States on the establishment of a new international court during the Second World War see Marston, Geoffrey, 'The London Committee and the Statute of the International Court of Justice', in: Lowe, Vaughan *et al.* (eds) *Fifty Years of the International Court of Justice: Essays in Honour of Sir Robert Jennings* (Cambridge University Press Cambridge 1996).

359 Oppenheim & Lauterpacht, *International Law, A Treatise – Disputes, War and Neutrality*, 263-264.

360 Art. 7(1) UNC.

361 United Nations, 'Report of the Inter-Allied Committee on the Future of the Permanent Court of International Justice, February 10, 1944', 4.

362 See the Report of the Rapporteur of Committee IV/1 in United Nations Information Organizations, *UNCIO XIII*, 381.

363 Another indication of this can be seen in the UNC's Art. 36(3) demand that the UNSC, when making recommendations on appropriate procedures or methods of adjustment in disputes the continuance of which is likely to endanger the maintenance of international peace and security "should also take into consideration that

and set out the proximity between the Court and the world organization can thus be observed, and it is the aim of the following parts of this chapter to show how this played out in practice.

The formula of "principal judicial organ", besides clearly granting the ICJ superior status among similar judicial bodies, signifies that the ICJ does not hold a judicial monopoly. This is in line with what applied to the PCIJ, which – pursuant to Art. 1 PCIJ Statute – was merely an addition to a potential community of courts and tribunals.[364] States Parties are thus allowed to submit disputes to other courts or tribunals or, based on State sovereignty governing much of inter-State dispute settlement, arbitration.[365] Furthermore, not only is the ICJ not the only judicial organ,[366] it is not even the only judicial organ under the auspices of the UN.[367] Much like the powers and procedures of the PCIJ, the ICJ is based on the aim of assisting in the fulfilment of the parent organization's objectives, and hence its rules of procedure are virtually identical to those of the PCIJ.[368] These similarities were considered necessary to safeguard the desired continuity in the development of the judicial process,[369] something which still today is mirrored in the ICJ's numerous references to decisions delivered by the PCIJ.[370] Moreover, the relationship between the ICJ and the UN is characterized by many of the details described

---

legal disputes should as a general rule be referred by the parties to the International Court of Justice".

364 Cf. *supra* Chapter D.II(2).

365 Cf. Art. 95 UNC which explicitly provides that "[n]othing in the present Charter shall prevent Members of the United Nations from entrusting the solution of their differences to other tribunals by virtue of agreements already in existence or which may be concluded in the future."

366 On the relationship between the ICJ and other international courts see, e.g., Gaya, Giorgio, 'Relationship of the ICJ with Other International Courts and Tribunals', in: Zimmermann, Andreas *et al.* (eds) *The Statute of the International Court of Justice – A Commentary* (Oxford University Press Oxford 2006).

367 This is meanwhile clearly exemplified by the creation of the two *ad hoc* criminal tribunals. Mosler, Hermann & Oellers-Frahm, Karin, 'Article 92 UNC', in: Simma, Bruno (ed) *The Charter of the United Nations: A Commentary – Volume II* (Oxford University Press Oxford 2nd edn. 2002), 1150; see *infra* Chapter G.

368 The Rules of Court underwent a significant revision in 1978: see Rosenne, 'Permanent Court of International Justice (PCIJ)', para. 11.

369 United Nations Information Organizations, *UNCIO XIII*, 384.

370 According to a study of the ICJ's case law up until 21 September 2009, the ICJ referred to the case law of the PCIJ in 117 instances. The last such reference was in *Certain Property (Liechtenstein v Germany) (Preliminary Objections)* ICJ Rep. 6 (2005).

above regarding the PCIJ. For example, both the UNSC and the United Nations General Assembly (UNGA) are the electoral organs for the Court,[371] the costs of the ICJ are borne by the UN with the UNGA being the decision-making body on financial issues,[372] the ICJ is to co-operate with the organs of the UN by providing advisory opinions whenever requested,[373] and the ICJ is an integral part of the overall effort to settle international disputes peacefully.[374]

Besides these characteristics, the ICJ also demonstrates certain proper features, which clearly underline the special and very close connection between the Court and the UN. The new Court was created by an instrument that remains an integral part of the constituting instrument of the political organization of the international community.[375],[376] Moreover, the members of that organization are *ipso facto* parties to the Court's Statute (cf. Art. 93(1) UNC). Even for those States that prefer not to be members of the UN but nevertheless desire to become parties to the Statute can do so only under the conditions set out by the UNGA and the UNSC.[377] Despite the small practical relevance that this constellation has, it is expressive of the intention behind the system. Phrased differently, it is virtually impossible to get involved with the ICJ without at the same time initiating some kind of activities from the remaining UN system. Another embodiment is Art. 36(3) UNC, according to which the UNSC is called upon to recommend that legal disputes should as a general rule be referred by the parties to the ICJ. The Covenant did not contain a similarly explicit embrace of the PCIJ as its "court of choice". Furthermore the ICJ Statute provides in Art. 69 that any amendment shall follow the procedure laid down by the UNC and applicable to that docu-

---

371 Art. 4(1) Statute of the International Court of Justice. See *infra* Chapter D.V(2).

372 Art. 33 ICJ Statute. See *infra* Chapter D.V(3).

373 Art. 65 ICJ Statute in combination with Art. 96 UNC.

374 See, e.g., Art. 33(1) UNC. See *infra* Chapter D.III(1).

375 Oppenheim & Lauterpacht, *International Law, A Treatise – Disputes, War and Neutrality*, 47.

376 One consequence of this is that the ICJ Statute is amended following the same procedure as is provided by the Charter of the UN (cf. Art. 69 ICJ Statute), whereas the Statute of the PCIJ did not include such an amendment clause, leading to the application of the consent principle under treaty law, i.e. the requirement of unanimous consent of all parties. See Karl, Wolfram, 'Article 69 ICJ Statute', in: Zimmermann, Andreas *et al.* (eds) *The Statute of the International Court of Justice – A Commentary* (Oxford University Press Oxford 2006), 1472.

377 Art. 93(2) UNC.

ment.[378] Finally, the ICJ's jurisdiction is explicitly to comprise "matters specially provided for in the Charter of the United Nations".[379] Although the Court itself has found there to be no such provision in the UNC,[380] the wording nevertheless bears witness to the drafters' intended close connection between the ICJ and the UN.[381]

3. Conclusions

> "The functioning of the United Nations depends not only on the institutional independence of its principal organs but also on their co-operation. The co-operation of the principal organs represents, in the same way as their independence, a constitutional principle of the Charter."[382]

As this statement reflects, the ICJ's independence, perceived in part as autonomy from the other organs of the UN,[383] must also be understood under the umbrella of (necessary) co-operation. From a historic perspective it appears that the drafters of the ICJ were less reluctant to ensure the separation of the Court from the world organization in the interest of strengthening its judicial mandate. The ICJ Statute included provisions from the PCIJ Statute which could have justified a description of the PCIJ–League relationship as "organic". These include the electoral system and the financial ties. But the organizational embedding of the ICJ goes beyond that of the PCIJ. Whereas the PCIJ Statute was a separate international treaty, such an attempt to

378 Art. 69-70 ICJ Statute.

379 Art. 36(1) ICJ Statute.

380 *Aerial Incident of 10 August 1999 (Pakistan v India) (Jurisdiction of the Court)* ICJ Rep. 12 (2000), para. 48.

381 These significant organizational ties have led some scholars to qualify the ICJ as a "quasi-constitutional" organ. Schwarzenberger, *International Law as Applied by International Courts and Tribunals – Vol. 4 – International Judicial Law*, 271. See Bassiouni, M. Cherif & Manikas, Peter, *The Law of the International Criminal Tribunal for the Former Yugoslavia* (Transnational Publ. New York 1996), 238 fn. 4 with further references.

382 President of the International Court of Justice, *Document transmitted by the President of the International Court of Justice to the Secretary-General on the implications of General Assembly resolution 61/262 in regard to certain provisions of the Statute of the Court* (2007) UN Doc. A/62/538 Annex II, 74.

383 A further indication of the fact that the ICJ itself does not consider itself absorbed by the UN is that it delivers its judgments not in the name of the organization, but in its own name: "The Court … delivers the judgment".

maintain at least the appearance of the Court's autonomy is lacking in the constitutive documents of both the ICJ and the UN. Instead the new constellation summarized in the ICJ's character as the "principal judicial organ" of the UN – as opposed to being another addition to other courts "to which States are always at liberty to submit their disputes for settlement"[384] – suggests the expected affinity of the ICJ to the broader agenda of the world organization and recognizes the political function necessarily played by the Court. If the ICJ is forced to operate in the political and legal environment shaped by the UN, however, it becomes relevant to what extent it can do so in an independent fashion so as to separate itself from the remaining UN system.[385]

III. The Functions Served by the ICJ

1. The Function of Dispute Settlement – The Dispute Settlement Mandate Rooted in the UNC

The main functions served by the ICJ are to settle (legal) disputes referred to it by States and to give advisory opinions in cases submitted to it by duly authorized international organizations, agencies and the UNGA. By exercising these functions, the ICJ makes a significant contribution to the development of international law, which in itself can be and has been interpreted as a separate function of the Court.[386] In particular the task of adjudicating on legal disputes is significantly shaped by the organizational context in which the ICJ operates, namely the close connection to the remaining organic structure of the UN. That the ICJ, pursuant to Art. 1 ICJ Statute and Arts. 7(1) and 92 UNC, is the principal judicial organ of the UN has two major implications:

---

384 Art. 1 PCIJ Statute.

385 According to G. Jaenicke, "[b]y virtue of its judicial independence, the ICJ, as the 'principal judicial organ' of the UN (Art. 92), clearly stands outside any hierarchical order, if indeed there is any, among the principal organs of the UN." Jaenicke, Günther, 'Article 7 UNC', in: Simma, Bruno (ed) *The Charter of the United Nations: A Commentary – Volume I* (Oxford University Press Oxford 2nd edn. 2002), 218.

386 See more on this *infra* Chapter D.III(2).

(I) The Court is obliged to operate within the wider framework created by the general objectives of the UN system.[387] According to Art. 1 lit. 1 UNC the maintenance of international peace and security is one of the primary and overarching purposes of the UN.[388] In consequence, the Preamble (and Art. 2 lit. 4 UNC in the form of a binding obligation) expresses the renunciation of armed force as a tool for inter-State dispute settlement.[389] Yet the fundamental prohibition of the threat and use of force necessitates the establishment not only of a system of collective sanctions against any offender and thus of strong international organizations able to reprimand any breach of the rule,[390] but also of viable alternative mechanisms for the settlement of conflicts. This is addressed by Art. 1 lit. 1 UNC, which promotes the settlement of international disputes by "peaceful means, and in conformity with the principles of justice and international law", followed by the principle set out in Art. 2 lit. 3 UNC, calling upon the UN and its members alike to "settle their international disputes by peaceful means in such a manner that international peace and security, and justice, are not endangered." The ICJ, in its capacity as one of six principal organs of the UN, is obliged to contribute to this common goal,[391] and can do so with the help of its special ability to apply legal techniques in the resolution of international dis-

---

387 Some of the implications of this contextualization will be dealt with in Chapter D.V *infra*. As stated above, the PCIJ was closely linked to a parent organization, the League of Nations, as was made clear *inter alia* by the first president of the court in his inaugural speech where he defined the court as being "one of the principal organs of the League" and occupying within the League "a place similar to that occupied in many States by the Judiciary"; PCIJ, *Acts and Documents concerning the Organisation of the Court: No. 2 Preparation of the Rules of Court*, 326 (15 February 1922). Nevertheless, the Covenant of the League of Nations did not contain any provision expressly classifying the PCIJ as an organ of the League, let alone its principal judicial organ.

388 Wolfrum, Rüdiger, 'Article 1 UNC', in: Simma, Bruno (ed) *The Charter of the United Nations: A Commentary – Volume I* (Oxford University Press Oxford 2nd edn. 2002), 42. See also the use of the formula "peace and security" throughout the ICJ Statute in e.g. the preamble, Arts. 1, 2 lits. 3 and 6, 11, 12, 24.

389 This was not the case with the League of Nations.

390 Cf. Randelzhofer, Albrecht, 'Article 2(4) UNC', in: Simma, Bruno (ed) *The Charter of the United Nations: A Commentary – Volume I* (Oxford University Press Oxford 2nd edn. 2002), 116-117.

391 Rosenne, Shabtai, *The World Court – What it is and how it Works* (Sythoff Leyden 1962), 36-38.

putes.[392] As early as in the *travaux préparatoires* to the ICJ Statute it was predicted that "[t]he *judicial* process will have a central place in … the settlement of international disputes by peaceful means" (emphasis added).[393] Peaceful settlement of disputes is in the UNC thus conceived not only as a political process but also as one characterized by legally substantiated methods.[394] The UNC mirrors this assessment in Art. 33(1) by listing judicial settlement as one of several equivalent[395] mechanisms for peaceful dispute settlement.

(II) The ICJ is not conceived as an organ subordinated to the other central organs of the UN,[396] and hence judicial settlement is formally on an equal footing with other means of dispute settlement. Due to the predominantly political nature of the UN as an inter-State organization of collective security, the settlement of disputes, and hence the maintenance of international peace and security, is mainly entrusted to the political organs of the UN, the UNGA[397] and the UNSC.[398] Yet the UNC establishes the ICJ as one of the enumerated "principal organs" of the UN, thus rejecting any hierarchical order among them. This balance and equality even seem to strip all the above-mentioned examples of how the UNGA can influence the Court of any real authority to influence the Court in its core activities (which of course equally applies *vice versa*). Instead the relationship between the principal organs is characterized by separate domains of competence where each principal organ "may act on its own initiative and where it is not subject to directives from the other organs."[399] Although this applies to the inter-relationship between all the principal organs of the UN, with respect to the ICJ this

392 Cf. Art. 92 UNC specifying the text of Art. 7(1) UNC by stating that the ICJ is the principal *judicial* organ of the UN.

393 United Nations Information Organizations, *UNCIO XIII*, 393.

394 Wolfrum, Rüdiger, 'Artikel 1 UNC', in: Simma, Bruno (ed) *Charta der Vereinten Nationen: Kommentar* (Beck München 1991), 9.

395 Tomuschat, Christian, 'Artikel 33 UNC', in: Simma, Bruno (ed) *Charta der Vereinten Nationen: Kommentar* (Beck München 1991), 476.

396 Art. 7(1) UNC does not place the principal organs of the UN in a hierarchical order. However, some Articles of the UNC allow for the (partial) control of one principal organ by another.

397 Cf. Art. 11 UNC.

398 The UNSC has the "primary responsibility" (cf. Art. 24(1) UNC) and the ability to bind the member States through and in the exercise of its functions (cf. Art. 25 UNC).

399 Jaenicke, 'Article 7 UNC', 218.

equality clearly cements the Court's judicial independence.[400] What is thus asked for, and to the degree just described even mandated, from the organs is a functional co-operation,[401] one where each organ focuses on its own competences, is not bound by the other organs' perception of how to solve a dispute but nevertheless is called upon to co-operate with them in the interest of the achievement of common goals.[402]

2. Contributing to the Development of International Law

a) The Power of the ICJ to Interpret International Law

Although the Court in the past has undoubtedly made contributions to the resolution of sensitive disputes, expecting this to be the main or even the only function of the Court would be to gravely overestimate both the influence the Court's decisions have and the significance ascribed to the Court by States.[403] But irrespective of the conflict-solving capacity of the Court, which in essence is a political feature and thus always competes with the activities of other UN organs, the ICJ through its proceedings interprets and hence contributes to the development of international law. The ICJ's prominent role in the progressive development of international law has been underlined in numerous resolutions of the UNGA.[404] The significance of and

---

400 Ibid.

401 Rosenne, Shabtai, *The Court and the United Nations* (Nijhoff Leiden 4th edn. 2006), 110.

402 Cf. *Legality of the Use by a State of Nuclear Weapons in Armed Conflict (Advisory Opinion)* ICJ Rep. 66 (1996), para. 25: "International organizations are governed by the 'principle of speciality', that is to say, they are invested by the States which create them with the powers, the limits of which are a function of the common interests whose promotion those States entrust them to."

403 See Steinberger, Helmut, 'The International Court of Justice', in: Mosler, Hermann *et al.* (eds) *Judicial Settlement of International Disputes – International Court of Justice, other Courts and Tribunals, Arbitration and Conciliation; an International Symposium* (Springer Berlin 1974), 207.

404 See, e.g., UNGA, *Need for Greater use by the United Nations and its Organs of the International Court of Justice* (14 November 1947) UN Doc. A/RES/171 (II). See also UNGA, *Declaration on the Occasion of the Twenty-Fifth Anniversary of the United Nations* (24 October 1970) UN Doc. A/RES/2627 (XXV) and UNGA, *Report of the International Law Commission* (16 December 1970) UN Doc. A/RES/2734 (XXV) and UNGA, *Peaceful Settlement of International Disputes* (12 December 1974) UN Doc. A/RES/3283 (XXIX).

the importance vested in this objective *per se* should not be underestimated, given the prominent mention of international law in subsection 3 of the preamble to the UNC[405] and Arts. 1(1), 13(1)(a) UNC.[406] The ICJ is well equipped to fulfil this task as it is the only international tribunal of a permanent character competent to decide upon any question of international law. At its disposal in developing international law the Court has the mechanisms of judicial dispute settlement among States, i.e. the contentious jurisdiction, and its function as a legal adviser to UN organs and agencies through its advisory jurisdiction.[407] As Judge Tanaka stated in his separate opinion in the *Barcelona Traction case*,

> "[t]he more important function of the Court as the principal judicial organ of the United Nations is to be found not only in the settlement of concrete disputes, but also in its reasoning, through which it may contribute to the development of international law."[408]

This is *prima facie* contradictory of the notion that "[t]he decision of the Court has no binding force except between the parties and in respect of that particular case,"[409] at least insofar as "development of international law" is not merely a side-effect of the settlement of concrete disputes but instead an original function with which the Court was entrusted. This concern is reinforced by the fact that decisions of the ICJ (or any other international court) are not recognized by the Statute or under general international law as sources of international law, but merely as subsidiary means that may contribute to

---

405 "[T]he peoples of the United Nations, determined to establish conditions under … respect for the obligations arising from treaties and other sources of international law can be maintained".

406 See also UNGA, *Need for Greater use by the United Nations and its Organs of the International Court of Justice*, where the UNGA calls upon the organs of the UN to request advisory opinions from the ICJ on questions of international law and recommends States to make more frequent use of the ICJ by submitting their legal disputes to the Court.

407 As opposed to the other means of dispute settlement laid down in Art. 33(1) UNC, namely negotiation, enquiry, mediation, conciliation, arbitration, resort to regional agencies or arrangements, or other peaceful means. Cf. Art. 96 UNC and Chapter IV Statute.

408 *Barcelona Traction, Light and Power Co Ltd (New Application: 1962) (Belgium v Spain) (Preliminary Objections) (Judge Tanaka Separate Opinion)* ICJ Rep. 65 (1964), 65-66.

409 Art. 59 ICJ Statute. See also Art. 94(1) UNC: "Each Member of the United Nations undertakes to comply with the decision of the International Court of Justice in any case to which it is a party."

the interpretation of other sources.[410] If the Court's decisions[411] were indeed not of any relevance beyond a particular case the ability of the Court to make a notable contribution to the development of international law would be rather limited. The rule of *sententia jus facit inter partes* expressed in Art. 59 ICJ Statute must be interpreted as limiting the precedential value of a decision of the ICJ in the sense that decisions are not *per se* binding on third parties or the Court itself.[412] This does not, however, mean that the Court does not also see a jurisprudential value in making references to and reaffirming points that have been made in previous decisions. As the Court has stated, it is striving to make use of its previous case law in the interest of "ensur[ing] consistency with its own past case law in order to provide predictability."[413] Hence the Court – by analogy with its predecessor – often cites its own decisions and advisory opinions,[414] despite the non-binding character of the latter.[415] As a consequence, although the principle of *stare decisis* is unknown to the ICJ,[416] the Court nevertheless refers to and is even hesitant to overrule its settled case law. The limited binding force of a judgment as stipulated in Art. 59 ICJ Statute is not violated by this practice, as the Court, by making use of its previous decisions, merely applies the law as developed in judicial

410 Cf. Art. 38 ICJ Statute. According to Art. 38(1)(d) ICJ Statute "judicial decisions ... [are] subsidiary means for the determination of rules of law." Attributing an ancillary role to judicial decisions in this way is consistent with the Romano-Germanic legal family and contrasts with the common-law legal family, where judicial precedents have binding character.

411 This obviously does not apply to advisory opinions which, by definition, are not binding.

412 Parry, Clive, *The Sources and Evidences of International Law* (Manchester University Press Manchester 1965), 92.

413 *Legality of Use of Force (Serbia and Montenegro v. Belgium) Joint declaration of Vice-President Ranjeva, Judges Guillaume, Higgins, Kooijmans, Al Khasawneh, Buergenthal and Elaraby* ICJ Rep. 330 (2004), para. 3. On the ECtHR's emphasis on the principles of certainty, foreseeability and equality before the law see Bernhardt, Rudolf, 'Article 59 ICJ Statute', in: Zimmermann, Andreas *et al.* (eds) *The Statute of the International Court of Justice – A Commentary* (Oxford University Press Oxford 2006), 1245 fn. 67.

414 On the practice of the PCIJ in this regard see Sørensen, Max, *Les sources du droit international: étude sur la jurisprudence de la Cour Permanente de Justice Internationale* (Munksgaard Kopenhagen 1946), 166.

415 Bernhardt, 'Article 59 ICJ Statute', 1244. See also Thirlway, Hugh, 'The International Court of Justice', in: Evans, Malcolm D. (ed) *International Law* (Oxford University Press Oxford 2nd edn 2006).

416 As it is to any other international court.

decisions.[417] Another dimension of the importance of referring to its own case law, even when the Court disagrees with its previous decisions, is the interest in maintaining the institution's prestige and authority. Particularly in the context of an increasingly proliferated institutional landscape with the inherent risk of diverging and contradicting jurisprudence, the Court's potential role as a centre of gravity for jurisprudential influence on the development of international law remains significant.[418]

b) Factors Influencing the Development of International Law through Adjudication

One limitation of the ICJ's role as an interpreter and promoter/driving force of international law stems from its lack of any power of initiative. The Court itself is unable, e.g. with the help of an autonomous prosecutor, (*ex officio*) to initiate proceedings on the basis of alleged violations of international law. This, in a negative sense, contributes to the earlier mentioned predictability of the Court. Whereas the contentious jurisdiction of the ICJ requires States to refer cases to it,[419] the issue of an advisory opinion demands a prior request by those (indirectly) enumerated bodies authorized to do so under the UNC.[420] But is this pre-determined circle of actors able to open the gates of the ICJ necessarily a limitation on the Court's ability to clarify and develop international law? It is the utilization of the Court by those who have been enabled to have recourse to it that determines the Court's contribution to the advancement of international law. Considering only the number of States which are members of the UN, and thus members of the Statute, the potential is considerable. However, it is the will of the States actually to seek the Court's advice which is decisive for the Court's role. This desire has fluctuated throughout the history of the ICJ and has in particular been influenced by political de-

---

417 Although this does arguably not mean that the Court, by interpreting international law, creates such law itself.

418 Oeter, Stefan, 'Vielfalt der Gerichte – Einheit des Prozessrechts?', in: Hofmann, Rainer *et al.* (eds) *Die Rechtskontrolle von Organen der Staatengemeinschaft: Vielfalt der Gerichte – Einheit des Prozessrechts?* (C.F. Müller Heidelberg 2007), 153.

419 Cf. Art. 36(1) ICJ Statute.

420 Art. 96 UNC; cf. Art. 65 ICJ Statute.

velopments, of which decolonization and the Cold War are but the two most prominent.[421]

Further relativizing the Court's ability decisively to influence the development of international law is the condition that neither Arts. 7(1) and 92 UNC nor any other provision in the UNC suggests any hierarchy among the principal organs of the UN. This suggests that the ICJ, just like the other organs of the UN, has an inherent and independent right to interpret the UNC or other international law as and when circumstances so require.[422] This in turn implies that the Court does not have supremacy over the other five main bodies of the UN even when it comes to authoritatively interpreting international law in general or UN law in particular.[423] Irrespective of this, it is undeniable that the ICJ has decided a number of important cases especially in the field of border delimitation,[424] regarding the use and allocation of natural resources,[425] and has furthermore been able to draw attention to and shape the rules pertaining to e.g. the sources of international law and elements of the *jus ad bellum* and *jus in bello*.[426]

3. Subsidiary Functions

The above-mentioned functions of dispute settlement and interpretation and development of international law are not the only roles ascribed to the ICJ.

---

421 Jennings, Robert Y., 'General Introduction (ICJ Statute)', in: Zimmermann, Andreas *et al.* (eds) *The Statute of the International Court of Justice – A Commentary* (Oxford University Press Oxford 2006), 13.

422 Rosenne, *The World Court – What it is and how it Works*, 39.

423 Steinberger, 'The International Court of Justice', 203.

424 See, e.g. *Frontier Dispute (Benin/Niger)* ICJ Rep. 90 (2005); *Land and Maritime Boundury between Cameroon and Nigeria (Cameroon v. Nigeria: Equatorial Guineu intervening)* ICJ Rep. 303 (2002); *Land, Island and Maritime Frontier Dispute (El Salvador/Honduras: Nicaragua intervening)* ICJ Rep. 351 (1992).

425 For example, in the *Gabčíkovo-Nagymaros Case*, the ICJ contributed significantly to the law of watercourses by emphasising the importance of "equitable utilization" as a principle for the use and allocation of international freshwater resources: *Gabčíkovo-Nagymaros Project (Hungary/Slovakia)* ICJ Rep. 7 (1997).

426 Seminal decisions are, e.g., *Military and Paramilitary Activities in and against Nicaragua (Nicaragua v. United States of America) (Jurisdiction and Admissibility) (Judgment)*; *Legality of the Threat or Use of Nuclear Weapons (Advisory Opinion)*; *Legal Consequences of the Construction of a Wall in the Occupied Palestinian Territory (Advisory Opinion)* ICJ Rep. 136 (2004).

It has occasionally been argued that the Court accepts, or should accept, further roles, such as preventing disputes from escalating into long-drawn-out and costly judicial proceedings,[427] the preservation of the unity of international law,[428] hearing judicial appeals,[429] engaging in judicial review,[430] and the interpretation and development of UN institutional law.[431] Whereas certain of these functions must be rejected as having little or no basis in the Statute, others are highly debated but have not thus far been acknowledged by the Court itself, and yet others can be labelled at least as subsidiary or variations of the two earlier-mentioned functions. Arguably, the ICJ as the principal judicial organ of the UN and by reason of its eminent role in the community of international courts is able to promote the unity of international law by contributing to the development of international law in particular directions and to counterbalance uncontrolled diversification and inconsistencies in international law. This all the more emphasizes the importance that the ICJ has for the international legal order, and consequently the likelihood

---

427 On this kind of "preventive diplomacy" role of the ICJ see Jennings, Robert Y., 'The United Nations at Fifty: The International Court of Justice after Fifty Years' (1995) 89 American Journal of International Law 3; Adede, Andrónico O., 'Judicial Settlement in Perspective', in: Muller, Sam *et al.* (eds) *The International Court of Justice: Its Future Role after Fifty Years* (Martinus Nijhoff The Hague 1997), 63-64.

428 Mosler, 'The International Judiciary from the Point of View of an International Judge', 170.

429 Amr, *The Role of the International Court of Justice as the Principal Judicial Organ of the United Nations*, 341 et seq.

430 The task of "constitutional interpretation" was mentioned as early as in the UNGA Resolution 171(II) of 14 November 1947 on a need for greater use by the United Nations and its organs of the International Court of Justice. The debate on the role of the ICJ as a quasi-constitutional court of the international legal order has been intense: see, e.g., Weeramantry, Christopher G., 'Expanding the Potential of the World Court', in: Jasentuliyana, Nandasiri (ed) *Perspectives on International Law* (Kluwer Law 1995), 344-45; Malanczuk, Peter, 'Reconsidering the Relationship between the ICJ and the Security Council', in: Heere, Wypo P. (ed) *International Law and The Hague's 750th Anniversary* (T.M.C. Asser Press 1999), 88-89; McWhinney, Edward, 'The International Court as Constitutional Court and the Blurring of the Arbitral/Judicial Processes', in: Muller, Sam (ed) *The Flame Rekindled – New Hopes for International Arbitration* (Nijhoff Dordrecht 1994), 81-89.

431 Amr, *The Role of the International Court of Justice as the Principal Judicial Organ of the United Nations*, 121 et seq.

that various actors may have a real interest in influencing the ICJ to further their needs.

4. Conclusions

Due to its organizational setting in the UN the ICJ has a variety of functions and expectations directed at it; more so than any other international court. The function of dispute settlement is at the core of the ICJ's tasks and opens the Court to the interests of States as (potential) parties to a dispute. As the principal judicial body of the UN, the ICJ is furthermore obliged to harmonize with the UN's political organs. This may create areas of friction between them, where political solutions do not conform to the judicial dispute settlement method promoted by the ICJ.

IV. The Notion of Judicial Independence in the Statute of the ICJ

1. Drafting Background of the Inclusion in Art. 2 ICJ Statute

A commitment by the ICJ to judicial independence follows from Art. 2 ICJ Statute, the wording of which is identical to that contained in Art. 2 PCIJ Statute: "The Court shall be composed of a body of independent judges ...." During the drafting of the Statute, Art. 2 was given scant attention and the question of the independence of the judges was on the whole largely neglected. Neither the Dumbarton Oaks Proposal nor the Informal Inter-Allied Committee proposed any amendment of Art. 2 PCIJ Statute in this regard.[432] Only three proposals – from Cuba, Honduras and the Netherlands – addressed the issue by demanding that more emphasis be placed on the independence of judges.[433] Cuba wished to connect the requirement to the court body instead of the individual judge;[434] Honduras formulated a necessity to guaran-

432 United Nations Information Organizations, *Volume XIV – United Nations Committee of Jurists* (United Nations Information Organizations London New York 1945), 397-398.

433 The two proposals for revised wordings of Art. 2 from Venezuela (ibid, 363) and Egypt (ibid, 301) submitted to the Committee of Jurists did not deal with the independence requirement.

434 Ibid, 397-398.

tee, in the most absolute manner, the independence of judges;[435] and the Netherlands considered it important that judges not only agree to be "impartial and independent" but that the Statute should also recognize this.[436] Arts. 1 and 2 were discussed neither during the meetings of the Committee of Jurists nor in the Subcommittee. Hence the Committee of Jurists in its *Official Comments Relating to the Statute of the Proposed International Court of Justice*[437] and later in the *Draft of Statute of an International Court of Justice*[438] submitted to the United Nations Conference on International Organization recommended the retention of Art. 2 in its wording from the PCIJ Statute.

At the San Francisco Conference the Committee IV/1 on the International Court of Justice considered the issue of the independence of the judges at its seventh meeting.[439] The suggestion to replace the word "independent" in Art. 2 PCIJ Statute with the word "impartiality" was rejected on the basis that it was important that judges "should be not only impartial but also independent of control of their own countries or the [UN]".[440] The drafting of the Statute of the PCIJ was equally characterized by a reserved analysis of the requirement of independence. Indeed the inclusion appears to be mainly based on tradition, especially that of arbitral tribunals.[441]

2. Basic Contents and Function of Art. 2 ICJ Statute

The requirement of independence of the ICJ judges enshrined in Art. 2 ICJ Statute is closely connected to the further requirements of international-mindedness, high moral character, and competence, as becomes apparent from the further wording of Art. 2.[442] But whereas the requirement to disreg-

---

435 Ibid, 398.

436 Ibid, 398. On the relationship between the two concepts of impartiality and independence within the framework of the ICJ see *infra* Chapter D.IV(4).

437 Reprinted in ibid, 384.

438 Reprinted in ibid, 756-776.

439 United Nations Information Organizations, *UNCIO XIII*, 173-174.

440 Ibid, 174. See *infra* Chapter D.IV(4).

441 Aznar-Gómez, Mariano, 'Article 2 ICJ Statute', in: Zimmermann, Andreas *et al.* (eds) *The Statute of the International Court of Justice – A Commentary* (Oxford University Press Oxford 2006), 207.

442 "The Court shall be composed of a body of independent judges, elected regardless of their nationality from among persons of high moral character, who possess the

ard the nationality of potential future judges is further qualified in Art. 3 Statute as an important element of the election process, and competence is elaborated with the description of jurisconsults and practitioners, the content and scope of the integrity, propriety and independence requirements remain "only subjectively determinable".[443] According to G. Schwarzenberger, the independence of the judges of the ICJ must to a certain degree be congruent with the independence of civil servants employed by the UN.[444] Art. 100 UNC provides that the United Nations Secretary General (UNSG) and the staff members "shall not seek or receive instructions from any government or from any other authority external to the [UN]."[445] Moreover, every Member State of the UN undertakes not to seek to influence members of the civil service in their work.[446] In view of the common objective of the organs of the UN to maintain peace and security it would stand to reason that this standard of autonomy attributed to the administrative sector – independence from external instructions – ought to be extended also to the judicial arm of the UN.[447]

---

qualifications required in their respective countries for appointment to the highest judicial offices, or are jurisconsults of recognized competence in international law."

443 Abi-Saab, Georges, 'Ensuring the Best Bench: Ways of Selecting Judges', in: Peck, Connie *et al.* (eds) *Increasing the Effectiveness of the International Court of Justice* (Martinus Nijhoff Publishers The Hague 1997), 167.

444 Cf. Schwarzenberger, *International Law as Applied by International Courts and Tribunals – Vol. 4 – International Judicial Law*, 277.

445 Art. 100(1) UNC is further substantiated by Staff Regulations, *inter alia* sections 1.1 and 1.2. Such regulations are not uncommon in international organizations; cf., e.g., Art. VII. F. of the Statute of the International Atomic Energy Agency (adopted 26 October 1956, entered into force 29 July 1957) 276 UNTS 3: "In the performance of their duties, the Director General and the staff shall not seek or receive instructions from any source external to the Agency."

446 This idea of an independent civil service reaches back to the League of Nations and is based on the desire to establish an international secretariat that would not be burdened in the fulfilment of its responsibilities by the influence of States. See, e.g., Schreuer, Christoph & Ebner, Christian, 'Article 100 UNC', in: Simma, Bruno (ed) *The Charter of the United Nations: A Commentary – Volume II* (Oxford University Press Oxford 2nd edn. 2002), 1231.

447 According to G. Schwarzenberger the independence from external instructions must be considered the "rock-bottom minimum of [the UN's] judicial sector." Schwarzenberger, *International Law as Applied by International Courts and Tribunals – Vol. 4 – International Judicial Law*, 277.

General guidance on the meaning of this requirement can also be obtained from the case law of the ICJ itself.[448] Without explicit reference to Art. 2 Statute the Court determined that it "acts only on the basis of the law, independently of all outside influence or interventions whatsoever".[449] In his dissenting opinion to the ICJ's order in the *Land, Island and Maritime Frontier Dispute*, Judge M. Shahabuddeen referred to the judgment of the ECtHR in the *Neumeister case*, where that Court stated that the term *court* "implies only that the authority called upon to decide … must possess judicial character, that is to say be independent both of the executive and of the parties to the case".[450] According to Judge Shahabuddeen, there is no reason why one should not also apply this to international courts.[451] Judge K. Tanaka in his separate opinion to the *Barcelona Traction Case* considered the independence of the judiciary to be a universally recognized principle, not only for the municipal legal systems but also for the international legal system, which consists of a safeguard from other branches of government[452] but also from any other external power against various courts and as between judges.[453] Judge B. Winiarski in 1956 restated Judge D. Anzilotti's statement that "it is … difficult to see how the Court's independence of the political organs of the League of Nations could be safeguarded, if it were in the power of the Assembly or the Council to oblige the Court to answer any question

---

448 On the importance of independence for the ICJ as a whole see, e.g., *Conditions of Admission of a State to Membership in the United Nations (Article 4 of the Charter) (Order) (Dissenting Opinion by M. Zoričič (translation))* ICJ Rep. 94 (1948), 95 and *Judgments of the Administrative Tribunal of the ILO upon Complaints Made against UNESCO (Advisory Opinion) (Separate Opinion of Judge Winiarski (translation))* ICJ Rep. 104 (1956), 104.

449 *Legal Consequences for States of the Continued Presence of South Africa in Namibia (South West Africa) notwithstanding Security Council Resolution 276 (1970) (Advisory Opinion)* ICJ Rep. 16 (1971), para. 29.

450 *Neumeister v. Austria* (ECtHR) Application No. 1936/63 (27 June 1968), para. 24.

451 *Land, Island and Maritime Frontier Dispute (El Salvador/Honduras: Nicaragua intervening) (Order) (Dissenting Opinion of Judge Shahabuddeen)* ICJ Rep. 18 (1990), 45.

452 With regard to the international level, independence from other branches of government must be understood functionally and adapted to the existing allocation of powers on the international level.

453 *Barcelona Traction, Light and Power Co Ltd (New Application: 1962) (Belgium v Spain) (Second Phase) (Separate Opinion of Judge Tanaka)* ICJ Rep. 114 (1970), 154.

which they might see fit to submit to it",[454] adding that this statement had lost none of its force.

Independence, as interpreted by the judges of the ICJ themselves, therefore encompasses first and foremost the absence of any pressure or influence being exerted on the judges from the political organs of the UN leading to a distortion of the decision making process, in the sense that a decision is based on or determined by factors other than facts and the law as applied by the ICJ. Further materialization of Art. 2's notion of independence of the judges follows only from the detailed provisions in the Statute, *inter alia* from the incompatible functions established in Arts. 16-17 Statute which will be dealt with below.[455]

3. The Temporal Reach of the Requirement of Judicial Independence

The question has been raised whether candidates for the bench of the ICJ must have fulfilled the requirements stipulated in Art. 2 in their activities before being chosen as candidates[456] or if this only applies to judges once elected.[457] Such an extension to earlier parts of a judge's career path would on the one hand surely help to emphasize the significance of independence of the Court and perhaps even increase, in the public eye, the moral standing of the Court. On the other hand, however, it would create almost insurmountable obstacles in the quest for suitable candidates. The more far-reaching understanding of the requirement could be interpreted as following directly from the Statute; Art. 9 requires the "*persons to be elected* … [to] possess the qualifications required" (emphasis added), i.e. *inter alia* independence

---

454 *Judgments of the Administrative Tribunal of the ILO upon Complaints Made against UNESCO (Advisory Opinion) (Separate Opinion of Judge Winiarski)* ICJ Rep. 104 (1956), 104-105.

455 Schenk von Stauffenberg, Berthold, *Statut et Règlement de la Cour Permanente de Justice Internationale – Eléments d'interprétation* (Heymann Berlin 1934), 18. See also G. Schwarzenberger who adopts a similar approach, Schwarzenberger, *International Law as Applied by International Courts and Tribunals – Vol. 4 – International Judicial Law*, 277. See also *infra* Chapter D.VI(5).

456 In this sense see Amerasinghe, Chittharanjan Felix, 'Judges of the International Court of Justice – Election and Qualifications' (2001) 14 Leiden Journal of International Law 2, 336.

457 Karg, Moritz, *IGH vs. ISGH – Die Beziehung zwischen zwei völkerrechtlichen Streitbeilegungsorganen* (Nomos Baden-Baden 2005), 118-119.

as set out in Art. 2. However, the wording of Art. 2 speaks against such an extension as it determines the criteria for the Court as such ("composed of a body of independent judges").

Furthermore, at least when the requirement is interpreted narrowly to mean independence for the purpose of serving on the ICJ, it would create tension – if not contradiction – with the requirements of "qualifications required in [the candidates'] respective countries for appointment to the highest judicial offices", experience as "juris-consults of recognized competence in international law"[458] or with the demand that the bench as a whole represent "the main forms of civilization and … the principal legal systems of the world". How can knowledge and experience enable an individual to qualify as a judge of the ICJ on the one hand and disqualify him due to a proven lack of independence on the other? If the independence criterion had to be satisfied by the candidates' careers before they became judges it would in practice mean that all judges of the Court would (have to) lack experience in the judicial settlement of international disputes, as *every* previous involvement with *any* dispute in many functions would render the candidate insufficiently autonomous and hence unfit to sit as a judge in proceedings of the Court.[459] This solution can hardly have been intended. Finally, the *travaux préparatoires* suggest, without wasting words of clarity, that the requirement of independence aims to protect judges from the control of States and the UN, and that it is thus linked only to the "judges of the court".[460] As a consequence, the requirement of Art. 2 Statute does not mean that judges in all their previous activities have necessarily been independent. Instead their moral character and qualifications must make it likely that they will behave independently once elected.

458 Art. 2 Statute.

459 Judge Carneiro in a dissenting opinion in the *Anglo-Iranian Oil Co. Case* said: "It is inevitable that everyone of us in this Court should retain some trace of his legal education and his former legal activities in his country of origin. This is inevitable, and even justified, because in its composition the Court is to be representative of 'the main forms of civilization and of the principal legal systems of the world' (Statute, Article g), and the Court is to apply 'the general principles of law recognized by civilized nations'. (Statute, Article 38 (1) (c).)" *Anglo-Iranian Oil Co. Case (Jurisdiction), Judgment of July 22nd, 1952 (Dissenting Opinion of Judge Levi Carneiro)* ICJ Rep. 93 (1952), para. 14.

460 United Nations Information Organizations, *UNCIO XIII*, 174.

4. The Distinction between Independence and Impartiality

It should not pass unnoticed that Art. 2 Statute does not expressly demand that judges be impartial. This may surprise, especially considering that the non-overlapping but equally important meaning of the two terms was acknowledged as early as during the drafting of the Statute. Nevertheless, pursuant to Art. 20 Statute impartiality is mentioned as one component of the solemn declaration that every member of the Court must make before taking up his duties.[461] Impartiality in this context is thus closely connected to the fulfilment of judges' judicial duties instead of being an express consideration in the nomination and election of candidates.[462] As a consequence, from the context of the Statute and the Rules of Court, it appears that the two concepts are at least not considered identical.

The drafting history reveals that the requirement of impartiality was considered to be implied in Art. 2.[463] During the San Francisco Conference it was highlighted that the judges of the ICJ "should be not only impartial but also independent of control of their own countries or the [UN]".[464] That ultimately no explicit mention was made of impartiality is owed to two considerations: first, the overall satisfaction with the wording and functioning of Art. 2 of the PCIJ Statute meant that as few changes as possible to Art. 2 were felt to be needed.[465] Second, several delegates at the San Francisco Conference felt that the deletion of the word "independent" in favour of the word "impartial" could lead to misinterpretations, as independence was considered to encompass impartiality, but not the other way round.[466] Thus

---

461 According to Art. 4(1) Rules of Court this declaration shall be as follows: "I solemnly declare that I will perform my duties and exercise my powers as judge honourably, faithfully, impartially and conscientiously."

462 It should be noted that the members of the Court are to make the declaration "in open court". This reveals an understanding by the drafters of the Statute that the assurance of justice and adherence to certain judicial standards are important not merely in essence, not merely factually, but have symbolic implications and that their visibility is equally important. It can also be assumed that the drafters here were guided by the often reiterated sentence that justice must not only be done, it must also be seen to be done. See *R. v. Sussex Justices, ex p. McCarthy (King's Bench Division)* (King's Bench Division) 1 K.B. 256 (1924), 259; *Delcourt v. Belgium* (ECtHR) Application No. 2689/65 (17 January 1970), para. 31.

463 See for the same interpretation, e.g., Aznar-Gómez, 'Article 2 ICJ Statute', 211.

464 United Nations Information Organizations, *UNCIO XIII*, 174.

465 Rosenne, *The Court and the United Nations*, 358.

466 United Nations Information Organizations, *UNCIO XIII*, 174.

although the exact meaning of the terms was not delimitated, at least the relationship between them was understood in the interest of the widest possible protection of the Court's activities.[467]

For the ICJ itself, impartiality is usually understood to require that a judge shall perform his duties without any favour, bias or prejudice.[468] However, the close relationship between independence and impartiality and an accompanying lack of terminological separation are often expressed in the decisions by the ICJ.[469] Judge H. Mosler in a separate opinion to the advisory opinion on the *Application for Review of Judgement No. 273 of the United Nations Administrative Tribunal* highlights the importance of both independence and impartiality for the issue of an advisory opinion, without providing any guidance on where a distinction between the two notions may be drawn: in justifying his support of the ICJ's decision to give an opinion, he referred to the conviction that "the Advisory Opinion can be given in full independence and impartiality, and by means of judicial proceedings before the Court governed by its Statutes and Rules".[470] Judge E. Lauterpacht is similarly vague when referring to the "traditional impartiality" which characterizes the work of the Court[471] and the "duty of impartiality" which binds *ad hoc* judges of the Court.[472] The only guidance one may find is a statement of Judge N. Tarassov, according to whom independence is more a bar to the involvement of external actors (e.g. the parties to a dispute), whereas impartiality appears to be used as a wider term.[473] Overall, the Court never expli-

467 The above-mentioned Netherlands' request to include in the provision every safeguard to ensure that judges are "impartial and independent" goes in the same direction of a separation of the two concepts; see United Nations Information Organizations, *UNCIO XIV*, 398.

468 Aznar-Gómez, 'Article 2 ICJ Statute', 211.

469 Although both independence and impartiality are almost exclusively mentioned by individual judges in their dissenting and/or separate opinions and not by the full Court.

470 *Application for Review of Judgement No. 273 of the United Nations Administrative Tribunal (Advisory Opinion) (Separate Opinion of Judge Mosler)* ICJ Rep. 325 (1982), para. 8.

471 *Application of the Convention on the Prevention and Punishment of the Crime of Genocide (Bosnia and Herzegovina v Serbia and Montenegro) (Order of 13 September 1993) (Separate Opinion of Judge Lauterpacht)* ICJ Rep. 407 (1993), para. 6.

472 Ibid, para. 6.

473 "In theory, there could not be any such impact as all the members of a chamber, including the judges ad hoc, are independent of the parties and preserve their full

citly explains its understanding of the relationship between independence and impartiality, which may be either because it lacks relevance for the proceedings of the Court or because the issue *per se* is not contentious before the Court.

V. Structural Independence

1. Issues Regarding the ICJ's Relationship Vis-À-Vis States

States play a significant role in the activities of the Court mainly by being the only subjects of international law permitted to appear as parties before it.[474] In particular, States appearing before the ICJ can influence the procedure in various ways pursuant to the Statute. Parties may e.g. ask the Court to decide the dispute on the basis of justice and equity, i.e. outside the realm of the law;[475] they may decide the language of the procedure;[476] and they may under certain conditions appoint national judges. In particular the right of a State to have a judge of its own nationality sit on a case before the Court,[477] i.e. the right to appoint *ad hoc* judges, is a considerable concession to the influence of States on the activities of the ICJ, which will be dealt with in greater detail below.[478] One must, however, be careful to distinguish between the necessary influences that help the parties or the Court to shape the procedure according to the needs of the individual case and stimuli that have the potential to influence unduly the decision-making of the Court. Cornerstones of the procedure, such as the indication of provisional measures,[479] the publicity of the procedure,[480] orders for the conduct of the case,

---

impartiality during the whole of the proceedings in the case." *Land, Island and Maritime Frontier Dispute (El Salvador/Honduras: Nicaragua intervening) (Order) (Dissenting Opinion of Judge Tarassov)* ICJ Rep. 11 (1990), 14-15.

474 Art. 34(1) ICJ Statute. "It is the sovereign State alone, the normal subject of international law, that can make use of [the Court]"; Singh, Nagendra, *The Role and Record of the International Court of Justice: 1946 to 1988; in Celebration of the 40th Anniversary* (Nijhoff Dordrecht 1989), 25.

475 Art. 38(2) ICJ Statute. Hudson, *The Permanent Court of International Justice 1920-1942 – A Treatise*, 620.

476 Art. 39 ICJ Statute.

477 Art. 31(1)-(2) ICJ Statute.

478 See further *infra* Chapter D.V(2)(d).

479 Art. 41 ICJ Statute.

480 Art. 46 ICJ Statute.

the form and time for the parties to conclude agreements, and the taking of evidence,[481] remain, for example, under the control of the Court. Threats to its independent functioning are rather to be found, for example, in States' influence on the nomination and election procedure where numerous opportunities facilitate the indirect exertion of influence which is not immediately motivated by the necessities of a case. The nomination and election procedure will therefore be analysed in greater detail below.

2. The Composition of the Court

a) The Normative Framework of the Nomination and Election Procedure

The process for the selection of ICJ judges is based on a split procedure of nomination and election. The procedure is begun by a request by the UNSG three months before the date of the election, inviting States to nominate in their respective national groups in the PCA[482] no more than four persons able to accept the duties of a member of the Court.[483] Before making its nominations, the national group is recommended to "consult its highest court of justice, its legal faculties and schools of law, and its national academies and national sections of international academies devoted to the study of law."[484] The lists thus submitted are assembled by the UNSG into a single, alphabetically ordered list, which is submitted to the electors.[485] The election itself is conducted by the UNGA and the UNSC,[486] whereas both organs shall proceed in the election independently from each other.[487] In doing this the electors are called upon to bear in mind that the persons to be elected

481 Arts. 48, 49, 52 ICJ Statute.

482 Art. 4(1) ICJ Statute.

483 Art. 5 ICJ Statute. Depending on whether the individual State is a member of the UN and/or is represented in the PCA, the list of nominated individuals is compiled differently. Whereas in the case of a UN member State represented in the PCA the national group in that court has the duty to nominate, UN members without representation in the PCA shall appoint *ad hoc* national groups for this purpose (following the Art. 44 Hague Convention for the Pacific Settlement of Disputes [1907]) and non-UN members shall follow either a special agreement or, in the absence of this, the rules laid down by the UNGA upon recommendation of the UNSC (see Art. 4).

484 Art. 6 ICJ Statute.

485 Art. 7 ICJ Statute.

486 Art. 4(1) ICJ Statute.

487 Art. 8 ICJ Statute.

possess the required qualifications individually and that the body of judges as a whole represents the main forms of civilization and the principal legal systems of the world.[488] The majority necessary for election is an absolute majority in both electoral organs.[489] With regard to the election in the UNSC, no distinction in the weight of votes is made between the permanent and non-permanent members of the UNSC.[490] The elected individual has to be approved by the UNGA and the UNSC respectively, something that is not subject to any formal procedure.

b) National Groups of the PCA as the Nominating Bodies

The national groups in the PCA are, pursuant to Art. 4(1) ICJ Statute, in charge of the nomination of candidates for the bench of the ICJ. The PCA national groups are at least formally separate from States, a factor which is intended to protect the nomination process from political influence.[491] Pursuant to Art. 44 1907 Hague Convention I "[e]ach Contracting Power selects

---

488 Art. 9 ICJ Statute.

489 Art. 10(1) ICJ Statute. In the elections that took place in November 2011, an absolute majority in the UNGA was ninety-seven votes and in the UNSC eight votes were necessary; UNGA & UNSC, *Election of five members of the International Court of Justice – Memorandum by the Secretary-General* (26 July 2011) A/66/182–S/2011/452, paras. 8-9.

490 Art. 10(2) ICJ Statute. The Statute provides for a second and, if necessary, third ballot if, after the first meeting held for the purpose of elections, one or more seats remain vacant (Art. 11 ICJ Statute). If after a third meeting seats still remain unfilled, Art. 12 ICJ Statute provides for a special procedure in which a joint conference, consisting of members appointed by the UNGA and the UNSC, may choose by absolute majority one name for each seat still vacant. If the joint conference is not successful in electing a new member of the Court, Art. 12(3) ICJ Statute provides for election by the Court itself.

491 "In order to insulate the process of nomination from political considerations, candidates are not nominated directly by governments but by the national groups in the Permanent Court of Arbitration (PCA) or, in the case of countries not participating in the PCA, by similarly constituted national groups." ICJ, *Press Release 2005/23 – United Nations General Assembly and Security Council proceed to the election of five Members of the Court* (8 November 2005) available at <http://www.icj-cij.org/presscom/index.php?pr=638&pt=&p1=6&p2=1> (last visited: 21 March 2014); ICJ, *Press Release 2002/27 – United Nations General Assembly and Security Council proceed to the election of five Members of the Court* (22 October 2002) available at <http://www.icj-cij.org/presscom/index.php?pr=105&pt=&p1=6&p2=1> (last visited: 21 March 2014).

four persons at the most, of known competency in questions of international law, of the highest moral reputation, and disposed to accept the duties of Arbitrator."[492] A member may be appointed by different States and States may even "agree on the selection in common of" a member.[493] Members of the national groups hold office for renewable six year terms.[494] Neither the 1907 Hague Convention I nor the 1899 Hague Convention I prescribes any election procedure for the members, and although not much is known about how States proceed, it appears that "members are normally appointed by the Minister of Foreign Affairs or the legal adviser".[495]

A first observation on the appointment of arbitrators is that due to the scarcity of the practice of forming arbitration tribunals under the 1907 Hague Convention I,[496] it can be assumed that one of the considerations flowing into the appointment process to the PCA is the idea that it has an immediate effect on the periodic elections to the ICJ.[497] The national groups could, if understood in this way, be perceived as mere catalysts of the opinions held by those who appoint the members. Secondly, and linked to this first observation, is that there has been a strong tendency of States appointing to the PCA current or former legal advisors to foreign ministries, or other current or former holders of political office.[498] This practice should surprise any

---

492 Cf. Art. 23 International Convention for the Pacific Settlement of International Disputes. The same requirements apply to those arbitrators that are members of *ad hoc* national groups (cf. Art. 4(2) ICJ Statute).

493 Art. 44(4)-(5) 1907 Hague Convention I.

494 Art. 44(5) 1907 Hague Convention I.

495 Mackenzie, et al., *Selecting International Judges: Principle, Process, and Politics*, 70. See also McWhinney, Edward, 'Law, Politics and "Regionalism" in the Nomination and Election of World Court Judges' (1986-1987) 13 Syracuse Journal of International Law and Commerce 1, 4-5.

496 According to the PCA's own statistics, between 1988 and 2007 23 cases were conducted under the auspices of the PCA or with the cooperation of the bureau of the PCA: see 'Permanent Court of Arbitration – Past Cases' available at <http://www.pca-cpa.org/showpage.asp?pag_id=1146> (last visited: 21 March 2014). Of the 85 arbitrators in total who were involved in these cases just 20 were members of the PCA.

497 Institut de Droit International, *Annuaire de l'Institut de Droit International 1954-I* (Verlag für Recht und Gesellschaft A G. Genève 1954), 460; see also McWhinney, 'The International Court as Constitutional Court and the Blurring of the Arbitral/Judicial Processes'.

498 Currently, according to the official listing of the PCA, of the 351 registered members of the PCA 168 (i.e. approximately 48 %) have or have had in the past some kind of political office, e.g. ambassador, legal advisor to the foreign ministry, or minister.

observer familiar with the drafting background of the ICJ Statute; the original idea behind the use of the PCA national groups as the nominating bodies, which goes back to the Statute for the PCIJ, was precisely based on the consideration of "preventing political intrigues in the elections, because of the 'moral weakness of all political bodies'".[499] In other words, the members of the PCA were intended to be independent of their respective governments. Whereas the existence of civil servants or even government officials in PCA national groups in no way *ipso facto* means that the national groups are unable to live up to their intended independent functionality, this practice might lead to questionable results. It is especially upheld by the US[500] but has more broadly been a characteristic of appointments by all permanent members of the UNSC. In particular it could be interpreted as a readiness of States to appoint to the PCA only those who can be expected to make nominations that are in line with government politics. Legal advisors to foreign ministries are not only familiar with the foreign policy agendas of their home States; they have often helped to draft it.[501] This makes them ideal sponsors for ad-

---

See 'Permanent Court of Arbitration – Members of the Permanent Court of Arbitration' available at <http://www.pca-cpa.org/showpage.asp?pag_id=1041> (last visited: 21 March 2014).

499 Hudson, *The Permanent Court of International Justice 1920-1942 – A Treatise*, 140. Abi-Saab, 'Ensuring the Best Bench: Ways of Selecting Judges', 193. "The drafters of the Statutes of the Permanent Court of International Justice and ICJ expected that PCA national groups would be independent of their states, as this was the reason why PCA national groups were accorded the sole right to nominate candidates to those courts"; Mackenzie, et al., *Selecting International Judges: Principle, Process, and Politics*, 71, at fn. 41.

500 Abi-Saab, 'Ensuring the Best Bench: Ways of Selecting Judges', 193, who refers to the "custom" that among the four members of the US national group one can "typically find at least one and sometimes two from each of the major political parties, usually including the incumbent Legal Advisor of the Department of State and one of the predecessors from the other party." As an example, at the time of writing, the US national group is made up of Harold Koh, legal advisor to the Obama Administration (Democratic Party), David R. Andrews, who held the same post under the second Clinton Administration (Democratic Party), John Bellinger III, who was legal advisor under the second Bush Administration (Republican) and judge Stephen M. Schwebel, who was a member of the ICJ between 1981 and 2000.

501 One practical example illustrating the difficulties that may be connected to the political background of a judge is provided by P. Sands: "In one ICJ case, the following was observed: whilst counsel for a state party to a case made comments criticizing a political decision of another state, the judge who was a national of the state being criticized (and formerly the legal advisor of its Ministry of Foreign Affairs) was seen to remove the headphones (through which simultaneous interpretation

vancing their home State's foreign policy agenda by making nominations that presumably further that goal. Thirdly, States usually choose to reappoint the members of the PCA once their first term has expired,[502] which testifies to States' strong reliance on the competence of the PCA members who were initially appointed.[503]

One way of preventing these influences from channelling political considerations into the nomination process to the ICJ would be to make compulsory the consultation of the highest courts of justice, legal faculties and schools of law, and national academies and national sections of international academies devoted to the study of law, which is now *recommended* in Art. 6 Statute.[504] Although little is known about the extent to which the recommendations in Art. 6 Statute are followed,[505] a fact which in itself is reason enough

was being provided) and place them on the table in front of him, not putting them back on until the counsel had moved on to his next (non-political) point. He appeared to be expressing a view on counsel's performance, indeed on the arguments of the state concerned, and this raised an issue of judicial propriety, and of judicial independence, since independence assumes that the international judge will listen to all arguments put to him." Sands, Philippe J., 'The Independence of the International Judiciary: Some Introductory Thoughts', in: Charnovitz, Steve *et al.* (eds) *Law in the Service of Human Dignity – Essays in Honour of Florentino Feliciano* (Cambridge University Press Cambridge 2005), 318.

502 McWhinney, 'Law, Politics and "Regionalism" in the Nomination and Election of World Court Judges', 4.

503 Another potentially problematic issue is the lack of any bar on members of the PCA being candidates for the ICJ. However, this has never caused any concern in the past and it would moreover seem that this possibility is a necessity flowing from the identical function of members of the PCA and the ICJ, namely competence regarding dispute settlement in international law.

504 According to judge Schwebel, the provisions on nomination through the national groups of the PCA and Art. 6 Statute, "have somewhat insulated the nomination process from political influence in a very few democracies …; more generally their influence is not apparent. The electoral processes in the General Assembly and Security Council are profoundly political." Schwebel, Stephen M., *Justice in International Law: Further Selected Writings* (Cambridge University Press Cambridge 2011), 23-24.

505 Georget, Patricia, et al., 'Article 6 ICJ Statute', in: Zimmermann, Andreas *et al.* (eds) *The Statute of the International Court of Justice – A Commentary* (Oxford University Press Oxford 2006), 250. According to G. Guillaume, rapporteur to the Sixth Commission of the Institut de Droit International on the topic of the position of the international judge: "Ces dispositions sont appliquées sous des formes diverses dans nombreux pays tels que le Canada, les Etats-Unis, la France ou le Royaume-Uni. Elles semblent en revanche avoir été perdues de vue dans d'autres pays." Institut de Droit International, *The Position of the International Judge – Rapporteur: Gilbert*

to doubt whether the candidates chosen are indeed those who can instil in the ICJ the greatest possible independence and legitimacy, it appears from anecdotal evidence on this subject that very few PCA national groups follow such consultations.[506] Lifting the nomination process out of an often informal or semi-structured procedure, which most States still follow and which is more prone to permit political influence,[507] by expanding the opinions and judgments on suitable candidates would surely bolster the standing of the nomination process, and in that way of the ICJ as a whole. In addition, it would add a mechanism that is able to create transparency and objectivity, and thus to promote independence.

It should finally be noted that the PCA national groups do not play any role in the selection of *ad hoc* judges. Pursuant to Art. 31(2) Statute such judges "shall be chosen preferably from among those persons who have been nominated as candidates as provided in Articles 4 and 5", i.e. including the process of nomination by the national groups provided for in Art. 4(1) Statute. However, Art. 31(2) Statute is phrased only as a recommendation ("preferably") and is thus not binding on States. In practice, States have taken this wording as an invitation to circumvent the national groups (or to avoid appointing *ad hoc* national groups), and instead entirely let governmental considerations steer the designation of an *ad hoc* judge.[508] However, the

---

Guillaume – 6th Resolution – Sixth Commission – Session de Rhodes (2011) available at <http://www.idi-iil.org/> (last visited: 21 March 2014), para. 21. Sir E. Lauterpacht, who himself was a member of the British national group, considered that "[t]he whole idea is to try and insulate the process of nomination a little bit from direct government pressure. In the case of the British group, it's quite true we do act quite independently of the Government. That may not be equally so in other countries. Some certainly respect the idea, others place their members under direct governmental pressure or indeed, their members may be legal advisers of their foreign office and so on." 'Conversations with Professor Sir Eli Lauterpacht – Fifth Interview (28 March 2008)' available at <http://www.squire.law.cam.ac.uk/eminent_scholars/professor_sir_elihu_lauterpacht_conversations_with_professor_sir_eli_lauterpacht.php> (last visited: 21 March 2014), 17.

506 Mackenzie, et al., *Selecting International Judges: Principle, Process, and Politics*, 142-144.

507 Cf. ibid, 84-95.

508 Cf. e.g. the designation of the Canadian *ad hoc* judge in the *Gulf of Maine Case*. In this case the Canadian national group was not consulted before an *ad hoc* judge for Canada was appointed. According to E. McWhinney this "seems to be the general international practice." McWhinney, 'Law, Politics and "Regionalism" in the Nomination and Election of World Court Judges', 8.

special role of *ad hoc* judges is an important one that will be expounded on in greater detail below.[509]

c) Politicization of the Election Process: a Legacy from the PCIJ

Next to the nomination process, the election procedure is of particular interest because it historically posed the most significant obstacle to the creation of a permanent international court.[510] Already under the Statute of the PCIJ the system of election of the judges, which was similar to that provided for by the ICJ Statute, was criticised for being overly politicised and in need of improvement.[511] *A fortiori* it hence strikes one as odd that the system was largely retained in the Statute for the ICJ. As already outlined,[512] judges of the ICJ are elected if an absolute majority of the members of the UNGA and the UNSC express their support.[513] When casting their votes, States are called upon not only to make sure that candidates have certain individual characteristics,[514] but "also that in the body as a whole the representation of the main forms of civilization and of the principal legal systems of the world should be assured."[515] These requirements are considered to be fulfilled if the States vote with an equitable geographical distribution in mind,[516] which translates into the bench of candidates being composed of people from each of the five UN regional groups.[517] While these regional groups are informal, they are of major importance for coordinating policies between States and for elections

509 See *infra* Chapter D.V(2)(d).

510 E.g. Abi-Saab, 'Ensuring the Best Bench: Ways of Selecting Judges', 176. See also Mackenzie, et al., *Selecting International Judges: Principle, Process, and Politics*, 10-17.

511 Lauterpacht, *The Function of Law in the International Community*, 239-240.

512 See *supra* Chapter D.V(2)(a).

513 Arts. 4 and 10(1) ICJ Statute.

514 See on Art. 2 ICJ Statute *infra* Chapter D.VI(1).

515 Art. 9 ICJ Statute.

516 Mackenzie, et al., *Selecting International Judges: Principle, Process, and Politics*, 27-29.

517 Fassbender, Bardo, 'Article 9 ICJ Statute', in: Zimmermann, Andreas *et al.* (eds) *The Statute of the International Court of Justice – A Commentary* (Oxford University Press Oxford 2006), 271. 'United Nations Regional Groups of Member States' available at <http://www.un.org/depts/DGACM/RegionalGroups.shtml> (last visited: 21 March 2014).

to UN organs and subsidiary bodies.[518] The role of these groups is mainly to support certain candidates who are considered to represent them, or to negotiate the withdrawal of other candidates.[519] Furthermore, there is a *tradition*[520] that the permanent members of the UNSC are always represented in the ICJ. These customs, together with the increased importance of individual campaigning by candidates,[521] lobbying[522] and vote-trading, has contributed to the strong politicization of the election process and to a focus on values unrelated to the personal qualifications of candidates.

From the perspective of the independence of the Court, it must for example be asked if a tradition that particular States, namely the permanent members of the UNSC, claim a right to have *their own* member on the Court does not leverage even the basic approach of wrapping the election procedure in a formal and objective structure to the point where it must be questioned whether it is indeed an *election*. Especially since such a tradition is in stark contrast to the underlying idea of having both the UNGA and the UNSC involved in the process of electing the judges, which was a compromise between the demand for representation of powerful States and the quest for a truly global judicial institution. Art. 10(2) ICJ Statute,[523] which formed an essential part of this compromise,[524] is thereby weakened considerably, since the role of the permanent members has been allowed to grow not only to support these States' own candidates but also significantly to influence the

518 Aust, Anthony, *Handbook of International Law* (Cambridge University Press Cambridge 2nd edn. 2010), 188; Fassbender, 'Article 9 ICJ Statute', 271-273.

519 Mackenzie, et al., *Selecting International Judges: Principle, Process, and Politics*, 106.

520 Rosenne, Shabtai, *The Law and Practice of the International Court – Vol. 1 The Court and the United Nations* (Nijhoff Leiden 2006), 370.

521 Mackenzie, et al., *Selecting International Judges: Principle, Process, and Politics*, 110.

522 A substantial amount of lobbying is required of the nominated individuals as it has proven that no person will be elected to the bench unless his State of nationality (i.e. its politicians) at least supports his candidacy. This was pointed out to the author in an interview conducted with a judge of one of the international courts the subject of this study.

523 "Any vote of the Security Council, whether for the election of judges or for the appointment of members of the conference envisaged in Article 12, shall be taken without any distinction between permanent and non-permanent members of the Security Council."

524 Fassbender, 'Article 10 ICJ Statute', 287.

voting decisions of the non-permanent members.[525] It is undeniable that this convention regarding the five permanent members of the UNSC is a question of political power only. Although it is difficult accurately and objectively to assess the real or perceived preferences such State actions might engender in the individual judge they are in any event antagonistic to an independent ethos.

As regards the campaigning of candidates for the bench of the ICJ, serious doubts must be raised whether this increasing practice can be reconciled with generating an independent bench. The risk of instead creating the perception or the reality that candidates are asked to make assurances and commit themselves on issues that may come before them as members of the Court is one that is not easily, if at all, dissipated by references to the otherwise high moral integrity of the individuals involved.[526] Overall, the task of repelling the potential political influence generated by overt politicization is aggravated by the fact that – as the ICJ put it when referring to the reasons that determine how a Member of the UN casts its vote under Art. 4 UNC – "such reasons, which enter into a mental process, are obviously subject to no control".[527] The different interests that may influence the behaviour of electors are many and may include solidarity or co-operation within a regional bloc of States, the timing of a candidacy, political skills in the conduct of a campaign, and knowledge of the procedural rules governing the elections.[528] The appropriateness of these elements in the election process shall not be exhaustively dealt with here. Instead, it suffices to note two further aspects, of relevance for the independence of the ICJ.

Firstly, the politicization of the election process is a threat to the Court's independence only if it leads to an actual dissociation from the individual selection criteria, which for the ICJ judges are expressed in Art. 2 ICJ Statute.[529] In other words, only if political factors rather than the individual merit of the candidates drive the election process to an extent that judges are elected who are unfit for the position and who are inclined to fold under

525 Cf. Mackenzie, et al., *Selecting International Judges: Principle, Process, and Politics*, 132.

526 For critical views in this regard see ibid, 119-120.

527 *Conditions of Admission of a State to Membership in the United Nations (Article 4 of the Charter) (Advisory Opinion)* ICJ Rep. 57 (1948), 60.

528 McWhinney, 'Law, Politics and "Regionalism" in the Nomination and Election of World Court Judges', 13-15.

529 See for a further evaluation of these individual selection criteria *infra* Chapter D.VI(1).

political pressure in their judicial exercise, can the election process be truly criticised in the current context. The information available for such an evaluation of the bench of the ICJ is rather scanty. According to anecdotal evidence gathered in a study conducted between 2006 and 2008,[530] opinions regarding the election process range from that it has provided "good results", "fairly okay" candidates to the contention that the current system could make it possible for an inadequately, or entirely unqualified candidate to be selected. Without doubt, the politicized character of the elections[531] risks the emergence of the kind of influence that may compromise the independent functioning of the Court. Although an entirely merit-based selection would also not provide definite protection against outside influence being exerted on the Court, it would guard the Court against the criticism of being a tool of the political forces that bring the cases before it; in other words, it would strengthen its standing as an authority that is pioneering in developing the international rule of law, and no lower aspiration should a body have that is made up of

> "a body of independent judges, elected regardless of their nationality from among persons of high moral character, who possess the qualifications required in their respective countries for appointment to the highest judicial offices, or are jurisconsults of recognized competence in international law."

The second consideration slightly narrows the expectations created by the first, namely the fact that to rid the election procedure of all political considerations would be "an idle undertaking".[532] As was mentioned already, the ICJ is but one of the main organs of the larger UN system, and elections to it will by necessity be perceived as a political exercise. However unpleasant the politicization of the election and even the nomination procedure may seem from the outside, the lesson to be learned from the small differences between the PCIJ and the ICJ and the lack of any real initiative to change the above-mentioned critical points throughout the lifetime of the ICJ, is that it appears unrealistic to expect any changes to be made. At least with regard

530 Mackenzie, et al., *Selecting International Judges: Principle, Process, and Politics.*

531 S. Rosenne asserts that "so long as the conduct of the elections is the business of political bodies, political considerations will prevail"; Rosenne, *The Court and the United Nations*, 390.

532 Elias, Taslim Olawale, 'Report', in: Mosler, Hermann *et al.* (eds) *Judicial Settlement of International Disputes – International Court of Justice, other Courts and Tribunals, Arbitration and Conciliation; an International Symposium* (Springer Berlin 1974), 280.

to a state-centred organ such as the ICJ, the time does not seem ripe for States to give up the influence they have over judicial elections to non-State bodies. Whether the barriers to reform can be attributed to the comparatively long lifespan of the ICJ and thus its anchorage in a system that "was very much conditioned by the earlier experience of the second Hague Peace Conference of 1907"[533] will be clarified in the following chapters, when other international courts are scrutinized.

d) The Special Problem of Ad Hoc Judges

(1) Ad Hoc Judges at the ICJ – Normative Framework and Rationale

Every State party appearing before the ICJ that does not already have a judge of its nationality sitting on the bench has the right to appoint an *ad hoc* judge. This applies not only to the situation where only one of the parties has a judge of its own nationality, in which case all other parties may choose a person to sit as a judge;[534] but also to the situation where none of the judges has the nationality of any of the parties.[535] Such *ad hoc* judges are, as a general rule, as equally bound by the requirements of independence and impartiality as regular members of the Court.[536] Pursuant to Art. 31(6) ICJ Statute read in conjunction with Art. 2 ICJ Statute *ad hoc* judges are required to have the same personal and professional skills laid down in Art. 2 ICJ Statute, including the prerequisite of independence. Moreover, *ad hoc* judges are equally required to make a solemn declaration in court on *inter alia* the

533 Abi-Saab, 'Ensuring the Best Bench: Ways of Selecting Judges', 175.

534 The judge thus chosen must not necessarily hold the same nationality as the appointing party: Art. 31(2) ICJ Statute.

535 Art. 31(3) ICJ Statute.

536 According to a dissenting opinion of judge Tarassov in the *Land, Island and Maritime Frontier Dispute (El Salvador/Honduras: Nicaragua intervening)* case, "[i]n theory, … all the members of a chamber, including the judges ad hoc, are independent of the parties and preserve their full impartiality during the whole of the proceedings in the case." *Land, Island and Maritime Frontier Dispute (El Salvador/Honduras: Nicaragua intervening) (Order) (Dissenting Opinion of Judge Tarassov)*, 14-15. For a similar view see also Judge Lauterpacht in his separate opinion in *Application of the Convention on the Prevention and Punishment of the Crime of Genocide (Bosnia and Herzegovina v Serbia and Montenegro) (Order of 13 September 1993) (Separate Opinion of Judge Lauterpacht)*, paras. 3 and 6.

impartial and conscientious exercise of their duties.[537] The wording of the declaration to be made is identical for *ad hoc* and regular judges, according to Art. 8(1) Rules of Court, thus again underlining the basic equality between the two categories.[538] However, certain differences are provided for and follow from the nature of *ad hoc* and ordinary judges. One significant one is that *ad hoc* judges are not prohibited from acting as agent, counsel, or advocate in a case before the ICJ but only from participating in the decision of a case in which they have previously taken part in any capacity.[539] This is based on the consideration that *ad hoc* judges exercise the function of a judge for only a limited period of time which renders it impractical also to demand of them not simultaneously to be acting as agents, counsel, or advocate in any other case before the Court. Furthermore, *ad hoc* judges are not prohibited from exercising political or administrative functions.[540]

The justification of the institution of *ad hoc* judges was – and still remains – to ensure "equality of the parties before the Court and in the Court."[541] Where does this aim emanate from? The Court itself, due to its nature as an organ dealing with international inter-State dispute settlement, is bound by the principle of sovereign equality of States.[542] On the level of the ICJ, this equality of States is translated into full procedural equality between all the members of the Court.[543] Understood in this way, *ad hoc* judges are formally to neutralize the national judge that already sits on a bench.[544] This reading implies the rather discouraging assumption that every national judge is considered a potential threat to independence by being potentially and in some way in favour or supportive of the interests of the party whose nationality

537 Art. 31(6) and Art. 20 ICJ Statute.

538 See also Art. 7(2) Rules of Court which provides that *ad hoc* judges "shall participate in the case in which they sit on terms of complete equality with the other judges of the bench."

539 Art. 31(6) read together with Art. 17(1)-(2) ICJ Statute.

540 Art. 31(6) read together with Art. 16 ICJ Statute.

541 President of the International Court of Justice, *Document transmitted by the President of the International Court of Justice to the Secretary-General on the implications of General Assembly resolution 61/262 in regard to certain provisions of the Statute of the Court*, para. 45 *in fine*. Cf. Art. 31(6) ICJ Statute and Art. 7 Rules of Court.

542 Cf. Art. 2(1) UNC.

543 See also Scobbie, Iain, '"Une hérésie en matière judiciaire"? The role of the judge ad hoc in the International Court' (2005) 4 The Law and Practice of International Courts and Tribunals 3, 431.

544 See, e.g., Rosenne, Shabtai, *The Law and Practice of the International Court – Vol. 3 Procedure* (Nijhoff Leiden 2006), 1224.

he has.[545] But the nationality of one party is not the sole triggering logic behind the right to appoint *ad hoc* judges. As stated above, even in the case of formal equality, namely "[i]f the Court includes upon the Bench no judge of the nationality of the parties, each of these parties may proceed to choose [an *ad hoc*] judge."[546] Hence the *ad hoc* judge is not just considered the formal advocate of a particular party but moreover assumes the wider function of adding considerations in the decision-making process of the ICJ which are important to a particular State and which might, were he not sitting on the bench, otherwise not be taken into account. Judge E. Lauterpacht phrased it the following way in his separate opinion in the case on the *Application of the Convention on the Prevention and Punishment of the Crime of Genocide*, which deserves to be cited in some length:

> "5. At the same time, it cannot be forgotten that the institution of the ad hoc judge was created for the purpose of giving a party, not otherwise having upon the Court a judge of its nationality, an opportunity to join in the work of this tribunal. The evidence in this regard of the attitude of those who participated in the drafting of the original Statute of the Permanent Court of International Justice can hardly be contradicted. This has led many to assume that an ad hoc judge must be regarded as a representative of the State that appoints him and, therefore, as necessarily pre-committed to the position that that State may adopt.
> 6. Nonetheless, consistently with the duty of impartiality by which the ad hoc judge is bound, there is still something specific that distinguishes his role. He has, I believe, the special obligation to endeavour to ensure that, so far as is reasonable, every relevant argument in favour of the party that has appointed him has been fully appreciated in the course of collegial consideration and, ultimately, is reflected – though not necessarily accepted – in any separate or dissenting opinion that he may write."[547]

---

545 In the same direction goes Art. 32(1) Rules of Court which states that "[i]f the President of the Court is a national of one of the parties in a case he shall not exercise the functions of the presidency in respect of that case", hence suggesting that nationality may in itself cause potential bias.

546 Art. 31(3) ICJ Statute.

547 *Application of the Convention on the Prevention and Punishment of the Crime of Genocide (Bosnia and Herzegovina v Serbia and Montenegro) (Order of 13 September 1993) (Separate Opinion of Judge Lauterpacht)*, paras. 5-6. P. Kooijmans expresses a similar opinion, when first discarding the image of *ad hoc* judges as representatives of the appointing State, but then affirming that they ought to "take care that during the deliberations and in the judgment the views and positions taken by the party which has appointed him or her will be duly reflected." Kooijmans, Pieter H., 'Article 31 ICJ Statute', in: Zimmermann, Andreas *et al.* (eds) *The Statute of the International Court of Justice – A Commentary* (Oxford University Press Oxford 2006), 498.

Following this line of argument, the *ad hoc* judge supports the Court in delivering accurate decisions which take into account the various, legitimate interests of the parties. But even if this special role of the *ad hoc* judge is accurate and, more importantly, actually honoured by the *ad hoc* judges themselves, it raises the more crucial question whether it is not already every (ordinary) judge's duty to ensure that every relevant argument supportive of all parties appearing before the ICJ "has been fully appreciated", and, if so, whether an *ad hoc* judge can be justified as an expert of his country of origin.

(2) Ad Hoc Judges and Independence – An Attempt to Harmonize Two Conflicting Concepts

> "... the whole institution of the ad hoc judge, within the setting of the World Court, acknowledges an important role for partiality in the very process of trying to achieve an adequate understanding and appreciation of what the parties in conflict really believe."[548]

The central question that must be posed is whether the above-mentioned considerations underlying the *ad hoc* judge system, namely that the special link between a judge and a party appearing before the ICJ has a legitimate value in itself, can be reconciled with the independence of the judge and, consequently, with that of the Court as a whole. *Prima facie* it is a concession to the lack of independence of a Court if every party appearing before it in one way or another is in need of its own judge. However, in much of the scholarly literature written on this subject, it appears that, at least with regard to an international court such as the ICJ, this can be justified. What is referred to in this context is usually that "international adjudication is not a decision which can be taken lightly",[549] and instead a national judge is able to inject confidence into the judicial body[550] and to allay fears that the process may

---

548 See remarks by R. Falk in American Society of International Law, 'The Independence and Impartiality of International Judges', 517.

549 Tomuschat, Christian, 'National Representation of Judges and Legitimacy of International Jurisdictions: Lessons from ICJ to ECJ', in: Pernice, Ingolf *et al.* (eds) *The Future of the European Judicial System in a Comparative Perspective* (Nomos Berlin 2006), 184.

550 According to B. Schenk von Stauffenberg, in addressing the issue of *ad hoc* judges in the context of the PCIJ, "[c]ountries will not in fact feel full confidence in the decision of the Court in a case in which they are concerned if the Court includes

"be viewed as some kind of neo-colonial usurpation of the basic political rights of the people".[551] The *ad hoc* judge can ensure that arguments relevant for the nominating State have been properly explained to the bench, that national jurisprudence, legislation and other circumstances are understood by the Court if and when relevant, and that such considerations are properly taken into account in the judicial decision. In other words, international judicial adjudication of the kind that takes place before the ICJ demands that political considerations be taken into account. Again, to quote Judge E. Lauterpacht:

> "The administration of justice within the State can afford to rely on purely formal and procedural grounds. It can also afford to disregard the susceptibilities of either of the parties by ignoring such of its arguments as are not indispensable to the decision. This cannot properly be done in international relations, where the parties are sovereign States, upon whose will the jurisdiction of the Court depends in the long run, and where it is of importance that justice should not only be done but that it should appear to have been done."[552]

But was not the contention that justice should not only be done but that it should also be seen to be done one of the central arguments in support of making (international) courts as independent as possible? That *ad hoc* judges pose a potential threat to independent decision-making is apparent from the above-mentioned normative framework. If these judges are exempt from rules that otherwise play a significant role in ensuring a court's independence, such as the prohibition on exercising simultaneously political or administrative functions, then attention is called for. The counter-argument of practical necessity for *ad hoc* judges to be able to make a living while exercising a function confined in time can provide only limited justification for neglecting judicial independence.

What can be said with some degree of certainty, because it is based on empirical evidence, is that there is no necessary connection between the country of origin of *ad hoc* judges and the country that they represent. As of July 2013, 110 individuals had served as *ad hoc* judges in 179 instances

---

no Judge of their nationality, particularly if it includes a Judge of the nationality of the other party." Schenk von Stauffenberg, *Statut et Règlement de la Cour Permanente de Justice Internationale – Eléments d'interprétation*, 181. See also Mackenzie, et al. (eds), *The Manual on International Courts and Tribunals*, 8.

551 Tomuschat, 'National Representation of Judges and Legitimacy of International Jurisdictions: Lessons from ICJ to ECJ', 184.

552 Lauterpacht, Hersch, *The Development of International Law by the International Court* (Stevens London 1958), 39.

at the ICJ.[553] This indicates that a rather limited number of individuals are repeatedly chosen to serve temporarily on the bench of the ICJ. These judges came from 51 different (original) countries but represented an overall 74 different countries.[554] In only 76 instances (i.e. approximately 42% of all instances where *ad hoc* judges have served) has the country of origin also been the country represented by the *ad hoc* judge. Conversely, a look at the voting behaviour of *ad hoc* judges suggests that their use indeed threatens the overall balance of an otherwise independent court.[555] If taken seriously, the function of *ad hoc* judges as channels serving the Court to acquire detailed knowledge of the appointing State's legal traditions and other individualities[556] could be fulfilled by equipping the Court with all tools necessary to gather country-specific expertise whenever needed, without allowing such expertise also to have an influence on the actual decision-taking. This is all the more to be recommended as the rationale of *ad hoc* judges functioning as experts suffers from a considerable flaw: it serves to dispel all threats to the Court's independence only if States Parties appoint judges for sole reason of their expertise. One alternative solution to the problem of inequality between States Parties before the Court but which puts to rest concerns for the Court's independent functioning could be seen not in the addition of a national judge for every party, but instead the subtraction of all (possible) national judges.[557] This solution can certainly be said to "deprive the bench

---

553 'The Court – All Judges *ad hoc*' available at <http://www.icj-cij.org/court/index.php?p1=1&p2=5&p3=2> (last visited: 21 March 2014).

554 For detailed statistics see the Annex: *Ad Hoc* Judges of the ICJ.

555 Empirical data suggest that *ad hoc* judges indeed vote in favour of *their* party to a greater extent than their regular colleagues. See *Application of the Convention on the Prevention and Punishment of the Crime of Genocide (Bosnia and Herzegovina v Serbia and Montenegro) (Order of 13 September 1993) (Separate Opinion of Judge Lauterpacht)*, 409, Schwebel, Stephen M., 'National Judges and Judges Ad Hoc of the International Court of Justice' (1999) 48 The International and Comparative Law Quarterly 4, 893. See also Karg, *IGH vs. ISGH – Die Beziehung zwischen zwei völkerrechtlichen Streitbeilegungsorganen*, 134.

556 Guillaume, Gilbert, 'Some Thoughts on the Independence of International Judges vis-à-vis States' (2003) 2 The Law and Practice of International Courts and Tribunals 1, 164. It is somewhat telling for our analysis here that Guillaume goes on to state that "thanks to this system, in those cases where there is a judge having the nationality of one of the parties on the Court, the other party need not feel itself to be in a weaker position."

557 The report on a future PCIJ presented by M. Léon Bourgeois on 5 August 1920 on the eighth meeting of the League Council, while addressing the question of national judges, already considered this resolution "as being … most in accordance with the

of some of the best experience and ability on it and would also upset the delicate balance of relationships between group members."[558] But whereas the problem of equipping the bench with special expertise could be solved in the above-mentioned way, the rupture of a balance of relationships between group members, which incidentally is merely a political value, is simply a necessary consequence of taking judicial independence seriously.

3. Financing the ICJ

The financing of the ICJ relies entirely on the UN.[559] Pursuant to Art. 33 ICJ Statute, the costs of the Court are to be borne by the UN. The budget is, according to Art. II, Regulation 2.14 of the Financial Regulations and Rules of the United Nations,[560] prepared by the Court in consultation with the

---

actual rules of justice." League of Nations, *Official Journal – Number 6, September 1920* (Imprimerie 'Sonor', S.A. Genève 1920), 320. See on this question League of Nations, *Official Journal – Number 8, November-December 1920* (Imprimerie 'Sonor', S.A. Genève 1920), 16.

558 Prott, Lyndel V., 'The Role of the Judge of the International Court of Justice' (1974) 10 Revue Belge de Droit International, 488.

559 According to the annual report of the ICJ the budget for the biennium (!) 2010-2011 amounted to 51,010,200 USD (approximately 36,635,800 EUR; International Court of Justice, *Report of the International Court of Justice, 1 August 2009-31 July 2010* (1 January 2010) UN Doc. A/65/4(SUPP)); for the biennium 2008-2009 it amounted to 45,737,700 USD (approximately 33,061,265 EUR; International Court of Justice, *Report of the International Court of Justice, 1 August 2008-31 July 2009* (1 August 2009) UN Doc. A/64/4(SUPP)), which was a slight increase compared to the biennium 2007-2008 (41,200,400 USD/29,772,000 EUR; International Court of Justice, *Report of the International Court of Justice, 1 August 2007-31 July 2008* (1 January 2008) UN Doc. A/63/4(SUPP)) but a considerable increase compared to the biennium 2006-2007 (36,785,000 USD/26,598,000 EUR; International Court of Justice, *Report of the International Court of Justice, 1 August 2006-31 July 2007* (1 January 2007) UN Doc. A/62/4(SUPP)). The proposed budget for the biennium 2010-2011 amounts to 48,754,100 USD/34,768,800 EUR (UNGA, *Proposed programme budget for the biennium 2010-2011 – Part III International justice and law – Section 7 International Court of Justice* (1 April 2009) UN Doc. A/64/6 (Sect. 7)).

560 "Regulation 2.14. The programme budget proposals of the International Court of Justice shall be prepared by the Court in consultation with the Secretary-General. These programme budget proposals shall be submitted to the General Assembly by the Secretary-General, together with such observations as he or she may deem desirable." UNSG, *Financial Regulations and Rules of the United Nations* (9 May 2003) UN Doc. ST/SGB/2003/7.

UNSG in the form of proposals to be submitted to the UNGA by the UNSG. The Registrar of the Court prepares a preliminary budget[561] which is sent to the Court's Budgetary and Administrative Committee for consideration. Hereafter, the Court itself has to approve the budget before it is sent to the UNSG. Until this stage of the process of determining the budget, the Court is thus largely in control. The approved budget is analysed by the Advisory Committee on Administrative and Budgetary Questions, which issues a report to the UNGA. The latter has its Fifth Committee examine the budget and, finally, in a plenary meeting adopts the budget together with resolutions regarding the overall budget of the UN.[562]

It could be argued that the UNGA pursuant to Art. 17(1) UNC has complete discretion whether or not to approve a budget after having considered it.[563] This would put the Court's independence at jeopardy since it would provide the UNGA with a powerful tool to influence the Court's operation. However, such a literal and isolated interpretation of the provision would seriously impair the functioning of the UN and ultimately jeopardize the fulfilment of the purposes set out in Art. 1 UNC.[564] Although the precise level of the budget may be open to discretion, and therefore may always be implemented in order to pressure the Court, the UNGA instead has a legal obligation not to withhold the necessary funding which the principal organs of the UN require in order to function.[565] Problems in this regard have not yet occurred, to the knowledge of the author. This can also be attributed to the clear expression of the ICJ's opinion that Art. 17(1) UNC does not mean that

---

561 Art. 26(1)(j) Rules of Court. See also Arts. 26-38 Instructions for the Registry (International Cour of Justice, *Instructions for the Registry* (October 1946) available at <http://www.icj-cij.org/registry/index.php?p1=2&p2=3&p3=2&PHPSESSID=5c407&PHPSESSID=5c407> (last visited: 21 March 2014)).

562 Thus the budget is part of the overall budget of the UN and derived from it. See also Meron, Theodor, 'Budget Approval by the General Assembly of the United Nations: Duty or Discretion' (1967) 42 The British Yearbook of International Law, 107-108.

563 Art. 17(1) UNC: "The General Assembly shall consider and approve the budget of the Organization."

564 Cf. Art. 31(1) Vienna Convention on the Law of Treaties: "A treaty shall be interpreted in good faith in accordance with the ordinary meaning to be given to the terms of the treaty in their *context* and in the light of its *object and purpose*." (Emphasis added.).

565 Meron, 'Budget Approval by the General Assembly of the United Nations: Duty or Discretion', 121.

"the General Assembly has an absolute power to approve or disapprove the expenditure proposed to it; for some part of that expenditure arises out of obligations already incurred by the Organization, and to this extent the General Assembly has no alternative but to honour these engagements."[566]

VI. Personal Independence

1. The Pre-Electoral Requirements of Integrity and Qualification

The Statute in its Art. 2 requires ICJ judges to be of high moral character and to "possess the qualifications required in their respective countries for appointment to the highest judicial offices" or to be "jurisconsults of recognized competence in international law". One advantage of these individual selection criteria is that they are characteristics of individuals which are not relativized by the countries of the judges' origin or by the passports they hold. In that sense, they may establish a counterweight against the abovementioned overly politicized election process. But how can these requirements in detail help to ensure the ICJ judges' independent and impartial fulfilment of their duties?

a) High Moral Character

The demand for high moral character was first mentioned in the 1899 and 1907 Hague Conventions on the pacific settlement of Disputes[567] and the Statute of the PCIJ included this requirement in its Art. 2. It was further elaborated in Art. 5 Rules of Court of the PCIJ by the demand that every new judge make a declaration that his duties as a judge would be performed "honourably" and "conscientiously".[568] The same rules were maintained in Art. 4 of the ICJ's Rules of Court. At the time of their inception, these for-

566 *Effect of Awards of Compensation Made by the United Nations Administrative Tribunal (Advisory Opinion)* ICJ Rep. 47 (1954), 59.

567 Cf. the wording in Arts. 23 and 44 Hague Convention (1899 and 1907), which demands that the chosen arbitrators be "of known competency in questions of international law, of the highest moral reputation".

568 PCIJ, *Rules of Court* (adopted 24 March 1922) available at <http://www.icj-cij.org/pcij/serie_D/D_01.pdf> (last visited: 21 March 2014).

mulations were considered to reflect the ethical standards of their time as common to "the main forms of civilization".[569] They were perceived as formulations of principle, and there was no intention or perceived need to specify them,[570] since the morals of a person are "only subjectively determinable",[571] i.e. they are shaped by the vast array of influences and emotions affecting a particular individual in his decision making, which makes them difficult to grasp.[572] Notwithstanding the difficulty of defining what constitutes high moral character,[573] the personality of a candidate for office will have to be holistically assessed by the members of the electoral bodies, which puts a significant burden on them to do their work conscientiously.

In essence, the "moral suitability"[574] of a judge refers to a certain state of mind enabling an individual to withstand pressure being exerted in different ways. In other words, it is an appeal directed at the individual judge to be prepared to behave according to the right standards if a conflict situation arises, e.g. if a judge has a position which might put into question his impartiality from a party or if a judge has close relations with a State acting as a party before the Court which could raise doubts about the independence of his judgment. It would be misleading, however, to equate the requirement of "high moral character" with either independence or impartiality, although there are certainly areas of overlap, in particular since "high moral character" and "independence" are treated as two different notions in the ICJ Statute itself, and "high moral character" and "impartiality" are mentioned simultaneously in other instances, e.g. in the Rome Statute of the ICC.[575] The notion of "high moral character" ultimately materializes only in combination with

---

569 Art. 9 ICJ Statute. Cf. Schwarzenberger, *International Law as Applied by International Courts and Tribunals – Vol. 4 – International Judicial Law*, 281.

570 According to M. Hudson, their virtual implicitness made their mentioning seem "to serve little purpose." Hudson, *The Permanent Court of International Justice 1920-1942 – A Treatise*, 146.

571 Abi-Saab, 'Ensuring the Best Bench: Ways of Selecting Judges', 167.

572 As Judge M. Lachs said, judges are human beings and as such "have their weaknesses and limitations ... [and] both their achievements and shortcomings they must be looked upon as individuals: it is their personality that matters." *Military and Paramilitary Activities in and against Nicaragua (Nicaragua v United States of America) (Merits) (Separate opinion of Judge Lachs) ICJ Rep. 14 (1986)*, 159.

573 'Oxford English Dictionary' available at <http://www.oed.com/> (last visited: 21 March 2014): "character": "The sum of the moral and mental qualities which distinguish an individual or a race".

574 Elias, 'Report', 21.

575 Cf. Art. 36(3) Rome Statute. See further *infra* Chapter F.IV(2)(a).

objective conditions such as incompatibilities with judicial office[576] or the situation where a judge "for some special reason" ought not to exercise his function on the bench.[577] Furthermore, it has been proposed that the integrity and propriety of the judges requires a certain loyalty towards the Court, e.g. in the choice of words when referring to the Court and/or its judges, inside and outside the Court.[578]

b) The Required Competence

Pursuant to Art. 2 Statute members of the Court shall either possess the qualifications necessary in the candidate's home country for appointment to the highest judicial office or be of recognized competence in international law. As the two requirements are not complementary,[579] two different categories of candidates are created, of whom only the latter, the jurisconsults,[580] have to have a profound knowledge of international law.[581] The reasons behind this dichotomy are attributable to the compromise that had to be found between views held by the founders. Depending on their respective legal education in a common law or civil law system, on certain qualities necessary in a good judge that could or could not be acquired only through seasoning by experience at the bar and by experience upon the bench in their respective countries.[582]

Because competence in international law is not a compulsory requirement – which for a court such as the ICJ is somewhat surprising – the question

576 Arts. 16-17 ICJ Statute.

577 Art. 24 ICJ Statute. See further *infra* Chapters D.VI(5).

578 Aznar-Gómez, 'Article 2 ICJ Statute', 215.

579 On this see Rosenne, *The Law and Practice of the International Court – Vol. 3 Procedure*, 358; Scott, *The Project of a Permanent Court of International Justice and Resolutions of the Advisory Committee of Jurists – Report and Commentary*, 51.

580 The term "jurisconsults" is not defined in the ICJ Statute.

581 A proposal to amend the Statute of the PCIJ so that all candidates possess recognized practical experience in international law was turned down in 1929. Cf. Mosler, 'The International Judiciary from the Point of View of an International Judge', 171.

582 Scott, *The Project of a Permanent Court of International Justice and Resolutions of the Advisory Committee of Jurists – Report and Commentary*, 51. In deserves to be pointed out in this context that Art. 2 does not require that a judge has previously actually served in the highest judicial office in his home country, but merely that he is qualified to do so.

ought to be raised whether competence in international law or the lack of it has any influence on the independent functioning of the Court. The application of international law, as a legal order which is genuinely distinct from the municipal legal systems, is a defining element of the Court.[583] Indeed, besides being made up of judges from different nationalities, the character of the ICJ as an international court flows from its applying (and being expected to apply) international law to settle disputes between States. If international law is not applied, e.g. due to a lacking knowledge, the way is opened up for other sources to fill this void, potentially to the detriment of an otherwise autonomous jurisprudence.[584] What are these sources and are they realistically a threat to the Court's independent functioning?

As Judge L. Carneiro pointed out in his dissenting opinion in the *Anglo-Iranian Oil Co. Case*, "[i]t is inevitable that everyone of us in this Court should retain some trace of his legal education and his former legal activities in his country of origin."[585] In this sense, the competence requirement in Art. 2 ICJ Statute should be regarded as a mere reflection of reality, where many candidates for the bench of the ICJ have experience pertaining to the legal system with which they grew up. In support of this assumption, the Statute itself in Art. 9 acknowledges the relevance of competence in national legal systems by suggesting that the electors of ICJ judges should keep in mind that the body as a whole represents "the principal legal systems of the world". Art. 9 ICJ Statute thus states that the Court is best served by ensuring a fusion of the principal legal systems rather than expressly demanding competence in international law of all its judges.[586] According to a teleological interpretation given to the notion of "principal legal systems of the world", the term aims to ensure that the Court – more generally – is equipped with the legal expertise needed to fulfil its functions.[587] In other words, al-

---

583 And a characteristic that sets it apart from the political organs of the UN. Cf. Art. 38 ICJ Statute.

584 Elias, 'Report', 32 goes even further by stating that "qualification in international law was a greater safeguard for independence than any conceivable method of selection."

585 *Anglo-Iranian Oil Co. Case (Jurisdiction), Judgment of July 22nd, 1952 (Dissenting Opinion of Judge Levi Carneiro)*, para. 14.

586 This could be interpreted as a potential area of conflict between Arts. 2 and 9, which shall not be dealt with in detail here. See further on this point Rosenne, Shabtai, *The Law and Practice of the International Court – Vol. 1* (Sijthoff Leyden 1965), 363.

587 Fassbender, 'Article 9 ICJ Statute', 275.

though the ICJ Statute does not expressly demand that every judge be of recognized competence in international law, although this would be desirable considering the unquestionable role that this body of law plays in the functioning of the Court, the Statute seeks to fill this void by allowing the Court to profit from the "principal legal systems of the world". Legal competence in one form or another is thus welcomed, and this ought to be considered a legitimate aim.

It appears instead that the threat posed by not requiring of all its judges competence in international law stems not so much from a conflict with judges' competence in municipal law, but from the possibility this creates for sending to the Court judges who are overly deeply anchored in their national legal and/or political systems. More pointedly, the real threat is that the above-mentioned void will be filled with undue influence from outside the realm of the law. As M. Aznar-Gómez outlined, the objective selection criteria in Art. 2 ICJ Statute have throughout the history of the Court led to the crystallization of three categories of judges: practitioners with long experience in domestic courts, experts in international law, and the diplomatic and civil servants of States and international organizations.[588] Although this could be criticized as being a rough and oversimplified representation of the bench of the Court, there appears to be some merit in the allegation that the wording of Art. 2 ICJ Statute contributes to the opening up of the Court to personnel from the diplomatic corps and civil servants.[589] As will be shown, the fact that more recent international courts include in their statements on judges' competence the requirement for expertise in (a field of) international law shows that Art. 2 ICJ Statute is very much a child of its time, and that its wording is owed more to the historical context which bears sign of a proximity to arbitration.[590]

---

588 Aznar-Gómez, 'Article 2 ICJ Statute', 216.

589 For a more detailed overview see e.g. Mackenzie, et al., *Selecting International Judges: Principle, Process, and Politics*, 51-60.

590 The Institut de Droit International in its resolution of 2011 on the position of international judges, stated in Art. 1(1) that "[States] shall also ensure that judges possess the required competence and that the court or tribunal is in a position effectively to deal with issues of general international law." The Institut went on to confirm in Art. 1(6) that "[t]he selection of judges should be carried out taking into consideration, first and foremost, the qualifications of candidates, of which political authorities should be fully apprised."

2. Tenure and Security of Tenure

a) Length of Office and the Possibility of Re-Election

Regular elections to the bench of the ICJ take place every three years when one third of the Court's seats are voted upon. In this regard the ICJ is different from the PCIJ where the seats of all judges were voted upon at the same time.[591] This system was changed due to the "complete break in the continuity and traditions of the Court" that such all-embracing elections meant.[592] The election of only part of the bench at one time was expected to have the potential "for the adaptation of the court to social change."[593] Pursuant to Art. 13 ICJ Statute judges of the Court are elected for nine years with the possibility of re-election. The Statute does not provide for any limitation regarding the number of possible re-elections, and thus judges may be, and often are, re-elected.[594] The date of commencement of the term of office is not laid down expressly in the Statute but follows from Art. 2 para. 1 Rules of Court for judges elected in regular elections.[595]

At the outset, it must be conceded that the optimal length of tenure for ensuring that judges can conduct their judicial duties independently is virtually impossible to determine. It has been suggested that judges should be

---

591 Yet even in the drafting of the Statute of the PCIJ many proposals envisaged an appointment for a set term of years. See, e.g., Permanent Court of International Justice & Advisory Committee of Jurists, *Procès-Verbaux of the Proceedings of the Committee, June 16th-July 24th 1920 with Annexes*, 209 and 251.

592 United Nations, 'Report of the Inter-Allied Committee on the Future of the Permanent Court of International Justice, February 10, 1944', para. 35. See also the criticism by Hudson, *The Permanent Court of International Justice 1920-1942 – A Treatise*, 242.

593 Prott, 'The Role of the Judge of the International Court of Justice', 486.

594 With Manfred Lachs, the longest serving judge to date, having been on the bench between 1967 and 1993.

595 According to Art. 2 para. 1 Rules of Court a judge begins his term on 6 February in the year in which the relevant vacancy occurred. This specific date leans on the beginning of the terms of office of the judges elected in the first elections to the Court, which took place between 6 and 9 February 1946. See Rosenne, *The Law and Practice of the International Court – Vol. 1 The Court and the United Nations*, 380. For a judge elected to the bench to replace a member whose term of office has not expired the term begins from the date of the election (Art. 3(2) Rules of Court).

allowed to serve for fifteen years in order to reinforce their independence,[596] and even life tenure has been considered.[597] However, it must be recognized that there is no logic that provides a necessary link between e.g. short tenure and greater susceptibility to undue influence. What can be said is that shorter tenure does increase the desire of the Court to provide for the possibility of re-election, in the interest of ensuring the Court's continuity and traditions while also "[preserving] the capacity of adapting itself to the legal and political evolution of the world, a capacity which is necessary for it to remain in contact with this development, and thus fulfil its high mission".[598] Re-electability, as opposed to short tenure *per se*, is a real threat to the Court's independent functioning. As the Institute of International Law observed as early as in 1954, "[t]he possibility of re-election affects the independence as judges may tailor their decisions to meet the expectations of their political constituency in the United Nations."[599] But the report went on to make the important point that "[t]he evidence in support of this criticism is inevitably uncertain, subjective and impressionistic." More recent studies, however, emphasize that a considerable amount of campaigning is done by judges seeking re-election, and therefore provide a better picture of the potential threats to independence flowing from campaigning by judges seeking re-election.[600] Such campaigning may range from judges writing to the PCA national groups asking for their support to spending time at the seat of the UN in New York, to direct requests to meet representatives of missions to the UN, i.e. contact with entities with influence in the electoral bodies.[601] What is said at such meetings is obviously concealed from the public, but some missions apparently ask sitting judges blatantly "what is going on in

596 Institut de Droit International, *Annuaire de l'Institut de Droit International – Session d'Aix-en-Provence Avril/Mai 1954 Tome II* (Verlag für Recht und Gesellschaft A G. Genève 1954), 297.

597 See remarks by T. Franck in American Society of International Law, 'The Independence and Impartiality of International Judges', 521.

598 Permanent Court of International Justice & Advisory Committee of Jurists, *Procès-Verbaux of the Proceedings of the Committee, June 16th-July 24th 1920 with Annexes*, 209 and 251.

599 Institut de Droit International, *Annuaire de l'Institut de Droit International – Session d'Aix-en-Provence Avril/Mai 1954 Tome II*, 83.

600 See Mackenzie, et al., *Selecting International Judges: Principle, Process, and Politics*, 120-122. This study also builds on and analyses interviews with, at the time, current ICJ judges.

601 Ibid, 120.

the court and how he sees the organization and whether there is anything that needs to be developed."[602] It deserves to be emphasized that such conversations, be they public or not, need not taint the independence of the judge who hears them. But considering the context in which they are made and, consequently, the effect they may have on the judge and his perception of the requirements as to re-election, the potential damage is considerable. Anecdotal evidence further suggests that there are occasional incidents where judges have received strong support from a State following e.g. their formulation of a dissenting opinion which favoured that State. Whereas it can be claimed that so particular an incident is an isolated case, coincidental or in any event not part of the binding decision of the Court, the existence of such a link, coupled with the difficulty of obtaining evidence of the frequency of comparable events, should be a warning sign. That in view of such interactions a judge may consciously or subconsciously be influenced by the desire to obtain support for re-election does not require further justification.

The question that ought to be raised is whether judges' involvement in lobbying and campaigning merits concrete actions. One measure that could be taken is to eliminate the ability to be re-elected, coupled with an increase in tenure in order not to jeopardize the Court's continuity and ability to develop a *jurisprudence constante*.[603] The possibility of re-election is indeed viewed critically and as not fully compatible with judicial independence in scholarly literature.[604] The Institut de Droit International in its sixth resolution of 2011 on the position of international judges also came to the conclusion that

602 Interview results in ibid, 120.

603 This proposal was first submitted by the Institute of International Law in its abovementioned report; Institut de Droit International, *Annuaire de l'Institut de Droit International – Session d'Aix-en-Provence Avril/Mai 1954 Tome II*, 296. For opinions of scholars and ICJ judges on this proposal see Dugard, John, 'Article 13 ICJ Statute', in: Zimmermann, Andreas *et al.* (eds) *The Statute of the International Court of Justice – A Commentary* (Oxford University Press Oxford 2006), 313.

604 Helfer & Slaughter, 'Why States Create International Tribunals – A Response to Professors Posner and Yoo', 950; Mackenzie & Sands, 'International Courts and Tribunals and the Independence of the International Judge', 276-279.

> "[i]n order to strengthen the independence of judges, it would be desirable that they be appointed for long terms of office, ranging between nine and twelve years [and] such terms of office should not be renewable."[605]

But whereas this proposal has certain advantages, it will certainly not have the result of eliminating all kinds of undue influence.[606] As Judge M. Lachs stated, judges are human beings, and as such "have their weaknesses and limitations … [and] both their achievements and shortcomings they must be looked upon as individuals: it is their personality that matters."[607] What can be said with some degree of certainty, based on a comparison with the situation at other international courts which will be analysed in what follows, is that the tenure at the ICJ is already considerable.[608] This observation coupled with the impossibility of determining the ideal length to best secure independence give reason not to overestimate the actual length but instead to consider e.g. the ways in which this tenure is secured.

b) Removal from Office

Judicial tenure, regardless of length, cannot secure judges' independence unless it is also protected against possibilities of facile removal from office. This makes the conditions under which removability is possible one of the main tests of judicial independence.[609] ICJ judges cannot be removed from office by an outside authority. Instead Art. 13(4) ICJ Statute provides that a judge may resign from his office by the submission of a resignation to the President of the Court and the transmission of such resignation to the UN-

---

605 Institut de Droit International, *The Position of the International Judge – 6th Resolution – Sixth Commission – Session de Rhodes* (2011) available at <http://www.idi-iil.org/> (last visited: 21 March 2014), Art. 2(1).

606 According to statements by a former judge, some judges think about how something could be received by the UNGA; Mackenzie, et al., *Selecting International Judges: Principle, Process, and Politics*, 121. As undesirable as such considerations may be, it is unlikely that they can ever be eliminated entirely.

607 *Military and Paramilitary Activities in and against Nicaragua (Nicaragua v United States of America) (Merits) (Separate opinion of Judge Lachs)*, 159.

608 The tenure of judges at (selected) other international courts is: nine years (ITLOS, ICC), six years (ECtHR, IACtHR, and ECJ), four years (ICTY, ICTR).

609 Elias, Taslim Olawale, *New Horizons in International Law* (Sijthoff & Noordhoff Alphen aan den Rijn 1979), 72; Anderson, David H., 'Article 18 ICJ Statute', in: Zimmermann, Andreas *et al.* (eds) *The Statute of the International Court of Justice – A Commentary* (Oxford University Press Oxford 2006), 352.

SG.[610] Moreover, the Statute in Art. 18, a provision that so far has never been used to its full effect,[611] provides for the possibility of removing a judge from office if, "in the *unanimous* opinion of the *other members*, he has ceased to fulfill the required conditions" (emphasis added). Art. 6 Rules of Court establishes the procedure to be followed once the application of Art. 18 ICJ Statute is under consideration.[612]

Although Art. 18 ICJ Statute does not qualify what "the required conditions" means, it can be assumed that this includes the conditions of eligibility for election (i.e. Arts. 2-3 ICJ Statute) as well as the rules of conduct contained in Arts. 16, 17 and 23 ICJ Statute.[613] This implies, for example, that if a judge were to lose his qualification of high moral character due to reprehensible conduct or cease to be (or appear to be) independent due to additional engagements of a professional nature, he may be removed from office by his colleagues. This system must be welcomed, although it can be questioned whether the requirement of unanimity among the other judges is too high a bar for this provision to have any practical value. Proposals for a two-thirds

---

610 Art. 13(4) ICJ Statute. The seat becomes vacant only with the transmission of the resignation to the UNSG.

611 The fact that so far no attempt to make use of the ability to dismiss a judge has been recorded should not be taken as sufficient evidence of the lack of actual attempts or the desire to influence the Court, and thus of threats to independence. States are unwilling to exert pressure overly openly and the desire to dismiss a judge would certainly not be beneficial to the perception of a State's adherence to international law; at least as long as subtler methods of achieving the same purpose are available (e.g. influencing the nomination through national groups). Thus even if "the issue of removability is nearly always and everywhere regarded as the main test of judicial independence" (Elias, *New Horizons in International Law*, 72) it should not, once basic irremovability had been acknowledged, be the basis of too far-reaching conclusions on the actual independence of the Court.

612 Accordingly, the affected member of the Court shall be informed by the President in writing about the grounds for the beginning of removal procedures and shall also share any relevant evidence. The judge concerned shall furthermore at a private meeting of the Court, which must be specially convened for this purpose, be afforded an opportunity to make a statement, to furnish any information or explanations he wishes to give, and supply answers to any questions put to him. A further meeting must be convened to discuss the matter among the other members of the Court. A vote shall be taken only if it is requested.

613 Anderson, 'Article 18 ICJ Statute', 356.

majority[614] were, interestingly, rejected during the drafting of the ICJ Statute on the basis that this would be less likely to protect the independence of the judges (the same was felt about the prescription of a set retirement age[615]).[616] Recently, however, voices have again been raised in support of introducing such a qualified majority.[617] Besides this, in this writer's opinion, the rather sophisticated procedure prescribed in Art. 6 Rules of Court, according to which e.g. the members of the Court after two private meetings shall make a decision on whether or not the member of the Court concerned should be dismissed from office must be considered a sufficient safeguard against abuse of the ability to remove a judge. This procedure, which in its entirety takes place inside the Court itself, clearly reflects the desire to keep the issue of security of tenure at the disposal of the Court without any outside influence. It also ought to be pointed out that even a minority of judges seeking the dismissal of a colleague could make the continuing service of the latter virtually and practically impossible.[618] But such a group, however strongly its opinion may affect the will of the colleague to continue to serve on the Court, is not sufficient to force the removal of a judge.

Art. 18 ICJ Statute does not explicitly determine who is allowed to initiate a potential dismissal investigation, and in particular if any outside organ, such as the UNGA, UNSC, UNSG or States Parties to the Statute of the Court, may exercise this power. But reading Art. 18 ICJ Statute in conjunction

614 See, e.g., the proposal by Chile to lower the unanimity requirement to a requirement of a two-thirds majority; United Nations Information Organizations, *UNCIO XIII*, 475.

615 Hudson, *The Permanent Court of International Justice 1920-1942 – A Treatise*, 168.

616 See on this Rosenne, *The Law and Practice of the International Court – Vol. 1 The Court and the United Nations*, 399; Hudson, *The Permanent Court of International Justice 1920-1942 – A Treatise*, 168; Anderson, 'Article 18 ICJ Statute', 353.

617 See, e.g., Art. 2(2) of the resolution of the Institut de Droit International on the position of the international judge of 2011: "During their entire term of office, judges shall enjoy irremovability. Judges may be removed from office only if they cease to meet the required conditions for the performance of the judicial function, and following a decision adopted by their peers in accordance with due process. Such a decision could be preceded, if necessary, by a suspension of the judge concerned. In addition, *these decisions should be taken by qualified majority voting, for example a three-quarters majority*." (Emphasis added.).

618 On this see Guyomar, Geneviève, *Commentaire du règlement de la Cour Internationale de Justice adopté le 14 avril 1978 – interpretation et pratique* (Pedone Paris 1983), 32.

with Art. 6 Rules of Court leads to the conclusion that the reasonable interpretation is that the Court itself determines whether or not to investigate a particular situation with a view to dismissing a sitting judge. Any other interpretation would strip the Court of its autonomy and the ability to deflect influences from external organs on its purposive functioning.[619] This does not mean that e.g. the UNGA or the UNSC is barred from making requests to the Court that Art. 18 ICJ Statute be applied in a particular instance. However, it does mean that such a request does not have binding effect on the Court and instead the Court is called upon to react (or not) in a manner it deems fit.[620]

3. Remuneration

a) Considerations Influencing the Level of Salary

The remuneration of judges, on both the national and international levels, is often identified as one of the weak points in the protection of judicial independence. For ICJ judges, salaries, allowances and compensation are laid down by the UNGA. The only condition laid down by the relevant provision in Art. 32(5) ICJ Statute is that the UNGA is prohibited from lowering his salary during a judge's term of office. For the purpose of this rule, the term of office also includes subsequent terms of office, at least if the new term is continuous with the previous one.[621] The guiding considerations regarding the level of judges' salaries hark back to the deliberations of the Preparatory Commission, which regarded it as essential to accord judges sufficient emoluments "such as to guarantee their absolute independence" and on a level that renders the office of judge acceptable to those who are qualified

619 Anderson, 'Article 18 ICJ Statute', 356 is of the same opinion.

620 The Government of India addressed a note to the Registrar of the Court concerning statements made by a member of the Court on 1 March 1968. In the note India addressed the other members of the Court,calling for the behaviour not to be accepted or tolerated by them. The note does not seem to have resulted in any action. Ibid, 356 with further references.

621 Cf. President of the International Court of Justice, *Document transmitted by the President of the International Court of Justice to the Secretary-General on the implications of General Assembly resolution 61/262 in regard to certain provisions of the Statute of the Court*, para. 56.

– in accordance with Art. 2 ICJ Statute – to hold such office.[622] It was moreover suggested that the real value of the salaries ought not to be lower than those of the judges of the PCIJ during the period 1936-1939. Since the first salary was set for ICJ judges several adjustments have been made by the UNGA, most prominently through UNGA Resolution 61/262 of 2007,[623] which included a major modification of the method of calculating the level of salaries. Due to the controversy this resolution caused among the judges of the Court, this development will be described in greater length and detail in what follows, to illustrate the potential dangers posed to the independence of the Court by the application of Art. 32 ICJ Statute and the mechanisms available to avert potential threats.[624]

b) The Importance of Equality – The Impact of UNGA Resolution 61/262

The UNGA in its Resolution 59/282 of 13 April 2005[625] set the salaries of members of the ICJ at 170,080 USD per annum, effective from 1 January 2005, which was an increase of 6.3% compared to the level that had been applicable since 1 January 1999.[626] This adjustment, which was based on a

622 Preparatory Commission of the United Nations, *Report of the Preparatory Commission of the United Nations* (23 December 1945) UN Doc. PC/20, 58.

623 UNGA, *Conditions of service and compensation for officials other than Secretariat officials: members of the International Court of Justice and judges and ad litem judges of the International Tribunal for the Former Yugoslavia and the International Criminal Tribunal for Rwanda* (3 May 2007) UN Doc. A/RES/61/262.

624 It should be emphasized already at this stage that the discussion concerning UNGA Resolution 61/262 is one that is peculiar to the ICJ as the problems raised by this resolution ultimately are attributable to the character of the ICJ as the principal judicial organ of the UN, the mission of which is to resolve disputes between sovereign States. President of the International Court of Justice, *Document transmitted by the President of the International Court of Justice to the Secretary-General on the implications of General Assembly resolution 61/262 in regard to certain provisions of the Statute of the Court*, para. 73.

625 UNGA, *Special subjects relating to the programme budget for the biennium 2004–2005* (13 April 2005) UN Doc. A/RES/59/282.

626 The Advisory Committee on Administrative and Budgetary Questions in its report of 10 November 1998 had suggested that the annual salary of ICJ judges be set at 160,000 USD, see Report of the Advisory Committee on Administrative and Budgetary Questions, *Seventh report: conditions of service and compensation for officials other than Secretariat officials: members of the International Court of Justice* (10 November 1998) UN Doc. A/53/7/Add.6, para. 8. The UNGA supported

draft resolution presented by the Fifth Committee,[627] was only an interim measure, and the UNGA resolution requested the UNSG to submit to the UNGA a comprehensive report with a proposal for a more flexible mechanism of remuneration, *inter alia* based on market exchange rates.[628] This report was presented by the UNSG on 2 November 2006[629] and it suggested a flexible model for the calculation of judges' salaries, composed of a net base salary and a post-adjustment amount calculated on the basis of the post-adjustment multiplier. At the time, such a system already applied for the calculation of the salaries of staff in the professional and higher categories of the UN. In the subsequent consideration of that report by the Advisory Committee on Administrative and Budgetary Questions, the Committee concluded that the proposal unduly inflated the remuneration.[630] Since any increase in judges' salaries had to be decided by the UNGA pursuant to Art. 32(5) ICJ Statute, and since merely a new method for the adjustment of remuneration according to market exchange rates was desired in order to protect the level of remuneration, the Committee suggested the elaboration of new methods.[631] On 27 March 2007 the Fifth Committee, on the basis of the reports by the UNSG and the Advisory Committee on Administrative and Budgetary Questions, proposed a draft resolution dealing with the conditions of service

---

this level in UNGA, *Questions relating to the programme budget for the biennium 1998–1999* (18 December 1998) UN Doc. A/RES/53/214, part VIII, and UNGA, *Conditions of service and compensation for officials other than Secretariat officials: members of the International Court of Justice, judges of the International Tribunal for the Former Yugoslavia, judges of the International Tribunal for Rwanda and ad litem judges of the International Tribunal for the Former Yugoslavia* (27 June 2002) UN Doc. A/RES/56/285.

627 Report of the Fifth Committee, *Programme budget for the biennium 2004-2005* (6 April 2005) UN Doc. A/59/448/Add.3.

628 UNGA, *Special subjects relating to the programme budget for the biennium 2004–2005*, para. 8.

629 UNSG, *Conditions of service and compensation for officials other than Secretariat officials* (2 November 2006) UN Doc. A/61/554.

630 Under the proposal of the UNSG, the salary would have increased by 14.9% due to the UNSG's adoption of the net remuneration thus far (170,080 USD) as the net basic salary: see Report of the Advisory Committee on Administrative and Budgetary Questions, *Conditions of service and compensation for officials other than Secretariat officials* (6 December 2006) UN Doc. A/61/612, para. 7.

631 Ibid, para. 10.

and compensation for members of the ICJ.[632, 633] The resolution envisaged the adoption of the flexible model suggested by the UNSG and set the net base salary of the members of the ICJ at 133,500 USD starting from 1 January 2007. In order not to violate the ban on the reduction of salaries, allowances and compensation during the term of office,[634] the Fifth Committee also added that the level of annual salary approved in UNGA Resolution 59/282 should be maintained for the current members of the ICJ "for the duration of their current term of office or until such a time as this amount is overtaken by the application of the revised annual salary system". In response to the draft resolution the President of the ICJ addressed a letter to the President of the UNGA to express the Court's "extremely serious and deep concern" that the envisaged proposals on emoluments would not be in conformity with the ICJ Statute.[635] The concerns expressed by the ICJ President on behalf of the Court related to two points. Firstly, the President referred to the fun-

---

632 Fifth Committee, *Conditions of service and compensation for officials other than Secretariat officials: members of the International Court of Justice and judges and ad litem judges of the International Tribunal for the Former Yugoslavia and the International Criminal Tribunal for Rwanda* (29 March 2007) UN Doc. A/C.5/61/L.40.

633 The draft resolution was made available to the UNGA prior to the 93rd plenary meeting of the 61st session of the UNGA in April 2007 through a report of the Fifth Committee entitled "Programme budget for the biennium 2006-2007". Report of the Fifth Committee, *Programme budget for the biennium 2006-2007* (10 April 2007) UN Doc. A/61/592/Add.4.

634 Art. 32(5) ICJ Statute.

635 President of the International Court of Justice, *Letter dated 3 April 2007 from the President of the International Court of Justice to the President of the General Assembly* (3 April 2007) UN Doc. A/61/837. The concerns were later reiterated in numerous speeches by the President of the Court, see, e.g., Higgins, Rosalyn, 'Speech by H.E. Judge Rosalyn Higgins, President of the International Court of Justice, at the Meeting of the Legal Advisers of the Ministry of Foreign Affairs' available at <http://www.icj-cij.org/presscom/files/7/14097.pdf> (last visited: 21 March 2014); Higgins, Rosalyn, 'Speech by H.E. Judge Rosalyn Higgins, President of the International Court of Justice, to the General Assembly of the United Nations' available at <http://www.icj-cij.org/presscom/files/7/14117.pdf> (last visited: 21 March 2014); Higgins, Rosalyn, 'Speech by H.E. Judge Rosalyn Higgins, President of the International Court of Justice, to the Sixth Committee of the General Assembly' available at <http://www.icj-cij.org/presscom/files/3/14123.pdf> (last visited: 21 March 2014).

damental principle of equality,[636] stating that the salary should be the same for all members of the Court. The new system, however, meant that the remuneration of newly elected judges would be substantially lower than that of the sitting judges, and thus would have resulted in the formation of two groups of judges. Secondly, the President of the ICJ asserted that the proposed method of determining salaries violated the prohibition on reducing salaries formulated in Art. 32(5) ICJ Statute. According to the President, the proposal would have amounted to a *de facto* reduction in emoluments as no further account of changes in the exchange rate and the cost of living would have been taken. The Court also referred to its special character as the principal judicial organ of the UN when emphasizing that the concerns mentioned could not be allayed by a mere reference to financial rules applicable to national courts. On a more general note, the Court criticized the fact that it had not been consulted before the new system of remuneration was submitted for approval by the UNGA.

Despite calls by some UNGA Member States for the UNSG to consult with the President of the ICJ on the concerns raised by him,[637] the resolution was adopted by the UNGA without a vote and without any changes being made.[638] Instead in a memorandum dated 6 June 2007 the Legal Counsel to the Office of Human Resources Management, upon a request from the Registrar of the ICJ, responded to the concerns raised by the ICJ President.[639] The memorandum stated that "a decrease in salary for future members of the Court would not be inconsistent with the Statute" as Art. 32(5) ICJ Statute prevented a decrease *during* the term in office.[640] The Legal Counsel con-

636 Art. 32(1) ICJ Statute ("Each member of the Court shall receive an annual salary.") read in conjunction with Art. 31(6) ICJ Statute establishing the full equality between *ad hoc* judges and the permanent bench.

637 The German representative speaking on behalf of the EU, the US American representative and the representative from Sierra Leone: see UNGA, *93rd plenary meeting Official Records* (4 April 2007) UN Doc. A/61/PV.93, 4.

638 UNGA, *Conditions of service and compensation for officials other than Secretariat officials: members of the International Court of Justice and judges and ad litem judges of the International Tribunal for the Former Yugoslavia and the International Criminal Tribunal for Rwanda.*

639 See Annex I to UNSG, *Conditions of service and compensation for officials other than Secretariat officials: members of the International Court of Justice and judges and ad litem judges of the International Tribunal for the Former Yugoslavia and the International Criminal Tribunal for Rwanda: Report of the Secretary General* (8 November 2007) UN Doc. A/62/538.

640 Ibid, Annex I, para. 10 *in fine*.

firmed the principle of equality, which is expressly stated for *ad hoc* judges in Art. 31(6) ICJ Statute, and which in his opinion *a fortiori* also applies to permanent members.[641] He went on to conclude that due to the application of this principle in combination with the fact that elections to the bench are staggered pursuant to Art. 13(1) ICJ Statute, the new system of salaries infringed the principle of equal treatment.[642] The Legal Counsel therefore called upon the UNSG to address these concerns and to suggest possible practical measures for resolving the issues and request the UNGA to take those concerns into consideration.[643] Subsequently, the UNSG in his report presented on 8 November 2007 expressed support for the concerns uttered by the ICJ and requested the Member States to take action to remedy the situation.[644] The UNSG himself made two proposals: the first included a change in the currency in which the salary was calculated, from US dollars to Euros, which is the applicable currency of the seat country of the ICJ. The second proposal meant that the system adopted by UNGA Resolution 61/262 would be maintained, namely a net base salary and a corresponding post-adjustment amount per index point equal to 1% of base salary. However, in order to maintain equality in the level of compensation paid to the judges, an adjustment in the level of the base salary was suggested resulting in an increase in salary for all judges. The Advisory Committee on Administrative and Budgetary Questions considered the report by the UNSG in its thirty-seventh report on the programme budget for the biennium 2008-2009 issued on 12 March 2008.[645] The Fifth Committee, taking this report into consideration, presented a draft decision in which the level of the net base salary was increased to 158,000 USD, effective from 1 April 2008, and which no longer differentiated between current and newly elected judges.[646] The decision

641 Ibid, Annex I, para. 11.

642 Ibid, Annex I, para. 13.

643 Ibid, Annex I, para. 23.

644 Ibid, para. 73.

645 Advisory Committee on Administrative and Budgetary Questions, *Conditions of service and compensation for officials other than Secretariat officials: members of the International Court of Justice and judges and ad litem judges of the International Tribunal for the Former Yugoslavia and the International Criminal Tribunal for Rwanda – Thirty-seventh report of the Advisory Committee on Administrative and Budgetary Questions on the programme budget for the biennium 2008-2009* (12 March 2008) UN Doc. A/62/7/Add.36.

646 Draft Decision by the Fifth Committee, *Conditions of service and compensation for officials other than Secretariat officials: members of the International Court of Justice and judges and ad litem judges of the International Tribunal for the Former*

was adopted by the UNGA without a vote during its 91st plenary meeting on 3 April 2008.[647]

c) The Assessment of the ICJ

The ICJ did not question the UNGA's authority to interpret the provisions of the ICJ Statute applicable to the functions of the UNGA, including Art. 32(5) ICJ Statute on the determination of the salaries, allowances, and compensation for judges. The Court nevertheless rightly reserves the right to interpret the Statute authoritatively.[648] According to the ICJ, UNGA Resolution 61/262 is not compatible with the basic principles underlying the ICJ Statute, in particular the general principle of equality[649] of all judges,[650] which is reflected in the Statute.[651] The principle is based on the sovereign equality of States appearing before the Court[652] and entails equality of status and income of the Court's members. The sovereign equality of the States is thus transported onto the bench of the ICJ.[653] This, in the Court's view, is elementary to international inter-State dispute resolution. The Court also underlines these arguments by reference to the *travaux préparatoires* of the Statute of the PCIJ, which forcefully illustrate that the principle already un-

---

Yugoslavia and the International Criminal Tribunal for Rwanda (27 March 2008) UN Doc. A/C.5/62/L.31.

647 UNGA, *91st plenary meeting Official Records* (3 April 2008) UN Doc. A/62/PV.91. The decision is published in UNGA, *Conditions of service and compensation for officials other than Secretariat officials: members of the International Court of Justice and judges and ad litem judges of the International Tribunal for the Former Yugoslavia and the International Criminal Tribunal for Rwanda* (3 April 2008) UN Doc. 62/547.

648 President of the International Court of Justice, *Document transmitted by the President of the International Court of Justice to the Secretary-General on the implications of General Assembly resolution 61/262 in regard to certain provisions of the Statute of the Court*, para. 32.

649 Ibid, para. 35.

650 Arts. 31(6) and 32(5) ICJ Statute.

651 Derived from Art. 32(1) ICJ Statute. See also Art. 3(1) Rules of Court: "The Members of the Court, in the exercise of their functions, are of equal status, irrespective of age, priority of election or length of service."

652 Cf. Art. 2 para. 1 UNC.

653 Cf. *supra* Chapter D.II(2).

derlay the PCIJ Statute[654] and, as Art. 92 UNC demands, that the new Court was to work on that same basis. Yet the principle of equality is not violated just by the determination of different levels of emoluments for sitting members and new members taking office after 1 January 2007. The same considerations apply *mutatis mutandis* to the relationship between ordinary judges and *ad hoc* judges; pursuant to Art. 31(6) ICJ Statute (and Art. 7(2) Rules) such judges are to sit in "complete equality". In the opinion of the ICJ similar problems of financial inequality arise due to the date of nomination between *ad hoc* judges and judges re-elected after the critical date of 1 January 2007.[655] In all such cases the resolution poses the risk of discriminating between the different members of the ICJ.

d) Appraisal

The above reveals that the calculation of the salaries of ICJ judges follows rather simple but nonetheless significant rules. One is that the level of remuneration is, pursuant to Art. 32(5) ICJ Statute, set by the UNGA. As a result, any attempt by a different organ, such as the UNSG,[656] even to suggest a different level of emoluments is met with justified resistance by the Court.[657]

---

654 See *inter alia* the statement made by Mr Hagerup at the 8th meeting of the Committee of Jurists: "in the domain of law there is one indisputable principle, that of the equality of sovereign states. ... The principle of the equality of States is the Magna Charta of the smaller States and it is an outstanding juridical argument. ... if one tried to introduce an element of inequality into the scheme for the Court of Justice, this scheme would fall to the ground". Permanent Court of International Justice & Advisory Committee of Jurists, *Procès-Verbaux of the Proceedings of the Committee, June 16th-July 24th 1920 with Annexes*, 103. One pertinent statement made during the 8th meeting of the Committee of Jurists seems, as it was not questioned, to indicate a general consensus, namely that made by Mr Loder: "Two judges sitting at the same time might receive different salaries. This would not be admissible." Ibid, 196.

655 President of the International Court of Justice, *Document transmitted by the President of the International Court of Justice to the Secretary-General on the implications of General Assembly resolution 61/262 in regard to certain provisions of the Statute of the Court*, paras. 47-52 and 55-59.

656 Cf. the UNSG, *Conditions of service and compensation for officials other than Secretariat officials*, para. 82.

657 Even the Advisory Committee considered it appropriate to emphasize that only the UNGA has the authority to set the judges' salary: "It is up to the General Assembly to decide whether an increase should be provided ..."; see Report of the Advisory

It ought to be emphasized that the Court also heavily criticized the fact that it was not consulted, as used to be the practice when preparing changes to the judges' emoluments. Art. 32(5) *in fine* ICJ Statute, the prohibition on decreasing the emoluments during a judge's term of office was interpreted broadly by the ICJ so as to encompass not only numerical reductions in salary but also *de facto* reductions that follow from the freezing of emoluments irrespective of any change of exchange rate or costs of living. This is to be welcomed in the interest of ensuring a decent salary as a tool to safeguard the judges' independence. Although it may be that a *de facto* reduction is a consequence of harmless circumstances which have no relation to the actual work of the Court and/or its judges, the risk that this is not so and the danger that financial pressure is used for political ends deserve to be taken serious in this way.

However, placing strong emphasis on the equality of the members of the Court, as the ICJ did, and focusing on the origin of that principle as a reflection of the sovereign equality between States[658] is not unproblematic from the viewpoint of the judges' independence of their State of origin.[659] Allowing the inter-State relationship to be formative in this way raises the question whether the personal character in which the judges sit on the bench is sufficiently honoured. Does not this consideration instead witness a rather far-reaching respect for the requirement of nationality which should not play such a role if the judges were truly independent? Yet, whereas it is true that influence being exerted from the State of origin does form a central threat to the independence of a judge, linking the equality of all judges to that of States in their mutual relations does not as such imply the greater susceptibility of the individual judge – or the bench – to influences from States. Instead, the equality of judges serves an interest that is enshrined in other places

Committee on Administrative and Budgetary Questions, *Conditions of service and compensation for officials other than Secretariat officials*, para. 9.

658 Cf. *supra* Chapter D.II.

659 Although the Court explicitly affirmed the independence of judges from their States of origin; President of the International Court of Justice, *Document transmitted by the President of the International Court of Justice to the Secretary-General on the implications of General Assembly resolution 61/262 in regard to certain provisions of the Statute of the Court*, para. 37: "Although members of the International Court of Justice, like those of its predecessor, are completely independent of their States of origin and sit as individuals, it would be inconceivable for there to be differences in the way in which they are treated."

in the Statute, e.g. Art. 9 ICJ Statute,[660] which is to pay tribute to the particular function of the ICJ, namely the resolution of disputes between States. One might even go further and state that the purpose is to establish an equality of arms between the parties, or to equip the Court with the necessary expertise to solve the various kinds of disputes that may be brought before it.

4. Privileges and Immunities

a) The Normative Framework

The question of immunities and privileges conceded to the individual judges of a court is an ideal determinant of the independence of the members of the Court.[661] As J. Simpson/H. Fox put it, members of international tribunals "must enjoy immunity from legal proceedings and other privileges" if they are to have complete freedom in the exercise of their duties.[662] If the individual judge cannot feel safe from sanctions for the decisions he makes on the bench, if he has to fear negative consequences that affect other aspects of his life, then the most competent individual will either decline to serve as a judge or be disposed to surrender to the pressure. This also sheds light on the central motive behind the stipulation of any privileges of a judge of the ICJ: the necessity of functional independence, directed especially against influence from States, which facilitates the free and autonomous fulfilment of the judges' tasks.[663] This conviction is also reflected in Art. 19 ICJ Statute, which has the same wording as Art. 19 of the Statute of the PCIJ providing that "[t]he members of the Court, when engaged on the business of the Court, shall enjoy diplomatic privileges and immunities." [664] The provision is, as

---

660 "At every election, the electors shall bear in mind … that in the body as a whole the representation of the main forms of civilization and of the principal legal systems of the world should be assured."

661 Anderson, 'Article 19 ICJ Statute', 367.

662 Simpson & Fox, *International Arbitration: Law and Practice*, 102.

663 Koster, Martina, *Immunität internationaler Richter – gemessen an derjenigen der Diplomaten und der internationalen Funktionäre* (Verlag Recht und Wirtschaft Heidelberg 2002), 121 with further references.

664 The diplomatic privileges and immunities today – although this was not the case at the time the ICJ Statute or the Statute of the PCIJ was drafted – are codified by the Vienna Convention on Diplomatic Relations. The convention, however, mainly

the term "diplomatic" indicates, based on the functional immunity enjoyed by representatives of the Members of the UN and its officials pursuant to Art. 105 UNC, which extends to what is "necessary for the independent exercise of their functions in connexion with the Organization."[665]

On 13 February 1946, shortly before the ICJ began its operations, the UNGA asked the members of the Court in their first session to consider the issue of immunities, "with a view to ensuring that the International Court of Justice shall enjoy the privileges, immunities and facilities necessary for the exercise of its functions and the fulfilment of its purposes, in the country of its seat and elsewhere".[666] At the same time, the UNGA adopted the Convention on the Privileges and Immunities of the United Nations[667] according to which *inter alia* officials of the UN are to enjoy certain privileges.[668] The UNGA's request was met with detailed provisions on the immunities and privileges of members of the Court, the Registrar, the Court's staff, and the agents, counsel and advocates of the parties, laid down in letters exchanged

---

codifies customary law, which, thus remains subsidiarily applicable (see, e.g., Vitzthum, Wolfgang Graf & Bothe, Michael (eds), *Völkerrecht* (De Gruyter Berlin 3rd edn. 2001), 184). If orientated on the immunities and privileges of the heads of diplomatic missions mentioned in the convention, the immunities and privileges enjoyed by ICJ judges are: exemption from taxes and dues (Arts. 23 and 34); freedom of movement and travel on the territory of the Netherlands (the seat of the Court; Art. 26); inviolability of the person (Art. 26); inviolability and protection of any private residence (Art. 30(1)) and of papers, correspondence and property (Art. 30(2)); immunity from criminal jurisdiction and – subject to certain restrictions – civil and administrative jurisdiction (Art. 31).

665 Cf. United Nations Information Organizations, *UNCIO XIII*, 316.

666 UNGA, *Resolution on the Privileges and Immunities of the International Court of Justice* (13 February 1946) UN Doc. A/RES/22(I)C.

667 Convention on the Privileges and Immunities of the United Nations (adopted 13 February 1946, entered into force 17 September 1946) 1 UNTS 15.

668 In particular its Art. V provides that "[o]fficials of the UN shall (a) Be immune from legal process in respect of words spoken or written and all acts performed by them in their official capacity; (b) Be exempt from taxation on the salaries and emoluments paid to them by the United Nations; (c) Be immune from national service obligations; (d) Be immune, together with their spouses and relatives dependent on them, from immigration restrictions and alien registration; (e) Be accorded the same privileges in respect of exchange facilities as are accorded to the officials of comparable ranks forming part of diplomatic missions to the Government concerned; (f) Be given, together with their spouses and relatives dependent on them, the same repatriation facilities in time of international crisis as diplomatic envoys; (g) Have the right to import free of duty their furniture and effects at the time of first taking up their post in the country in question."

between the president of the ICJ and the Minister for Foreign Affairs of the host State, the Netherlands. Annexed to the initial letter from the ICJ president to the Minister for Foreign Affairs[669] are general principles according to which the members of the Court are *inter alia* to be treated as heads of diplomatic missions accredited to Her Majesty the Queen of the Netherlands.[670] From this exchange of letters it follows further that the privileges and immunities thus granted are not to serve the personal interest of the beneficiary, but instead the interest of the administration of international justice.[671] In a resolution dated 11 December 1946, the UNGA elaborated on this further by adopting a functional approach conferring on officials of the ICJ – i.e. not just the judges – "such privileges, immunities and facilities for residence and travel as may be necessary for the independent exercise of their functions".[672] By comparison, Art. 19 ICJ Statute stands out as more concise, especially if compared to similar provisions in more recent court documents,[673] a consideration mainly attributable to its historical origin.[674] However, systematically Art. 19 ICJ Statute must be read in conjunction not only with the above legal sources but also with the functional and broader

669 President of the International Court of Justice, *Letter from the President of the International Court of Justice to the Minister for Foreign Affairs of the Netherlands* (26 June 1946) available <http://www.icj-cij.org/documents/index.php?p1=4&p2=5&p3=3> (last visited: 21 March 2014).

670 See paragraph I(a) of the *Letter from the President of the International Court of Justice to the Minister for Foreign Affairs of the Netherlands* (26 June 1946). The letter was confirmed by the Minister for Foreign Affairs of the Netherlands on 26 June 1946.

671 Paragraph IV of the General Principles attached to the *Letter from the President of the International Court of Justice to the Minister for Foreign Affairs of the Netherlands* (26 June 1946) provides: "IV. Privileges and immunities are granted in the interests of the administration of international justice and not in the personal interest of the beneficiary."

672 UNGA, *Privileges and Immunities of Members of the International Court of Justice, the Registrar, Officials of the Registry, Assessors, the Agents and Counsel of the Parties and of the Witnesses and Experts* (11 December 1946) UN Doc. A/RES/90 (I), para. 4(a).

673 Cf. e.g. Art. 48(2) Rome Statute: "The judges … shall, when engaged on or with respect to the business of the Court, enjoy the same privileges and immunities as are accorded to heads of diplomatic missions and shall, after the expiry of their terms of office, continue to be accorded immunity from legal process of every kind in respect of words spoken or written and acts performed by them in their official capacity."

674 Art. 19 PCIJ Statute was also never amended and remained in the wording of 1920.

approach adopted in Art. 105 UNC, which establishes that the UN shall enjoy such privileges and immunities as are necessary for the fulfilment of its purpose.[675] Because the ICJ pursuant to Art. 7 UNC is one of the principal organs of the UN, this stipulation must also apply to the Court and its members.[676] As Art. 105 UNC is more general in scope than Art. 19 ICJ Statute, any possible conflict between the two provisions must nonetheless be resolved in favour of the latter.[677]

b) Does Art. 19 ICJ Statute Provide the Necessary Protection?

Whereas it is a strength of Art. 19 ICJ Statute that it equates judges with diplomatic agents for the purpose of determining the scope of privileges,[678] as it facilitates access to a codified set of rules which have been proven in practice, this equation can at the same time be the provision's weakness. Paragraph 4 of the preamble to the Vienna Convention on Diplomatic Relations (VCDR) describes the purpose of diplomatic privileges and immunities as "not to benefit individuals but to ensure the efficient performance of the functions of diplomatic missions as *representing States*" (emphasis added). The role of international judges, however, must not be confused with that of a diplomat. As follows from Arts. 16-17 ICJ Statute, an ICJ judge is barred from exercising the duties of a diplomat, and hence for that reason cannot be considered such an agent.[679] Thus, even if the immunities and privileges

---

675 With this functional connotation Art. 105 UNC resembles Art. 42 ICJ Statute, according to which agents, counsel and advocates appearing before the ICJ "shall enjoy the privileges and immunities necessary to the independent exercise of their duties."

676 Rosenne, *The Court and the United Nations*, 415.

677 I.e. by application of the rule of *lex specialis derogat generali*. See on this Rosenne, *The Law and Practice of the International Court – Vol. 1 The Court and the United Nations*, 415.

678 Cf. Art. 1(1)(b) Convention on the Prevention and Punishment of Crimes against Internationally Protected Persons, Including Diplomatic Agents (adopted 14 December 1973, entered into force 20 February 1977) 1035 UNTS 167, according to which the judges of the ICJ are equated with both Heads of States and representatives and officials of a State in the sense that they all are "internationally protected persons" for the purpose of the convention.

679 The reason for the reference to "diplomatic" privileges and immunities is also attributable to the fact that the law on diplomatic relations was codified only in 1969, long after the Statute of the ICJ was drafted.

of both judges and diplomats serve the same fundamental purpose, namely to safeguard their functionality, and even if the immunities arising from Art. 19 ICJ Statute are likely to be congruent with those following from the VCDR and granted to heads of diplomatic missions, there are certain distinctive features. The difference is unfortunately not just a formal one. It is precisely the different functions that merit the reading of different content into the immunity of judges and diplomats respectively.

The (ICJ) judge is not the representative of a (sending) State. Instead, he is a "servant of international law",[680] someone who is to perform his duties "conscientiously",[681] who has to "deal justice to their own countries as to the others"[682] and who is a representative only of the international court in question. This certainly does not exclude all ties the individual judge may, and is very likely to, have due to political, cultural and religious convictions and his bond with a particular home country. But the judge's special position is certainly incompatible with any sort of duty or loyalty towards a particular State – let alone government – such as is essential and truly defining for a diplomat's role.[683] In fact, for this very reason the individual judge also needs immunity towards his State of his origin,[684] a kind of protection a diplomat does not have under the rules on diplomatic relations, and arguably does not need since he is merely a servant, hence at the mercy, of his home State.[685]

---

680 Schücking, Walther & Wehberg, Hans, *Die Satzung des Völkerbundes – Band 1* (Vahlen Berlin 3rd edn. 1931), 402. See also Koster, *Immunität internationaler Richter – gemessen an derjenigen der Diplomaten und der internationalen Funktionäre*, 123 with further references.

681 Cf. Art. 4(1) Rules of Court: "I solemnly declare that I will perform my duties and exercise my powers as judge honourably, faithfully, impartially and *conscientiously*." (Emphasis added.).

682 Bustamante y Sirven, *La Cour Permanente de Justice Internationale*, 138.

683 In support of this it should also be stated that the State does not have a direct influence on the election of the judges, which are instead chosen by separate bodies.

684 "While the immunities and privileges of international judges are almost as developed as those of the national judge, they are not as effectual against his own country as against others: social pressure, e.g. sending to Coventry or loss of prestige and refusal to renominate as candidate at the election of judges are only two of the possible methods of exercising pressure."; Prott, 'The Role of the Judge of the International Court of Justice', 489.

685 Cf. Art. 31(4) Vienna Convention on Diplomatic Relations. Doehring, Karl, 'Zur Rechtsstellung internationaler Richter', in: Arndt, Hans-Wolfgang *et al.* (eds) *Völkerrecht und deutsches Recht: Festschrift für Walter Rudolf zum 70. Geburtstag* (Beck München 2001), 40.

Art. 19 ICJ Statute does not expressly provide for this protection.[686] And although the *travaux préparatoires* of the ICJ Statute speak out against a wide interpretation of Art. 19 encompassing such protection, this reading deserves to be supported for the sole reason that it is only this extension of applicability of privileges and immunities that enables the ICJ judge truly to fulfil his task.[687] In other words, the stipulation that ICJ judges enjoy "diplomatic privileges and immunities" can only be descriptive;[688] it is to be interpreted as a reference to the applicable material law substantiating the privileges and immunities of diplomatic missions, which then have to be read in light of the special function of international judges. Any other understanding would imply a considerable threat to the independent functioning of judges.[689]

A further point must be stressed, namely that the wording of Art. 19 ICJ Statute suggests that the immunities and privileges enjoyed are limited both *ratione materiae* and *ratione temporis* ("when engaged on the business of the Court").[690] The material aspect indicates that judges enjoy immunity only with regard to the work of the Court, but not regarding personal matters that are unconnected to the institution or the duties of the office. This could lead to the assumption that judges suffer from an undue limitation, where they might feel a need not to act in certain ways because of uncertainty whether or not the relevant action is covered by the immunities otherwise conceded. However, this uncertainty can never be ruled out altogether and it would furthermore mean an undue increase in prerogatives if they were to reach beyond functional justifications and relieve the judge of any common reticence. Furthermore, the temporal limitation of privileges and immunities

---

686 Anderson, 'Article 19 ICJ Statute', 367. See also the criticism in this regard from Doehring, 'Zur Rechtsstellung internationaler Richter', 40.

687 Doehring, *Völkerrecht – Ein Lehrbuch*, 298. To this effect see also the draft of a catalogue of immunities in Koster, *Immunität internationaler Richter – gemessen an derjenigen der Diplomaten und der internationalen Funktionäre*, 250 et seq., where as early as in the preamble it is laid down that the listed privileges are conceded in every State party to a court statute, including the State where the court has its seat and the home States of the judges.

688 See Anderson, 'Article 19 ICJ Statute', 362; Rosenne, *The Court and the United Nations*, 415.

689 Koster, *Immunität internationaler Richter – gemessen an derjenigen der Diplomaten und der internationalen Funktionäre*, 120 and 136-137.

690 French: "dans l'exercice de leurs fonctions"; German: "bei der Wahrnehmung ihres Amtes".

pursuant to Art. 19 ICJ Statute is relatively vague. A reasonable interpretation of Art. 19 ICJ Statute in conjunction with Art. 13(3) ICJ Statute[691] suggests that judges enjoy privileges and immunities as long as their place has not been filled and at any event until a case which they have begun to work on has been closed. However, this is but one interpretation of the provision and it should be considered a deficiency, similar to the unspecified geographic reach of privileges and immunities accorded to ICJ judges, and indeed a latent threat to the independent exercise of the judges' function,[692] that such uncertainty and room for interpretation exists.

c) The Waiver of Immunities

Neither the ICJ Statute nor the exchange of letters between the president of the ICJ and the Minister for Foreign Affairs of the Netherlands contains a provision on States' right to waive judges' immunities.[693] This is consistent, considering the above-mentioned differentiation between international judges and diplomats; whereas the latter's fundamental function is to "represent the sending State in the receiving State" and "[p]rotecting in the receiving State the interests of the sending State",[694] hence necessitating a right for the sending State to have direct control over its representatives, the international judge does not fulfil his tasks on behalf of any State and his service should thus not be at the discretion of States. But considering the above-mentioned affirmative stance on an application of the immunities and privileges towards judges' home States, the question arises who else should have the competence to waive these prerogatives in order not to establish a legal vacuum (i.e. judges equipped with privileges and immunities which cannot be waived in any situation and towards every entity). Although this issue is far from settled it is appropriate to assume that the organization, for which the affected agent works, in the case of the ICJ judges the ICJ itself, and for which the immunit-

691 "3. The members of the Court shall continue to discharge their duties until their places have been filled. Though replaced, they shall finish any cases which they may have begun."

692 Koster, *Immunität internationaler Richter – gemessen an derjenigen der Diplomaten und der internationalen Funktionäre*, 140.

693 Anderson, 'Article 19 ICJ Statute', 365.

694 Art. 3(1)(a)-(b) Vienna Convention on Diplomatic Relations.

ies and privileges thus function, has such a right.[695] The absence of any regulation to this effect in the Statute must be seen as a deficiency as it opens up the possibility of conflicts and leaves the position in favour of a solution supportive of the judges' independence with fewer arguments than necessary. It remains to be seen in the following chapters of this study whether additional arguments can be derived from a comparative view of other international courts.

5. Incompatible Activities

a) Simultaneous Side Activities and Prior Involvement – The Legal Framework

In the context of the PCIJ, provisions on incompatible the functions and disqualification of judges were already described as assurances of the independence of the judges.[696] As such provisions, like those relating to judges' remuneration and privileges and immunities, depending on their configuration are well suited to making a direct attack on independence appear a legitimate measure, the provisions in Arts. 16-17 ICJ Statute on the incompatibility of certain activities with the position of an ICJ judge are central to the protection of the independence of ICJ judges. More than most provisions, they provide "substance to the principle of the independence of the judges",[697] due to the immediate effect additional (or side) activities may have on the exercise of the judges' duties by creating deflecting dependences.

According to Art. 16(1) ICJ Statute "[n]o member of the Court may exercise any political or administrative function, or engage in any other occupation of a professional nature."[698] This provision follows as a logical consequence

---

695 Doehring, *Völkerrecht – Ein Lehrbuch*, 298. As regards the procedure, it would make sense to allow the procedural rules for the removal from office described above (see *supra* Chapter D.VI(2)(b)) to apply analogously.

696 They have been described as the main assurances of judicial independence at the ICJ. See, e.g., Schenk von Stauffenberg, *Statut et Règlement de la Cour Permanente de Justice Internationale – Eléments d'interprétation*, 18; Schwarzenberger, *International Law as Applied by International Courts and Tribunals – Vol. 4 – International Judicial Law*, 277.

697 Rosenne, *The Court and the United Nations*, 400.

698 The wording of Art. 16 has undergone only minor changes: see Couvreur, Philippe, 'Article 16 ICJ Statute', in: Zimmermann, Andreas *et al.* (eds) *The Statute of the*

from the various stipulations on the nature of the judges' position, which is supposed to be an exclusive and full-time occupation. The wording "any other occupation of a professional nature"[699] suggests a broad understanding of functions which are unacceptable alongside the position of judge, with the exercise of political and administrative functions to be merely two apparent examples.[700] Any decision on the scope of this provision is made by the Court itself.[701] Art. 17 ICJ Statute further extends the catalogue of undesirable functions to any *current* involvement as agent, counsel, or advocate in *any* case, or *prior* involvement in any capacity with a *pending* case; all these activities are condemned as potential threats to the independence of the Court. Also in the application of Art. 17 ICJ Statute it is primarily the individual judge who is called upon to recuse himself in relevant instances, and doubts are to be settled by decision of the Court without interference from outside.

b) Incompatible Activities in the Practice of the ICJ as Threats to Independence

The practice so far has shown a certain willingness by judges to recuse themselves when prior activities may question their independence in a particular case.[702] For example, in *Certain Phosphate Lands in Nauru (Nauru v. Australia)* one judge recused himself because he had chaired a committee of inquiry into the matter of substance.[703] Another judge recused himself in *Arbitral Award of 31 July 1989 (Guinea-Bissau v. Senegal)* because he had served on the panel which had delivered the challenged award.[704] In *Anglo-*

International Court of Justice – A Commentary (Oxford University Press Oxford 2006), 324-329.

699 These words were added to the provision in the revised wording accepted in 1929, based on a recommendation from the Committee of Jurists: see Rosenne, *The Law and Practice of the International Court – Vol. 1 The Court and the United Nations*, 400.

700 When adopting this amendment in 1929 the Conference of Signatories gave the example of "such an activity as being director of a company"; see on this ibid, 401.

701 Art. 16(2) ICJ Statute.

702 For a list of voluntary recusals and situations where members of the Court did not recuse themselves see Rosenne, *The Law and Practice of the International Court – Vol. 3 Procedure*, 1062-1065.

703 *Certain Phosphate Lands in Nauru (Nauru v. Australia)* ICJ Rep. 240 (1992).

704 *Arbitral Award of 31 July 1989 (Guinea-Bissau v Senegal)* ICJ Rep. 53 (1991).

Iranian Oil Co. (United Kingdom v. Iran), Sir B. Rau chose not to sit on the basis that he had been India's representative to the UNSC as it was considering the issue which was later brought before the Court.[705] In *South West Africa (Ethiopia v. South Africa; Liberia v. South Africa)* Sir M. Zafrullah Khan recused himself because he had been a member of the UNSC as it voted against South Africa on issues relating to South West Africa.[706] However, in the same *South West Africa* case the Court rejected an attempt by South Africa to seek the recusal of Judge P. Nervo due to his participation in the UNSC. The practice of the Court is extensive,[707] yet it is difficult to deduce any red threads as decisions are made without reasons being given. What can be said with some certainty is that judges themselves take seriously the importance of keeping prior engagements connected to a particular case away from the bench.

Whether or not a particular side activity may be considered a threat to the independence of the Court, and thus violate Art. 16 ICJ Statute, depends to some degree on the political aspects linked to such an activity and on the circumstances in which the occupation is exercised. Whereas occasional scholarly activities have traditionally been accepted and even encouraged as being helpful in expanding and understanding the role of the ICJ,[708] the function of members of the Court as arbitrators and conciliators is highly delicate as it may require them to make political judgments on issues that may later appear before the Court and which may easily develop into a perceived political bias of judges, utterly irreconcilable with the ICJ's independent functioning. Nevertheless, the Court has by tradition accepted that its members also act as arbitrators, which has led to a continuous contribution of ICJ judges to important inter-State arbitrations of recent time.[709] The Court itself provided a rare glimpse of its own practice of interpreting Art. 16

705 *Anglo-Iranian Oil Co. (United Kingdom v. Iran)* ICJ Rep. 93 (1952).

706 *South West Africa (Ethiopia v. South Africa; Liberia v. South Africa) (Second Phase)* ICJ Rep. 6 (1966). See also Prott, 'The Role of the Judge of the International Court of Justice', 487.

707 Vagts, Detlev F., 'The International Legal Profession: A Need for More Governance?' (1996) 90 American Journal of International Law 2, 255-258. See also Guyomar, *Commentaire du règlement de la Cour Internationale de Justice adopté le 14 avril 1978 – interpretation et pratique*, 182-200.

708 Couvreur, 'Article 16 ICJ Statute', 334.

709 For an overview see ibid, 333-334.

ICJ Statute[710] in a response that was given to a request by the Advisory Committee on Administrative and Budgetary Questions for an "analysis of the practice of the Court with respect to Art. 16, paragraph 1, of its Statute".[711] In order to scrutinize the Court's practice in some greater detail, the summary of the Court's opinion regarding Art. 16 ICJ Statute deserves to be cited in some greater detail:

> "31. Under the authority vested in the Court under Article 16, paragraph 2, of its Statute, ICJ has, in view of the judicial character of the activities involved, interpreted the bar to the members of the Court engaging in other occupations of a professional nature as not debarring a limited participation of Judges in other judicial or quasi-judicial activities of an occasional nature, as well as scholarly pursuits in the sphere of international law as members of learned societies or as occasional lecturers. The Judges accepting such occasional activities give the fullest precedence to their supervening duties as members of the Court. Based on a long-standing tradition of the Permanent Court of International Justice founded in 1922, as well as the recorded intention of the United Nations Conference on International Organization that adopted the text of Article 16 of the Statute, the Court further interpreted Article 16 as permitting the members to accept occasional appointments as arbitrators. In doing so, the Court referred to a similar practice existing in the courts of a number of Member States, such as Australia, Canada, Denmark, France, Germany, India, the Libyan Arab Jamahiriya, the Netherlands, Norway, Sweden and Tunisia, as well as some states of the United States of America.
> 32. The Court has consistently taken the position that contributions by its members to third-party settlement of disputes by legal processes in other forums, as by occasional service as arbitrators, are compatible with the Judges' functions as members of the Court. These activities are subject, however, to two conditions: the first is that the Judges must give absolute precedence to their obligations as members of the Court; and the second is that they should not accept appointment in an arbitral case, which, in another phase, is subject to being submitted to the Court.
> 33. The Court will continue to keep under review any questions that may arise of the compatibility of the functions of judges with the Statute of ICJ and with their supervening obligations."[712]

---

710 Two reports of 1947 and 1967 of three-member Committees dealing with the issue of incompatibilities of functions have not been published by the Court.

711 Advisory Committee on Administrative and Budgetary Questions, *Twelfth report of the Advisory Committee on Administrative and Budgetary Questions – Programme Budget for the Biennium 1994-1995 – Conditions of service and compensation for officials other than Secretariat officials, Pension scheme for the members of the International Court of Justice* (8 March 1995) UN Doc. A/49/7/Add.11, para. 8.

712 UNSG, *Report of the Secretary-General – Proposed Programme Budget for the Biennium 1996-1997 – Conditions of service and compensation for officials other*

Following from the above, in the opinion of the Court and based on pertinent practice of the PCIJ and national courts as well as the *travaux préparatoires* of the ICJ Statute, members' limited participation in other judicial or quasi-judicial activities of an occasional nature is compatible with their functions as members of the Court. This was again confirmed in the Court's Annual Report to the UNGA for the period 1 August 1995 to 31 July 1996, in which the judges' occasional functioning as arbitrators in *inter alia* inter-State arbitrations is viewed as evidence of the "awareness of the contribution that the Members of the Court may, by this function, make to the development of international law, and of the benefits deriving therefrom for all institutions concerned."[713] Whereas it may be accurate to consider that side activities of ICJ judges may lend a certain authority to the entities involved, this neither rebuts the concerns of a threat to judicial independence, nor is it an argument that is particularly apt to justify involvement in other forms of pacific dispute settlement. The same holds true for the idea that ICJ judges form a small group of individuals "capable of settling an international dispute by arbitration",[714] although the correctness of this argument appears highly questionable in view of the current number of 353 members of the PCA,[715] who by definition are of "known competency in questions of international law, of the highest moral reputation and *disposed to accept the duties of arbitrators*" (Art. 44 1907 Hague Convention I; emphasis added). In particular, most arguments presented in favour of ICJ judges' role as arbitrators are unable to dispel the central concern that if such a role is assumed, the judge is subject to the political mechanisms that steer arbitration and thus becomes a potential vehicle for these mechanisms to influence the work of the ICJ. The attempt to control these mechanisms by demanding that judges should not accept appointment in an arbitral case which may also be submitted to the Court can put to rest only some of these concerns, since it may not always be accurately predicted how the Court may be affected.

---

than Secretariat officials, Members of the International Court of Justice (2 November 1995) UN Doc. A/C.5/50/18, paras. 31-33.

713 International Court of Justice, *Report of the International Court of Justice, 1 August 1995-31 July 1996* (1 January 1996) UN Doc. A/51/4, para. 199.

714 Couvreur, 'Article 16 ICJ Statute', 333.

715 Cf. 'Permanent Court of Arbitration – Members of the Permanent Court of Arbitration' available at <http://www.pca-cpa.org/showpage.asp?pag_id=1041> (last visited: 21 March 2014).

One decisive argument may be that involvement in international arbitration is but another means of fulfilling the ICJ's proper function of achieving the peacekeeping goal of the UN, which it is committed to contribute to as the principal judicial organ of the UN.[716] Yet this is hardly convincing. External arbitration, e.g. of the kind performed under the 1907 Hague Convention I, is precisely *not* dispute settlement by an international court such as the ICJ.[717] The ICJ furthermore neither is responsible for the conduct of the individual arbitrators, nor is it in control of the arbitration. It appears to be an overly optimistic interpretation to consider that if an arbitration was successful and has thus contributed to the pacific settlement of disputes in general, automatically the ICJ's contribution to achieving the UNC's goals[718] has been advanced. Whereas the ICJ certainly does not need to win any external laurel wreaths, the much more unpleasant question ought to be asked whether the failure of an arbitral tribunal formed under the PCA or even the failure to form such a tribunal with the participation of ICJ judges should consequently be interpreted as a betrayal of the functions of the ICJ. Not at least the harmful light this indirect entanglement of the ICJ with arbitration casts on the independence of the ICJ, an issue which arbitration is not made to contemplate in the same way; these kinds of side activities should be seen as critical. In this regard it is unfortunate that the ICJ Statute, in particular Art. 16(1) ICJ Statute, not more directly provides for the service of ICJ judges in arbitral tribunals,[719] and that not more is known under what conditions and to what extent members of the Court are involved in arbitration.

716 Art. 92 UNC read in conjunction with Art. 1(1) UNC. Cf. Couvreur, 'Article 16 ICJ Statute', 333.

717 Cf. *supra* on the functions served by the ICJ in Chapter D.III.

718 In particular Art. 1(1) UNC seems to be called upon in this context: "1. To maintain international peace and security, and to that end: ... to bring about by peaceful means, and in conformity with the principles of justice and international law, adjustment or settlement of international disputes or situations which might lead to a breach of the peace".

719 Cf. in this regard *infra* on the position taken by Judge Buergenthal in *Legal Consequences of the Construction of a Wall in the Occupied Palestinian Territory*, where he criticized the "formalistic and narrow construction" of Art. 17(2) ICJ Statute, and instead demanded that a wide, teleological interpretation, orientated by the fair and impartial administration of justice underlying every court of law should be utilized.

c) Assessing Prior Involvement in a Case – The Application of Art. 17(2) ICJ Statute

(1) The Order on the Composition of the ICJ in the Case of Legal Consequences of a Wall in the Occupied Palestinian Territory – Facts of the Case

In early 2004 the ICJ was called upon to decide whether one of its judges, Judge N. Elaraby from Egypt, was precluded from participating in a case as a consequence of his prior activities, performed in the discharge of his diplomatic and governmental functions at the time, or as a result of statements made in his personal capacity after being an official of his government but prior to his appointment as an ICJ judge. Specifically, Judge Elaraby had participated as a representative of Egypt in the Tenth Emergency Special Session of the UNGA – which dealt with Israeli actions in occupied East Jerusalem and the rest of the occupied Palestinian territory and which had requested the advisory opinion of the ICJ regarding legal consequences of the construction of a wall in the occupied Palestinian territory.[720] He was furthermore a Legal Adviser to the Egyptian Ministry of Foreign Affairs, a Legal Adviser to the Egyptian Delegation to the Camp David Middle East Peace Conference in 1978, involved in initiatives following the signing of the Israel-Egypt Peace Treaty in 1979 and had given an interview to an Egyptian newspaper where his views on questions regarding Israel were elaborated. As a consequence of this account, the government of Israel on 31 December 2003 addressed a letter to the Registrar of the Court in which the government – without naming the judge in question – drew the Court's attention to Judge Elaraby's earlier participation in the Tenth Emergency Special Session, stressing that it would be "inappropriate for a Member of the Court to participate in decisions in a case in which he has previously played an active, official and public role as an advocate for a cause that is in contention in this case".[721] A confidential letter was subsequently addressed

720 The tenth Emergency Special Session of the UNGA was convened for the first time on 24 April 1997, following a request from the Permanent Representative of Qatar after a series of UNSC and UNGA meetings regarding the Israeli decision to build Har Homa, a 6,500 unit housing project, in the Jabal Abu Ghneim area of East Jerusalem.

721 Letter reproduced in part in *Legal Consequences of the Construction of a Wall in the Occupied Palestinian Territory (Order)* ICJ Rep. 3 (2004), 4.

to the President of the Court pursuant to Art. 32(2) Rules of Court,[722] in which Israel elaborated on the conditions it considered to be relevant regarding the participation of Judge Elaraby in the present case.

(2) The Majority's Order

By a majority of thirteen votes to one the Court did not find the conditions brought to its attention by Israel to be of such a nature as to preclude Judge Elaraby's participation in the case pursuant to Art. 17(2) ICJ Statute. The Court focused on the role Judge Elaraby had played as a diplomatic representative, which in accordance with the Court's earlier case law[723] was not considered capable of triggering the application of Art. 17(2) ICJ Statute.[724] The majority went on to state that the earlier activities of Judge Elaraby were performed before the substantive issue of the requested advisory opinion, namely the construction of a wall in the occupied Palestinian territory, arose. As he did not even on other occasions – particularly in the above-mentioned newspaper interview – express an opinion on the question pending before

722 Art. 32(2) Rules of Court: "The Member of the Court who is presiding in a case on the date on which the Court convenes for the oral proceedings shall continue to preside in that case until completion of the current phase of the case, notwithstanding the election in the meantime of a new President or Vice-President. If he should become unable to act, the presidency for the case shall be determined in accordance with Article 13 of these Rules, and on the basis of the composition of the Court on the date on which it convened for the oral proceedings."

723 *Legal Consequences for States of the Continued Presence of South Africa in Namibia (South West Africa) notwithstanding Security Council Resolution 276 (1970) (Advisory Opinion)*, para. 9. See also *South West Africa (Ethiopia v. South Africa; Liberia v. South Africa) (Order of 18 March 1965)* ICJ Rep. 3 (1965); *The 'Wimbledon' (Government of His Britannic Majesty v German Empire)* PCIJ Series A No. 1 (1922), 11. As Judge Buergenthal pointed out in his dissenting opinion, the general rule that prior activities, performed in the discharge of a judge's diplomatic and governmental functions, do not fall within the scope of Art. 17(2) cannot be considered to be without exception: *Legal Consequences of the Construction of a Wall in the Occupied Palestinian Territory (Order) (Dissenting Opinion of Judge Buergenthal)*, para. 6. One such situation would be where a judge can be said to have gone beyond representing his Government, e.g. by mixing his own opinions with those officially held by the home Government.

724 *Legal Consequences of the Construction of a Wall in the Occupied Palestinian Territory (Order)*, para. 8.

the ICJ in the present case, he could not be considered to have "previously taken part [in the case] in any capacity".[725]

(3) The Dissenting Opinion of Judge Buergenthal

Judge T. Buergenthal agreed with the majority in acknowledging that Judge Elaraby's earlier statements, made during his discharge of diplomatic and governmental functions, should be seen as the views of his government rather than his personal opinions.[726] However, he had a different view as regards the interview given by Judge Elaraby when he was no longer an official and thus only could have spoken in his personal capacity. Judge Buergenthal, in his dissenting opinion, concedes that a strictly literal interpretation of Art. 17(2) ICJ Statute, which the majority had followed in emphasizing that Judge Elaraby had not "previously taken part [in the case] in any capacity" would render this provision inapplicable. Yet in the opinion of Judge Buergenthal, Art. 17(2) ICJ Statute does not establish the only basis for disqualification, but instead merely refers to "the most egregious violations of judicial ethics."[727] He further elaborated that the Court must also consider whether a judge's views can create the impression of unfairness or partiality, irrespective of whether the Statute or other constitutive documents provide for this. In the opinion of Judge Buergenthal, this obligation derives from the dictum that justice must not only be done, but that it also must be seen to be done, which is binding on every court.[728] In other words, Art. 17(2) ICJ Statute ought to be given, instead of a "formalistic and narrow construction",[729] a wide, teleological interpretation, orientated by the idea of fair and proper administration of justice underlying every court of law. The standard that should be applied is whether the opinions expressed by a judge refer to questions that the Court has to examine or take into account, or to arguments presented by the interested parties. The credibility or validity of such opinions is for the Court to assess, against the standard that they may create an appearance of bias. A positive answer to this test is sufficient to make Art. 17(2)

725 Art. 17(2) ICJ Statute. Ibid, 5.

726 *Legal Consequences of the Construction of a Wall in the Occupied Palestinian Territory (Order) (Dissenting Opinion of Judge Buergenthal)*, para. 6.

727 Ibid, para. 10.

728 Ibid, para. 11.

729 Ibid, para. 13.

ICJ Statute applicable and hence to preclude the judge in question from participating in the proceedings. In the case at hand, Judge Buergenthal reached the conclusion that although Judge Elaraby did not express an opinion on the specific question that was referred to the ICJ by the UNGA, some of the arguments expressed by him related to the broader context of the Israeli -Palestinian conflict in such a way that they created an appearance of bias which precluded Judge Elaraby from participating in the proceedings.

(4) Assessment – Formalism versus Judicial Policy in the Interest of Impartial Administration of Justice

It must be welcomed that the majority opinion clarifies that Art. 17(2) ICJ Statute does not *ex officio* disqualify a judge who has publicly taken a position on an issue that arises in a particular case.[730] Such an interpretation would make it particularly difficult to attract to the bench individuals who possessed recognized competence in international law or even the qualifications required in their respective countries for appointment to the highest judicial office.[731] Yet the opinion adopted by the majority, that only the manifestation of an opinion on the question pending before the ICJ in the present case would have been relevant, makes Art. 17(2) ICJ Statute rather inflexible for addressing positions taken or statements made by a judge that may raise legitimate concern about that judge's impartiality. On the other hand, Judge Buergenthal's rather wide interpretation of Art. 17(2) ICJ Statute in the case of Judge Elaraby, whereas obviously being more sensitive to the concern of the Court's independence, is not covered by the wording of that provision; he even concedes that himself.[732] In this sense, the majority's determination is easier to defend in light of the general rules of interpretation prescribed in Art. 31(1) Vienna Convention on the Law of Treaties (VCLT).[733] Yet adherence to a broader standard of justice and fairness as suggested by Judge Buergenthal

730 UNSC, *Statute of the International Tribunal for the Former Yugoslavia*, 510.

731 As requested by Art. 2 ICJ Statute.

732 "It is clear, of course, that the language of Article 17, paragraph 2, does not apply in so many words to the views Judge Elaraby expressed in the *supra* interview." *Legal Consequences of the Construction of a Wall in the Occupied Palestinian Territory (Order) (Dissenting Opinion of Judge Buergenthal)*, para. 10.

733 Art. 31(1) VCLT: "1. A treaty shall be interpreted in good faith in accordance with the ordinary meaning to be given to the terms of the treaty in their context and in the light of its object and purpose."

is reasonably well supported by the dictum established in most municipal legal orders and increasingly also in the self-conception and case law of international courts:[734] that justice must not only be done but also be seen to be done.[735] In other words, the need to be more sensitive to concerns of the Court's independence increases, and with it will the expectation that such concerns are taken more seriously. The same progressive and forward-looking approach to applying the ICJ Statute, unbound by a rigid adherence to its wording, is moreover not unfamiliar to the Court itself; as was shown above, the ICJ has chosen to interpret the wording of Art. 16 ICJ Statute benevolently when practical considerations are considered to call for it. At the same time, the rather hidden remark that a wider interpretation of Art. 17(2) ICJ Statute which allows the Court freely to consider whether one of its judges has expressed views or taken positions "that create the impression that he will not be able to [be] fair and impartial", might be considered "judicial policy",[736] is very probably the deciding reason for the majority's relatively cautious, but in the end overly rigid, interpretation.

VII. Conclusions

The ICJ is arguably the most important judicial dispute settlement body in the international legal order. Its establishment is the blueprint against which any court established since has been and will be tested. Its decisions have considerable weight when determining the current and future state of international law, despite – and perhaps even because of – the growing proliferation of international courts in recent decades. As a permanent court competent to decide upon any question of international law and through its integration in a world organization of collective security it resolves concrete legal problems and clarifies and, within the limits of its judicial function, develops international law. As peace and security, the maintenance of which is the main goal of the UN, thrive in a political climate of law-mindedness, the ICJ

734 "Since the international judge, if he is to be effective, must perforce work less under the protection and guidance of 'black-letter law' than his colleagues in a national court, he must be *seen to be the more impartial.*" (Emphasis in the original.) Franck, Thomas M., *The Structure of Impartiality: Examining the Riddle of one Law in a Fragmented World* (Macmillan New York 1968), 169.

735 Cf. *Legal Consequences of the Construction of a Wall in the Occupied Palestinian Territory (Order) (Dissenting Opinion of Judge Buergenthal)*, para. 11.

736 Ibid, para. 11 *in fine*.

can make a significant contribution by the fulfilment of its judicial functions. But the accomplishment of this task is possible only when the Court is able to operate independently, without mingling beyond recognition with and being made a tool of the political forces that operate around it and with which it has, as the principal judicial organ of the UN, to harmonize.

The judicial independence of the ICJ is recognized as an important feature of the Court and the judges by the main instruments of the Court, most prominently Art. 2 ICJ Statute. Various safeguards affecting the procedure before the Court, such as the Court's discretion to give advisory opinions,[737] the obligation to decide in accordance with international law, the long tenure of judges coupled with the impossibility for outside authorities to remove a judge from office, the granted immunities and the prohibition on judges exercising other occupations of a professional nature or having previously been unduly involved in a case in any other capacity, help to ensure its independent functioning. However, as has been shown above, the protection of judicial independence at the ICJ suffers from numerous compromises due primarily to the respect for State sovereignty and the interest of co-operation between organs within the UN.

Many of the elements of independence just mentioned are directly based on the necessities arising from the main functions of the ICJ, judicial dispute settlement and the interpretation and development of international law. For example, although States do not elect ICJ judges directly, there are nevertheless various opportunities for States to influence the selection process; to the extent that the processes of both nomination and election are considered to be highly politicised. One further such significant impairment of the independence of the Court is the institution of *ad hoc* judges. It lies obviously in such judges' nature (and they are expected) to ensure that special considerations of a particular State are taken into account by the Court. Although this might appear to be a legitimate concern which serves the objective interest of ensuring that "every relevant argument in favour of the party that

737 Art. 65(1) ICJ Statute: "The Court *may* give an advisory opinion on any legal question at the request of whatever body may be authorized by or in accordance with the Charter of the United Nations to make such a request." (Emphasis added.) See also Art. 96(a) UNC according to which the UNGA or the UNSC may *request* the ICJ to give an advisory opinion on any legal question.

has appointed him has been fully appreciated",[738] the question why such a person, who takes on the legitimate function of an expert, should then have the right to take part in the decision-making is not readily answerable. Granted that the complete abolition of the system of *ad hoc* judges would not be accepted by the States who still are "the normal subject of international law, that can make use of [the court]"[739] and that the system may have the function of neutralizing certain inequalities on the bench; yet in order to protect the Court from momentary and case-specific political influences exerted on it, it would be desirable to prohibit its use, at least when no judge has the nationality of any of the parties appearing before the Court.[740]

Whereas the functions of the Court obviously necessitate the Court's autonomy – since it would not otherwise make its judicial contribution to the corpus of principal organs of the UN – absolute independence is not in the interest of the fulfilment of the purposes of the Court. The activities of the Court must be co-ordinated with those of the other organs of the UN. The system regulating the apportionment of financial resources within the UN, a part of which is the budget of the ICJ together with the salaries of the judges, is a vivid indication of this. In these contexts it is necessary for the Court to be equipped not with full autonomy, but rather with the necessary means to present and articulate its concerns.

The Court, and the normative framework which ultimately ensures its independence, always oscillates between obedience to State sovereignty and the political character of the international legal order on the one hand, and exhaustive sovereignty from any other organ(s) on the other. Overall it has to be emphasized that the system of safeguards of the independence of judges seems to have functioned fairly well throughout the history of the Court. There are very few cases where the Court has had to discuss any possible lack of independence or impartiality and, more importantly, there has not so far been any open attempt to remove a judge from the Court and judges display a readiness to recuse themselves if special reasons occur that could allow the presumption of bias. This does not imply, however, that the Court has not often been criticised for displaying a lack of independence. But much of

738 *Application of the Convention on the Prevention and Punishment of the Crime of Genocide (Bosnia and Herzegovina v Serbia and Montenegro) (Order of 13 September 1993) (Separate Opinion of Judge Lauterpacht)*, para. 6.

739 Singh, *The Role and Record of the International Court of Justice: 1946 to 1988; in Celebration of the 40th Anniversary*, 25.

740 Art. 31(2) ICJ Statute.

this must be soberly attributed to the political nature of many of the disputes the Court is called upon to settle.[741]

741 One recent example illustrating the political nature of cases before the Court but also revealing the sometimes blatant ignorance of the Court's independence is the report about the warning by the Russian foreign minister to the Court "not to grapple with Georgia's lawsuit against Russia" (Online edition, 'Lavrov warns UN court against tackling Georgia's lawsuit' *The Voice of Russia* (16 September 2010); on 12 August 2008 Georgia filed an action with the ICJ accusing Russia of discriminating against the Georgian population in South Ossetia and Abkhazia, which Russia recognized as independent States following the Caucasus war in August 2008). Another example is the official statement issued by Serbia's Crown Prince Aleksandar Karađorđević on the ICJ's advisory opinion on the compatibility with international law of the unilateral declaration of independence in respect of Kosovo, which was said to "clearly [show] that force has prevailed over International Justice!" 'The Public Relations Office of HRH Crown Prince Alexander II: Crown Prince Alexander's Statement Regarding Decision by International Court of Justice on Kosovo' <http://www.royalfamily.org/statements/state-det/state-2274.html> (last visited: 21 March 2014).

Chapter E: Judicial Independence in the International Tribunal for the Law of the Sea

I. Introduction

The independence of the ITLOS[742] is of particular interest to a broader study on the independence of international courts, since the traditional preference of States for utilizing arbitration instead of adjudication by a standing international tribunal in the field of the law of the sea is notable. This is attributable to the flexibility of arbitration, *inter alia* to States' capacity to determine the arbitrators, the issue for resolution and the applicable law.[743] The ITLOS is one of the – if not *the*[744] – most significant achievements of a lengthy, yet ultimately very successful process of codification in the field of the law of the sea. It is conceived as a permanent judicial body available to all States Parties to the UNCLOS and other States and non-State entities in certain cases. The ITLOS is a specialized international tribunal in that it has general jurisdiction over all disputes relating to the law of the sea.[745] Its non-mandatory jurisdiction *ratione materiae*[746] is shared with dispute settlement by the

---

742 Hereinafter also referred to as "the Tribunal".

743 See for a broader (historic) overview Rothwell, Donald, 'The International Tribunal for the Law of the Sea and Marine Environmental Protection – Expanding the Horizons of International Oceans Governance' (2003) 17 Ocean Yearbook, 30. The *penchant* for arbitration has been pointedly summarized as follows: "Arbitration is believed to constitute a smaller exception to State sovereignty as parties exercise more control on the adjudicating body." Rah, Sicco and Wallrabenstein, Tilo, 'The International Tribunal for the Law of the Sea and its Future' (2007) Ocean Yearbook, 53.

744 Rothwell, Donald, 'Building on the Strengths and Addressing the Challenges: The Role of Law of the Sea Institutions' (2004) 35 Ocean Development and International Law 2, 132.

745 Pursuant to Art. 288(2) UNCLOS, the Tribunal may offer dispute settlement services relating to the interpretation and application of all international agreements, as long as such agreements provide for the exercise of the ITLOS' jurisdiction and relate to the purposes of UNCLOS.

746 Art. 288 UNCLOS. A dispute between States Parties must be submitted to compulsory procedures entailing binding decisions under Section 2 of Part XV of UNCLOS only when no settlement has been reached using the non-judicial dispute settlement

ICJ, arbitration tribunals and special arbitral tribunals.[747] Thus the Tribunal forms part of a dispute settlement system provided for by UNCLOS. Coupled with its limited compulsory jurisdiction[748] and in conjunction with the fact that the ITLOS is not an organ of a standing international organization, but rather an autonomous treaty body,[749] poses particular and distinct questions with regard to the protection of its independence. These questions have to be resolved in an area of tension between organizational autonomy, which *prima facie* plays out favourably for the Tribunal's independence, and integration into a competitive system of judicial dispute settlement mechanisms, which facilitates forum shopping and a need for self-assertion as potential long term negative effects on the Tribunal's independence.[750] Considering the relatively low workload of the Tribunal so far[751] it is questionable whether the protection of judicial independence may itself influence the willingness of States to make use of the Tribunal.

mechanisms envisaged in Art. 33(1) UNC or any other means of the parties' choice (cf. Art. 280 UNCLOS).

747 Constituted either in accordance with Annex VII UNCLOS or in accordance with Annex VIII UNCLOS.

748 In three different fields the Tribunal enjoys compulsory jurisdiction over the States Parties to UNCLOS: with regard to disputes relating to activities in the deep seabed area (Art. 187 UNCLOS), the prompt release of detained vessels and crews (Art. 292(1) UNCLOS) and requests for provisional measures pending the constitution of an arbitral tribunal to which a dispute is being submitted (Art. 290(5) UNCLOS).

749 Treves, Tullio, 'The Law of the Sea "System" of Institutions', in: von Bogdandy, Armin *et al.* (eds) *Max Planck Yearbook of United Nations Law – Volume 2* (Martinus Nijhoff Publishers Leiden 1998), 336.

750 Cf. Rothwell, 'Building on the Strengths and Addressing the Challenges: The Role of Law of the Sea Institutions', 146.

751 As of March 2014 the Tribunal had concluded 22 contentious cases, provided one advisory opinion and had two cases in its list; 'International Tribunal for the Law of the Sea – Cases' available at <http://www.itlos.org/index.php?id=10> (last visited: 21 March 2014).

II. Genesis and Organizational Setting of the ITLOS

1. The First and Second UN Conferences on the Law of the Sea (1958 and 1960)

In a resolution of 21 February 1957, the UNGA convened the first United Nations Conference on the Law of the Sea[752] to deal with the substantive law of the sea, which it was able partially to codify in four conventions.[753] Regarding the issue of dispute settlement, the conference was unable to agree on an obligatory procedure but instead settled on the Optional Protocol of Signature Concerning the Compulsory Settlement of Disputes.[754] Although the possibility of the submission of disputes to arbitral tribunals was raised throughout the conference,[755] the Protocol did not provide for a comprehensive and obligatory dispute settlement mechanism. Instead it envisaged optional dispute settlement by the ICJ for certain parts of the (then) codified law of the sea. The creation of a separate tribunal for the law of the sea was not discussed.[756] Although the negotiations at the first conference and its

---

752 UNGA, *International Conference of Plenipotentiaries to Examine the Law of the Sea* (21 February 1957) UN Doc. A/RES/1105 (XI).

753 Convention on the Territorial Sea and the Contiguous Zone (adopted 29 April 1958, entered into force on 10 September 1964) 516 UNTS 205; Convention on the High Seas (adopted 29 April 1958, entered into force 30 September 1962) 450 UNTS 11; Convention on Fishing and Conservation of the Living Resources of the High Seas (adopted 29 April 1958, entered into force 20 March 1966) 559 UNTS 285; Convention on the Continental Shelf (adopted 29 April 1958, entered into force 10 June 1964) 499 UNTS 311. The conference could resort to the preparatory work by the ILC, which in its first to eighth session between 1949 and 1956 drafted rules on issues such as the continental shelf, fisheries, the contiguous zone and the territorial sea.

754 Optional Protocol of Signature Concerning the Compulsory Settlement of Disputes (adopted 29 April 1958, entered into force 30 September 1962) 450 UNTS 169.

755 See, e.g., the suggested amendment by the Netherlands on the inclusion in the convention of an article on the settlement of dispute, UNGA, *Convening of a second international conference of plenipotentiaries: letter dated 24 April 1958 from the Chairman of the Delegation of Cuba to the President of the Conference* (14 April 1958) UN Doc. A/CONF.13/L.25, 112.

756 This holds true even for the second conference on the law of the sea, convened between 17 March and 26 April 1960 and based on a request from the UNGA; see UNGA, *Convening of a Second UN Conference on the Law of the Sea* (10 December 1958) UN Doc. A/RES/1307 (XIII); UNGA, *Report of the Committee of the Whole* (14 April 1960) UN Doc. A/CONF.19/L.4. The second conference was instead

outcome can be considered to bear witness to the fundamental willingness of States to subject disputes under the law of the sea regime to institutional judicial dispute settlement, the ICJ and arbitration were still considered sufficient mechanisms at the time, not at least because of the control they gave States over dispute settlement.

2. The Third UN Conference on the Law of the Sea (1973-1982)

Although dispute settlement was not initially on the agenda of the third conference, this changed as it became clear that the law of the sea was in need of a holistic approach in the form of a "convention dealing with *all matters* relating to the law of the sea" (emphasis added).[757] Early initiatives to create a law of the sea tribunal include proposals from Malta,[758] Canada,[759] and the United Kingdom.[760] These proposals envisaged the Tribunal to be

confined to the consideration of the breadth of the territorial sea and fishery limits, although both topics were ultimately postponed indefinitely.

757 See UNGA, *Reservation Exclusively for Peaceful Purposes of the Sea-Bed and the Ocean Floor, and the Subsoil Thereof, Underlying the High Seas beyond the Limits of Present National Jurisdiction and use of their Resources in the Interests of Mankind, and Convening of the Third United Nations Conference on the Law of the Sea* (16 November 1973) UN Doc. A/RES/3067 (XXVIII), paras. 3 and 7.

758 Malta considered it a "[b]asic prerequisite to an orderly economic development of ocean space beyond national jurisdiction and hence to the equitable sharing by all States in the benefits derived from the exploitation of its natural resources" that "certainty in international law and mechanisms for the peaceful and certain settlement of disputes" be guaranteed. This was considered to necessarily involve "the creation of an international court with binding powers of adjudication". See Report of the Committee on the Peaceful uses of the Sea-Bed and the Ocean Floor Beyond the Limits of National Jurisdiction, *Draft Ocean Space Treaty – Working Paper Submitted by Malta* (16 July 1971) UN Doc. A/AC.138/53, 111-112; Committee on the Peaceful Uses of the Sea-Bed and the Ocean Floor Beyond the Limits of National jurisdiction, *Report of the Committee on the Peaceful Uses of the Sea-Bed and the Ocean Floor Beyond the Limits of National jurisdiction* (1971) UN Doc. A/8421, 105.

759 Report of the Committee on the Peaceful uses of the Sea-Bed and the Ocean Floor Beyond the Limits of National Jurisdiction, *International Sea-Bed Régime and Machinery Working Paper, submitted by the Delegation of Canada* (24 August 1971) UN Doc. A/AC.138/59, 222.

760 Report of the Committee on the Peaceful uses of the Sea-Bed and the Ocean Floor Beyond the Limits of National Jurisdiction, *International Sea-Bed Régime: United*

composed of a small body of legal (and possibly technical) experts and to be empowered to seek advisory opinions from the ICJ.[761] The British proposal explicitly provided that the tribunal "would have to be entirely independent". However, the composition of the proposed tribunal in each individual case reminds much of conventional arbitration, with every party having the right to designate one person from a list and the people thus designated selecting the chairman of the arbitration tribunal. It was only by a proposal submitted by the USA in 1973 that the nomination and election of judges to a new law of the sea tribunal was suggested, following the procedure applicable to ICJ judges.[762]

Already during the initial stages of the conference the variety of possible dispute settlement mechanisms, among them numerous judicial dispute settlement mechanisms, posed a problem. Whereas consent was swiftly reached on lending the political dispute settlement mechanisms priority over any form of judicial procedure potentially entailing binding decisions,[763] the arrangement among the latter generated intensive debate among States' representatives. To be available were *ad hoc* arbitral tribunals, a new law of the sea tribunal or the ICJ. The question was ultimately resolved in the so-called Montreux formula, which enabled States Parties to the future convention to choose, when ratifying or otherwise expressing consent to be bound by the convention, one or more of the jurisdictions of the three fora.[764] The informal single negotiating text prepared by the chairman of the first committee in-

---

Kingdom Proposals for Elements of a Convention (30 July 1971) UN Doc. A/AC.138/46, 89-90.

761 Consideration was also given to the possibility of allowing appeals from the Tribunal to the ICJ on questions relating to international law.

762 Report of the Committee on the Peaceful uses of the Sea-Bed and the Ocean Floor Beyond the Limits of National Jurisdiction, *Draft Articles for a Chapter on the Settlement of Disputes: submitted by the United States of America* (21 August 1973) UN Doc. A/AC.138/97, 22-23.

763 See, e.g., Australia, Belgium, Bolivia, Colombia, El Salvador, Luxembourg, Netherlands, Singapore and United States of America,, *Working paper on the settlement of law of the sea disputes* (27 August 1974) UN Doc. A/CONF.62/L.7. Even the Optional Protocol on Compulsory Settlement of Disputes stemming from the first conference, provided for compulsory jurisdiction by the ICJ only "unless some other form of settlement is provided in … or has been agreed upon by the parties within a reasonable period".

764 Adede, Andrónico O., *The System for Settlement of Disputes under the United Nations Convention on the Law of the Sea – A Drafting History and a Commentary* (Nijhoff Dordrecht 1987), 53-54. See now Art. 287 UNCLOS.

cluded in Part III the establishment of a tribunal as an organ of the International Seabed Authority (ISA); it was to be composed of a body of independent judges and equipped with extensive jurisdiction relating to the future convention.[765] At the fourth session of the conference the question of dispute settlement was for the first time included in a formal debate by the plenary.[766] At this stage of the deliberations the establishment of a new tribunal was agreed, but the delimitation towards other judicial dispute settlement mechanisms, in particular the ICJ, remained unclear.[767] A negotiating group was established under the chairmanship of A. Adede and entrusted with considering the specific issues relating to dispute settlement under UNCLOS.[768]

765 See Third United Nations Conference on the Law of the Sea, *Informal single negotiating text, part I* (7 May 1975) UN Doc. A/CONF.62/WP.8/Part I, Arts. 32-34.

766 See the records of the 58th-65th Plenary meeting, Third United Nations Conference on the Law of the Sea, *58th Plenary meeting* (5 April 1976) UN Doc. A/CONF.62/SR.58-Third United Nations Conference on the Law of the Sea, *65th Plenary meeting* (12 April 1976) UN Doc. A/CONF.62/SR.65.

767 Representative of this general impression are e.g. the statements made by the representative of Australia ("it was desirable to establish a new tribunal as an alternative to the International Court of Justice in order to settle disputes relating to the interpretation of the convention"; Third United Nations Conference on the Law of the Sea, *58th Plenary meeting*, para. 15) and Sweden ("[Sweden] acknowledged the need for the establishment of a judicial organ within the framework of the convention."; Third United Nations Conference on the Law of the Sea, *61th Plenary meeting* (6 April 1976) UN Doc. A/CONF.62/SR.61, para. 5). Even States that opposed the creation of a new tribunal declared their willingness to support the establishment if the majority of States preferred its creation, see, e.g., Canada, Third United Nations Conference on the Law of the Sea, *65th Plenary meeting*, para. 7; Venezuela, Third United Nations Conference on the Law of the Sea, *62nd Plenary meeting* (7 April 1976) UN Doc. A/CONF.62/SR.62, para. 79.

768 Unfortunately, beginning with the fifth session of the conference the dispute settlement system was the object of merely informal meetings of which no formal records were produced, and the evolution of the various provisions on the dispute settlement system, including the Tribunal for the law of the sea, can thus be reconstructed only with the help of drafts prepared by the chairmen of the committees or the president of the conference. The advantage of this procedure was considered to be the increased focus on actual participation in the conference negotiations. Adede, *The System for Settlement of Disputes under the United Nations Convention on the Law of the Sea – A Drafting History and a Commentary*, 4.

3. The Rationale Underlying the ITLOS

In the course of the proceedings the positions of the States Parties had polarised around two different positions. Whereas the *generalists* supported the establishment of a uniform dispute settlement mechanism under the future convention, e.g. in the shape of a law of the sea tribunal, the *functionalists* opted for *ad hoc* dispute settlement procedures chosen according to the character of the individual dispute and which would entail decisions by technical rather than legal experts.[769] The above-mentioned Montreux formula ultimately provided a combination of applicable fora: the ICJ, arbitration and a new law of the sea tribunal. A major concern in the generalists' approach was the interest in uniformity in the interpretation of the future law of the sea convention.[770] This argument of unity and non-contradicting development of international law was speaking out in favour of recourse to the ICJ, which already possessed the potential to produce harmonized and non-contradicting jurisprudence even on topics relating to the law of the sea.[771] But the extended use of the ICJ was also seen critically especially by developing States and new States that had not been able to shape the creation and functioning of the ICJ. Opting for extensive usage of arbitration as the main

769 This classification was first mentioned by the representative of Spain, Third United Nations Conference on the Law of the Sea, *60th Plenary meeting* (6 April 1976) UN Doc. A/CONF.62/SR.60, para. 23. Further on this classification see Dupuy, René-Jean & Vignes, Daniel (eds), *A Handbook on the New Law of the Sea – Volume 2* (Nijhoff Dordrecht 1991), 1334-1338.

770 See point II of the four fundamental points summarized by the representative from El Salvador from the draft articles of the Working Group; Third United Nations Conference on the Law of the Sea, *51st Plenary meeting* (29 August 1974) UN Doc. A/CONF.62/SR.51, paras. 7-13. Nordquist, Myron H. (ed) *United Nations Convention on the Law of the Sea 1982: A Commentary – Volume V* (Nijhoff Dordrecht 1989), 8.

771 See, e.g., Third United Nations Conference on the Law of the Sea, *60th Plenary meeting*, para. 24; Third United Nations Conference on the Law of the Sea, *61th Plenary meeting*, paras. 5-6; Third United Nations Conference on the Law of the Sea, *62nd Plenary meeting*, para. 12. Moreover, the ICJ had already accumulated a significant body of case law addressing issues of the law of the sea. Cf. Nordquist (ed) *United Nations Convention on the Law of the Sea 1982: A Commentary – Volume V*, 41 with further references. For an overview of the ICJ's marine-related case law see Yankov, Alexander, 'The International Tribunal for the Law of the Sea and the Comprehensive Dispute Settlement System of the Law of the Sea', in: Chandrasekhara Rao, P. *et al.* (eds) *The International Tribunal for the Law of the Sea – Law and Practice* (Kluwer Law International The Hague 2001), 39-40.

dispute settlement mechanism was criticized by some representatives as jeopardizing the uniformity of jurisprudence, particularly as arbitration did not follow a set and common procedure, and thus by its very nature was not striving for institutional or even jurisprudential consistency.[772] This despite the fact that arbitration was often the method favoured by States for the resolution of international disputes,[773] which was consistent with the traditional favouring of consent-based and non-compulsory methods of dispute settlement.[774]

The advantage of the establishment of a law of the sea tribunal was the special competence that could be accumulated by placing on the bench individuals who were highly skilled not only in legal but also technical issues relating to the law of the sea.[775] In the view of many State representatives this made the Tribunal particularly well suited to adjudicating cases involving specialized fields of law such as the law of the sea, pollution and scientific research.[776] Moreover, establishing a new tribunal was sometimes seen as a tribute to the sovereignty of States, in the sense that it would provide them with a wider choice of mechanisms for dispute settlement.[777] Furthermore a new tribunal compared to arbitration had the advantage of potentially reducing the costs for the parties involved,[778] producing decisions more swiftly

772 Third United Nations Conference on the Law of the Sea, *59th Plenary meeting* (5 April 1976) UN Doc. A/CONF.62/SR.59, para. 12.

773 See, e.g., Third United Nations Conference on the Law of the Sea, *62nd Plenary meeting*, para. 12.

774 Klein, Natalie, *Dispute Settlement in the UN Convention on the Law of the Sea* (Cambridge University Press Cambridge 2005), 17.

775 Third United Nations Conference on the Law of the Sea, *61th Plenary meeting*, para. 26.

776 Third United Nations Conference on the Law of the Sea, *60th Plenary meeting*, para. 52.

777 See, e.g., Third United Nations Conference on the Law of the Sea, *58th Plenary meeting*, para. 6; Third United Nations Conference on the Law of the Sea, *60th Plenary meeting*, para. 52. This argument must be seen in conjunction with the criticism by some (developing and new) States that the ICJ did not represent the entire world community.

778 The relatively high initial costs of establishing a new tribunal was mentioned in criticism; see, e.g., Third United Nations Conference on the Law of the Sea, *59th Plenary meeting*, para. 15; Third United Nations Conference on the Law of the Sea, *62nd Plenary meeting*, para. 38; Third United Nations Conference on the Law of the Sea, *64th Plenary meeting* (9 April 1976) UN Doc. A/CONF.62/SR.64, para. 9.

and creating little in the way of organizational burden.[779] Another frequently mentioned yet not undisputed prospect was the opportunity to open the tribunal to subjects other than States in their capacity as parties to a dispute.[780] The idea of a new tribunal also incorporated the expectations of many smaller States of playing a role comparable to that of larger States.[781] The desire for more respect for the equality of States was *inter alia* substantiated by the demand for a more equal system of election of international judges and the equitable distribution of the seats on the bench among the various regions of the world; something many States considered to be lacking in the ICJ.

4. Conclusions

As shown by the brief outline of the history of origin of the ITLOS, the Tribunal is the result of a necessary compromise between a lack of confidence in the existing judicial dispute settlement mechanisms and the imperatives flowing from the technical nature of UNCLOS.

States did not desire to adopt a model similar to that of the ICJ, namely an international tribunal closely linked to an international organization. Since the law of the sea can hardly be said to be so specialized as to be beyond the tribunals of the time, the creation of the ITLOS indicates a certain lack of

---

779 In the course of the conference the new tribunal was also seen as a means to avert differing interpretations of the prospective convention and to combine technical and legal issues, as would seen to be necessary in law of the sea disputes; Third United Nations Conference on the Law of the Sea, *61th Plenary meeting*, para. 38.

780 See, e.g., Third United Nations Conference on the Law of the Sea, *60th Plenary meeting*, paras. 10, 35. Some States even advocated amending the ICJ Statute as well as the UNC to the effect of allowing those other entities access to the ICJ with regard to law of the sea disputes: see ibid, para. 16. The Sea-Bed Committee dealt extensively with the question of disputes with regard to sea-bed mining; disputes between States and also between seabed institutions and private and public corporations. See Sohn, L, 'A Tribunal for the Sea-Bed or the Ocean' (1972) 32 Zeitschrift für ausländisches öffentliches Recht und Völkerrecht. For the counter-argument that such an innovation regarding the jurisdiction *ratione personae* would not be in conformity with the state of international law at the time see, e.g., Third United Nations Conference on the Law of the Sea, *58th Plenary meeting*, paras. 11, 29.

781 Third United Nations Conference on the Law of the Sea, *63rd Plenary meeting* (8 April 1976) UN Doc. A/CONF.62/SR.63, paras. 4-5; Third United Nations Conference on the Law of the Sea, *64th Plenary meeting*, para. 28.

confidence in the ICJ, at least an inadequacy of arbitration,[782] or even a desire to advance institutionalized judicial dispute settlement. Being created by an international agreement that is the result of an international diplomatic conference, the ITLOS is independent of any international organization, e.g. with regard to the selection of its judges. Instead the Tribunal relies on the States that created it through their ratification of UNCLOS.[783] Based on the special character of the law of the sea as a comprehensive and technical field of law, involving not only States but also other actors, the ITLOS has several advantages as regards the two alternative systems of judicial dispute settlement. Among them is the special expertise available at the Tribunal, the ability to extend its jurisdiction *ratione personae*, and the expedience and promptness with which the proceedings before it can be conducted.

III. The Functions Served by the ITLOS

1. The Mandate of Dispute Settlement as the Main Function of the ITLOS

The central function of the ITLOS is the settlement of disputes relating to the law of the sea. Whereas Art. 279 UNCLOS obliges States Parties to "settle any dispute between them … by peaceful means",[784] Art. 286 UNCLOS refers any dispute concerning the interpretation or application of UNCLOS that could not be settled by other means to compulsory procedures entailing binding decisions. The question of what constitutes a *dispute* under UNCLOS was not discussed during the third conference, and it is thus reasonable to assume it to have the same meaning as that adopted by the ICJ.[785]

782 Merrills, John G., *International Dispute Settlement* (Cambridge University Press Cambridge 3rd edn. 1998), 185.

783 As of March 2014 UNCLOS has 166 parties; 'United Nations Convention on the Law of the Sea – Status' available at <http://treaties.un.org/Pages/ViewDetailsIII.aspx?&src=TREATY&mtdsg_no=XXI~6&chapter=21&Temp=mtdsg3&lang=en#1> (last visited: 21 March 2014).

784 And hence in principal opens up for numerous procedures for the settlement of disputes, cf. the reference to Art. 33(1) UNC.

785 "Considering that, in the view of the Tribunal, a dispute is a 'disagreement on a point of law or fact, a conflict of legal views or of interests' (Mavrommatis Palestine Concessions, Judgment No. 2, 1924, P.C.I.J., Series A, No. 2, p. 11), and '[i]t must be shown that the claim of one party is positively opposed by the other' (South West Africa, Preliminary Objections, Judgment, I.C.J. Reports 1962, p. 328)." *Southern Bluefin Tuna Cases (New Zealand v. Japan; Australia v. Japan) Requests*

The Tribunal itself determines when a justiciable dispute is before it.[786] In making such a decision, the ITLOS is not bound by similar decisions of any other court or institution,[787] and in particular not by States.[788] Whereas it is conceivable that the UNGA or the UNSC would deal simultaneously with a situation that is before the ITLOS (for example if one of the parties brings the dispute to the attention of one of these political organs), since the Tribunal is not part of the organizational structure of the UN it is in principal not compelled to take the UN organs' potentially relevant decisions or opinions into consideration. This is emphasized by Art. 1(1) Agreement on Cooperation and Relationship between the United Nations and the International Tribunal for the Law of the Sea, which provides as follows:[789]

> "The United Nations recognizes the International Tribunal for the Law of the Sea as an autonomous international judicial body with jurisdiction as provided for in the relevant provisions of the Convention and the statute of the International Tribunal annexed thereto."

This is a significant difference from the ICJ and one that can have a substantial impact on the independence of decision-making of the Tribunal, where fewer conscious and unconscious considerations of any political organ have come to play.[790]

Nevertheless, it is to be expected that the ITLOS is not entirely indifferent towards the activities of the UN, including its purely political organs. Pursuant to UNGA Resolution 51/204, the Tribunal has observer status with the

---

for provisional measures (Order) ITLOS Cases Nos 3 and 4 (27 August 1999), para. 44. Of this same opinion see, e.g., Dupuy & Vignes (eds), *A Handbook on the New Law of the Sea – Volume 2*, 1340 and Nordquist (ed) *United Nations Convention on the Law of the Sea 1982: A Commentary – Volume V*, 18-19.

786 Cf. Art. 288(4) UNCLOS. On the question of the Tribunal's *Kompetenz-Kompetenz* see the early statement made by the Greek representative, Third United Nations Conference on the Law of the Sea, *65th Plenary meeting*, para. 17: "The International Court of Justice or the law of the sea tribunal must have 'the competence of the competence'".

787 Although it has a tendency to decide in conformity with settled case law by the ICJ. See, e.g., the above-mentioned *Southern Bluefin Tuna Cases (New Zealand v. Japan; Australia v. Japan) Requests for provisional measures (Order)*, para. 44.

788 See, however, the prescriptions in Section 3 of Part XV UNCLOS.

789 Agreement on Cooperation and Relationship between the United Nations and the International Tribunal for the Law of the Sea (adopted 18 December 1997, entered into force 12 March 1998) 2000 UNTS 467.

790 Cf. the above-mentioned statement that some judges of the ICJ think about how something could be received by the UNGA before making a decision.

UNGA, allowing it to "participate in the sessions and the work of the General Assembly" in such capacity.[791] Thus e.g. the President of the ITLOS regularly addresses the plenary meeting of the UNGA to report on the work of the Tribunal.[792] Moreover, the UN on its side has established the Division of Ocean Affairs and the Law of the Sea which has been given the function of monitoring developments, reporting to the UNGA on matters relating to the law of the sea, formulating recommendations aimed at promoting a better understanding of UNCLOS, and ensuring that the UN has the capacity to respond to requests for advice and assistance from States in the implementation of UNCLOS.[793] The Division serves as the secretariat of UNCLOS and provides secretariat functions to the Meetings of States Parties to UNCLOS.[794] Although it can be questioned whether the Division can be used by the UNGA as a tool to exert influence on the decision-making of the Tribunal, its limited administrative competencies, which are mostly not directly related to the ITLOS, do not suggest that this could be the case.

The advantage of this treaty based system is that the Tribunal itself has the discretion to decide to what extent it will take into consideration actions by the UN. Much of the co-operation between the Tribunal and the UN thus, at least on the surface, takes place under the conditions to be established by the Tribunal. One exception is the provision in Art. 298(1)(c) UNCLOS which allows States to exempt themselves from the jurisdiction of the Court in "disputes in respect of which the Security Council of the United Nations is exercising the functions assigned to it by the [UNC]". But here it is instead the State, the potential party to a dispute before the Tribunal, and not the UN itself, which may influence to what extent the Tribunal can exercise its jur-

791 UNGA, *Observer status for the International Tribunal for the Law of the Sea in the General Assembly* (17 December 1996) UN Doc. A/RES/51/204, para. 1. This observer status was also codified in Art. 3(1) Agreement on Cooperation and Relationship between the United Nations and the International Tribunal for the Law of the Sea.

792 See, e.g., United Nations Convention on the Law of the Sea – Meeting of States Parties, *Annual report of the International Tribunal for the Law of the Sea for 2010* (4 April 2011) SPLOS/222, para. 67.

793 See 'The Division for Ocean Affairs and the Law of the Sea' available at <http://www.un.org/Depts/los/doalos_activities/about_doalos.htm> (last visited: 21 March 2014).

794 Which in turn is the body entrusted with *inter alia* electing the members of the Tribunal, considering its annual report and dealing with its budgetary and administrative matters. See *infra* Chapter E.IV(4).

isdiction. Such State conduct is unproblematic as it lies equally in the discretion of States to subject themselves to the jurisdiction of the ITLOS in the first place.

2. The Auxiliary Task of Enforcing Environmental Concerns

An important point in the understanding of the ITLOS as an independent judicial body flows from its ability to operate independently of the parties appearing before it, in particular States. One such indicator is that the Tribunal has been equipped with the power to prescribe provisional measures not only to preserve the rights of the parties involved in a particular dispute,[795] but also to avert "serious harm to the marine environment".[796] The reason for this extended rationale for provisional measures is to be found in the specialized character of a law of the sea tribunal. Even the very early arbitral awards handed down by international courts and tribunals dealing with environmental issues, such as the *Bering Sea (Fur Seal) Arbitration (United Kingdom v United States of America)*,[797] the *Trail Smelter Case (United States of America v Canada)*[798] and the *Lake Lancoux Arbitration (Spain v France)*,[799] proved that in disputes between States and also increasingly between States and non-State entities there is a potential for conflict between economic and

795 Traditionally, the interests of the parties to the dispute are the central basis for prescribing provisional measure in international litigation. See Wolfrum, Rüdiger, 'Interim (Provisional) Measures of Protection', in: Wolfrum, Rüdiger (ed) *The Max Planck Encyclopedia of Public International Law* (Oxford University Press Online Edition 2012), paras. 4-18.

796 Art. 290(1) *in fine* UNLCOS. Cf. also the ability of "the court or tribunal to which the dispute has been submitted [to] prescribe any provisional measures which it considers appropriate under the circumstances to preserve the respective rights of the parties to the dispute *or to prevent damage to the stocks in question*" (emphasis added); Art. 31(2) Agreement for the Implementation of the Provisions of the United Nations Convention on the Law of the Sea of 10 December 1982 Relating to the Conservation and Management of Straddling Fish Stocks and Highly Migratory Fish Stocks (adopted 4 August 1995, entered into force 11 December 2001) 2167 UNTS 3.

797 *Bering Sea (Fur Seal) Arbitration (United Kingdom v United States of America)* (Arbitration Tribunal) International Environmental Law Reports, Vol. I, 43 (1893).

798 *Trail Smelter Case (United States of America v Canada)* (Arbitral Tribunal) 3 RIAA 1907 (1941).

799 *Lake Lancoux Arbitration (Spain v France)* (Arbitral Tribunal) 12 RIAA 281 (1957).

ecological interests,[800] which makes such questions relevant for international courts and tribunals.

This rationale must particularly apply to a tribunal that is to oversee adherence to the law of the sea regime. UNLOS has such significant environmental impact that it has been classified not only as a regulatory instrument for the oceans but also as a "multilateral environmental instrument for the oceans".[801] Indeed the protection and preservation of the environment is a concern that forms an integral part of UNLOS. Indicative of this is already section 3 of the preamble to UNCLOS, in which the States Parties declare that they are conscious, when signing the UNCLOS, "that the problems of ocean space are closely interrelated and need to be considered as a whole". The connection between the law of the sea and protection of the environment is more concretely set out in Art. 192 UNCLOS, where States acknowledge their "obligation to protect and preserve the marine environment." To that extent, when interpreting and applying the UNCLOS, the ITLOS is called upon to take environmental concerns into account. If this analysis is accurate, and if the Tribunal is thus obliged to help implement the protection of the marine environment, then this presupposes a far-reaching independence from States, which can be expected to be more in favour of seeing their own (e.g. economic) interests enforced than those of the world community as a whole. It thus becomes relevant to analyse further to what extent the Tribunal is able independently to concede environmental interests a major role, especially when these interests are opposed.

---

800 Sands, Philippe J., 'Litigating Environmental Disputes – Courts, Tribunals and the Progressive Development of International Environmental Law', in: Ndiaye, Tafsir Malick *et al.* (eds) *Law of the Sea, Environmental Law and Settlement of Disputes; Liber Amicorum Judge Thomas A. Mensah* (Nijhoff Leiden 2007), 314.

801 Rothwell, 'The International Tribunal for the Law of the Sea and Marine Environmental Protection – Expanding the Horizons of International Oceans Governance', 27. The reason for this is that the development of modern international environmental law took place almost in parallel to the development of the modern law of the sea, beginning in the late 1950s. According to V. Frank, "[t]he protection of the marine environment is an area where the jurisdictional rules of the law of the sea and the objectives, principles and approaches of international environmental law meet and influence each other to form the 'international environmental law of the sea'." Frank, Veronica, *The European Community and Marine Environmental Protection in the International Law of the Sea – Implementing Global Obligations at the Regional Level* (Nijhoff Leiden 2007), 9.

3. The Emergency Powers of the ITLOS

The ITLOS was equipped with extensive powers to rule on issues that do not immediately affect the merits of a contentious case but that have an effect on the practical conditions surrounding it or that may have a bearing on the formation of a dispute. The Tribunal may decide on provisional measures where it itself has *prima facie* jurisdiction over the dispute[802] and in cases to be referred to arbitration, pending the constitution of an arbitration tribunal.[803] In this regard it is significant that Art. 290 UNCLOS enables the Tribunal not only to decide or indicate[804] provisional measures but indeed to "prescribe" them.[805] Moreover, the Tribunal has reserved the right to recommend certain actions to be taken or to be omitted in combination with the prescription of provisional measures.[806] The binding character of provisional measures prescribed by the ITLOS[807] witnesses the far-reaching subjection of States to the rule of the Tribunal in the particular area of protecting rights and interests, including the party-independent interest of protecting the marine environment, until a final decision has been able to settle them.[808] How far-reaching is this regime in the case of the Tribunal?

Art. 290(1) UNCLOS prescribes that the Tribunal is at liberty to decide on "*any* provisional measures *which it considers* appropriate under the cir-

---

802 Art. 290(1) UNCLOS.

803 Art. 290(5) UNCLOS. Cf. Art. 25 Statute of the Tribunal.

804 Cf. Art. 41(1) ICJ Statute: "The Court shall have the power to *indicate*, if it considers that circumstances so require, any provisional measures which ought to be taken to preserve the respective rights of either party." (Emphasis added.).

805 Moreover, pursuant to Art. 290(6) UNCLOS, the parties to a dispute are obliged to comply promptly with any provisional measures: "6. The parties to the dispute shall comply promptly with any provisional measures prescribed under this article."

806 See, e.g., *The M/V 'SAIGA' (No 2) Case (Saint Vincent and the Grenadines v Guinea) Request for provisional measures (Order)* ITLOS Case No. 2 (11 March 1998), para. 43: "Considering that, in order to prevent aggravation or extension of the dispute, the parties should endeavour to find an arrangement to be applied pending the final decision, without prejudice to their contentions on jurisdiction or merits".

807 Cf. Art. 89(5) Rules of the Tribunal.

808 It is widely assumed that this feature also influenced the ICJ in its decision in the *LaGrand* case in which it ruled that its own provisional measures are binding (see *LaGrand Case (Germany v United States of America) (Judgment)* ICJ Rep. 466 (2001), para. 102), see, e.g., Oellers-Frahm, Karin, 'Article 41 ICJ Statute', in: Zimmermann, Andreas *et al.* (eds) *The Statute of the International Court of Justice – A Commentary* (Oxford University Press Oxford 2006), 953-958.

cumstances" (emphasis added). Although this power can only be exercised after a dispute has been "duly submitted" to the Tribunal, the latter is at liberty to decide which measures ought to apply and what intensity they ought to have. Thus the ITLOS does not consider itself bound by the request of a party, at least as regards the final decision on the substantive scope of the measures prescribed.[809]

This ability of the Tribunal to act independently of the parties' requests at first glance amounts to a departure from the rule of *non ultra petita.*[810] However, it is motivated by the interest in efficiency and expediency not only inherent in the nature of the concept of provisional measures in general[811] but also underlying the conception of the ITLOS as a cost-efficient Tribunal able to provide expeditious and efficient procedures.[812] The Tribunal is thus, at least in direct comparison with the ICJ, less of a State/party controlled organ,[813] and instead conceptualized as operating in the interest of the community of States.[814] However, the discretionary power of the Tribunal with regard to provisional measures is limited by the prohibition on prescribing them *proprio motu.*[815] Pursuant to Art. 290(3) UNCLOS the Tribunal

---

809 This is reflected in Art. 89(5) Rules of the Tribunal: "When a request for provisional measures has been made, the Tribunal may prescribe measures different in whole or in part from those requested". See also *Case concerning Land Reclamation by Singapore in and around the Straits of Johor (Malaysia v Singapore) Request for provisional measures (Order)* ITLOS Case No. 12 (8 October 2003), para. 101.

810 The rule that an adjudicating body cannot decide more than it has been asked to do.

811 See, e.g., Permanent Court of International Justice, *Series D. Acts and Documents Concerning the Organization of the Court – Second Addendum to No 2. Modification of the Rules* (A.W. Sijthoff's Leyden 1931), 185.

812 Laing, Edward A., 'Automation of International Judicial Bodies: A Preliminary Analysis', in: Chandrasekhara Rao, P. *et al.* (eds) *The International Tribunal for the Law of the Sea – Law and Practice* (Kluwer Law International The Hague 2001), 222-223.

813 Cf. Art. 41 ICJ Statute, which provides that "provisional measures … ought to be taken to preserve the respective *rights of either party.*" (Emphasis added.).

814 This reflects the broader shift in international law from a system of cooperation to a mechanism recognizing and preserving common values of the community of States. Wolfrum, Rüdiger, 'Provisional Measures of the International Tribunal for the Law of the Sea', in: Chandrasekhara Rao, P. *et al.* (eds) *The International Tribunal for the Law of the Sea – Law and Practice* (Kluwer Law International The Hague 2001), 176.

815 This question was the subject of intensive debate during the negotiations at the third conference: see Dupuy & Vignes (eds), *A Handbook on the New Law of the Sea – Volume 2*, 1379-1381.

may adopt these measures only "at the request of a party to the dispute", which reflects the rationale underlying all dispute settlement under UNCLOS, namely that only parties to a dispute may bring a case before the Tribunal.[816] A true compulsory judicial procedure before the ITLOS, in the sense of activating its jurisdiction even without States' subjection to it in every case, was never able to gather sufficient support among States' representatives at the third conference. There was nevertheless agreement that the Tribunal should be given independence, and in particular be able to operate independently of the parties.[817] In other words, the powers of the Tribunal, although comparatively extensive and progressive in the field of international law, are still ultimately bound by the initiative of the parties to a dispute.

Parallel to the authority to prescribe provisional measures the Tribunal, pursuant to Art. 292 UNCLOS, is entrusted (along with the other fora potentially applicable under Part XV UNCLOS) with the task of deciding on the prompt release of detained vessels and crews. This procedure enables the Tribunal to strike a balance between the internationalization of the regime governing navigation in the Exclusive Economic Zone and the protection of the rights of coastal States. As with the procedure regarding the prescription of provisional measures, although the spark must come from the States which may be parties in a prospective, but still at this stage avoidable, dispute, the influence of States over this power is limited, since an application for release may also be made "on behalf of" a State.[818]

4. Conclusions

In exercising its main function of settling disputes, the Tribunal itself determines whether a justiciable dispute is before it. The ITLOS is not institutionally linked to the UN. Instead it is part of a wider settlement system under UNCLOS, which also takes into account non-judicial dispute settlement mechanisms. The Tribunal may nevertheless in the exercise of its dispute settlement function touch upon issues that are simultaneously dealt with by one of the principal organs of the UN. In order to balance this overlap the relationship

816 Wolfrum, 'Provisional Measures of the International Tribunal for the Law of the Sea', 181. Cf. Art. 75 Rules of the ICJ which explicitly permits the ICJ "to examine *proprio motu* … the indication of provisional measures".

817 Dupuy & Vignes (eds), *A Handbook on the New Law of the Sea – Volume 2*, 1374.

818 Art. 292(2) UNCLOS.

between the UN and the ITLOS is based on *inter alia* an agreement pursuant to which the UN recognizes the Tribunal as an autonomous international judicial body. What is more, the ITLOS is a specialized Tribunal which does not aim at contributing to the further development of international law in general,[819] but instead is expected to settle disputes that may arise in the application of the law of the sea. This merits special procedures in which the Tribunal enjoys compulsory jurisdiction, namely interim measures of protection and the prompt release of crews and vessels. Here the decisions of the Tribunal serve the interests underlying the area of law which the Tribunal has been called upon to serve rather than any interests of the parties to a (potential) dispute.

IV. Structural Independence

1. The Relationship with other Organs Established under UNCLOS – the ITLOS and the ISA

The institutional structure established under UNCLOS reveals that the ITLOS was envisaged as an independent organ. The Tribunal is created under UNCLOS, an agreement resulting from a conference convened by the UN, but is nevertheless not an organ of the UN.[820] The relationship with the remaining organizational structure of the Convention is slightly more complicated. The principal body established by UNCLOS is the ISA[821],[822] which pursuant to Art. 157(1) UNCLOS is the "organization through which States Parties shall … organize and control activities in the Area [i.e. the area of the seabed and

819 Beyond the value the decisions have pursuant to Art. 38 ICJ Statute.

820 See *infra* Chapter E.IV(3).

821 The Authority consists of an Assembly, a Council and a Secretariat as its principal organs, and the Enterprise, which shall carry out activities in the Area directly, as well as the transporting, processing and marketing of minerals recovered from the Area. See further 'International Seabed Authority' available at <http://www.isa.org.jm/en/home> (last visited: 21 March 2014). See also Wood, Michael, 'International Seabed Authority (ISA)', in: Wolfrum, Rüdiger (ed) *The Max Planck Encyclopedia of Public International Law* (Oxford University Press Online Edition 2012).

822 Fleischhauer, Carl-August, 'The Relationship Between the International Court of Justice and the Newly Created International Tribunal for the Law of the Sea in Hamburg', in: von Bogdandy, Armin *et al.* (eds) *Max Planck Yearbook of United Nations Law – Volume 1* (Martinus Nijhoff Publishers Leiden 1997), 629.

ocean floor and subsoil thereof, beyond the limits of national jurisdiction[823]], particularly with a view to administering the resources of the Area."[824]

The Authority is itself an autonomous international organization,[825] distinct from any political or organizational superstructure, and in particular autonomous from the organizational set-up of the UN.[826] For long during the negotiations of the third conference the Authority was envisaged to be equipped with four organs, an Assembly, a Council, a Tribunal and a Secretariat.[827] The Tribunal thus envisaged to be linked to the Authority was to have special jurisdiction over disputes arising from the application of the part of the convention relating to the Area,[828] and was initially planned together with and in parallel to a new tribunal with more general jurisdiction regarding law of the sea disputes.[829] The main consideration in support of a separate tribunal for disputes relating to the Area was that a distinct forum for the adjudication of the new and rather complex, yet important, regime of the Area was able to guarantee the consistent and uniform interpretation of this law.[830] Eventually, it was not until a revised single negotiating text was presented on 23 November 1976 that this parallel of two new, separate judicial dispute settlement mechanisms was rejected in favour of the establishment of one new law of the sea tribunal with a treaty based, thus standing,

---

823 Art. 1(1)(1) UNCLOS.

824 See also Section 1 Subsection 1 Annex to the Agreement relating to the Implementation of Part XI of the United Nations Convention on the Law of the Sea of 10 December 1982 (adopted 28 July 1994, entered into force 28 July 1996) 1836 UNTS 41.

825 Wood, 'International Seabed Authority (ISA)', para. 1.

826 Wood, Michael, 'The International Seabed Authority – Fifth to Twelfth Sessions (1999-2006)', in: von Bogdandy, Armin *et al.* (eds) *Max Planck Yearbook of United Nations Law – Volume 11* (Martinus Nijhoff Publishers Leiden 2007), 49. Cf. the self-characterization of the ISA provided on its website (as of 21 March 2009): "The International Seabed Authority is an autonomous international organization established under the 1982 United Nations Convention on the Law of the Sea and the 1994 Agreement relating to the Implementation of Part XI of the United Nations Convention on the Law of the Sea."

827 See Third United Nations Conference on the Law of the Sea, *Revised single negotiating text (part I)* (6 May 1976) UN Doc. A/CONF.62/WP.8/REV.1/Part I, Art. 24.

828 Ibid, Art. 33(1)(a).

829 Cf. Third United Nations Conference on the Law of the Sea, *Informal single negotiating text, part I*, Art. 32.

830 Vitzthum, Wolfgang Graf, 'International Seabed Area', in: Wolfrum, Rüdiger (ed) *The Max Planck Encyclopedia of Public International Law* (Oxford University Press Online Edition 2012), para. 5.

seabed disputes chamber.[831] The establishment of a Seabed Disputes Chamber is provided for in Art. 186 UNCLOS and in Art. 14 Statute, which dissolves the Chamber as a judicial organ of the Authority and instead makes it a part of the new Tribunal.[832] The Tribunal itself stands independently of the Authority.[833] This is emphasized by the fact that the Authority does not have any functions relating to the ITLOS similar e.g. to those of the UNGA as regards the ICJ. The only possible point of contact between the two organs is that the Authority may in the future, pursuant to Art. 19 Statute, contribute to the costs of the Tribunal. This potential addition to the sources of financing of the Tribunal is, however, dependant on the prior approval of and determination by the primary financiers, the States Parties to UNCLOS.[834]

2. A Court Within the Court – The Special Status of the Seabed Disputes Chamber

As described above, the Seabed Dispute Chamber is not a separate international court. However, while the Chamber, as is suggested by its name, is part of the Tribunal and e.g. its members are selected by and from the members of the Tribunal,[835] it fulfils functions that are significantly different from those of the ITLOS at large. This special status testifies to the significance that UNCLOS attributes to the seabed regime. The Chamber is composed of 11 members, selected by a majority of the elected members of the Tribunal and from among them.[836] This ensures that members of the Chamber, like their colleagues on the Tribunal, are subject to the requirements regarding candidacy, election and qualification set out in the Statute. All members of the Chamber are selected every three years and may serve on the Chamber for only a maximum of two terms.[837] It is noteworthy that the Assembly of

---

831 Third United Nations Conference on the Law of the Sea, *Revised single negotiating text (part IV)* (3 November 1976) UN Doc. A/CONF.62/WP.9/REV.2, Art. 9, Art. 15 Annex II.

832 Nordquist (ed) *United Nations Convention on the Law of the Sea 1982: A Commentary – Volume V*, 361.

833 Fleischhauer, 'The Relationship Between the International Court of Justice and the Newly Created International Tribunal for the Law of the Sea in Hamburg', 629-630.

834 See on this *infra* Chapter E.IV(4).

835 Art. 35 Statute.

836 Art. 35(1) Statute.

837 Art. 35(2) Statute.

the Authority may adopt suggestions relating to the representation of the principal legal systems of the world and equitable geographical distribution in the composition of the Chamber.[838] In this sense, the Assembly takes on a function which for the ICJ is served by the electors, i.e. the UNGA and the UNSC.[839] It may also be interpreted as a remnant from the original idea of the Chamber as the judicial organ of the Authority, i.e. as a tribunal responsible for disputes concerning the interpretation and application of the seabed regime. Yet the recommendations on the composition of the Chamber – which so far have not been formulated – cannot *prima facie* be said to have a negative influence on the independence of the Chamber as they are merely "recommendations", thus not binding on the actual electoral body. They are moreover intended to be of only a general nature, which is likely to exclude references to individuals.[840]

Further links between the Authority and the Chamber are established through the right for the Authority to appear before the Chamber,[841] and that its rules, regulations and procedures shall be applicable law before the Chamber.[842] The potential exercise of a right to *locus standi* of the Authority before the organ entrusted with the adjudication of seabed disputes was one of the main reasons for dislocating the specialized seabed tribunal under the Authority and transforming it into a chamber of the Tribunal. Under the earlier model, the Authority might have appeared before its own judicial organ as a party, which would seriously have called into question the impartiality of the procedures.[843] Under the current model, however, the Chamber is not part of the organizational set-up of the Authority, a fact which allays

838 Art. 35(2) Statute.

839 Cf. Art. 9 ICJ Statute.

840 Art. 35(2) Statute reads as follows: "In the selection of the members of the Chamber, the representation of the principal legal systems of the world and equitable geographical distribution shall be assured. The Assembly of the Authority may adopt *recommendations of a general nature* relating to such representation and distribution." (Emphasis added.).

841 Art. 37 Statute.

842 Art. 38(a) Statute.

843 Interestingly, the lack of a separation of adjudication and administration was a problem encountered for long in some European municipal legal systems, such as the Scandinavian ones. See further, Nergelius, Joakim & Zimmermann, Dominik, 'Judicial Independence in Sweden', in: Seibert-Fohr, Anja (ed) *Judicial Independence in Transition: Strengthening the Rule of Law in the OSCE Region* (Springer Heidelberg 2012).

all *prima facie* threats to impartiality potentially arising from the appearance of the Authority before the Chamber.

In principal, the Chamber is the compulsory forum for disputes regarding the Area, to which the Authority, which is responsible for the administration and protection of the seabed area, can bring actions against Member States in order to settle disputes concerning the seabed. The exclusive jurisdiction *ratione materiae* of the Chamber encompasses the following:

(I) disputes between contracting States concerning the interpretation or application of Part XI of UNCLOS and the Annexes relating thereto, subject to the ability of the dispute to be referred to a special chamber of the ITLOS;[844]

(II) disputes between a contracting State and the Authority, regarding acts or omissions that violate Part XI of UNCLOS or the Annexes relating thereto or of rules, regulations and procedures of the Authority;[845]

(III) disputes between a contracting State and the Authority regarding the latter's acts alleged to be in excess of jurisdiction or a misuse of power;[846]

(IV) disputes between parties to a contract concerning either the interpretation or application of a relevant contract or a plan of work[847] or acts or omissions of a party to the contract relating to activities in the Area and directed to the other party or directly affecting its legitimate interests;[848]

(V) disputes between the Authority and a prospective contractor concerning the refusal of a contract or a legal issue arising in the negotiation of the contract;[849] or

(VI) disputes between a contracting Party and the Authority concerning the latter's responsibility or liability for any damage arising out of wrongful acts in the conduct of its operations.[850]

When these variations of exclusive jurisdiction are read together, the impression arises that the Chamber's jurisdiction is strikingly similar to that of ad-

---

844 Art. 187(a) UNCLOS, read in conjunction with Art. 188(1)(a) UNCLOS.

845 Art. 187(b)(i) UNCLOS.

846 Art. 187(b)(ii) UNCLOS.

847 At the request of any party such a dispute may be referred to binding commercial arbitration; cf. Art. 188(2) UNCLOS.

848 Art. 187(c) UNCLOS.

849 Art. 187(d) UNCLOS.

850 Art. 187(e) UNCLOS, read in conjunction with Annex III, Art. 22 UNCLOS.

ministrative courts in civil law countries, in particular regarding paragraphs (II), (III), (V), and (VI) above: specialization in settling disputes concerning the exercise of public power, and particularly ascertaining whether official acts of a global administrative body (the Authority) are consistent with applicable law (UNCLOS). The evaluation of whether the Authority's rules, regulations and procedures are in conformity with the provisions of the UNCLOS, an exercise which may become necessary for the Chamber, is furthermore analogous to the judicial review (*Normenkontrolle*) that is part of the remit of many national judiciaries. Seen from this perspective, it is all the more important that the Chamber was conceived as a court within the Tribunal which is itself autonomous, and not part of the Authority, the decisions of which it may be called upon to review.

In this context, it must be emphasised that pursuant to Art. 189 UNCLOS the Chamber "shall have no jurisdiction with regard to the exercise by the Authority of its discretionary powers", and that it in no case shall "substitute its discretion for that of the Authority" when exercising its jurisdiction regarding the Area. This disconnection between its administrative and judicial roles should be welcomed in the interest of a clear separation of political execution of discretionary power in the exercise of the Authority's functions and the judicial function served by the Chamber.

Finally, the above-mentioned widening of the applicable law also to include rules, regulations and procedures adopted by the Authority[851] cannot be seen as an infringement of or potential threat to the independence of the Chamber/the ITLOS in the administration of justice, as all interpretation and application of the law remains within the discretion of the Chamber. Art. 38(a) Statute instead must be interpreted as a practical necessity due to the Chamber's quasi administrative jurisdiction pursuant to Art. 187(b)(i) Statute, i.e. the jurisdiction over disputes between a State Party and the Authority concerning acts or omissions of either one alleged to be in violation of *inter alia* rules, regulations and procedures of the Authority. The same holds true for the obligation of the Chamber to apply "the terms of contracts concerning activities in the Area in matters relating to those contracts".[852]

In sum, there are no direct dependencies between the Chamber and the Authority. Instead an analysis of the history of the origins of the Tribunal and the Authority reveals that the final solution of a separate seabed disputes

851 Art. 38(a) Statute.
852 Art. 38(b) Statute, read in conjunction with Art. 187(c) Statute.

chamber within the ITLOS was to a large extent, besides financial reasons and the interest in uniform and consistent jurisprudence in this field, based on eliminating concerns of a lack of independence.

3. The ITLOS as Part of an Independent Treaty Regime – Consequences for its Self-Conception as an Independent Tribunal

UNCLOS – and with it the establishment of UNCLOS' comprehensive dispute settlement system contained in part XV – is the result of diplomatic conferences of plenipotentiaries specifically convened for that purpose.[853] Although the three conferences on the law of the sea were convened by the UN, more precisely by the UNGA,[854] and carried the reference to their initiator in the official name of the conferences,[855] they cannot be seen as organs of the UN.[856] The conferences are on the contrary to be understood as international conferences governed by international law, and as such independent bodies in the sense that they possessed temporary powers and authorities that are independent of the convening organization.[857] All organs of the conferences (such as the committees and the negotiating groups) reported

853 See generally Rosenne, Shabtai & Gebhard, Julia, 'Conferences on the Law of the Sea', in: Wolfrum, Rüdiger (ed) *The Max Planck Encyclopedia of Public International Law* (Oxford University Press Online Edition 2012).

854 See UNGA, *International Conference of Plenipotentiaries to Examine the Law of the Sea*; UNGA, *Convening of a Second UN Conference on the Law of the Sea*; UNGA, *Reservation Exclusively for Peaceful Purposes of the Sea-Bed and the Ocean Floor, and the Subsoil Thereof, Underlying the High Seas beyond the Limits of Present National Jurisdiction and Use of their Resources in the Interests of Mankind, and Convening of a Conference on the Law of the Sea* (17 December 1970) UN Doc. A/RES/2750 (XXV).

855 Beginning with the first plenary meeting the conference had the official name of a "Third United Nations Conference on the Law of the Sea"; cf. Third United Nations Conference on the Law of the Sea, *1st Plenary meeting* (3 December 1973) UN Doc. A/CONF.62/SR.1, para. 1.

856 On the rationale of utilizing the UN, and in particular the UNGA, as the convening body for international conferences see Schermers, Henry G. & Blokker, Niels, *International Institutional Law: Unity within Diversity* (Nijhoff Boston 4th edn. 2003), 1186-1187.

857 Sabel, Robbie, 'Conferences and Congresses, International', in: Wolfrum, Rüdiger (ed) *The Max Planck Encyclopedia of Public International Law* (Oxford University Press Online Edition 2012), para. 7.

to the Plenary of the conference only.[858] Furthermore, all three law of the sea conferences were governed by their own rules of procedure and general international law, and thus followed the established premise that international conferences have an independent right to adopt their own rules of procedure.[859] Indeed the president of the third law of the sea conference proposed that the UNGA rules of procedure be applied to the conference only as long as it had not itself adopted its own rules of procedure. Several statements by States' representatives further confirm the view that the conference was indeed going to adopt and apply its own rules and not be subject to rules stemming from the UN[860] which, if at all, were to be applied following a case-by-case decision taken by consensus among the representatives.[861]

The functional autonomy from any organizational framework in general, and the UN in particular, is further reflected in the condition that the invitation to the third conference on the law of the sea was not restricted to the members of the UN[862] but was instead based on an *ad hoc* determination and explicitly included Member States of specialized agencies or the International Atomic Energy Agency, States Parties to the ICJ Statute, the Republic of Guinea-Bissau and the Democratic Republic of Viet-Nam.[863] This was not least a

858 Dupuy & Vignes (eds), *A Handbook on the New Law of the Sea – Volume 1*, 165.

859 Cf. Dunn, Frederick Sherwood, *The Practice and Procedure of International Conferences* (Johns Hopkins Press Baltimore 1929), 17; Sabel, Robbie, *Procedure at International Conferences: A Study of the Rules of Procedure at the UN and at Inter-Governmental Conferences* (Cambridge University Press Cambridge 2006), 22-26.

860 See, e.g., the statement made by the representative of Japan, Third United Nations Conference on the Law of the Sea, 5th *Plenary meeting* (11 December 1973) UN Doc. A/CONF.62/SR.5, para. 18: Mr. Ogiso (Japan) recalled that the President had stated, at the end of the previous meeting, that the rules of procedure of the UNGA would automatically apply until the Conference had adopted its own rules of procedure. He wished to make it clear that, since the Conference was totally independent of the UNGA, and that since no understanding had been reached on the provisional application of the rules of procedure of the UNGA, such a procedure would be acceptable only if the Conference as a whole agreed to the President's proposal.

861 Ibid, paras. 18-19, 41.

862 This is of interest insofar as at the time of the first plenary meeting of the conference, the UN had 131 member States, compared to today's 193; 'United Nations Member States – Growth in United Nations Membership, 1945-Present' available at <http://www.un.org/en/members/growth.shtml> (last visited: 21 March 2014).

863 See UNGA, *Reservation Exclusively for Peaceful Purposes of the Sea-Bed and the Ocean Floor, and the Subsoil Thereof, Underlying the High Seas beyond the Limits of Present National Jurisdiction and use of their Resources in the Interests of*

tribute to the "desirability of achieving universality of participation in the Conference" serving the overall mandate "to adopt a convention dealing with *all matters* relating to the law of the sea" (emphasis added).[864] In addition to those invited to participate actively in the conference, numerous other actors, such as inter-governmental and non-governmental organizations and the United Nations Council for Namibia, were given observer status pursuant to UNGA Resolution 3067. Furthermore, various other actors, such as trust territories, associated States and national liberation movements, were allowed to participate at the conference.[865] Thus the group of participants was not restricted by the criterion of statehood. Using the conventional categorization in international law, the third conference may thus be classified as a diplomatic conference with universal participation convened for the purpose of drafting a multilateral agreement.

Whereas the conference itself did not have the power legally to bind States, any treaty adopted upon its completion was nevertheless an independent treaty regime which bound those States that fulfilled all relevant requirements under national and international law to be bound by an international agreement. Moreover, any organ established under such a treaty is – in principle – equally independent and in particular independent of any organization convening the treaty conference.[866] In other words, the ITLOS, which was established by UNCLOS, is independent of the various (principal) organs of the UN. This does not imply, however, that the principal organs of the UN will not play any role in the activities of the ITLOS. For example, the exercise of the UNSC's functions under the UNC enables a State to declare that it does not accept procedures to be taken before the ITLOS in an affected

Mankind, and Convening of the Third United Nations Conference on the Law of the Sea, para. 7.

864 See ibid, paras. 3, 7.

865 See Dupuy & Vignes (eds), *A Handbook on the New Law of the Sea – Volume 1*, 165.

866 It should be noted that with the signing of the Agreement on Cooperation and Relationship between the United Nations and the International Tribunal for the Law of the Sea, the ITLOS could have been declared a specialized agency of the UN. Yet such a relationship was not considered to be appropriate for the Tribunal; see Nordquist, Myron H. & Moore, John Norton (eds), *Current marine environmental issues and the International Tribunal for the Law of the Sea – twenty-fifth annual conference of the Center for Oceans Law and Policy, University of Virginia School of Law, held from March 16 – 19, 2001, in Hamburg, Germany* (Nijhoff Publishers The Hague 2001), 46.

dispute.[867] Furthermore, the geographical groups established by the UNGA are used in determining the distribution of seats on the Tribunal's bench,[868] and contributions to the budget of the Tribunal are based on existing UN arrangements.[869] Further, the President of the Tribunal regularly reports to the plenary meetings of the UNGA, usually under the agenda item "Oceans and the law of the sea".[870] But the above-mentioned independence does mean that influence of a more direct kind exerted by the principal organs or the UN, for example on the composition of the bench of the Tribunal by the implicit guarantee that permanent members of the UNSC will be reserved a seat, can and must be excluded.

4. The Composition of the Tribunal

a) The Elected Members of the Tribunal

The central provision establishing the composition of the ITLOS is Art. 2 Statute which lays down that the Tribunal is to be "composed of a body of 21 independent members, elected from among persons enjoying the highest reputation for fairness and integrity and of recognized competence in the field of the law of the sea." The size of the Tribunal's bench is considerably larger than the 15 judges constituting the bench of the ICJ[871] and even than

867 See Art. 298(1)(c) UNCLOS.

868 Art. 3(2) ITLOS Statute. Cf. *infra* Chapter E.IV(5)(b)(3).

869 Furthermore, much like in the first meetings of the ICTY, the UNSG through his representative, the Legal Counsel of the UN, presided over the meetings of the ITLOS until a president had been elected in accordance with Art. 12 Statute; Nordquist & Moore (eds), *Current marine environmental issues and the International Tribunal for the Law of the Sea – twenty-fifth annual conference of the Center for Oceans Law and Policy, University of Virginia School of Law, held from March 16 – 19, 2001, in Hamburg, Germany*, 48.

870 E.g. the President of the Tribunal delivered a statement to the plenary meeting of the UNGA on 7 December 2010, In his statement, the President referred to the "developments which had taken place with respect to the Tribunal since the previous session of the Assembly, ... reported on the Tribunal's capacity-building programmes, including regional workshops on dispute settlement and the law of the sea, an annual training programme for government officials and researchers on dispute settlement under the Convention, and the Tribunal's internship programme." United Nations Convention on the Law of the Sea – Meeting of States Parties, *Annual report of the International Tribunal for the Law of the Sea for 2010*, para. 67.

871 Art. 3 ICJ Statute.

the 18 judges of the ICC.[872] But whereas the increase in the number of judges can be interpreted as a development characterizing the continued proliferation of international courts – where newer courts tend to be composed of a higher number of judges – and attributable e.g. to the increase in the number of actors involved in shaping international law, the composition of the ITLOS' bench has a more specific explanation. During the drafting of UNCLOS, the number of judges on the ITLOS was gradually raised from nine,[873] 11,[874] 15[875] to finally be agreed at 21.[876] The constant justification for this increase was the consideration that a larger number of judges is better suited to ensuring the speedy dispatch of the work of the Tribunal and to enabling the forming of the Seabed Dispute Chamber and other standing *ad hoc* chambers. As mentioned earlier, the Tribunal is a specialized court dealing with issues relating to the law of the sea, which is reflected in the demand for competence in the field of the law of the sea that every judge must possess.[877] The highly technical nature of this area of law, which involves difficult scientific and practically relevant questions, makes it necessary to make the Tribunal as flexible as possible. In no other way can the Tribunal meet the expectations of efficiency that the parties have of it. A Tribunal which does not provide for this flexibility, which would not of itself be able to meet the needs inherent in many of the cases brought before it, would be more prone to political influences that come in the guise of remedies for practical hardships.[878] The earlier mentioned Seabed Dispute Chamber which, according to Art. 35(1) Statute, is to be composed of 11 judges, would, in times of a high workload, already commit a majority of the judges and in effect leave merely 10 judges

872 Art. 36 Rome Statute. Cf. *infra* Appendix: International Courts – A Chart.

873 See Third United Nations Conference on the Law of the Sea, *Informal single negotiating text, part I*, Art. 32(4).

874 See Third United Nations Conference on the Law of the Sea, *Revised single negotiating text (part I)*, Art. 33(5).

875 See Third United Nations Conference on the Law of the Sea, *Informal single negotiating text (part IV)* (21 July 1975) UN Doc. A/CONF.62/WP.9, Art. 2(1).

876 See Third United Nations Conference on the Law of the Sea, *Revised single negotiating text (part IV)*, Art. 2(1).

877 Art. 2(1) *in fine* Statute. See on this requirement *infra* Chapter E.IV(3)(b)(1).

878 The Rules of the Tribunal address the concerns regarding its effectiveness for example in Rule 46 ("Time-limits for the completion of steps in the proceedings may be fixed by assigning a specified period but shall always indicate definite dates. *Such time-limits shall be as short as the character of the case permits*." Emphasis added.) and Rule 49 ("The proceedings before the Tribunal shall be conducted without unnecessary delay or expense.").

for the Tribunal itself. This would make the simultaneous sitting of the chamber and the Tribunal in their full required composition (the quorum of the Tribunal is 11 judges)[879] impossible, unless the quorum of the chamber were not at the same time limited in Art. 35(7) Statute to seven judges. Yet it must furthermore be taken into account that additional chambers may become necessary (both special chambers of the ITLOS[880] and *ad hoc* chambers under the Seabed Disputes Chamber[881]), and indeed have been established at the Tribunal.[882] Currently the Tribunal has the following chambers:

(I) an annually constituted chamber of summary procedure, composed of five judges;[883]

(II) a chamber for fisheries disputes, composed of nine members;[884]

(III) the chamber for marine environment disputes, composed of seven members;[885]

(IV) the chamber for maritime delimitation disputes, composed of 11 members;[886] and

(V) the special chamber to deal with the *Case concerning the Conservation and Sustainable Exploitation of Swordfish Stocks in the South-Eastern Pacific Ocean (Chile/European Community)*[887] consisting of five judges.[888]

Further *ad hoc* chambers may be established in particular cases and are to be composed of three or more of the Tribunal's members.[889] Due to the relatively low workload of the Tribunal so far this option has not been used extensively. Yet in view of these considerations and in the interest of maintaining the Tribunal's efficient functioning the number of 21 judges must at least be considered not to be an unduly high number.

879 Art. 13(1) Statute.
880 Art. 15 Statute.
881 Art. 36 Statute.
882 Although the caseload of the Tribunal, at least at the time of writing, does not appear to highlight this problem.
883 Art. 15(3)-(4) Statute.
884 Art. 15(1) Statute.
885 Art. 15(1) Statute.
886 Art. 15(1) Statute.
887 *Case concerning the Conservation and Sustainable Exploitation of Swordfish Stocks in the South-Eastern Pacific Ocean (Chile/European Union) Order 2009/1* ITLOS Case No. 7 (16 December 2009).
888 Art. 15(2) Statute.
889 Art. 15(2) Statute.

Another reason for the size of the ITLOS' bench is linked to the requirement of attaining "representation of the principal legal systems of the world and equitable geographical distribution" of the seats.[890] Whereas the demand for an equitable geographical distribution reminds of the provision in Art. 9 ICJ Statute,[891] the ITLOS' Statute is more detailed when demanding that "[t]here shall be no fewer than three members from each geographical group as established by the [UNGA]."[892] This provision, which is a component in the election process and thus deserves to be analysed in greater detail later, makes a certain number of judges unavoidable. The UNGA has established five different geographical groups,[893] which thus fixes the minimum number of ITLOS judges at 15; yet in this calculation still no considerations have been taken into account other than mere equal representation between the groups. Thus, if the bench of the ITLOS is to follow the geographical distribution of the UNGA and be a representation of those regions, the number of judges must necessarily exceed 15.

It is questionable whether such considerations can at all, not just in regard to the ITLOS, be brought into conformity with a desire to establish a court as an independent organ. If representation of legal systems is to be taken seriously, it implies particular expectations by those who have established this requirement; expectations that are likely to be unrelated to the particular needs of the cases that come before the Tribunal. It must be hoped that judges do not consider this as a calling which would conflict with and supersede the law the Tribunal is actually called upon to apply and limited to applying.[894]

890 Art. 2(2) Statute. Nordquist (ed) *United Nations Convention on the Law of the Sea 1982: A Commentary – Volume V*, 341.

891 "[R]epresentation of the main forms of civilization and of the principal legal systems of the world should be assured".

892 Art. 3(2) Statute.

893 'United Nations Regional Groups of Member States' available at <http://www.un.org/depts/DGACM/RegionalGroups.shtml> (last visited: 21 March 2014).

894 According to Art. 293 UNCLOS the applicable law for the ITLOS is "this Convention and other rules of international law not incompatible with this Convention." The Tribunal also has the power "to decide a case ex aequo et bono, *if the parties so agree*." (Emphasis added.)

b) The Nomination and Election Procedure – Normative Framework and Practical Implementation

(1) The Required Qualifications of Judges

The system of nomination and election of judges to the ITLOS is similar to that with regard to the ICJ. Yet certain particularities stand out and provide for a special conceptualization with regard to the ITLOS. As stated, Art. 2 Statute requires that the judges be independent, enjoy the highest reputation for fairness and integrity and hold recognized competence in the field of the law of the sea. The ITLOS is the only court studied here which does not require that its judges also hold competences necessary for national judicial office.[895]

It may be questioned whether limiting the legal requirement for membership to "recognized competence in the law of the sea" is too narrow,[896] considering the importance of general international law in the work of the Tribunal. Insofar as knowledge of the applicable law may be considered a deterrent to allowing undue influence on the judicial exercise, this issue is relevant also when assessing the actual independence of the judges of the ITLOS. The impression arises that this limited demand for legal expertise is not only an overt accentuation of the special character of the ITLOS, but perhaps also a hidden attempt to allow for the inclusion on the bench of individuals who have "competence in the field of the law of the sea" but who are nonetheless not fully qualified jurists. Without suggesting that only trained lawyers are capable of being independent, expectations regarding concrete protection mechanisms undoubtedly grow considerably if individuals with a more *political* vitae are allowed to serve on the Tribunal. Such covert politicization is detrimental to the perceived independence of a judicial organ, due to the connoted link between a pertinent candidate and the political entities responsible for nominating and electing the judges.

The requirement of independence in Art. 2 Statute is, like its corresponding inclusion in Art. 2 ICJ Statute, above all a declaratory provision. But whereas few substantive guidelines can be deduced from the requirement when analysing the wording alone, some conclusions can be drawn from a

895 See Appendix: International Courts – A Chart.

896 For a critical assessment see Wood, Michael, 'The International Tribunal for the Law of the Sea and General International Law' (2007) 22 International Journal of Marine and Coastal Law 3.

systematic interpretation. Firstly, it must be understood as a confirmation of the existence of a fundamental requirement of independence being addressed to every individual agreeing to become a member of the ITLOS' bench. Secondly, it is suggested that the requirement of independence is one that is primarily, yet logically not exclusively, a requirement for the individual judge, his personality and individual performance, and not for the Tribunal as an institution. Thirdly, the use of the general term *independence* in an early provision of the Statute implies that some suggestions as to its concretization may be expected from the following provisions of the Statute, as well as from the rules of procedure that assist the Tribunal in creating the framework for the effective exercise of its functions. Hence it is necessary to look at the concretizations of this criterion, in particular the regulation of incompatible activities and fundamental irremovability during tenure, a task that will be undertaken in the following sections.

As with the system applied with regard to the ICJ, there is no direct mechanism that can enforce compliance with these personal requirements. Instead the criteria in Art. 2 Statute must be interpreted as mere guidelines and suggestions for States when they make their nominations and subsequently elect the members. In other words, they ultimately amount to non-binding instructions. The only mechanism that may lend some force to the criteria and which provides the Tribunal with a power autonomously to ensure that its members fulfil them is the ability to remove a judge form office in accordance with the requirements laid down in Art. 9 Statute. This provision will thus be expounded in greater detail below.[897]

(2) The Procedure for the Making of Nominations – The Discretion of States

Each State Party to UNCLOS may nominate a maximum of two people for election to the bench of the ITLOS.[898] The only limitation that the Statute lays upon States Parties in choosing those candidates is that they have the qualifications prescribed in Art. 2 Statute. Neither the Statute nor the Rules of the Tribunal contain further provisions or even restrictions on how and/or who the States should choose as their nominees. This system thus appears

897 See *infra* Chapter E.V(2).
898 Art. 4(1) Statute.

to be still more in favour of allowing direct effect for States' interest than the system of nominations made for the bench of the ICJ, which interposes the national groups in the PCA. The inclusion of the national groups as an additional level between the nominating States and the UNGA, as shown above,[899] served the desire to make the nominations less dependent on the momentary political constellations within a State and to guarantee the choosing of individuals who indeed possess the necessary personal qualifications.[900] Although the national groups fulfil few tasks other than making the nominations and thus still provide idle ground for the direct influence of States, the nomination procedure with regard to the ITLOS is still more rigidly in the hands of States and almost wholly undisturbed by external guidelines. As the qualifications prescribed in Art. 2 Statute must be seen as minimum requirements, there is in particular no guarantee that nominations are made with the prime concern of the functioning of an organ of the international legal system in mind. Instead the system pays tribute to the important role that States play (as parties) as regards the ITLOS.

Essentially, the result of an unregulated national nomination process is excessive discretion for States: on the one hand, if a State is willing to subject its own nomination process to transparent, objective or even just law-based procedures, then an important step is taken towards ensuring that the bench of the ITLOS is made up of independent judges. On the other hand, if a State sees in the scantily regulated nomination procedure pursuant to the Statute an invitation to propose politically motivated nominees, then it will be almost impossible to guarantee that the Tribunal is an independent judicial institution. Although little is known about national nomination processes for international judicial office, studies have shown that most countries follow informal nominations in which few criteria are mentioned and even fewer followed, that little outside consultation takes place and that a lack of transparency limits the knowledge about the entire process to a few insiders.[901] This path is all the more dangerous as "[t]he approach of each state is influenced by

---

899 *Supra* Chapter D.V(2)(b).

900 Cf. e.g. Rosenne, *The World Court – What it is and how it Works*, 55.

901 For a broad overview see Mackenzie, et al., *Selecting International Judges: Principle, Process, and Politics*, 63-99. Some countries have gone so far as to legislate to regulate the nomination process. See, e.g., the Slovenian 'Law on Nomination of Judges from the Republic of Slovenia to International Tribunals/Courts (17 July 2001)' available at <http://www.iccnow.org/documents/SloveniaLaw.pdf> (last visited: 21 March 2014).

its domestic political culture and the structure of its domestic institutions",[902] leading to a dilution of the standards applied to finding the judges for the same court. Studies have further indicated that the right political affiliations do indeed make it more likely to obtain a nomination to an international court, that access to the diplomatic corps enables individuals to form relationships supportive of nominations and that party politics can be essential.[903] But is then the lack of transparency in and the state-centeredness of the national nomination procedure a threat to the independent functioning of the Tribunal? To the extent that the goal of independence is the ideal of adjudication without any political influence, this question must be answered in the affirmative. Although there is no necessary connection between a state-controlled nomination process and a dependent judge, individuals who have been chosen pursuant to such a system are instilled with the incitement to feel commitments *vis-à-vis* this system for their nomination, rather than attributing their position to the objective competences and accomplishments over which they had the major personal influence through their professional career path.

It may be that, like what applies to the ICJ, the functioning of the ITLOS, being largely based on the willingness of States to subject themselves to the Tribunal's rule, mandates certain trade-offs.[904] Conversations between the author and judges of international courts suggest that international judges attribute major importance to the fact that in particular the procedures before

902 Centre for International Courts and Tribunals & University College London, *Selecting International Judges: Principle, Process and Politics – Discussion Paper* (2008) available at <http://www.ucl.ac.uk/laws/cict/docs/Selecting_Int_Judges.pdf> (last visited: 21 March 2014), para. 5.2.

903 Mackenzie, et al., *Selecting International Judges: Principle, Process, and Politics*, 78-84; Terris, et al., *The International Judge – An Introduction to the Men and Women who Decide the World's Cases*, 23-26.

904 This is also a conclusion which the author has made from an interview with a judge of one of the international courts the subject of the present study (who will remain anonymous). According to this judge, the procedures before the ICJ and the ITLOS in particular are based on consensus between States. It would not be feasible to force upon States a judge whom that State is not in favour of. Any attempt to do so would result in an increased recourse to arbitration, where the possibilities for the parties to influence both the composition and the procedure are much larger. It must thus be acknowledged that there is competition between institutionalized international judicial adjudication and arbitration. This competitive condition must have a formative impact on institutionalized dispute settlement, unless this arbitration (again) becomes the main form of judicial dispute settlement.

the ICJ and the ITLOS are based on consensus between States and that it thus would not be feasible to force upon States a judge they are not in favour of. Any attempt to do so would result in an increased recourse to arbitration, where the chances for the parties to influence both the composition and the procedure are far greater. Whereas it must be acknowledged that there is competition between institutionalized international judicial adjudication and arbitration, and that the success of international courts is historically linked to the fate of arbitration, such an argument is not able to justify the lack of structured national nomination procedures and the nearness of politics and (potential) candidates for the bench of international courts in general. The competitive condition must instead have a formative impact on institutionalized dispute settlement, unless arbitration is (again) strengthened as the judicial dispute settlement form of choice for States.

Since the relevance of a wide discretion for States to shape their nomination systems, and the consequential risks for arbitrariness and politicization, is a recurring issue, it will be dealt with in more detail in a later context where more material and especially practice is available for evaluation, namely regarding nominations to the ECtHR.[905]

(3) The Election of Judges – Regulating the Influence of States on the Composition of the ITLOS

The system of elections to the bench of the ITLOS reminds one in many ways of the system used at the ICJ, and may therefore be subjected to the same criticism that was raised in that context. Like ICJ judges, the judges of the ITLOS are elected for a renewable period of nine years.[906] Whereas Art. 2 Statute establishes the personal qualifications that are required of the

905 See further *infra* Chapter H.IV(3).

906 Art. 5(1) Statute. At the first elections to the tribunal, however, one third of the members (i.e. seven judges) were elected for six years, and one third for three years. The names of the judges affected by this regulation were chosen by lot (Art. 15(2) Statute). This system was inherited from the ICJ and serves the purpose of facilitating elections every three years of one third of the members. By this system the Tribunal avoids having to remove and change the entire bench, which would run counter to the interest of the continuity and reliability of the Tribunal.

members of the bench,[907] the nomination and election procedure itself is laid down in Art. 4 Statute and further clarified by the Rules of the Tribunal. That provision makes the distinction, with regard to the pre-election phase, between initial and subsequent elections to the Tribunal's bench. Only in the pre-election phase of first elections is the UNSG involved in the process. All the functions that he holds in this regard, the written invitation to the States Parties to submit their nominations, the preparation of a list of all nominated persons, and the submission of that list to the States Parties,[908] are in subsequent elections taken over by the Registrar of the Tribunal. Only the convening of the meetings, including the regular meetings for the elections, pursuant to Rules 3(1), 4(1) and 5(1) Rules of Procedure for Meetings of States Parties[909] read together with Art. 319(2)(e) UNCLOS[910] is still notified by the UNSG.[911] The change that is envisaged in the administration of the pre-election phase of the elections between the first and following elections shows the Tribunal's intention to move as far as possible away from reliance on outside authorities for the purpose of administrative services. This must be welcomed as continued administration by an external body would unnecessarily question the autonomous standing of the Tribunal *vis-à-vis* an organ that otherwise has no affiliation with the Tribunal and raise the question why the Tribunal was not equipped with the necessary infrastructure and financial means to supervise elections.

The election itself is conducted by secret ballot during a meeting of the States Parties,[912] which follows the usual practice in international courts but

---

907 The Statute uses the terms *members* and *judges* without distinction, see Nordquist (ed) *United Nations Convention on the Law of the Sea 1982: A Commentary – Volume V*, 342.

908 Art. 4(2) Statute.

909 United Nations Convention on the Law of the Sea – Meeting of States Parties, *Rules of Procedure for Meetings of States Parties* (24 January 2005) SPLOS/2/Rev. 4.

910 "In addition to his functions as depositary, the Secretary-General shall: … (e) convene necessary meetings of States Parties in accordance with this Convention."

911 Art. 4(4) Statute provided the States Parties to UNCLOS with the ability to change the system of the UNSG as the entity convening the meetings for the purpose of the elections. This may be explained by the fact that the States Parties still wanted the UNSG to play a certain role, especially when it came to cooperation between the ITLOS and the UN. As expressed by the Agreement on Cooperation and Relationship between the United Nations and the International Tribunal for the Law of the Sea certain cooperation between the UN (through the UNSG) and the ITLOS is provided for in order to coordinate the overlapping jurisdiction between the two.

912 Art. 4(4) Statute.

is not e.g. expressly mentioned in the Statute of the ICJ. States Parties alone are allowed to vote, and every State Party has one vote for every seat that is vacant and balloted upon.[913] Only if two-thirds of the States Parties are present at the meeting can elections be held. The necessary majority to be elected is the largest number of votes and a two-thirds majority of the States Parties present and voting, provided that such majority includes a majority of the States Parties.[914] If a seat cannot be filled at a first round of balloting, further rounds will follow. However, in this regard it must be noted that the ITLOS' Statute does not provide for detailed regulation of these follow-up procedures, as e.g. the ICJ Statute does.[915] Instead, pursuant to Art. 4(4) Statute the procedure of subsequent elections is to be decided by the States Parties.[916] However, as for example the majority requirements for elections are established in the Statute itself, they may be interpreted as being exempt from States' ability to decide on the procedure. So far no attempts have been made to change the majority requirements in subsequent rounds of voting, although several rounds of elections do occur.[917] The procedure for filling vacancies is regulated in Art. 6 Statute, which provides that the method is to follow that of the first elections with the alteration that the Registrar shall proceed to issue the invitations to the States Parties.

The distribution of seats between States follows established rules. No two members of the Tribunal may be nationals of the same State,[918] which assists in adhering to the requirements of Art. 2(2) Statute, that the principal legal systems of the world are represented on the Tribunal and that an equitable geographical distribution is assured. Furthermore, Art. 3(2) Statute establishes a certain minimum representation of the geographical groups, by stating that

---

913 United Nations Convention on the Law of the Sea – Meeting of States Parties, *First Elections of the Members of the International Tribunal for the Law of the Sea* (31 July 1996) SPLOS/L.3/REV.1, paras. 7 and 10.

914 Art. 4(4) *in fine* Statute.

915 Cf. Arts. 11-12 ICJ Statute.

916 Nordquist (ed) *United Nations Convention on the Law of the Sea 1982: A Commentary – Volume V*, 347.

917 During the last triennial elections on 13 June 2008, the two judges for the African States were elected only in the second and third rounds of elections (see 'States Parties to the Convention on Law of the Sea Elect Seven Members of International Tribunal as They Begin Eighteenth Meeting' <http://www.un.org/News/Press/docs/2008/sea1901.doc.htm> (last visited: 21 March 2014)). None of the candidates put forward in the first round and only one candidate suggested in the second round was able to obtain a two-thirds majority of the votes.

918 Art. 3(1) Statute.

the Tribunal shall have "no fewer than three members from each geographical group as established by the General Assembly of the United Nations." This concretisation of Art. 2(2) Statute does not exist in the ICJ Statute, which may be justified by the lower number of judges serving on that court and thus the smaller risk of a shift in the majority ratios of geographical distribution. The exact distribution between the geographical groups further follows a key laid down by the meeting of the States Parties for the purpose of the first elections,[919] which was changed in a decision by the Meeting of States Parties of 26 June 2009[920] and became effective with the triennial elections held in 2011 to be the following:

(I) five members from the Group of African States;
(II) five members from the Group of Asian States;
(III) three members from the Group of Eastern European States;
(IV) four members from the Group of Latin American and Caribbean States (GRULAC);
(V) three members from the Group of Western European and other States (WEOG); and
(VI) the remaining one member from among the Group of African States, the Group of Asian States and the Group of Western European and other States.

These rather detailed regulations are intended to provide a certain minimum representation on the bench of the different regions. In view of the significant majorities that are necessary for the election of a judge (see above) it was feared that the developing nations otherwise could block the election of judges from the developed/industrialized States.[921] The distribution key

---

919 United Nations Convention on the Law of the Sea – Meeting of States Parties, *First Elections of the Members of the International Tribunal for the Law of the Sea*: "(a) Five judges from the African Group; (b) Five judges from the Asian Group; (c) Four judges from the Latin American and Caribbean Group; (d) Four judges from the Western European and Other States Group; (e) Three judges from the Eastern European Group."

920 One of the judges of the WEOG became a "shared member" to be elected from among the Group of African States, the Group of Asian States and the WEOG; see United Nations Convention on the Law of the Sea – Meeting of States Parties, *Arrangement for the allocation of seats on the International Tribunal for the Law of the Sea and the Commission on the Limits of the Continental Shelf* (26 June 2009) SPLOS/201.

921 United Nations Convention on the Law of the Sea – Meeting of States Parties, *First Elections of the Members of the International Tribunal for the Law of the Sea*, paras. 7 and 10.

prevents this and puts in the place of political determination on distribution a set of formal and predictable rules that cannot be transgressed unless they are amended following the regular procedure of amendments established in Art. 41 Statute.[922]

(4) The Selection Process in Practice Thus Far

The above sections have focused on a review and assessment of the legal framework for both the nomination and election process to the ITLOS, and it was possible to point out some unsatisfactory circumstances enshrined in the applicable legal system. Turning now to the implementation of this regulatory system, additional drawbacks come to light. In what follows, we shall concentrate on the problematic practice of presenting a "clean slate", i.e. that a regional group nominates exactly as many candidates as there are geographical seats available. This procedure emerges from an analysis of the practice hitherto of the triennial nomination and election of members of the ITLOS. The practice, which is known also from elections to the ICJ and the ICC,[923] is problematic insofar as it leaves the electors, the remaining States Parties, no choice but to elect the proposed candidates. This is, of course, also the reason it is used by Member States, namely to ensure that the desired candidate takes office. Although it may be motivated by relevant and appropriate considerations, such as the competence of some candidate, not to nominate further individuals "in vain", the consensus in academic circles and among practitioners is that this behaviour has more often than not been motivated by purely political reasons and thus is aimed unduly to disrupt the critical scrutiny that elections are supposed to warrant. To make this observation tangible, as an example, see the election of seven members

922 Amendments to Sections 1-3 of the Statute may be adopted pursuant to the simplified procedure established in Art. 313 UNCLOS, i.e. the amendment is considered adopted if no State Party has objected to it within 12 months from the date on which the proposed amendment was circulated by the UNSG, or by consensus at a conference convened in accordance with UNCLOS. The Tribunal itself may also propose such amendments to the Statute as it may consider necessary.

923 Cf. Mackenzie, et al., *Selecting International Judges: Principle, Process, and Politics*, 35.

of the ITLOS during the twenty-first Meeting of States Parties, followed the following regional allocation of seats:[924]

(I) one (1) member from the African States;
(II) one (1) member from the Asian States;
(III) one (1) member from the Eastern European States;
(IV) two (2) members from the Latin American and Caribbean States;
(V) one (1) member from the Western European and Other States; and
(VI) one (1) member of the Tribunal elected from among the African, Asian and Western European and other States.

The list of candidates for the election, compiled by the Registrar of the Tribunal pursuant to Art. 4(2) Statute, provided the following regarding nominees, their nationality/supporting country and their affiliation with regional groups:[925]

Nominee	Nationality/Nominated by	Regional Group
Attard, David Joseph	Malta	WEOG
Ayensu, Kathleen Quartey	Ghana	African Group
Bula-Bula, Sayeman	Democratic Republic of the Congo	African Group
Cot, Jean-Pierre	France	WEOG
Gao, Zhiguo	China	Asia-Pacific Group
Kelly, Elsa	Argentina	GRULAC
Kulyk, Markiyan Z.	Ukraine	Eastern European Group
Lokossa, Francis	Benin	African Group
Lucky, Anthony Amos	Trinidad and Tobago	GRULAC
Ndiaye, Tafsir Malick	Senegal	African Group

When comparing the above list of nominees with the regional allocation of seats to be balloted upon, it becomes apparent that only the African Group proposed more nominees than the number of geographical seats available to

924 United Nations Convention on the Law of the Sea – Meeting of States Parties, *Report of the twenty-first Meeting of States Parties* (29 June 2011) SPLOS/231, paras. 57-68.

925 United Nations Convention on the Law of the Sea – Meeting of States Parties, *Election of seven members of the International Tribunal for the Law of the Sea – List of candidates nominated by States Parties* (15 March 2011) SPLOS/219. The Meeting of States Parties eventually elected Jean-Pierre Cot (France), Zhiguo Gao (China), Elsa Kelly (Argentina), Markiyan Z. Kulyk (Ukraine), Anthony Amos Lucky (Trinidad and Tobago) and Tafsir Malick Ndiaye (Senegal), and Joseph Attard (Malta); United Nations Convention on the Law of the Sea – Meeting of States Parties, *Report of the twenty-first Meeting of States Parties*, paras. 66-67.

it (four candidates for one seat, plus the seat shared between the African, Asian and Western European and other States). Both the Eastern European Group and the Latin American and Caribbean Group submitted as many nominations as there were seats available for the group in question (one and two respectively), thus effectively eliminating real choice in the eventual election during the Meeting of States Parties. The Western European and Others Group submitted two nominees for one seat, plus the seat shared between the African, Asian and Western European and other States. Since the shared seat was indeed filled by the WEOG, the number of nominations again fitted the number of seats possibly available for that group to fill. One seat allocated to the Asia-Pacific Group was vacant and one nominee was proposed; no nomination was even made for the seat shared between the African, Asian and Western European and other States. In view of these observations, it is no surprise that a glance at the election results provides an equally monotonous picture: the candidate of the Asia-Pacific Group was elected by 141 of 149 votes cast; the candidates from the Latin American and Caribbean Group were elected by 142 and 137 votes respectively; and the nominee from the Eastern European Group was able to obtain 143 out of 149 possible votes.[926]

For the regular elections that took place between 1996 and 2008, the following table shows, organized by the five geographical groups, the number of seats that were available each time for (re-)election and the number of nominations that were submitted by States Parties.[927]

	Seats available for election					Nominations submitted by States Parties				
Group	2008	2005	2002	1999	1996	2008	2005	2002	1999	1996
African Group	1+1*	2	1*	1+1*	5	9	5	5	3	10
Asia-Pacific Group	1+1*	1+1*	1*	2*	5	3	4**	1	3	8
Eastern European Group	1	1	1*	1*	3	1	1	2	2	3
GRULAC	1*	1*	1+1*	1*	4	1	1	2	1	4
WEOG	1*	1	1+1*	1*	4	1	4**	3	1	8

* Seat was up for re-election.

** At least one nominee was supported by more than one country, from one or more geographical groups.

926 United Nations Convention on the Law of the Sea – Meeting of States Parties, *Report of the twenty-first Meeting of States Parties*, para. 66.

927 All information was assembled from the Lists of candidates submitted by Governments of States Parties, submitted to the Meeting of States Parties by the Registrar of the ITLOS, and the annual reports of the ITLOS, available at 'Documents of the

What becomes apparent from the above figures is that for every triennial election, including for the first election in 1996, the Latin American and Caribbean Group has chosen to submit a number of nominees that exactly matches the number of seats available for (re-)election for that group. The willingness to re-elect a sitting judge from that group can only in some cases provide a rational explanation of why the group effectively excluded a real choice between candidates. Instead it appears that the group managed to coordinate its nominations to allow it to have a decisive effect on the subsequent elections. The African Group, instead, appears to have little or no coordination of its nominations, submitting in every election at least twice as many nominees as there are seats available to vote upon for that group.[928] In the Asia-Pacific Group, the number of nominees and available seats for election match fairly well and usually provide for only one more candidate than the available seats, thus permitting only the smallest possible *choice* for the electors. That the elections in 1996 for every geographical group indicate a considerably larger number of nominees than seats available is explained by the fact that these were the first elections to the bench. The Eastern European Group's practice deviates in one important respect from that of the other groups. Although the number of nominees and available seats for that group are fairly congruent, it is striking that the group chose to nominate more individuals than seats available every time those seats were up for re-election. Since the group did not choose to submit a higher number of nominees than available seats in all other elections, including the constituting

---

Meeting of States Parties to the United Nations Convention on the Law of the Sea (SPLOS)' available at <http://www.un.org/depts/los/meeting_states_parties/SPLOS_documents.htm> (last visited: 21 March 2014).

928 As another sign of this lack of prior coordination within the African Group it may be noted that the Government of Nigeria chose to withdraw its nomination of Justice Emmanuel Oladeinde Sanyaolu from the list of candidates for the triennial election to the Tribunal in 2008, "in order to respect the decision of the African Union ministerial meeting on candidature and the spirit of brotherhood within the continent" (United Nations Convention on the Law of the Sea – Meeting of States Parties, *Election of seven members of the International Tribunal for the Law of the Sea – List of candidates nominated by States Parties: withdrawal of a candidate* (2 April 2008) SPLOS/171/Add.1, Annex, Note Verbale dated 26 March 2008 from the Embassy of the Federal Republic of Nigeria addressed to the Registrar of the International Tribunal for the Law of the Sea). See also United Nations Convention on the Law of the Sea – Meeting of States Parties, *Election of seven members of the International Tribunal for the Law of the Sea – List of candidates nominated by States Parties* (11 March 2008) SPLOS/171.

elections in 1996, this phenomenon cannot be explained by a will to allow the electors to have a *choice*. Instead it may, objectively, be interpreted as a subtle attempt to exert pressure on the sitting judge, or at the very least to erase, indeed counteract, any sense of assurance that service on the Tribunal guarantees re-nomination or re/-election. The same could be said regarding at least one instance of the nomination behaviour of the Western European and Others Group (elections in 2002), although that group's data indicate a relative concordance between the number of nominated individuals and seats available for election.

These empirical observations suggest at the very least that most relevant decisions have already been taken when the States Parties move to cast their votes in elections or, put more critically, that the actual decision-making process by which the Meeting of States Parties chooses an individual to hold judicial office is mostly lacking in determinant content. It would go too far directly to deduce from the above-mentioned data and observations a threat to the independent functioning of the Tribunal. However, what can be said with some degree of certainty is that by levering the filtering mechanisms of real competition and a real choice in the elections increases the likelihood that a candidate is elected who does not meet the individual selection criteria.[929] Furthermore, clean slates in general witness an apparent politicization of both the nomination and election processes.[930] If the nomination effectively becomes the election, then the appointment of judges to the ITLOS becomes dangerously close to the appointment of arbitrators. To the extent that a clean slate is motivated by the consideration that a particular seat *belongs* to the nominating group and that the nominee thus shall categorically represent that group, the prospect of assembling an independent bench rests on a crumbling foundation. These fears are enforced by the fact that it is not possible to vote explicitly against a clean slate, but merely to abstain from voting.[931] Yet due to the balance the equitable geographical distribution rule seeks to establish, it is highly unlikely that the remaining membership would

929 Mackenzie, et al., *Selecting International Judges: Principle, Process, and Politics*, 110.

930 In view of the empirical data presented, it shall not be emphasized here how this politicization can come about, e.g. by consensus, due to pressure from a powerful State in a particular regional group, or because of the (unintentional) order in which the nominations were presented.

931 On the ability to abstain from voting to protest a clean slate see Mackenzie, et al., *Selecting International Judges: Principle, Process, and Politics*, 35, 110.

opt to refuse to elect a clean slate. One possible way to prevent clean slates would be to provide the Tribunal with more control over the nomination process, e.g. by requiring that a minimum number of nominations are submitted every time, which must be higher than the number of seats available.[932]

(5) Conclusions

The selection process to the bench of the Tribunal is, with the exception of the rules pertaining to the distribution of seats, less regulated than that applicable to the ICJ. At the same time, the involvement of external entities is more limited with regard to the pre-election phase, but also regarding nomination and election, which is performed by the States Parties only. Overall there are fewer provisions that nevertheless establish a process that in many regards reminds of that at the ICJ. A significant adverse difference has to be seen in the direct nomination of the ITLOS judges by the States, without the influence of a critical, scrutinizing organ such as the national groups of the PCA. However, in view of the stated questionable ability of those national groups to exclude political influence exerted by the States the difference, and possible advantage of the ICJ system in this regard should not be overstated. The impression must remain that States may and do have considerable influence over the composition of the bench; a right that in view of the role States play in international law in general cannot be entirely overlooked even in favour of the idealistic goal of making the Tribunal function as independently as possible.

The practice of presenting a clean slate, which also occurs at the ICJ, tangibly indicates that States wish to maintain control over the appointment process as far as this is possible. That this practice is to the detriment of the observance of the individual selection criteria and, as a consequence, with its straightforward influence from States a potential threat to the independent functioning of the Tribunal, is obvious. On the other hand, with its commitment to equitable geographical distribution and the distribution following the geographical group, the election process at the ITLOS provides a minimum guarantee that is not surmountable by momentary political influence from States or even groups of States. The personal requirements established

932 As referred to above, the current restriction is of a different kind and sets only as an upper limit of two nominations per State Party; Art. 4(1) Statute.

by the Statute, as well as the requirement of representation of the principal legal systems of the world, are similar to those asked for by the ICJ Statute.

c) The Role of Ad Hoc Judges at the ITLOS

(1) The Legal Framework

Under the heading of "Nationality of Members" the Statute in Art. 17 provides for the use of the national judge as well as for the appointment of *ad hoc* judges. The legal regime surrounding the work of the ITLOS rejects neither of these institutions but instead affirms the customary perception, which is that both can be of certain value for the Tribunal's proper functioning. Pursuant to Art. 17(1) Statute the members of the Tribunal who have the nationality of any of the parties in a particular dispute are not obliged to vacate their seats on the bench, but retain the right to participate as members of the Tribunal. If, however, any (or both)[933] of the parties lacks a member of its nationality on the bench in a particular dispute, the Statute grants that party the right to choose a person to participate, for the purpose of that dispute, as a member of the Tribunal.[934] Where several parties in the opinion of the Tribunal, i.e. irrespective of the estimation of the parties concerned,[935] are joined by the same interest, they retain the right to appoint only one joint *ad hoc* judge for that dispute.[936] This right is granted only if none of the parties joined by the common interest has a judge of its nationality on the bench.[937]

National as well as *ad hoc* judges pursuant to Art. 17(6) Statute are required, like regular members of the bench, to fulfil the conditions of independence, highest reputation for fairness and integrity and recognized competence in the field of the law of the sea,[938] the requirement of not having been involved with the case in certain functions[939] and having made the solemn declaration required by any judge.[940] Pursuant to Art. 19(5) Rules it

933 See Art. 17(3) Statute.
934 Art. 17(2) Statute.
935 Cf. Art. 20(2) Rules.
936 Art. 17(5) Statute.
937 Art. 20(1) Rules.
938 Art. 2 Statute.
939 Art. 8 Statute.
940 Art. 11 Statute. The declaration is to have the same wording as for regular judges, Art. 9(1) Rules.

is for the Tribunal to decide when these conditions are no longer fulfilled, with the consequence that the judge in question "shall cease to sit on the bench". It should be noted that parties to a dispute have the right to raise objections against the choice made by other parties,[941] which provides a formal procedure for making the criticism that e.g. a chosen *ad hoc* judge does not fulfil the requirements in Art. 2 Statute as regards personal qualifications. The final decision on such objections, and thus on the chosen individual's suitability for judgeship, is made by the Tribunal itself.[942]

(2) The Particularities of Ad Hoc Judges at the ITLOS

At a closer reading, Art. 17(6) Statute indicates a certain restrictiveness in establishing criteria which *ad hoc* judges have to fulfil before they can "participate in the decision on terms of complete equality with their colleagues".[943] It may for example be noted that certain criteria which are considered to be important in ensuring the bench's independence are apparently not required to be fulfilled by national or *ad hoc* judges. In line with what applies to those judges at the ICJ, they do not have to fulfil the requirements with regard to incompatible activities established for regular judges.[944] In other words, although an *ad hoc* judge may not have previously participated in a case as agent, counsel or advocate for one of the parties, or as a member of a national or international court or tribunal, or in any other capacity, he is not barred from

> "exercise[ing] any political or administrative function, or associat[ing] actively with or be[ing] financially interested in any of the operations of any enterprise concerned with the exploration for or exploitation of the resources of the sea or the seabed or other commercial use of the sea or the seabed".

From the point of view of avoiding conflicting interests in the mind of a judge in order to enable him to make decisions independently, this must be

941 Art. 19(3) Rules.

942 Art. 19(3) *in fine* Statute. Cf. Art. 35(3)-(4) Rules of the ICJ.

943 Art. 17(6) *in fine* Statute.

944 While Art. 17(6) Statute does refer to Art. 8 Statute, on the "[c]onditions relating to participation of members in a particular case", Art. 17(6) does not refer to Art. 7 Statute.

criticized as highly problematic.[945] It may be invoked, as was done in the context of the ICJ, that these judges fulfil a mandate that is limited in time, and that they do not have e.g. the financial stability that would be necessary in order to rationalize the exclusion of any parallel side activities. A certain degree of affiliation and dependence of the national/*ad hoc* judges may thus be unavoidable and remain a feature which distinguishes between them and their colleagues on the bench. Yet the failure to include even a weakened reference to Art. 7 Statute creates a risk by unnecessarily relying on the benevolence of Member States and the integrity of individuals, even more so than as regards ordinary members. Since Art. 17(6) Statute also does not make applicable to *ad hoc* judges the provision in Art. 7(2) Statute, it furthermore follows that the Statute, while rejecting prior involvement in a case as agent, counsel or advocate, considers it legitimate that *ad hoc* judges may simultaneously act as agent, counsel or advocate in a different case before the Tribunal. If the function of an agent, counsel or advocate is considered irreconcilable with the functions of an ordinary member of the Tribunal, why should this assessment differ for *ad hoc* judges? Again, practical reasons may be put forward, in light of a limited community of legal scholars with expertise in the law of the sea. Although it must be considered a blatant clash with the idea of an independent Tribunal, an interpretation of the interplay between Arts. 17(6) and 7(2) Statute can, however, also lead to the conclusion that the drafters acknowledged the function of *ad hoc* judges to be to "act as agent, counsel or advocate".

Art. 8 Rules, which mirrors Art. 17(6) Statute,[946] establishes that the main function of *ad hoc* judges is to participate in the relevant case on terms of

945 The restrictiveness of Art. 17(6) Statute in establishing requirements that have to be fulfilled by the national judge or *ad hoc* judge, and which thus have to be observed by the appointing State, is also mirrored in the lack of any suggestion, as is contained in Art. 31 ICJ Statute, that the *ad hoc* judge "preferably" be chosen from among those previously nominated for election to the Tribunal. As this stipulation in the ICJ Statute was already drafted in non-binding terms and in reality proved to be of little practical relevance (cf. Art. 31 ICJ Statute), and since in the nomination process for the ITLOS there are no lists of nominees similar to those drafted by the national groups for the purpose of ICJ elections (cf. Art. 4(1) ICJ Statute), the ITLOS' Statute has learned a lesson and supports the discretion of States to appoint any person, within the limits mentioned above, they may deem fit at any particular time.

946 A difference between the two provisions is that Art. 17(6) mentions that *ad hoc* judges "shall participate *in the decision* on terms of complete equality with their colleagues", whereas Art. 8 Rules refers to a complete equality of *ad hoc* judges with the other judges to "participate *in the case* in which they sit" (emphasis added).

complete equality with the other judges, i.e. to participate in the decision-making of the Tribunal. Pursuant to Art. 41(3) *in fine* Rules *ad hoc* judges are not, however, to be taken into account for the calculation of the quorum of the ITLOS.[947] A similar provision was included in Art. 20(3) Rules of the ICJ.[948] This means that *ad hoc* judges are certainly equal with other judges in that they may take part in the decisions handed down by the Tribunal in a particular case, but not for the purpose of establishing whether the Tribunal is functional in the first place. Hence, *ad hoc* judges are valuable in influencing the outcome of decision-making in a case but not for determining the functionality of the Tribunal. This once again underlines that *ad hoc* judges are merely a concession to the interest of parties before the Tribunal. Their remit is to provide a voice for the interests of a party in a dispute, but at the same time there is the concern of protecting the independence of the Tribunal, in the sense of not allowing such judges to influence more of its (internal) functioning.

The question of parties' right and need to appoint an *ad hoc* judge and having a judge of one's own nationality on the bench acquires another dimension before the ITLOS with the extension of the Tribunal's jurisdiction *ratione personae* to entities other than States.[949] The right to appoint an *ad hoc* judge is restricted to cases where at least one of the potential other parties is a State party and that State has a national judge on the bench or has appointed an *ad hoc* judge, or where an international organization is a party and a sitting judge has the nationality of one of the organization's Member States.[950] If the other party is not a State or an international organization, then the entity retains the right of appointment only if there is a judge with the nationality of a sponsoring State of that party.[951] Judges having the nationality of a Member State of an international organization or that of a sponsoring State of a natural or juridical person or State enterprise preclude the right of such

---

No substantial difference can be implied as both provisions in essence refer to the fulfilment of the functions that are being referred to the *ad hoc* judge; cf. Chandrasekhara Rao, P. & Gautier, Philippe (eds), *The Rules of the International Tribunal for the Law of the Sea – A Commentary* (Nijhoff Leiden 2006), 26.

947 This already follows from the formulation in Art. 13 Statute, according to which "a quorum of 11 *elected members* shall be required to constitute the Tribunal" (emphasis added).

948 However not in the Statute, cf. Art. 25(3) ICJ Statute.

949 Cf. Art. 20(2) Statute.

950 Art. 22(1)(a) Rules.

951 Art. 22(1)(b) Rules.

parties to appoint *ad hoc* judges.[952] A sitting judge who has the nationality of a Member State of an international organization that is a party to a dispute has the same function as a judge of the nationality of a State party for the purpose of the right of any other party to appoint an *ad hoc* judge.[953] It thus follows that a judge who holds the nationality of a Member State of an international organization that is a party before the ITLOS is able and qualified to assume the interests of that entire organization. The interest of not overstepping the influence that such party judges may have is expressed in Art. 22(4) Rules which provides that only one such judge is allowed to sit on a case. This rule testifies not only to the acknowledgment of the *ad hoc* judges' potentially negative influence on the Tribunal's independence but also to a certain will to limit this influence. The aim of that provision is to rule out any bias in the composition of the bench in favour of merely one party to the dispute.

Finally, if the premise of the *ad hoc* judge as a representative of his country of origin is accepted, then the rule that an international organization which is a party in a dispute before the ITLOS should not have more than one judge with the nationality of one of its Member States[954] poses a problem in light of the EC's membership of UNCLOS. The EC area is granted a minimum of three judges pursuant to Art. 3(2) Statute and a maximum of six pursuant to the key established in 2009 for the distribution of seats among geographical groups.[955] The disqualification of all but one of these judges according to Art. 22 of the Rules would not only imply a significant change in the composition of the bench but also have the risk of underrepresentation of European States and of opening the situation up for disproportionate influence of non-European judges on the Tribunal's decision-making in cases where the EC is involved and affected. That this problem is not merely theoretical is shown by the EC's signature of the UNCLOS. Moreover, in the *Swordfish Case* the EC was already a party to a dispute before the Tribunal, and the transfer of competences in the area of fisheries and high-sea fisher-

952 Art. 22(2) Rules.

953 Art. 22(3) Rules.

954 Art. 22(4) Rules.

955 United Nations Convention on the Law of the Sea – Meeting of States Parties, *Arrangement for the allocation of seats on the International Tribunal for the Law of the Sea and the Commission on the Limits of the Continental Shelf.* See also *supra* Chapter E.IV(4)(b)(3).

ies[956] from the Member States to the EC and the enlargement of the EC/EU permit the prediction that further disputes involving the EC will arise in the future. In addition, it cannot be ruled out that other international organizations, e.g. NAFTA, MERCOSUR, ASEAN, may also join the UNCLOS in the near future.[957] A solution to this problem might be the utilization of *ad hoc* chambers upon the request of the parties[958] or decided by the Tribunal *ex officio*,[959] which allow the *ad hoc* adjustment of the number of judges participating in the decision-making process. Although the Tribunal can decide on the number of judges to sit on a particular case in any event, subject to the limitation in Art. 13(1) Statute (a quorum consists of 11 elected members), the forming of *ad hoc* chambers has the advantage of greater flexibility in deciding the Tribunal's composition in a particular case. On the other hand, it would again be a concession to the political nature of the relevant dispute.

d) The Use of Scientific and Technical Experts

From the beginning of the negotiations leading to the adoption of the UNCLOS, and of part XV in particular, the consensus subsisted that any disputes arising under the new regime of the law of the sea could be of a highly technical nature. Although this concern was a contributing factor to eventually including regular arbitration among the various mechanisms available for dispute settlement,[960] the issue had to be taken into account with regard to the new law of the sea tribunal as well. One of the consequences is the requirement contained in Art. 2(1) Statute that every judge be of recognized competence in the field of the law of the sea. Yet this is ultimately a requirement of legal expertise and not of pertinent technical knowledge. Thus Art. 289 UNCLOS fills a void by providing the ITLOS with the ability in consultation with the parties to a dispute to select two or more scientific or

---

956 Art. 3(1) lit. e and Art. 32 Consolidated Version of the Treaty establishing the European Community (adopted 25 March 1957, entered into force 1 January 1958) OJ C 321E; Art. 80(2) and Art. 71 ECT. Cf. *Case concerning the Conservation and Sustainable Exploitation of Swordfish Stocks in the South-Eastern Pacific Ocean (Chile/European Union) Order 2009/1*.

957 It should be noted that this problem never occurred at the ICJ as the jurisdiction *ratione personae* of the ICJ does not extend to non-State entities.

958 Art. 15(2) Statute.

959 Art. 15(1) Statute.

960 See Art. 287 UNCLOS.

technical experts to sit with the Tribunal. At first glance, this provision is able to contribute considerably to the strengthening of the independence of the Tribunal in particular as regards the parties to a dispute, since the Tribunal with the assistance of such experts does not have to rely on the parties for necessary information. The institution is strengthened by the discretion the Tribunal has to have recourse to such experts; it *may* select them but can also choose to refrain from appointing them. Furthermore, the Tribunal has the right *proprio motu* to appoint such experts. The ITLOS is thus provided with a tool to seek and receive additional knowledge and expertise which helps it to reach decisions that are factually correct even in matters that are of a highly complicated scientific and/or technical nature. At the same time, those experts do not have the right to vote, but merely to provide the Tribunal with expert opinions, and are thus not able to influence the decision-making of the Tribunal directly. It still remains the obligation of the judges to translate the technical expertise into an application of the law in a particular case.

The precise implementation of the right to appoint experts pursuant to Art. 289 UNCLOS is codified in the Rules of the Tribunal. In accordance with Art. 15 Rules, parties may request the appointment of experts at any time before the closure of the written proceedings; later requests, if made prior to the closure of the oral proceedings, may be considered by the Tribunal if appropriate in the circumstances of the case. The Tribunal retains the right in any situation to reject the appointment of experts.[961] The selection of an expert is made after the president of the Tribunal has made a proposal, following consultation with the parties.[962] The Tribunal is free to choose any expert it deems fit, but in doing so is called to observe the following provisions.

(I) Experts in the fields of fisheries protection and preservation of the marine environment, marine scientific research, and navigation, including pollution from vessels and by dumping, shall be chosen preferably from a list prepared for the purpose of supporting special arbitration.[963]

---

961 Eiriksson, Gudmundur *The International Tribunal for the Law of the Sea* (Nijhoff The Hague 2000), 66.

962 Art. 15(2) Rules.

963 Art. 15(3) Rules read in conjunction with Art. 2 Annex VIII UNCLOS. The information provided on the website of the ITLOS states that the selection of experts "*should* be based on the relevant list prepared according to article 2 of Annex VIII to the Convention." (Emphasis added.) 'International Tribunal for the Law of the Sea – Experts under article 289 of the Convention' available at <http://www.itlos.org/index.php?id=20> (last visited: 21 March 2014).

This list is based on two nominees submitted by every State party to UNCLOS.[964] Whereas it may be argued that this nomination limits the choice of the Tribunal in obtaining independent expert advice, the influence from States is relativized by the fact that the Tribunal is not bound to select from those candidates; experts are only preferably to be chosen from this list.

(II) Every expert shall be independent and enjoy the highest reputation for fairness, competence and integrity.[965] It remains, as part of the Tribunal's right to select, entirely in the discretion of the ITLOS whether a person does or does not meet those requirements. Every expert before taking up his duties is furthermore required to make a declaration in which he *inter alia* declares that he has the will to perform such duties impartially.

Experts appointed pursuant to Art. 289 UNCLOS have to be distinguished from those experts that serve the purpose of providing evidence, giving advisory opinions or the answering appropriate questions during proceedings, and who may be called by either the parties or the Tribunal itself.[966] The opinions of those experts may be challenged by the parties or contradicted by another expert opinion. The Art. 289-expert is, however, merely an advisor to the judges and not challengeable in the same way for the reason that parties often may not be aware of the precise contribution those experts make. From the perspective of the standard of a fair trial this can be justified only by excluding the expert from the right to vote. On the other hand, in order to facilitate the work of such experts, the Tribunal has established in its Resolution establishing the Internal Judicial Practice that such experts shall be sent copies of the written pleadings and other notes and documents in the case, that they sit with the judges during the oral proceedings and take part in the deliberations in accordance with article 42 of the Rules.[967] Overall, since disputes before the Tribunal are likely to affect questions of a complicated non-legal nature which the judges themselves may not be able to assess

---

964 Art. 2(3) Annex VIII UNCLOS. Also the chambers of the Tribunal have the right to appoint such experts, Art. 15(4) Rules.

965 Art. 15(3) Rules.

966 Arts. 77-78 Rules; cf. Art. 27 Statute which provides the Tribunal with the power to "make orders for the conduct of the case" and "make all arrangements connected with the taking of evidence."

967 See Art. 10 ITLOS, *Resolution on the Internal Judicial Practice of the International Tribunal for the Law of the Sea* (31 October 1997) ITLOS/10.

appropriately, the institution of independent experts gains real significance.[968] In those circumstances it is important that the Tribunal is equipped with the tools to gain the necessary knowledge on its own, without having to rely on either the parties to the relevant case or any other external entity.

5. Financing the Tribunal

The regular costs of the Tribunal shall, according to Art. 19 of the Statute, "be borne by the States Parties [of UNCLOS] and by the Authority on such terms and in such a manner as shall be decided at meetings of the States Parties."[969] In the situation where any entity other than a State Party becomes a party to a dispute before the Tribunal, which pursuant to Art. 20(2) Statute is possible, such entity shall contribute towards the costs of the Tribunal to the extent that the Tribunal itself considers appropriate.[970]

Two initial conclusions can be drawn from this balancing of the financial burden of the Tribunal. First, this system of financing pays tribute to the specialized character of the ITLOS. Since the Tribunal's jurisdiction *ratione personae* not only extends to States Parties to UNCLOS it is only consequen-

968 It may be noted that Art. 289 UNCLOS does not apply only to the ITLOS, but also to the ICJ where experts also contribute to excluding technical errors from decisions and to the conformity of decisions with the latest scientific knowledge. Here the experts are called assessors and regulated by Art. 30(2) ICJ Statute and Art. 9 ICJ Rules.

969 According to the Meeting of States Parties Decision on budgetary matters of the International Tribunal for the Law of the Sea for 2011-2012, the approved budget of the ITLOS for the biennium 2011-2012 amounts to 20,398,600 EUR (United Nations Convention on the Law of the Sea – Meeting of States Parties, *Decisions on Budgetary Matters of the International Tribunal for the Law of the Sea for 2011-2012* (9 July 2010) SPLOS/217), which is a considerable increase compared to the preceding biennium where the budget was set at 17,515,000 EUR (United Nations Convention on the Law of the Sea – Meeting of States Parties, *Decision on budgetary matters of the International Tribunal for the Law of the Sea for 2009-2010* (20 June 2008) SPLOS/180). The reason for this increase in the total costs of the ITLOS is mainly an increase in special allowances to judges (which was raised with 1,037,500 EUR), staff costs (the expenses for temporary assistance for meetings amounted to 606,800 EUR), and expenditures in the pension scheme (raising by 314,200 EUR): see United Nations Convention on the Law of the Sea – Meeting of States Parties, *Decisions on Budgetary Matters of the International Tribunal for the Law of the Sea for 2011-2012*, 2.

970 Art. 19(2) Statute.

tial that the costs of the Tribunal are also borne by all those entities that may become parties before the Tribunal. For the same reason, it can hardly be considered a (possible) infringement of the independence of the Tribunal that its funding is in this way purposively tailored. Second, linking the central part of the financing of the Tribunal to the States Parties rather than any international organization, such as the UNGA in the case of the ICJ, only *prima facie* suggests that the Tribunal's independence is guaranteed to a wider extent.[971] In reality, the power of the Meeting of States Parties to adopt the budget of the Tribunal gives it "considerable weight in shaping the way the Tribunal works."[972] A practical example of this is that the Meeting authorized the Tribunal to hold only two meetings in 1998 due to financial considerations, while the Tribunal had proposed that there should be three. This minor issue cannot be considered a threat to the Tribunal's autonomous functioning, as occasional financial constraints do affect even (international) courts, and it merely serves to underline that non-judicial and external considerations cannot be entirely prevented from exerting influence on the work of the Tribunal. The more significant conclusion, especially in comparison to the ICJ, is that the political entity which takes the decision is not distracted and thus less likely to be guided by undue political considerations. The Meeting of States Parties is instead entirely devoted to the law of the sea and the dispute settlement mechanism under UNCLOS.[973]

The source of financing is different from that of the ICJ where the budget is borne by the UN as decided by the UNGA. The limited number of tasks

971 Of a different opinion see Nordquist (ed) *United Nations Convention on the Law of the Sea 1982: A Commentary – Volume V*, 372, who seems to see in this system of financing an entirely greater independence of the Tribunal compared to e.g. the ICJ.

972 Treves, 'The Law of the Sea "System" of Institutions', 331.

973 The Meeting of States Parties, among other things, elects the members of the ITLOS and the members of the Commission on the Limits of the Continental Shelf; it considers the annual report of the ITLOS and deals with the Tribunal's budgetary and administrative matters; It receives information provided by the Secretary-General of the International Seabed Authority and the Chairman of the Commission on the Limits of the Continental Shelf on the activities of these bodies and also receives the Report of the UNSG pursuant to Art. 319 UNCLOS for the information of States Parties on issues of a general nature, relevant to them, that have arisen with respect to the UNCLOS.

that have to be performed by the Meeting[974] make it more likely for the States Parties to analyse and discuss in more detail the functioning of the Tribunal, compared with the ICJ budget which is discussed as part of the entire UN budget. It may be said that the ICJ is thus merely indirectly influenced by the financial decisions made by States, in their capacity as UN Member States, whereas the States Parties to UNLCOS have direct influence without the intermediary of an international organization. However, in both systems, the budget can be agreed upon only by reaching a decision acceptable to a majority. The only advantage is that the budget of the ITLOS does not have to compete directly within the broader framework of the budget of a super-ordinate organization. Whereas the ICJ budget is part of the broader UN budget and the raising of funds thus has to compete with other costs, the ITLOS' budget is not in a similar competitive situation. However, the budget of the UNGA is governed by similar State interests to decision-making within the Meeting of States Parties.

The meeting of the States Parties to UNCLOS is merely an administrative organ in charge of the election of judges and budgetary and administrative matters.[975] The Tribunal itself is to some extent involved in the budget process: Pursuant to the Tribunal's Financial Regulations and Rules,[976] a draft budget is prepared by the Registrar.[977] It is then referred to the Committee on Budget and Finance – established by the Tribunal – which is expected to give its comments and recommendations on the draft. Then the draft is transmitted to the Tribunal which is to "consider and approve the draft budget"[978] and sends it to the Secretariat of the UN. This step merely serves the purpose of making the draft budget available to all States Parties and international organizations prior to the opening of the Meeting of States Parties, which has finally to approve it. Supplementary budget proposals

974 The election of the members of the Tribunal (Art. 4(4) Statute; and of the Commission on the Limits of the Continental Shelf, Art. 2(2) Annex II UNCLOS) and the decision on the expenses of the Tribunal (Art. 19(1) Statute).

975 See 'Meeting of States Parties to the Convention' available at <http://www.un.org/Depts/los/meeting_states_parties/meeting_states_parties.htm> (last visited: 21 March 2014).

976 Financial Regulations and Rules of the International Tribunal for the Law of the Sea – Prepared by the Tribunal (1 January 2005) available at <http://www.itlos.org/fileadmin/itlos/documents/basic_texts/Financial.Regs.Rules.E.pdf> (last visited: 21 March 2014).

977 Rule 103.1.

978 Rule 103.4.

may be made by the Registrar in exceptional cases, and by the Meeting of States Parties.[979] A point of criticism in the composition of the budget is that the Meeting of States Parties determines in its decisions on budgetary matters regarding the ITLOS an "amount for case-related costs" which, according to the Meeting, is to provide the Tribunal with the financial means necessary to consider cases in a particular biennium. This amount is sometimes allocated generally,[980] but sometimes with express reference to a particular case before the Tribunal.[981] Although it cannot be a general criticism that the Meeting of States Parties makes decisions on how the budget is spent, since it is the organ that has been entrusted by the States Parties with settling administrative matters affecting the Tribunal, making reference to particular cases may unduly influence the way in which the Tribunal exercises its judicial work.

As mentioned, according to Art. 19(1) Statute the Tribunal may rely on two different yet mutually exclusive complementary sources of funds, the States Parties and the ISA. This dispersion of possible sources is certainly in the interest of the Tribunal's independence of the States Parties. Adding the Authority as another source of funding will lessen the risk of the decision on funds being utilized by States as a mechanism for exerting pressure on the Tribunal.[982] The ISA is itself an independent treaty organization estab-

---

979 Rule 3.6 and Rule 103.4(c).

980 See, e.g., United Nations Convention on the Law of the Sea – Meeting of States Parties, *Decision on budgetary matters of the International Tribunal for the Law of the Sea for 2009-2010*, para. 3: "With a view to providing the Tribunal with the financial means necessary to consider cases in 2009-2010, in particular those requiring expeditious proceedings, the Meeting of States Parties approves an amount of 2,564,700 EUR for case-related costs of the Tribunal. This amount is included in the total appropriation … The case-related costs shall be used only in the event of cases being submitted to the Tribunal."

981 See, e.g., United Nations Convention on the Law of the Sea – Meeting of States Parties, *Decisions on Budgetary Matters of the International Tribunal for the Law of the Sea for 2011-2012*, para. 3: "With a view to providing the Tribunal with the financial means necessary to consider cases in 2011-2012, in particular Case No. 16 and cases requiring expeditious proceedings, the Meeting of States Parties approves an amount of 4,519,200 EUR for case-related costs of the Tribunal. That amount is included in the total appropriation … The case-related costs shall be used only in the event of cases being submitted to the Tribunal."

982 As is regularly stated in the decisions on budgetary matters of the ITLOS made by the Meetings of States Parties, the budgets have so far been financed by the contributions of all States and international organizations that are parties to UNCLOS, and the opportunity of the Authority to make a contribution is kept open for future budgets. See, e.g., United Nations Convention on the Law of the Sea – Meeting of

lished under UNCLOS and is funded by a variety of financial sources. It is the Assembly, the supreme organ of the ISA,[983] which ultimately decides on the budget of the Authority.[984] The funds of the Authority, pursuant to Art. 171 UNCLOS, include assessed contributions from members of the Authority, funds originating in the administration of organizing and controlling all mineral-related activities in the international seabed area, funds from the Enterprise, borrowed funds pursuant to Art. 174 UNCLOS, voluntary funds, and payments to a compensation fund pursuant to Art. 151(10) UNCLOS. It is in particular the funds originating in the administration of organizing and controlling all mineral-related activities in the international seabed area that have the potential to become a truly State-independent source of financing from which the Tribunal then may benefit. So far, however, the Authority has entered into just 11 contracts for exploration for polymetallic nodules in the deep seabed.[985]

V. Personal Independence

1. The Pre-Electoral Requirements of Integrity and Qualification

As regards personal qualifications, the Statute of the ITLOS is more precise than the ICJ Statute and demands of its members that they enjoy "the highest

States Parties, *Decision on budgetary matters of the International Tribunal for the Law of the Sea for 2005-2006* (23 June 2004) SPLOS/117, para. 4; United Nations Convention on the Law of the Sea – Meeting of States Parties, *Decision on budgetary matters of the International Tribunal for the Law of the Sea for 2007-2008* (23 June 2006) SPLOS/145, para. 3; United Nations Convention on the Law of the Sea – Meeting of States Parties, *Decision on budgetary matters of the International Tribunal for the Law of the Sea for 2009-2010*, para. 4: "Without prejudice to the application of the provisions of article 19 of annex VI to the United Nations Convention on the Law of the Sea in respect of future budgets of the Tribunal regarding the contribution to be made by the International Seabed Authority, the budget of the Tribunal for [2009-2010] will be financed by all States and international organizations that are parties to the Convention."

983 Art. 160 UNCLOS.

984 Art. 172 UNCLOS.

985 See 'Contractors – International Seabed Authority' available at <http://www.isa.org.jm/en/scientific/exploration/contractors> (last visited: 21 March 2014).

reputation for fairness and integrity".[986] This requirement, although phrased differently, is unlikely to have any different content from the requirement established by Art. 2 ICJ Statute, that ICJ judges be of high moral character.[987] It amounts to an important safeguard of the independence of the Tribunal as the moral suitability of the individual member of the Tribunal is the gatekeeper to political influence on decision-making. As such the moral requirements established in Art. 2 Statute have to be understood as demands directed primarily at the States Parties, setting up a framework within which they are expected to make their nominations, but also at the Meetings of States Parties for the time at which they conduct elections.

As regards the demands Art. 2 Statute raises, it is unfortunate that the provision lacks autonomous enforcement or, at the very least, a control mechanism. As it is now, compliance with these requirements is left up to the States Parties alone, in particular when States make their nominations. This is of particular concern regarding the ITLOS where the competences required of judges are particularly significant as the ITLOS is a specialized Tribunal compared to e.g. the ICJ.[988] The Tribunal has the jurisdiction *ratione materiae* of providing dispute settlement that entails the interpretation and application of UNCLOS and any other agreement that relates to the purpose of UNCLOS, i.e. disputes relating to the codified law of the sea.[989] In this spirit, Art. 2 Statute requires of the members of the Tribunal that they have "recognized competence in the field of the law of the sea". This demand *prima facie* goes even further than what the ICJ Statute demands of ICJ

---

986 In its entirety Art. 2 Statute reads as follows: "1. The Tribunal shall be composed of a body of 21 independent members, elected from among persons enjoying the highest reputation for fairness and integrity and of recognized competence in the field of the law of the sea." The case specific allocation of parts of the budget seems to remain uncriticized by the judges themselves, see United Nations Convention on the Law of the Sea – Meeting of States Parties, *Meeting of States Parties to Law of Sea Convention 136th-137th Meetings (AM & PM) – States Parties to Convention on Law of the Sea Hear Briefing by International Tribunal President, on Draft Budget Proposals, Other Financial Matters* (15 June 2010) SEA/1941.

987 The ITLOS judges have to make a solemn declaration upon taking office (Art. 11 Statute). According to Art. 5 Rules, this declaration shall have the following wording: "I solemnly declare that I will perform my duties and exercise my powers as judge honorably, faithfully, impartially and conscientiously". It is thus identical with the one to be given by ICJ judges (cf. *supra* Chapter D.VI(1)).

988 Oellers-Frahm, 'International Courts and Tribunals, Judges and Arbitrators', para. 10.

989 Art. 288(1) Statute and Art. 21 Rules.

judges, who do not overall have to prove their competence in international law to be eligible for election to the bench. The establishment of the criterion that the ITLOS judges have to have a particular recognized legal competence serves the Tribunal's independence in the sense that, if such competence is available, judges may appreciate to a greater extent the value of serving this field of law. In other words, greater commitment to the law of the sea limits the opportunity for any rational void to appear that may, given a particular moral state of mind favourable to outside influence, be filled by off-topic political rather than legal considerations.

2. Tenure and Security of Tenure

The rules applicable to tenure and its security at the ITLOS are similar to those applicable to ICJ judges. Pursuant to Art. 5 Statute every judge has tenure of nine years,[990] and it thus follows the general practice for international courts that has developed in recent decades.[991] Judges are to fulfil their duties until a successor has been chosen and has begun to assume his judicial functions, which serves the purpose of ensuring that there is always a full complement of judges at the Tribunal.[992] Judges are obliged to finish any proceedings which they have begun to take part in before the date of their replacement. According to Art. 5(3) Statute,

> "[t]he members of the Tribunal shall continue to discharge their duties until their places have been filled. Though replaced, they shall finish any proceedings which they may have begun before the date of their replacement."[993]

---

990 With certain exceptions being made for two-thirds of the judges that are elected at the first election.

991 Cf. *infra* Appendix: International Courts – A Chart.

992 Nordquist (ed) *United Nations Convention on the Law of the Sea 1982: A Commentary – Volume V*, 348.

993 Art. 5(3) Statute. The use of the term *proceedings*, as opposed to the term *cases* used in Art. 13(3) ICJ Statute might give reason for a different assessment of a judge's duty to fulfil certain tasks before leaving office. The Rules of the Tribunal use the term proceedings in a more specialized way in order to circumscribe the bringing of a dispute to the Tribunal ("When proceedings before the Tribunal are instituted by means of an application ..."; Art. 54 Rules) and in order to address the different stages of a dispute that is before the Tribunal (subsection 2 and subsection 4 Rules differ between the written and the oral proceedings). It is thus to be assumed that a judge at the ITLOS has more limited obligations to fulfil certain duties before stepping down from his office, for example contributing to the conclu-

The security of tenure of the ITLOS judges is established somewhat differently from that of the judges of the ICJ. According to the wording of the pertinent provision, Art. 9 Statute ("Consequence of ceasing to fulfil required conditions"), only the preconditions for declaring a seat vacant are established. These are that a judge in the unanimous opinion of the other members of the Tribunal has ceased to fulfil the required conditions. It is notable, although it is unlikely to have real significance, that the exceptional nature of the removal of a judge from office before his tenure has expired is not expressly stated as it is in Art. 18(1) ICJ Statute.[994] Yet the exceptional nature of such an action must be assumed to be implicit. This is *inter alia* supported by the requirement that only the unanimous decision of the other members of the Tribunal can bring about such a result. Thus in essence, it can be assumed that ITLOS judges have the same protection of tenure as their colleagues at the ICJ.

The strengthening of their independence, by not being tempted to make decisions based on what helps them secure their tenure, must thus also be considered to be the same. The term "required conditions", which in earlier drafts of UNCLOS was merely "conditions",[995] is not defined anywhere in the Statute. The lack of practice from the ITLOS, but also from the ICJ which in Art. 18(1) ICJ Statute contains the same wording in this regard, contributes to complicating the interpretation. It must be assumed, however, that primarily the requirements enabling a person to be considered for judgeship, i.e. Arts. 2, 3, 7, 8 Statute, are meant.[996] These include the lack of independence of any judge as this is a requirement set out in Art. 2(1) Statute. The wording of Art. 2(1) already suggests that the requirement of independence is not just one which has to be fulfilled at the time judges are elected, but that the bench must continue to be composed of members demonstrating

---

sion of the written stage of a case but not having to remain in office for the oral proceedings. *Prima facie* this is a more liberal provision that enables the Tribunal to more directly react to the challenges posed to it.

994 "No member of the Court can be dismissed unless …".

995 See Third United Nations Conference on the Law of the Sea, *Informal single negotiating text (part IV)* (6 May 1976) UN Doc. A/CONF.62/WP.9/Rev. 1, 194, Heading of Art. 9.

996 Nordquist (ed) *United Nations Convention on the Law of the Sea 1982: A Commentary – Volume V*, 354 is of the same opinion. It has furthermore been assumed that reasons of health or permanent incapacity to exercise functions may be subsumed under this wording: Chandrasekhara Rao & Gautier (eds), *The Rules of the International Tribunal for the Law of the Sea – A Commentary*, 23.

independence. Reading Art. 9 Statute in conjunction with the second half sentence of Art. 2 Statute, where the criteria of "highest reputation for fairness and integrity and of recognized competence in the field of the law of the sea" are established, emphasizes that judges must live up to these standards not just at the time of their election but throughout their careers. This is a valuable extension of the scope of Art. 2 Statute, not only in light of the long period during which a judge may serve on the ITLOS.

The procedure to be followed when applying Art. 9 Statute is established in Art. 7 Rules and provides for extensive opportunities to investigate the question of a loss of required conditions among the members of the Tribunal, i.e. internally. Whenever the application of Art. 9 Statute is under consideration, the Member concerned shall be so informed by the President or Vice-President of the Tribunal in a written statement which shall include the grounds therefor and any relevant evidence. A private meeting is to be convened at which the affected member shall have the opportunity to make statements and provide answers to questions put to him by the other members. In a second meeting, which is to take place without the member concerned, the matter shall be discussed by the other members, who may state their opinions, and a vote shall be taken if requested. Of prime importance from the perspective of the independence of the Tribunal is that only a unanimous decision by the other members of the Tribunal may have the effect of removing a judge from office. In this respect Art. 9 Statute corresponds to Art. 18(1) ICJ Statute, but differs from the pertinent provisions relating to the other courts that remain to be analysed in what follows. Equally similarly to what applies at the ICJ, no outside intervention which may be motivated by political considerations seeking to influence the decision-making of the Tribunal may have the same effect.

3. Remuneration

The remuneration of ITLOS judges follows a different system from that of the ICJ, although the Meetings of States Parties have made it clear that in respect of the level of remuneration of ITLOS members, there shall be equivalence with the levels of pay of members of the ICJ,[997] and the overall

---

997 This was first established during the fourth Meeting of the States Parties, see United Nations Convention on the Law of the Sea – Meeting of States Parties, *Revised Budget Estimates for the International Tribunal for the Law of the Sea Covering*

remuneration of the members of the ITLOS shall not exceed the level of remuneration of judges of the ICJ.[998] Pursuant to Art. 18(1) Statute each member of the Tribunal shall receive a set annual allowance, plus a special allowance determined according to the number of days on which the individual judge exercises his judicial functions. On average, and based on the approved budgets and with various other benefits not included, judges of the ITLOS received an annual allowance of approximately 68,000 EUR per annum in 2009-2010, plus an average special allowance of approximately 19,200 EUR, resulting in an annual salary of approximately 87,200 EUR.[999] In comparison, ICJ judges received an annual salary amounting to 179,000 EUR in 2008, 186,700 EUR in 2009 and 205,000 EUR in 2010.[1000] Available statistical data for the years between 1999-2009 show that the development has been relatively steady, but that the special allowance did not increase much between 2000 and 2009. The reason for this is the comparatively low but relatively constant number of cases before the ITLOS.

A special safeguard against the reduction of salaries, allowances and compensation is contained in Art. 18(5) Statute and applies throughout judges' terms of office.[1001] The fact that the determination of ITLOS judges' salary depends, to some degree, on their actual service on the Tribunal, and that at any rate the salary is lower than that of e.g. ICJ judges, may be seen

the Period 1996-1997 (10 April 1996) SPLOS/WP.3/Rev. 1, para. 17. It is also repeated continuously, see, e.g., United Nations Convention on the Law of the Sea – Meeting of States Parties, *Decision on adjustment of the remuneration of members of the International Tribunal for the Law of the Sea* (21 June 2005) SPLOS/132. This particular decision of the Meeting of States Parties was a reaction to the UNGA Resolution 59/282 of 13 April 2005, in which the UNGA decided, with retroactive effect from 1 January 2005, to increase the annual salary and pensions of the members of the ICJ by 6.3 per cent as an interim measure.

998 United Nations Convention on the Law of the Sea – Meeting of States Parties, *Revised Budget Estimates for the International Tribunal for the Law of the Sea Covering the Period 1996-1997*, para. 13.

999 United Nations Convention on the Law of the Sea – Meeting of States Parties, *Decisions on Budgetary Matters of the International Tribunal for the Law of the Sea for 2011-2012*. This is a slight increase *vis-à-vis* the biennium of 2009-2010, when the annual allowance was approximately 136,100 EUR.

1000 UNSG, *Conditions of service and compensation for officials other than Secretariat officials: members of the International Court of Justice and judges and ad litem judges of the International Tribunal for the Former Yugoslavia and the International Criminal Tribunal for Rwanda: Report of the Secretary General* (15 July 2010) UN Doc. A/65/134, para. 66 and Annex I.

1001 "They may not be decreased during the term of office."

as an element of insecurity for the judges. In particular, the rather low salary, apart from not being an incentive to attract competent individuals to serve on the ITLOS' bench, creates the danger that individuals who have been elected also have greater motivation to seek additional sources of income.[1002] This insecurity, however, is on the one hand a necessity following from the specialized nature of the Tribunal, making a judgeship not a full-time occupation in the first place. On the other hand, from the perspective of the independence of the judges, this problematic constellation can be justified only by allowing judges to be engaged in other activities that are at least not inappropriate but nevertheless able to raise their income and to allow them to build their reputations and standing in the international law community.[1003] Only if the ability to exercise auxiliary functions is balanced against the assurance of the judges' independence by making them unsusceptible to pressure linked to financial concerns can membership of the ITLOS bench be appealing enough to attract the most competent international lawyers in the field of the law of the sea.

The right to receive a retirement pension is regulated by the special Pension Scheme Regulations for Members of the International Tribunal for the Law of the Sea adopted by the ninth Meeting of States Parties.[1004] The amount of the pension is determined on the basis of the number of years served on the Tribunal; a minimum of three years on the bench is required. Theoretically, the minimum number of years that a judge must have served in order to be eligible for a pension could be an incentive for judges to seek re-election and thus be a potential threat to independent decision-making. However, since the tenure of the judges is already considerably longer than the minimum requirement for receiving a pension, no conflict can be seen to arise.

1002 This is certainly not only a problem connected to the level of income provided by the ITLOS but rather also an issue linked to the overall workload of the Tribunal, creating an incitement for judges to "seek other challenges".

1003 See *infra* Chapter E.V(5) on incompatible activities.

1004 United Nations Convention on the Law of the Sea – Meeting of States Parties, *Decision on Pension Scheme Regulations for Members of the International Tribunal for the Law of the Sea* (7 June 1999) SPLOS/47.

4. Immunities and Privileges

Equipping the judges of the ITLOS with immunities and privileges is important in furnishing them with protection against undue influence, and thus an assurance of the independent fulfilment of their functions as judges. Art. 10 Statute corresponds to Art. 19 ICJ Statute and provides the ITLOS' judges with a status that is equal to that of a diplomat. The provision is relatively short and does not e.g. provide a definition of what is meant by conceding the rights "when [judges are] engaged on the business of the Tribunal". It is to be assumed that only judges acting in their official capacity can have recourse to the provision, although this may in practice lead to difficulties of delimitation. However, other sources pertinent to the ITLOS help to define what is meant by "diplomatic privileges and immunities". In particular, Art. 13 Agreement on the Privileges and Immunities of the International Tribunal for the Law of the Sea, which otherwise merely refers to the Tribunal as an institution, states that members of the Tribunal shall "enjoy the privileges, immunities, facilities and prerogatives accorded to heads of diplomatic missions in accordance with the Vienna Convention." This equivalence between judges and heads of diplomatic missions pursuant to the Vienna Convention on Diplomatic Relations was already assumed for ICJ judges and amounts in essence to the following protections: exemption from taxes and dues;[1005] freedom of movement and travel on the territory of the Netherlands, as the seat of the Court;[1006] inviolability of the person;[1007] inviolability and protection of any private residence[1008] and of papers, correspondence and property;[1009] immunity from criminal jurisdiction and – subject to certain restrictions – civil and administrative jurisdiction.[1010] Essentially, what was mentioned as criticism in the context of the ICJ, namely that the international judge is not a political representative and thus needs further or more far-reaching privileges and immunities, e.g. also freedom of movement and travel on the territory of the judge's home country, for the protection of his independence applies *mutatis mutandis* to judges of the ITLOS. Giving IT-

1005 Arts. 23 and 34 VCDR; cf. Art. 18(8) Statute: "The salaries, allowances, and compensation shall be free of all taxation."
1006 Art. 26 VCDR.
1007 Art. 26 VCDR.
1008 Art. 30(1) VCDR.
1009 Art. 30(2) VCDR.
1010 Art. 31 VCDR.

LOS judges the same status as diplomats ignores the fact that the latter do not have, and arguably do not need, special immunities as regards their States of origin.[1011]

Yet Art. 13(3) Agreement on the Privileges and Immunities of the International Tribunal for the Law of the Sea does go further than Art. 19 ICJ Statute by stating that the members of the ITLOS, as well as their immediate families, "shall be accorded every facility for *leaving the country where they may happen to be* and for entering and leaving the country where the Tribunal is sitting." (Emphasis added.) In other words, it is acknowledged that the members shall have the right to leave any country, including that of their own origin, if it is linked to the exercise of their function. Art. 13(2) continues to accord privileges and immunities irrespective of the judges' nationality by providing:

> "On journeys in connection with the exercise of their functions, they shall in all countries through which they may have to pass enjoy all the privileges, immunities and facilities granted by these countries to diplomatic agents in similar circumstances."

Again the provision detaches the granting of privileges and immunities from the nationality of the individual judge, and thereby extends them in a way that pays tribute to the function of an international judge as a representative of the international court he is a member of. Art. 13 of the Agreement also establishes other rights, such as insurance against third-party risks. An important provision in support of judges' independence must be seen in Art. 13(7) which provides that judges shall have "immunity from legal process in respect of words spoken or written and all acts done by them in discharging their functions" even after they have ceased to be members of the Tribunal. An equivalent provision is not available to guard ICJ judges' independence from fear of reprisals after their tenure has ended.

The immunities and privileges mentioned so far, and in particular Art. 10 Statute, apply to the individual judge and not to the Tribunal as an institution. The granting of privileges and immunities for the ICJ as an institution is

---

1011 Cf. the comments made on this system at the ICJ, *supra* Chapter D.VI(4).

derived from the UNC[1012] and substantiated by UNGA Resolution 90(I).[1013] For the ITLOS, a different path was chosen, namely the conclusion of the Agreement on the Privileges and Immunities of the International Tribunal for the Law of the Sea mentioned earlier. This has the advantage compared to the ICJ system that a binding international document is available. The UNGA resolution does not have this compelling quality and can be considered binding on States only insofar as it codifies customary international law.

5. Incompatible Activities

The declarations that have to be made by any member before taking office confirm the commitment that members of the Tribunal be impartial in the exercise of their functions.[1014] From this requirement of impartiality flows the fundamental necessity for the judges to stand above the parties to a dispute in order to settle such dispute without crediting the parties as such, but merely with reference to the applicable law and the facts as presented during the proceedings.

The regulation of the activities a judge may perform while serving on the bench of the ITLOS is a central issue in this context, as other activities may in fact make the judge or make him merely seem to be a spokesperson for a particular cause. Art. 7 Statute, which is the central provision in this regard, is more liberal in its wording than the equivalent provision applicable to ICJ judges. Whereas Art. 16 ICJ Statute demands the rejection of any occupation of a professional nature parallel to the membership of the ICJ, Art. 7 Statute is more selective and merely rejects three different categories of activities: (I) political or administrative functions;[1015] (II) active or financial association

---

1012 Art. 105 UNC ("The Organization shall enjoy in the territory of each of its Members such privileges and immunities as are necessary for the fulfilment of its purposes.") read together with Art. 92 UNC ("The International Court of Justice shall be the principal judicial organ of the United Nations. It shall function in accordance with the annexed Statute, which is based upon the Statute of the Permanent Court of International Justice and forms an integral part of the present Charter.").

1013 UNGA, *Privileges and Immunities of Members of the International Court of Justice, the Registrar, Officials of the Registry, Assessors, the Agents and Counsel of the Parties and of the Witnesses and Experts*.

1014 Art. 11 Statute in conjunction with Art. 5(1) Rules; this also applies to *ad hoc* judges, see Art. 9(1) Rules.

1015 Art. 7(1) Statute.

in the operations of any enterprise concerned with the exploration for or exploitation of the resources of the sea or the seabed or other commercial use of the sea or the seabed;[1016] and (III) acting as agent, counsel or advocate in a case before the Tribunal[1017].

The first and third categories of incompatible activities are hardly surprising. It is at the core of the independence of any (international) court that its activities not be unduly associated with political functions, and there would be an apparent conflict of interests if a judge during his service on the bench also appeared as a representative of a party in a case before the same Tribunal.[1018] The second category, active association with or financial interest in the commercial use of the sea or the seabed, is necessary as the judges of the ITLOS, being experts in the law of the sea, may be expected to be of interest to such enterprises. This exposure of the judges to commercial interests justifies the explicit mention of the unacceptability of such activities.

What is more important, however, is the omission in the ITLOS' Statute of a broader provision on incompatible activities. *Prima facie*, this lacuna may be interpreted as a potential threat to the guarantee of the impartiality of the judges. In contrast, however, it is motivated and indeed dictated by the already mentioned fact that membership cannot be considered a full-time occupation, despite the requirement of permanent availability of judges,[1019] which also justifies the lower payment the judges receive. Thus Art. 7 Statute

---

1016 Ibid.

1017 Art. 7(2) Statute. The *prior* involvement of a judge in a case before the Tribunal concerns the second kind of potential violations of a promise of impartiality. The pertinent provision, Art. 8 Statute, corresponds to Art. 17 ICJ Statute. It deserves to be underlined that the determination on any doubts with regard to the conditions relating to participation of members in a particular case follows what applies to similar determinations on incompatible activities, namely that the uncertainties shall be resolved by decision of the majority of the other members of the Tribunal present (Art. 8(4) Statute). Hence also in this context, the Tribunal retains the sole decision-making power.

1018 An agent is the diplomatic representative of a State Party to a case in the relations between that State and the Tribunal (cf. Art. 53(1) Rules of ITLOS), which makes it inherently irreconcilable with the simultaneous exercise of a judicial function. The role of counsel and advocates is not much different, as they act as assistants to a State Party (Art. 53(2) Rules of ITLOS). See on this issue also Valencia-Ospina, Eduardo, 'International Courts and Tribunals, Agents, Counsel and Advocates', in: Wolfrum, Rüdiger (ed) *The Max Planck Encyclopedia of Public International Law* (Oxford University Press Online Edition 2012), paras. 12-14.

1019 Art. 41(2) Rules.

constitutes a necessary compromise between the requirement of guaranteeing independence on the one hand and the conceding of a right to exercise side activities appropriate and necessary for persons of the standing of the ITLOS judges on the other. As membership is not a full-time occupation, the provision should also be applied with some flexibility.[1020]

Favouring the Tribunal's autonomy is the fact that the Tribunal itself decides, with the majority of the other members of the Tribunal,[1021] i.e. without external intervention, on any doubts regarding the application of Art. 7 Statute. An example of a rather unproblematic side activity of the ITLOS judges is service as an academic, whereas acting as an arbitrator on the PCA must be subjected to the same critical scrutiny as in the case of ICJ judges.[1022] In contrast, and following what Art. 7 Statute already indicates, occupations that include financial interests in the commercial use of the sea or the seabed are very likely to run counter to the judges' independence. A review of the current side activities of judges, labeled "professional experiences" and as reported by the judges and the Tribunal themselves, are the following: a director of a consulting company; a professorship; an advisor to NGOs; the presidency of a regional branch of the International Law Association; membership of editorial boards and the position of editor-in-chief of a law journal; the head of a research institute; a partner in a law firm; a consultant to the oil industry; ambassador/counsel in the cabinet of the Minister of Foreign Affairs; and an expert for the Organization for Security and Co-operation in Europe (OSCE).[1023] Whereas most of these activities do not counter the aim of Art. 7 Statute, others appear to teeter on the edge of liberal interpretation and blatant violation of that provision.

1020 Nordquist (ed) *United Nations Convention on the Law of the Sea 1982: A Commentary – Volume V*, 351.

1021 Art. 7(3) Statute.

1022 It must be kept in mind that the occupation of member of the PCA is also bound by at least a customary commitment to independence. Cf. the website of the PCA, stating that "[t]he PCA has a three-part organizational structure consisting of an Administrative Council that oversees its policies and budgets, a panel of *independent* potential arbitrators known as the Members of the Court, and its Secretariat, known as the International Bureau, headed by the Secretary-General." (Emphasis added.) See 'Permanent Court of Arbitration – Structure' available at <http://www.pca-cpa.org/showpage.asp?pag_id=1039> (last visited: 21 March 2014).

1023 All information available at 'International Tribunal for the Law of the Sea – Members' available at <http://www.itlos.org/index.php?id=96> (last visited: 21 March 2014).

As already mentioned, judges of the ITLOS are required to keep themselves permanently available to exercise their judicial functions and are likewise obliged to attend all meetings, but are not required to be permanently at the Tribunal.[1024] Because judges of the ICJ are not only required to hold themselves permanently available to the Court[1025] but are also expected to be permanently at the Court, the operation of the ICJ is more rigorous still as the ICJ is also in permanent session pursuant to Art. 23(1) ICJ Statute. A similar provision for the ITLOS does not exist, and instead the Tribunal holds sessions according to the administrative workload and that relating to cases before the Tribunal.[1026] Members of the Tribunal are required to attend all meetings that are held, and exceptions may be made only in specific cases listed in Art. 41(2) Rules; e.g. when a member is absent on leave or prevented from attending by illness or for other serious reasons duly explained to the President. Thus the obligation of the judges to fulfil their functions at the ITLOS, and specifically their obligation to attend the meetings of the Tribunal, override any other obligations that they may have.[1027] This special regulation follows from the consideration that the Tribunal is a specialized Tribunal with a limited jurisdiction, a fact which would make it unreasonable, both economically and practically, to require it to be permanently in session and/or the judges to be permanently at (the seat of) the Tribunal. Instead the individual judge's position at the ITLOS is a part-time occupation.[1028] Only

1024 Art. 41(2) Rules. See on the interpretation of this requirement Anderson, David H., 'The Internal Judicial Practice of the International Tribunal for the Law of the Sea', in: Chandrasekhara Rao, P. *et al.* (eds) *The International Tribunal for the Law of the Sea – Law and Practice* (Kluwer Law International The Hague 2001), 199.

1025 Cf. Art. 23(3) ICJ Statute.

1026 With regard to administrative sessions the Tribunal has established the practice of holding two such sessions every year for the purpose of preparing the budget proposals, the adoption of an annual report to the Meetings of States Parties, the consideration of organizational and procedural matters relating to the Tribunal and the preparation of further reports and publications (see 'ITLOS General Information – Sessions' available at <http://www.itlos.org/index.php?id=22> (last visited: 21 March 2014)).

1027 Chandrasekhara Rao & Gautier (eds), *The Rules of the International Tribunal for the Law of the Sea – A Commentary*, 119. This is of interest when it comes to the other activities the ITLOS judge may or may not exercise during his membership of the bench, see Art. 7 Statute.

1028 Karg, *IGH vs. ISGH – Die Beziehung zwischen zwei völkerrechtlichen Streitbeilegungsorganen*, 131.

the President and the Registrar of the Tribunal are, pursuant to Art. 12(3) Statute, obliged to reside at its seat,[1029] which is necessary already from an administrative perspective to guarantee the Tribunal's functioning.

VI. Conclusions

The ITLOS is a specialized Tribunal with the task of settling disputes arising under the regime of the law of the sea as established by UNLOS and other rules of international law not incompatible with UNCLOS. The rationale underlying its creation was the need to provide a forum for dispute settlement in an area of law that at times is highly technical and characterized by the presupposition of scientific knowledge. The Tribunal is also a result of the assessment of the adequacy of other dispute settlement bodies, such as the ICJ and arbitration, which had thus far been used in the area of the law of the sea. Whereas both of these fora had their advantages (e.g. a standing non-contradictory jurisprudence in the field, or an organizational and procedural flexibility serving the interests of the parties) they also exhibited serious deficiencies that could be effectively corrected by the setting up of a new standing tribunal (e.g. reducing costs, predictability of the procedure, special competence on the bench, the availability of dispute settlement to non-State entities, better identification between the organ, its rules and procedures, and the various interests immanent in a diversified world community).

The assessment of the Tribunal has led to the following result regarding its independence. The ITLOS is conceived as an independent organ as it was established by a diplomatic conference with universal participation convened for the purpose of drafting a multilateral agreement. This independence in particular refers to the Tribunal's relationship with the UN and its organs, in relation to which it is autonomous.[1030] Whereas for example this implies that the Tribunal does not have to compete directly with other organs for its financing and that it is not required to harmonize with the (political) activities of the principal organs of the UN, still the Tribunal is called upon, as a result of the overlapping jurisdictions *ratione materiae*, to take into consideration

1029 I.e. in Hamburg, Germany; cf. Art. 1(2) Statute.

1030 See the statement in Art. 1(1) Agreement on Cooperation and Relationship between the United Nations and the International Tribunal for the Law of the Sea: "The United Nations recognizes the International Tribunal for the Law of the Sea as an autonomous international judicial body …".

actions by the UN. A mutual willingness to co-operate is e.g. illustrated by the ITLOS' observer status to the UNGA, and the UN's establishment of a Division of Ocean Affairs and the Law of the Sea.

The specialized function of settling law of the sea disputes, coupled with the fundamental availability of the Tribunal to all States of the world and even certain additional entities, characterizes the framework for its judicial independence. Whereas the number of judges constituting the bench is comparatively high, the Tribunal has the ability *proprio motu* further to extend its ranks by appointing technical and scientific experts, detaching it from reliance on the parties to a dispute. The qualifications required of judges are similar to those applicable to judges of the ICJ, being generally referred to in the beginning of the Statute but defined by subsequent provisions. As with the standards known from the ICJ, any requirements that are established are recommendations to those engaged in the nomination and election process, which in the case of the ITLOS are States. However, an enforcement mechanism is not available, a fact which is owed to the state-centeredness that affects the ITLOS. Nominations are reserved for the States Parties that established the Tribunal and which make use of it. A separate organ with the responsibility for nominations, such as the national groups of the PCA, is not envisaged. From the perspective of limiting the influence of fleeting political considerations on nominations this is problematic; although the real effect of the national groups at the PCA is equally questionable for the reasons elaborated on above, and thus does not serve as a conducive alternative. The elections provide for high majority requirements, which, together with detailed safeguards for the adequate representation of geographical groups, contribute to giving the bench a diverse composition, preventing the predominance of a particular (legal) culture and the suppression of others. Yet numerous circumstances, of which the practice of presenting a clean slate is one, indicate that the election process is overly politicised. For its financing the ITLOS mainly relies on the States Parties; any adverse effect, such as a directing by States, can be mitigated by future partial financing through the ISA.

The position of the individual judge has particular similarities with that of the ICJ judge, although the part-time position of the ITLOS judge sometimes merits questionable deviations. Removal from office is possible only if the unanimous opinion of the other members of the bench supports it, a requirement which amounts to an important safeguard for the independent functioning of the Tribunal. The benefit is that this mechanism keeps the control of the observation of the requirements with the Tribunal itself, rather than placing it with any external body. This mechanism of removal from office is also the only appropriate equivalent to an enforcement mechanism for compliance with the earlier stated personal requirements that is not susceptible to direct external influence. Remuneration is limited, configured flexibly but protected against any reduction during the tenure of each individual judge. This less than satisfactory condition is however closely linked to the protection of the judges' impartiality, which, as a consequence, is more liberal. Immunities and privileges are, by and large, equal to those granted to heads of diplomatic missions, although providing for enhanced protection against home States.

Chapter F: Judicial Independence in the International Criminal Court

I. Introduction

The ICC[1031] is a permanent international court established to try those accused of having committed the most serious crimes of international concern. It is, similar to both the ICJ and the ITLOS, a permanent international judicial institution and must therefore be distinguished from the two *ad hoc* criminal Tribunals, which will be addressed later. Through its establishment by an international treaty, the Rome Statute, the ICC avoids the legitimacy concerns that were repeatedly raised regarding its *ad hoc* predecessors.[1032]

The independence of the ICC was highlighted as a separate issue throughout the drafting of the Rome Statute and was prominently codified in the ninth recital of its preamble.[1033] Whereas the ICC certainly encapsulates the idealistic visions of previous, current and future generations, its remit implies that it is condemned sometimes to interfere in the interests of States, but also possibly in the exercise of its functions to collide with the international organization entrusted with the primary responsibility for the maintenance of international peace and security. Bringing to justice individuals who have caused crimes that are usually committed on a large scale and often are State-sponsored inevitably pushes the ICC into the realm of the political sphere which is largely and traditionally governed by States' interests: many

---

1031 Hereinafter also referred to as "the Court".

1032 See *infra* Chapter G.II.

1033 The recitals of a preamble usually reflect the considerations that have played a role in the drafting of the treaty, see Gardiner, Richard K., *Treaty Interpretation* (Oxford University Press Oxford 2008), 186-187. They are of both textual and teleological significance. The latter function is laid down in Art. 31(2) Vienna Convention on the Law of Treaties, according to which "[t]he context for the purpose of the interpretation of a treaty shall [include] its preamble and annexes". The purpose of the preamble to the Rome Statute is to describe the main purposes of the Statute and to reiterate the obligations of States: Triffterer, Otto (ed) *Commentary on the Rome Statute of the International Criminal Court – Observers' Notes, Article by Article* (Beck München 2nd edn. 2008), 4. It must therefore be taken into account when interpreting the Statute.

of the crimes adjudicated upon by the ICC have been committed in the course of armed conflicts with high political stakes, and hence suspects may even involve (former) ministers or even heads of State. The balancing of the independent exercise of its jurisdiction and the taking into consideration of (legitimate) interests of other actors in the shaping of political processes are thus at the core of the ICC.

II. Genesis and Organizational Setting of the ICC

1. Early Beginnings and the Hurdle of State Interests

The ICC is the result of a lengthy codification process which effectively began after the IMT and the International Military Tribunal for the Far East in Tokyo went down in history as the first modern examples of international criminal tribunals.[1034] Even before the IMT and the Tokyo Tribunal took up their work, attempts were made to establish organs able to prosecute individuals on an international level for serious crimes.[1035] Apart from the need to remove the prosecution of such crimes from the national judiciary, which had proven unsuccessful after the First World War, it was understood from the criminal trials held after World War Two that any such international prosecution had to avoid being perceived as victor's justice and a mere product of momentous political considerations.[1036] This led to the conviction

---

1034 Bassiouni, M. Cherif (ed) *The Legislative History of the International Criminal Court: Volume 1 – Introduction, Analysis, and Integrated Text of the Statute, Elements of Crimes and Rules of Procedure and Evidence* (Transnational Publishers New York 2005), 26.

1035 The first *modern* proposal for an international criminal court was presented in 1871 by G. Moynier: see Hall, Christopher Keith, 'The First Proposal for a Permanent International Criminal Court' (1998) 322 International Review of the Red Cross. For an historical overview of the attempts to establish a standing international criminal court see, e.g., Bassiouni (ed) *The Legislative History of the International Criminal Court: Volume 1 – Introduction, Analysis, and Integrated Text of the Statute, Elements of Crimes and Rules of Procedure and Evidence*, 54-75.

1036 The problem of "prosecution and judgment … by victor nations over vanquished foes" was also acknowledged by the IMT itself: "We must summon such detachment and intellectual integrity to our task that this Trial will commend itself to posterity as fulfilling humanity's aspirations to do justice." See the opening address of the US Chief Prosecutor at the IMT in Nuremberg, Justice R. H. Jackson, reprinted in 'The Avalon Project: Nuremberg Trial Proceedings Vol. 2 – Second Day,

that an international criminal jurisdiction ought to be a permanent body[1037] and that it should not be limited to a particular faction of individuals or a particular conflict.[1038]

After the UNGA adopted the Genocide Convention of 1948, which contained the call for an international penal tribunal able to try those charged with committing genocide,[1039] it also invited the International Law Commission (ILC) to examine the prospect of establishing an international criminal tribunal.[1040] While the ILC itself began the formulation of the principles enshrined in the Charter of the IMT[1041] and the drafting of a code of offences against the peace and security of mankind, a special rapporteur was entrusted with the task of drafting a statute for an international criminal court.[1042] At the same time, the UNGA set up a special committee,[1043] which submitted a draft statute for an international criminal court in 1952.[1044] This report envisaged a permanent court, which would function only on the basis of

---

Wednesday, 21 November 1945, Morning Session' available at <http://avalon.law.yale.edu/imt/11-21-45.asp> (last visited: 21 March 2014).

1037 Schabas, William A., *An Introduction to the International Criminal Court* (Cambridge University Press Cambridge 3rd edn. 2007), 6.

1038 E.g. the judges of the IMT refused to convict with regard to some war crimes after hearing evidence that showed similar behaviour from British and American soldiers; ibid, 6.

1039 See Art. 6 Genocide Convention: "Persons charged with genocide or any of the other acts enumerated in article III shall be tried by a competent tribunal of the State in the territory of which the act was committed, or by such international penal tribunal as may have jurisdiction with respect to those Contracting Parties which shall have accepted its jurisdiction."

1040 UNGA, *Study by the International Law Commission of the Question of an International Criminal Jurisdiction* (9 December 1948) UN Doc. A/RES/260 (III) B.

1041 Remit established in UNGA, *Formulation of the Principles Recognized in the Charter of the Nurnberg Tribunal and in the Judgment of the Tribunal* (21 November 1947) UN Doc. A/RES/177 (II), paragraph (a), and the principles adopted by the ILC in International Law Commission, *Report of the International Law Commission on its Second Session, 5 June to 29 July 1950, Official Records of the General Assembly, Fifth session, Supplement No.12 (A/1316)* (July 1950) UN Doc. A/CN.4/34.

1042 His report was submitted in March 1950: Ricardo J. Alfaro, *Report on the Question of International Criminal Jurisdiction by Ricardo J. Alfaro, Special Rapporteur* (3 March 1950) UN Doc. A/CN.4/15 (1950).

1043 The Committee on International Criminal Jurisdiction; UNGA, *International Criminal Jurisdiction* (12 December 1950) UN Doc. A/RES/489 (V).

1044 Committee on International Criminal Jurisdiction, *Report of the 1951 Committee on International Criminal Jurisdiction* (1 – 31 August 1951) UN Doc. A/2136.

cases being submitted to it. A second committee established by the UNGA[1045] presented its final report in 1954.[1046] However, partly due to the difficulty of reaching a satisfactory definition of the crime of aggression, the UNGA suspended the mandates of both committees.[1047]

Despite the adoption of a definition of aggression in 1974,[1048] the work on a proposed international criminal court was not to be resumed until 1981, when the UNGA requested the ILC to continue its work on the draft code of offences.[1049] In 1989 the UNGA again requested the ILC "to address the question of establishing an international criminal court".[1050] A first draft statute was submitted to the UNGA in 1993,[1051] and a final version was presented to the sixth committee of the UNGA the following year.[1052] In order to review the ILC draft statute and "to consider arrangements for the convening of an international conference of plenipotentiaries", an *ad hoc* committee was convened.[1053] The work on the draft code of crimes, of which the ILC had presented a first draft in 1991,[1054] continued at the same time.[1055]

1045 UNGA, *International Criminal Jurisdiction* (5 December 1952) UN Doc. A/RES/687 (VII).

1046 See the text of the draft in Johnson, D.H.N., 'The Draft Code of Offences Against the Peace and Security of Mankind' (1955) 4 The International and Comparative Law Quarterly 3, 466-468.

1047 Meanwhile, the ILC submitted a draft on a code of crimes the same year; International Law Commission, *Yearbook of the International Law Commission* (United Nations New York 1954), 129-134.

1048 UNGA, *Definition of Aggression* (14 December 1974) UN Doc. A/RES/3314 (XXIX).

1049 UNGA, *Draft Code of Offences against the Peace and Security of Mankind* (10 December 1981) UN Doc. A/RES/36/106.

1050 UNGA, *International criminal responsibility of individuals and entities engaged in illicit trafficking in narcotic drugs across national frontiers and other transnational criminal activities* (4 December 1989) UN Doc. A/RES/44/39.

1051 International Law Commission, *Revised Report of the Working Group on the Draft Statute for an International Criminal Court* (19 July 1993) UN Doc. A/CN.4/L.490.

1052 See International Law Commission, *Report of the International Law Commission on the work of its forty-sixth session* (22 July 1994) UN Doc. A/49/10; see also Crawford, James, 'The ILC's Draft Statute for an International Criminal Tribunal' (1994) 88 American Journal of International Law 1.

1053 UNGA, *Establishment of an International Criminal Court* (9 December 1994) UN Doc. A/RES/49/53.

1054 International Law Commission, *Report of the International Law Commission on the work of its forty-third session* (29 April – 19 July 1991) UN Doc. A/46/10.

1055 The draft code was discussed and ultimately adopted by the ILC in a revised form in 1996.

The report of the *ad hoc* committee[1056] made some significant departures from the ILC draft. Whereas the ILC draft still built on the distinction between the statute and the code of crimes, the first was merely to contain a list of the crimes subject to the court's jurisdiction and thus be "primarily procedural and adjectival",[1057] the *ad hoc* committee instead opted for a more detailed definition of the jurisdiction *ratione materiae* in the statute itself.[1058] Some issues in the ILC draft were retained; the court was still to be a permanent and independent organ established by an international treaty. Others were adopted but amended; the principle of complementarity was introduced by the ILC draft but streamlined considerably by the *ad hoc* committee.

Due to profound differences of opinion between States regarding the structure and functioning of the future criminal court, hopes of convening an international conference following the *ad hoc* committee vanished. Instead the UNGA established the Preparatory Committee on the Establishment of an International Criminal Court (PrepCom) to continue the drafting work of the *ad hoc* committee and further to discuss the ILC draft.[1059] The decision to establish the PrepCom instead of extending the mandate of the *ad hoc* committee indicated a shift from non-binding discussions to a more serious phase of drafting.[1060] The two meetings held by the PrepCom in 1996 dealt in particular with issues relating to the general principles of criminal law, the jurisdiction of the court, the definition of crimes, the principle of complementarity, and the role of the UNSC.[1061] On the basis of three further sessions

---

1056 Ad Hoc Committee on the Establishment of an International Criminal Court, *Report of the Ad Hoc Committee on the Establishment of an International Criminal Court* (6 September 1995) UN Doc. A/50/22.

1057 International Law Commission, *Report of the International Law Commission on the work of its forty-sixth session*, 66.

1058 In other words, the longstanding distinction between the statute for an international criminal court and the substantive code of crimes was finally dropped: Schabas, *An Introduction to the International Criminal Court*, 16.

1059 UNGA, *Establishment of an International Criminal Court* (11 December 1995) UN Doc. A/RES/50/46.

1060 Cassese, Antonio (ed) *The Rome Statute of the International Criminal Court: A Commentary – Volume I* (Oxford University Press Oxford 2002), 46.

1061 The most important conclusion from these negotiations was that the debate had shifted from whether it would be desirable and possible to establish an international court to the kind of court that would attract the broadest support and best serve the interests of the international community. See the statements made by Adriaan Bos, chairman of the Preparatory Committee, reprinted in Morris, Virginia & Bourloyannis-Vrailas, M.-Christiane, 'The Work of the Sixth Committee at the

held in 1997, the PrepCom was able to submit a draft statute,[1062] comprising 166 pages and still a large number of brackets indicating undecided passages and issues, which was to function as the starting point for an ensuing diplomatic conference.[1063] Although the PrepCom was able to refer real substantive suggestions to the international conference on numerous issues, some were considered to be in need of political solutions, among them those relating to the powers of the permanent members of the UNSC and those affecting the sovereignty of States.

2. The Rome Conference

The United Nations Diplomatic Conference of Plenipotentiaries on the Establishment of an International Criminal Court[1064] was held in Rome between 15 June and 17 July 1998 and proceeded to adopt the provisions of the Rome Statute "by general agreement" in the working groups, i.e. without a vote.[1065] Some of the core issues, however, were not allocated to a working group but instead remained with the chair of the Committee of the Whole.[1066] This included the role of the UNSC, the list of crimes over which the court was to have inherent jurisdiction and jurisdiction over those persons not nationals of Member States. The reason is to be found in the political delicacy of these issues, many States fearing to make too far-reaching concessions too early. Those core issues were not resolved until the final day of the conference, when the president of the Committee of the Whole submitted his final proposal under the pressure of not allowing the conference to fail. At the same time as the Statute was adopted, a Preparatory Commission was established

---

Fifty-First Session of the UN General Assembly' (1997) 91 American Journal of International Law 3, 548.

1062 Schabas, *An Introduction to the International Criminal Court*, 17.

1063 Preparatory Committee on the Establishment of an International Criminal Court, *Report of the Preparatory Committee on the Establishment of an International Criminal Court* (14 April 1998) UN Doc. A/CONF.183/2/Add.1.

1064 UNGA, *Establishment of an International Criminal Court* (15 December 1997) UN Doc. A/RES/52/160.

1065 The Rome Statute was signed by 120 States, with 21 abstentions and seven votes against. United Nations Diplomatic Conference of Plenipotentiaries on the Establishment of an International Criminal Court, *Summary Record of the 9th Plenary Meeting* (17 July 1998) UN Doc. A/CONF.183/SR.9, para. 10.

1066 Schabas, *An Introduction to the International Criminal Court*, 20.

entrusted with making the necessary arrangements for the Court to start its work.[1067] By the time the Commission had concluded its work and mandate[1068] in July 2002, after holding ten sessions[1069] and only days after the ICC came into effect, it had adopted draft texts of a number of important instruments, including the Rules of Procedure and Evidence,[1070] the Elements of Crimes,[1071] a relationship agreement between the Court and the UN,[1072] basic principles governing a headquarters agreement to be negotiated between the Court and the host country,[1073] financial regulations and rules,[1074] an agreement on the privileges and immunities of the Court,[1075] a budget for the first financial year,[1076] and the rules of procedure of the Assembly of States Parties (ASP).[1077]

1067 See Resolution F of the United Nations Diplomatic Conference of Plenipotentiaries on the Establishment of an International Criminal Court, *Final Act of the United Nations Diplomatic Conference of Plenipotentiaries on the Establishment of an International Criminal Court* (17 July 1998) UN Doc. A/CONF.183/10.

1068 UNGA, *Establishment of the International Criminal Court* (12 December 2001) UN Doc. A/RES/56/85.

1069 For an overview of the progress made at the different sessions see Bassiouni (ed) *The Legislative History of the International Criminal Court: Volume 1 – Introduction, Analysis, and Integrated Text of the Statute, Elements of Crimes and Rules of Procedure and Evidence*, 103-110.

1070 Rules of Procedure and Evidence (adopted 9 September 2002, entered into force 9 September 2002) Official Records ICC-ASP/1/3 (Part II-A).

1071 Elements of Crimes (adopted 9 September 2002, entered into force 9 September 2002) Official Records ICC-ASP/1/3 (Part II-B).

1072 Negotiated Relationship Agreement between the International Criminal Court and the United Nations (adopted 4 October 2004, entered into force 22 July 2004) Official Records ICC-ASP/3/Res.1.

1073 Headquarters Agreement between the International Criminal Court and the Host State (adopted 7 June 2007, entered into force 1 March 2008) Official Records ICC-BD/04-01-08.

1074 Financial Regulations and Rules (latest amendment adopted on 22 November 2008) (adopted 9 September 2002) Official Records ICC-ASP/7/5 (Part. II-D).

1075 Agreement on the Privileges and Immunities of the International Criminal Court (adopted 9 September 2002, entered into force 22 July 2004) Official Records ICC-ASP/1/3 (Part II-E).

1076 Budget appropriations for the first financial period and financing of appropriations for the first financial period (adopted 3 September 2002) Official Records ICC-ASP/1/Res.12.

1077 Rules of Procedure of the Assembly of States Parties (adopted 8-12 September 2002) Official Records ICC-ASP/1/3/Part.II-A.

Numerous actors besides State delegates significantly influenced the preparation phase leading up to the Rome conference, the outcome of the Rome conference itself and the preparation following immediately after the adoption of the Rome Statute. They contributed significantly towards equipping the ICC with a mandate and tools that could touch upon the interests of States, such as its complementary function in relation to national jurisdictions. NGOs were able to influence the various stages of the work leading up to the creation of the ICC[1078] and have continued to influence the way the court is perceived, working for the universal adoption and ratification of the Statute and implementation of the complementarity principle by lobbying for broad implementation of the substantive provisions of the Rome Statute in national legal systems. At times the driving force behind the negotiations was individual States, or consortiums of States, such as the group of like-minded States, which had decisively influenced the negotiations at Rome and played a significant role in providing the momentum needed to resolve some of the most fiercely debated topics.

The role of the UNSC, and in particular the question whether or not the UNSC ought to influence when and if a person may be tried by the Court, was not settled until the very end of the Rome conference. And the final outcome on this issue was an "uneasy compromise" which preserved a role for the UNSC but without entirely subordinating the Court to the filter of the UNSC. One characteristic feature of the ICC, its complementary function in relation to national jurisdictions, was settled as early as during the drafting of the PrepCom, and the solution was kept until the last draft of the Statute was adopted at Rome. This principle provided an important compromise which even today is opposed in view of the ICC's ability to evaluate national judicial systems.[1079] It is important to emphasize that the Rome Statute ulti-

---

1078 Triffterer, Otto, 'Der Ständige Internationale Strafgerichtshof – Anspruch und Wirklichkeit', in: Gössel, Karl Heinz *et al.* (eds) *Gedächtnisschrift für Heinz Zipf* (Müller Heidelberg 1999), 498. See, e.g., the Coalition for the International Criminal Court which was formed in 1995 and which had an influence on the decision-making process from the preparatory committee to the Rome Conference and beyond.

1079 Although it is a general misconception to believe that the Court would truly assess the entire national judicial system, since the pertinent provision in Art. 17(2) refers to "a particular case". Yet the fact that the ICC may prosecute crimes which *prima facie* fall within the ambit of national judiciaries is not always welcomed: 'Judicial Independence: Colombia should leave the International Criminal Court' available at <http://colombiareports.com/opinion/131-gustavo-silva-cano/6673-judicial-in

mately provided for a stronger judicial institution than that sketched by the ILC draft.[1080] Exactly how strong the ICC is, in terms of its autonomy from other actors, must be assessed on the basis of an understanding of the functions it is envisaged as fulfilling and the capacities given to it under the main legal instruments, in particular the Rome Statute.

III. The Functions Served by the ICC

The preamble to the Rome Statute acts as the starting point for analysing the functions served by the ICC, as it sets the tone and explains the rational basis for the ICC.[1081] Pursuant to the fifth recital of the preamble the States Parties are "[d]etermined to put an end to impunity" for perpetrators of the most serious crimes of concern to the international community. In combination with the preamble's ninth recital,[1082] the fight against impunity circumscribes the central function of the ICC. Besides the immediate purpose of trying those who may be charged with committing crimes pursuant to the Statute,[1083] the preamble in recital seven, read together with recital nine, acknowledges the ICC's function of reaffirming the purposes and principles of the UNC, in particular the prohibition of the threat or use of force inconsistent with the purposes of the UN. Finally, recital eleven bears witness to the States Parties' intent that the adoption of the Rome Statute should guarantee lasting respect for and the enforcement of international justice.[1084] In what follows, the two first-mentioned functions will be scrutinized in greater detail to help

---

dependence-colombia-should-leave-the-international-criminal-court.html> (last visited: 21 March 2014).

1080 E.g. whereas the ILC draft anticipated a court with subject matter jurisdiction based on existing international criminal law and no independent triggering mechanism through the Court's own prosecutor, the Rome Statute provides for its own definitions of crimes and has as one of three different triggering mechanisms an independent prosecutor.

1081 Lee, Roy S. (ed) *The International Criminal Court: The Making of the Rome Statute; Issues, Negotiations, Results* (Kluwer Law International The Hague 1999), 425.

1082 "Determined to these ends … to establish an independent permanent International Criminal Court …".

1083 International Law Commission, *Report of the International Law Commission on the work of its forty-sixth session*, 70.

1084 "Resolved to guarantee lasting respect for and the enforcement of international justice …".

delimit the sources of influence on and thus threat to the independence of the Court.

1. On the Need for a Permanent International Criminal Jurisdiction

The ICC is a manifestation of the acceptance that the international legal order is no longer a field of law the only objective of which is to regulate the relationships between sovereign States. International law, like any other legal order, has the overall aim of protecting certain common values and interests.[1085] On the national level as well as on the international plane, criminal law serves to protect such values and interests by penalizing certain behaviour that violates values considered to be inherent in the respective legal order.[1086] Among such values and interests are those that affect the international legal order as such, shared by the entire international community and thus entitled to protection by its organs. This category includes in particular international peace and security as expressed e.g. in the UNC.[1087] International criminal law acknowledges this; the Rome Statute in recitals 3-5 of the preamble and Art. 1 explicitly states that the crimes formulated in Art. 5 "threaten the peace, security and well-being of the world" and thus are "of concern to the international community as a whole". Eradicating the impunity of perpetrators of such crimes "contribute[s] to the prevention of such crimes." But the need for institutions to prosecute individuals for the violation of international criminal law is not based just on the protection of values and interests characterizing the international community. Beyond this, international law has come to provide additional protection for values that are primarily safeguarded by national authorities, as they are originally conceived as limitations on the exercise of public authority on a national level and by national authorities. Examples of this are particular human rights, which

---

1085 Frowein, Jochen Abr., 'Ius Cogens', in: Wolfrum, Rüdiger (ed) *The Max Planck Encyclopedia of Public International Law* (Oxford University Press Online Edition 2012), para. 3. See also J. Kokott and F. Hoffmeister on the concept of *international public order*, Kokott, Juliane & Hoffmeister, Frank, 'International Public Order', in: Wolfrum, Rüdiger (ed) *The Max Planck Encyclopedia of Public International Law* (Oxford University Press Online Edition 2012).

1086 Cf. Triffterer, 'Der Ständige Internationale Strafgerichtshof – Anspruch und Wirklichkeit', 503: "Jedem Rechtssystem obliegt ein *eigenständiger* Schutz der von ihm anerkannten Rechtsgüter und Interessen."

1087 Arts. 2(6), 11, 12, 18 and Chapter VII UNC.

have been considered to be of such existential importance that any violation of them concerns not only the individual(s) directly affected but the international community as a whole, thus triggering their protection under international law irrespective of where such a violation has taken place.[1088] In this sense, international criminal law provides an additional protection of values and interests, which ought to derive their primary protection from national legal orders. The progressive recognition of human rights has proceeded beyond a mere demand for their protection at the national level. Instead the development has shown that due to infringements of such rights by States themselves, effective protection of those rights needs to rise above the national level of protection by means of the addition of international enforcement instruments. Examples of this are human rights commissions and regional human rights courts in Europe and the Americas. But whereas these bodies focus on the recognition of the individual victim, international criminal courts add the further consideration that in every such violation the entire world community is a victim.

2. The Fight against Impunity as the Core Function of the ICC

The fundamental task of the ICC is to provide the legal community in which it is embedded with the ability to hold persons responsible for the violations they have committed of certain protected values held by this community.[1089] Whereas the violations of international rules by States were for some time triable by international jurisdictions,[1090] the prosecution of individuals by an international court was prevented by the reluctance of States to subject their own citizens to any uncontrollable jurisdiction. In particular, since the major crimes for which the international community might develop an interest in prosecuting are crimes that are often state-sponsored, committed on a large scale or otherwise directly affect the interests of States, international criminal prosecutions of individuals is impeded. Even if only an individual

---

1088 Triffterer, 'Der Ständige Internationale Strafgerichtshof – Anspruch und Wirklichkeit', 504-505.

1089 Triffterer (ed) *Commentary on the Rome Statute of the International Criminal Court – Observers' Notes, Article by Article*, 21.

1090 Maogoto, Jackson Nyamuya, 'Early Efforts to Establish an International Criminal Court', in: Doria, José *et al.* (eds) *The Legal Regime of the International Criminal Court – Essays in Honour of Professor Igor Blishchenko* (Martinus Nijhoff Publishers Leiden 2009), 5.

stands trial, his home State nevertheless has an interest in the appraisal of the acts and might even want to avoid any objective assessment of those actions being made. The desire to end impunity is thus closely linked to the context in which international crimes are being committed. The early development of international criminal law focused on the criminalization of war crimes, i.e. acts committed during war and which violated the rules that all States considered limited the conduct of war (*jus ad bellum*). The substantive elements developed further but was never entirely detached from the close link to military conflicts. Thus enabling international prosecution and making individuals responsible for their own violations of international criminal law before an international tribunal implies breaking through the veil of State sovereignty.[1091]

For the ICC this implies that even at an early stage, namely the decision on whether or not a particular situation may be dealt with by the Court with a view to prosecuting individuals, politically highly delicate decisions are required to be made. Despite a certain reluctance of at least the States that supported the establishment of the Court to interfere with the functioning of the Court, it is likely that States will attempt to prevent it from becoming active or even to induce the Court to become active if it furthers their needs. This in itself does not necessarily infringe upon the independence of the Court. As will be shown below, the ICC is based on the jurisdictional scope that the States Parties agreed upon in Rome, and it is the Court's duty to maintain this framework. Furthermore, the early stages of proceedings primarily affect the actions of the Prosecutor and not, strictly speaking, the judicial function of the judges. Although the Prosecutor, especially at the beginning of the Court's existence, has been its "public face"[1092] and although his office is an organ of the Court and thus may not be organizationally separated from the ICC as an institution, judicial independence as understood in the present context relates to the judicial capacity of a court. Understood in this sense, the Prosecutor is merely the counterpart to the accused and not an indispensable part of the judicial arm of the Court. The office of the Prosecutor should thus be separated from the Court for the purpose of the following study.

A further concern that ought to be highlighted is that the fight against impunity, in which the ICC takes a central role, is by no means a battle fought

1091 Ibid, 22.

1092 Ratnesar, Romesh, 'The Don Quixote of Darfur' *Time* (2 November 2007).

by the ICC alone. Instead the ICC, as for example shown by the principle of complementarity,[1093] is a careful compromise between the national interest into prosecuting crimes committed on States' territory or by or against States' nationals on the one hand, and the interest of the international community into protecting certain common values on the other. This implies that a close interaction between the international and the national levels is at the heart of the ICC's activities, at least when it comes to deciding whether or not the Court should become active in a particular situation. This develops not only a close relationship but also necessitates close co-operation between the two levels, in a way that is significantly different from the conceptualization of e.g. the *ad hoc* Tribunals.

3. The Contribution to the Preservation of Peace

> "Trials take place in the face of political realities of ongoing wars, delicate peace negotiations and uncooperative governments; criminal proceedings against individuals may not always be a priority for the United Nations."[1094]

The most serious human rights violations take place during armed conflicts, be they international or internal conflicts. Maintaining and restoring international peace and security, therefore, bears directly on the need for international judicial intervention in the face of crimes of international concern.[1095] It may be open for discussion whether and to what extent international criminal jurisdictions can indeed develop a pacifying effect through prosecuting individuals.[1096] But beyond this debate, which largely centres round empirical and sociological arguments, it cannot be denied that the drafters of the Rome Statute had this function in mind when they conceptualized the Court. Pursuant to the preamble to the Rome Statute the Court is set to "put

---

1093 Bergsmo, Morten & Webb, Philippa, 'International Criminal Courts and Tribunals, Complementarity and Jurisdiction', in: Wolfrum, Rüdiger (ed) *The Max Planck Encyclopedia of Public International Law* (Oxford University Press Online Edition 2012).

1094 Bertodano, Sylvia de, 'Judicial Independence in the International Criminal Court' (2002) 15 Leiden Journal of International Law 2, 409.

1095 Triffterer (ed) *Commentary on the Rome Statute of the International Criminal Court – Observers' Notes, Article by Article*, 12.

1096 For an overview of this discussion see Nitsche, Dennis, *Der Internationale Strafgerichtshof ICC und der Frieden – eine vergleichende Analyse der Befriedungsfunktion internationaler Straftribunale* (Nomos Baden-Baden 2007).

an end to impunity for the perpetrators of [the most serious crimes of concern to the international community]", which "threaten the peace, security and well-being of the world". In other words, and put in more idealistic terms befitting the ICC, the Court aims to contribute to peace through justice.[1097]

In reality, numerous political concerns and strategic interests pursued by States, the UN and other actors on the international plane influence the achievement of peace in a particular setting. The addition of the ICC may not always be reconcilable with these concerns and interests; *realpolitik* may not always be aligned with the pursuit of justice. This fundamental truth is of concern to any attempt to strengthen international criminal justice, and it is the paramount concern which affects the question of the independence of the ICC. It is thus highly desirable to create effective mechanisms enabling the Court to repel any exertion of improper influence on the administration of justice that flows from a potential conflict between such interests.

4. Conclusions

The analysis of the functions of the ICC must take its vantage point in the preamble of the Rome Statute. The functions thus expressed define what legitimate expectations can (and should) be put to the ICC and thus can be served by the independent functioning of the Court. Two central functions can be identified: (I) the enforcement of international criminal law serving to end impunity,[1098] and (II) the pacifying function. Both these functions can be said to help establish respect for and enforcement of international justice, which has to be balanced against the interests of States and other actors on the international plane. Since those latter interests often do not conform to, but indeed sometimes contradict, the interest of criminal prosecution, a clash between the actors involved is pre-programmed. Furthermore, due to the nature of the crimes prosecuted by the ICC, it is likely that this clash will take on harsher forms. Through the above definition of the ICC's

1097 Yet the preamble also expresses recognition of the Court's limitations. Whereas it is acknowledged that a variety of "unimaginable atrocities", namely "grave crimes", threaten the peace and security of the world, the ICC provides a forum for the punishment of those who committed the most serious crimes of concern to the international community.

1098 Triffterer (ed) *Commentary on the Rome Statute of the International Criminal Court – Observers' Notes, Article by Article*, 10.

functions it may be construed as the main goal of the ICC to uphold the interests of justice while neither pursuing nor allowing any political goals to be followed.[1099] Finally, another argument in favour of a high level of protection for the Court's independence becomes apparent from the above, which did not arise earlier in the case of the ICJ and the ITLOS: the ICC prosecutes individuals and thereby takes on a significant responsibility in a way which would not exist if the parties before it had more or less subjected themselves to the jurisdiction being exercised. As a consequence, if the Court is to pursue the aim of ending impunity and establishing respect for international justice, it must ensure fair trials and not just provide the international community with convictions, which may be welcomed by actors such as the media, politicians and NGOs but do not comply with a more fundamental request for fair procedures that is linked to human nature.[1100]

IV. Structural Independence

1. The Legal Nature of the ICC

Although the Rome Statute was drafted under the close monitoring and auspices of the UN, the ICC is not integrated into the organizational structure of the UN. This is not altered by the initial assistance provided by the UN Secretariat in the first elections to the Court and in the administration of the first sessions of the Meeting of States Parties.[1101] On the contrary, the pre-

---

1099 Skinnider, Eileen, 'Ensuring the Independence of the International Criminal Court' (2006) 7 Global International Courts Review 2, 25.

1100 Bertodano, 'Judicial Independence in the International Criminal Court', 410. More on this *infra* Chapter G.IV(1)(b)(2)-(3).

1101 In this, the ICC resembles the ITLOS, with regard to which the UN also initially provided certain administrative services. Following a decision of the Preparatory Commission, the first session of the ASP to the Rome Statute was held at UN Headquarters and from 3 to 10 September 2002 and the UNSG invited States Parties to the meeting. Regarding the full extent of the role taken by the UN, see Assembly of States Parties to the Rome Statute of the International Criminal Court – First session, New York, 3-10 September 2002 (adopted 9 September 2002, entered into force 22 July 2004) Official Records ICC-ASP/1/3. On its website, the ICC makes it very clear that it is to be understood as an "independent institution" which "is *not* part of the United Nations, but it maintains a cooperative relationship with the U.N." (Emphasis added.) 'ICC – Structure of the Court' available

amble to the Statute in recital nine states that the body thus established is "an independent permanent International Criminal Court in relationship with the United Nations system".[1102] Art. 4 Rome Statute ("Legal status and powers of the Court") further defines the legal nature of the ICC by providing that it shall have international legal personality.[1103]

From a first reading, the legal personality thus granted is not circumscribed or limited, even by the exercise of the functions of the Court. Comparing this to e.g. the legal nature of the ICJ, it highlights the distinction that although the ICJ was equally equipped with legal personality, this characteristic is linked and limited to the functions of the ICJ.[1104] In what follows, this legal nature of the ICC will be analysed in greater detail to provide a framework for the later overall assessment of the degree to which the Court is able to function independently from other subjects of international law.

a) The ICC as a Subject of International Law

Subjects of international law enjoy rights and are obliged to carry out duties directly under international law and possess the general capacity to act on the international plane, without being dependent on other subjects.[1105] The

at <http://www.icc-cpi.int/en_menus/icc/structure%20of%20the%20court/Pages/structure%20of%20the%20court.aspx> (last visited: 21 March 2014).

1102 Cf. Art. 1 Statute ("An International Criminal Court is hereby established. It shall be a permanent institution …") and Art. 2 Statute ("The Court shall be brought into relationship with the United Nations through an agreement to be approved by the ASP to this Statute and thereafter concluded by the President of the Court on its behalf.").

1103 "Article 4 – Legal status and powers of the Court
1. The Court shall have international legal personality. It shall also have such legal capacity as may be necessary for the exercise of its functions and the fulfilment of its purposes.
2. The Court may exercise its functions and powers, as provided in this Statute, on the territory of any State Party and, by special agreement, on the territory of any other State."

1104 Oellers-Frahm, Karin, 'Der institutionelle Rahmen: Status, Ausstattung und Personalhoheit internationaler Gerichte – Der IGH, der Internationale Strafgerichtshof und das Jugoslawien-Tribunal im Vergleich' (2003) 30 Europäische Grundrechte-Zeitschrift 4/6, 108.

1105 Ipsen, Knut, *Völkerrecht – ein Studienbuch* (Beck München 3rd edn. 1990), 52; Vitzthum & Bothe (eds), *Völkerrecht*, 169; Verdross, Alfred & Simma, Bruno,

extent of the rights and duties follows from the nature of the relevant subject and its positioning in the broader framework of the international legal order. For the ICC it is mentioned explicitly in Art. 4(1) Rome Statute that the Court shall have international legal personality. This provision is helpful due to its clarity but, with regard to the States Parties to the Statute, does not add much to the state of the law that applies even without such a provision. Can the legal personality of the ICC thus be assumed even when the binding force of Art. 4(1) Rome Statute is disregarded and, if so, what does it imply?

Following the argument first developed by the ICJ in the case of *Reparation for Injuries Suffered in the Service of the United Nations*, the international legal personality can be implied by the attribution of functions and rights to an extent that only the possession of international personality would enable it to carry out the intentions of its founders.[1106] To extend this argument of implied powers,[1107] which by the ICJ was developed with regard to the UN as the "supreme type of international organization",[1108] to the ICC demands that that Court too is equipped with functions that necessitate the possession of a competence enabling those functions to be effectively discharged. The Statute indeed contains a number of provisions that presuppose the international treaty making power of the ICC. For example, Art. 2 Rome Statute envisages that the Court is brought into a legal relationship with the UN by an agreement.[1109] Pursuant to Art. 3(2) Rome Statute the Court shall itself enter into a headquarters agreement with the Netherlands.[1110] The possibility

---

Universelles Völkerrecht – Theorie und Praxis (Duncker & Humblot Berlin 3rd edn. 1984), 22.

1106 *Reparation for injuries suffered in the service of the United Nations (Advisory Opinion)* ICJ Rep. 174 (1949), 178-179.

1107 On the notion of implied powers see Blokker, Niels, 'International Organizations or Institutions, Implied Powers', in: Wolfrum, Rüdiger (ed) *The Max Planck Encyclopedia of Public International Law* (Oxford University Press Online Edition 2012).

1108 *Reparation for injuries suffered in the service of the United Nations (Advisory Opinion)*, 179.

1109 "Article 2 (Relationship of the Court with the United Nations)
The Court shall be brought into relationship with the United Nations through an agreement to be approved by the ASP to this Statute and thereafter concluded by the President of the Court on its behalf."

1110 The headquarters agreement was concluded on 7 June 2007, with the signature by President P. Kirsch of the ICC and the Dutch Minister of Foreign Affairs, H. E. Verhagen; Headquarters Agreement between the International Criminal Court and the Host State.

of non-State parties to the Rome Statute providing co-operation and judicial assistance to the Court may follow on the basis of agreements between the Court and such States.[1111] Additionally, Rule 16(4) of the Rules of Procedure and Evidence[1112] and Art. 4(2) Rome Statute[1113] provide for further functions the effective discharge of which demand international legal personality. In sum, therefore, even if Art. 4(1) had not been included in the Statute, the legal subjectivity of the Court in relation to States Parties would nevertheless have had to be affirmed.[1114]

b) The Question of Objective International Personality

This reasoning as well as the wording of Art. 4(1) Rome Statute does not immediately reveal whether this legal personality exists only in relation to States Parties or if it is also applicable in relation to non-State Parties. This is important insofar as the Rome Statute, being an international treaty, primarily binds only those States that have signed and ratified it, but not third States.[1115] However, the ICC is dependent on the co-operation of States, including non-Member States, and it would be seriously hampered in the exercise of its functions if it had to rely on the recognition of its legal personality by individual States. As mentioned, as a rule treaty provisions bind only States party to that treaty and can create no obligations for third actors.[1116] This also applies to the constituent instruments of an international institution such as the Rome Statute. As regards non-Member States legal

---

1111 Art. 87(5)(a) Rome Statute.

1112 Agreements on relocation and provision of support services on the territory of a State of traumatized or threatened persons.

1113 "The Court may exercise its functions and powers, as provided in this Statute, on the territory of any State Party and, by special agreement, on the territory of any other State."

1114 It should be noted that the ILC draft did not contain an explicit provision on the legal personality of the court since at that stage the means of establishment of the court was still uncertain.

1115 Cf. Art. 6 Vienna Convention on the Law of Treaties: "Every treaty in force is binding upon the parties to it and must be performed by them in good faith" and Art. 34(1): "A treaty does not create either obligations or rights for a third State without its consent."

1116 On this general rule see Vukas, Budislav, 'Treaties, Third-Party Effect', in: Wolfrum, Rüdiger (ed) *The Max Planck Encyclopedia of Public International Law* (Oxford University Press Online Edition 2012), paras. 8-15.

personality would thus demand explicit or implicit recognition. However, in exceptional cases international legal personality has been acknowledged as developing *erga omnes* effect. The ICJ in its advisory opinion in *Reparation for Injuries Suffered in the Service of the United Nations* developed the so-called doctrine of objective international personality with regard to the UN.[1117] On the crucial point the ICJ established the following standard which has since been interpreted as a test for determining the applicability of legal personality in relation to non-Member States:

> "fifty States, representing the vast majority of the members of the international community, had the power, in conformity with international law, to bring into being an entity possessing objective international personality, and not merely personality recognized by them alone".[1118]

Can this reasoning be applied to the ICC?[1119] Following the above quote, the ICJ considers the number of States supporting the establishment of the institution in question to be the crucial point. In other words, the support an international institution has in the international community is decisive. Strictly speaking, this number must represent the "vast majority of the members of the international community" in order for legal personality to extend to the international community. Pursuant to Art. 125(1) and (3) the Rome Statute shall be open to accession by all States. As of March 2014, 122 States had joined the constituting instrument of the Court, bringing the Court gradually closer to being supported by an overwhelming majority of the world's

---

1117 *Reparation for injuries suffered in the service of the United Nations (Advisory Opinion).*

1118 Ibid, 185.

1119 The applicability of the doctrine of objective international personality beyond the UN is disputed in scholarly writing. Whereas W. Graf Vitzthum is of the opinion that it is tailor made for the UN and does not apply to other international organizations (Vitzthum & Bothe (eds), *Völkerrecht*, 306), M. Shaw considers that "in principle it is now well established that international organizations may indeed possess objective international legal personality." (Shaw, *International Law*, 259.) M. Shaw also refers to the case of *Interpretation of the Agreement of 25 March 1951 between the WHO and Egypt* in which the ICJ, with regard to the World Health Assembly, confirmed that "international organizations are subjects of international law and, as such, are bound by any obligations incumbent upon them under general rules of international law, under their constitutions or under international agreements to which they are parties." (*Interpretation of the Agreement of 25 March 1951 between the WHO and Egypt (Advisory Opinion)* ICJ Rep. 73 (1980), 89-90).

States.[1120] This global approach is furthermore mirrored in the function of the Court as described in the preamble to the Rome Statute, where recital nine establishes ICC's jurisdiction over the most serious crimes "of concern to the international community as a whole". It may thus be argued that the ICC has international legal personality not only pursuant to Art. 4(1) Statute in relation to the States Parties to the Rome Statute but also following from the application of the doctrine of objective international personality, and thus provides a criminal justice system that complements, yet stands independent of, the collective security system of the UN.

Closely linked to the question of international legal personality of the ICC, and partly as a consequence of it, is the classification of the ICC as an international organization. In order for an institution to be an international organization it must be based on an agreement between subjects of international law (usually States), have an organic structure, and be equipped with legal powers exercisable on the international plane for the purpose of advancing common purposes.[1121] The ICC was established by an international treaty and shall function as a permanent institution.[1122] It is composed of several organs[1123] which do not follow the instructions of the States Parties but instead function on the basis of a complex interaction within the Court and the occasional assistance of States. Thus the ICC is to be seen as an international organization which e.g. brings it to eye level, from an organizational viewpoint, with the UN.

c) The Role of the Prosecutor

(1) Distinguishing Between the Court and the Office of the Prosecutor?

The existence of the Office of the Prosecutor (OTP) is a pivotal characteristic of the ICC and one that clearly separates it from the courts dealt with so far,

1120 See 'ICC – The States Parties to the Rome Statute' available at <http://www.icc-cpi.int/en_menus/asp/states%20parties/Pages/the%20states%20parties%20to%20the%20rome%20statute.aspx> (last visited: 21 March 2014).

1121 See, e.g., Vitzthum & Bothe (eds), *Völkerrecht*, 277; Schmalenbach, Kirsten, 'International Organizations or Institutions, General Aspects', in: Wolfrum, Rüdiger (ed) *The Max Planck Encyclopedia of Public International Law* (Oxford University Press Online Edition 2012), paras. 3-10.

1122 Art. 1 Rome Statute.

1123 Art. 34 Rome Statute.

the ICJ and the ITLOS. Through the Prosecutor the Court can be called upon to adjudicate on cases without the support or even against the will of States. Hence it comes as no surprise that the creation of an independent prosecutorial authority was one of the topics most discussed during the preparation of the Rome Statute, as many States were not willing to allow the initiation of investigations and prosecutions by an entity over which no immediate control could be exercised.[1124] But what is the relationship between the OTP and the rest of the Court based upon?

As regards the status of the OTP under the Rome Statute, Art. 34 determines that the OTP is an "organ" of the Court, at the same level as the Presidency, the Registry, the Appeals Division, the Trial Division and the Pre-Trial Division. Indeed the very existence of a prosecutorial arm of the Court follows from functional necessity[1125] and may be deduced from general rules that can be said to govern international trials.[1126] International criminal law has established a number of basic guarantees and rights of the accused, founded on statutes of current and past international criminal courts,[1127] judicial practice, fundamental standards of human rights as laid down in international (including regional) treaties[1128] and supported by general principles upheld in most countries of the world. These include *inter alia* the presumption of innocence and the principle of a fair and expeditious trial.[1129] In particular, and following the opinion of human rights bodies, the right to a

1124 Wouters, Jan, et al., 'The International Courts's Office of the Prosecutor – Navigating between Independence and Accountability', in: Doria, José *et al.* (eds) *The Legal Regime of the International Criminal Court – Essays in Honour of Professor Igor Blishchenko* (Martinus Nijhoff Publishers Leiden 2009), 349.

1125 Triffterer (ed) *Commentary on the Rome Statute of the International Criminal Court – Observers' Notes, Article by Article*, 932.

1126 Due to the youth of international criminal law and in particular its organizational arm (international courts), there are not yet any general international rules on international criminal proceedings, but instead each international court establishes its own rules of procedure and evidence. See Cassese, Antonio, *International Criminal Law* (Oxford University Press Oxford 2005), 389; Schomburg, Wolfgang & Nemitz, Jan Christoph, 'International Criminal Courts and Tribunals, Procedure', in: Wolfrum, Rüdiger (ed) *The Max Planck Encyclopedia of Public International Law* (Oxford University Press Online Edition 2012), paras. 1-4.

1127 See, e.g., Art. 21 ICTY Statute, Art. 20 ICTR Statute.

1128 Cf., e.g., Art. 14 ICCPR, Art. 6 ECHR.

1129 Cassese, Antonio, *International Criminal Law* (Oxford University Press Oxford 2nd edn. 2008), 389. On this principle, see Doswald-Beck, 'Fair Trial, Right to, International Protection '.

fair trial implies that there must be equality of arms between the parties to proceedings.[1130] This by definition entails that the procedure must be conceived as a dispute between the accused and the prosecution held before the judges. The UNSG, when considering the establishment of an international tribunal for the atrocities committed in the former Yugoslavia, stated that "the organization of the International Tribunal should reflect the functions to be performed by it" and the function of prosecuting persons responsible for serious violations of international humanitarian law "presupposes an international tribunal composed of a judicial organ, a prosecutorial organ and a secretariat".[1131] The UNSG went on to state that the function of the prosecutorial organ would be to "investigate cases, prepare indictments and prosecute persons responsible for committing the violations", whereas the judicial organ would hear the cases. The UNSG thus formulated his conception based on the assumption of a functional separation of the prosecutorial and judicial arms of the *ad hoc* criminal tribunal. The organization of the ICC is similar to that of the *ad hoc* Tribunals and it thus builds on the adversarial system,[1132] but includes numerous elements from the inquisitorial system as well.[1133] In this unique model, the Prosecutor must be conceived as a distinct "organ of justice",[1134] entrusted with far-reaching responsibilities for gathering evidence on behalf of both the prosecution and the defence.[1135]

Art. 42(1) Rome Statute takes up these concepts by stating that the OTP is a separate and independent organ,[1136] the basic function of which is to receive referrals and any substantiated information on crimes within the

---

1130 See, e.g., *Anni Äärelä and Jouni Näkkäläjärvi v. Finland* (Human Rights Committee) Communication No. 779/1997 (4 February 1997), para. 7.4; *Avocats Sans Frontières (on behalf of Bwampamye) v. Burundi* (African Commission on Human and Peoples' Rights) Communication No. 231/99 (6 November 2000), paras. 26–27; Doswald-Beck, 'Fair Trial, Right to, International Protection ', para. 29.

1131 UNSG, *Report of the Secretary-General Pursuant to Paragraph 2 of Security Council Resolution 808 (1993)* (3 May 1993) UN Doc. S/25704, para. 4.

1132 Cassese, *International Criminal Law*, 384; Schabas, *An Introduction to the International Criminal Court*, 237.

1133 See Kreß, Claus, 'The Procedural Law of the International Criminal Court in Outline: Anatomy of a Unique Compromise' (2003) 1 Journal of International Criminal Justice 3.

1134 Cassese, *International Criminal Law*, 387.

1135 Ibid, 387. Kaul, Hans-Peter, 'International Criminal Court (ICC)', in: Wolfrum, Rüdiger (ed) *The Max Planck Encyclopedia of Public International Law* (Oxford University Press Online Edition 2012), paras. 31-33.

1136 Schabas, *An Introduction to the International Criminal Court*, 351.

jurisdiction of the Court, to examine them and to conduct investigations and prosecutions before the Court. The administrative component of its independence, as established in Art. 42(2) Rome Statute,[1137] was added after the ILC draft.[1138] This functional independence, if it is to have any substance, must apply not only in relation to e.g. the ASP and individual States, but also in relation to the other organs of the Court, primarily the judges, the judicial organ. Prosecutorial independence is strengthened by the requirement that no member of the OTP shall seek or act on instructions from any external source. The Prosecutor is elected directly by the ASP and only a majority in the ASP may remove him;[1139] he may – like the judges[1140] – not be re-elected.[1141] The salaries of the Prosecutor, and of the Deputy Prosecutors, are determined by the ASP.[1142] The prosecutorial independence as perceived in the description of the Prosecutor's function in Arts. 42(1)-(2) Rome Statute is not absolute,[1143] and especially at various stages is subject to the judicial control of the Chambers of the Court.[1144] W. Schabas makes an overall negative assessment of the actual independence of the Prosecutor:

"And yet the Prosecutor's so-called independence is everywhere constrained. Much of the initial litigation at the Court has involved attempts to trim the wings of the Prosecutor. He has vigorously defended his independence, but not always successfully. Many of the checks on the prosecutorial independence are the result of negotiated compromises in the Statute. The

---

1137 Art. 42(2) Rome Statute: "The Prosecutor shall have full authority over the management and administration of the Office, including the staff, facilities and other resources thereof."

1138 Cassese (ed) *The Rome Statute of the International Criminal Court: A Commentary – Volume I*, 270.

1139 Art. 42(4) and Art. 46 Rome Statute.

1140 See *infra* Chapter F.V(1)(b).

1141 "[A] measure designed to ensure their independence at the personal level by removing any incentive to curry favour with States in order to promote a second mandate." Schabas, *An Introduction to the International Criminal Court*, 352.

1142 Art. 49 Rome Statute.

1143 He is e.g. subject to the Pre-Trial Chamber from the earliest stage of proceedings through the authorization to proceed pursuant to Art. 15(3) Rome Statute; if a situation is referred to the Court by a State or the UNSC, that referrer defines the scope of the prosecution (see also Art. 53(3) Rome Statute).

1144 The Prosecutor's autonomous role in the proceedings before the Court does not imply that his prerogatives are not framed by other actors such as the Pre-Trial Chamber, the Trial-Chamber or even the UNSC (see the right to defer investigations under Art. 16).

concept of a genuinely independent prosecutor, with freedom to select cases and suspects for prosecution, was radical and unprecedented. … In effect, the Rome Statute limits the actions of the Prosecutor in several important ways."

Yet the OTP holds functions that are significantly different from those of the judicial organ of the Court. This finding is also not altered by the observation that numerous provisions in the Rome Statute apply to both the Prosecutor and one (or more) other Court organ.[1145]

(2) Does the Independent Prosecutor Enhance the Court's Independence?

What does this role of the OTP mean for the independent functioning of the Court's judicial organ? Throughout the drafting of the Rome Statute, even including at the Rome Conference itself, the inclusion of a Prosecutor equipped with *propriu motu* powers to initiate an investigation was put forward by NGOs and a number of States, primarily the like-minded States. It was praised as an important step towards the establishment of an effective, impartial and credible ICC,[1146] and as "indispensable of an independent and effective Criminal Court".[1147] According to H.-P. Kaul "[t]he *proprio motu* powers of the Prosecutor are of paramount importance to the idea of independent international justice in criminal matters." These arguments first and foremost rely on the OTP as a tool to increase the Court's efficiency in pursuing the aims for which it was established. Enabling the Court to function on behalf of the international community instead of having to rely on complaints by States or the UNSC may certainly do that, since it may be assumed

1145 See also Rule 9 Rules of Procedure and Evidence ("Operation of the Office of the Prosecutor"). Wouters, et al., 'The International Courts's Office of the Prosecutor – Navigating between Independence and Accountability', 346. According to J. Jones one may even get the impression that the Prosecutor and Deputy Prosecutor are "judicial officers, possessing the same qualities and conduct as that of judges": Cassese (ed) *The Rome Statute of the International Criminal Court: A Commentary – Volume I*, 271.

1146 Fernández De Gurmendi, Silvia A, 'The Role of the Prosecutor', in: Lee, Roy S. (ed) *The International Criminal Court: The Making of the Rome Statute; Issues, Negotiations, Results* (Kluwer Law International The Hague 1999), 176-180 with further references.

1147 Fernández De Gurmendi, Silvia A, 'The Role of the Prosecutor', in: Politi, Mauro *et al.* (eds) *The Rome Statute of the International Criminal Court: A Challenge to Impunity* (Ashgate u.a. Aldershot 2001), 55.

that States and the UNSC would, for political considerations, refrain from referring certain cases to the Court. But what the *proprio motu* power of the Prosecutor does not influence directly is the ability of the ICC's judicial arm to adjudicate independently once the Court has been seized of a case. However, it is conceivable that judicial independence understood as the autonomous functioning of the judicial arm of the Court may benefit from the independent functioning of the OTP in one particular way. By relying on the OTP to receive referrals, examine them and conduct investigations and prosecutions before the Court, most of the attention of political actors is directed towards the OTP, instead of the judges. In particular the delicate situation in the early phase of a case, including the significant decision to begin investigating at all in a particular situation, is likely to provoke States to vent their irritation which, with this system, is filtered away from the judges.[1148] By directing these sentiments to an organ which is distinct from the one which has to make the judicial decisions in the case, those decisions are more likely to be sheltered to some degree against these influences.

d) Summary

In summary, the ICC is an international organization equipped with (objective) international legal personality. It can carry out its rights and duties directly under international law, has the general capacity to act on the international plane and must not follow any instructions from other institutions, unless this is provided for in its Statute (and other instruments) or general international law. As a consequence, the ICC has been equipped with important tools to make the exercise of its activities largely autonomous in relation to all those subjects of international law that might seek to influence the Court. By being provided with an independent OTP the Court is not only able to determine more independently in which situations prosecutions will be initiated but also to redirect any possible exerted influence away from the judicial organ responsible for making the final decisions.

1148 In support of this one may refer to the fact that the OTP is perceived as the public face of the Court: see, e.g., Simons, Marlise, 'Argentine Prosecutor Turns Focus to New War Crimes Court' *The New York Times* (29 September 2003); Getz, Arlene, 'Rocking The Courtroom – The ICC Prosecutor on His Work, Human Rights and Sudan' *Newsweek* (21 March 2009); Musoke, Cyprian, 'ICC boss launches war victims office' *The New Vision* (4 June 2010).

2. The Composition of the Court

a) The Required Qualifications of Judges

Art. 36 Rome Statute regulates the procedure of the nomination and election of ICC judges but also contains the main provisions on the qualifications that any judge on the bench of the ICC must possess.[1149] The ICC bench is composed of 18 judges, making it the third largest court studied here, behind only the ITLOS and the ECtHR. Art. 36(2) Rome Statute even provides the possibility for the Presidency[1150] to suggest an increase in the number of judges, with the final decision upon such a suggestion being taken by the ASP with a two-thirds majority of its members. It is thus likely that only the practical needs of the Court itself may initiate an increase in the number of judges,[1151] and the broad support of the States Parties to the Rome Statute may implement it. In particular, the ASP does not have the ability of its own motion to reduce the bench, e.g. in order to impede the Court in exercising its functions.

The qualifications to be taken into account when selecting judges are set out in Art. 36(3)(a) Rome Statute, and include high moral character, impartiality, integrity, and the qualifications required in their respective States for appointment to the highest judicial office. These requirements thus do not differ significantly from those which apply to ICJ or ITLOS judges. The *travaux préparatoires* do not reveal why the requirement of impartiality was included rather than that of independence, which was included in both the ICJ Statute[1152] and the ITLOS Statute[1153]. In view of the lack of support in the *travaux préparatoires* it would go too far to assume this to be a consequence of either a broader or narrower understanding of impartiality *vis-à-vis* independence. But it does suggest that it was felt to be significant to underline that the Court is not only free from reliance on any organ or insti-

---

1149 The present analysis will follow this structure and thus address the qualification requirements in the present context instead of in Chapter F.V.

1150 See on the Presidency *infra* Chapter F.IV(2)(d).

1151 This rationale is supported by Art. 36(2)(c)(ii) Rome Statute which mentions as the sole reason for a subsequent proposal to reduce the number of judges that the "workload of the Court justifies it". The decision to reduce the number of judges, provided it is not reduced below the original size of the bench, is taken by the Court alone, through its Presidency.

1152 Art. 2 ICJ Statute.

1153 Art. 2(1) ITLOS Statute.

tution, as mentioned above, but that it also does not take sides in a particular case before it. It may not be a surprise that the Rome Statute, like the Statutes of the *ad hoc* Tribunals and the ECtHR, all being courts before which individuals appear, emphasizes the element of autonomy that is non-involvement with the parties to a case, the unequal treatment of the like, and equal treatment of the unlike.[1154]

As regards the required technical expertise that ICC judges must possess,[1155] Art. 36(3)(a) Rome Statute demands the qualifications required of judges in their respective States for appointment to the highest judicial office, wording strikingly similar to that of Art. 2 ICJ Statute. However, Art. 36(3)(b) Rome Statute further creates two different categories of candidates: those with experience in criminal law and procedure (known as "List A" candidates) and those with relevant international law experience (known as "List B" candidates):

> "Every candidate for election to the Court shall:
> (i) Have established competence in criminal law and procedure, and the necessary relevant experience, whether as judge, prosecutor, advocate or in other similar capacity, in criminal proceedings; or
> (ii) Have established competence in relevant areas of international law such as international humanitarian law and the law of human rights, and extensive experience in a professional legal capacity which is of relevance to the judicial work of the Court"

Since the ICC's ability fairly and effectively to adjudicate on cases rests not only on the psychological quality of its judges but also on the intellectual aptness of judges, it ought to be welcomed that the Rome Statute sets out the standards explicitly. Furthermore, it should be welcomed that such emphasis is placed on the legal expertise of judges. Although Art. 36(3)(b)(ii) Rome Statute in particular is not a perfect guard against candidates with mainly political experience, it nevertheless focuses on legal expertise by demanding that judges being elected from List B have competence in international law as well as "extensive experience in a professional legal capacity". Since the Court adjudicates on cases potentially involving deprivation of individual liberty and because it needs to assure States Parties and individuals

1154 Cf. *supra* Chapter B.IV(5)(d)(1).

1155 Judges are also explicitly required to "have an excellent knowledge of and be fluent in at least one of the working languages of the Court" (Art. 36(3)(c) Rome Statute), something that in other courts appears to be taken for granted. See on this subject, Mackenzie, et al., *Selecting International Judges: Principle, Process, and Politics*, 43-45.

that fair trials are being held, adherence to these qualification requirements is of paramount importance. In addition, considering that the ICC is a rather young institution with a more complex procedural framework than both the ICJ and the ITLOS, allowing for more opportunity for influence from the outside to influence how cases are being processed, the more detailed provision on selection criteria which thus gives States much less latitude is called for.

b) The Two Procedures for Making Nominations

The nomination procedure is initiated when the ASP circulates through diplomatic channels the invitations to States Parties to submit nominations for candidates to the ICC's bench.[1156] Nominations are to be made by the States Parties to the Rome Statute.[1157] Non-State parties, but also NGOs and IGOs which have had a significant influence on the establishment of the Court, do not have the right to make formal suggestions. Every State Party may nominate one candidate, who does not need to be a national of the nominating State but must be a national of one of the States Parties.[1158] Nominations are required to be accompanied by a statement that *inter alia* outlines how the candidate fulfils the requirements in Art. 36(3)(a)-(c) Rome Statute, whether he is nominated under List A or B, how representation of the principal legal systems in the world, equitable geographical representation and gender balance are affected, and whether he has legal expertise on special issues.[1159] A feature that is certain to contribute to the transparency of the nomination process is the requirement that the secretariat of the ASP make all nominations and the accompanying statements available on the website of the ICC.[1160]

In making nominations, States Parties have a choice between two methods: they may choose either to follow the nomination procedure used at the ICJ, i.e. nomination through the national groups at the PCA, or to utilize the same

1156 Procedure for the Nomination and Election of Judges of the International Criminal Court (adopted 10 September 2004) Official Records Resolution ICC-ASP/3/Res.6, para. 1.

1157 Art. 36(4)(a) Rome Statute.

1158 Art. 36(4)(b) Rome Statute.

1159 Art. 36(4)(a) *in fine* Rome Statute and Procedure for the Nomination and Election of Judges of the International Criminal Court, para. 6.

1160 Ibid, para. 8.

procedure as is used for appointment to the highest judicial office in the relevant State.[1161] This choice was based partly on a compromise between States which sought unlimited control over the nomination process and others that preferred to have in place a more rigorous institutional framework, and partly in order better to enable the selection of candidates who hold the "qualifications required in their respective States for appointment to the highest judicial offices".[1162] According to the *travaux préparatoires*, the reference to the ICJ's nomination system was made "to ensure that merit would be a paramount consideration in the election of judges".[1163] But in view of the above-mentioned dangers inherent in a procedure based on the national groups at the PCA, this explanation is based on a flawed appreciation of that system. It is not automatic that nominations by the PCA national groups comply with the requirements in Art. 36(3)(a)-(c) Rome Statute. Instead, allowing nominations through those groups raises the issues that have been addressed in earlier chapters; although such groups are formally independent and themselves have an expertise that is helpful in proposing the right candidates to the ICC's bench, the real independence of these groups must be questioned as they in some cases are little more than an intermediary for States. In contrast, permitting nominations to be made according to the "procedure for the nomination of candidates for appointment to the highest judicial offices in the State in question" implies submission to a multitude of nomination procedures, including direct nominations by governments, which can be more or less open for politicization but in any event enhance States' control over the process.[1164] Only in instances where the national selection process follows transparent and balanced rules in practice and in theory can the procedure for the nomination of candidates for appointment

1161 Art. 36(4)(a) Rome Statute.

1162 For a summary of the background see Mackenzie, et al., *Selecting International Judges: Principle, Process, and Politics*, 19-22.

1163 Preparatory Committee on the Establishment of an International Criminal Court, *Report of the Preparatory Committee on the Establishment of an International Criminal Court, Volume I (Proceedings of the Preparatory Committee during March-April and August 1996)* (13 September 1996) UN Doc. A/51/22, para. 37.

1164 For an overview of the possible national selection procedures see Ten Brinke, Daniel & Deml, Hans-Michael (eds), *Judges in the Service of the State? Procedures, Criteria and Political Influence on National Selection of Judges for the Highest Judicial Offices and their Possible Influence on the International Criminal Court* (Shaker Aachen 2002).

to the highest judicial office in the States[1165] provide for a more rigorous vetting process of nominees, and thus provide a better safeguard for compliance with any merit requirement. As a matter of principle, if the Rome Statute wishes to establish an independent international court, which is undoubtedly the case, then every concession to greater control by States has to be compensated for by mechanisms that restrain the exercise of such control. The Advisory Committee on Nominations may be one such mechanism.

c) The Advisory Committee on Nominations – Real Defence of Judicial Independence or a Paper Tiger?

Of particular interest when seeking to ensure that nominations are based on merit rather than on political considerations, as a safeguard of the independence of the Court from political influence on its decision-making, is the possibility provided in Art. 36(4)(c) that an Advisory Committee on Nominations be established.[1166] *Prima facie*, this organ provides a most helpful tool for objectively facilitating compliance with the requirements in Art. 36(a)-(c) Rome Statute, something that none of the other courts dealt with in this study have access to. Such a mechanism would bring obvious advantages as it would, if established accordingly, allow the scrutiny of nominations by practitioners and academics inclined to make recommendations based on the candidates' experience and quality of work, as required by the Rome Statute. But the high expectations that are easily vested in the Committee rely on the assumption of further conditions, which, when analysing the drafting history of this provision, must unfortunately be viewed more pessimistically.

1165 It was explicitly chosen not to leave the procedure and criteria entirely to a State's internal law, but to link them to a specific (hopefully established) procedure, namely one for appointment to the highest judicial office; see Lee (ed) *The International Criminal Court: The Making of the Rome Statute; Issues, Negotiations, Results*, 161-162.

1166 Also NGOs chose to approach States Parties and give recommendations on the nomination process. See, e.g., Human Rights Watch, 'ICC: Recommendations for Nominating and Electing Candidates to Serve as Judges – Letter to Foreign Ministers of ICC States Parties (18 May 2011)' available at <http://www.hrw.org/news/2011/05/18/icc-recommendations-nominating-and-electing-candidates-serve-judges> (last visited: 21 March 2014).

The idea of the establishment of an Advisory Committee on Nominations was introduced by the United Kingdom delegation during the Rome Conference.[1167] Other proposals were also discussed, but could not obtain majority support.[1168] Overall the intention to ensure a more objective procedure for the nomination process was obvious throughout the drafting process, yet the interest of States in retaining control over the process was stronger. The Committee's function, according to the United Kingdom's proposal, was to gather further information on the candidates, and on this basis make proposals and recommendations to the States Parties before the elections, in order to prevent their politicization.[1169] However, to give due recognition to the integrity of States, the conference could only agree to allow the Committee's decisions to be of an advisory nature and it was moreover not to have the capacity, if established at all, to delete a candidate from the list of nominees. One further weakness of the provision ultimately included in the Rome Statute is that it does not establish the procedure or composition of the committee. The original United Kingdom proposal envisaged that the chief justices of the Member States would sit on this Committee.[1170] Any such guideline was omitted from the adopted Rome Statute, which also does not provide for any procedural framework for the Committee. In sum, as the composition and mandate of the Committee are to be determined by the ASP, and in addition any decisions by the Committee would still remain non-

1167 Lee (ed) *The International Criminal Court: The Making of the Rome Statute; Issues, Negotiations, Results*, 163; Bassiouni (ed) *The Legislative History of the International Criminal Court: Volume 2 – Article-by-Article Evolution of the Statute*, 263.

1168 It deserves mentioning that the US made a proposal which was included in the 1998 report of the Preparatory Committee as Option 2 of Art. 37(4), and which envisaged that the nominations were to be made by a Nominating Committee (see Bassiouni (ed) *The Legislative History of the International Criminal Court: Volume 2 – Article-by-Article Evolution of the Statute*, 256). Although the Committee was to be composed of the members of the ASP, and thus granted the member States significant influence over the nomination process comparable to the custom of the national groups at the PCA for the purpose of nominations to the ICJ, the proposal in essence meant that any individuals meeting the formal qualification requirements and irrespective of nationality could be nominated. This was perceived as an infringement of the sovereign right of States freely to nominate candidates of their own choice (Lee (ed) *The International Criminal Court: The Making of the Rome Statute; Issues, Negotiations, Results*, 162-163).

1169 Lee (ed) *The International Criminal Court: The Making of the Rome Statute; Issues, Negotiations, Results*, 164.

1170 Ibid, 163.

binding on States, the initial proposal was broken down to almost redundant lip service to more transparency and objectivity in the nomination procedure.

The ASP on 10 December 2010 requested its Bureau to "prepare a report to the Assembly for its tenth session on the potential implementation of article 36, paragraph 4(c), of the Rome Statute".[1171] In response, the Bureau on 30 November 2011 issued a report on the establishment of a Committee for the consideration of the ASP, suggesting that the Committee be established and attaching draft terms of reference.[1172] The report was drafted on the basis of just two informal consultations, and found its vantage point in restating the applicable provisions in the Rome Statute and the pertinent provisions of resolution ICC-ASP/3/Res.6 ("Procedure for the Nomination and Election of Judges of the International Criminal Court"). It outlined that according to the Rome Statute the States Parties are responsible for the statutory requirements, and that this should be complemented by "an independent organism in the very structure of the Assembly in order to facilitate the process of election of the judges."[1173] In the opinion of the Bureau, whereas the Committee "would enjoy legitimacy" and "be responsible to the Assembly", it would neither remove States Parties from their role in the nomination of the candidates nor "duplicate the Assembly in its role of election."[1174] In essence, the Bureau mirrored the fact that the Committee, pursuant to Art. 36(4)(c) Rome Statute, would have only an advisory role, that its function would be of "mere technical assessment, without altering the process of decision-making by these organisms." Considering that the Committee is thus envisaged as working under the control of the ASP, which is merely an intergovernmental body composed of the States Parties to the Rome Statute, it is indeed unlikely that a profound conflict of competence between the Committee and the States Parties would occur in the election process. As regards the composition of the Committee, the terms of reference suggested by the

---

1171 Strengthening the International Criminal Court and the Assembly of States Parties (adopted 10 December 2010) Official Records Resolution ICC-ASP/9/Res.3, para. 24. In this context, the ASP emphasized "the importance of nominating and electing the most highly qualified judges in accordance with article 36 of the Rome Statute and encourages States Parties to conduct thorough and transparent processes to identify the best candidates".

1172 Assembly of States Parties – Report of the Bureau on the establishment of an Advisory Committee on nominations of judges of the International Criminal Court (adopted 30 November 2011) Official Records Resolution ICC-ASP/10/36.

1173 Ibid, para. 10.

1174 Ibid, para. 12.

Bureau propose that there shall be nine members, who are nationals of States Parties,

> "designated by the Assembly of States Parties by consensus on recommendation made by the Bureau of the Assembly also made by consensus, reflecting the principal legal systems of the world and an equitable geographical representation, as well as a fair representation of both genders, based on the number of States Parties to the Rome Statute."[1175]

The Committee is thus configured very much like the ICC itself, following the requirements for the composition established in Art. 36(8)(a) Rome Statute. The Bureau does not justify why the composition should be subjected to the same requirements as apply to the ICC itself. In particular, the requirement that all members of the Committee must find support from a double consensus from within the ASP and the Bureau may be expected to ensure that no controversial individuals will be admitted. This caution seems unwarranted, however, in view of the merely advisory function of the Committee. The fact that the members would not be considered "representatives of States or other organizations" and that they "would serve in their personal capacity, and would not take instructions from States Parties, States or any other organizations or persons" is a welcome provision in the attempt to prohibit the Committee from channelling the political considerations of States. Yet it remains that, as long as the Committee is not strengthened in its mandate, the real impact the Committee's work might have will rely on the electoral organ, i.e. the ASP.[1176] The elections to the first Committee took place from 14 to 22 September 2012 and it held its first meeting on 19 April 2013,[1177]

1175 Ibid, Annex, para. 1.

1176 It deserves to be mentioned that the Coalition for the International Criminal Court, an NGO working to ensure the ICC's fair, effective and independent functioning, in December 2010 established the so-called "Independent Panel on International Criminal Court Judicial Elections". The Panel is supposed to "raise awareness of the qualifications for judicial candidates required by the Rome Statute and to encourage States Parties to nominate the most qualified candidates to be judges of the [ICC]." The Panel is intended to contribute to these goals "through making public its assessment process as well as its assessments of individual candidates." See 'Independent Panel on International Criminal Court Judicial Elections – Terms of Reference, adopted 12 May 2011' <http://www.iccindependentpanel.org/content/terms-reference-independent-panel> (last visited: 21 March 2014).

1177 See Report of the Advisory Committee on Nominations of Judges on the work of its first meeting (adopted 31 May 2013) Official Records Resolution ICC-ASP/12/23.

adopting provisional rules of procedure and recommending that costs relating to future meetings of the Committee should be borne by the ASP as of 2014.

d) The Election Procedure

The procedure prescribed by the Rome Statute for the election of judges contains few novelties compared with the system used with regard to the ITLOS. For the purpose of the elections two lists of nominated candidates are compiled, containing on List A those candidates holding criminal law experience and on List B those with competence in international law.[1178] The reason for this twin-track system was to more easily ensure that the bench of the ICC would have an acceptable division of skills and experience and to accommodate the different views held by States on the necessary competence of a judge of the ICC.[1179] There is *prima facie* no reason to consider the flexibility of this system to be a threat to equipping the Court with judges able to free themselves from off-topic influences, as candidates on both lists are required to have legal competence, in either criminal or international law.[1180] Both provide strong protection against bringing to the bench individuals with a questionable distance to purely judicial processes. Elections are held by secret ballot cast by the members of the ASP. The majority required is "the highest number of votes and a two-thirds majority of the States Parties present and voting",[1181] which is a higher requirement than that which applies with newer courts such as the ITLOS.[1182] According to Art. 36(7) Rome Statute no two judges may be of the same nationality. Besides the personal qualifications laid down in Art. 36(3) Rome Statute and which are a matter of concern primarily for the nomination process, Art. 36(8)(a)-(b) Rome Statute prescribes the requirements on the composition of the bench and which limit the States in the election process. States are thus called upon to "take into account" the representation of the principal

---

1178 A candidate can be included in only one of the lists, even if he possesses the qualifications required for both, Art. 36(5) Rome Statute. Cf. *supra* Chapter F.IV(2)(a).

1179 Lee (ed) *The International Criminal Court: The Making of the Rome Statute; Issues, Negotiations, Results*, 164.

1180 See *supra*, Chapter F.IV(2)(d).

1181 Art. 36(6)(a) Rome Statute.

1182 This majority requirement applies to all decisions on matters of substance to be taken by the ASP: see Art. 112(7)(a) Rome Statute.

legal systems of the world, an equitable geographical representation, fair gender representation, and the need for legal expertise on certain specific issues. With regard to the independence of the Court it should be welcomed that this provision is phrased as a non-binding guideline.[1183] Whereas the aims established in Art. 36(8) without doubt are legitimate, any prescription of e.g. a particular geographical representation on the bench could be interpreted as an attempt to control the direction of the Court's decision-making. The Court does not provide for *ad hoc* judges, and the only possible extension of the bench is regulated in Art. 36(2) Rome Statute.[1184]

The first elections took place during the first resumed session of the ASP on 3-7 March 2003.[1185] These elections were characterized by a significantly higher level of transparency and public interest than is usual for elections to international courts.[1186] The second round of elections followed on 26-27 January 2006 during the fourth resumed session of the ASP, at which six seats were voted upon pursuant to Art. 36(9)(c).[1187] Five of the judges elected were those who had held office since the first elections.[1188] All seats were assigned after the first round of voting. In 2007 a third round of elections occurred following the resignations of three judges.[1189] The elections took

1183 It may be noted that the requirement of ensuring representation of the principal legal systems of the world and equitable geographical distribution is formulated less stringently than e.g. in the Statute of the ITLOS, which has a similar provision. In the latter case the mentioned requirements "shall be assured" (Art. 2(2) ITLOS Statute).

1184 See on the ability to suggest an increase in the number of judges serving on the bench *supra* Chapter F.IV(2).

1185 The swearing in ceremony followed on 11 March 2003 at which each judge made a solemn declaration pursuant to Art. 45 Rome Statute and rule 5 Rule of Procedure and Evidence.

1186 Mackenzie, Ruth & Sands, Philippe J., 'Judicial Selection for International Courts: Towards Common Principles and Practices', in: Malleson, Kate (ed) *Appointing Judges in an Age of Judicial Power – Critical Perspectives from Around the World* (University of Toronto Press Toronto 2006), 228.

1187 'Second Election of Judges of the International Criminal Court – Resumed Fourth Session of the Assembly of States Parties, held from 26 to 27 January 2006 at United Nations Headquarters' available at <http://www.icc-cpi.int/NR/rdonlyres/9F5E7613-DF43-4DE6-BD97-D32BFB4E645E/277233/E_totalelectionresults_26jan1630.pdf> (last visited: 21 March 2014).

1188 Judge Ekaterina Trendafilova was newly elected.

1189 The vacancies resulted from the 10 December 2006 resignation of Judge Maureen Harding Clark (Ireland), the resignation of Judge Karl T. Hudson-Phillips (Trinidad

place at the sixth session of the ASP held between 30 November and 14 December 2007. After the first round, two posts had been assigned,[1190] but the third seat on the bench could be filled only after the fourth round.[1191] In January 2009 six new seats had to be filled and elections were held during the resumed seventh session of the ASP from 19 to 23 January 2009 at UN Headquarters. Another round of elections took place during the eighth session of the ASP held on 18 November 2009 in The Hague, where two seats were balloted upon. The latest elections were held during the tenth session of the ASP, between 12 and 21 December 2011.

A recent study has shown that the electoral process is highly politicized at the ICC as well, and that neither the separation of the electoral organ from the wider "vote-trading industry of UN elections" nor the more detailed legal framework of the Rome Statute has been able to prevent this.[1192] Whether this, however, also has the impact of making the ICC prone to influence on its activities is not clear. Even if the election process itself is still subjected to political influence, the level of detail of the legal framework nevertheless appears to provide more checks against which misconduct can be identified.

e) The Administrative Functions of the Presidency of the ICC

The Rome Statute in Art. 34 establishes the Presidency as a separate organ of the Court, which is unknown in other international courts. The Presidency is composed of judges only, and it is responsible for the administration of the Court.[1193] This is different from the situation at the two *ad hoc* Tribunals where the administration of the court is the responsibility of the Registrar

---

and Tobago), effective as of 30 September 2007, and the resignation of Judge Claude Jorda (France), effective as of 12 August 2007.

1190 'Assembly of States Parties to the Rome Statute of the International Criminal Court – Election of the Judges of the International Criminal Court – Election to Fill Three Judicial Vacancies (Sixth Session of the Assembly of States Parties, held from 30 November to 14 December 2007) – Results' available at <http://www.icc-cpi.int/NR/rdonlyres/1A306C85-5B10-486C-8644-9F16E7476C56/277120/Election_of_Judgesbasic30Nov 2100.pdf> (last visited: 21 March 2014).

1191 Ibid.

1192 See Mackenzie, et al., *Selecting International Judges: Principle, Process, and Politics*, 100-136.

1193 Art. 38(3) Rome Statute.

who is directly accountable to the UNGA. The Presidency has the power to decide to what extent judges, who do not serve the Presidency, shall be required to serve on a full-time basis.[1194] As all judges are elected as full-time members of the Court already and must hold themselves available to serve on that basis from the commencement of their terms of office, the real significance of this provision is limited. However, since judges who are required to serve on a full-time basis are not to engage in any other occupation of a professional nature,[1195] and thus are subject to a more far-reaching rule on prohibited side activities (in fact similar to the one applicable to ICJ judges), the Presidency may effect the degree of protection against external influences stemming from incompatible activities. Nonetheless, the Presidency is allowed to use this tool only if the workload of the Court so requires and in consultation with its members. The power of the Presidency to excuse a judge from the exercise of a function under the Rome Statute will be dealt with in a later section.[1196]

The Court Presidency also has the power to assign both trial and Pre-Trial Chambers.[1197] There is no real risk of the parties being able to influence the composition of a particular panel hearing a case. But the risk of a judge lobbying for participation in a particular case or the President's tendency to appoint certain judges taking into account subjective considerations does arise when no system of random assignment of cases to judges or benches is used. The central argument in favour of this system is that it creates more flexibility and the ability to react swiftly to the requirements of efficiency and complication that may be found in each case; in short the ability to respond to the practical and current needs of the Court. For this it may be considered impractical to use random assignment of cases,[1198] and even if the Presidency is granted the power over the composition of the panels it may not be making such decisions according to arbitrary discretion, but rather for practical considerations, a "controlled randomness".[1199] This argu-

1194 Art. 35(3) Rome Statute.

1195 Art. 40(3) Rome Statute.

1196 See *infra* Chapter F.V(3).

1197 Art. 61(11) Rome Statute; Art. 46 Regulations of the Court (Regulations of the Court (as amended on 14 June and 14 November 2007) (adopted 26 Mai 2004, entered into force 26 Mai 2004, date of entry into force of amendments 18 December 2007) Official Records ICC-BD/01-02-07).

1198 Meron, Theodor, 'Judicial Independence and Impartiality in International Criminal Tribunals' (2005) 99 American Journal of International Law 2, 364.

1199 Ibid, 364.

ment is not persuasive. It is not convincing that no practical mechanism can be elaborated which merges objective randomness with practical flexibility so as to adapt the assignment of cases to the available judges, taking into account the overall workload at any particular time. It is in particular not conclusive why the unpredictability of the case load would necessitate case assignment by the Court's Presidency.

3. Financing the Court

a) Outline of the System of Financing

As with other (international) courts the mode of financing is important when it comes to safeguarding judicial independence, as the injection or withholding of funds is an effective and subtle way of influencing the activities of a Court according to political considerations. The rules governing the financing of the ICC are laid down in Part XII of the Rome Statute and further detailed in the Financial Regulations and the Rules.[1200] The system provides for three sources of financial support to the Court: contributions by States Parties, funds provided by the UN[1201] and voluntary contributions.[1202] The organiz-

---

1200 The programme budget for the year 2012 was 108,800,000 EUR (Programme budget for 2012, the Working Capital Fund for 2012, scale of assessments for the apportionment of expenses of the International Criminal Court, financing appropriations for 2012 and the Contingency Fund (adopted 21 December 2011) Official Records Resolution ICC-ASP/10/Res.4), 103,607,900 EUR for 2011 (Programme budget for 2011, the Working Capital Fund for 2011, scale of assessments for the apportionment of expenses of the International Criminal Court, financing appropriations for 2011 and the Contingency Fund (adopted 10 December 2010) Official Records Resolution ICC-ASP/9/Res.4), 103,623,300 EUR for 2010 (Programme budget for 2010, the Working Capital Fund for 2010, scale of assessments for the apportionment of expenses of the International Criminal Court, financing appropriations for the year 2010, the Contingency Fund, conversion of a GTA psychologist post to an established one, Legal aid (defence) and the Addis Ababa Liaison Office (adopted 26 November 2009) Official Records Resolution ICC-ASP/8/Res.7), which was only slightly higher than the programme budget for 2009 of 101,229,900 EUR (Programme budget for 2009, the Working Capital Fund for 2009, scale of assessments for the apportionment of expenses of the International Criminal Court, financing appropriations for the year 2009 and the Contingency Fund (adopted 21 November 2008) Official Records Resolution ICC-ASP/7/Res.4).

1201 Art. 115 Rome Statute.

1202 Art. 116 Rome Statute.

ation of the system was throughout the preparatory work in Rome closely linked to the broader question of the relationship between the ICC and the UN. Although the proposal was made that the UN should be the sole supplier of the Court's funds, i.e. a system similar to the one applied to the ICJ, this was soon rejected due to the risk of the ICC becoming the victim of across-the-board cuts which have occurred – and will continue to occur – for the ICJ and the *ad hoc* criminal tribunals. Since these courts are part of the organizational structure of the UN, any financial hardship that the UN experiences, even if not caused by the courts themselves, is likely to have consequences for their budgets. The option of financing the ICC solely through States was supported by some State representatives in Rome due to the better protection of the independence of the Court.[1203] What was meant was apparently the independence of the Court from the UN; yet in effect such a system would have merely exchanged the (possible) dependence on an international organization for increased dependence from States. However, supporters could with some confidence point to the recently established ITLOS and ISA, which are both financed autonomously from the UN and merely by the contributions of States Parties.

The ICC budget thus does not have to be immediately co-ordinated with that of the UN, but is instead decided by the ASP, i.e. the organ made up of only the representatives of the States Parties.[1204] Whether or not this provides for more stable payment of the funds necessary for the exercise of the functions of the Court and thus better enables the Court to operate independently without having to invest time and effort in lobbying for additional funds is doubtful. Whereas it is true that the ICC's budget far outstrips that of the ICJ, despite the fact that the latter has more cases on its docket,[1205] and the

1203 Lee (ed) *The International Criminal Court: The Making of the Rome Statute; Issues, Negotiations, Results*, 402-403.

1204 Art. 115 Rome Statute and rule 90 of the Rules of Procedure and Evidence.

1205 In direct comparison, the discrepancy becomes rather obvious: the budget of the ICC for 2009 (Programme budget for the year 2009: Programme budget for 2009, the Working Capital Fund for 2009, scale of assessments for the apportionment of expenses of the International Criminal Court, financing appropriations for the year 2009 and the Contingency Fund) was 101,229,900 EUR whereas the budget of the ICJ for the biennium (!) 2010-2011 amounted to 36,635,800 EUR (International Court of Justice, *Report of the International Court of Justice, 1 August 2009-31 July 2010*). However, it must be noted that of the ICC budget, the judiciary merely occupies 10,332,100 EUR, i.e. approximately 10 %. About 25 % of the budget was costs of the OTP, which the ICJ does not have, and about 60 % of the budget was costs of the Registry, which in the ICC's case has functions unknown

staffing of the ICJ (114)[1206] thus is only a fraction of that of the ICC (766),[1207] these numbers may not just be a result of the funding and organizational embedding of the ICC but ought also to be seen as a result of the function and jurisdiction of the courts. For example, the ICC budget pursuant to Art. 114 Rome Statute is to be used for all the expenses of the Court and the ASP. The Court is not able to require the parties to pay the costs of proceedings, as the ICJ can.[1208] The Committee on Budget and Finance is also responsible only for the ICC, which better ensures that the needs of the Court are addressed adequately and can be voiced *vis-à-vis* States. In the interest of the Court's independence it should also be emphasized that the ICC does have a certain enforcement tool at its disposal which helps it to gather the assessed contributions. Pursuant to Art. 112(8) Rome Statute a State Party which is in arrears in the payment of its financial contributions towards the costs of the ICC can lose its vote in the ASP.

b) Funds Provided by the UN – The Example of the Darfur Referral

As mentioned, the ICC has a close co-operative relationship with the UN as envisaged in Art. 2 Rome Statute and spelt out in the Relationship Agreement between the International Criminal Court and the United Nations.[1209] One such aspect of co-operation is the already mentioned referral of a situation by the UNSC to the Court pursuant to Art. 13(b) Rome Statute. As the first referral made by the UNSC shows, the contribution of funds by the UN

---

to the ICJ (e.g. establishing and maintaining a Victims and Witnesses Unit pursuant to Art. 43(6) Rome Statute).

1206 UNGA, *Proposed programme budget for the biennium 2012-2013 – Part III International justice and law – Section 7 International Court of Justice* (17 March 2011) UN Doc. A/66/6 (Sect. 7).

1207 Programme budget for 2012, the Working Capital Fund for 2012, scale of assessments for the apportionment of expenses of the International Criminal Court, financing appropriations for 2012 and the Contingency Fund, para. 2.

1208 Cf. Art. 33 ICJ Statute which provides that the expenses of the Court shall be borne by the UN, i.e. the States Parties to the Statute; see Mackenzie, et al. (eds), *The Manual on International Courts and Tribunals*, 33. Pursuant to Art. 64 ICJ Statute each party shall bear its own costs unless otherwise decided by the ICJ.

1209 Negotiated Relationship Agreement between the International Criminal Court and the United Nations.

pursuant to Art. 115(b) Rome Statute[1210] is voluntary. When the situation in Darfur was forwarded to the ICC the UNSC explicitly excluded any financial commitment to the investigation of the crimes that had occurred in that conflict.[1211] According to para. 7 of the pertinent Resolution 1593 the UNSC recognized "that none of the expenses incurred in connection with the referral including expenses related to investigations or prosecutions in connection with that referral, shall be borne by the United Nations" but instead by the other means of financing envisaged in the Statute, namely the parties to the Statute and voluntary contributions. It may be argued that the Court is provided with sufficient financial means by way of the regular budget, and that it thus ought to be able to cover the costs which may arise through its various activities. Yet the budget is always drafted with regard to planned and foreseen activities in mind, and the referral of the Darfur situation was certainly not one of those in the 2004 budget. However, this particular situation did not lead to any significant hardships for the Court, since the workload and therefore the available funding remained on a reasonable level. Yet under more straitened conditions the Court could find itself either unable to meet the requests to exercise its jurisdiction, which from the perspective of its independent functioning would still be tolerable,[1212] or able to conduct investigations but substantially guided by the aim of not creating additional burdens for the Court, i.e. in neglect of its obligations as an independent and impartial arbiter.

c) Voluntary Contributions as a Means of Influencing the Court's Activities?

Pursuant to Art. 116 Rome Statute the ICC may receive voluntary contributions, both in financial assets and in kind, from governments, international organizations, individuals, corporations and other entities. Voluntary contributions, if thought of as being conditional by the provider, pose a potential

1210 "Funds provided by the United Nations, subject to the approval of the General Assembly, in particular in relation to the expenses incurred due to referrals by the Security Council."

1211 UNSC, *Reports of the Secretary-General on the Sudan* (31 March 2005) UN Doc. S/RES/1593 (2005).

1212 After all, according to Art. 13 Rome Statute "[t]he Court *may* exercise its jurisdiction" if a situation is referred to the Prosecutor by the UNSC." (Emphasis added.).

threat to the independence of the Court, although they may at times be necessary when the regular funds pursuant to Art. 115 Rome Statute, i.e. mainly assessed contributions from States Parties, would leave the Court underfinanced for the tasks it is expected to fulfil. Irrespective of this, voluntary contributions are not to be seen as funds of the Court and the ASP. This is emphasized by the fact that Art. 115 ("Funds of the Court and of the Assembly of States Parties") Rome Statute does not mention such contributions and because Art. 116 Rome Statute speaks of them as "additional funds". During the deliberations in the Preparatory Committee voluntary funds evoked strong opinions both in favour of and against their use. Whereas some representatives considered them to provide the Court with "real independence" in the sense of autonomy from the traditional sources of funding,[1213] the same argument can and was reversed. Art. 116 Rome Statute reflects the States Parties' awareness of the potential risk for the independence of the Court that may arise from such contributions by providing that these funds may be received and used only "in accordance with relevant criteria adopted by the Assembly of States Parties", e.g. regarding the purpose for which they are made, how they are used and how/if they are accounted for.[1214]

Concerning the purpose for which contributions may be made, Regulation 7.2 of the Court's Financial Regulations and Rules provides that they may only be accepted if they are consistent with the "nature and functions" of the ICC and follow the other criteria adopted by the ASP for this purpose.[1215] Two such criteria have so far been established in the governing instruments of the Court. Regulation 7.2 itself mandates that "contributions which directly or indirectly involve additional financial liability for the Court shall require the prior consent of the Assembly of States Parties" before they can be accepted. A second criterion is found in a resolution of the ASP on relevant criteria for voluntary contributions to the ICC.[1216] This resolution demands of the contributing entities that they make a declaration that the contributions

1213 Lee (ed) *The International Criminal Court: The Making of the Rome Statute; Issues, Negotiations, Results*, 404.

1214 Triffterer (ed) *Commentary on the Rome Statute of the International Criminal Court – Observers' Notes, Article by Article*, 1718.

1215 Financial Regulations and Rules (latest amendment adopted on 22 November 2008).

1216 Relevant criteria for voluntary contributions to the International Criminal Court (adopted 3 September 2002) Official Records ICC-ASP/1/Res.11.

are not intended to affect the independence of the Court and entrusts the Registrar with the task of ensuring that independence is not affected or that any other applicable criteria established by the ASP are violated. Since voluntary contributions are unlikely to be made without being tied to a particular (and rarely altruistic) purpose, it is possible to imagine that the Court could receive a donation only under preconditions which ran counter to the aims of the ICC.[1217] In such cases the Registrar would be barred from accepting the donation. No such cases have been registered so far, and considering that the ASP has refrained from adopting any further criteria for the receipt and use of voluntary contributions the matter is of manageable proportions.

Yet it remains to be stated that in the interest of the independence of the Court and considering that voluntary contributions must never become more than an additional form of funding for the Court, the Registrar ought to interpret his controlling task under ICC-ASP/1/Res.11 rather broadly so as to prevent any potential infringement of the Court's independence.[1218] In case

---

1217 Regulations 7.3-7.4 provide that voluntary contributions that are being accepted for purposes specified by the donors shall be treated as trust funds or special accounts and contributions for which no purpose has been specified shall be reported as gifts. Trust funds may be established (and closed) only by the Registrar (see Regulation 6.5) and shall be reported both to the Presidency and the ASP, which thus control the Registrar in his exercise of this function. One such fund – although a particular kind as it has its legal basis in Art. 79 Statute – that has been set up is the trust fund for the benefit of victims of crimes within the jurisdiction of the Court, and of the families of such victims (established by Resolution ICC-ASP/1/Res.6 Establishment of a fund for the benefit of victims of crimes within the jurisdiction of the Court, and of the families of such victims). The fund is governed by the Regulations of the Trust Fund for Victims (Regulations of the Trust Fund for Victims (adopted 3 December 2005) Official Records ICC-ASP/4/Res.3) which establish a number of safeguards. One such safeguard is that contributions from governments shall not be earmarked (ibid, para. 27) but shall instead be beneficial to victims. Yet the Trust Fund for Victims is special not only because it is mandated in the Statute (Art. 79 Rome Statute) but also because it derives its funds from a variety of sources and thus does not just rely on voluntary contributions. To bind voluntary contributions to a particular purpose established by the Court itself and to combine those voluntary contributions with other sources of funding as in the case of the Trust Fund for Victims may indeed be the appropriate way of ensuring that the Court may function independently of any political influence despite the obvious background of voluntary contributions in particular motivations and intentions held by the respective donor.

1218 See on this Relevant criteria for voluntary contributions to the International Criminal Court which in para. 3 determines that "the Registrar shall report to the

of doubt he ought to refuse the contribution.[1219] It must also be emphasized that pursuant to above-mentioned Regulation 7.2 only the Registrar of the Court may receive voluntary contributions, and not the judicial organ of the Court. If judges were allowed to accept such contributions it would seriously damage the perceived independence and impartiality of the entire Court.

d) Appraisal of the System of Financing

Neither sole financing through States (either States Parties to the Statute or States referring cases to the Court) or by the UN would have been a wise solution from the viewpoint of protecting the ICC's independence. The prosecution of the most serious crimes, which often are intrinsically linked to the same politics that directly or indirectly form the agenda of States and international organizations involved in ensuring and protecting international peace, must function with as little friction as possible *vis-à-vis* those actors. Yet the ICC is also compelled to have recourse to those entities in one form or another for its funding, since only they have the necessary resources that may be made available to the Court. It is rather obvious that the Court is unable to generate sufficient income itself.[1220] Thus the current system of mixed financing from both States Parties and the UN is an appropriate compromise which has the advantage of making the ICC less susceptible to threats from one-sided dependence. Voluntary contributions should be kept merely as an additional source of financing that does not affect the way in which the costs of the Court are met and shall in particular not drive the Court into dependence on the donor by e.g. creating a lower assessment of the contributions to be made by the States Parties to the budget.[1221] In addition, voluntary contributions should be made subject to extensive regulations that ensure transparency in the process of their adoption and utilization.

Assembly of States Parties all offered voluntary contributions, regardless of whether they were accepted or refused."

1219 According to judge Sang-Hyun Song, the Registrar is obliged to refuse the money in case of doubt: see Song, Sang-Hyun, 'The Independence of the ICC and Safeguards against Political Influence', Symposium on the International Criminal Court, Conference in Beijing, China (3-4 February 2007).

1220 The only possible income is the ordering of a fine pursuant to Art. 77(2) Rome Statute. But any further powers in this regard would also seriously question the Court's independence.

1221 See the wording of Art. 116 Rome Statute: "Without prejudice to article 115 …".

V. Personal Independence

1. Tenure and Security of Tenure

a) Can Non-Renewable Terms Strengthen Judges' Independence?

Pursuant to Art. 36(9)(a) Rome Statute the judges of the ICC hold office for a nine year non-renewable term.[1222] The length of the judges' term of office thus reflects the length of tenure for ICJ judges and is also similar to that of judges at the ITLOS. In comparison to the other international criminal jurisdictions, the ICTY and ICTR both have four year terms, and the ECtHR, where judges hold office for six years, the Rome Statute grants the ICC judges a relatively long term in office. However, the choice of a longer term appears to come at the price of the possibility of re-election and can only be understood when seen in this broader context.

The *travaux préparatoires* indicate that the ILC opted for a tenure of 12 years in its first draft submitted in 1993.[1223] Already here the relatively long term was seen in the light of the two supplementing rules, namely the non-renewability of the term and the ability to continue in office to finish any case the hearing of which had already begun.[1224] According to the working group of the ILC, the long tenure was "a sort of trade-off for the prohibition

---

1222 Both longer and shorter terms are possible only during the initial phase of the ICC's existence, namely pursuant to Arts. 36(9)(b)-(c) and 37(2) Rome Statute. Art. 36(9)(b) Rome Statute in combination with Art. 36(9)(c) provides for the exception that judges selected to serve for a term of three years at the first election shall be eligible for re-election. Furthermore, Art. 37(2) Rome Statute provides that judges who have been elected to fill a vacancy which lasted three years or less shall equally be eligible for re-election. Of the initial eighteen judges, six were to serve for a full nine year term, six were to serve for six years and six members were to serve for only three years. According to some commentators, the granting of a possibility of re-election for those judges that initially only served for six years would have meant the potential opening up of the Court to political influence: see Triffterer (ed) *Commentary on the Rome Statute of the International Criminal Court – Observers' Notes, Article by Article*, 947.

1223 See International Law Commission, *Revised Report of the Working Group on the Draft Statute for an International Criminal Court*, 51.

1224 Art. 36(10) Rome Statute: "Notwithstanding paragraph 9, a judge assigned to a Trial or Appeals Chamber in accordance with article 39 shall continue in office to complete any trial or appeal the hearing of which has already commenced before that Chamber."

of their re-election".[1225] Following the criticism from some States that 12 year tenures would be too long, the ILC opted for the nine year term in its 1994 Draft Statute, which was seen to be still compatible with the all-important principle of non-eligibility for re-election.[1226] The length of tenure, which was also favoured because it meant concurrence with the ICJ,[1227] therefore was a reaction to the need to prevent re-election, which in turn was perceived necessary due to the special nature of an international criminal institution. In academia non-eligibility for re-election is mostly approved of as a means of strengthening the Court's independence and described as progressive compared to systems of other international courts.[1228] For example, according to A. Cassese the prohibition of re-election is "[a] wise manner of further strengthening the independence of judges".[1229] With this system, any politicisation that may flow from overt campaigning is suppressed in the first place. This not only ensures the actual independence of the Court but moreover guarantees that even the Court's perceived independence is not infringed upon due to judges engaging in re-election campaigns. Eliminating the re-election of judges altogether also avoids the almost insurmountable difficulties relating to trying to shape re-elections in ways most supportive of the Court's independence.

Yet the predominantly affirmative assessment of the non-renewable terms is somewhat blurred by a practical consideration that should not be ignored. The independence of the Court, and indeed that of any court, is closely linked to its efficient functioning. Whereas campaigning of judges may have an adverse effect on the work of the Court, by leading to distracting the judges or, in the worst case, to decision-making which is formulated accordingly, the prevention of re-electability also has the negative effect of stripping the Court of valuable experience and expertise. This is certainly not a problem inherent in the debate on the possibility to re-elect judges alone, since longer terms may also contribute to the maintenance of the collective experience

---

1225 International Law Commission, *Revised Report of the Working Group on the Draft Statute for an International Criminal Court*, 13.

1226 This remained unchallenged by the Preparatory Committee and the Rome Conference; International Law Commission, *Report of the International Law Commission on the work of its forty-sixth session*, 51-52.

1227 Lee (ed) *The International Criminal Court: The Making of the Rome Statute; Issues, Negotiations, Results*, 156.

1228 Meron, 'Judicial Independence and Impartiality in International Criminal Tribunals', 362.

1229 Cassese, *International Criminal Law*, 379.

on the bench. But the rather static limitation imposed by non-renewability is somewhat more artificial than e.g. the limitation imposed by a mandatory retirement age.[1230]

A related provision that contributes to the efficient functioning of the Court but which does not directly affect external influence on the Court is Art. 36(10) Rome Statute, providing that a judge assigned to a Trial or Appeals Chamber shall continue in office to complete trials and appeals which have already begun.[1231] Interestingly this does not apply to pre-trial judges, although e.g. both the 1993[1232] and 1994[1233] ILC Drafts still provided for this. Yet Art. 39(3)(a) Rome Statute states that "[j]udges assigned to the Trial and Pre-Trial Divisions shall serve in those divisions for a period of three years, and thereafter until the completion of any case the hearing of which has already commenced in the division concerned." Although this provision explicitly only affects the term for which a judge serves in a trial or Pre-Trial Chamber, rather than his entire tenure, the continuity on the bench and the minimization of the risk of undue influence on the proceedings which are pursued by this provision would be subjected to a significant limitation if this did not extend beyond the ordinary tenure of judges.

b) Removal from Office

The possibility to remove ICC judges from their office is structured differently from what applies at the ICJ or the ITLOS. Yet more important is the fact that it is addressed in the Rome Statute at all, which is an improvement on the *ad hoc* Tribunals that were established prior to the ICC but which did

---

1230 The introduction of an age limit was discussed in the preparatory process but ultimately rejected as being arbitrary and lacking support in both international and national practice regarding the term of office of judges; see Lee (ed) *The International Criminal Court: The Making of the Rome Statute; Issues, Negotiations, Results*, 157.

1231 This for example means that Judge Blattmann, although his tenure expired in 2009, remains in office until Trial Chamber I gives its decision in the Lubanga trial.

1232 Art. 7(6) 1993 ILC Draft, see International Law Commission, *Revised Report of the Working Group on the Draft Statute for an International Criminal Court*, 11.

1233 Art. 6(6) 1994 ILC Draft, see International Law Commission, *Report of the International Law Commission on the work of its forty-sixth session*, 50.

not deal with the matter.[1234] According to W. Schabas, the mere existence of Art. 46 Rome Statute is an improvement

> "because a judge or other senior judicial official, whose independence and impartiality is fundamental to the integrity of the institution, should know precisely the grounds, conditions, and procedure for removal from office. Leaving this unstated, and therefore implicit, can only nurture fears of the arbitrary, and thereby impact negatively."[1235]

A judge may only be removed for one of the three reasons set out in Art. 46(1)(a)-(b) Rome Statute: for serious misconduct, a serious breach of the judge's duties under the Statute, or due to incapacity to exercise the functions required under the Statute. The Rules of Procedure and Evidence exemplify serious misconduct with behaviour manifesting itself both within and outside the course of official duties.[1236] The former, which is considered negatively to affect the administration of justice, includes the disclosure of facts or information which would be seriously prejudicial to the proceedings or to a person.[1237] Outside the course of official duties serious misconduct is characterized by causing or being likely to cause serious harm to the standing of the Court.[1238] A serious breach of duty is gross negligence in the performance or knowingly acting in contravention of duties.[1239]

The procedure for dealing with a request for removal from office is laid down in Art. 46 Rome Statute and is detailed in the Rules of the Court and the Regulations of the Court.[1240] Procedures are initiated by confidential

---

1234 On the excusing and disqualification of judges see *infra* Chapter F.V(3).

1235 Schabas, William A., *The International Criminal Court: A Commentary on the Rome Statute* (Oxford University Press Oxford 2010), 610.

1236 The same applies to misconduct of a less serious nature giving rise to disciplinary measures, cf. *infra* Chapter F.V(4).

1237 Rule 24(1)(a) Rules of Procedure and Evidence.

1238 Rule 24(1)(b) Rules of Procedure and Evidence.

1239 Rule 24(2) Rules of Procedure and Evidence. The rules provide the example of a judge not complying with the duty to request that he be excused despite knowing the grounds for such recusal. See on this *infra* Chapter F.V(3).

1240 It must certainly be welcomed that the procedure is established in great detail in the Rules of Procedure and Evidence and the Regulations of the Court, but this is no real advantage *vis-à-vis* e.g. the ICJ. The lack of detailed provisions concerning the handling of incoming complaints against judges contained in the governing instruments of either the ICJ or the ITLOS does not imply that those courts do not appropriately address such complaints.

complaint transmitted to the Presidency,[1241] which may also initiate proceedings on its own motion.[1242] The Presidency has a regulatory function through its duty to set aside anonymous and manifestly unfounded, i.e. inadmissible, complaints.[1243] The removal itself is decided by the ASP upon the recommendation of the *other* judges, whose decision is to be taken at a plenary session.[1244] Both decisions have to gather support by a two-thirds majority.[1245] During the drafting of the Rome Statute suggestions were also made that only a decision of the judges themselves could remove one of their peers from the bench.[1246] It must be considered a regrettable concession to the control over the new ICC being sought by States that the ASP, an organ plainly driven by State interests, was ultimately determined to be involved in the decision-making process. The reason this right in other courts is reserved for the judges themselves is precisely to avoid any possible external influence that may manifest itself through the removal of or attempt to remove a judge.[1247] It can be assumed that the main reason for the procedure at the ICC is based on the desire to establish the accountability of the Court towards the appointing body.[1248] What may be advanced as a justification in the case of the ICC is that individuals, not States, appear before the Court. In line with the development of individuals' subjectivity in international law, there ought to be checks in place upon the organs that are able to implement directly, and without the mediation of any State, the obligations that international

---

1241 Rule 26 Rules of Procedure and Evidence; Regulation 119(1) Regulations of the Court (as amended on 14 June and 14 November 2007).

1242 Rule 26 Rules of Procedure and Evidence.

1243 In order to make this determination, the Presidency is assisted by three judges (Regulation 120 Regulations of the Court) who shall make a recommendation to the Presidency on both the two grounds of admissibility, as well as the assessment of serious misconduct and serious breach of duties. Cf. *infra* on the procedure in the event of a request for disciplinary measure, Chapter F.V(4).

1244 Rule 29(1) Rules of Procedure and Evidence.

1245 Art. 46(2)(a) Rome Statute.

1246 See Schabas, *The International Criminal Court: A Commentary on the Rome Statute*, 610.

1247 The interest of avoiding this tool to be implemented to allow political considerations to influence the Court's judicial functions is also not served by allowing the ASP to make such a decision by secret ballot: see Art. 46(2) Rome Statute.

1248 Triffterer (ed) *Commentary on the Rome Statute of the International Criminal Court – Observers' Notes, Article by Article*, 1003. Although this notion apparently did not affect the removal procedures for other international courts such as the ICJ or the ITLOS, where only the judges themselves could remove one of their colleagues from office; cf. *supra* Chapter D.VI(2)(b) and Chapter E.V(2).

law puts upon them.[1249] Yet there is little reason to allow these checks to be in the hands of States.

Removal of a judge from office is sanctioned only by a double two-thirds majority, which is considerably less than the requirement of unanimity applicable at the ICJ[1250] and the ITLOS. Yet it is not easy to decide whether an opinion in favour of either unanimity or a two-thirds majority is the most appropriate system to protect independence. It may e.g. be argued that the higher hurdle for state-centred courts is justified, as States have already made a decision to subject themselves to that court's jurisdiction, whereas individuals before the ICC have not had a similar choice, and that therefore there must be more opportunities to influence the procedure before the Court. The lower majority requirement may also find support because it better ensures the functioning of the Court; if and when a two-thirds majority of the bench is convinced that a judge ought to be removed from office, the basis for the continued service of that judge may be irrevocably destroyed.

As with the procedures outlined with respect to the ICJ and the ITLOS, the affected judge must be informed of the initiated procedure[1251] and must be given the opportunity to present and receive evidence, to make submissions and to supply answers to questions put to him.[1252] A judge may further be suspended from his duties pending the final decision.[1253] Such a decision may, according to Regulation 124(1) Regulations of the Court, be made following the Presidency's decision of admissibility of the complaint "by the organ competent to make a decision under article 46, paragraphs 2 and 3." This is a rather unfortunate formulation as both the ASP and the other judges under Art. 46(2) Rome Statute are competent to make decisions, even though they are different. Thus suspension by the ASP appears to be possible, albeit only after the Court (i.e. the Presidency) has determined that a complaint is admissible. The calamitous nature of this provision is reinforced by the fact that Rule 28 Rules of Procedure and Evidence does not provide conclusive instructions on what triggers a suspension. The provisions states

1249 Walter, 'Subjects of International Law', paras. 15-18.

1250 Proposals for a two-thirds majority to remove a judge from office were, interestingly, rejected in the drafting of the ICJ Statute on the basis that this would be less suited to protecting the independence of the judges.

1251 Rule 27(1) Rules of Procedure and Evidence.

1252 Art. 46(4) Rome Statute and Rule 27(2) Rules of Procedure and Evidence.

1253 Rule 28 Rules of Procedure and Evidence and Regulation 124 Regulations of the Court.

that a judge may be suspended "[w]here an allegation … is of a sufficiently serious nature". Considering that suspension is an option only after a complaint has been determined to be admissible, i.e. not manifestly unfounded, the standard must lie somewhere between this threshold and one of the grounds for removal from office, i.e. serious misconduct and serious breach of duty. It would have been advisable at least for the ICC itself in the Regulations of the Court to establish clearer standards so as to avoid the potential criticism of being arbitrary in any future practice. In this context it may be noted that if the plenary session finds that conduct does not amount to serious misconduct or a serious breach of duty, i.e. where it cannot lead to removal of the relevant judge, the plenary session may still decide that the relevant judge engaged in misconduct of a less serious nature and that a disciplinary measure needs to be imposed.[1254] In such a case, the ASP is no longer involved.

2. Incompatible Activities – Inclusion of the Appearance as a Criterion

The provision relating to incompatible activities in the Rome Statute, Art. 40(2), explicitly makes the connection between extra-judicial activities and judges' independence. Not only is the title of Art. 40 Rome Statute "Independence of the judges", but Art. 40(1) Rome Statute explicitly declares that "[t]he judges shall be independent in the performance of their functions." The limitation upon ICC judges expressed in Art. 40(2) Rome Statute also states that they "shall not engage in any activity which is likely to interfere with their judicial functions or to affect confidence in their independence." Judges required to serve on a full-time basis, i.e. those making up the Presidency and other judges who have been required *ad hoc* to serve on a full-time basis,[1255] shall not engage in any other occupation of a professional nature.[1256] Further safeguards include that any doubts about the application of Art. 40 Rome Statute shall be resolved by a decision of an absolute majority of the judges,[1257] which is a lesser requirement than applies at the ICJ and the ITLOS.

1254 See on disciplinary measures *infra* Chapter F.V(4).
1255 Art. 35(2)-(3) Rome Statute.
1256 Art. 40(3) Rome Statute.
1257 Art. 40(4) Rome Statute. The affected judge shall not take part in the decision.

The formulation "likely ... to affect confidence in their independence" is rather broad; almost all professional occupations can be interpreted as having an effect on the confidence that an observer may have in a judge's independence. The same criticism must be raised with respect to the prohibition of activities that are likely to interfere with judges' judicial functions. The formulations are vague and depend on an interpretation of terms such as "affect", "confidence", "interfere" and, most importantly, "independence". At least from the viewpoint of providing the judges with guidance on what side activities are compatible with their service on the ICC, the Rome Conference would have been well advised to opt for suggesting a provision similar to Art. 16(1) ICJ Statute, which excludes any political or administrative function, and any other occupation of a professional nature. From the *travaux préparatoires* it at least follows that activities such as part-time teaching and writing for publication were considered compatible with judges' functions,[1258] which would also be in line with the interpretation usually given to Art. 16(1) ICJ Statute. Yet this does not necessarily mean that every such activity cannot destroy confidence in judges' independence. The only reliable indication of permitted side activities follows from a reading of Art. 40(3) Rome Statute: if judges serving on a full-time basis at the seat of the Court are prohibited from exercising "any other occupation of a professional nature", then any other judge who merely has to hold himself available to serve on that basis is not explicitly barred from practising a second occupation of a professional nature. For a Court that was never expected to have too little work for its bench, this is a rather unfortunate condition, and it is doubtful whether this result was intended by the drafters of the Rome Statute.

Further guidance on the interpretation of Art. 40(2) Rome Statute may be received from the Code of Judicial Ethics which the judges themselves adopted in 2005.[1259] The purpose of the Code is to "contribute to judicial independence and impartiality ... with a view to ensuring the legitimacy and effectiveness of the international judicial process". Art. 10 of the Code describes certain activities of ICC judges as potentially posing a threat to the independence and impartiality:

1258 Cf. Preparatory Committee on the Establishment of an International Criminal Court, *Report of the Preparatory Committee on the Establishment of an International Criminal Court, Volume I (Proceedings of the Preparatory Committee during March-April and August 1996)*, 13.

1259 Code of Judicial Ethics (adopted 9 March 2005, entered into force 9 March 2005) Official Records ICC-BD/02-01-05.

> "1. Judges shall not engage in any extra-judicial activity that is incompatible with their judicial function or the efficient and timely functioning of the Court, or that may affect or may reasonably appear to affect their independence or impartiality.
> 2. Judges shall not exercise any political function."

The formulation "may reasonably appear to affect their independence or impartiality" is very similar to the above-mentioned wording "likely to ... affect confidence in their independence", in the sense that it is the *appearance* of independence (and impartiality) that is the point of reference. The ICC system thereby, to a greater degree than both the ICJ and the ITLOS, pays tribute to the perception of its independence from outside. This is desirable as this standard has also developed in national judicial systems, where individuals appear before the courts.[1260] As regards conclusive indications as to side activities that are prohibited, the provision is not overly expressive. Art. 10(2) of the Code merely states that the judges consider political functions to be incompatible with service on the bench, seemingly both for judges serving full-time and those merely available to do so. Although it is laudable that the provision in its entirety exempts from an assessment pursuant to Art. 40(2) Rome Statute and Art. 10(1) of the Code those side activities which most obviously appear to be a threat to independence and impartiality, it is not convincing why professional administrative functions were not also included in this category. In the case of the ICC, there are no compelling financial or career-related concerns that motivate this lacuna or vagueness, especially as the annual remuneration of ICC judges is relatively high compared to the salaries of judges of other international courts.[1261] In this context it

1260 The first time real significance was attributed to the appearance was in *R. v. Sussex Justices, ex p. McCarthy (King's Bench Division)*, 259: "But while that is so, a long line of cases shows that it is not merely of some importance but is of fundamental importance that justice should not only be done, but should manifestly and undoubtedly be seen to be done." See also *Delcourt v. Belgium*, para. 31.

1261 The salaries and entitlements of the judges are governed by the Conditions of Service and Compensation of the Judges of the International Criminal Court, as adopted by the ASP to the Rome Statute at its 4th meeting. According to these Conditions of Service, the remuneration of a judge working on a full-time basis at the Court has been established at 180,000 EUR net per annum. Assembly of States Parties to the Rome Statute of the International Criminal Court – Second Session, Official Records, Part III – Conditions of Service and Compensation and Staff Regulations (8-12 September 2003) Official Records Resolution ICC-ASP/2/10, para. A.I.A.1. See also Strengthening the International Criminal Court

deserves to be mentioned that the salaries and allowances are not to be reduced during judges' terms of office.[1262]

3. Excusing and Disqualification

The ICC Presidency has the power to excuse a judge from the exercise of a function upon his own request.[1263] The individual judge is called upon to recuse himself where his impartiality might reasonably be doubted on any ground.[1264] As an example of when a judge shall be disqualified from a case, the Rome Statute lists a "judge has previously been involved in any capacity in that case before the Court or in a related criminal case at the national level involving the person being investigated or prosecuted". The grounds for disqualification are further set out in Rule 34 Rules of Procedure and Evidence. However, the judge also has an obligation to make a request to be excused where he has reason to believe that a ground for disqualification exists in relation to him, and he must not wait for a request for disqualification to be made. Such requests for disqualification can be made by the Prosecutor or the person being investigated or prosecuted by the ICC.[1265] Like what applies at the ICJ and the ITLOS the challenged judge shall be entitled to present his comments on the matter, but shall not take part in the decision. It must be welcomed in the interest of not unduly using disqualification procedures to influence the Court's decision-making that an absolute majority of the judges has to decide on any question arising from the application of pertinent provisions. However, again the majority requirement is considerably lower than at the ICJ and the ITLOS. This could be motivated by the interest in keeping proceedings involving individuals more flexible, in order to honour the rights of those individuals that entities appearing before the ICJ and the ITLOS usually do not have, among them the right to a fair trial.

---

and the Assembly of States Parties (adopted 10 September 2004) Official Records Resolution ICC-ASP/3/Res.3, Annex, Part III, para. 1.

1262 Art. 49 Rome Statute.

1263 Art. 41 Rome Statute and Rule 33 Rules of Procedure and Evidence.

1264 Art. 41(2)(a) Rome Statute.

1265 Art. 41(2)(b) Rome Statute.

4. Disciplinary Measures

Besides the possibility to remove a judge for having committed serious misconduct or a serious breach of his duties under the Rome Statute pursuant to Art. 46 Rome Statute, it is also possible according to Art. 47 Rome Statute to take disciplinary measures against a judge for the commission of misconduct of a less serious nature. What constitutes "misconduct of a less serious nature" is defined in Rule 25 Rules of Procedure and Evidence. It includes conduct that takes place in the course of official duties, if it "causes or is likely to cause harm to the proper administration of justice before the Court or the proper internal functioning of the Court", and conduct outside the course of official duties if it "causes or is likely to cause harm to the standing of the Court". One example of the former is repeatedly failing to comply with requests made by the Presidency.[1266] According to Rule 30 decisions to impose a disciplinary measure shall be taken by the Presidency. Such disciplinary measures are limited to either reprimands or pecuniary sanctions.[1267]

The regulation of disciplinary measures against judges is unique among the instruments governing the various international courts included in this study. Neither the Statutes or Rules of the *ad hoc* Tribunals nor the instruments of the ICJ deal with this topic. Disciplinary measures must be seen as a pre-stage to the ability to request the removal of a judge, i.e. as a sanction for behaviour that is detrimental to the administration of justice or the internal or external functioning of the Court. This is supported by the parallelism of many procedural issues, vividly illustrated by the fact that the Presidency has the discretion to treat an alleged "less serious" breach as if it were a case of removal from office[1268] and vice versa.[1269] All complaints for misconduct of a less serious nature are reviewed by the Presidency which may also initiate proceedings of its own motion.[1270] Anonymous or manifestly unfounded complaints shall be set aside.[1271] In conducting this initial review of the ad-

1266 Rule 25(1)(a)(ii) Rules of Procedure and Evidence. The definitions in Rule 25(1)(a) are not exhaustive.

1267 Rule 32 Rules of Procedure and Evidence.

1268 Rule 25(2) Rules of Procedure and Evidence.

1269 Regulation 121(1) Regulations of the Court (as amended on 14 June and 14 November 2007).

1270 Rule 26(1) Rules of Procedure and Evidence.

1271 Rule 26(2) Rules of Procedure and Evidence.

missibility of a complaint, the Presidency is assisted by "one or more judges, appointed on the basis of automatic rotation, in accordance with the Regulations".[1272] According to Regulation 120, this form of "inquiry commission"[1273] shall "seek additional comments from either the person being complained against or the complainant and shall make a recommendation to the Presidency on" the admissibility. The Presidency then decides whether it accepts any such recommendation.[1274] In a next step, i.e. when the Presidency considers the complaint to be neither anonymous nor manifestly unfounded but that it manifestly falls outside the scope of serious misconduct and serious breach of duty giving rise to removal,[1275] the Presidency is free to deal with the complaint on the merits,[1276] including deciding the sanction to be imposed.[1277] One important difference between less serious breaches, potentially leading to disciplinary measures, and misconduct that may lead to removal from office is that the proceedings concerning the latter involve the ASP and are not "without prejudice to any additional procedure to be followed by the Assembly".[1278] The fact that decisions to impose a disciplinary measure shall be taken by the Presidency without external influence[1279] makes it less likely for this tool to be used to influence the bench unduly. In contrast, the fact that reprimands, which is one of the two kinds of possible disciplinary measures, according to Rule 30(4) Rules of Procedure and Evidence "shall be recorded in writing and shall be transmitted to the President of the Bureau of the Assembly of States Parties" should call for caution. Intended or not, this provision appears to allow the ASP to take disciplinary measures into account when deciding on actions directly affecting the judges, e.g. their election.

1272 Ibid.
1273 Schabas, *The International Criminal Court: A Commentary on the Rome Statute*, 617.
1274 Regulation 120(3) Regulations of the Court.
1275 Rule 24 Rules of Procedure and Evidence.
1276 Regulation 121(1) Regulations of the Court.
1277 Rule 30(1) Rules of Procedure and Evidence.
1278 Regulation 123(2) Regulations of the Court.
1279 Cf. on decisions of removal from office, *supra* Chapter F.V(1)(b).

VI. Conclusions

The ICC has the aim of ending the selectivity and political motivation that have been characteristic of past international criminal prosecutions. This necessarily implies that it has to be free from – or at least to a considerably lesser degree dependent upon – influence exerted by political actors. The ability of the Court to become active through its independent Prosecutor and despite the inactivity of States is one of the characteristics of the Court and one which makes the ICC both into a powerful tool in the fight against impunity and a potential antagonist to State interests. Whether the ICC will succeed where its predecessors and State inactivity have failed is to a large extent determined by the degree to which it is able to operate independent. The ability of the ICC Prosecutor to initiate investigations *propriu motu* is one important tool to allow the Court to function autonomously. But even if situations are referred to it, by States or the UNSC, the Court remains the master of the prosecutions, as it is not compelled to exercise its jurisdiction. Instead the referral of situations to the ICC is helpful to allow the efforts of the Court to be co-ordinated (subject to the terms of the Court itself) with activities of the UN in order to give the aims of fighting impunity and establishing respect for and enforce international justice a realistic opportunity.

According to Judge S.-H. Song, the answer to the question whether the ICC will withstand the political pressure and act completely independently is to be answered in the affirmative, "because the Rome Statute provides robust mechanisms to protect fully the independence of the Court and to safeguard it from political influence."[1280] As the analysis above has shown, numerous such efforts to uphold the independence of the Court can indeed be distinguished in its founding and regulating instruments. Most prominently, the judges have adopted a Code of Judicial Ethics which contains guidelines on essential ethical standards and is meant to help the judges (who are thus the addressees of the Code) to deal with ethical and professional issues that may arise. In the Code the judges are called upon to "not only uphold the independence of their office and act impartially, but [also] to further confidence in their independence and the appearance of impartiality."[1281] The Code testifies to the importance that the judges have accorded to their independence. Furthermore, in providing for the ability to establish an Advisory

1280 Song, 'The Independence of the ICC and Safeguards against Political Influence'.
1281 Kaul, 'International Criminal Court (ICC)', para. 15.

Committee to review nominations to the bench, the Rome Statute addresses one of the recurring concerns in the quest for increased judicial independence, namely the opaque authority of States to nominate individuals to the bench. The long tenure of judges coupled with the inability to be re-elected to the bench presents the highest standard of any international court analysed in this study. These features and others provide an entirely different approach to the protection of judicial independence than e.g. at the ICJ or the ITLOS. It is suggested here that the explanation for this is the fact that individuals and not States appear before the Court. Whereas States have different instruments at their disposal to influence how and if at all they are subjecting themselves to international adjudication, individuals prosecuted before the ICC do not have similar opportunities to escape international prosecution. This raises the demand, similar to that which prevails on the national level, that the ICC act in ways that do not violate the rights of individuals as and insofar as they are protected under international law.

However, despite the predominantly positive resumé portrayed above, certain concerns must nevertheless be raised. The praised Code of Judicial Ethics merely contains guidelines and is not addressed to individuals who stand trial before the Court and who thus could have an interest in using it as a basis for challenging the behaviour of judges. Furthermore, the Advisory Committee on Nominations is not a standing organ; it may be established by the ASP and even then holds only the powers it has *ad hoc* been equipped with. As suggested already by its name, however, the Committee was never envisaged to have the authority to reject the nominations of States Parties. Finally, the procedures surrounding removal from office, excusing, disqualification and disciplinary measures follow rather detailed rules. Yet the majorities necessary for taking decisions are considerably lower than corresponding majorities required at the ICJ or the ITLOS and the involvement of the ASP in the removal of a judge from office, even if it serves only to approve a recommendation of the judges themselves, raises doubt whether the praised appreciation of the confidence in independence and assurance of appearance of impartiality is taken seriously in this context. Overall it deserves to be supported when Judge H.-P. Kaul concludes that "[i]t remains essential that the ICC continues to show – through the way it conducts all [its] activities – that it is a purely judicial, objective, neutral, and non-political institution",[1282] in other words that the partially new tools which the Court has been equipped with are tested and proven of value in practice.

1282 Ibid, para. 118.

Chapter G: Judicial Independence in the Ad Hoc International Criminal Tribunals for the Former Yugoslavia and Rwanda

I. Introduction

The fundamental difference between the ICTY and the ICTR[1283] on the one hand, and the other international courts analysed in this study on the other, is the mode of establishment of the two *ad hoc* Tribunals. Whereas the ICJ, the ITLOS, the ICC and the ECtHR were established on the basis of agreements concluded between States, usually formulated at a conference of the States Parties, the *ad hoc* Tribunals originate in resolutions of the UNSC, acting under Chapter VII UNC. This gives the Tribunals a political connotation; indeed observers have been tempted to apply the stigma of embodying selective justice.[1284] *Prima facie* the very notion of special tribunals, i.e. judicial bodies established for the sole purpose of trying the alleged perpetrators of crimes committed in a particular situation, raises concerns regarding the ability of those tribunals to be independent and impartial.[1285] Furthermore, it is enough to perform the thought experiment that an *ad hoc* Tribunal would conduct investigations into actions of nationals of one of the UNSC veto powers in order to grasp the array of questions that would arise and appreciate how delicate the relationship between justice and political considerations is

1283 Hereinafter collectively also referred to as "the [*ad hoc*] Tribunals".

1284 On the notion of "selective justice" see Byrne, Rosemary, 'Promises of Peace and Reconciliation: Previewing the Legacy of the International Criminal Tribunal for Rwanda' (2006) 14 European Review 4, 493. On the selectivity of international criminal law see Cryer, Robert, *Prosecuting International Crimes – Selectivity and the International Criminal Law Regime* (Cambridge University Press Cambridge 2005), 191 et seq.

1285 Morris, Virginia & Scharf, Michael P., *The International Criminal Tribunal for Rwanda – Volume 1* (Transnational Publishers New York 1996), 76. Cf., e.g., Rule 5(b) UN Special Rapporteur on the Study on the Independence of the Judiciary, *Draft Universal Declaration on the Independence of Justice ("Singhvi Declaration")* (1989) E/CN.4/Sub.2/1985/18/Add.5/Rev. 1: "No ad hoc jurisdiction shall be established to displace jurisdiction properly vested in the courts."

in the case of *ad hoc* Tribunals.[1286] Indeed one of the first challenges to the legality of the *ad hoc* Tribunals was a challenge to the UNSC's power to establish the ICTY on the basis of the lack of impartiality of the Tribunal and the contention that "[n]o independent tribunal, particularly an international tribunal, can be a subsidiary organ of any body, including the Security Council."[1287] An example of a question that other courts do not have to address and which considerably influences the Tribunals' independence is their impending closure, which is currently being organized and implemented under the umbrella of the so-called completion strategy.[1288] In what way and to what extent does the Tribunals' temporary existence influence their independence will be one of the focuses of the following analysis.

II. Genesis and Organizational Setting of the ICTY and ICTR

1. The Establishment of the ICTY

Establishing an international criminal court with the remit of trying individuals responsible for serious violations of international humanitarian law became an expectation after armed conflict erupted and continued for several years in Yugoslavia in the early 1990s. The country had on several occasions been the scene of conflicts and wars, e.g. the Balkan Wars fought in 1912 and 1913, which were often shaped by ethnic antagonism. The region was further characterized by tensions between ethnic and religious groups that had been patchworked together in the wake of the end of the First World War, and in particular following the collapse of the Ottoman and Austrian

1286 Cf. Goldstone, Richard J., 'International Jurisdiction and Prosecutorial Crimes' (1999) 47 Cleveland State Law Review 4, 479.

1287 UNGA, *Letter dated 19 May 1993 from the Chargé dàffaires a.i. of the Permanent Mission of Yugoslavia to the United Nations addressed to the Secretary-General* (21 May 1993) UN Doc. A/48/170 S/25801.

1288 Neither the so-called completion strategies nor the IRMCT, established by UNSC, will be dealt with separately here. Many questions that would arise in those contexts with regard to the independent functioning of the *ad hoc* Tribunals, such as the tenure of judges and the relationship between the Tribunals and the remaining UN system, will instead be made a subject of discussion in other forms. For an overview and assessment of the IRMCT, see Frolich, 'Introductory Note to the United Nations Security Council Resolution 1966: International Residual Mechanism for ICTY and ICTR'.

empires. After the death of President Tito and further incited by the end of the Cold War, the country began to fall victim to the secessionist ambitions of several of its regions.[1289] Driven by the territorial ambitions of the various ethnic groups, the secession of States soon led to "ethnic cleansing" followed by terror, persecution and inhumane acts predominantly directed against the civilian population. In particular European politicians, who had a common interest in preventing the conflict from escalating further, gradually realized that the atrocities also called for criminal accountability and prosecution. Following calls in the press for the establishment of an international criminal tribunal to address those atrocities,[1290] the German Foreign Minister K. Kinkel reiterated his previous call for the establishment of an international criminal court, drew attention to an earlier proposal to establish an international crimes tribunal, and called for a mandate for the ILC to draft a statute.[1291] After three rapporteurs in October 1992 presented a report supporting the idea of an international war crimes tribunal,[1292] the UNSC began to take its own initiatives, and in UNSC Resolution 764 reaffirmed that "persons who committed or order the commission of grave breaches of the [Geneva Conventions of 12 August 1949] are individually responsible".[1293] However,

---

1289 On the historic background see Bassiouni & Manikas, *The Law of the International Criminal Tribunal for the Former Yugoslavia*, 11-64.

1290 See, e.g., the newspaper articles of M. Klarin in the Belgrade newspaper *Borda* of 16 May 1991, where it was suggested that a new Nuremberg tribunal should be established to judge crimes against peace and crimes against humanity in the former Yugoslavia (reprinted in Cassese, Antonio (ed) *The Path to the Hague: Selected Documents on the Origins of the ICTY* (ICTY The Hague 1997), 43-45) and Stone, Norman, 'Dubrovnik: the case for a war crime trial – why not restore the Nuremberg Tribunal?' *Guardian* (13 November 1991).

1291 UNGA, *Provisional Verbatim Record of the 8th Meeting, Held at Headquarters, New York, on Wednesday, 23 September 1992* (23 September 1992) UN Doc. A/47/PV.8, 61.

1292 See Corell, Hans, et al., *Proposal for an International War Crimes Tribunal for the Former Yugoslavia by Rapporteurs (Corell – Türk – Thune) under the CSCE Moscow Human Rights Dimension to Bosnia-Hergegovina and Croatia* (9 February 1993) UN Doc. S/25307. See also Morris, Virginia & Scharf, Michael P., *An Insider's Duide to the International Criminal Tribunal for the Former Yugoslavia – A Documentary History and Analysis* (Transnational Publishers New York 1996), 27. See also Corell, et al., *Proposal for an International War Crimes Tribunal for the Former Yugoslavia by Rapporteurs (Corell – Türk – Thune) under the CSCE Moscow Human Rights Dimension to Bosnia-Hergegovina and Croatia.*

1293 UNSC, *Additional deployment to Sarajevo airport* (13 July 1992) UN Doc. S/RES/764 (1992), para. 10.

the increased attention on obligations of individuals rather than States[1294] suggested a possible lacuna in the then existing international judicial landscape. The subsequent UNSC Resolution 771 of 13 August 1992 called upon States and international organizations "to collate substantiated information ... relating to the violations of international humanitarian law".[1295] In a following resolution the UNSC especially requested the UNSG to establish a Commission of Experts to examine and analyse the information thus gathered.[1296] The Commission,[1297] headed by M. Cherif Bassiouni, in an interim report to the UNSC called for the establishment of an international tribunal. This was preceded by resolutions in which the UNGA expressed its conviction that "those who commit or order the commission of acts of 'ethnic cleansing' are individually responsible and should be brought to justice"[1298] and, two days later, urging the UNSC to "consider recommending the establishment of an *ad hoc* international war crimes tribunal".[1299] Finally and decisively, the UNSC in a resolution dated 22 February 1993 determined that the situation in the territory of the former Yugoslavia constituted "a threat to international peace and security" and hence decided that:

> "an international tribunal shall be established for the prosecution of persons responsible for serious violations of international humanitarian law committed in the territory of the former Yugoslavia since 1991".[1300]

1294 O'Brien, James, 'The International Tribunal for Violations of International Humanitarian Law in the Former Yugoslavia' (1993) 87 American Journal of International Law 4, 640.

1295 UNSC, *Former Yugoslavia* (13 August 1992) UN Doc. S/RES/771 (1992), para. 5.

1296 UNSC, *Former Yugoslavia* (6 October 1992) UN Doc. S/RES/780 (1992), para. 2.

1297 The Commission was established in UNSG, *Report of the Secretary-General Pursuant to Paragraph 2 of Security Council Resolution 808 (1993)*. Generally on the work of the Commission of Experts see Bassiouni, M. Cherif, 'The United Nations Commission of Experts Established Pursuant to Security Council Resolution 780 (1992)' (1994) 88 American Journal of International Law 4.

1298 UNGA, *"Ethnic Cleansing" and Racial Hatred* (15 March 1993) UN Doc. A/RES/47/80, para. 4.

1299 UNGA, *The situation in Bosnia and Herzegovina* (18 December 1992) UN Doc. A/RES/47/121, para. 10.

1300 UNSC, *Tribunal (Former Yugoslavia)* (22 February 1993) UN Doc. S/RES/808 (1993), para. 1. The resolution was adopted unanimously, see UNSC, *Provisional Verbatim Record of the 3175th Meeting, Held at Headquarters, New York, on Monday, 22 February 1993* (22 February 1993) UN Doc. S/PV.3175, 8.

The debate preceding the adoption of this resolution was characterized by scepticism based mainly on political considerations, such as the influence of an international criminal tribunal on the on-going negotiations to find a political settlement for the underlying dispute.[1301] A look at the verbatim record of the 3175th meeting of the UNSC, at which Resolution 808 was debated, reveals both general enthusiasm among the permanent members of the UNSC for the proposal for an international criminal tribunal and also voices emphasising the *ad hoc* and non-permanent nature of the institution,[1302] as well as its necessary role in reaching a negotiated peace settlement.[1303] The competence of the UNSC to establish the Tribunal was questioned by

---

1301 Bassiouni & Manikas, *The Law of the International Criminal Tribunal for the Former Yugoslavia*, 202.

1302 According to the report of the UNSG, "as an enforcement measure under Chapter VII … the life span of the international tribunal would be linked to the restoration and maintenance of international peace and security in the territory of the former Yugoslavia, and Security Council decisions related thereto." UNSG, *Report of the Secretary-General Pursuant to Paragraph 2 of Security Council Resolution 808 (1993)*, 28.

1303 UNSC, *Provisional Verbatim Record of the 3175th Meeting, Held at Headquarters, New York, on Monday, 22 February 1993*. J.-B. Mérimée, France's ambassador to the UN saw in the establishment of a tribunal the possibility "to do justice to the victims and to the international community" and to "send a clear message to those who continue to commit these crimes that they will be held responsible for their acts." (At 8.) Moreover, the prosecution of those responsible for serious violations of international humanitarian law is for the UN and in particular the UNSC "a matter of doing their duty to maintain and restore peace." Mr. Mérimée called for a further decision under chapter VII UNC "which establishes its competence in the maintenance and restoration of international peace and security." (At 10.) M. Albright, then United States ambassador to the UN, stated that the new tribunal would be "no victor's tribunal." (At 11.) She expressed the US's strong support for the tribunal. The UK representative, M. Richardson, expressed his countries support for the creation of a tribunal but underlined its character as an "*ad hoc* legal framework to deal with war crimes committed only in the territory of the former Yugoslavia." (At 15.) The assessment by the Russian Federation was less enthusiastic and rather highlighted the interaction between the future tribunal and other means to reach a negotiated peace settlement: "We believe that the Security Council's adoption of a resolution deciding that an international tribunal shall be established for the prosecution of persons responsible for serious violations of international humanitarian law committed in the territory of the former Yugoslavia reflects the international community's will to exert its influence on all parties to the conflict in order to accelerate the peace process." (At 16.) See on this Scharf, Michael, 'Indicted for War Crimes, the What?' *Washington Post* (3 October 1999).

some States,[1304] but this did not ultimately prevent the UNSC from unanimously supporting its creation. The UNSG was requested to report to the UNSC proposals on the establishment of such a tribunal and on 3 May 1993 the UNSG submitted his report, which included an annotated draft statute for the Tribunal.[1305] The UNSC adopted the statute unanimously and without modification in its Resolution 827 on 25 May 1993,[1306] yet again referring explicitly to Chapter VII of the UNC. On 20 August 1993 the UNSC accepted the UNSG's list of 23 nominations for judges,[1307] and on 15 September 1993 the UNGA, in accordance with Art. 13 Statute of the ICTY (ICTY-S) (now Art. 13 *bis*), elected the first 11 judges for a term of four years.[1308] In early 1994 the judges drafted the Rules of Procedure and Evidence and dealt with practical matters, e.g. the establishment of a detention centre.[1309] The first indictment was issued on 4 November 1994.[1310]

2. The Establishment of the ICTR

Before the ICTY was able to begin its work another crisis caught the attention of the world and raised the question of establishing yet another *ad hoc* judicial

---

1304 Schabas, William A., *The UN International Criminal Tribunals – The Former Yugoslavia, Rwanda and Sierra Leone* (Cambridge University Press Cambridge 2006), 22.

1305 UNSG, *Report of the Secretary-General Pursuant to Paragraph 2 of Security Council Resolution 808 (1993)*, Annex.

1306 UNSC, *Statute of the International Tribunal for the Former Yugoslavia.*

1307 UNSC, *Tribunal (Former Yugoslavia)* (20 August 1993) UN Doc. S/RES/857 (1993).

1308 UNGA, *United Nations Press Release* (17 September 1993) UN Doc. GA/8500.

1309 Schabas, *The UN International Criminal Tribunals – The Former Yugoslavia, Rwanda and Sierra Leone*, 23. A first Prosecutor was appointed on 21 October 1993 by the UNSC upon nomination from the UNSG (UNSC, *Tribunal (Former Yugoslavia)* (21 October 1993) UN Doc. S/RES/877 (1993)). The first Prosecutor resigned before taking up his work, only to be replaced by R. Goldstone from South Africa; UNSC, *On the appointment of the Prosecutor of the International Tribunal for the Prosecution of Persons Responsible for Serious Violations of International Humanitarian Law Committed in the Territory of the Former Yugoslavia since 1991* (8 July 1994) UN Doc. S/RES/936 (1994).

1310 *The Prosecutor of the Tribunal against Dragan Nikolić* (ICTY) Case No. IT-94-2-I (4 November 1994).

institution.[1311] After the assassination of President J. Habyarimana of the Central African Republic of Rwanda reports of terrible atrocities started to circulate in the international media in April 1994.[1312] The assassination was merely the catalyst which awakened the historic conflict between the two ethnic groups, the majority Hutu and the minority Tutsi. Over the course of 100 days several hundred thousand Tutsis and moderate Hutu were murdered,[1313] often in full view of the UN.[1314] When the calls from the UNSC to the parties to the conflict to respect international humanitarian law were not complied with,[1315] the President of the UNSC on 30 April 1994 chose to emphasize individual responsibility for the brutal crimes that were reported.[1316] Numerous resolutions were subsequently adopted which qualified the actions in Rwanda as crimes punishable under international law.[1317]

1311 Generally on the establishment of the ICTR see Karhilo, Jaana, 'The Establishment of the International Tribunal for Rwanda' (1995) 64 Nordic Journal of International Law 4; Morris & Scharf, *The International Criminal Tribunal for Rwanda – Volume 1*, 75-116.

1312 There is a wealth of literature on the Rwandan genocide and only a few works should be mentioned here: Gourevitch, Philip, *We wish to inform you that tomorrow we will be killed with our families* (Farrar, Straus and Giroux New York 1998); Prunier, Gérard, *The Rwanda crisis – 1959-1994: History of a Genocide* (Hurst London 1995); Mukagasana, Yolande & Kazinierakis, Alain, *Les blessures du silence* (Actes Sud Arles 2001).

1313 The estimated total number of victims in the conflict varies from 500,000 to 1,000,000 or more: see *The Prosecutor v. Jean-Paul Akayesu* (ICTR) Case No. ICTR-96-4-T (2 September 1998), para. 111.

1314 Following the killing of ten members of the Belgian 2nd Commando Battalion, the Paracommando Regiment, which operated as a part of United Nations Assistance Mission for Rwanda (UNAMIR) the UNSC decided the reduction of the UN peacekeeping force from 1,500 to 270, see UNSC, *Adjustment of the mandate of the UN Assistance Mission for Rwanda due to the current situation in Rwanda and settlement of the Rwandan conflict* (21 April 1994) UN Doc. S/RES/912 (1994).

1315 See ibid, para. 5.

1316 UNSG, *Statement by the President of the Security Council Condemning Slaughter of Civilians in Kigali and Other Parts of Rwanda* (30 April 1994) UN Doc. S/PRST/1994/21.

1317 E.g. UNSC, *The expansion of the mandate of the UN Assistance Mission for Rwanda and imposition of an arms embargo on Rwanda* (17 May 1994) UN Doc. S/RES/918 (1994); UNSC, *Extension of the mandate and deployment of the 2 additional battalions of the UN Assistance Mission for Rwanda and settlement of the conflict in Rwanda* (8 June 1994) UN Doc. S/RES/925 (1994); UNSC, *Requesting the Secretary-General to establish a Commission of Experts to examine violations of international humanitarian law committed in Rwanda* (1 July 1994) UN Doc.

The first voices in support of an *ad hoc* international war crimes tribunal for Rwanda were raised,[1318] including a request from the new government of Rwanda that had formed in the meantime, calling for the UN to establish a tribunal.[1319] The new tribunal was born with the adoption of UNSC Resolution 955 on 8 November 1994.[1320] Despite the initial request from Rwanda to establish a tribunal, the resolution made explicit reference to Chapter VII UNC; thus the ICTR was not based on the co-operative achievement of the UN and the affected State.[1321] The statute of the new tribunal was annexed to the resolution and was, in most parts, identical to that of the ICTY. The first judges were elected in May 1995[1322] and the first indictments were issued on 28 November 1995.[1323] The new tribunal met with criticism, not just due

---

S/RES/935 (1994). The resolution of 8 June 1994 was the first one in which the UNSC used the word genocide with regard to the atrocities in Rwanda; see Schabas, *The UN International Criminal Tribunals – The Former Yugoslavia, Rwanda and Sierra Leone*, 25-26.

1318 Apparently, US Secretary of State W. Christopher had expressed his government's support for such a tribunal at the end of June 1994, Greenhouse, Steven, 'US, Having Won Changes, Is Set to Sign Law of the Sea' *New York Times* (1 July 1994), 1.

1319 UNGA, *Letter Dated 94/09/28 From the Permanent Representative of Rwanda to the United Nations Addressed to the President of the Security Council* (29 September 1994) UN Doc. S/1994/1115. See also on the address of the Rwandan President to the UNGA, UNSC, *Security Council 3453rd Meeting, Tuesday, 8 November 1994* (8 November 1994) UN Doc. S/PV.3453, 14.

1320 UNSC, *Tribunal (Rwanda)* (8 November 1994) UN Doc. S/RES/955 (1994). The resolution was adopted with one dissenting vote (Rwanda) and one abstention (China). On the reasons behind the voting behaviour see Morris & Scharf, *The International Criminal Tribunal for Rwanda – Volume 1*, 72-72; Shraga, Daphna & Zacklin, Ralph, 'The International Criminal Tribunal for Rwanda' (1996) 7 European Journal of International Law 4, 504; Schabas, *The UN International Criminal Tribunals – The Former Yugoslavia, Rwanda and Sierra Leone*, 29.

1321 Cf. the SCSL, which is based on an agreement between the UN and the Government of Sierra Leone, Agreement between the United Nations and the Government of Sierra Leone on the Establishment of a Special Court for Sierra Leone (adopted 16 January 2002, entered into force 12 April 2002) 2178 UNTS 138.

1322 ICTY, *Report of the International Criminal Tribunal for the Prosecution of Persons Responsible for Genocide and Other Serious Violations of International Humanitarian Law Committed in the Territory of Rwanda and Rwandan Citizens Responsible for Genocide and Other Such Violations Committed in the Territory of Neighbouring States Between 1 January and 31 December 1994* (24 September 1996) UN Doc. A/51/399-S/1996/778, para. 7.

1323 Ibid, para. 31; ICTR, *ICTR Press Release* (12 December 1995) available at <http://www.unictr.org/tabid/155/Default.aspx?id=617> (last visited: 21 March 2014).

to the questioned authority of the UNSC to establish an *ad hoc* international criminal tribunal, but also because the Rwandan government ultimately opposed its establishment due in particular to the omission of capital punishment as a penalty that could be imposed by the Tribunal.[1324] Although Rwanda did – at times – demonstrate its willingness to prosecute those responsible for the atrocities, the judicial system of the country had been largely destroyed and several leaders suspected of having committed crimes were in neighbouring countries reluctant to extradite them.[1325] Moreover, the special character of the crimes that had been committed led to the conclusion that international prosecutions were less likely to be perceived as revenge and be better suited to contributing to political reconciliation.

3. Conclusions

Two main conclusions, which are of relevance for the following appraisal of the Tribunals' ability to an independent operation, can be drawn from the events that led up to their creation. Firstly, it cannot be denied that the ICTY and ICTR were established to address particular events that occurred in the framework of a – more or less – delimitable conflict, and that the majority of acts that could be prosecuted ended before the Tribunals were able to take up their activities.[1326] Thus it was predictable that the Tribunals would see themselves confronted with the allegation of being victor's justice[1327] and blamed for their retroactivity.[1328] The allegation underlying these two accusations is that the Tribunals were not independent from the outset, as they were established with the set agenda of holding individuals responsible for the atrocities that had been committed. Acquittals would surely be avoided, as they would denigrate the reasons for the political decision to establish the Tribunals in the first place. This promised, irrespective of the merit of any such argument, to lead to immense scrutiny of the *ad hoc* Tribunals from

1324 Morris & Scharf, *The International Criminal Tribunal for Rwanda – Volume 1*, 67-72.

1325 Ibid, 66.

1326 This already follows from the jurisdiction *ratione temporis*, which, however, at least fort he ICTR allows for the prosecution of crimes committed after the date of the tribunal's establishment.

1327 Schabas, *The UN International Criminal Tribunals – The Former Yugoslavia, Rwanda and Sierra Leone*, 48 with further references.

1328 On this subject generally see ibid, 60-67.

the day of their inception, not just from States but also from the general public. If the Tribunals could prove that they were able to function independently, of States and the UN, this would significantly contribute to quieting any doubts about the legitimacy or legality of their establishment. Secondly, the *ad hoc* Tribunals were established from within the UN system, not just with the participation of the UN, as in the case of the Special Tribunal for Sierra Leone, but they are part and parcel of the organizational structure of the UN.[1329] This raises the question of the appropriate and at times even necessary relationship between the various organs of the UN, in particular the UNSC as the principal organ establishing the Tribunals, and the Tribunals in their work.

III. The Functions Served by the ICTY and ICTR

1. Conviction and Punishment of Individuals for Criminal Responsibility

The purposes for which the ICTY and the ICTR were established are clearly characterized by the institutions' nature as *ad hoc* criminal bodies, namely to prosecute those responsible for serious violations of international humanitarian law in a particular geographical and temporal context. Pursuant to Art. 1 of the Tribunals' Statutes, they "shall have the power to prosecute persons responsible for serious violations of international humanitarian law committed in the territory of" the respective underlying conflict. This was also emphasised in the relevant UNSC resolutions, which stated that the Tribunals are established for the "sole purpose" of prosecuting those responsible for serious violations of international humanitarian law.[1330] The formulation "sole purpose" must be read in conjunction with the overall classification of the Tribunals in those resolutions. The institutions were international tribunals in the wider sense, but vested only with the ability to undertake individual criminal prosecution. By formulating individual criminal responsibility as the "sole purpose", the UNSC underlined the centrality of the function of individual criminal prosecutions and the special character of the Tribunals, which should not be seen as general international criminal courts

1329 For more details see *infra* Chapter G.IV(1)(a).

1330 UNSC, *Tribunal (Former Yugoslavia)* (25 May 1993) UN Doc. S/RES/827 (1993), para. 2; UNSC, *Tribunal (Rwanda)*, para. 1.

but as exceptions from within the organizational structure of the UN.[1331] The UNSC did not pursue the opportunity to form a general international criminal jurisdiction,[1332] but was also not seeking to create a precedent for future such institutions. With the aim of establishing jurisdiction over natural persons only[1333] it was furthermore apparent that the Tribunals would not be allowed to judge States' behaviour or disputes between States.[1334]

Placing the individual at the centre of attention for the activities of the Tribunals necessarily heightened their obligation to respect human rights safeguards. Traditionally the individual was not a subject of public international law and could be affected only by enforcement and individual rights through the mediation of the State.[1335] But due to the impressive evolution of international human rights norms since the end of the Second World War,[1336] international instruments provide for the protection of individual rights in municipal criminal trials,[1337] in particular the right to a fair trial, which is relevant in the present context and which amounts to "a common core of meaning of sufficient dimensions as to permit a detailed statement of the scope of that right which can command widespread international

---

1331 The resolutions emphasize this further in the preambles which speak of "the particular circumstances" of the former Yugoslavia and Rwanda and the character of the ICTY as an "ad hoc measure" justifying this step by the UN (UNSC Resolution 827, recital VI; UNSC Resolution 955, recital VII).

1332 Not least since the preparations for the ICC were simultaneously underway; UNSG, *Report of the Secretary-General Pursuant to Paragraph 2 of Security Council Resolution 808 (1993)*, para. 12. The UNSC would arguably be barred from establishing a broader international criminal jurisdiction as this could not be considered a measure for the maintenance and restoration of peace and security (cf. Arts. 39 and 42 UNC) and would furthermore encroach upon the competences of the UNGA under Art. 13 UNC.

1333 Art. 6 ICTY-S; Art. 5 ICTR-S.

1334 The relationship between the *ad hoc* Tribunals and the ICJ was thus clear; whereas the ICJ has no jurisdiction over individuals and thus would not be the forum to adjudicate on individual criminal responsibility, the *ad hoc* Tribunals would likewise not have the jurisdiction that influences the settlement of inter-State disputes.

1335 Verdross & Simma, *Universelles Völkerrecht – Theorie und Praxis*, No. 47; Walter, 'Subjects of International Law', para. 15.

1336 Buergenthal, Thomas, 'Human Rights', in: Wolfrum, Rüdiger (ed) *The Max Planck Encyclopedia of Public International Law* (Oxford University Press Online Edition 2012), paras. 3-7.

1337 See, e.g., Art. 14 ICCPR, Art. 6 ECHR, Art. 8 ACHR, Art. 40 Convention on the Rights of the Child.

consent".[1338] Yet even if the nation-State, as the central subject of international law, thus can be claimed to be restrained by international human rights,[1339] the question arises whether this applies equally to international organisations in general and international criminal tribunals in particular. To provide for the slightest consistency the UNSC, together with the organs it establishes, must be bound by UN standards.[1340] Moreover, international criminal courts exercise judicial powers over individuals by analogy to national courts. Indeed it may be argued in the case of the *ad hoc* Tribunals, which exercise concurrent jurisdiction and have primacy over national jurisdictions,[1341] that they must operate under the same restraints as the national courts they replace in order not to be discriminatory.[1342] Furthermore, although it is still a largely open question to what extent human rights bind the UN generally and the UNSC in particular, if the *ad hoc* Tribunals were not bound by human rights restraints this would enable the UNSC to circumvent its own human rights obligations. In addition, there is no reason to assume that human rights, which have evolved with the purpose of creating protection for the individual from State interference and the abuse of power by governments,[1343] would not also apply in the international setting, i.e. when the individual is subject to the exercise of similar powers by organs on the international level. These reasons, mentioned in support of an extension of human rights restraints to international courts, suggest that the right to a fair trial, which is often mentioned as one of the core human rights, and the incorporated right to an independent and impartial tribunal, would have to be observed on the sole basis that individuals are being prosecuted before the *ad hoc* Tribunals.

1338 Harris, David, 'The Right to a Fair Trial in Criminal Proceedings as a Human Right' (1967) 16 The International and Comparative Law Quarterly 2, 378.

1339 Safferling, Christoph Johannes Maria, *Towards an International Criminal Procedure* (Oxford University Press Oxford 2001), 39.

1340 Cf. Zappalà, Salvatore, *Human Rights in International Criminal Proceedings* (Oxford University Press Oxford 2003), 5.

1341 Cf. Art. 9 ICTY-S; Art. 8 ICTR-S.

1342 Cf. Safferling, *Towards an International Criminal Procedure*, 40.

1343 Malanczuk, *Akehurst's Modern Introduction to International Law*, 209.

2. Restoring and Maintaining International Peace and Security

Referring to the prosecution of individuals for serious violations of international humanitarian law as the sole purpose of the Tribunals cannot suffice as the sole objective of the Tribunals, as this could equally well have been achieved by either strengthening the pertinent national judiciaries or by establishing the Tribunals on the basis of agreements rather than UNSC resolutions.[1344] UNSC Resolutions 827 and 955, after determining that the situations in Rwanda and the former Yugoslavia continued to "constitute a threat to international peace and security",[1345] express the UNSC's conviction that the *ad hoc* measures "would contribute to the restoration and maintenance of peace".[1346] Irrespective of whether international criminal justice may actually contribute to the restoration and/or maintenance of international peace and security in (post-)conflict situations,[1347] this aim was clearly expressed as a reason for the Tribunals' establishment, and is considered by some scholars to be the central objective of the Tribunals.[1348] It is based on the consideration that the atrocities that occurred in the former Yugoslavia as well as in Rwanda may give rise to feelings of revenge, which manifest themselves in further and future crimes, and that continued conflicts can be avoided only by prosecuting those allegedly responsible before independent and impartial tribunals, applying a fair procedure and providing for the punishment of those who are found guilty.[1349] The independence and impar-

---

1344 Schabas, *The UN International Criminal Tribunals – The Former Yugoslavia, Rwanda and Sierra Leone*, 68. The option of establishing the Tribunals through agreements in particular is illustrated by the SCSL, which is also an *ad hoc* Tribunal but based on a treaty concluded between the UN and the government of Sierra Leone; Agreement between the United Nations and the Government of Sierra Leone on the Establishment of a Special Court for Sierra Leone.

1345 As the UNSC had stated in other earlier resolutions, e.g. UNSC Resolution 808.

1346 Recitals 4 and 6 ICTY-S; recitals 5 and 7 ICTR-S. With respect to the situation in the former Yugoslavia the determination that it constituted a threat to international peace and security was already made in UNSC Resolution 808.

1347 For a political analysis of this topic see Nitsche, *Der Internationale Strafgerichtshof ICC und der Frieden – eine vergleichende Analyse der Befriedungsfunktion internationaler Straftribunale*.

1348 Schabas, *The UN International Criminal Tribunals – The Former Yugoslavia, Rwanda and Sierra Leone*, 68.

1349 Kamardi, Christiane, *Die Ausformung einer Prozessordnung "sui generis" durch das ICTY unter Berücksichtigung des Fair-Trial-Prinzips* (Springer Berlin; Heidelberg 2009), 19.

tiality of the Tribunals may here communicate the necessary trust in the criminal prosecution that may suffocate feelings of revenge and prevent them from materializing in additional crimes.

However, the function of restoring and maintaining international peace and security necessarily invites the critique that the Tribunals are little more than instruments implementing the objectives of the UN in general and the UNSC in particular.[1350] If indeed the Tribunals were quasi-political tools in this sense, this would seriously jeopardize their ability to be accepted in the countries where the conflicts were happening. Political bias is what originally caused the conflicts and the affected societies would be likely to react by rejecting the Tribunals if political bias were also to characterize international criminal justice. From the perspective of the general public that is affected by the underlying conflicts, the prosecution of individuals for criminal responsibility for acts in these conflicts can thus appropriately be performed only by an independent and impartial tribunal. Indeed it was considered one of the major advantages of an international tribunal that the prosecution could take place detached from the national judicial and political system. Thus the independence and impartiality of the Tribunals is a core feature of their conceptualization. It is moreover apparent that the function of the *ad hoc* Tribunals to restore and maintain peace may bring them into a peculiar relationship with the UNSC. On the one hand the UNSC is the principal UN organ vested with the "primary responsibility for the maintenance of international peace and security",[1351] but on the other the Tribunals exercise adjudicatory functions which the UNSC could not exercise itself[1352] and should

---

1350 This criticism is fuelled by allegations that the Tribunals focus their prosecutions on the individuals most responsible for the military or political decision-making processes, in order to advance peace initiatives. See, e.g., *Prosecutor v. Momir Nikolić, Sentencing Judgement* (ICTY) Case No. IT-02-60/1-S (2 December 2003), para. 60.

1351 Art. 24(1) UNC. It was in exercise of this function that the *ad hoc* Tribunals were established: "The Security Council has resorted to the establishment of a judicial organ in the form of an international criminal tribunal as an instrument for the exercise of its own principal function of maintenance of peace and security, i.e., as a measure contributing to the restoration and maintenance of peace in the former Yugoslavia." *Prosecutor v. Duško Tadić, Appeals Chamber, Decision on the defence motion for interlocutory appeal on jurisdiction*, para. 38.

1352 "Plainly, the Security Council is not a judicial organ and is not provided with judicial powers (though it may incidentally perform certain quasi-judicial activities such as effecting determinations or findings). The principal function of the Security Council is the maintenance of international peace and security, in the discharge

thus not interfere with. The analysis of possible safeguards for the Tribunals' independence and impartiality will show whether the necessary separation is provided for.

3. Ancillary Functions

a) Deterring Future Crimes – Ad Hoc Prosecution Taken Serious

Although UNSC Resolutions 827 and 955 do not mention the deterrent effect of the Tribunals, it must be concluded that they serve the purpose of deterring future serious violations of international humanitarian law by reason of their retroactive jurisdiction *ratione temporis*[1353].[1354] The report of the UNSG preparing for the establishment of the ICTY reiterates what the UNSC mentioned in UNSC Resolution 808, namely that one of the aims of the new Tribunal would be to put an end to serious violations of international humanitarian law.[1355] This function of ending such crimes is seen by some commentators as an indication that the UNSC pursued a deterrent purpose with the establishment of the ICTY.[1356] The Tribunals themselves have time and again referred to deterrence as an important role. One of the earliest recognitions is to be found in the *Tadić* case where the ICTY Appeals Chamber noted:

> "In adopting resolution 827, the Security Council established the International Tribunal with the stated purpose of bringing to justice persons responsible for serious violations of international humanitarian law in the former Yugoslavia,

---

of which the Security Council exercises both decision-making and executive powers." Ibid, para. 37.

1353 The jurisdiction of the tribunals is limited to crimes committed after the 1 January 1991 in the case of the ICTY and to crimes committed between 1 January 1994 and 31 December 1994 in the case of the ICTR. Art. 8 ICTY-S, Art. 7 ICTR-S.

1354 Bassiouni & Manikas, *The Law of the International Criminal Tribunal for the Former Yugoslavia*, 251 with the statement that the view was reaffirmed in UNSC Resolution 827 and throughout "that such a process of international justice will lead not only to justice, but also to deterrence."

1355 UNSG, *Report of the Secretary-General Pursuant to Paragraph 2 of Security Council Resolution 808 (1993)*, para. 26. See also UNSC Resolution 827.

1356 See, e.g., Kamardi, *Die Ausformung einer Prozessordnung "sui generis" durch das ICTY unter Berücksichtigung des Fair-Trial-Prinzips*, 18.

thereby deterring future violations and contributing to the re-establishment of peace and security in the region."[1357]

The quoted passage emphasizes that the deterrent function is closely linked to the constitutive function of restoring and maintaining peace. In that context the above-mentioned rationale regarding independence, as a factor that enhances the ability to restore and maintain peace, may have the same role with regard to deterrence. If prosecutions attract the necessary trust of the societies involved in the underlying conflicts but also of the broader world public, then politically motivated selectivity of punishments can be traded for a more intolerable stance of the world community on the committing of serious crimes.

b) Reconciliation – The Value of Independently Establishing the Truth

The function of reconciliation is also closely linked to the restoration and maintenance of international peace and security, and thus played a part when this was formulated as an objective for the Tribunals' establishment. Whereas the resolution establishing the ICTY does not refer to the concept of national reconciliation, UNSC Resolution 955 establishing the ICTR expresses the UNSC's conviction that the prosecution of people "would contribute to the process of national reconciliation".[1358] One element of the attempt to support reconciliation through international criminal law and appro-

---

1357 *Prosecutor v. Duško Tadić, Appeals Chamber, Decision on the defence motion for interlocutory appeal on jurisdiction*, para. 72. See also *Prosecutor v. Dragan Nikolić, Judgement on Sentencing Appeal* (ICTY) Case No. IT-94-2-I (4 February 2005), para. 46; *Prosecutor v. Zejnil Delalić, Zdravko Mucić (aka "Pavo"), Hazim Delić and Esad Landžo (aka "Zenga")* (ICTY) Case No. IT-96-21-A (20 February 2001), paras. 800-801.

1358 UNSC Resolution 955, recital 7. It may also be mentioned that the UNSC resolution calling for the SCSL also referred to the importance of a national process of reconciliation: "Noting also the steps taken by the Government of Sierra Leone in creating a national truth and reconciliation process … to contribute to the promotion of the rule of law"; "Recognizing that, in the particular circumstances of Sierra Leone, a credible system of justice and accountability for the very serious crimes committed there would end impunity and would contribute to the process of national reconciliation and to the restoration and maintenance of peace", "Acknowledging the important contribution that can be made … to expedite the process of bringing justice and reconciliation to Sierra Leone and the region." See UNSC Resolution 1315, paras. 4, 7, 12.

priate institutions is to establish the truth behind the crimes and also the wider context of the underlying conflict. Statements made by the US representative to the UN during the preparation of the establishment of the ICTY indicate this:

> "Truth is the cornerstone of the rule of law, and it will point towards individuals, not peoples, as perpetrators of war crimes. And it is only the truth that can cleanse the ethnic and religious hatreds and begin the healing process."[1359]

Moreover, Judge P. Wald described one goal of the ICTY as being the "truth in fact finding for history's sake".[1360] With their activities the Tribunals develop a historical record surrounding the underlying conflict and thus guard against revisionism.[1361] Although the truth-seeking function as such was not mentioned by the UNSC when establishing the Tribunals, the ICTY and ICTR themselves have identified this in their case law as one important function of their activities.[1362] The objective establishment of the truth presupposes decisions being made by an entity that is independent of undue influence and undue favouritism. In particular it assumes that prosecutions are conducted under the applicable law and without allowing influence from

---

1359 ICTY, *Report of the International Criminal Tribunal for the Prosecution of Persons Responsible for Genocide and Other Serious Violations of International Humanitarian Law Committed in the Territory of Rwanda and Rwandan Citizens Responsible for Genocide and Other Such Violations Committed in the Territory of Neighbouring States Between 1 January and 31 December 1994*, 12. Cf. also earlier statements made in UNSC, *Provisional Verbatim Record of the 3175th Meeting, Held at Headquarters, New York, on Monday, 22 February 1993*, 11: "This will be no victors' tribunal. The only victor that will prevail in this endeavour is the truth."

1360 Wald, Patricia M., 'Judging War Crimes' (2000) 1 Chicago Journal of International Law 1, 196.

1361 MacDonald, Gabrielle Kirk, 'Crimes of Sexual Violence: The Experience of the International Criminal Tribunal' (2000) 39 Columbia Journal of Transnational Law 1, 7-8. "The judgments provide an incontrovertible record of how the communities became so divided, how neighbours raped and killed neighbours, how friends forgot their friendship, and how intermarriages meant nothing when one ethnic group was pitted against another by incessant, virulent propaganda."

1362 *Prosecutor v. Dragan Nikolić, Sentencing Judgement* (ICTY) Case No. IT-94-2-S (18 December 2003), para. 3 ("In confessing his guilt and admitting all factual details contained in the Third Amended Indictment in open court on 4 September 2003 Dragan Nikolić has helped further a process of Reconciliation. He has guided the international community closer to the truth in an area not yet subject of any judgement rendered by this Tribunal, truth being one prerequisite for peace.").

e.g. the UNSC, seeking to direct the prosecution in a way favourable to its own agenda, to determine their outcome.

An important factor in the Tribunals' ability to fulfil a mandate of reconciliation is the choice of their seat. Although it was not uncontroversial to establish both the ICTY and the ICTR outside the countries where the crimes were committed,[1363] the UN considered it a value in and of itself to locate the Tribunals in The Hague and Arusha respectively. According to the UNSG:

> "[t]he location of the Yugoslavia and Rwanda tribunals outside the countries where the crimes were committed has allowed them to benefit from more adequate operational facilities and has helped protect their security and independence."[1364]

What shines through in this argument is the fact that the countries in which the crimes took place were not considered suitable for an independent judiciary, even if it was to function under the control of the international community. The fact that past and current hybrid or internationalized criminal tribunals, such as the Serious Crimes Panels in the District Court of Dili (East Timor), 'Regulations 34 and 64' Panels in the courts of Kosovo and the SCSL, have had to struggle to ensure cooperation from governments seems to bear this argument out.[1365]

1363 In particular in the case of the seat of the ICTR, Rwanda strongly favoured locating the Tribunal in the country in order "to teach the Rwandese people a lesson, to fight against the impunity to which it had become accustomed since 1959 and to promote national reconciliation." UNSC, *Security Council 3453rd Meeting, Tuesday, 8 November 1994*, 16. The representative of Rwanda to the UNSC further argued that the Tribunal "will have to deal with Rwandese suspects, responsible for crimes committed in Rwanda against the Rwandese" and that "establishing the seat of the Tribunal on Rwandese soil would promote the harmonization of international and national jurisprudence." However, the UNSG in a report to the UNSC stated that "the choice of Rwanda as the location of the seat would not be feasible or appropriate" and that following an examination of "the considerations of justice and fairness as well as administrative efficiency, including access to witnesses, and economy" instead Arusha, Tanzania be designated. UNSG, *Report of the Secretary-General Pursuant to Paragraph 5 of Security Council Resolution 955 (1994)* (13 February 1995) UN Doc. S/1995/134, para. 45. The UNSC supported the suggestion, UNSC, *On the decision to designate Arusha as the seat of the International Tribunal for Rwanda* (22 February 1995) UN Doc. S/RES/977 (1995).

1364 UNSG, *Report of the Secretary-General – The rule of law and transitional justice in conflict and post-conflict societies* (23 August 2004) UN Doc. S/2004/616, para. 44.

1365 See, e.g., Romano, Cesare P. R., 'Mixed Criminal Tribunals (Sierra Leone, East Timor, Kosovo, Cambodia)', in: Wolfrum, Rüdiger (ed) *The Max Planck Encyclo-*

c) The Role of Victims

The role of victims has received growing importance in international criminal law and international human rights law since the Tribunals began their work. In its sentencing judgment of 18 December 2003 the Trial Chamber noted that

> "[a]cting under Chapter VII of the Charter of the United Nations, this Tribunal is not only mandated to search for and record, as far as possible, the truth of what happened in the former Yugoslavia, but also to bring justice to both victims and their relatives and to perpetrators."[1366]

In its first annual report to the UNGA the ICTY affirmed that one should not be blind to the victim's point of view, according to which there should be public disclosure of the inhuman acts from which he or she has suffered and that the actual perpetrator of the crime be tried and, if found guilty, punished.[1367] Although the accentuation of the role of the victims was not one of the primary purposes for which the *ad hoc* Tribunals were established, it nevertheless is a concern that permeates several of the objectives underlying their work, such as the impartial determination of the truth and the documenting of the events for the future.[1368] Highlighting the interests of the victims once again puts the individual in the centre of attention of the Tribunals. In the tradition of the purposes for which the human rights of the individual were established it is reasonable to assume that only Tribunals that are independent of the organs that exercise executive powers can best protect the interests of an individual victim.

---

pedia of Public International Law (Oxford University Press Online Edition 2012), para. 68.

1366 *Prosecutor v. Dragan Nikolić, Sentencing Judgement*, para. 120.

1367 The *ad hoc* Tribunals did not yet go beyond the recognition of suffering and loss of victims also to give them rights before the tribunals; this is something that came first with the ICC. Cf. Art. 15(3) Rome Statute according to which victims may make representations to the Pre-Trial Chamber after it has received a request for authorization of an investigation from the prosecutor; Rules 89-93 Rules of Procedure of the ICC which provides for the possibility of victims participating in proceedings *inter alia* through written applications to the Registrar to be submitted to the (Rule 89) and the attendance and participation in the proceedings of legal representatives of a victim (Rule 91). See also Art. 53(1)(c) Rome Statute according to which the interests of the victims shall be taken into account when a decision is made by the prosecutor on the initiation of an investigation.

1368 Kamardi, *Die Ausformung einer Prozessordnung "sui generis" durch das ICTY unter Berücksichtigung des Fair-Trial-Prinzips*, 21-22.

4. Summary

Compared to earlier international criminal jurisdictions as well as the subsequently established ICC, the *ad hoc* Tribunals were conceived of and justified by a utilitarian rather than a retributive premise.[1369] Overall the *travaux préparatoires* as well as statements from the Tribunals themselves reveal that the primary aims served by the Tribunals are the conviction and punishment of individuals for their criminal responsibility and the restoration of peace by providing criminal proceedings detached from the parties to the conflict. For both of these functions the Tribunals' independence plays an important role: if individuals are to be tried and this judicial exercise is to be credible, then the Tribunals have to comply with fair trial standards recognized by international human rights law, and if peace is to be achieved their independent functioning could generate the necessary trust in the affected societies as well as in the international community. However, as the Tribunals' *ad hoc* nature reveals, their independence is questioned at the outset through allegations that they were pursuing whatever political aims the parent organization had in establishing the two jurisdictions. The ICTY and ICTR may defy this criticism effectively only by functioning autonomously, independently of outside influence on their core, judicial activities and without favouritism that may lead to adjudication deviating from fair and objective application of the applicable law.

In particular as the function of restoring and maintaining international peace and security is, and remains, the overarching function of the UNSC it is essential to analyse how the responsibilities between the Tribunals and the UNSC have been distributed and where frictions could arise that may compromise the independent functioning of the Tribunals.

1369 Schabas, *The UN International Criminal Tribunals – The Former Yugoslavia, Rwanda and Sierra Leone*, 8.

IV. Structural Independence

1. The Legal Framework of the Establishment of the Ad Hoc Tribunals and its Relevance for the Tribunals' Independence

According to the resolutions establishing the *ad hoc* Tribunals, the UNSC acted under chapter VII of the UNC[1370] and in pursuit of its main purpose of maintaining international peace and security.[1371] In order to fulfil its function Art. 39 UNC provides that the UNSC shall – after having determined the existence of any threat or breach of the peace or any act of aggression – make recommendations or decide measures pursuant to Arts. 41-42 UNC to maintain or restore international peace and security.[1372] As a consequence, the Tribunals must be seen as legitimate measures "to maintain and restore international peace and security". In the organizational structure of the UN they are to be classified as subsidiary organs,[1373] which the UNSC may establish "as it deems necessary for the performance of its functions."[1374] The following section will analyse what consequences this classification has for the legal relationship between the Tribunals and the UN, and in particular the ability of the former to operate independently of the latter.

An obligation for the UNSC to respect the autonomy of the *ad hoc* Tribunals, despite the fact that the Tribunals are established by the UNSC and thus are in an inferior position to it, could also derive from the fact that the UNSC as well as the Tribunals is bound by the internationally recognized

1370 Last preambular paragraphs of UNSC Resolution 827; UNSC Resolution 955: "Acting under Chapter VII of the Charter of the United Nations".

1371 Art. 24(1) UNC.

1372 The resolutions do not identify whether either Art. 41 or Art. 42 UNC is the legal basis in the view of the UNSC; however this is relatively unproblematic as Art. 39 UNC leaves it open to the UNSC to determine what measures shall be taken in order to maintain or restore international peace and security. *Prosecutor v. Duško Tadić, Appeals Chamber, Decision on the defence motion for interlocutory appeal on jurisdiction*, para. 39; *The Prosecutor versus Joseph Kanyabashi* (ICTR) Case No. ICTR-96-15-T (18 June 1997), para. 20.

1373 Paulus, Andreas, 'Article 29 UNC', in: Simma, Bruno (ed) *The Charter of the United Nations: A Commentary – Volume I* (Oxford University Press Oxford 2nd edn. 2002), 540-541, 556-563.

1374 Art. 29 UNC. See also Art. 7(2) UNC which provides that besides the principle organs of the UN, "[s]uch subsidiary organs as may be found necessary may be established in accordance with the present Charter." However, Art. 29 UNC is *lex specialis* in relation to Art. 7(2) UNC, ibid, 541.

right of individuals standing criminal trial to a "hearing by a competent, independent and impartial tribunal established by law".[1375] Whether there is such a right binding upon the UNSC and/or the Tribunals, even notwithstanding the exercise of the UNSC's functions under Chapter VII UNC, will therefore be analysed further below.[1376]

a) The Relationship Between the UNSC and the Tribunals Due to the Latter's Classification as Subsidiary Organs

> "No independent tribunal, particularly an international tribunal, can be a subsidiary organ of any body, including the Security Council."[1377]

(1) The Legal Framework Governing Subsidiary Organs

As already mentioned, Art. 7(2) UNC provides a general authority for principal organs of the UN to establish subsidiary organs,[1378] and Art. 29 UNC more specifically allows the UNSC to establish subsidiary organs.[1379] The practical impact of whether Art. 7(2) or Art. 29 UNC is applicable as the procedural provision on which the establishment of the Tribunals is based is limited. As shown by the ICJ in its opinions in *Effect of Awards of Compensation Made by the United Nations Administrative Tribunal*[1380] and in *Application for Review of Judgement No. 158 of the United Nations Admin-*

1375 See, e.g., Art. 14(1) ICCPR.

1376 See *infra* Chapter G.IV(1)(b).

1377 UNGA, *Letter dated 19 May 1993 from the Chargé dàffaires a.i. of the Permanent Mission of Yugoslavia to the United Nations addressed to the Secretary-General.*

1378 "Such subsidiary organs as may be found necessary may be established in accordance with the present Charter." Cf. *Effect of Awards of Compensation Made by the United Nations Administrative Tribunal (Advisory Opinion)*, 58-61; *Application for Review of Judgement No. 158 of the United Nations Administrative Tribunal (Advisory Opinion)* ICJ Rep. 166 (1973), 172. It must be noted that the ICJ in the advisory opinion *Effect of Awards of Compensation Made by the United Nations Administrative Tribunal* gave its view on the possibility of the UNGA, and not the UNSC, establishing a subsidiary organ. However, the provision conceding such a right for the UNGA, Art. 22 UNC, is identical with Art. 29 UNC.

1379 "The Security Council may establish such subsidiary organs as it deems necessary for the performance of its functions."

1380 *Effect of Awards of Compensation Made by the United Nations Administrative Tribunal (Advisory Opinion)*, 58.

istrative Tribunal,[1381] the ICJ finds no difference between Art. 7(2) UNC as the more general and Art. 29 UNC as the more precise provision containing the competence to establish subsidiary organs.[1382] This is consequential insofar as the wording of the two provisions is almost identical, both demanding that the established organ be "subsidiary" and that the establishment must be "found/deemed necessary".[1383] The criterion that every subsidiary organ

---

1381 *Application for Review of Judgement No. 158 of the United Nations Administrative Tribunal (Advisory Opinion)*, para. 16.

1382 Cf. Paulus, 'Article 29 UNC', 541-542.

1383 The only difference, which however is not relevant for the analysis here, is the additional demand contained in Art. 29 UNC that UNSC subsidiary bodies must be deemed "necessary for the performance of its functions." This requirement has two aspects. Firstly, Art. 29 UNC demands a substantive competence to establish any organ that supports the realisation of the powers and functions of the UNSC. This competence can be found e.g. in Art. 24 UNC and Chapter VII UNC. As mentioned earlier, the *ad hoc* Tribunals were established to maintain international peace and security (cf. *Prosecutor v. Duško Tadić, Appeals Chamber, Decision on the defence motion for interlocutory appeal on jurisdiction*, paras. 33 et seq.), and hence the UNSC's substantive competence is beyond doubt in the case of the *ad hoc* Tribunals. Secondly, however, the functional limitation in Art. 29 UNC seems to hint at that the UNSC must (and can only) have delegated to its subsidiary organ(s) the exercise of its own competences and functions (cf. Kelsen who interprets this, Kelsen, Hans, *The Law of the United Nations: A Critical Analysis of its Fundamental Problems* (Stevens London 1950), 137, 142: "It stands to reason that an organ can delegate only the power conferred upon it by the constitution."). Arguably and as stated in the Tadić decision, the UNSC is not a judicial organ and is thus not provided with judicial powers (*Prosecutor v. Duško Tadić, Appeals Chamber, Decision on the defence motion for interlocutory appeal on jurisdiction*, para. 37). However, A. Paulus suggests that Art. 29 UNC by no means requests an express power or function but merely demands that the scope of the powers or functions of the subsidiary organ "must remain within the competences and functions of the [UNSC]." (Paulus, 'Article 29 UNC', 542. Of a different opinion see Sarooshi, Dan, 'The Legal Framework Governing United Nations Subsidiary Organs' (1996) 67 The British Yearbook of International Law, 424). Furthermore, if the UNSC delegates competences which it does not possess itself, it must, according to the implied powers doctrine (see, e.g., M Blokker, Niels, 'International Organizations or Institutions, Implied Powers', in: Wolfrum, Rüdiger (ed) *The Max Planck Encyclopedia of Public International Law* (Oxford University Press Online Edition 2012)), be authorized to do so by a substantive provision of the UNC which at least requires that the UNSC has the substantive competence to adopt measures relating to the affected area (*Effect of Awards of Compensation Made by the United Nations Administrative Tribunal (Advisory Opinion)*, 61). The UNSC undoubtedly has the competence to adopt measures relating to the maintenance of peace and security.

must be deemed "necessary for the performance of [the UNSC's] functions" is also the sole restriction placed by Art. 29 UNC on the UNSC's power to establish a subsidiary organ.[1384]

(2) The Relationship Between Principal and Subsidiary Organs – Issues of Definition

The notion "subsidiary organ" is not defined in the UNC itself, and the drafting history of the UNC is equally silent on the meaning of this terminology. From the wording it can be inferred that the subsidiary organ has been established (or otherwise recognized) by one of the principal organs of the UN,[1385] and that it must be furnishing assistance to the *principal* organ. The Dumbarton Oaks Proposal initially used the term "auxiliary organ"[1386] which later, without any reasons being given, was replaced by "subsidiary organ"[1387]. With regard to the usage of "subsidiary organs" in Art. 22 UNC, i.e. as organs established by the UNGA,[1388] the Dumbarton Oaks Proposal even referred to the yet more general and vacuous terms "bodies and agencies" of the UNGA.[1389] According to M. Hilf and D.-E. Kahn, both "auxiliary" and "subsidiary" organs have in common the element of institutional assignment and subordination, as both do not participate in the exercise of the external powers of the parent organ.[1390] They nevertheless suggest that the term "subsidiary organ" implies that the relevant body discharges its functions independently of the main organ, whereas "auxiliary organs" have a more dependent and subordinated position. This picture is somewhat blurred by an observation which the UN itself made in 1955, namely that "[i]n the

1384 Cf. *Application for Review of Judgement No. 158 of the United Nations Administrative Tribunal (Advisory Opinion)*, para. 16 *in fine*.

1385 Jaenicke, 'Article 7 UNC', 218.

1386 French: "*organe auxiliaire*".

1387 French: "*organe subsidiaire*".

1388 In this regard usually no difference is made between subsidiary organs established pursuant to Art. 22 UNC or Art. 29 UNC, let alone between these provisions and Art. 7(2) UNC.

1389 Goodrich, Leland M. & Hambro, Edvard, *Charter of the United Nations – Commentary and Documents* (Columbia University Press New York 3rd edn. and rev. 1969), 665, 667.

1390 Hilf, Meinhard & Khan, Daniel-Erasmus, 'Article 22 UNC', in: Simma, Bruno (ed) *The Charter of the United Nations: A Commentary – Volume I* (Oxford University Press Oxford 2nd edn. 2002), 423.

practice of the United Nations such expressions as 'Commissions', 'committees', 'subsidiary organs', 'subsidiary bodies' and 'subordinate bodies' have been used interchangeably."[1391] B. Rudolf appears to agree in part when asserting that "[t]he UN system of committees is characterized by its lack of coherence, both in terms of structure and of terminology."[1392] This would suggest that no difference in substance is necessarily intended between those terms when used to describe organs established by the principal organs of the UN; indeed any name, be it commission or committee or otherwise, could be given to them.[1393] According to G. Jaenicke,

> "the term 'subsidiary organ' does not necessarily imply any presumption as to the measure of control that the principal organ may exercise over the subsidiary organ it has established, or as to the measure of autonomy this subsidiary organ may enjoy *vis-à-vis* the principal organ."[1394]

He thus stresses the need for restraint when drawing any conclusions based solely on the terminology. In order to gain insight into the actual degree of independence stemming from the character of an organ labelled a "subsidiary organ" it is thus more fruitful to analyse on a case-by-case basis the relationship between subsidiary organs and the principal organs that established them.

(3) Features Prescribing Structural Independence Following from the Classification of the Ad Hoc Tribunals as Subsidiary Organs

In some UN documents attempts to define the characteristics of subsidiary organs have been undertaken based on the subsidiary organs established hitherto. Whereas some of these characteristics are considered to be necessary requirements for the lawful establishment of a subsidiary organ, others are characteristics that instead help to distinguish them from other organs in the

---

1391 United Nations, *Repertory of Practice of United Nations Organs – Repertory of Practice (1945-1954), Volume 1 – Extracts relating to Article 7 of the Charter of the United Nations* (United Nations New York 1955), 224.

1392 Rudolf, Beate, 'United Nations Committees and Subsidiary Bodies, System of', in: Wolfrum, Rüdiger (ed) *The Max Planck Encyclopedia of Public International Law* (Oxford University Press Online Edition 2012), para. 4.

1393 Kelsen, *The Law of the United Nations: A Critical Analysis of its Fundamental Problems*, 138.

1394 Jaenicke, 'Article 7 UNC', 218.

UN system.[1395] The Repertory of Practice of United Nations Organs lists the following characteristics, which even today find support in academic writing and which thus deserve to be looked at in more detail.[1396]

(I) *Membership*: Subsidiary organs may be composed of either States[1397] or individuals.[1398] If the latter is the case it is assumed that members function in their personal capacity and are not subject to instructions from their governments.[1399] Where the number of members of a subsidiary organ is limited, an equitable geographical distribution is usually maintained.

(II) *Structure*: Although the majority of subsidiary organs lack permanent machinery, some do have their own organizational structure.[1400]

(III) *Scope of activities*: The functions served by subsidiary organs are vast and cannot be listed exhaustively. Among them are the preparation of studies to be submitted to UN principal organs, assistance in the discharge of financial and budgetary questions, and execution of relief and rehabilitation and judicial functions.[1401]

1395 Sarooshi, 'The Legal Framework Governing United Nations Subsidiary Organs', 421.

1396 United Nations, *Repertory of Practice of United Nations Organs – Repertory of Practice (1945-1954), Volume 1 – Extracts relating to Article 7 of the Charter of the United Nations*, 226-228.

1397 E.g. the Interim Committee of the General Assembly; UNGA, *Establishment of an Interim Committee of the General Assembly* (13 November 1947) UN Doc. A/RES/111 (II), UNGA, *Re-establishment of the Interim Committee of the General Assembly* (3 December 1948) UN Doc. A/RES/196 (III) and UNGA, *Re-establishment of the Interim Committee of the General Assembly* (21 November 1949) UN Doc. A/RES/295 (IV).

1398 E.g. the UN Mediator in Palestine; UNGA, *Appointment and terms of reference of a United Nations Mediator in Palestine* (14 May 1948) UN Doc. A/RES/186 (S-2).

1399 Jaenicke, 'Article 7 UNC', 219.

1400 The Repertory of Practice of United Nations Organs here referred to e.g. UNICEF, UNRWA, UNKRA and the High Commissioner for Refugees; United Nations, *Repertory of Practice of United Nations Organs – Repertory of Practice (1945-1954), Volume 1 – Extracts relating to Article 7 of the Charter of the United Nations*, 226.

1401 Early example of organs exercising the judicial function are the UN Tribunals in Libya and Eritrea and the UN Administrative Tribunal; ibid, 227. G. Jaenicke in his non-exhaustive overview over functions exercised by subsidiary organs lists institutions with judicial functions besides numerous others; see Jaenicke, 'Article 7 UNC', 220-223.

(IV) *Powers*: The powers exercised by subsidiary organs include the reporting and making of recommendations to UN principal organs, the establishment of their own subsidiary organs, the adoption of rules of procedure, entering into agreements with governments,[1402] suing or taking legal action or even making decisions binding on the UN.[1403] The principal organ is generally free to determine the nature and scope of the powers to be exercised and the degree of autonomy in that exercise by the relevant subsidiary organ, provided that the principal organ acts within the limits of its own competences.[1404] In the opinion of the ICJ in *Effect of Awards of Compensation Made by the United Nations Administrative Tribunal*, the classification of a body as a subsidiary organ (in that particular context the UN Administrative Tribunal) does not mean that that body is subordinate to the principal organ establishing it (the UNGA) and that it cannot bind that principal organ. According to the ICJ, the UN Administrative Tribunal exercises functions which the principal organs, both the UNSC and the UNGA, do not themselves possess under the UNC, namely the judicial functions.[1405] Accordingly, although the principal organ has the power to establish a subsidiary *judicial* organ as a tool to fulfil its own functions under the UNC, it may not interfere in that organ's adjudication. This same line of argument must also apply to the relationship between the *ad hoc* Tribunals and the UNSC; the UNSC is prohibited from interfering in the conduct of individual cases[1406] and it may not change individual

---

1402 The legal capacity to act on the international or national plane follows from the subsidiary organs' status as organs of the UN, the internationally recognized legal personality of the UN, the application of Arts. 104-105 UNC and of the Convention on the Privileges and Immunities of the UN. See Jaenicke, 'Article 7 UNC', 224.

1403 The ICJ for the first time endorsed the possibility of a subsidiary organ (the UN Administrative Tribunal) to bind the body which had established it (the UNGA) in the advisory opinion *Effect of Awards of Compensation Made by the United Nations Administrative Tribunal (Advisory Opinion)*.

1404 Jaenicke, 'Article 7 UNC', 223.

1405 *Effect of Awards of Compensation Made by the United Nations Administrative Tribunal (Advisory Opinion)*, 61 and *Prosecutor v. Duško Tadić, Appeals Chamber, Decision on the defence motion for interlocutory appeal on jurisdiction*, para. 37.

1406 Cf. Sarooshi, 'The Legal Framework Governing United Nations Subsidiary Organs', 453.

decisions of the Tribunals since they are an exercise of powers that the UNSC itself does not possess.[1407]

(V) *Method of Reporting*: Whereas some subsidiary organs report solely to the principal organ that established them, others report to more than one principal organ.

(VI) *Duration*: Some subsidiary organs, such as the Advisory Committee on Administrative and Budgetary Questions, operate on a permanent basis, others function only during sessions of their parent principal organ, and yet others are established merely for the fulfilment of a particular task and are terminated after that task has been completed. Irrespective of the intended life span of the organ, the principal organ retains the inherent power to suspend or discontinue it.[1408]

In addition to the core characteristics of establishment by a principal organ, the authority and control exercised by it over the subsidiary organ and the decision on the termination of the subsidiary organ,[1409] D. Sarooshi adds the further element that subsidiary organs necessarily possess a certain degree of independence from their principal organ.[1410] This element, he argues, is necessary as the subsidiary organ otherwise would be merely a part of the establishing principal organ.[1411] This view, while conforming to the diversity

1407 As concluded by the ICJ in the Administrative Tribunal Advisory Opinion, decisions of the tribunal that is established by the principal organ, is binding on that organ; see *Effect of Awards of Compensation Made by the United Nations Administrative Tribunal (Advisory Opinion)*, 53.

1408 Jaenicke, 'Article 7 UNC', 223.

1409 Supporting the view that these three features are common to all subsidiary organs: United Nations, *Repertory of Practice of United Nations Organs – Repertory of Practice (1945-1954), Volume 1 – Extracts relating to Article 7 of the Charter of the United Nations*, 228; Hilf & Khan, 'Article 22 UNC', 423; UNGA, *Summary of internal Secretariat studies of constitutional questions relating to agencies within the framework of the United Nations* (15 November 1954) UN Doc. A/C.1/758, paras. 1-2.

1410 Sarooshi, 'The Legal Framework Governing United Nations Subsidiary Organs', 416. This view is supported by Hilf & Khan, 'Article 22 UNC', 423.

1411 Cf. Dupuy, René-Jean & Recht, Haagse Academie voor Internationaal, *Manuel sur les organisations internationales* (Nijhoff Dordrecht 1988), 130.See also the discussion in the 6th Committee on whether committees of the UNGA are to be seen as subsidiary organs or rather as integral parts of the UNGA. The discussion reached the conclusion that subsidiary organs are exercising functions in a manner which is distinct from the internal workings of the principal organ, that they are usually active even between the sessions of the UNGA and/or if it exercises functions which the principal organ does not possess; see Sarooshi, 'The Legal

in membership, structure and scope of activities outlined above, deserves support for a reason which is particularly important for the *ad hoc* Tribunals; as mentioned earlier, subsidiary organs can and often do exercise functions which the parent principal organ itself does not possess.[1412] Were the principal organ still allowed to interfere with this function or even to have substantial influence on how it was exercised when performed by the subsidiary organ it established, this would go beyond the competences it has under the UNC and thus circumvent and violate the delimitation of the powers between principal organs enshrined in the UNC.[1413] It should be emphasised that this additional requirement could potentially stand in contradiction to the second requirement mentioned above, namely the authority and control exercised by the principal organ over the subsidiary organ.[1414] Therefore, when concluding that a certain level of independence towards the establishing principal organ is innate in the nature of a UN subsidiary organ, the question arises where the exact border is drawn between this independence and the legitimate (and necessary) authority and control exercised by the principal organ. It is reasonable, owing to the wide variety of different types of subsidiary organs established so far,[1415] that this assessment cannot be made across the board for all bodies, but instead must be based on an assessment of the individual situation, taking into consideration the intention of the principal organ at the

---

Framework Governing United Nations Subsidiary Organs', 417 with further references.

1412 This is what the ICJ established in the *Awards* case, stating that "the Charter does not confer judicial functions on the General Assembly ... By establishing the Administrative Tribunal, the General Assembly was not delegating the performance of its own functions: it was exercising a power which it had under the Charter to regulate staff relations." See *Effect of Awards of Compensation Made by the United Nations Administrative Tribunal (Advisory Opinion)*, 61. For the UNSC, and in particular with regard to the ICTY, this is reiterated in *Prosecutor v. Duško Tadić, Appeals Chamber, Decision on the defence motion for interlocutory appeal on jurisdiction*, para. 38.

1413 For more on this issue see Sarooshi, 'The Legal Framework Governing United Nations Subsidiary Organs', 458 et seq. and Paulus, 'Article 29 UNC', 543.

1414 N. Blokker describes the authority and control exercised by the UNSC over its subsidiary organs "an essential characteristic of subsidiary organs", see Blokker, Niels, 'Is the Authorization Authorized? Powers and Practice of the UN Security Council to Authorize the Use of Force by "Coalitions of the Able and Willing"' (2000) 11 European Journal of International Law 3, 551.

1415 For an overview see Jaenicke, 'Article 7 UNC', 219-224.

time of establishment and the nature of functions conferred on the subsidiary body.[1416]

(4) Conclusions

The *ad hoc* Tribunals, following their classification as subsidiary organs, are in a subordinate position in relation to the UNSC which established them.[1417] This subordination amounts to the UNSC's capacity to decide to establish the Tribunals, the authority to determine the nature and scope of the powers to be exercised and the degree of autonomy in that exercise by them, and the decision on the termination of the Tribunals.[1418] However, irrespective of these powers, certain inalienable characteristics flow from the Tribunals' nature as subsidiary organs. The judges making up the Tribunals function in their personal capacity and are not subject to instructions from their governments or the UN. The Tribunals are granted the power to adopt rules of procedure, to enter into agreements, to sue or to take legal action and to make binding decisions. The UNSC is prohibited from interfering in the conduct of individual cases,[1419] and is also unable to change individual decisions of the Tribunals as they are an exercise of powers that the UNSC itself does not possess.[1420] However, it ought to be asked whether the powers the UNSC has under Chapter VII UNC may penetrate these delimitations, in particular as the conclusions of the ICJ in the Administrative Tribunal Advisory Opinion were made with regard to the UNGA, which does not have similar enforcement powers. This shall be examined in what follows.

1416 Cf. *Effect of Awards of Compensation Made by the United Nations Administrative Tribunal (Advisory Opinion)*, 61. See also Paulus, 'Article 29 UNC', 542.

1417 Jaenicke, 'Article 7 UNC', 219; Boven, Theodoor C. van, 'Autonomy and Independence of United Nations Judicial Institutions: A Comparative Note', in: Wellens, Karel (ed) *International Law: Theory and Practice: Essays in Honour of Eric Suy* (Nijhoff The Hague 1998), 681.

1418 The termination process of the *ad hoc* Tribunals has already been initiated by the completion strategies.

1419 Cf. Sarooshi, 'The Legal Framework Governing United Nations Subsidiary Organs', 453.

1420 As concluded by the ICJ in the Administrative Tribunal Advisory Opinion, decisions of the tribunal that is established by the principal organ, is binding on that organ; see *Effect of Awards of Compensation Made by the United Nations Administrative Tribunal (Advisory Opinion)*, 53.

b) Limits to the Exercise of Powers under Chapter VII UNC

(1) Generally on Limits to the UNSC's Powers Under Chapter VII UNC

As a cornerstone of the system of collective security of the UN, Art. 41 UNC allows the UNSC to decide on non-military enforcement measures, and it is under the umbrella of this legal framework that the *ad hoc* Tribunals were established. Despite the discretion the UNSC has in determining the appropriate action to be taken under Art. 41 UNC,[1421] this discretion is not unlimited. Like any other organ of the UN the UNSC has to act in accordance with the purposes and principles of the UN,[1422] with other substantive rules of the Charter and with general principles of international law,[1423] in particular *ius cogens*.[1424] To the extent that non-*ius cogens* norms of humanitarian law and human rights norms form part of the purposes of the UN[1425] they must equally be observed. This raises the question whether either human rights law or *ius cogens* contains the right to a trial before an independent[1426] court or tribunal, and thus whether the UNSC would also be called upon to have to respect the independence of any tribunal it establishes under Chapter VII UNC.

1421 Art. 41 UNC: "The Security Council may decide *what measures … are to be employed* to give effect to its decisions, and it may call upon the Members of the United Nations to apply such measures." (Emphasis added.).

1422 Art. 24(2) UNC.

1423 Martenczuk, Bernd, *Rechtsbindung und Rechtskontrolle des Weltsicherheitsrats – Die Überprüfung nichtmilitärischer Zwangsmaßnahmen durch den Internationalen Gerichtshof* (Duncker & Humblot Berlin 1996), 281-282; Frowein, Jochen Abr. & Krisch, Nico, 'Introduction to Chapter VII UNC', in: Simma, Bruno (ed) *The Charter of the United Nations: A Commentary – Volume I* (Oxford University Press Oxford 2nd edn. 2002), 711.

1424 Paulus, 'Article 29 UNC', 541. Cf. the statement contained in the Report of the Rapporteur of Committee 1 to Commission I preparing the draft of the preamble, purposes and principles of the UNC: "When the [UN] has used the power given to it and the force at its disposal to stop war, then it can find the latitude to apply the principles of justice and international law". See United Nations Information Organizations, *Volume VI – Commission I – General Provisions* (United Nations Information Organizations London New York 1945), 453.

1425 See Art. 1(3) UNC.

1426 Only the independence, considered as undue influence exerted from a separate (external) organ, will be considered in the following. The question of impartiality is one that primarily is considered on the level of the personal independence of judges.

(2) The Right to be Judged by an Independent Tribunal as a Human Right

Numerous international human rights instruments and provisions contain the right to be judged by an independent and impartial tribunal, in particular with regard to criminal proceedings. This is codified e.g. in Art. 10 Universal Declaration of Human Rights (UDHR),[1427] Art. 6 ECHR,[1428] Art. 8(1) ACHR,[1429] Art. 7(1)(d) African Charter on Human and Peoples' Rights (AChHPR).[1430] Art. 14(1) ICCPR states that:

> "[i]n the determination of any criminal charge against him, or of his rights and obligations in a suit at law, everyone shall be entitled to a fair and public hearing by a competent, independent and impartial tribunal established by law."

In addition, a number of non-binding instruments equally restate this principle,[1431] and it is a requirement that can be found in many national constitutions.[1432] The wide basis that the right to a hearing by an independent and impartial tribunal thus appears to have has led the Special Rapporteur on the Independence of Judges and Lawyers to assert it as "general principles of law recognized by civilized nations in the sense of Article 38(1)(c) of the Statute of the International Court of Justice."[1433] In view of these sources

---

1427 "Everyone is entitled in full equality to a fair and public hearing by an independent and impartial tribunal, in the determination of his rights and obligations and of any criminal charge against him."

1428 "In the determination of his civil rights and obligations or of any criminal charge against him, everyone is entitled to a fair and public hearing within a reasonable time by an independent and impartial tribunal established by law."

1429 "Every person has the right to a hearing, with due guarantees and within a reasonable time, by a competent, independent, and impartial tribunal, previously established by law, in the substantiation of any accusation of a criminal nature made against him or for the determination of his rights and obligations of a civil, labour, fiscal, or any other nature."

1430 "Every individual shall have the right to have his cause heard. This comprises: … (d) the right to be tried within a reasonable time by an impartial court or tribunal."

1431 E.g. Seventh United Nations Congress on the Prevention of Crime and the Treatment of Offenders, *United Nations Basic Principles on the Independence of the Judiciary*.

1432 For an overview see Bassiouni, M. Cherif, 'Human Rights in the Context of Criminal Justice. Identifying International Procedural Protections and Equivalent Protections in National Constitutions' (1993) 3 Duke Journal of Comparative and International Law 2, 270.

1433 Special Rapporteur on the Independence of Judges and Lawyers, *Independence and Impartiality of the Judiciary, Jurors and Assessors and the Independence of Lawyers: Report of the Special Rapporteur, Param Cumaraswamy, Submitted in*

the right to an independent and impartial tribunal must be considered a human right enshrined in general international law. However, human rights are binding on the UNSC only insofar as the UNSC does not override their application by reference to the primary goal to establish peace. As the maintenance of peace was the main objective pursued by the UNSC when establishing the *ad hoc* Tribunals, it is plausible that their independent functioning would be compromised whenever it was deemed necessary.[1434] In particular, since the situations in Yugoslavia and Rwanda were the subject of political discussions in and decisions by the UNSC even after the establishment of the *ad hoc* Tribunals. It thus should be asked whether the right to be judged by an independent and impartial tribunal has a more far reaching binding effect, either as an individual right from which no derogation is allowed or from its quality as a peremptory norm.

(3) Judicial Independence as a Non-Derogable Right?

(i) Non-Derogability of the Right to Judicial Independence in the ICCPR

Art. 4(2) ICCPR lists the rights from which no derogation may be made, but this does not include Art. 14(1) ICCPR on the right to independent and impartial proceedings. This could lead to the *e contrario* conclusion that Art. 14(1) ICCPR may be derogated from and that the provision thus does not retain special protection. Such a conclusion is, however, not compulsory,[1435] and it in particular provides a loose ground for a wider argument reaching beyond the ICCPR.[1436] The same conclusion was reached by the HRC in its General Comment on Art. 4 ICCPR of July 2001.[1437] The Com-

---

Accordance with Commission on Human Rights Resolution 1994/41 (6 February 1995) UN Doc. E/CN.4/1995/39, para. 34.

1434 “Peace takes precedent over justice.” Frowein & Krisch, 'Introduction to Chapter VII UNC', 711.

1435 From a logical viewpoint, the lack of a prohibition on derogating does not consequentially imply a right to derogate.

1436 S. Oeter seems to be of the same view: see Oeter, Stefan, 'Ius cogens und der Schutz der Menschenrechte', in: Ehrenzeller, Bernhard *et al.* (eds) *Menschenrechte, Demokratie und Rechtsstaat – Liber Amicorum Luzius Wildhaber* (Dike/Nomos Zürich/Baden-Baden 2007), 509-510.

1437 Human Rights Committee, *General Comment 29, States of Emergency (Article 4)* (31 August 2001) UN Doc. CCPR/C/21/Rev. 1/Add.11, para. 6.

mittee instead suggests an individual assessment of the derogability of the rights protected under the ICCPR, and states that "the principles of legality and the rule of law require that fundamental requirements of fair trial must be respected during a state of emergency." The Committee does not expressly clarify whether it considers the rights under Art. 14(1) ICCPR to be subsumed under this, but instead states that it includes the right that "[o]nly a court of law may try and convict a person for a criminal offence."[1438]

The Committee makes more specific statements in its decisions on complaints brought by individuals. In *Gonzalez del Rio v. Peru* it recalled "that the right to be tried by an independent and impartial tribunal is an absolute right that may suffer no exception."[1439] The decisions (views) of the HRC are not considered to be binding[1440] although the opinion has been expressed in academic writing that the affected State has an obligation to implement its views.[1441] An argument that goes against including Art. 14(1) ICCPR among non-derogable provisions is that the HRC explicitly turned down a suggestion made by the Sub-Commission on Prevention of Discrimination and Protection of Minorities to add Art. 14 ICCPR to the list of non-derogable provisions in the form of an optional protocol.[1442] In this regard the HRC stated:

> "that it would simply not be feasible to expect that *all provisions of article 14* can remain fully in force in any kind of emergency. Thus, the inclusion of article 14 *as such* into the list of non-derogable provisions would not be appropriate."[1443] (Emphasis added.)

To be precise, the wording does not rule out the fact that the various parts of Art. 14 ICCPR would be non-derogable, but it merely states that the inclusion of the *entire* Art. 14 ICCPR would not be feasible. Moreover, a further reading of the opinion of the HRC reveals the reasons for this statement. The HRC feared, justifiably, that such an optional protocol would invite

---

1438 Ibid, para. 16.

1439 Human Rights Committee, *González del Río v. Peru, Communication No. 263/1987* (2 November 1992) UN Doc. CCPR/C/46/D/263/1987, para. 5.2.

1440 On the binding character of the views of the HRC see Wense, Wolf von der, *Der UN-Menschenrechtsausschuß und sein Beitrag zum universellen Schutz der Menschenrechte* (Springer Berlin 1999), 52. See further *supra* Chapter C.IV(2)(e) at fn. 322.

1441 Ibid, 52.

1442 Human Rights Committee, *Report of the Human Rights Committee (Volume II)* (21 September 1994) UN Doc. A/49/40, 119.

1443 Ibid, 119.

States not to sign and thereby consider themselves able to derogate from Art. 14(1) ICCPR. In other words, the offer to sign the optional protocol would have invited the interpretation of the absence of doing so as if Art. 14 ICCPR was derogable. As a consequence, the position taken and statement made by the HRC do not support the view that Art. 14(1) ICCPR, and in particular the provision on independence, may be derogated from in times of emergency. On the contrary, it suggests that parts of Art. 14(1) ICCPR are non-derogable, and in view of the earlier statements made by the HRC the independence of courts ought to be included among them.

Finally, a number of statements made by the Special Rapporteur on the Independence of Judges and Lawyers also assume the non-derogable nature of the independence of courts. As Special Rapporteur P. Cumaraswamy stated, the requirement of an independent and impartial judiciary is necessary for the realization of other rights, especially such rights which prescribe judicial supervision.[1444] Among these are Art. 6 ICCPR (Right to Life), which demands that "[n]o one shall be arbitrarily deprived of his life" and which is itself non-derogable.[1445] If the necessary precondition of an independent and impartial judiciary were derogable, this would enable derogation from the right to life.[1446] In their final report "The right to a fair trial: Current recognition and measures necessary for its strengthening" the Special Rapporteurs S. Chernichenko and W. Treat list numerous sources (regional human rights treaties as well as non-binding instruments) which consider the inde-

1444 Special Rapporteur on the Independence of Judges and Lawyers, *Independence and Impartiality of the Judiciary, Jurors and Assessors and the Independence of Lawyers: Report of the Special Rapporteur, Param Cumaraswamy, Submitted in Accordance with Commission on Human Rights Resolution 1994/41*, para. 42.

1445 Art. 6 ICCPR read in conjunction with Art. 4(2) ICCPR.

1446 Meron, Theodor, 'On a Hierarchy of International Human Rights' (1986) 80 American Journal of International Law 1, 11 is of the same view. See also de Zayas, Alfred, 'The United Nations and the Guarantee of a Fair Trial in the International Covenant on Civil and Political Rights and the Convention Against Torture and Other Cruela, Inhuman or Degrading Treatment or Punishment', in: Weissbrodt, David *et al.* (eds) *The Right to a Fair Trial* (Springer 1998), 674; McGoldrick, Dominic, 'The Interface between Public Emergency Powers and International Law' (2004) 2 International Journal of Constitutional Law 2, 418; Svensson-McCarthy, Anna-Lena, *The International Law of Human Rights and States of Exception. With Special Reference to the Travaux Préparatoires and Case-Law of the International Monitoring Organs* (Nijhoff Den Haag 1998), 448.

pendence and impartiality of the judiciary.[1447] On this empirical basis they make the suggestion that fair trial guarantees, and in particular the right enshrined in Art. 14(1) ICCPR, are non-derogable rights. As the Special Rapporteurs also refer to regional human rights regimes, it is prudent to analyse the approach of those instruments regarding the question of the derogability of the right to an independent tribunal.

(ii) Non-Derogability of the Right to Judicial Independence in the ECHR

The ECHR in Art. 15(2) lists the rights which States Parties may not derogate from even in times of public emergency and these do not include the right to fair trial,[1448] which comprises the right to an independent and impartial judiciary. However, the jurisprudence of the ECtHR has stated that even in situations where national security is at stake:

> "the concepts of lawfulness and the rule of law in a democratic society require that measures affecting fundamental human rights must be subject to some form of adversarial proceedings before an independent body competent to review the reasons for the decision and relevant evidence."[1449]

Although the decisions are binding only for the States Parties which are immediately affected and have recognized the jurisdiction of the ECtHR,[1450] the ECtHR has repeated this jurisprudence on occasion.[1451] Furthermore it is by now generally accepted that the judgments of the ECtHR establish a guiding effect,[1452] meaning that they have quasi-binding effect for all

---

1447 Commission on Human Rights, *The Administration of Justice and the Human Rights of Detainees – The right to a fair trial: Current recognition and measures necessary for its strengthening, Final report prepared by Mr. Stanislav Chernichenko and Mr. William Treat* (3 June 1994) UN Doc. E/CN.4/Sub.2/1994/24, paras. 127-140.

1448 Art. 6 ECHR.

1449 *Al-Nashif v. Bulgaria* (ECtHR) Application No. 50963/99 (20 June 2002), para. 123.

1450 Art. 46 ECHR.

1451 See, e.g., *Case of Liu v. Russia* (ECtHR) Application No. 42086/05 (6 December 2007), para. 59; *C.G. and Others v. Bulgaria* (ECtHR) Application No. 1365/07 (24 April 2008), para. 40.

1452 German: "*Orientierungswirkung*". See on this Grabenwarter, Christoph, *Europäische Menschenrechtskonvention – Ein Studienbuch* (Beck München 4th edn. 2009), 98 with further references; Busch, Christoph, 'Fundamental Rights and Private Law in the EU Member States', in: Busch, Christoph *et al.* (eds) *EU*

Member States established through the anticipation that any non-compliance with the judgment could lead to a conclusion by the ECtHR that the State has violated its obligations under the ECHR. In summary therefore, it must be affirmed that the non-derogable nature of the right to an independent and impartial tribunal is also recognized under the ECHR.

(iii) Non-Derogability of the Right to Judicial Independence in the ACHR

According to Art. 27(2) ACHR the derogation from the obligations under the ACHR is not possible with regard to *inter alia* "judicial guarantees essential for the protection of" certain enumerated fundamental rights.[1453] The IACtHR has on several occasions stated that these judicial guarantees include "the active involvement of an independent and impartial judicial body having the power to pass on the lawfulness of measures adopted in a state of emergency."[1454] The Inter-American Commission on Human Rights (IACommHR) has in a similar fashion considered that:

Compendium – Fundamental Rights and Private Law (Walter de Gruyter München 2010), 9-10. "Die Wirkungen der Entscheidungen des EGMR bestehen in einer völkerrechtlichen Befolgungspflicht der Staaten gem. Art. 46 I EMRK. … es besteht keine Bindungswirkung (= keine stare decisis), nur eine völkerrechtliche Befolgungspflicht des Vertragsstaats. Es besteht aber darüber Einigkeit, dass Ihnen eine Orientierungswirkung zukommt: Entscheidungen deutscher Gerichte sind daran auszurichten, um der späteren Feststellung einer Konventionswidrigkeit vorzubeugen." Kilian, Michael, 'Der Einfluss der EMRK auf die deutsche Verfassungsrechtsprechung', in: Höland, Armin (ed) *Wirkungen der Rechtsprechung des Europäischen Gerichtshofs für Menschenrecht im deutschen Recht* (BWV Verlag Berlin 2012), 126.

1453 Art. 27(2) ACHR reads: "2. The foregoing provision does not authorize any suspension of the following articles: Article 3 (Right to Juridical Personality), Article 4 (Right to Life), Article 5 (Right to Humane Treatment), Article 6 (Freedom from Slavery), Article 9 (Freedom from Ex Post Facto Laws), Article 12 (Freedom of Conscience and Religion), Article 17 (Rights of the Family), Article 18 (Right to a Name), Article 19 (Rights of the Child), Article 20 (Right to Nationality), and Article 23 (Right to Participate in Government), or of the judicial guarantees essential for the protection of such rights."

1454 *Judicial Guarantees in States of Emergency (Arts. 27(2), 25 and 8 of the American Convention on Human Rights), Advisory Opinion*, para. 20; *Habeas Corpus in Emergency Situations (Arts. 27(2), 25(1) and 7(6) American Convention on Human Rights), Advisory Opinion* (IACtHR) OC-8/87 (30 January 1987), paras. 29-30. To the same effect Commission on Human Rights, *The Administration of Justice and the Human Rights of Detainees – The right to a fair trial: Current recognition*

> "due process rights form an integral part of the judicial guarantees essential for the protection of non-derogable rights and may therefore be considered non-derogable under the express terms of Article 27(2) of the American Convention."[1455]

The IACommHR went on to conclude that the basic components of the right to a fair trial cannot be justifiably suspended, and that these "include in particular the right to a fair trial by a competent, independent and impartial court for persons charged with criminal offenses".[1456] It may thus be concluded that the right to an independent and impartial tribunal is considered a non-derogable right under the ACHR.[1457]

(iv) Non-Derogability of the Right to Judicial Independence in the Arab Charter on Human Rights and the African Charter on Human and Peoples' Rights

The Arab Charter on Human Rights considers the fair trial guarantees to be non-derogable in exceptional situations of emergency, and thus seems to codify what the ECtHR established in its jurisprudence regarding Art. 15(2) ECHR.[1458] The AChHPR does not list the rights from which derogations may be made. Instead provisions on individual rights contain the possibility that they are derogated from, e.g. Art. 8 on freedom of conscience and the profession and free practice of religion.[1459] Neither Art. 7, providing for the

---

and measures necessary for its strengthening, Final report prepared by Mr. Stanislav Chernichenko and Mr. William Treat, para. 136.

1455 Inter-American Commission on Human Rights, *Report on Terrorism and Human Rights* (22 October 2002) OAS Official Records OEA/Ser.L/V/II.116, Doc. 5 rev. 1 corr, para. 246.

1456 Ibid, para. 247.

1457 Olivier, Clémentine, 'Revisiting General Comment No. 29 of the United Nations Human Rights Committee about Fair Trial Rights and Derogations in Times of Public Emergency' (2004) 17 Leiden Journal of International Law 2, 418-419 is of the same view. See also Svensson-McCarthy, *The International Law of Human Rights and States of Exception. With Special Reference to the Travaux Préparatoires and Case-Law of the International Monitoring Organs*, 495.

1458 Art. 4(1)-(2), read in conjunction with Art. 13 League of Arab States, Arab Charter on Human Rights (revised).

1459 "Freedom of conscience, the profession and free practice of religion shall be guaranteed. No one may, *subject to law and order*, be submitted to measures restricting the exercise of these freedoms." (Emphasis added.).

right to access to the judiciary including access to an impartial court or tribunal, nor Art. 26, prescribing the "duty to guarantee the independence of the Courts", contains such a possibility. Considering also the significant role international human rights instruments such as the ICCPR played in the development of the African Charter,[1460] this leads to the assumption that the African Charter, too, regards the right to an independent judiciary to be non-derogable. This is confirmed by decision of the African Commission on Human and Peoples' Rights (ACommHR).[1461]

(v) The Right to be Judged by an Independent Tribunal as a Peremptory Norm?

Independently of the above conclusion on the question of non-derogability, but also possibly supporting it, the right to have access to an independent and impartial judiciary may have the quality of a peremptory norm, in which case the UNSC would be bound by it even when acting under Chapter VII UNC.[1462] According to Art. 53 VCLT a peremptory norm of general international law

> "is a norm accepted and recognized by the international community of States as a whole as a norm from which no derogation is permitted and which can be modified only by a subsequent norm of general international law having the same character."[1463]

1460 Ouguergouz, Fatsah, 'African Charter on Human and Peoples' Rights (1981)', in: Wolfrum, Rüdiger (ed) *The Max Planck Encyclopedia of Public International Law* (Oxford University Press Online Edition 2012), paras. 7-9.

1461 *Civil Liberties Organisation, Legal Defence Centre, Legal Defence and Assistance Project v. Nigeria* (African Commission on Human and Peoples' Rights) Comm. No. 218/98 (1998), para. 27: "It is our view that the provisions of Article 7 should be considered non-derogable providing as they do the minimum protection to citizens and military officers alike especially under an unaccountable, undemocratic military regime."

1462 See *Application of the Convention on the Prevention and Punishment of the Crime of Genocide (Bosnia and Herzegovina v Serbia and Montenegro) (Order of 13 September 1993) (Separate Opinion of Judge Lauterpacht)*, 440.

1463 Vienna Convention on the Law of Treaties. This provision explicitly applies only for the purpose of the VCLT, i.e. between treaty parties; however, it can be said that the principle of jus cogens is applicable beyond this also to non-member States of the UN. See Kadelbach, Stefan, *Zwingendes Völkerrecht* (Duncker und Humblot Berlin 1992), 177.

Following this definition, the right to an independent and impartial court would have to be (I) accepted and recognized by the international community of States as a whole and (II) accepted as peremptory. The widespread ratification that the above-mentioned Art. 14 ICCPR has received[1464] is but one suggestion for a broad acceptance of the independence of courts as a right by the international community.[1465] It can nevertheless not be deduced from those sources that this right is also perceived by the international community as peremptory. Whereas the non-derogable nature of a right is a strong indication also of its peremptory character, it is not a necessary characteristic.[1466] The instruments mentioned above do not provide the required basis for a conclusion that States would consider the right to an independent judiciary as a peremptory norm. Indeed very few norms have been given this status,[1467] and although some voices have been raised in favour of considering due process guarantees[1468] and the right to fair trial[1469] as peremptory, this can only be considered a development in progress but not finite.

1464 At the time of writing the ICCPR had 167 parties. See 'International Covenant on Civil and Political Rights – Statuts as at 21 March 2014' available at <http://treaties.un.org/Pages/ViewDetails.aspx?src=TREATY&mtdsg_no=IV-4&chapter=4&lang=en> (last visited: 21 March 2014).

1465 The term *international community of States* does not demand that all existing States support the norm in question. Instead it is sufficient that all the essential components of the international community recognize it, which in practice would mean nearly all States: see Hannikainen, Lauri, *Peremptory Norms (Jus Cogens) in International Law – Historical Development, Criteria, Present Status* (Lakimiesliiton Kustannus Helsinki 1988), 211. See also Frowein, 'Ius Cogens'.

1466 Orakhelashvili, Alexander, 'The Impact of Peremptory Norms on the Interpretation and Application of United Nations Security Council Resolutions' (2005) 16 European Journal of International Law 1, 65. The human rights documents mentioned above without doubt contain rights that are not accepted as ius cogens norms.

1467 Malanczuk, *Akehurst's Modern Introduction to International Law*, 57-58.

1468 According to Herdegen: "Even if 'due process' as enshrined in universal and regional instruments of human rights has not fully emerged as jus cogens, the total denial of protection against random sanctions would not conform to peremptory standards." Herdegen, Matthias, 'Review of the Security Council by National Courts: A Constitutional Perspective', in: De Wet, Erika *et al.* (eds) *Review of the Security Council by Member States* (Intersentia Antwerpen 2003), 79.

1469 De Wet, Erika, 'The Role of Human Rights in Limiting the Enforcement Power of the Security Council: A Principled View', in: Wet, Erika de *et al.* (eds) *Review of the Security Council by Member States* (Intersentia Antwerp 2003), 22; Orakhelashvili, Alexander, *Peremptory Norms in International Law* (Oxford University Press Oxford 2006), 60. E. De Wet goes even as far as stating that: "it

(4) Conclusions

As the above analyses has shown, the right to a hearing by an independent and impartial court is a human right which has the character of a non-derogable right but which has not gained the status of a peremptory norm. As a consequence the UNSC is not only called upon to respect the independence of the *ad hoc* Tribunals pursuant to Art. 24(2) UNC,[1470] but is bound by it and has to respect it even when exercising its powers under Chapter VII UNC. This is in accordance with what the UNSG stated in his report preparing for the establishment of the ICTY, namely that the Tribunal

> "would, of course, have to perform its functions independently of political considerations; it would not be subject to the authority or control of the Security Council with regard to the performance of its judicial functions."[1471]

Only in exceptional cases may the UNSC strike a balance in an individual case between the overarching aim of maintaining peace and the observance of the independence of the Tribunals in favour of the former. This could be avoided in its entirety only if and when the principle of independence in criminal proceedings had also gained the character of a peremptory norm. Although the development points in this direction, this is not the case yet. By way of conclusion, it may also be questioned if the necessary majorities would be reached in the UNSC for decisions that overtly violate the *ad hoc* Tribunals' independence.

2. The Composition of the Tribunals

a) The Organs of the Tribunals

According to Art. 11 ICTY-S and Art. 10 Statute of the ICTR (ICTR-S) the *ad hoc* Tribunals consist of three main organs: (I) the Chambers, which comprise three Trial Chambers for each of the Tribunals and one shared Appeals Chamber; (II) the Prosecutor, which office was until 15 September

---

is submitted that any measure by the Security Council that undermined the principles of independence, impartiality and even-handedness during criminal proceedings would violate a jus cogens norm."

1470 Read in conjunction with Art. 1(3) UNC.

1471 UNSG, *Report of the Secretary-General Pursuant to Paragraph 2 of Security Council Resolution 808 (1993)*, para. 28.

2003 shared between the two *ad hoc* Tribunals;[1472] and (III) a Registry for each Tribunal, responsible for the administration and servicing of the Tribunals. The Prosecutor is a distinct and independent organ of the Tribunal(s),[1473] and it is the only organ that may initiate proceedings before the Tribunals.

When comparing the structure of the organs of the *ad hoc* Tribunals with that of the ICC it becomes obvious that the former do not have a Presidency as a separate organ. Instead the Statutes and Rules of Procedure and Evidence distribute the functions between the President and the Bureaus of the Tribunals. The Presidents of the Tribunals shall primarily "preside at all plenary meetings of the Tribunal, co-ordinate the work of the Chambers and supervise the activities of the Registry".[1474] He shall further exercise the functions which the Statute or the Rules of Procedure and Evidence confer on him, among which are that he is consulted by the UNSG when the Registrar is appointed,[1475] decisions are made, in consultation with the judges, on pardon or commutation of a sentence,[1476] Trial Chambers are designated,[1477] judges are assigned[1478] and *ad litem* judges designated.[1479] Important functions which are similar to those exercised by the Presidency of the ICC are further performed by the Bureau, an organ which is not provided for by the Statute of the *ad hoc* Tribunals but instead by the Rules of Procedure and Evidence. According to Rule 23 ICTY-S and ICTR-S, the Bureau is composed of the President, the Vice-President and the Presiding Judges of the Trial Chambers. Its purpose is to assist the President in "all major questions relating to the functioning of the Tribunal",[1480] i.e. including those where the President makes the final decision. The Tribunals have thus themselves

1472 On 15 September 2003 a separate Prosecutor's office was installed for the ICTR: see UNSC Resolution 1503. Prior to this establishment a Deputy Prosecutor based in Kigali/Arusha ensured a continuous presence of the OTP on the ground.

1473 Cf. Art. 16(2) ICTY-S and Art. 15(2) ICTR-S.

1474 Rule 19(A) Rules of Procedure and Evidence of the ICTY and Rule 19 Rules of Procedure and Evidence of the ICTR.

1475 Art. 17(3) ICTY-S and Art. 16(3) ICTR-S.

1476 Art. 28 ICTY-S and Art. 27 ICTR-S.

1477 See, e.g., Rules 9 and 62 Rules of Procedure and Evidence of the ICTY and Rules 9 and 15(A), (B) Rules of Procedure and Evidence of the ICTR.

1478 Art. 14(3) ICTY-S and Rules 15(A), 15bis(C) and (D), 27, 28, 50(A), 51 (A), 72(E), 77(K), 119(A) Rules of Procedure and Evidence of the ICTY.

1479 Art. 14(5) ICTY-S. The President of the ICTR may only request the appointment of ad litem judges through the UNSG, Art. 12*ter*(2) ICTR-S.

1480 Rule 23(B) ICTY-S and ICTR-S.

opted to spread the responsibility for the functioning of the Tribunals among the judges, instead of gathering this duty in the person of the President and as intended by the Statutes. This way the Tribunals become less susceptible to undue influence, albeit that the functions of the Bureau are of a consultative nature only.

b) Election and Nomination of the Judges

(1) The Legal Framework for the Selection of Permanent Judges

Whereas the procedure for the election of judges to the ICJ can be described as a simultaneous and independent exercise of the UNGA and the UNSC, with regard to the *ad hoc* Tribunals the procedure is successive and interrelated, although both principal organs of the UN are equally responsible for elections to the bench of the Tribunals. The election procedure is initiated by the UNSG who invites Member States and non-Member States maintaining permanent observer missions at the UN to make nominations.[1481] These nominations are forwarded to the UNSC, which establishes a list of between twenty-two and thirty-three candidates for the ICTR and twenty-eight to forty-two candidates for the ICTY. This narrower list is subsequently submitted to the UNGA which elects the judges by an absolute majority.

Assessments of past elections to the *ad hoc* Tribunals have usually led to a rather pessimistic verdict, often citing much of the criticism that has been referred to in previous chapters on other courts. According to W. Schabas

> "[t]he elections themselves do not show the most glorious side of international justice. They involve complex negotiations, often insincere pledges to vote for certain candidates, and commitments by States based on considerations that are far from judicial excellence and the need for the most qualified judges at the international tribunals."[1482]

The strength of the arguments, which are critical of the election process through the UN organs, is enforced by the fact that judges of the *ad hoc* Tribunals serve for only four years, a term which is considerably shorter than that of the other courts analysed in this study and which makes (re-)

1481 Art. 12 bis ICTR-S and Art. 13 bis ICTY-S.

1482 Schabas, *The UN International Criminal Tribunals – The Former Yugoslavia, Rwanda and Sierra Leone*, 595.

election a practically relevant concern.[1483] An indication of the political influence on the selection process is to be found in the nomination procedure. For the election of 14 permanent judges at the ICTY in 2005, the UNSG received a total of 19 nominations.[1484] Not only is this number surprisingly close to the number of vacant seats to be voted on and thus leaves both the UNGA and the UNSC a rather narrow choice. It is also considerably lower than the maximum number of the two nominations every Member State of the UN and non-member State maintaining permanent observer missions at UN Headquarters may make pursuant to Art. 13 bis ICTY-S. The same discrepancy can be observed in numerous other elections to the bench of both the ICTY[1485] and the ICTR.[1486] This indicates that considerable consultations

---

1483 The length of tenure will be addressed in a later section, see *infra* Chapter G.V(1).

1484 UNSG, *Election of judges of the International Tribunal for the Prosecution of Persons Responsible for Serious Violations of International Humanitarian Law Committed in the Territory of the Former Yugoslavia since 1991 – Memorandum by the Secretary-General* (21 October 2004) UN Doc. A/59/438.

1485 Three additional posts on the bench of the ICTY in 1998 were met by 13 nominations (UNSG, *Election of judges of the International Tribunal for the Prosecution of Persons Responsible for Serious Violations of International Humanitarian Law Committed in the Territory of the Former Yugoslavia since 1991 – Memorandum by the Secretary-General* (16 September 1998) UN Doc. A/53/351), for the election of 11 new judges the UNSG received 19 nominations in 1997 (UNSG, *Election of judges of the International Tribunal for the Prosecution of Persons Responsible for Serious Violations of International Humanitarian Law Committed in the Territory of the Former Yugoslavia since 1991 – Memorandum by the Secretary-General* (18 April 1997) UN Doc. A/51/877). For the election of 11 new judges in 1993, the UNSC forwarded a list of 23 nominees to the UNGA (UNSG, *Election of judges of the International Tribunal for the Prosecution of Persons Responsible for Serious Violations of International Humanitarian Law Committed in the Territory of the Former Yugoslavia since 1991 – Memorandum by the Secretary-General* (26 August 1996) UN Doc. A/47/1005).

1486 For elections in 2003 to fill 11 posts on the ICTR the UNSG received only 17 nominations (UNSG, *Election of judges of the International Criminal Tribunal for the Prosecution of Persons Responsible for Genocide and Other Serious Violations of International Humanitarian Law Committed in the Territory of Rwanda and Rwandan Citizens Responsible for Genocide and Other Such Violations Committed in the Territory of Neighbouring States between 1 January and 31 December 1994 – Memorandum by the Secretary-General* (13 December 2002) UN Doc. A/57/492); the posts of two additional judges attracted only five nominations, all from African States (UNSG, *Election of judges of the International Criminal Tribunal for the Prosecution of Persons Responsible for Genocide and Other Serious Violations of International Humanitarian Law Committed in the Territory of Rwanda and Rwandan Citizens Responsible for Genocide and Other*

and collusion must have taken place between States, a fact which must be considered far from the ideal manner of choosing the most suitable individuals for the office.

The prescribed qualifications that a person has to fulfil in order to become a judge at the *ad hoc* Tribunals are rather detailed when it comes to the spelling out of special expertise in the fields of international humanitarian law and human rights law, but are incidentally in conformity with the requirements established at other international courts. Pursuant to Art. 13 ICTY-S and Art. 12 ICTR-S both permanent and *ad litem* judges

> "shall be persons of high moral character, impartiality and integrity who possess the qualifications required in their respective countries for appointment to the highest judicial offices."

Furthermore the Statutes require that, in the overall composition of the Chambers and sections of the Tribunals, due account is taken of the experience of the judges in criminal law, international law, including international humanitarian law and human rights law.[1487]

The selection procedure demonstrates that although the Tribunals are subsidiary organs of the UNSC they are nevertheless closely linked to the representative principal organ of the UN,[1488] the UNGA. It is only the UNGA that conducts a vote in order to select permanent judges to the Tribunals; the UNSC merely has the ability to narrow the list of nominations. This implies

---

Such Violations Committed in the Territory of Neighbouring States between 1 January and 31 December 1994 – Memorandum by the Secretary-General (3 April 2001) UN Doc. A/55/872), nine vacancies were met with 18 nominations in 1998 (UNSG, *Election of judges of the International Criminal Tribunal for the Prosecutionof Persons Responsible for Genocide and Other Serious Violations of International Humanitarian Law Committed inthe Territory of Rwanda and Rwandan Citizens Responsible for Genocide and Other Such Violations Committed inthe Territory of Neighbouring States between 1 January and 31 December 1994 – Memorandum by the Secretary-General* (1 October 1998) UN Doc. A/53/443), six vacant posts were met with 12 nominations submitted by the UNSC to the UNGA (UNSG, *Election of judges of the International Criminal Tribunal for the Prosecution of Persons Responsible for Genocide and Other Serious Violations of International Humanitarian Law Committed inthe Territory of Rwanda and Rwandan Citizens Responsible for Genocide and Other Such Violations Committed inthe Territory of Neighbouring States between 1 January and 31 December 1994 – Memorandum by the Secretary-General* (2 May 1995) UN Doc. A/49/893).

1487 Art. 13 Sentence 2 ICTY-S and Art. 12 Sentence 2 ICTR-S.

1488 *Prosecutor v. Duško Tadić, Appeals Chamber, Decision on the defence motion for interlocutory appeal on jurisdiction*, para. 44.

that the Tribunals do in fact represent more than only a judicial extension of the UNSC and indeed attempt to represent the broader aims of the UN. Consequently, the ICTY has on occasion emphasized the support it receives not only from the UNSC but also from the UNGA,[1489] which participated in the establishment of the Tribunal, takes part in the election of the judges and approves the budget, and which repeatedly encourages the activities of the Tribunal.[1490] The fact that curricula vitae of the candidates are circulated publicly before any selection takes place ensures that candidates are scrutinized by States and NGOs, making the nomination of an unqualified or inappropriate candidate an "unbearable embarrassment for any State".[1491] But even if pre-selection by the UNSC is *prima facie* in accordance with the role of the UNSC as the organ establishing the Tribunals, the function of the UNSC is somewhat more problematic as it can hardly be seen as a neutral third party with relation to the conflicts that gave rise to the creation of the Tribunals. This raises the question of the appropriateness of the influence of the UNSC on the composition of the Tribunals' benches through the ability to exclude certain individuals from the list of nominees to be forwarded to the election body, the UNGA.[1492] The question is legitimate if an organ that has imposed sanctions on parties to the Yugoslav conflict in the past is the right body also to pre-select judges and whether this influence may distort the aim of equipping the Tribunals with the best qualified judges, as demanded by the Statutes.[1493] At least compared to the SCSL, which also functions under the close supervision of the UN, the system for the selection of judges

---

1489 Ibid, para. 44.

1490 See, e.g., UNGA, *The situation in Bosnia and Herzegovina* (20 December 1993) UN Doc. A/RES/48/88 and UNGA, *Rape and abuse of women in the areas of armed conflict in the former Yugoslavia* (20 December 1993) UN Doc. A/RES/48/143, UNGA, *The situation in Bosnia and Herzegovina* (8 November 1994) UN Doc. A/RES/49/10 and UNGA, *Rape and abuse of women in the areas of armed conflict in the former Yugoslavia* (6 March 1995) UN Doc. A/RES/49/205.

1491 According to W. Schabas, this process ensures that the selection process has quality control built into it. Schabas, *The UN International Criminal Tribunals – The Former Yugoslavia, Rwanda and Sierra Leone*, 507.

1492 Kamardi, *Die Ausformung einer Prozessordnung "sui generis" durch das ICTY unter Berücksichtigung des Fair-Trial-Prinzips*, 97.

1493 Critical in this regard are e.g. Schabas, *The UN International Criminal Tribunals – The Former Yugoslavia, Rwanda and Sierra Leone*, 506-507, Kamardi, *Die Ausformung einer Prozessordnung "sui generis" durch das ICTY unter Berücksichtigung des Fair-Trial-Prinzips*, 92 and 98.

is more transparent and there is, although pruned, an election rather than a straightforward appointment of the judges.

(2) The Practice of not Appointing to the Bench Nationals of the Parties to the Underlying Conflict

With regard to the composition of subsidiary bodies the establishing organ usually follows the principle of equitable geographical distribution or in other ways seeks to achieve a balanced composition. Concerning the *ad hoc* Tribunals this is reflected in the demand for "adequate representation of the principal legal systems of the world" expressed in the Statutes[1494] and, regarding the election of *ad litem* judges, additionally requiring the bearing in mind of "equitable geographical distribution".[1495] Thus the requirements are less far-reaching than those established by Art. 9 ICJ Statute, where besides the representation of the principal legal systems the representation of the main forms of civilization is also a separate requirement.[1496]

At the outset, the requirements formulated in the Statutes deserve the same critical assessment as their counterparts enshrined in e.g. the ICJ Statute as a potential threat to independence. The attention that was paid in academic literature to the fact that in the first elections to the ICTY held in 1993 and 1997 no judge was elected to represent the Eastern European Group of States[1497] underlines the fragility of the question of the composition of the *ad hoc* Tribunals.

According to V. Morris and M. Scharf the understanding of the drafters of Art. 13 ICTY-S was that judges should be impartial to the "Yugoslav situation".[1498] As a result of this interpretation, no judges from the Balkan region have been appointed as ICTY judges and no judges from any of the countries involved in the Rwandan conflict in the mid-1990s have been ap-

---

1494 Art. 13bis(1)(c) ICTY-S and Art. 12bis(1)(c) ICTR-S for permanent judges.

1495 Art. 13ter(1)(c) ICTY-S and Art. 12ter(1)(c) ICTR-S.

1496 It has been argued that it could be beneficial for the perceived impartiality of a tribunal if the cultural background is not given any relevance. Kamardi, *Die Ausformung einer Prozessordnung "sui generis" durch das ICTY unter Berücksichtigung des Fair-Trial-Prinzips*, 87-89.

1497 To this group used to belong the former Yugoslavia.

1498 Morris & Scharf, *The International Criminal Tribunal for Rwanda – Volume 1*, 143.

pointed to the ICTR.[1499] Although this approach is, *prima facie*, consistent with the requirement of maintaining the impartiality of the Tribunals it does not accord with the objective requirements posed in the Statute;[1500] if indeed the judges of the Tribunals were to "be persons of high moral character, impartiality and integrity", would it not be a necessary consequence that their nationality does not influence their ability to adjudicate on cases impartially? The choice not to select judges from certain nationalities thus appears to tackle the problem of independence from the wrong end. It should be emphasized that neither the Statutes nor the Rules of Procedure and Evidence contain a nationality requirement to this effect; the question of nationality is usually one that arises only when the question is about *ad hoc* judges, national judges, and appointment of judges of the same nationality. Focusing on the nationality, even if it is done covertly, seems disconcerting for a court where individuals, not States, stand accused of having violated international humanitarian law. This should hold true at least as long as the formulation of the qualifications of judges laid down in the Statutes was intended by the drafters to be more than mere lip service which was expected not to be complied with. Finally, if Art. 13 ICTY-S is interpreted as meaning impartiality from the "Yugoslav situation", which in turn is understood to disqualify judges from the Balkan region on the mere basis of their nationality, it could with some justification be asked if further nationalities could not be disqualified from the bench due to the involvement of the State in question in the "Yugoslav situation", e.g. through the UNSC. The impression must remain that the qualification hurdles established in the Statutes were even by the drafters never expected to be total safeguards for what they demanded.

(3) The Determination of the Composition and Structure of the Chambers by the UNSC

By UNSC Resolution 1166 of 1998[1501] the UNSC decided to increase the number of judges in the Trial Chambers of the ICTY by three permanent

1499 Swart, Mia, 'To Recuse or not to Recuse? How Independent are the Judges of International Criminal Tribunals?' (2003) 28 South African Yearbook of International Law, 187.

1500 Art. 13 ICTY-S; Art. 12 ICTR-S.

1501 UNSC, *The International Tribunal for the former Yugoslavia (ICTY)* (13 May 1998) UN Doc. S/RES/1166.

judges and to establish a third Trial Chamber. Both actions were undertaken with explicit reference to Chapter VII UNC. According to the preamble to the resolution the reason for both the increase in the number of judges and the establishment of an additional Trial Chamber was to enable the ICTY to try without delay the large number of accused and to allow the ICTY to continue its effort to improve its procedures.[1502] In view of this involvement of the UNSC it could be asked whether the UNSC, or any outside organ, should have the authority to change the composition in this way. The mere reference to an obligation of the UNSC to ensure that the ICTY is able to fulfil its judicial function cannot suffice, as even a decrease in the number of judges, and thus the removal of judges, could *prima facie* be justified by the same argument. Furthermore, the UNSC in Resolution 808 expressly stated that the ICTY would be independent of the UNSC "with regard to the performance of its judicial functions." This was based on the earlier assessment made by the UNSG with regard to the legal basis for the establishment of the ICTY. According to the UNSG:

> "[t]he Security Council would be establishing, as an enforcement measure under Chapter VII, a subsidiary organ within the terms of Article 29 of the Charter, but one of a judicial nature. This organ would, of course, have to perform its functions independently of political considerations; it would not be subject to the authority or control of the Security Council *with regard to the performance of its judicial functions*. As an enforcement measure under Chapter VII, however, the life span of the international tribunal would be linked to the restoration and maintenance of international peace and security in the territory of the former Yugoslavia, and Security Council decisions related thereto."[1503] (Emphasis added.)

It can be argued that the UNSC's decision to increase the number of judges and to establish a third Trial Chamber violated those recommendations of the UNSG, and that the UNSC interfered in the performance of the ICTY's judicial functions and thus violated the standard set for its independence.

1502 "Convinced of the need to increase the number of judges and Trial Chambers, in order to enable the International Tribunal for the Prosecution of Persons Responsible for Serious Violations of International Humanitarian Law Committed in the Territory of the Former Yugoslavia since 1991 ("the International Tribunal") to try without delay the large number of accused awaiting trial,
Noting the significant progress being made in improving the procedures of the International Tribunal, and convinced of the need for its organs to continue their efforts to further such progress."

1503 UNSG, *Report of the Secretary-General Pursuant to Paragraph 2 of Security Council Resolution 808 (1993)*, para. 28.

Yet that standard for the independence of the ICTY, and for the ICTR, has to be measured by other yardsticks as well. As stated earlier, the *ad hoc* Tribunals are in a particular relationship as subsidiary organs operating under the supervision of a principal organ. As such, they depend in some regards, e.g. concerning the staffing, on the UNSC. As such the aim of changing the staffing, in particular when made to enable the court to fulfil its functions, is still within the authority of the UNSC pursuant to the relationship between a principal organ and its subsidiary.[1504] Since the effect of this amendment was merely to add three judges to the bench it is unlikely to have affected the Tribunal in its independent decision-making; it nevertheless demonstrates that the UNSC is prepared actively to influence the working conditions of the ICTY.[1505] Furthermore, the actions decided by the UNSC in its Resolution 1166 were preceded by a repeated request from the President of the ICTY, Judge G. Kirk McDonald. In her letter of 16 April 1998 to the UNSG, the President reiterated a request made earlier directly before the UNSC "for an additional Trial Chamber of three judges" in order "to provide accused persons in custody with an expeditious trial and to utilize fully the court".[1506] Seen from this perspective, any inaction – rather than the actual step taken by the UNSC – would have been a far greater involvement in the performance of the Tribunal's judicial functions.

c) Appointment of the Registry and of Registry Staff

According to Art. 17(3)-(4) ICTY-S[1507] the Registrar, who is responsible for the administration and servicing of the Tribunal, shall be appointed by the UNSG after consultation with the President of the ICTY, and the staff of the Registry shall be appointed by the UNSG upon the recommendation of the Registrar. This procedure is further detailed in the Rules of the Tribunal,

---

1504 See *supra* Chapter G.IV(1)(a).

1505 See M. Swart who considers this to be calling the institution's independence into question, Swart, 'To Recuse or not to Recuse? How Independent are the Judges of International Criminal Tribunals?', 188.

1506 UNSG, *Identical letters dated 5 May 1998 from the Secretary-General addressed to the President of the General Assembly and the President of the Security Council* (6 May 1998) UN Doc. S/1998/376, Annex: Letter dated 16 April 1998 from the President of the International Tribunal for the Former Yugoslavia addressed to the Secretary-General.

1507 The following applies *mutatis mutandis* to the ICTR, cf. Art. 16(3)-(4) ICTR-S.

which prescribe that the President of the Tribunal shall seek the opinion of the other permanent judges on any candidates for the post of Registrar before consulting with the UNSG.[1508] With regard to the appointment of the Deputy Registrar and the Registry staff the Registrar is called upon to consult with the Bureau, i.e. the body composed of the President, the Vice-President and the Presiding Judges of the Trial Chambers,[1509] before making his recommendations for appointments to the UNSG.[1510]

As a result, although the President of the ICTY as well as the other (permanent) judges are to be consulted in the appointment of the Registrar, Deputy Registrar and the Registry staff, the ultimate decision on their appointment lies with a body that is external to the Tribunal itself. There is furthermore no duty on the UNSG to comply with the submissions of the President of the Tribunal or of the Registrar, as they are mere recommendations. Hence the staff of the Registry, including the Registrar himself and his deputy, are part of the UN Secretariat, and as such come under the chief administrative officer, i.e. the UNSG.

Moreover, the staff of the Tribunal(s) are not subject to special regulations, conceived only for the purpose of the Tribunal, such as the Staff Regulations for the International Criminal Court or the Staff Regulations for the Registry of the International Court of Justice,[1511] but instead the Staff Regulations and Staff Rules of the UN apply. Although the staff do not have to follow any instructions other than those of the Registrar,[1512] and although the Registry operates under the supervision of the President of the Tribunal,[1513] formally separating the staff from the Tribunal and thus stripping the Tribunal of autonomy in personnel matters is not supportive of but indeed detrimental

1508 Rule 30 ICTY Rules. Cf. Rule 30 ICTR Rules.

1509 Rule 23(A) ICTY Rules; cf. Rule 23(A) ICTR Rules.

1510 Rule 31 ICTY Rules. Cf. Rule 31 ICTR Rules which only demands the Registrar's consultation with the President before making recommendations to the UNSG.

1511 Staff Regulations (adopted 12 September 2003, entered into force 12 September 2003) Official Records ICC-ASP/2/Res.2 and ICJ, *Staff Regulations for the Registry of the International Court of Justice* (approved 7 March 1979, last amended 20 March 2012) available at <http://www.icj-cij.org/registry/en/regulations.pdf> (last visited: 21 March 2014). However, both were modelled on the basis of the Staff Regulations of the United Nations.

1512 Oellers-Frahm, 'Der institutionelle Rahmen: Status, Ausstattung und Personalhoheit internationaler Gerichte – Der IGH, der Internationale Strafgerichtshof und das Jugoslawien-Tribunal im Vergleich', 116.

1513 Rule 19(A) ICTY Rules; Rule 19(A) ICTR Rules.

to the conception of a Tribunal functioning independently of outside influence. In particular, the Staff Rules of the UN merely provide that the staff members in the performance of their duties "shall neither seek nor accept instructions from any government or from any other source external to the [UN]",[1514] which neither excludes instructions from the UNSG nor in other ways refers the staff members only to the subordination of their respective (subsidiary) organ.[1515] This finding is all the more alarming considering the sometimes far-reaching influence exerted by the UNSG in the sense of not merely participating in formulating and developing the objectives of the UN[1516] but also contributing to the political objectives.[1517]

From the perspective of an independent court, the administration of which should not be under the direct influence of any external authority, this constellation is less favourable than, for example, that of the Registrar and Registry staff at the ICC. In the latter case, the Registrar and the Registry staff are part of their own institution and subordinate only to the court president and the other judges. This does not automatically mean that the staff of the Tribunals' Registries are in fact less independent or would pay undue attention in their work to the actions and policies of the UNSG which would influence the Tribunal in question in its decision-making. However, two concerns must be raised. Firstly, this constellation does create the appearance that the Tribunals are not, at least from the perspective of their administrative implementation, functioning independently of the organization that presided over their creation.[1518] Secondly, appointment through an external body creates an obligation for that body to respect the independent functioning of the staff, as they are personnel of an independent judicial institution, and in

---

1514 Regulation 1.2(d) UNGA, *Staff Regulations of the United Nations and provisional Staff Rules* (21 October 2009) UN Doc. ST/SGB/2009/7.

1515 According to K. Oellers-Frahm only the Registrar is allowed to give instructions: Oellers-Frahm, 'Der institutionelle Rahmen: Status, Ausstattung und Personalhoheit internationaler Gerichte – Der IGH, der Internationale Strafgerichtshof und das Jugoslawien-Tribunal im Vergleich', 116.

1516 Cf. e.g. Art. 99 UNC.

1517 Göttelmann, Wolfgang & Münch, Wolfgang, 'Article 101 UNC', in: Simma, Bruno (ed) *The Charter of the United Nations: A Commentary – Volume II* (Oxford University Press Oxford 2nd edn. 2002), 1259; Seidl-Hohenveldern, Ignaz & Loibl, Gerhard, *Das Recht der internationalen Organisationen einschließlich der supranationalen Gemeinschaften* (Heymann Köln 4th edn. 1984), 102-106.

1518 It deserves to be underlined that this system is not mandated by the relationship between a principal organ and its subsidiary organs; cf. *supra* Chapter G.IV(1)(a).

particular a duty not to make use of the administrative powers of the chief administrative officer of the UN, the UNSG, in a way which is detrimental to the independent functioning of the Tribunals.

3. Financing the Ad Hoc Tribunals

The costs of the ICTY and the ICTR "shall be borne by the regular budget of the United Nations in accordance with Article 17 of the Charter of the United Nations";[1519] hence the questions raised in the context of the ICJ's budget apply. A consequence of the fact that the *ad hoc* Tribunals depend on the usual process for adoption of the regular UN budget is that they do not rely solely on the organ that established them, i.e. the UNSC, but also on the UNGA. This direct subordination of the Tribunals to the UNGA in budgetary matters speaks out in favour of a certain degree of autonomy towards the UNSC, and even implies that the Tribunals operate on the same level in the discharge of their responsibilities as the main organ.[1520] The inclusion of a court in the budgetary framework of a political organization has the potential of creating friction, due to the likely discrepancy between needs of the judiciary on the one hand, and the practical possibilities and/or political interests of the organization on the other. Despite such drawbacks, the system does have its obvious advantages compared to the financing of the SCSL, which is entirely based on voluntary contributions, a fact which has created financial shortages and makes the court vulnerable to inappropriate influences and even manipulation.[1521]

Pursuant to Arts. 7(2) and 29 UNC the only limitation on the UNSC in establishing a subsidiary organ such as the *ad hoc* Tribunals is that it deems the establishment necessary. The UNSC was under no obligation to ensure sufficient funding for the *ad hoc* Tribunals before their creation, and thus it would, in theory, be possible to establish *ad hoc* tribunals for which it turns out that no sufficient funds can be made available under the already strained UN budget. However, scholarly writing usually affirms the existence of an obligation on the UN to finance those subsidiary bodies that are being cre-

1519 Art. 32 ICTY-S. See also Art. 30 ICTR-S.
1520 Hilf & Khan, 'Article 22 UNC', 423 fn. 23.
1521 Schabas, *The UN International Criminal Tribunals – The Former Yugoslavia, Rwanda and Sierra Leone*, 623.

ated.[1522] Still the subsidiary organs remain, in this sense, part of the larger UN system, and as such are not immune to the fact that the strained UN budget may lead to the allocation of insufficient funds. However, at least from a comparative perspective, the budgets of the *ad hoc* Tribunals have been relatively high and the Tribunals' budgets are individually far larger than those of the ICJ, the ICC, the ITLOS and the ECtHR.[1523]

Regular Budget					
ICJ	ITLOS	ICC	ICTY	ICTR	ECtHR
46,605,800 USD (2010-2011)	20,398,600 EUR (2011-2012)	111,000,000 EUR (2012)	301,895,900 USD (2010-2011)	245,295,800 USD (2010-2011)	65,810,300 EUR (2012)

V. Personal Independence

1. Tenure and Security of Tenure

a) The Short Tenure of ICTY and ICTR Judges

Permanent judges of the *ad hoc* Tribunals sit for a renewable term of four years.[1524] With this the *ad hoc* Tribunals provide the shortest judicial tenure of all the courts analysed in this study; at least when possible re-election is left out. This condition was criticized early on as being potentially detrimental to the Tribunals' judicial independence,[1525] and it was a decisive reason, coupled with the concerns for independence and impartiality flowing from short terms,[1526] why the Rome Statute set the terms at nine years. The reason

1522 Rudolf, 'United Nations Committees and Subsidiary Bodies, System of', para. 7.
1523 The budget for the biennium 2010-2011 amounts to 301,895,900 USD of the ICTY (217,901,200 EUR; 'ICTY – The Cost of Justice' available at <http://www.icty.org/sid/325> (last visited: 21 March 2014)) and to 245,295,800 USD for the ICTR (177,040,800 EUR; 'ICTR Budget and Staff' available at <http://www.unictr.org/AboutICTR/GeneralInformation/tabid/101/Default.aspx> (last visited: 21 March 2014)). The reasons for the high budgets must certainly be seen in the considerably higher workload of the *ad hoc* Tribunals at least in comparison to the ICJ, the ITLOS and the ICC.
1524 Art. 13bis ICTY-S; Art. 12bis ICTR-S.
1525 Bassiouni & Manikas, *The Law of the International Criminal Tribunal for the Former Yugoslavia*, 806.
1526 Schabas, William A., 'Independence and Impartiality of the International Criminal Judiciary', in: Decaux, Emmanuel (ed) *From Human Rights to International*

behind this short tenure, which it should be noted is considerably shorter not only than that of ICC judges but also of e.g. judges at the ECtHR (nine years), is primarily the *ad hoc* nature of the Tribunals.[1527] When elaborating on the functioning of the Tribunals, members of the UNSC felt that greater weight ought to be given to the possibility of having the "principal legal systems of the world" represented on the Tribunals despite their limited lifespan.

In particular the short term of office combined with the possibility of re-election must be seen as detrimental to the independence of the judges. The shorter the term of office, the greater the legitimate incitement for both the Tribunals (in order to maintain an institutional memory and to provide consistency) and the individual judges (to allow for career perspectives) to seek re-election. An increased number of (re-)elections in turn increases the likelihood that the earlier mentioned risks to independence which are represented by politicised nomination and election procedures eventually materialize into undue influence on the judicial functioning of the Tribunals. In this regard it is unfortunate that the regulation of the tenure of permanent judges does not at least have a ceiling of either the total number of years an individual may serve on the Tribunal,[1528] or the number of permissible re-elections.

There can be little doubt that the tenure of four years is rather too short to enable one to make any substantial contribution to the work of the Tribunals, which on the subjective level of the judges creates pressure to seek re-election.[1529] The system can thus be said to anticipate that judges will seek re-election and hence increases the necessity to be able to rely on the individual judge's integrity as a bar to any improper influence being al-

---

Criminal Law: Studies in Honour of an African Jurist, the Late Judge Laïty Kama (Brill Leiden 2007), 577.

1527 Bassiouni & Manikas, *The Law of the International Criminal Tribunal for the Former Yugoslavia*, 806.

1528 This would remind one of what already applies for *ad litem* judges at the *ad hoc* Tribunals. Pursuant to Art. 13ter ICTY-S and Art. 12ter ICTR-S, *ad litem* judges shall be elected for a term of four years and may be re-elected. However, they are appointed by the UNSG, upon request of the President of the ICTY/ICTR, to serve in the Trial Chambers for one or more trials, for a cumulative period of up to three years. This system was motivated by the interest of not allowing *ad litem* judges to be eligible for UN retirement pensions (Schabas, 'Independence and Impartiality of the International Criminal Judiciary', 508).

1529 Schabas, *The UN International Criminal Tribunals – The Former Yugoslavia, Rwanda and Sierra Leone*, 508.

lowed to have an impact on the decision-making in a particular case in order to please the organs responsible for re-election. Despite these concerns, two reasons that suggest that the risk for the Tribunals' independence may be exaggerated should be addressed. First, the re-election of judges is by no means automatic, and several failed candidatures suggest that there is a functioning control mechanism in place that might separate partial judges from the bench.[1530] However, it cannot with any certainty be claimed that a failed re-election campaign is actually due to shortcomings in the sitting judge or benefits, in the eye of the electoral organs, of the preferred individual.[1531] Second, as highlighted by Judge P. Wald, "[b]ecause the judges will within relatively short periods return to their native countries, they do not appear to invest primary career ambitions in their Tribunal tenure".[1532] As she rightly points out, "many have already completed their main judicial careers; others are performing a public service but do not see their current stint as the launching pad for the next judicial promotion." Following this reasoning the short tenure may have the effect of increasing the utilitarian perception that service on the bench of the Tribunals would mean. The short tenure might be perceived as a signal that any service on the bench is too short for any career ambitions to arise, and instead it is indeed service for the causes underlying the Tribunals' establishment. This argument would, if pushed to its limits, lead to the somewhat unrealistic suggestion that permanent judges should be completely abolished in favour of the use of *ad litem* judges.

1530 Examples include judge Mohamed Amin El-Abbassi El Mahdi from Egypt who was nominated for re-election in 2005 but was not elected (UNSG, *Election of judges of the International Tribunal for the Prosecution of Persons Responsible for Serious Violations of International Humanitarian Law Committed in the Territory of the Former Yugoslavia since 1991 – Memorandum by the Secretary-General*).

1531 Schabas, 'Independence and Impartiality of the International Criminal Judiciary', 508.

1532 Wald, 'Judging War Crimes', 196.

b) The Ad Hoc Extension of Tenure by the UNSC – Exercise of Administrative Authority or Violation of the Tribunals' Independence?

Unlike the ICJ Statute, which allows for judges to conclude any cases which they may have begun,[1533] the Statutes of the *ad hoc* Tribunals do not provide for a similar possibility. This lacuna arose as a problem in the *Čelebići* case[1534] and led to the UNSC interfering and adopting Resolution 1126, according to which three judges were explicitly allowed to "finish the Čelebići case which they have begun before expiry of their terms of office."[1535] The decision cannot just be seen as an indication that it was a mistake for the statute not to allow for continued service to finalize cases, but also as an admission that the four-year tenure was rather short. The same holds true of the numerous cases where the UNSC has decided to extend the terms of office of individual judges, in order to increase the effectiveness of trial proceedings.[1536]

1533 Art. 13(3) ICJ Statute.

1534 See Swart, 'To Recuse or not to Recuse? How Independent are the Judges of International Criminal Tribunals?', 192.

1535 UNSC Resolution 1126: "Endorses the recommendation of the Secretary-General that Judges Karibi-Whyte, Odio Benito and Jan, once replaced as members of the Tribunal, finish the Celebici case which they have begun before expiry of their terms of office; and takes note of the intention of the International Tribunal to finish the case before November 1998." UNSC, *Establishment of an international tribunal for the prosecution of persons responsible for serious violations of international humanitarian law committed in the territory of the former Yugoslavia* (27 August 1997) UN Doc. S/RES/1126 (1997). A further example are judges K. Prost (Canada) and O.-B. Støle (Norway) who were allowed to complete the Popović case which they began before the expiry of their terms of office; UNSC, *International Tribunal for the Prosecution of Persons Responsible for Serious Violations of International Humanitarian Law Committed in the Territory of the Former Yugoslavia since 1991* (16 December 2009) UN Doc. S/RES/1900 (2009). For the ICTR, see, e.g., UNSC, *International Criminal Tribunal for Rwanda* (19 May 2003) UN Doc. S/RES/1482 (2003).

1536 The fact that the completion strategy has put additional pressure on the Tribunals in recent years can only serve as a limited explanation and it is instead another emphasis for the overly short tenure. See, for the ICTY, UNSC, *International Tribunal for the Prosecution of Persons Responsible for Serious Violations of International Humanitarian Law Committed in the Territory of the Former Yugoslavia since 1991* (29 September 2008) UN Doc. S/RES/1837 (2008), UNSC, *International Tribunal for the Prosecution of Persons Responsible for Serious Violations of International Humanitarian Law Committed in the Territory of the Former Yugoslavia since 1991* (7 July 2009) UN Doc. S/RES/1877 (2009), UNSC, *Inter-*

Although the suggestion to let the three judges sit on the case beyond the expiry of their tenure came from the UNSG, and thus not from the organ that has the power to change the working conditions of the ICTY, this example nevertheless bears witness to the rather far-reaching competence of the UNSC to interfere with the work of the Tribunals. There is little doubt that the UNSC does have the power to change the tenure of the judges by way of amendment of the Statutes; the Statutes were both adopted in the resolutions establishing the *ad hoc* Tribunals and are thus open for amend-

---

national Tribunal for the Prosecution of Persons Responsible for Serious Violations of International Humanitarian Law Committed in the Territory of the Former Yugoslavia since 1991, UNSC, *International Tribunal for the Prosecution of Persons Responsible for Serious Violations of International Humanitarian Law Committed in the Territory of the Former Yugoslavia since 1991* (29 June 2010) UN Doc. S/RES/1931 (2010), UNSC, *International Tribunal for the Prosecution of Persons Responsible for Serious Violations of International Humanitarian Law Committed in the Territory of the Former Yugoslavia since 1991* (29 June 2011) UN Doc. S/RES/1993 (2011). For the ICTR, see UNSC, *International Criminal Tribunal for the Prosecution of Persons Responsible for Genocide and Other Serious Violations of International Humanitarian Law Committed in the Territory of Rwanda and Rwandan Citizens Responsible for Genocide and Other Such Violations Committed in the Territory of Neighbouring States between 1 January and 31 December 1994* (13 June 2006) UN Doc. S/RES/1684 (2006), UNSC, *International Criminal Tribunal for the Prosecution of Persons Responsible for Genocide and Other Serious Violations of International Humanitarian Law Committed in the Territory of Rwanda and Rwandan Citizens Responsible for Genocide and Other Such Violations Committed in the Territory of Neighbouring States between 1 January and 31 December 1994* (18 July 2008) UN Doc. S/RES/1824 (2008), UNSC, *International Criminal Tribunal for the Prosecution of Persons Responsible for Genocide and Other Serious Violations of International Humanitarian Law Committed in the Territory of Rwanda and Rwandan Citizens Responsible for Genocide and Other Such Violations Committed in the Territory of Neighbouring States between 1 January and 31 December 1994* (7 July 2009) UN Doc. S/RES/1878 (2009), UNSC, *International Criminal Tribunal for the Prosecution of Persons Responsible for Genocide and Other Serious Violations of International Humanitarian Law Committed in the Territory of Rwanda and Rwandan Citizens Responsible for Genocide and Other Such Violations Committed in the Territory of Neighbouring States between 1 January and 31 December 1994* (29 June 2010) UN Doc. S/RES/1932 (2010), UNSC, *International Criminal Tribunal for the Prosecution of Persons Responsible for Genocide and Other Serious Violations of International Humanitarian Law Committed in the Territory of Rwanda and Rwandan Citizens Responsible for Genocide and Other Such Violations Committed in the Territory of Neighbouring States between 1 January and 31 December 1994* (21 December 2011) UN Doc. S/RES/2029 (2011).

ment following the same procedure.[1537] However, to interfere in an individual case might raise questions regarding the degree of respect the UNSC has for the working of the Tribunals. It can be argued that the above-mentioned example was not detrimental to the functioning of the Tribunal in the particular case. On the contrary, the decision might even have increased it by allowing judges most familiar with the circumstances of the case to continue and take part in the decision-making. But it raises the question whether the UNSC could for example decide to replace an individual judge, or the entire bench, in a particular case for (apparent or hidden) political reasons. If it can be shown that the UNSC actually intended to interfere with the judicial function rather than make an administrative decision as in the above-mentioned example, this would violate the judicial independence of the Tribunals it is called upon to respect.[1538]

The extensive practice of recent years in prolonging the terms of office of *ad litem* judges, i.e. judges who are appointed by the UNSG at the request of the Presidents of the Tribunals to sit on one or more specific trials, points in the same direction.[1539] Some such *ad litem* judges have served considerably longer on the Tribunals than was originally envisaged, in part due to the increased need for their services in order for the Tribunals to achieve the goal of the completion strategies. By extending their terms of office, and even to allow for their re-election, the independence of *ad litem* judges, who are effectively employed on a contractual basis, is put under increasing pressure. Overall, by having to request the political organs of the UN for support in this way in order to maintain even a basic judicial need such as sufficient capacity at the Tribunals, the *ad hoc* Tribunals become unduly dependent

---

1537 Cf. also what was said above on the powers of the UNSC in its capacity as the mother organ to the *ad hoc* Tribunals as subsidiary organs, *supra* Chapter G.IV(1)(a).

1538 Cf. UNSG, *Report of the Secretary-General Pursuant to Paragraph 2 of Security Council Resolution 808 (1993)*, para. 28.

1539 As examples may be mentioned, for the ICTY, UNSC, *International Tribunal for the Prosecution of Persons Responsible for Serious Violations of International Humanitarian Law Committed in the Territory of the Former Yugoslavia since 1991*, and, for the ICTR, UNSC, *International Criminal Tribunal for the Prosecution of Persons Responsible for Genocide and Other Serious Violations of International Humanitarian Law Committed in the Territory of Rwanda and Rwandan Citizens Responsible for Genocide and Other Such Violations Committed in the Territory of Neighbouring States between 1 January and 31 December 1994*.

on an outside decision-making process for actions that should be rather self-evident.

c) Removal from Office

Although it is frequently considered one of the most significant indications of the assurance of judges' independence, the Statutes of the *ad hoc* Tribunals do not address the issue of dismissal or removal from office.[1540] Important questions such as which organ is authorized to decide such steps and under what preconditions are hence left unregulated and leave an uncomfortable opening for diverse interpretations that potentially threaten the judicial independence of those Tribunals. The lack of clarity with respect to the legal framework of the *ad hoc* Tribunals must therefore be seen as a significant lacuna in the Statutes. Seen from the perspective of the individual judges it would in particular have been important to anticipate what might constitute sufficient grounds for removal from office in order for them to take the necessary steps *ex officio*. From the perspective of the court as a whole, and its perceived independence, it is all the more important that the *ad hoc* Tribunals are equipped with the procedure necessary to deal adequately with any obstacles to its efficient functioning. This does not inevitably mean that the Tribunal itself, i.e. the other judges, must be the responsible organ. But it does imply that procedures and the grounds for such swift procedures should be in place in order for them to be utilized when and if it becomes necessary.

The question of dismissal was raised before the ICTY but the Tribunal did not decide it at the time. In the case of *Delalić et al.*[1541] the defence had argued that the UNSC had the authority to dismiss judges. Whereas the majority of the Bureau avoided a decision on the issue, Judge M. Shahabuddeen in a separate declaration rejected the argument that the ICTY, as a subsidiary organ, would with respect to the removal of judges be under the authority of the UNSC. As a matter of fact, there is indeed nothing in the ICTY-S, or

1540 Disqualifying judges from sitting in individual cases will be dealt with separately: see *infra* Chapter G.V(3).

1541 *Prosecutor v. Zejnil Delalić, Zdravko Mucić (aka "Pavo"), Hazim Delić and Esad Landžo (aka "Zenga"), Decision of the Bureau on Motion to disqualify Judges pursuant to Rule 15 or in the Alternative that certain Judges recuse themselves* (ICTY) Case No. IT-96-21-A (25 October 1999).

the ICTR-S, to attribute the responsibility for removing judges due to a loss of essential qualifications either to the UNSC or to the UNGA. Judge M. Shahabuddeen in his declaration concludes that the UNSC, despite having established the Tribunal and despite its power to amend the ICTY-S, cannot remove a judge without authorization in the Statute and, more importantly, without amending it. Any other interpretation would, in his opinion, violate the nature of the ICTY "as an independent and truly judicial body."[1542] A contrary view is formulated by W. Schabas in his treatise on the UN's international criminal tribunals, where he states that it is "probably a general principle of law that where no mechanism is established to remove an office-holder, the authority for removal resides with the body that appointed the office-holder".[1543] Whereas this position might be applicable regarding political institutions, such as international organisations, it does not pay tribute to the special nature of the *ad hoc* Tribunals, which, as outlined above,[1544] merits special treatment. Two reasons in particular contradict this. First, the other international courts analysed in this study have not opted for a system whereby the appointing organ would also be the one responsible, and authorized, to dismiss a judge. Instead the common practice appears to be a rule according to which such questions are left to the relevant court itself, above all to the *other* judges.[1545] Secondly, even if one were to refer this responsibility to the UNGA, which is the appointing organ in the case of the *ad hoc* Tribunals, one is still left with the task of determining the procedure to be observed in removing a particular judge, including the majority requirements for such decisions and whether the appointing organ's decision shall be the sole basis for a finding on the removal of a judge. In this regard, no

---

1542 *Prosecutor v. Zejnil Delalić, Zdravko Mucić (aka "Pavo"), Hazim Delić and Esad Landžo (aka "Zenga"), Decision of the Bureau on Motion to disqualify Judges pursuant to Rule 15 or in the Alternative that certain Judges recuse themselves, Declaration of Judge Shahabuddeen* (ICTY) Case No. IT-96-21-A (25 October 1999), 4. Judge M. Shahabuddeen here cites the ICJ, *Effect of Awards of Compensation Made by the United Nations Administrative Tribunal (Advisory Opinion)*, 53.

1543 Schabas, *The UN International Criminal Tribunals – The Former Yugoslavia, Rwanda and Sierra Leone*, 510. According to W. Schabas, if the ICTY and ICTR judges could be removed by the UNGA, this "would probably not shock the 'ordinary person'".

1544 See above on the consequences flowing from the characterization of the Tribunals as subsidiary organs, *supra* Chapter G.IV(1)(a).

1545 Even in the system of the ICC, where the ASP is involved, the removal must at least be recommended by the judges.

general rule can be identified, although based on the requirements applicable at the courts analysed so far in this study, at the very least a two-thirds majority must be required.

Overall, the opinion of Judge M. Shahabuddeen that neither the UNSC nor the UNGA should have the authority to dismiss a particular judge deserves to be supported. Yet it raises the necessary follow-up question what other organ might have this authority, as it would seem escapist to pretend that removal could never become relevant. As mentioned, a comparative analysis of the courts studied so far reveals a practice that the colleagues of the affected judge, sometimes followed by an additional decision of the appointing body, hold the power of removal. In the case of the *ad hoc* Tribunals, however, the legal framework does little to support this assumption. Rule 24 of the Rules of Procedure and Evidence of the ICTY,[1546] addressing the functions of the plenary, provides that the judges shall "decide upon matters relating to the internal functioning of the Chambers and the Tribunal [and] exercise any other functions provided for in the Statute or in the Rules." The removal of a judge due to a loss of independence can hardly be labelled as a matter affecting only the internal functioning of the Tribunal. But even if the Rules were interpreted in this wider sense, the Statutes of the *ad hoc* Tribunals do not confer on the judges the authority to decide on this issue, and thus a conflict would arise between the Statute and the Rules, which would have to be resolved in favour of the former.[1547] Art. 15 ICTY-S, which establishes the framework within which the Rules of Procedure and Evidence have to operate, provides that:

> "[t]he judges of the International Tribunal shall adopt rules of procedure and evidence for the conduct of the pre-trial phase of the proceedings, trials and appeals, the admission of evidence, the protection of victims and witnesses and other appropriate matters."

Judge M. Shahabuddeen, in his above-mentioned declaration, states that a rule prescribing a judge's loss of tenure due to loss of independence could

1546 Cf. Rule 24 Rules of Procedure and Evidence of the ICTR.

1547 "The rules of international criminal tribunals are an instrument for the application of their statutes to which they are subsidiary; thus, they have to be interpreted in the light of the latter. While these statutes contain only a restricted number of provisions dealing with procedural issues, the rules clarify the relevant norms and set out in detail the applicable procedural law. This is particularly so with respect to the statutes of the ICTR, the ICTY, the SCSL, and the STL." Schomburg & Nemitz, 'International Criminal Courts and Tribunals, Procedure', para. 4.

qualify under the requirement of "other appropriate matters", but that it can "scarcely be regarded as part of any 'rules of procedure and evidence'".[1548] This argument gains support by the fact that Art. 14 ICTR-S emphasizes the procedural link by requiring that the judges shall adopt Rules of Procedure and Evidence "for the purpose of proceedings before the" ICTR. Furthermore, a look at the documents in which the same situation is regulated in the case of the other courts dealt with in this study confirms that the Rules of Procedure and Evidence, which are the instruments in which strictly procedural issues are to be addressed, are indeed not the appropriate setting.[1549]

What remains is the argument that the Statutes of the *ad hoc* Tribunals, although not containing an express provision to this effect, imply that the judges, i.e. the Plenary, are empowered to make decisions as to the tenure of individual judges. However, the fact that Art. 18(1) ICJ Statute, Art. 9 ITLOS Statute, Art. 46(2) Rome Statute and Art. 3(5) Statute of the United Nations Administrative Tribunal[1550] are provisions which deal with the issue of the removal of judges suggests that the absence of such a provision cannot readily be interpreted in the same way. However, the limited comparative overview as well as the fact that the ICJ in its advisory opinion on *Effect of Awards of Compensation Made by the United Nations Administrative*

1548 *Prosecutor v. Zejnil Delalić, Zdravko Mucić (aka "Pavo"), Hazim Delić and Esad Landžo (aka "Zenga"), Decision of the Bureau on Motion to disqualify Judges pursuant to Rule 15 or in the Alternative that certain Judges recuse themselves, Declaration of Judge Shahabuddeen*, 2.

1549 According to W. Schomburg and J. Nemitz, the Rules of Procedure and Evidence deal with "the investigation period, rights of suspects and accused, conduct of pre-trial proceedings, trials and appeals, admission of evidence, protection of victims and witnesses, review proceedings, and general standards for granting pardon or commutation of sentence." Schomburg & Nemitz, 'International Criminal Courts and Tribunals, Procedure', para. 1. It is further important to note that the experience of the Rules of Procedure and Evidence of the *ad hoc* Tribunals, which were changed numerous times by the judges themselves, prompted the creation of a preparatory commission to draft the procedures for the ICC, rather than the judges themselves. See Sorel, 'International Courts and Tribunals, Procedure', para. 16.

1550 Like the Rome Statute, Art. 3(5) Statute of the United Nations Administrative Tribunal provides for double security: "No member of the Tribunal can be dismissed by the General Assembly unless the other members are of the unanimous opinion that he or she is unsuited for further service." UNGA, *Statute of the Administrative Tribunal of the United Nations (as amended by resolution 782 B (VIII) on 9 December 1953, 957 (X) on 8 November 1955, 50/54 on 11 December 1995, 52/166 on 15 December 1997, 55/159 on 12 December 2000, 58/87 on 9 December 2003, 59/283 of 13 April 2005)* (24 November 1949) UN Doc. A/RES/351 A (IV).

Tribunal confirmed that decisions from the (other) judges as well as of an external body are required to remove a judge from office and that only such stipulations assure the independence of the members of a court (in that particular case the UNAT)[1551] emphasizes that this is the most convincing interpretation of the lacuna in the Statutes of the *ad hoc* Tribunals.

d) Excursus: Removal from Office at the SCSL

The legal framework referred to above for the removal of judges from their office is regulated in a similar way in the SCSL. Neither the Statute of the Court nor its Rules of Procedure and Evidence expressly address the question of dismissal or removal of a judge. Although this does not exclusively relate to removal procedures the Rules do, however, state that a judge "may not sit at a trial or appeal in any case in which his impartiality might reasonably be doubted on any substantial ground."[1552] Where it has thus been alleged that a judge is not fit to sit on the bench of the SCSL, the following procedure is provided for. According to Rule 15 *bis* (A) the President of the Court may refer the matter to the Council of Judges, which is the organ of the Court that must be consulted by the President of the Court "on all major questions or matter relating to the functioning of the [SCSL]."[1553] Where the Council determines that the allegation is of a serious nature and is substantiated, the matter shall be referred to the Plenary Meeting which may "make a recommendation to the body which appointed the Judge."[1554] This important provision, which was included by the Court in the Rules at a late stage, to be precise on 24 November 2006, has its legal basis in Rule 24 (iii) which has the same wording as the above-mentioned Rule 24 of the Rules of Procedure and Evidence of the ICTY, namely that the judges shall "decide upon matters relating to the internal functioning of the Chambers and the [Court and] exercise any other functions provided for in the" Statute or in the Rules.

1551 *Effect of Awards of Compensation Made by the United Nations Administrative Tribunal (Advisory Opinion)*, 52.

1552 Rule 15(A) Special Court for Sierra Leone, *Rules of Procedure and Evidence* (adopted 16 June 2002, last amended 16 November 2011) available at <http://www.sc-sl.org/DOCUMENTS/tabid/176/Default.aspx> (last visited: 21 March 2014). As regards the procedure to disqualify a judge, cf. Rule 15 of the Rules of Procedure and Evidence of the ICTY, which will be dealt with *infra* Chapter G.V(3).

1553 Rule 23(B) Rules of Procedure and Evidence.

1554 Rule 15 *bis* (B) Rules of Procedure and Evidence.

The above legal provisions have been put to the test in a case where Judge M. Sow was appointed by the UNSG to sit as an alternate judge in Trial Chamber II of the SCSL, which was responsible for the case against C. G. Taylor. When the Trial Chamber delivered its long awaited judgment in the case on 26 April 2012, Judge M. Sow, apparently without giving any prior notice to his colleagues, made a public objection containing his own rather negative opinions on the judgment that had just been delivered, the proceedings and on the SCSL itself. This behaviour was, in accordance with Rule 15 *bis* (A), referred to the Council of Judges which considered the allegation to be of a serious nature and to have been substantiated, so it was decided further to refer the matter to the Plenary Meeting. The Plenary Meeting issued a resolution "on complaint by Trial Chamber II against Justice Malick Sow",[1555] according to which it decided *pursuant to Rule 24 (iii)*, that the behaviour of Judge M. Sow amounted to "misconduct rendering him unfit to sit as an Alternate Judge of the Special Court", suspended him from sitting in further proceedings and called upon the appointing authority to decide upon the further status of Judge M. Sow "pursuant to Rule 15 *bis* (B)".[1556]

This legal framework and its application emphasize that the other judges are not explicitly authorized to make a decision about the removal of a judge. But the SCSL has apparently considered it justifiable to regulate, in Rule 15 *bis*, that the colleagues of the judge alleged to be unfit to sit on the Court may make a recommendation to the appointing organ. In other words, that the recommendation to the appointing organ is necessary to trigger a removal. It deserves to be emphasised that Rule 15 *bis* (B) is silent as to whether the appointing body can remove a judge; it merely states that the matter can be referred to it. However, as shown in the case of Judge M. Sow referred to above, the SCSL appears to be of the opinion that the UNSG is the body that can "decide upon the further status of" the judge.[1557] Although there are significant differences between the *ad hoc* Tribunals and hybrid international criminal tribunals such as the SCSL, and thus the drawing of comparisons should be made with caution, some lessons can be learned from this. It is

---

1555 Special Court for Sierra Leone, *Transcript: Case No. SCSL-2003-01-T The Prosecutor of the Special Court v. Charles Ghankay Taylor, Wednesday, 16 May 2012, 09.30 a.m, Sentencing Hearing, Trial Chamber II* (16 May 2012) available at <http://www.sc-sl.org/CASES/ProsecutorvsCharlesTaylor/Transcripts/tabid/160/Default.aspx> (last visited: 21 March 2014), 49682.

1556 Ibid, 49683. At the time of writing a decision from the UNSG is still outstanding.

1557 Ibid, 49683.

particularly surprising that the SCSL did not even itself consider that it was authorized to remove one of its judges, irrespective of the close connection between the judges and the UNSG who appoints them. Instead one chose to adopt, in some sense, an overly careful and balanced approach where the collegiate of the judges co-operate with the appointing organ in removing a judge. The Court could instead have based itself on the situation at other international courts and have reserved to itself the right to decide on the removal of its judges from office. It should further be mentioned that the application of Rule 24 (iii) is not just, due to its vagueness, problematic as a justification to remove a judge but also to suspend a judge from sitting, as happened in the case referred to above.

2. Remuneration

For judges of the ICTY and ICTR remuneration, including a pension, follows the system applicable at the ICJ.[1558] The same applies for *ad litem* judges, who for the period during which they are appointed to serve on a Tribunal shall benefit from the same terms and conditions of service *mutatis mutandis* as the permanent judges.[1559] As such the judges are generally well paid and there is, for example, no financial incentive to engage in side activities in order to earn an appropriate income. Linking the terms and conditions of ICTY/ICTR judges to those of ICJ judges is a logical consequence of the *ad hoc* Tribunals being integral parts of the UN system. It means for example that the prohibition on reducing the salary during the term of office of judges equally applies for ICTY/ICTR judges,[1560] since this has not been addressed in the Statutes of the *ad hoc* Tribunals.

1558 "The terms and conditions of service shall be those of the judges of the International Court of Justice." (Art. 13bis(3) ICTY-S) and "The terms and conditions of service shall be those of the permanent judges of the International Tribunal for the Former Yugoslavia." (Art. 12bis(3) ICTR-S.).

1559 Art. 13quarter(1)(a) ICTY-S; Art. 12quarter(1)(a) ICTR-S.

1560 Art. 13bis(3) ICTY-S and Art. 12bis(3) ICTR-S read in conjunction with Art. 32(5) ICJ Statute.

3. Recusal and Disqualification – The Tribunals' Standard of Impartiality

a) The Legal Framework for Disqualification

According to Rule 15 of the Rules of Procedure and Evidence of the ICTY and the Rules of Procedure and Evidence of the ICTR a "[j]udge may not sit in any case in which he has a personal interest or concerning which he has or has had any association which might affect his impartiality." Like ICC judges, the Tribunal judges are primarily called upon to recuse themselves and withdraw from any such case, in which situation the President of the Tribunal shall assign another judge. If a judge does not recuse himself, every party to a relevant case may apply to the presiding judge for the disqualification of that judge. The procedure that follows resembles that at the ICC: the presiding judge is to discuss the matter with the affected judge, after which the question is, in the case of the ICTY, referred to the President of the Tribunal who may, if necessary, appoint a panel of three judges to make a binding decision.[1561] In the case of the ICTR, the Bureau is to make a decision and, if the application is upheld, the presiding judge shall appoint another judge to replace the disqualified judge.[1562] The *ad hoc* Tribunals, together with the ICC, thus provide for a mechanism according to which the parties themselves are able to raise the issue of recusal. This mechanism has been used diligently and has for example led to a change in the previous practice of the Tribunals to allow regular rotation of judges between trial and appellate chambers.[1563] In the *Prosecutor v. Furundžija* judgment the Appeals Chamber of the ICTY established the fundamental test that would apply pursuant to Rule 15 of the Rules of Procedure and Evidence of the ICTY on inappropriate personal interest and association.[1564] Due to the importance of this case as the basis for all subsequent decisions pertaining to the application of Rule 15, the Appeals Chamber's judgment deserves to be analysed in more detail.

1561 Rule 15(B)(i)-(ii) Rules of Procedure and Evidence of the ICTY.

1562 Rule 15(B) Rules of Procedure and Evidence of the ICTR.

1563 See on this Wald, 'Judging War Crimes', 195.

1564 *Prosecutor v. Furundžija, Appeals Chamber, Judgement.*

b) The Test of Impartiality Developed by the ICTY – Factual Background of Prosecutor v. Furundžija

The question put before the Appeals Chamber was whether Judge F. Mumba, the presiding judge of the Trial Chamber in *Prosecutor v. Furundžija*,[1565] was impartial or gave the appearance of bias. The factual basis of the Appellant's allegations was not disputed in essence by the Prosecutor,[1566] but instead there was a difference of opinion on the interpretation of the facts and the relevance of these facts to the appeal.[1567] Judge F. Mumba, who was from Zambia, was elected a judge at the ICTY on 20 May 1997.[1568] Between 1992 and 1995 she was a member of the United Nations Commission on the Status of Women (UNCSW).[1569] During her tenure at the UNCSW, the Commission *inter alia* urged UN Member States to bring to justice individuals involved in rape during conflict in the former Yugoslavia.[1570] The Commission furthermore sought the establishment of a special unit in the OTP of the ICTY that would deal mainly with war-related violence against wo-

1565 *Prosecutor v. Furundžija, Trial Chamber, Judgement* (ICTY) Case No. IT-95-17/1-T (10 December 1998).

1566 However, the prosecution did address some issues that lie on the border between factual basis and assessment of the facts; e.g. the prosecution contends that Judge F. Mumba attended UNCSW sessions in her capacity as a representative of Zambia and not in a personal capacity (*Prosecutor v. Furundžija, Respondent's Brief of the Prosecution (Public Version)* (ICTY) Case No. IT-95-17/1-A (30 September 1999 (public version on 28 June 2000)), para. 6.15).

1567 *Prosecutor v. Furundžija, Appeals Chamber, Judgement*, para. 168. The assessment of the facts will not be described in greater detail here, unless they are of immediate importance for the legal principles applied to those facts.

1568 See the biography of Judge F. Mumba in International Tribunal for the Prosecution of Persons Responsible for Serious Violations of International Humanitarian Law Committed in the Territory of the Former Yugoslavia since 1991, *Yearbook 1997* (United Nations New York 1997), 26-27.

1569 'Commission on the Status of Women – Follow-up to Beijing and Beijing +5' available at <http://www.un.org/womenwatch/daw/csw/index.html#terms> (last visited: 21 March 2014). The UNCSW's mandate is to promote the objectives of equality, development and peace, and to monitor the implementation of measures for the advancement of women.

1570 Resolution 38/9. *Rape and abuse of women in the areas of armed conflict in the former Yugoslavia*, para. 6, reprinted in Commission on the Status of Women, *Commission on the Status of Women, Report on the 38th Session, 7-18 March 1994* (1 January 1994) UN Doc. E/1994/27, 27.

men.[1571] In a number of resolutions the UNCSW addressed the war in the former Yugoslavia, and in particular the allegations of mass and systematic rape.[1572] In particular, the Commission in several resolutions urged the ICTY to prosecute those allegedly responsible for practices of mass and systematic rape and to give these cases priority.[1573] The UNCSW also helped to prepare for the UN Fourth World Conference on Women in Beijing in 1995 and assisted in drafting the "Platform for Action",[1574] the outcome document of that conference. In that document a number of "critical areas of concern" were identified, some of which had special relevance for the conflict in the former Yugoslavia.[1575]

c) The Submissions of the Appellant and the Respondent

The Appellant did not allege that Judge F. Mumba was actually biased or that she would be generally disqualified from sitting as a judge.[1576] However, pursuant to Rule 15 actual bias is not required for disqualification, but instead a personal interest or any past association which might affect a judge's im-

---

1571 For example, in Resolution 38/9, entitled *Rape and abuse of women in the areas of armed conflict in the former Yugoslavia*, the Commission strongly condemns the practice of rape and abuse of women and children, declares it to be a heinous crime, demands its immediate cessation, urges punishment of the perpetrators, especially through the ICTY, with full cooperation of States, and requests support to victims of the practice. Ibid.

1572 Ibid.

1573 E.g. Resolutions 37/3. *Rape and abuse of women in the territory of the former Yugoslavia* (reprinted in Commission on the Status of Women, *Commission on the Status of Women, Report on the 37th Session, 17-26 March 1993* (28 May 1993) UN Doc. E/1993/27) and 39/4. *Rape and abuse of women in the areas of armed conflict in the former Yugoslavia* (reprinted in Commission on the Status of Women, *Commission on the Status of Women, Report on the 39th Session, 15 March-7 April 1995* (1 January 1995) UN Doc. E/1995/26).

1574 United Nations Commission on the Status of Women, *Fourth World Conference on Women, Platform for Action* (17 October 1995) UN Doc. A/CONF.177/20.

1575 These areas included "Violence against women", "The effects of armed or other kinds of conflict on women, including those living under foreign occupation" (i.e. women and armed conflict), and "Lack of respect for and inadequate promotion and protection of the human rights of women" (i.e. women and human rights).

1576 *Prosecutor v. Furundžija, Appellant's Reply Brief (Public Version)* (ICTY) Case No. IT-95-17/1-A (23 June 2000), 48. The defense was careful to underline that the facts in the present case were "very special and very unusual".

partiality is enough. Thus the defence submitted that Judge F. Mumba had a personal interest in and association with the UNCSW, the Platform of Action of the 1995 UN Fourth World Conference on Women and individuals linked to it and therefore should have been disqualified pursuant to Rule 15.[1577] According to the Appellant, in order to determine whether a judge has or has had any association which might affect his impartiality, it must be asked whether a reasonable member of the public, knowing all the facts, would come to an affirmative conclusion in this regard.[1578] In the opinion of the Appellant, the application of this test to the background of Judge F. Mumba would lead to an appearance that she sat in a case "that could advance, and in fact advanced, a legal and political agenda which she helped to create while a member of the [UNCSW]."[1579] The main basis for the claim of perceived bias was that judge F. Mumba was closely linked to the Platform of Action, which called for judicial action by the end of 1998 to reaffirm that rape is a war crime.[1580] As a judgment in *Prosecutor v. Furundžija* would have provided the first opportunity for both *ad hoc* Tribunals to "reaffirm that rape is a war crime",[1581] this was a sufficient basis for holding Judge F. Mumba's impartiality to be in doubt.[1582] Moreover, the Appellant saw in

---

1577 *Prosecutor v. Furundžija, Defendant's Amended Appellate Brief (Public Version)* (ICTY) Case No. IT-95-17/1-A (23 June 2000), 121.

1578 Ibid, 138; *Prosecutor v. Furundžija, Appellant's Reply Brief (Public Version)*, 46. This standard ("well settled principle of law"; *Prosecutor v. Furundžija, Defendant's Amended Appellate Brief (Public Version)*, 136) was derived from American, British, Canadian and Australian case law, citing *inter alia Judges* 46 Am.Jur. 2d (1994); *Decision by the Appellate Committee of the House of Lords, Lead Opinion of Lord Browne-Wilkinson* (House of Lords) 2 W.L.R. 272 (15 January 1999), 12-13 (citing *R. v. Sussex Justices, ex p. McCarthy (King's Bench Division)*, 259); *R.D.S. v. The Queen* (Supreme Court of Canada) 3 S.C.R. 484 (27 September 1997), 103; *Webb v. The Queen* (High Court of Australia) 181 CLR 41 (30 June 1994), 10.

1579 *Prosecutor v. Furundžija, Defendant's Amended Appellate Brief (Public Version)*, 121.

1580 United Nations Commission on the Status of Women, *Fourth World Conference on Women, Platform for Action*, para. 145.

1581 With reference to the Čelebići case by the ICTY (*Prosecutor v. Zejnil Delalic, Zdravko Mucic (aka "Pavo"), Hazim Delic and Esad Landžo (aka "Zenga") ("Čelebići Case"), Judgement* (ICTY) Case No. IT-96-21-A (20 February 2001), paras. 478-479) and the case of *The Prosecutor v. Jean-Paul Akayesu*, para. 598; this was later refuted by the Appeals Chamber; *Prosecutor v. Furundžija, Appeals Chamber, Judgement*, para. 209-210.

1582 *Prosecutor v. Furundžija, Appellant's Reply Brief (Public Version)*, 47.

her participation as judge in the case a direct continuation of the promotion of the goals and interests of the UNCSW and its Platform for Action.[1583]

The prosecution instead submitted that the Appellant had advanced neither any evidence that Judge F. Mumba had a personal interest in the case nor evidence in support of actual bias or partiality.[1584] The prosecution emphasized that the attribution of bias to Judge F. Mumba for her experience from work in the UNCSW would raise a more fundamental problem, namely that it would be in contradiction with the views expressed in the Rome Statute of the ICC, where Art. 36(8) states that "States Parties shall also take into account the need to include judges with *legal expertise on specific issues, including, but not limited to, violence against women or children.*" (Emphasis added.) The Prosecution suggested that this principle ought to apply also to the judges of the ICTY. The legal expertise gained by Judge F. Mumba in her work for the UNCSW was thus not incompatible with her subsequent service as judge at the ICTY, but indeed an asset.[1585] The prosecution went further by claiming that any expertise gained from prior associations and activities could not in itself be a ground for disqualification "when they are in fact part of the very personal qualifications which make a person a suitable candidate for election as Judge."[1586] It was also not conceded that the test for disqualification developed and presented by the Appellant, and which was largely derived from case law from national courts, might be read into Rule 15(A).[1587] That test was, in the view of the Prosecutor, too wide and if, *arguendo*, Rule 15(A) did include such a test, it was not satisfied in the present case.[1588] The prosecution as an alternative developed its own test, which it elaborated on the basis of the *Pinochet* judgment of the House of

1583 *Prosecutor v. Furundžija, Appeals Chamber, Judgement*, para. 170.
1584 *Prosecutor v. Furundžija, Respondent's Brief of the Prosecution (Public Version)*, para. 6.33.
1585 Ibid, paras. 6.2 and 6.54.
1586 Ibid, para. 6.3.
1587 Ibid, para. 6.41.
1588 Ibid, para. 6.41.

Lords[1589] and a case from the Constitutional Court of South African.[1590] According to the prosecution, the standard ought to be whether there was a "reasonable apprehension of bias".[1591] The Prosecutor extended the test by assuming that legal officers are impartial, that their office demands a certain level of legal training and experience and that personal views on general matters, which a judge may have expressed in the past, do not as such constitute a ground for recusal. This taken together, in the view of the Prosecutor, raised the level of proof that had to be provided in order to be successful in an allegation of perceived judicial bias.[1592]

d) The Appraisal by the Appeals Chamber

The judgment in *Prosecutor v. Furundžija* was the first time that the Appeals Chamber of the ICTY was seized of the issue of impartiality concerning one of the Tribunal's judges, and the Appeals Chamber rightly considered the matter to be of "general importance".[1593] In other words, the resolution of

1589 Here in particular the distinction made by the House of Lords between two different types of cases was relevant, namely (1) those where a judge is in fact a party to the litigation or has a relevant interest in its outcome, in which case disqualification is automatic; and (2) those where in some other way a judge's conduct or behaviour may give rise to a suspicion that he is not impartial (*R v. Bow Street Metropolitan Stipendiary Magistrate and others, ex parte Pinochet Ugarte (No 2)* (House of Lords (England and Wales)) 1 All ER 577 (1999), 586c-d (RP A444)).

1590 *President of the Republic of South Africa and Others v. South African Rugby Football Union and Others, Judgement on Recusal Application* (Constitutional Court of South Africa) (7) BCLR 725 (CC) (3 June 1999). The Constitutional Court of South African in turn considered case law from South Africa, England and Wales, Australia and Canada: see paras. 37-38.

1591 *Prosecutor v. Furundžija, Respondent's Brief of the Prosecution (Public Version)*, para. 6.48. *President of the Republic of South Africa and Others v. South African Rugby Football Union and Others, Judgement on Recusal Application*, paras. 37-38.

1592 *Prosecutor v. Furundžija, Respondent's Brief of the Prosecution (Public Version)*, para. 6.49.

1593 *Prosecutor v. Furundžija, Appeals Chamber, Judgement*, para. 173. This determination has not only an intuitive meaning but also a legal one. As stated in the case of *Prosecutor v. Tadić*, the Appeals Chamber has recurrently used this formulation as the threshold for a matter to be addressed by the Chamber even if for strictly procedural reasons a ground for appeal would be lacking, *Prosecutor v. Duško Tadić, Appeals Chamber, Judgement* (ICTY) Case No. IT-94-1-A (15 July 1999), paras. 247, 281.

the matter was deemed to be important for the development of the case law of the ICTY as it involved an important point of law.[1594] The Appeals Chamber initially stated that it was a fundamental human right of an accused to be tried by an independent and impartial tribunal, which is part of the right to a fair trial.[1595] This is reflected in Art. 13(1) ICTY-S, through the requirement that judges shall have high moral character, be impartial and be of integrity,[1596] and in Art. 21 ICTY-S, where the rights of the accused and the right to a fair trial have their basis for the ICTY.[1597] After having referred to a number of international instruments containing a similar requirement of access to an independent and impartial judiciary,[1598] the Chamber turned to an analysis of the extensive case law of the ECtHR on the interpretation of Art. 6 ECHR. Impartiality may, according to the jurisprudence of the ECtHR, be considered from a subjective perspective, comprising the personal conviction(s) of a judge in a particular case, and from an objective perspective, comprising guarantees to exclude any legitimate doubt.[1599] The latter test comprises not only the question whether a judge is "genuinely impartial"

1594 Cf. *Prosecutor v. Milorad Krnojelac, Judgement* (ICTY) Case No. IT-97-25-A (17 September 2003), paras. 6-7. See also *Prosecutor v. Dario Kordić & Mario Čerkez, Judgement* (ICTY) Case No. IT-95-14/2-A (17 December 2004), para. 1031. See also Human Rights Watch, *Genocide, War Crimes and Crimes Against Humanity – A Topical Digest of the Case Law of the International Criminal Tribunal for the Former Yugoslavia* (Human Rights Watch New York 2006), 771-772.

1595 *Prosecutor v. Furundžija, Appeals Chamber, Judgement*, para. 177.

1596 The Chamber here refers to Arts. 2 and 11 Statute of the International Tribunal for the Law of the Sea; Art. 19 Statute of the Inter-American Court of Human Rights; Arts. 36(3)(a), 40 and 41 of the Rome Statute.

1597 The Chamber furthermore refers to the Report of the UNSG on the establishment of the ICTY, in which it is stated that "[i]t is axiomatic that the International Tribunal must fully respect internationally recognized standards regarding the rights of the accused at all stages of its proceedings. In the view of the Secretary-General, such internationally recognized standards are, in particular, contained in Article 14 of the International Covenant on Civil and Political Rights." UNSG, *Report of the Secretary-General Pursuant to Paragraph 2 of Security Council Resolution 808 (1993)*, para. 106.

1598 Art. 10 UDHR, as well as several regional human rights treaties, Art. 6(1) ECHR, Art. 8(1) ACHR, Art. 7(1)(d) AChHPR.

1599 According to the ECtHR in *Piersack v. Belgium*, "[a] distinction can be drawn … between a subjective approach, that is endeavouring to ascertain the personal conviction of a given Judge in a given case, and an objective approach, that is determining whether he offered guarantees sufficient to exclude any legitimate doubt in this respect." *Piersack v. Belgium*, para. 30.

but also whether the judge "appears to be impartial".[1600] Indeed, even if no actual bias can be proven, but it is just appearances which raise doubts about a judge's impartiality, this has been considered sufficient to establish a violation of Art. 6 ECHR. In making this assessment the viewpoint of the accused is important, but it is decisive if the doubts about impartiality are objectively justified, i.e. if one can apprehend an appearance of bias. The Chamber finds that the interpretation of an appearance of bias is somewhat different in various national legal systems. Whereas courts in the UK tend to request a "real danger of bias rather than a real likelihood",[1601] on the basis of an assertion of the relevant circumstances from the available evidence, and thus leave out the perspective of a reasonable person, courts of other common law systems, such as the Supreme Court of South Africa,[1602] the High Court of Australia[1603] and the Supreme Court of Canada,[1604] contemplate whether the relevant circumstances would give a "reasonable" and "informed" person a "reasonable apprehension of bias".[1605] On this basis, the Chamber developed the following standard for the interpretation of the impartiality requirement in Rule 15:

> "A. A Judge is not impartial if it is shown that actual bias exists.
>
> B. There is an unacceptable appearance of bias if:
>
> i) a Judge is a party to the case, or has a financial or proprietary interest in the outcome of a case, or if the Judge's decision will lead to the promotion of a cause in which he or she is involved, together with one of the parties. Under these circumstances, a Judge's disqualification from the case is automatic; or

1600 *Prosecutor v. Furundžija, Appeals Chamber, Judgement*, para. 182.

1601 *R v. Gough* (House of Lords) A.C. 646 (1993), 661.

1602 *President of the Republic of South Africa and Others v. South African Rugby Football Union and Others, Judgement on Recusal Application.*

1603 *Webb v. The Queen.*

1604 *R.D.S. v. The Queen.*

1605 To support this test further, the Appeals Chamber refers to the test adopted by the US Supreme Court in *U.S. v. Bremers et al.* where it was stated that a federal judge is disqualified for lack of impartiality where "a reasonable man, cognizant of the relevant circumstances surrounding a Judge's failure to recuse himself, would harbour legitimate doubts about the Judge's impartiality." (*U.S. v. Bremers et al.* (US Supreme Court) 195 F. 3d 221, 226 [5th Cir.] (1999).) Furthermore the Chamber refers to civil law jurisdictions (namely Germany and Sweden), where not only actual bias may lead to disqualification, but also the fear of bias suffices to challenge a judge. See Arts. 22-23 of the German Code of Criminal Procedure and Sections 13 and 14 of the Swedish Code of Judicial Procedure.

ii) the circumstances would lead a reasonable observer, properly informed, to reasonably apprehend bias."[1606]

In the case of Judge F. Mumba, the question of actual bias was not alleged by the Appellant, and thus no conclusion on the basis of paragraph A could be made. Analysis of the first branch of paragraph B, whether Judge F. Mumba was a party to the cause or had a disqualifying interest therein, according to the Appeals Chamber did not lead to the apprehension of an unacceptable appearance of bias. Judge F. Mumba had not been a member of the UNCSW contemporaneously with her service as judge in the present case,[1607] and the link between her and the organization was in any case not close.[1608] With regard to whether the circumstances of Judge F. Mumba's membership of the UNCSW would lead a "reasonable" and "informed" observer to apprehend bias the Appeals Chamber determined that the threshold for proving an unacceptable appearance of bias must be high.[1609] The Chamber was of the view that a presumption of impartiality attaches to every judge,[1610] and that it is for the Appellant to adduce sufficient evidence to satisfy the Appeals Chamber of the opposite.[1611] In its assessment of the facts the Appeals Chamber was of the view that Judge F. Mumba, when a member of the UNCSW, acted as a representative of her country. Hence she was subject to the instructions and control of her country, and thus any views presented by her before the UNCSW ought to be treated as the views of her government. Furthermore, her prior membership of the UNCSW should be

---

1606 *Prosecutor v. Furundžija, Appeals Chamber, Judgement*, para. 189.

1607 She served as a member of the UNCSW between 1992-1995.

1608 In this case, in the view of the Appeals Chamber, differed from the *Pinochet* case, where Lord Hoffmann while hearing the case was director of Amnesty International Charity Limited, a capacity that was considered to manifest a disqualifying interest. *R v. Bow Street Metropolitan Stipendiary Magistrate and others, ex parte Pinochet Ugarte (No 2)*. The Pinochet Case was referred to extensively by the Appellant, see *Prosecutor v. Furundžija, Defendant's Amended Appellate Brief (Public Version)*, 129-138.

1609 *Prosecutor v. Furundžija, Appeals Chamber, Judgement*, para. 197.

1610 The presumption of impartiality had been recognized by the Tribunal before; in a decision in the case *Prosecutor v. Dario Kordić et al* the Bureau stated that "[a] judge is presumed to be impartial." (*Prosecutor v. Dario Kordić & Mario Čerkez, Bureau Decision "Prosecution's Motion regarding the Trial Chamber's Decision of 12 June 2003"* (ICTY) IT-95-14/2-PT (4 May 1998), 2.).

1611 *Prosecutor v. Furundžija, Appeals Chamber, Judgement*, para. 197.

seen in the light of Art. 13(1) ICTY-S,[1612] namely as indicating experience in international law, including human rights law. According to the Chamber "[i]t would be an odd result if the operation of an eligibility requirement were to lead to an inference of bias."[1613]

e) Appraisal of the Standard Developed by the Appeals Chamber

The two-pronged test for challenges to judicial impartiality developed by the Appeals Chamber has a number of difficulties regarding its application in practice, such as showing "that actual bias exists".[1614] However, these difficulties must be seen as unavoidable and as a necessary consequence of the subjective elements involved in the assessment at various stages. The presumption of impartiality is a central part. The Chamber does not describe what this presumption should be derived from, but the legal basis must be assumed to follow from the preconditions for office as a judge[1615] and are further detailed by the oath of office that every judge has to take.[1616] It would indeed be inconsistent not to adopt a presumption of impartiality in light of the scrutiny that every judge has to go through in the selection process with regard to his ability to divest himself of any irrelevant personal beliefs or predispositions. This of course conversely increases the pressure to have truly functioning "quality control", to use the terminology of W. Schabas,[1617] built into the selection process. In light of the criticism that was raised in earlier chapters of the ability of the selection process, both for the *ad hoc* Tribunals and other international courts, to ensure an independent bench, it is doubtful whether this standard is actually met.

1612 "In the overall composition of the Chambers and sections of the Trial Chambers, due account shall be taken of the experience of the judges in criminal law, international law, including international humanitarian law and human rights law."

1613 *Prosecutor v. Furundžija, Appeals Chamber, Judgement*, para. 205.

1614 Since the Rules of Procedure and Evidence in this part are identical for the two Tribunals, the following conclusions apply to the ICTR *mutatis mutandis*.

1615 Art. 13(1) ICTY-S.

1616 Rule 14(A) Rules of Procedure and Evidence of the ICTY and ICTR respectively: Before taking up duties each judge shall make the following solemn declaration: "I solemnly declare that I will perform my duties and exercise my powers as a Judge of the [ICTY or ICTR] honourably, faithfully, impartially and conscientiously."

1617 Schabas, *The UN International Criminal Tribunals – The Former Yugoslavia, Rwanda and Sierra Leone*, 507.

The presumption of impartiality can primarily be rebutted by demonstrating actual bias. However, as in *Prosecutor v. Furundžija*, parties will be reluctant to claim any actual bias, as this would require dealing with an overwhelming evidential burden. This increases the temptation and relevance of the second principle, the assertion of an unacceptable appearance of bias. Of particular concern will be the test of subjecting the circumstances in a case to the review of an imaginary "reasonable person". This standard obviously seeks to incorporate the traditionally phrased need that justice be seen to be done.[1618] It should be questioned, however, why the Chamber adopts the perspective of an observer who not only knows the facts and relevant circumstances of the case, but who is also aware of the "traditions of integrity and impartiality that form part of the background and apprised also of the facts that impartiality is one of the duties that Judges swear to uphold."[1619] Is not this standard too high, considering the effect the Tribunal has and is supposed to have on the general public? In particular, in light of the difficulty for even the international judiciary to characterize what impartiality entails in its own context, it appears rather ambitious to demand that a reasonable observer know the "traditions of integrity and impartiality that form part of the background". In particular the second half of that quotation, the "background" of which impartiality forms a part, should have been documented as referring to a national legal system, as it was taken from a judgment of the Supreme Court of Canada, which obviously can fall back on traditions and circumstances that are not readily applicable to an international court.

A further point of criticism must be raised with regard to the determination of the threshold that must be met by an Appellant who seeks to rebut the presumption of impartiality attached to a judge. In this context, the Appeals Chamber stated that reasonable apprehension of bias must be "firmly established".[1620] However, this standard of proof is not mentioned in the later parts of the decision, and it is thus unclear not only what an Appellant has to provide in support of his allegation but also whether the Chamber suggests

1618 *Prosecutor v. Furundžija, Appeals Chamber, Judgement*, para. 195.

1619 Ibid, para. 190, citing *R.D.S. v. The Queen.*

1620 Reference is made to *Re JRL; Ex parte CJL* (Supreme Court of Canada) CLR 343, 352 (1986) and *Re Polities; Ex parte Hoyts Corporation Pty Ltd* (High Court of Australia) 173 CLR 78 (1991).

this threshold to be the applicable standard of proof.[1621] Except for a clear statement to this effect, another reason to question this is that the Chamber also used the formulation "high threshold".[1622]

4. Incompatible Activities

The Statutes of both *ad hoc* Tribunals lack any explicit mention of the right or prohibition of judges to exercise simultaneous side activities. Again it is a surprising lacuna which poses a serious threat to the independent functioning of the Tribunals. In particular when tenure, as was addressed earlier, is comparatively short, this increases the need for judges to ensure that their careers do not suffer from a temporary and foreseeably short service in the name of international criminal justice. The lack of a provision on incompatible activities can nevertheless be explained, in part, by the uncertainty that prevailed in the early to mid-1990s as to how an international criminal tribunal established from within the UN system should be structured. Irrespective of this, a review of the legal framework as well as of the documents surrounding the activities of the *ad hoc* Tribunals suggests that the side activities of Tribunal judges are not entirely unregulated and were not even entirely neglected at the time when the *ad hoc* Tribunals began their operations.

The references contained in Art. 13bis(3) ICTY-S, that the "terms and conditions of service ... of the judges of the International Court of Justice" shall apply to ICTY judges, and in Art. 12bis(3) ICTR-S, that "[t]he terms and conditions of service shall be those of the permanent judges of the" ICTY, suggest that Art. 16(1) ICJ Statute is applied to both *ad hoc* Tribunals by analogy.[1623] This means that judges of the *ad hoc* Tribunals are prohibited from "exercis[ing] any political or administrative function, or engag[ing] in any other occupation of a professional nature." This appears rational at least as long as no other special rule overrides such an interpretation. In further support of this, the Advisory Committee on Administrative and Budgetary Questions as early as 29 March 1994, in its review of the UNSG's report on

---

1621 The Bureau picked up this formulation in a decision of 11 June 2003 (*Prosecutor v. Radoslav Brdjanin, Decision on Application for Disqualification* (ICTY) Case No. IT-99-36-R77 (11 June 2003)).

1622 *Prosecutor v. Furundžija, Appeals Chamber, Judgement*, para. 197.

1623 Brubaker, Joseph R., 'The Judge who Knew too Much: Issue Conflicts in International Adjudication' (2008) 26 Berkeley Journal of International Law 1, 120.

conditions of service and allowances of the members of the ICTY, referred to the Under-Secretary-General for Legal Affairs, the Legal Counsel, who "indicated that the judges of the Tribunal were to serve on a full-time basis and thus might not engage in *any other occupation of a professional nature* during their tenure in office." (Emphasis added.)[1624] The Advisory Committee went even further and explicitly demanded the application of Art. 16(1) ICJ Statute in its subsequent report one year later,[1625] which was supported by the UNGA.[1626]

That judges of the *ad hoc* Tribunals are prohibited from exercising any occupation of a professional nature, in particular any political or administrative function, is a demand that abundantly serves to protect judicial independence. In view of the sufficient and secure remuneration of the judges, this requirement is also not too burdensome from the perspective of any private ambitions that the judges may hold.

1624 Report of the Advisory Committee on Administrative and Budgetary Questions, *Financing of the International Tribunal for the Prosecution of Persons Responsible for Serious Violations of International Humanitarian Law Committed in the Territory of the Former Yugoslavia since 1991* (29 March 1994) UN Doc. A/48/915, para. 6. The same statement was made by the Legal Counsel before the first elections of judges to the ICTR: "the Legal Counsel stated that the judges of the International Tribunal for Rwanda were to serve on a full-time basis and thus could not engage in any other occupation of a professional nature during their tenure." UNSG, *Election of judges of the International Criminal Tribunal for the Prosecution of Persons Responsible for Genocide and Other Serious Violations of International Humanitarian Law Committed inthe Territory of Rwanda and Rwandan Citizens Responsible for Genocide and Other Such Violations Committed inthe Territory of Neighbouring States between 1 January and 31 December 1994 – Memorandum by the Secretary-General*, para. 5.

1625 Report of the Advisory Committee on Administrative and Budgetary Questions, *Programme Budget for the Biennium 1994-1995 – Financing of the International Tribunal for the Prosecution of Persons Responsible for Serious Violations of International Humanitarian Law Committed in the Territory of the Former Yugoslavia since 1991* (10 March 1995) UN Doc. A/49/7/Add.12, para. 7.

1626 UNSG, *Report of the Secretary-General – Conditions of service for the judges of the International Criminal Tribunal for the Former Yugoslavia and the International Criminal Tribunal for Rwanda* (22 October 1997) UN Doc. A/52/520, para. 14.

5. Privileges and Immunities of the Judges

That the *ad hoc* Tribunals are part of the wider UN system is also reflected in the regulation of the privileges and immunities of the judges as well as of the Tribunals as such. Pursuant to Art. 30(2) ICTY-S and Art. 29(2) ICTR-S, the judges shall enjoy the privileges and immunities, exemptions and facilities accorded to diplomatic envoys.[1627] The criticism that was raised in the context of Art. 19 ICJ Statute, namely that diplomatic privileges and immunities do not take into account the special position of an international judge, which cannot be equated with that of a diplomatic envoy who represents a government and thus does not need protection from it, applies *mutatis mutandis* in this context. In addition, however, the Tribunals as well as the judges shall enjoy the protection of the Convention on the Privileges and Immunities of the United Nations.[1628] Since pursuant to the Convention the privileges and immunities of individuals are accorded *vis-à-vis* every Member State of the UN, the Tribunal judges enjoy explicit protection that goes beyond that of e.g. ICJ judges.[1629]

VI. Conclusions

The question of judicial independence is particularly relevant at the *ad hoc* Tribunals as their establishment can be traced back to political considerations which have significantly shaped their close organizational affiliation with the UN. The Tribunals were vested with the function of ending impunity, and thus contributing to restoring and maintaining peace in a conflict situation which the UN sought to master with all possible tools, including judicial means. But whereas the duty to harmonize with the remaining UN system

---

1627 According to the UNSG, the judges, the Prosecutor and the Registrar "have the status of diplomatic agents", a terminology that does not appear to be used in a wider or narrower sense than "diplomatic envoys". UNSG, *Report of the International Tribunal for the Prosecution of Persons Responsible for Serious Violations of International Humanitarian Law Committed in the Territory of the Former Yugoslavia since 1991 – Note by the Secretary-General* (29 August 1994) UN Doc. A/49/342, para. 169.

1628 Art. 30(1) ICTY-S and Art. 29(1) ICTR-S.

1629 See Art. V Section 17 Convention on the Privileges and Immunities of the United Nations, which establishes the privileges and immunities of officials *vis-à-vis* "the Governments of all Members."

is one pole towards which the Tribunals are pulled, obligations stemming from *inter alia* international human rights and owed to the individuals who stand trial before them represent a different but no less relevant pole. This ambivalence precipitates not least in the need for the Tribunals themselves to deal with questions of independence and in their public perception.[1630]

As was shown, the right to a hearing by an independent and impartial court is a human right which has the character of a non-derogable right that binds any organ that interacts with the Tribunals, including the Tribunals themselves. On the other hand, the Tribunals are in various ways, and due to their conception as subsidiary organs in the UN system, dependant on the UNGA and the UNSC, be it for administrative purposes such as the extension of judges' tenure when practically necessary, or for their financing. This opens up opportunities for possible adverse influence on the independence of the Tribunals, as it cannot be guaranteed that the influence that is being exerted is merely a fulfilment of necessary functions attributed to a principal organ *vis-à-vis* its subsidiary organ or a hidden attempt to have political considerations influence the judicial work of the Tribunals.

1630 Another example of a case where the impartiality of a judge of an *ad hoc* Tribunal caught the broader public's eye concerned remarks on the legal definition of genocide made by Judge C. Flügge. In an interview with the German newspaper Der Spiegel, Judge C. Flügge (who at the time of the interview was a member of the Trial Chamber of the ICTY in the *Karadžić* case) replied as follows when asked if the Srebrenica massacre could be defined as genocide: "I don't want to discuss this specific case. More generally, however, I do ask myself whether we even need the term genocide to characterize such crimes. Why do we have to draw this distinction in the first place? Does it make it more or less unjust when a group of people is killed, not for national, ethnic, racist or religious reasons, as regulated in our statute, but merely because these people all happened to be in a certain location? … I believe that we should consider devising a new definition of the crime. Perhaps the term mass murder would eliminate some of the difficulties we face in arriving at legal." Flügge, Christoph, 'UN Tribunal Judge on the Karadžić Trial: 'A Victory for Justice'' *Der Spiegel* (7 September 2009). The comments were discussed extensively in the press (see, e.g., Congress of North American Bosniaks, 'CNAB Demands Removal of ICTY Judge Christoph Flügge (10 July 2009)' available at <http://www.bosniak.org/cnab-demands-removal-of-icty-judge-christoph-flugge/> (last visited: 21 March 2014)) and following pressure from different interest groups, Judge C. Flügge was removed from the *Karadžić* case. Yet it is highly questionable whether there was any reason to consider his impartiality to be in doubt. First, he mentioned explicitly that he did not "want to discuss this specific case". Secondly, the reflection on the scope of the term genocide is something that should be expected of a judge, and not surprise.

Something that stands out in the analysis of the protection of judicial independence in the ICTY and the ICTR is that in many regards, such as the regulation of incompatible activities exercised by sitting judges, or the conditions and procedures for the removal of judges, the Tribunals' Statutes and Rules of Procedure and Evidence are fragmentary. In some cases, the Tribunals have been able to fill the lacuna with their own judicature, for example as regards the authority to remove a judge due to a loss of judicial independence. In others, such as the remuneration of judges, a reference to the applicability of the rules of the ICJ system clarifies the legal framework. Whereas the study of the protection of judicial independence at the Tribunals has occasionally revealed high and modern standards, e.g. the transparency of the vetting process of nominations to the bench, in other instances, such as the short and renewable tenure, the chosen system was worthy of criticism. Due to their high workload, the Tribunals have been able to provide an illuminating example of how disqualification due to bias can be assessed in the context of an international court. Whether this standard will be able to establish itself in other international jurisdictions, especially those whose decisions have an immediate effect on individuals, remains to be seen.

Finally, it should not be ignored that the independence of the Tribunals on several occasions has been put to the test. One example is the call of Judge A. Cassese (then president of the ICTY) to the International Olympic Committee not to allow Serbia to participate in the Games unless it helped to arrest Karadžić and Mladić, whom he referred to as "war criminals".[1631] Whereas it is not realistic to demand of judges, even if they are actively engaged in a case, to refrain from commenting on that case in the public, for a judge to describe as guilty a man who has not yet been tried by the Tribunals may seriously question the impartiality that must be displayed by every judge.

1631 Bertodano, 'Judicial Independence in the International Criminal Court', 417.

Chapter H: Judicial Independence in the European Court of Human Rights

I. Introduction

The ECtHR[1632] is in many ways significantly different from the ICJ, the ITLOS, and the different international criminal jurisdictions analysed so far. Not only is the ECtHR different in the sense that it is a human rights court, at the centre of attention in which is the protection of individuals' human rights. But, more importantly, the ECtHR can be categorized as a regional court, very similar to its sister court in the Americas, the IACtHR.[1633] It is based on the will of a group of States which have certain legal traditions in common, such as, on a very basic level, the separation of powers and adherence to the rule of law. As these traditions have a major influence on the consolidation of the principle of judicial independence, this is certain to have implications for the way judicial independence is seen and protected in the common human rights court.[1634] Another reason why judicial independence in relation to the ECtHR deserves special attention is that the Court decides on adherence to that standard for municipal judiciaries in its jurisprudence on Art. 6 ECHR. In this function, the Court has produced a very detailed, although not always consistent, case law on the content of the principle of judicial independence. The importance of this case law is strengthened by sheer numbers: in 2011 more than a third of the judgments in which the Court found a violation included a violation of Art. 6 ECHR.[1635] And it

---

1632 Hereinafter also referred to as "the Court".

1633 The IACtHR will not be dealt with separately in this study. However, due to the resemblance in some respects between the ECtHR and its American counterpart/Sister, reference will be made to the latter where it is helpful to highlight important issues or to refer to alternative solutions.

1634 The same argument of regionalism influencing the arrangement of judicial independence has also been made with respect to e.g. the ECJ, which, however, will not be dealt with in this thesis.

1635 These violations relate to both the fairness and the length of the proceedings before national courts. 'European Court of Human Rights – The European Court of Human Rights in Facts and Figures 2011' available at <http://www.echr.coe.int/Documents/Facts_Figures_2011_ENG.pdf> (last visited: 21 March 2014), 9.

would be contradictory if the Court did not follow the standards it developed for national jurisdictions, in particular as the same individuals appear before both. Furthermore, a court that delivers judgments on respect for human rights by national authorities is inevitably being pushed into the spotlight of political attention. The large number of applications overall, but especially from particular States such as Russia and Turkey,[1636] suggests that the Court's adjudication has real political importance, making it the target of harsh criticism and of allegations of rendering politically motivated judgments.[1637] It is thus desirable to have effective measures in place that protect the Court from any sort of influence that directly or indirectly may be exerted upon it in order to influence its adjudication.

II. Genesis and Organizational Setting of the ECtHR

1. Adoption of the ECHR and the Vision of a Regional Human Rights Court

The first steps in preparation for the ECHR were taken by the Congress of Europe, convened by the International Committee of Movements for European Unity.[1638] There demands for a European human rights convention as the basis for the future community were raised, and included the creation

---

1636 Of the total number of 64,547 applications in the year 2011, 14,465 (i.e. 22.4%) were from Russia, and 8,702 (i.e. 13.5%) were from Turkey. See ibid, 10.

1637 Following the ruling of the Grand Chamber in the *Kononov* case, where the ECtHR decided that a Latvian judgment convicting a Soviet World War II veteran, Vasily Kononov, for genocide did not violate Art. 7 ECHR, the ECtHR was accused of being partial and against Russia. See, e.g., Vermin, J, 'Crossing the line' *Russia Law Online* (26 May 2010). It is also not to uncommon that the ECtHR and its judges are alleged to be "unwilling or unable to understand the concerns of" a particular people, or interferes in the affairs of a country; see, e.g., Slack, James, 'UK judge who went native in Strasbourg' *Daily Mail* (25 January 2012). The headlines of some media reports already reveal the strong emotions that surface when the ECtHR is involved: see, e.g., Morris, Harvey, 'Britain vs. the European Court of Human Rights' *International Herald Tribune* (19 April 2012); Lyle, Tara, 'Is the European Court of Human Rights the Villain it is Being Presented as?' *The Independent* (19 April 2012); Patrick, Angela, 'Don't believe the myth: Strasbourg is doing a good job' *The Guardian* (17 April 2012).

1638 The European Movement was a federation of peace movements after the end of Second World War, cf. The European Movement, *European Movement and the Council of Europe* (Hutchinson London 1949), 38-39.

of a European court to which claims of violations of fundamental rights could be brought. The Political Sub-Committee of the International Committee suggested that members of a future Council of Europe (CoE) should subscribe to a declaration of fundamental rights,[1639] and "[a]n *independent European Court* should be created, to which any member of the Council could refer cases of alleged infringement of the Declaration" (emphasis added).[1640] The Cultural Sub-Committee also considered it "essential for the safeguarding of [human rights] that there should be established a Supreme Court with supra-State jurisdiction to which citizens and groups can appeal, and which is capable of assuring the implementation of the Charter."[1641] From the beginning it was considered "essential to secure the absolute independence of the Supreme Court from all political and economic pressure."[1642] Work in the European Movement was heavily influenced by the UDHR[1643] and, as far as the European Court was concerned, by the ICJ Statute[1644] and the Nuremberg Trials.[1645]

The International Council of the European Movement proposed at its February 1949 Brussels Conference that two institutions, a human rights commission and a court, should be established.[1646] The underlying reason for this suggested dichotomy was a compromise that had to be struck between

---

1639 Congress of Europe, *Europe Unites: The Story of the Campaign for European Unity, Including a Full Report of the Congress of Europe, held at The Hague, May 1948* (Hollis & Carter London 1949), 25.

1640 Ibid, 25. The Sub-Committee reiterated in its final resolution the called for the adoption of a Charter of Human Rights and for the establishment of a Court of Justice to which "any citizen ... shall have redress ... of any violation of his rights as formulated in the Charter." Ibid, 39.

1641 Resolution reprinted in ibid, 89.

1642 See the statements by A. Marc, member of the French Federalist Movement, during the debate in the Cultural Sub-Committee, reprinted in ibid, 81.

1643 Which was adopted in the meantime by the UNGA; Universal Declaration of Human Rights 10 December 1948 GA Res. 217A (III), UN Doc. A/810 at 71 (1948).

1644 Weil, Gordon L., *The European Convention on Human Rights: Background, Development and Prospects* (Sythoff Leyden 1963), 26.

1645 These Trials to the organizers of the European Movement established "a new conception of international responsibility [that] did more than any other event to undermine and shake the notion that the sovereignty of the State within its own territory is unlimited." The European Movement, *European Movement and the Council of Europe*, 113.

1646 Weiss, Claus, *Die Europäische Konvention zum Schutze der Menschenrechte und Grundfreiheiten* (Metzner Frankfurt am Main 1954), 4.

fears that either the court could become or the States remain too influential.[1647] A first draft European convention on human rights and a statute for the future court were thus submitted to the CoM of the CoE,[1648] which on 16 August 1949 referred the task of formulating a convention to the Parliamentary Assembly of the Council of Europe (PACE).[1649] A majority of the members of the PACE supported the view that a judicial organ should make judicial rulings on petitions by individuals and that only the most important cases should be referred to a court.[1650] When the draft was discussed in the plenary session of the PACE the form of judicial protection was discussed in great detail, with some members even rejecting altogether the idea of the creation of a special European human rights court.[1651] These rejections were largely rebutted; and the establishment of the court was justified by the need to enforce individuals' rights.[1652] However, it was conceded that individuals

---

1647 Ibid.

1648 Both are reprinted in Council of Europe, *Collected Edition of the "Travaux Préparatoires" of the European Convention on Human Rights – Volume I – Preparatory Commission of the Council of Europe, Committee of Ministers, Consultative Assembly, 11 May – 8 September 1949* (Martinus Nijhoff The Hague 1975), 296-321.

1649 It began its consideration of the convention on 19 August 1949 in particular in the Assembly's Legal Committee lead by P.-H. Teitgen and Sir D. Maxwell-Fyfe. Ibid, 36 *et seq*. See also Weiss, *Die Europäische Konvention zum Schutze der Menschenrechte und Grundfreiheiten*, 5.

1650 Cf. Council of Europe, *Collected Edition of the "Travaux Préparatoires" of the European Convention on Human Rights – Volume I – Preparatory Commission of the Council of Europe, Committee of Ministers, Consultative Assembly, 11 May – 8 September 1949*, 46-48. The Legal Committee rejected the idea that rights and freedoms under the future convention could be protected by a right of petition to the CoM or to a special committee (see Weil, *The European Convention on Human Rights: Background, Development and Prospects*, 29; Weiss, *Die Europäische Konvention zum Schutze der Menschenrechte und Grundfreiheiten*, 5-6).

1651 For example, M. Rolin, who was chairman of the Committee on Legal and Administrative Questions and between 1959 and 1971 was himself to be a judge at the ECtHR (between 27 September 1968 and 5 May 1971 even as its president), was of the opinion that States could have recourse to the ICJ whereas individuals were in no real need of judicial protection. Partsch, Karl Josef, 'Die Entstehung der Europäischen Menschenrechtskonvention' (1953) 1953/54 Zeitschrift für ausländisches öffentliches Recht und Völkerrecht 15, 645.

1652 See the report by M. Teitgen, Rapporteur of the Committee on Legal and Administrative Questions, reprinted in Council of Europe, *Collected Edition of the "Travaux Préparatoires" of the European Convention on Human Rights – Volume*

should first have to bring their cases to a commission which could decide whether or not to refer the complaint to the full court.[1653] On 8 September 1949 the PACE adopted a draft which was submitted to the CoM,[1654] which forwarded it to the specially established Committee of Legal Experts. The Committee proceeded in its work from the basis of the PACE draft[1655] and the preparatory work of the UNCHR, which throughout 1950 had been working on a draft convention containing binding commitments.[1656] As the Committee was of the opinion that the establishment of a court would be a political choice it was not competent to make,[1657] the PACE's draft was retained without any major changes. The Committee of Senior Government Officials,[1658] convened by the CoM, finally presented the compromise of an optional clause allowing, but not requiring, States to recognize the competence of the court and giving individuals access to a commission.[1659] This draft was again submitted to the CoM and to the PACE, and the latter seized the opportunity *inter alia* to criticise the fact that individuals, groups and NGOs could have access to the court (or commission) only if the State against

I – Preparatory Commission of the Council of Europe, Committee of Ministers, Consultative Assembly, 11 May – 8 September 1949, 282.

1653 Ibid, 284.

1654 Council of Europe, *Collected Edition of the "Travaux Préparatoires" of the European Convention on Human Rights – Volume II – Consultative Assembly, Second Session of the Committee of Ministers, Standing Committee of the Assembly, 10 August – 18 November 1949* (Martinus Nijhoff The Hague 1975), 274-285.

1655 Weiss, *Die Europäische Konvention zum Schutze der Menschenrechte und Grundfreiheiten*, 7.

1656 This work was ultimately to result in the adoption of the ICCPR and the ICESCR.

1657 Council of Europe, *Collected Edition of the "Travaux Préparatoires" of the European Convention on Human Rights – Volume IV – Committee of Experts, Committee of Ministers, Conference of Senior Officials, 30 March – June 1950* (Martinus Nijhoff The Hague 1977), 84; Weil, *The European Convention on Human Rights: Background, Development and Prospects*, 31.

1658 Meetings were held between 8 and 17 June 1950.

1659 It was based on a proposal from Sweden: see Council of Europe, *Collected Edition of the "Travaux Préparatoires" of the European Convention on Human Rights – Volume IV – Committee of Experts, Committee of Ministers, Conference of Senior Officials, 30 March – June 1950*, 212. However, still several countries raised their objection to the establishment of a European Court of Human Rights, e.g. Denmark, Greece, Norway, the Netherlands, the United Kingdom and Turkey, see ibid, 210-212.

which the complaint was directed had accepted such complaints.[1660] Furthermore the court was considered to have fallen victim to excessive respect for the interests of States: the number of judges was to be equal to the number of members of the CoE, they were to be nominated by the States and only one judge was allowed for every State Party. The PACE thus demanded that States should subordinate their sovereignty to a court that provided all necessary safeguards on equity, impartiality and conscience.[1661] Nevertheless a "partial, even inadequate guarantee of human rights and freedoms, [was considered] better than having no guarantee at all",[1662] and thus a new draft was submitted to the CoM, which on 3 November 1950 was adopted by the ministers during their 6th session. The convention entered into force on 3 September 1953 after Luxembourg had deposited the tenth and last necessary instrument of ratification.[1663]

2. Initial Steps – From a Two-Tiered Control Mechanism to a Single Court

The original control mechanism of the ECHR consisted of two judicial organs: First was a ECommHR entrusted with the task of deciding on the admissibility of applications. The goal of this apparatus was to seek a friendly settlement between the parties, and eventually the drawing up of a report on the facts containing its opinion as to whether a breach of the ECHR had occurred.[1664] Second was a court that was to decide on all cases concerning

---

1660 Sir D. M. Fyfe, who in the discussions of the CoM on 7 August 1950 had favoured direct access to the commission for individuals (see Partsch, 'Die Entstehung der Europäischen Menschenrechtskonvention', 650-651) criticized the CoM draft in this regard, calling it "a retrogressive step in that the general tendency of international law has been to emphasize the rights and duties of an individual as a subject of international law." See Council of Europe, *Collected Edition of the "Travaux Préparatoires" of the European Convention on Human Rights – Volume V – Legal committee – Ad hoc joint committee – Committee of ministers – Consultative assembly 23 June – 28 August 1950* (Martinus Nijhoff The Hague 1978), 226.

1661 Council of Europe, *Collected Edition of the "Travaux Préparatoires" of the European Convention on Human Rights – Volume V – Legal committee – Ad hoc joint committee – Committee of ministers – Consultative assembly 23 June – 28 August 1950*, 296.

1662 Ibid, 282.

1663 Cf. Art. 59(2) ECHR.

1664 Cf. Arts. 24-25 ECHR first edition. The final text of the convention signed at Rome on 4th November 1950 is reprinted in Council of Europe, *Collected Edition of the*

the interpretation and application of the ECHR.[1665] After the required eight recognitions of the compulsory jurisdiction of the court had been registered, the first elections to the bench of the ECtHR took place on 21 January 1959.[1666] Pursuant to Art. 55 ECHR first edition the ECtHR on 18 September 1959 adopted its own Rules,[1667] and on 14 November 1960 it handed down its first judgment.[1668]

A number of optional protocols were added to the ECHR,[1669] some that amended it in its substantive provisions,[1670] and some affecting the control machinery under the ECHR. The latter included e.g. the second protocol, conferring upon the ECtHR the competence to give advisory opinions.[1671] Protocol No. 5 introduced a system for altering the term of office of judges of the ECtHR when their home State became a member of the ECHR at a later stage.[1672] More importantly, Protocol No. 8 significantly extended the

---

"Travaux Préparatoires" of the European Convention on Human Rights – Volume VII – Standing Committee of the Consultative Assembly, Consultative Assembly, Committee of Experts, Committee of Ministers, Legal Committee, 3 November 1950 – 15 May 1951 (Martinus Nijhoff The Hague 1985), 48-81.

1665 Cf. Art. 45 ECHR first edition.

1666 Cf. Arts. 56(1) ECHR first edition. On the first elections see European Commission of Human Rights & European Court of Human Rights, *Yearbook of the European convention on Human Rights – 1958-1959* (Nijhoff The Hague 1960), 118-131.

1667 ECtHR, *Rules of the European Court of Human Rights* (adopted 18 September 1959, last amended 6 May 2013, entered into force 1 January 2014) available at <http://www.echr.coe.int/Documents/Rules_Court_ENG.pdf> (last visited: 21 March 2014).

1668 *Lawless v. Ireland* (ECtHR) Application No. 332/57 (14 November 1960).

1669 For an overview see 'Council of Europe – Human Rights (Convention and Protocols only)' available at <http://conventions.coe.int/Treaty/Commun/ListeTraites.asp?MA=3&CM=7&CL=ENG> (last visited: 21 March 2014).

1670 Such as the first protocol adding the protection of property, right to education, and right to free elections, Protocol to the Convention for the Protection of Human Rights and Fundamental Freedoms as amended by Protocol No. 11, adding the protection of property, right to education, and right to free elections.

1671 Protocol No. 2 to the Convention for the Protection of Human Rights and Fundamental Freedoms, conferring upon the European Court of Human Rights competence to give advisory opinions (adopted 6 May 1963, entered into force 21 September 1970) CETS No. 044.

1672 The amendment can be traced back to the Court's proposal of a system whereby one third of the membership of the Court shall be renewed every three years in order to increase the stability on the bench. The previous system led to too large a fluctuation on the bench: see Protocol No. 5 to the Convention for the Protection of Human Rights and Fundamental Freedoms, amending Articles 22 and 40 of the

rules pertaining to the criteria for office and prescribed the individual capacity in which members of the ECommHR sit and established the rule on allowed auxiliary functions such members may serve.[1673] With regard to the ECtHR specifically, Protocol No. 8 added a provision that members of the Court should also sit in an individual capacity and included a limitation on the peripheral positions that a judge might hold, as long as they were not incompatible with his independence and impartiality as a member of the Court or the demands of that office.[1674] These changes were, interestingly, not based on a need for change stemming from the functioning of the ECtHR as such, but instead it was the desire to attain consistency between the ECommHR and the Court that was the driving force behind the amendments.[1675] But the Court still played a rather hidden role and to some extent operated in the shadow of the ECommHR. As far as the clarification that judges would sit in their individual capacity was concerned, the authors of the Protocol acknowledged that the Court had already provided for this in its Rules in the interest of its independence and impartiality.[1676] Protocol No. 8 also extended the size of the chambers of the Court, from seven to nine members, in order to make the chambers more representative of the Court as a whole.[1677] The structural development of the ECtHR[1678] was based to a large extent on considerations of its effectiveness and was often pushed forward by the PACE, which was interested not only in creating the preconditions for the

---

Convention (adopted 20 January, entered into force 20 December 1971) CETS No. 055, paras. 1-5.

1673 Protocol No. 8 to the Convention for the Protection of Human Rights and Fundamental Freedoms (adopted 19 March 1985, entered into force 1 January 1990) CETS No. 118.

1674 Art. 9 Protocol No. 8.

1675 Cf. Council of Europe, *Protocol No. 8 to the Convention for the Protection of Human Rights and Fundamental Freedoms, Explanatory Report* (19 March 1985) available at <http://conventions.coe.int/Treaty/en/Reports/Html/118.htm> (last visited: 21 March 2014), paras. 11 and 43. The reasons for the change of the provisions relating to the ECommHR were the aim to increase the efficiency of the control mechanism, see id., para. 29.

1676 Ibid, para. 43 and Rule 4 of the Rules of Court (which developed over time and was extended to include both independence and impartiality after the Court amended the Rules).

1677 Ibid, para. 45.

1678 Besides the earlier Protocols, Protocol 9 allowed individuals to refer cases to the Court and Protocol 10 adapted the majority requirement for the determination of the CoM of a violation of the ECHR to that of the decision-making in the ECommHR and the ECtHR.

Court to work effectively but also in gradually transforming the Court into a more *judicial* institution.[1679] It must be remembered in this context that the ECtHR until the entry into force of Protocol No. 11 was only one part of the (and not *the*) judicial control mechanism under the ECHR. Besides the ECommHR the CoM itself had a quasi-judicial role, in that it could decide on violations of the ECHR in cases that were neither settled by the Commission nor referred to the ECtHR.[1680] There was thus still a political element inherent in the control mechanism. The most significant amendment to the control machinery under the ECHR followed from Protocol No. 11.

3. The Restructuring of the Control Machinery Through Protocol No. 11

Protocol No. 11, adopted on 20 April 1994, was not an optional protocol like the previous ones, but instead it amended the ECHR and would come into force only upon ratification by *all* Member States.[1681] The reason for choosing an amending protocol was the profound nature of the changes that were suggested to be made to the ECHR control system, which effectively prevented the parallelism of two different mechanisms.[1682] The driving forces behind the adoption of the protocol were twofold: firstly, to reduce the length of proceedings and, secondly, to reinforce their judicial character. The main changes were the establishment of a single, full-time Court; recognition of the right of individual petition; and the jurisdiction of the Court being made compulsory and indefinite for participating States.

The need for reform of the control machinery gradually arose over the decades and became urgent in the 1980s. The early system was designed with the initial membership of ten States of the CoE in mind, and relying on the option for States to accept the right of individual petition[1683] and to accept

1679 Hence Protocol No. 2, on the competence of the Court to give advisory opinions, was initiated by Recommendation 232 of 22nd January 1960 adopted by the Consultative Assembly ("extension of the competence of the European Court of Human Rights as regards the interpretation of the Convention on Human Rights").

1680 See Art. 32 ECHR old version.

1681 This occurred on 1 November 1998 upon ratification of Russia, on 5 May 1998.

1682 Council of Europe, *Protocol No. 11 to the Convention for the Protection of Human Rights and Fundamental Freedoms, restructuring the control machinary established thereby, Explanatory Report* (11 May 1994) available at <http://conventions.coe.int/treaty/en/Reports/Html/155.htm> (last visited: 21 March 2014), paras. 55-56.

1683 Cf. Art. 25 ECHR old version.

the jurisdiction of the court.[1684] However, with the increase in membership of the CoE[1685] and the wider cultural differences among CoE Member States, the number[1686] and complexity of cases referred to the Commission, and hence also to the Court, increased considerably.[1687] Whereas in the early days of the Commission and Court most cases were matters of criminal law, an increasing number of situations adjudicated on by the two bodies dealt with non-criminal matters, such as rights of migrants, property rights, social security and the protection of privacy. Merging the Commission and the Court into one permanent court was seen as a tool to handle the increasing backlog of cases,[1688] to make the supervisory system more homogenous and provide it with a "markedly more judicial character".[1689]

1684 Cf. Art. 46 ECHR old version.

1685 Especially the end of the Cold War and the membership applications of East and Central European countries, for which the human rights system of the ECHR constituted "an important element for the building-up of fundamental rights, democracy and the rule of law", put strains on the system. See Parliamentary Assembly of the Council of Europe, *Recommendation 1194 – on the reform of the control mechanism of the European Convention on Human Rights* (1992) available at <http://assembly.coe.int/Mainf.asp?link=/Documents/AdoptedText/ta92/EREC1194.htm> (last visited: 21 March 2014).

1686 The number of admitted applications to the ECommHR increased in the following way: 5 in the 1950s; 54 in the 1960s; 168 in the 1970s; 455 in the 1980s. Similar increases were registered for the ECtHR and the CoM, see Council of Europe, *Protocol No. 11 to the Convention for the Protection of Human Rights and Fundamental Freedoms, restructuring the control machinary established thereby, Explanatory Report*, para. 21. Cf. Janis, Mark Weston, et al., *European Human Rights Law: Text and Materials* (Clarendon Press Oxford 2nd edn. 1995), 113.

1687 Council of Europe, *Protocol No. 11 to the Convention for the Protection of Human Rights and Fundamental Freedoms, restructuring the control machinary established thereby, Explanatory Report*, para. 19.

1688 The first suggestion to establish a single, full-time court, came from the PACE (Parliamentary Assembly of the Council of Europe, *Recommendation 1087 – on the improvement of the procedures of the European Convention on Human Rights* (1988) available at <http://assembly.coe.int/main.asp?Link=/documents/adoptedtext/ta88/erec1087.htm> (last visited: 21 March 2014)).

1689 Parliamentary Assembly of the Council of Europe, *The reform of the control mechanism of the European Convention on Human Rights, Report, Rapporteur: Mr Vogel, Germany* (15 September 1992) Doc. 6659, para. 5.4: "Finally, this Protocol aims at strengthening the judicial elements of the system." Council of Europe, *Protocol No. 11 to the Convention for the Protection of Human Rights and Fundamental Freedoms, restructuring the control machinary established thereby, Explanatory Report*, para. 25.

However, the reform was not free from scepticism, some of which deserves to be mentioned here. In particular, the fear subsisted that the Court could be inundated with frivolous litigation and exploited for political ends.[1690] The new ECtHR, which although retaining the name of the old court was considered a new institution,[1691] was to function on a permanent basis. The initial worry that the judges of a full-time, permanent court would lose contact with their national roots was refuted by reference to the situation at the ECJ, where the judges have frequent contact at least within their own countries.[1692] The ECommHR was abolished and the quasi-judicial function of the CoM omitted; thus only a purely judicial complaint process was retained.[1693] The Court was vested with jurisdiction in all matters concerning the interpretation and application of the Convention, including inter-State cases, individual applications and the authority to provide advisory opinions. As to the Court's internal structure the number of judges was made equal to that of the States Parties to the ECHR, instead of that of the members of the CoE.[1694] This was primarily symbolic[1695] and emphasized that the Court was an ECHR organ and not a CoE organ.[1696] The rule that no two judges may have the same nationality was omitted with the peculiar result that the nationality of

1690 Council of Europe, *Protocol No. 11 to the Convention for the Protection of Human Rights and Fundamental Freedoms, restructuring the control machinary established thereby, Explanatory Report*, para. 7.

1691 Ibid, para. 58.

1692 Cf. statements by the British ECtHR judge F. Jacobs, Jacobs, Francis, 'Seminar on International Law and European Law at the University of Neuchâtel, 14-15 March 1986: Merger of the European Commission and the European Court of Human Rights' (1987) 8 Human Rights Law Journal, 195.

1693 The CoM retained only the task of monitoring the implementation of judgments: see Miller, Vaughne, 'Protocol 11 and the New European Court of Human Rights' (4 December 1998) House of Commons Library Research Papers, 11-12.

1694 Council of Europe, *Protocol No. 11 to the Convention for the Protection of Human Rights and Fundamental Freedoms, restructuring the control machinary established thereby, Explanatory Report*, para. 29.

1695 As the number of States Parties to the Statute of the CoE ('Statute of the Council of Europe – State of Ratification' available at <http://conventions.coe.int/Treaty/Commun/ChercheSig.asp?NT=001&CM=8&DF=11/07/2010&CL=ENG> (last visited: 21 March 2014)) and that of the ECHR ('Convention for the Protection of Human Rights and Fundamental Freedoms – State of Ratification' available at <http://conventions.coe.int/Treaty/Commun/ChercheSig.asp?NT=005&CM=1&DF=11/07/2010&CL=ENG> (last visited: 21 March 2014)) are the same (47 as of March 2014).

1696 See on the relations between the ECtHR and the CoE *infra* Chapter H.IV(1)(b).

a candidate could amount to a quasi-criterion for election.[1697] The term of office was reduced to a renewable six years in order to increase the rotation on the bench; for the same reason a retirement age of 70 was introduced.[1698] Due to the increased workload, the judges were allowed to be assisted by legal secretaries (i.e. law clerks).[1699] In sum, Protocol No. 11 reinforced the judicial nature of the enforcement system under the Convention.[1700]

4. Functioning of the New Court and the Need for Further Changes

Despite, or perhaps because of, the institutional and procedural changes introduced by Protocol No. 11 the exorbitant increase in the workload of the Court could not be contained, let alone reduced. As a result further changes became necessary and inevitable. In a first step the CoM agreed in principle to additional budgetary appropriations for the period from 2003 to 2005, to allow the Court to recruit a significant number of extra lawyers, as well as administrative and auxiliary staff.[1701] After preparation by the Steering Committee for Human Rights a new draft additional protocol was submitted to the CoM[1702]and eventually opened for signature by Member States on 13 May 2004, and it entered into force on 1 June 2010.[1703] Unlike Protocol No. 11, Protocol No. 14, instead of changing the structure, introduced changes

1697 Krüger, Hans Christian, 'Selecting Judges for the New European Court of Human Rights' (1996) 17 Human Rights Law Journal 11/12, 401.

1698 Council of Europe, *Protocol No. 11 to the Convention for the Protection of Human Rights and Fundamental Freedoms, restructuring the control machinary established thereby, Explanatory Report*, para. 63.

1699 Ibid, para. 31.

1700 Mahoney, Paul, 'Separation of Powers in the Council of Europe: The Status of the European Court of Human Rights vis-à-vis the Authorities of the Council of Europe' (2003) 24 Human Rights Law Journal 5/8, 159.

1701 Council of Europe, *Protocol No. 14 to the Convention for the Protection of Human Rights and Fundamental Freedoms, amending the control system of the Convention, Explanatory Report* (13 June 2004) available at <http://conventions.coe.int/Treaty/EN/Reports/Html/194.htm> (last visited: 21 March 2014), para. 23. These additional funds of 35 million Euro were granted in a decision of the CoM of 17 July 2002, Decision of the CoM, 17 July 2002, 805th Session of the CoM.

1702 Document CM(2004)65) in April 2004.

1703 After ratification of Russia, on 18 February 2010.

to the functioning of the existing control system of the ECHR.[1704] It essentially introduced amendments in three main areas: (I) reinforcement of the Court's filtering capacity by making a single judge competent to declare inadmissible or to strike out an individual application;[1705] (II) a new admissibility criterion concerning cases in which the applicant had not suffered a significant disadvantage;[1706] and (III) measures for dealing with repetitive cases.[1707] These changes, which significantly increase the role and responsibility of the individual judge, are complemented by a number of important amendments such as the extended tenure of judges, the omission of the chance of being re-elected,[1708] the replacement of legal secretaries[1709] with Rapporteurs who form part of a new Registry and who shall assist the single Judge[1710] and a new function for the Grand Chamber relating to the question whether a High Contracting Party has failed to fulfil its obligation to comply with a judgment.[1711] Beyond these changes it is also important to note what was not changed and thus makes the control mechanism vulnerable to influence. One such question is the status of the Registry of the Court and the connection between the Registry staff and the CoE.[1712]

1704 See Council of Europe, *Protocol No. 14 to the Convention for the Protection of Human Rights and Fundamental Freedoms, amending the control system of the Convention, Explanatory Report*, paras. 35-36.

1705 See Art. 27 ECHR.

1706 See Art. 35(3)(b) ECHR.

1707 Scc Art. 28(1)(b) ECHR.

1708 See *infra* Chapter H.V(2).

1709 Legal secretaries under the previous second sentence of Art. 25 ECHR never in practice had an existence of their own, independently of the registry, since the Court was equipped with scientific staff even before the introduction of this provision by Protocol No. 11. See Korinek, Karl & Holoubek, Michael (eds), *Österreichisches Bundesverfassungsrecht: Textsammlung und Kommentar* (Springer Wien 2007), Art. 25 para. 2; Council of Europe, *Protocol No. 14 to the Convention for the Protection of Human Rights and Fundamental Freedoms, amending the control system of the Convention, Explanatory Report*, para. 58.

1710 See *infra* Chapter H.IV(6).

1711 Art. 46(4) ECHR.

1712 See *infra* Chapter H.IV(2)(d).

5. Conclusions

The concept of the protection of human rights was one of the reasons for the establishment of new European institutions rather than one of the effects of their establishment.[1713] A look at the negotiations leading up to the creation of the ECHR and the ECtHR reveals that to a large extent they are built on initiatives by parliamentarians and on idealistic motives.[1714] The negotiations were characterized by a struggle between the CoM and the Parliamentary Assembly, where the former was keen to ensure that it had influence over the future control mechanism. In this sense, the conception of the Court with the influence of the national governments on the composition of the bench was a victory of the CoM.[1715] Conversely, the later revision of the system, including the structural changes brought about by Protocol No. 11, was a significant step towards making the Court a more judicial and independent institution. Despite these efforts, the Court is currently confronted with significant challenges: the number of cases as well as the backlog of cases is steadily increasing; as of January 2012, approximately 151,600 cases were pending before the ECtHR,[1716] an increase of 20% compared to two years earlier.[1717] And although the number of judgments delivered in 2011 (1,157) was considerably smaller than in 2010 (1,499) and 2009 (1,625), this reduction is explained by the Court's new routine of especially examining complex

1713 Weil, *The European Convention on Human Rights: Background, Development and Prospects*, 23.

1714 Ibid, 27.

1715 Cf. the discussions in the sittings of the Consultative Assembly, held from 11 to 16 August 1950, of the report of the CoM, Council of Europe, *Collected Edition of the "Travaux Préparatoires" of the European Convention on Human Rights – Volume V – Legal committee – Ad hoc joint committee – Committee of ministers – Consultative assembly 23 June – 28 August 1950*, 210-351.

1716 'European Court of Human Rights – The European Court of Human Rights in Facts and Figures 2011' available at <http://www.echr.coe.int/Documents/Facts_Figures_2011_ENG.pdf> (last visited: 21 March 2014), 5.

1717 'European Court of Human Rights – Statistics 1/1-30/9/2010' available at <http://www.echr.coe.int/NR/rdonlyres/8699082A-A7B9-47E2-893F-5685A72B78FB/0/Statistics_2010.pdf> (last visited: 21 March 2014) or 'European Court of Human Rights – Pending Applications Allocated to a Judicial Formation – 30/09/2010' available at <http://www.echr.coe.int/NR/rdonlyres/99F89D38-902E-4725-9D3D-4A8BB74A7401/0/Pending_applications_chart.pdf> (last visited: 21 March 2014).

cases and to join applications which raise similar legal questions.[1718] New reforms are thus necessary and envisaged,[1719] but these have to be scrutinized carefully in order not to infringe upon the independence of the Court in favour of (potentially) increased efficiency.

III. The Functions Served by the ECtHR

1. The ECtHR as a Guardian of Human Rights

The ECtHR is a human rights court. It rules on individual or State applications alleging violations of the civil and political rights set out in the ECHR. Its main function is well described in Art. 19 ECHR as "[t]o ensure the observance of the engagements undertaken by the High Contracting Parties in the Convention and the Protocols thereto ..." The ECHR is an international treaty under which Contracting States are committed to securing fundamental civil and political rights, both to their own citizens and moreover to any person within their jurisdiction.[1720] By including in the ECHR an extensive list of rights and freedoms which the Contracting States have committed themselves to ensure, the States have expressed their will to create a common law in the fields of human rights.[1721] In order to ensure this common standard, the ECtHR is established as a control mechanism. The Court functions by

---

1718 'European Court of Human Rights – The European Court of Human Rights in Facts and Figures 2011' available at <http://www.echr.coe.int/Documents/Facts_Figures_2011_ENG.pdf> (last visited: 21 March 2014), 8.

1719 See, e.g., the Conference on the future of the European Court of Human Rights held in Interlaken (Switzerland), 18-19 February 2010, the High level Conference on the Future of the European Court of Human Rights in Izmir (Turkey), 26-27 April 2011, and the High Level Conference on the Future of the European Court of Human Rights in Brighton (United Kingdom), 18-20 April 2012. Some such reforms that have been discussed are the increase of the number of judges on the Court (Tomuschat, Christian, 'The European Court of Human Rights Overwhelmed by Applications: Problems and Possible Solutions', in: Wolfrum, Rüdiger *et al.* (eds) *The European Court of Human Rights overwhelmed by applications: problems and possible solutions – international workshop, Heidelberg, December 17 – 18, 2007* (Springer Berlin 2009), 14) and the limitation of access to the Court (ibid, 15).

1720 Art. 1 ECHR.

1721 Mahoney, Paul & Prebensen, Sørensen, 'The European Court of Human Rights', in: Macdonald, Ronald St. J. (ed) *The European System for the Protection of Human Rights* (Nijhoff Dordrecht 1993), 621.

handing down judgments on the basis of individual applications brought under Art. 34 ECHR and State applications brought under Art. 33 ECHR. The Court's judgments are binding on respondent Parties,[1722] and their execution is supervised by the CoM.[1723] In more than fifty years the Court has delivered more than 10,000 judgments which have had an impact on the human rights situation in all Contracting States, often leading governments to alter their legislation and administrative practices so as to bring them into conformity with the common law under the ECHR. Its nature as a human rights court brings with it two important consequences for the understanding of its judicial independence.

Firstly, the Court, by giving judgments on individual applications, i.e. judgments affecting individuals, is obliged to provide a fair trial as regards the parties and the individual in particular. Borrowing from the reasoning proposed above in the context of the *ad hoc* Tribunals,[1724] on the value of the human right to a fair trial as a customary rule from which no derogation is possible, including access to an independent court, the Court is obliged to be both independent and impartial and thus necessary safeguards need to be in place to ensure this. As a further concern, the expectation of many individuals that recourse to an international court will deliver justice, is remarkably higher in the case of the ECtHR compared to the international criminal courts, and can thus be severely damaged. Whereas individuals can appear before the international criminal courts as accused or witnesses, an international human rights court such as the ECtHR is activated at the initiative of individuals.

The second consequence is that the ECtHR monitors compliance with the human rights laid down in the ECHR, which includes the right to a fair trial by an independent and impartial court (Art. 6(1) ECHR)[1725] as one of the

---

1722 Art. 46(1) ECHR.

1723 Council of Europe, *Protocol No. 14 to the Convention for the Protection of Human Rights and Fundamental Freedoms, amending the control system of the Convention, Explanatory Report*, para. 11.

1724 See *supra* Chapter G.IV(1)(b).

1725 Art. 6(1) ECHR: "In the determination of his civil rights and obligations or of any criminal charge against him, everyone is entitled to a fair and public hearing within a reasonable time by an independent and impartial tribunal established by law. Judgment shall be pronounced publicly but the press and public may be excluded from all or part of the trial in the interests of morals, public order or national security in a democratic society, where the interests of juveniles or the protection of the private life of the parties so require, or to the extent strictly necessary in the

most prominent provisions. The large number of cases where the Court therefore in detail establishes the various components of an independent and impartial judiciary bears witness to the importance that the Court attaches to the principle of judicial independence and impartiality for the assurance of individual rights.[1726] It would be inconsistent and contradictory if the Court did not also follow this standard, especially as the same individuals that appear before the national judiciaries that allegedly violated Art. 6 ECHR also appear before the ECtHR.[1727]

2. The Quasi-Constitutional Character of the ECtHR

It is no coincidence that pertinent academic writing observes that there is a "constitutional component" to the Court,[1728] with some commentators being inclined to call the ECtHR a constitutional court,[1729] a quasi-constitutional court *sui generis*,[1730] and the ECHR, to use the words of the ECtHR itself

---

opinion of the court in special circumstances where publicity would prejudice the interests of justice."

1726 See on the Court's case law on the independence and impartiality of national judiciaries, in Van Dijk, Pieter, 'Article 6 § 1 of the Convention and the Concept of "Objective Impartiality"', in: Mahoney, Paul *et al.* (eds) *Protection des droits de l'homme: la perspective européenne – Mélanges à la mémoire de Rolv Ryssdal* (Heymann Köln 2000); Korinek & Holoubek (eds), *Österreichisches Bundesverfassungsrecht: Textsammlung und Kommentar*, Art. 6, paras. 50-67.

1727 Cf. on this point Council of Europe, *Protocol No. 8 to the Convention for the Protection of Human Rights and Fundamental Freedoms, Explanatory Report*, para. 29: "The second sentence added to the text of Article 23 highlights the qualities of independence and impartiality required of members of the Commission. Article 6 of the Convention lays down the right of access to an independent and impartial tribunal, and it is appropriate that the Convention should also contain similar express guarantees as regards proceedings before the Commission."

1728 Garlickl, Lech, 'Judicial Deliberations: The Strasbourg Perspective', in: Huls, Nick *et al.* (eds) *The Legitimacy of Highest Courts' Rulings: Judicial Deliberations and Beyond* (Asser The Hague 2009), 390.

1729 Bruinsma, Fred J. & Parmentier, Stephen, 'Interview with Mr Luzius Wildhaber, President of the ECHR' (2003) 21 Netherlands Quarterly of Human Rights 2, 185.

1730 Wildhaber, Luzius, 'A Constitutional Future for the European Court of Human Rights' (2002) 23 Human Rights Law Journal 5-7, 161; Alkema, Evert Albert, 'The European Convention as a Constitution and its Court as a Constitutional Court', in: Mahoney, Paul *et al.* (eds) *Protection des droits de l'homme: la perspective européenne – Mélanges à la mémoire de Rolv Ryssdal* (Heymann Köln 2000), 41; Schermers, Henry G., 'A European Supreme Court', in: Mahoney, Paul *et al.*

from the *Loizidou* case, "a constitutional instrument of European public order".[1731] Irrespective of whether one assumes the classification of the Court as a "constitutional court" in an orthodox or in a functional/descriptive sense, it cannot be denied that the ECtHR over the years has gathered recognition for its constitutional function insofar as the Court is charged with the interpretation and application of a constitutional instrument in a specialist field.[1732] This observation is indicative of the compelling need to define the Court's independence as regards States, for whom this constitutional adjudication means a considerable intrusion into their traditional sovereignty. How does this constitutional function materialize?

The ECtHR cannot invalidate national legislation since its core function remains the determination of violations of the ECHR. Yet that does not imply that the enforcement system of the ECHR is solely individual-relief based.[1733] Instead the Court establishes the existence of a violation of the ECHR, after which the enforcement of this finding is left to the bodies of the CoE.[1734] The Court itself has no power of intervention or regulatory power, or the ability to suggest certain solutions to the (national) legislative branches. Judgments of the Court are not formative judgments or annulment judgments but are instead only of a declaratory nature in determining a violation of the obligations under the ECHR.[1735] Judgments sometimes may have the result

---

(eds) *Protection des droits de l'homme: la perspective européenne – Mélanges à la mémoire de Rolv Ryssdal* (Heymann Köln 2000), 1271; Greer, Steven, *The European Convention on Human Rights. Achievements, Problems and Prospects* (Cambridge University Press Cambridge 2006), 167–192.

1731 *Case of Loizidou v. Turkey (Preliminary Objections)* (ECtHR) Application No. 15318/89 (23 March 1995), para. 75. This terminology was repeated in the Bosphorus Airways v Ireland 2005-IV; 42 EHRR 1, para. 156. See also the concurring opinion of Judge Jambrek in *Fischer v. Austria* (ECtHR) Application No. 16922/90 (26 April 1995); and the partly dissenting opinion of Judge Martens, joined by Judge Foighel in *Ahmet Sadik v. Greece* (ECtHR) Application No. 18877/91 (15 November 1996). See further e.g. Ress, Georg, 'Rechtsstellung, Aufgabenbereich und Legitimation des Europäischen Gerichtshofs für Menschenrechte', in: Holoubek, Michael *et al.* (eds) *Dimensionen des modernen Verfassungsstaates: Symposion zum 60. Geburtstag von Karl Korinek* (Springer Wien 2002), 132-133.

1732 White, Robin C.A. & Boussiakou, Iris, 'Separate Opinions in the European Court of Human Rights' (2009) 9 Human Rights Law Review 1, 56.

1733 Wildhaber, 'A Constitutional Future for the European Court of Human Rights', 163.

1734 Cf. Art. 46 ECHR.

1735 See, e.g. *Marckx v. Belgium* (ECtHR) Application No. 6833/74 (13 June 1979), para. 58; *Norris v. Ireland* (ECtHR) Application No. 10581/83 (26 October 1988),

that a State adapts its constitution or constitutional structure, and these are consequences that are typical for decisions by a constitutional court; but they are not necessary consequences. As the Court stated in its *Marckx* judgment of 1979, "[i]t is for the respondent State, and the respondent State alone, to take the measures it considers appropriate to ensure that its domestic law is coherent and consistent."[1736] The domestic laws' coherence and consistency is the goal demanded by the Court; the means to achieve it are left to the respective State. In effect therefore, although a judgment of the ECtHR may, and often does, result in legislative action this is not a necessary or binding effect of judgments in general, making a comparison between the ECtHR and a constitutional court problematic.[1737] But although the effects of judgments may differ from one State to another,[1738] the Court's case law does progress in establishing a common standard for substantive or procedural fundamental rights in the ECHR area, which makes it not only a powerful controller of the exercise of public authority, but an additional proponent of individuals' rights.

IV. Structural Independence

1. The Status of the ECtHR

The legal status of the ECtHR has been unclear ever since the Court's inception. The lack of any clear provisions in the fundamental legal documents on either its status *vis-à-vis* the CoE or its legal personality independent of both Contracting States of the ECHR and the organs and bodies of the CoE,

---

para. 50; Villiger, Mark Eugen, *Handbuch der europäischen Menschenrechtskonvention (EMRK): unter besonderer Berücksichtigung der schweizerischen Rechtslage* (Schulthess Zürich 2nd edn. 1999), 144.

1736 *Marckx v. Belgium*, para. 42.

1737 Ress, 'Rechtsstellung, Aufgabenbereich und Legitimation des Europäischen Gerichtshofs für Menschenrechte', 133.

1738 However, "neither Article 13 (art. 13) nor the Convention in general lays down for the Contracting States any given manner for ensuring within their internal law the effective implementation of any of the provisions of the Convention" See *James and others v. The United Kingdom* (ECtHR) Application No. 8793/79 (21 February 1986), para. 84. See also *Ireland v. The United Kingdom* (ECtHR) Application No. 5310/71 (18 January 1978), paras. 238-239 and *Swedish Engine Drivers' Union v. Sweden* (ECtHR) Application No. 5614/72 (6 February 1976), para. 50.

has been considered unique among comparable international courts,[1739] and it complicates the estimation of the degree to which the independence of its judges may be threatened through possible links to other organs or entities. In particular it blurs the distinction between organizational links that are necessary for the functioning of the Court and undue influences that instead threaten the fulfilment of the judicial remit of the Court. Although the principle of separation of powers may not be transposed in all its aspects from the national context to the international level in general[1740] and the intergovernmental context of the CoE in particular,[1741] the insularity of the ECtHR from encroachment of executive, political organs is nevertheless an important constant for a judicial organ such as the ECtHR.

a) The Legal Capacity of the ECtHR

The first step in assessing the structural independence of the ECtHR is to determine whether the Court has the capacity to be a subject of international law, i.e. the general capacity to fulfil its functions and to act on the international plane, to enjoy rights and be obliged to carry out duties directly under international law.[1742] If this subjectivity was lacking, the Court would have to rely entirely on either the Contracting States of the ECHR or the CoE[1743] to solve important matters such as financing, staff administration or the conclusion of necessary agreements and treaties on topics such as the Court's immunities.

The extent of the rights and duties for any subject of international law follow from the nature of the relevant subject and its positioning in the broader framework of the international legal order. For the ECtHR this legal personality is not mentioned explicitly in any of the documents relevant for

---

1739 Mahoney, 'Separation of Powers in the Council of Europe: The Status of the European Court of Human Rights vis-à-vis the Authorities of the Council of Europe', 152.

1740 Cf. on this *supra* Chapter B.IV(3)(b).

1741 Mahoney, 'Separation of Powers in the Council of Europe: The Status of the European Court of Human Rights vis-à-vis the Authorities of the Council of Europe', 157.

1742 Ipsen, *Völkerrecht – ein Studienbuch*, 52; Vitzthum & Bothe (eds), *Völkerrecht*, 169; Verdross & Simma, *Universelles Völkerrecht – Theorie und Praxis*, 22.

1743 As the international organization under the auspices of which the ECHR was drafted.

the Court's functioning, in particular the ECHR and the Rules of Court.[1744] To the extent that the legal personality of the Court derives from its constitution by an international organization, this Court would also have to be denied this capacity. Without doubt it was not the intention of the Contracting States of the ECHR for the ECHR to establish an international organization the only organ of which would be the ECtHR.[1745] It is moreover not in conformity with the aims of the ECHR, as a treaty that was drafted under the auspices of the CoE and which was not intended to establish a separate (concurring) international organization alongside the CoE.[1746] A further basis for the international legal personality of the ECtHR could be, pursuant to the reasoning of the ICJ in the case of *Reparation for Injuries Suffered in the Service of the United Nations*, that it is implied by the attribution of functions and rights to an extent that only the possession of international personality would enable it to carry out the intentions of its founders.[1747] It is difficult to apply this argument of implied powers to the ECtHR. The necessary equipment of the Court with functions that necessitate the possession of a competence enabling those functions to be effectively discharged, i.e. provisions that presuppose international treaty making power of the ECtHR, is not discernible in the documents relating to the Court. There is no provision either in the ECHR or the Rules of Court that demands that the Court be brought into a relationship with the CoE through an agreement. It is also not mandated that the Court itself enter into a headquarters agreement with France, regulating the seat of the Court in Strasbourg.[1748] Instead it is assumed that the Court profits from the agreements that the CoE has concluded in support of the protection of its privileges and immunities and the inviolability of the buildings and premises of the CoE.[1749] The Court is furthermore not

---

1744 The Rules of Court could not be the source as they are drafted by the Court itself: see Art. 25(d) ECHR.

1745 Ress, Georg, 'Die Organisationsstruktur internationaler Gerichte, insbesondere des neuen Europäischen Gerichtshofs für Menschenrechte', in: Hafner, Gerhard (ed) *Liber amicorum: Professor Ignaz Seidl-Hohenveldern in honour of his 80*th *birthday* (Kluwer The Hague 1998), 546.

1746 Cf. the preamble to the ECHR, where the contracting States in the first sentence describe themselves as "being members of the Council of Europe".

1747 *Reparation for injuries suffered in the service of the United Nations (Advisory Opinion)*, 178-179. Cf. *supra* Chapter F.IV(1)(a) on the ICC as a subject of international law.

1748 Instead the seat of the Court is laid down in Rule 19(1) Rules of Court.

1749 See the General agreement on privileges and immunities of the Council of Europe (adopted 2 September 1949, entered into force 10 September 1952) CETS No. 2;

enabled to enter (and has not entered) into agreements with Contracting Parties to the ECHR in order to ensure co-operation and judicial assistance to it;[1750] instead it relies on the duty to co-operate, as established mainly in the ECHR.[1751] In comparison, the Rome Statute explicitly states that the ICC "shall have international legal personality" and describes it further as the "legal capacity ... necessary for the exercise of its functions and the fulfilment of its purposes."[1752] Furthermore, the Statute of the IACtHR provides that the Court "is an autonomous judicial institution"[1753] and that the relations of the Court with the host country, with governments, with the Organization of American States (OAS) and its organs, agencies and entities and with other international governmental organizations shall be governed through special agreements.[1754] These agreements are concluded between the Court itself and the other party in question. In sum, therefore, the legal subjectivity of the ECtHR cannot be affirmed, which results in the Court not being able, or not considering itself authorized, to enter into agreements with the CoE or States Parties to the ECHR. One practical example where this insufficient regulatory framework becomes apparent is with regard to the non-existence of an agreement similar to that between the Secretariat of the OAS and the Inter-American Court of Human Rights on the Administrative Operation of the Secretariat of the Court.[1755] This particular question will be dealt with in more detail below.

Special Agreement relating to the Seat of the Council of Europe (adopted 2 September 1949, entered into force 28 November 1949) CETS No. 3; see Boer-Buquicchio, Maud de, 'Klarstellung zum Status des Europäischen Gerichtshofs für Menschenrechte und seiner Beziehungen zum Europarat' (2003) 30 Europäische Grundrechte-Zeitschrift 17/20, 562.

1750 Cf. Art. 87(5)(a) Rome Statute.

1751 Art. 38 ECHR: "The Court shall examine the case together with the representatives of the parties and, if need be, undertake an investigation, for the effective conduct of which the High Contracting Parties concerned shall furnish all necessary facilities." Rule 44A of the Rules of Court and as reiterated in resolutions by the CoM (see, e.g., Committee of Ministers of the CoE, *States' obligation to co-operate with the European Court of Human Rights* (adopted 26 June 2001) Resolution ResDH(2001)66); Committee of Ministers of the CoE, *States' obligation to co-operate with the European Court of Human Rights* (adopted 4 July 2006) Resolution ResDH(2006)45).

1752 Art. 4(1) Rome Statute.

1753 Art. 1 Statute of the Inter-American Court of Human Rights (adopted 31 October 1979, entered into force 1 January 1980) 1144 UNTS 123.

1754 Art. 27 IACtHR Statute.

1755 See for a comparison with the IACtHR *infra* Chapter H.IV(2)(f).

b) The Status of the ECtHR Vis-À-Vis the CoE

According to the prevailing opinion represented in academic writing, the ECtHR at least formally is no organ of the CoE.[1756] This is supported by Art. 10 CoE Statute, according to which the organs of the CoE are listed as being the CoM and the PACE.[1757] Including the ECtHR in the organizational structure of the CoE could be construed by reference to the acceptance, pursuant to Art. 3 CoE Statute, by every Member State of the CoE (of the rule of law and) of the principle of the enjoyment of human rights and the aim of the CoE, pursuant to Art. 1(b) CoE Statute, to pursue such principles "by agreements". However, it is a weak argument to state that this constitutes recognition of the ECHR and implicitly of the ECtHR, resulting in the qualification of the ECtHR as a – formal – organ of the CoE.[1758] The argument does also not gain force by statements made during the drafting of the ECHR, where it was said that "[i]f a European Court is set up, this Court should be an organ of the Council of Europe, whose Member States should participate in the election of its members."[1759] These statements were made

---

1756 Korinek & Holoubek (eds), *Österreichisches Bundesverfassungsrecht: Textsammlung und Kommentar*, Art. 19 para. 18; Engel, Norbert Paul, 'Status, Ausstattung und Personalhoheit des Inter-Amerikanischen und des Europäischen Gerichtshofs für Menschenrechte: Facetten und Wirkungen des institutionellen Rahmens' (2003) 30 Europäische Grundrechte-Zeitschrift 4/6, 127; Ress, 'Die Organisationsstruktur internationaler Gerichte, insbesondere des neuen Europäischen Gerichtshofs für Menschenrechte', 544; Ress, Georg, 'Der Europäische Gerichtshof für Menschenrechte, seine Reform und die Rolle der nationalen Gerichte', in: Karl, Wolfram (ed) *Internationale Gerichtshöfe und nationale Rechtsordnung – Internationales Symposium am Österreichischen Institut für Menschenrechte am 28. und 29. November 2003 in Salzburg zu Ehren von em.o.Univ.-Prof. DDr. Dr. h.c. Franz Matscher* (N. P. Engel Kehl 2005), 43. See Golsong, Heribert, 'Implementation of International Protection of Human Rights' (1963) 110 Recueil des Cours / Académie de Droit International de La Haye 3, para. 12, who is of a different opinion, citing other authors who go even further by classifying the ECtHR as an autonomous organ of the CoE in the same way that the ICJ is an autonomous organ of the UN.

1757 Both these organs are served by the Secretariat of the CoE; Art. 10(2) Statute CoE.

1758 Korinek & Holoubek (eds), *Österreichisches Bundesverfassungsrecht: Textsammlung und Kommentar*, Art. 19 para. 18.

1759 Council of Europe, *Collected Edition of the "Travaux Préparatoires" of the European Convention on Human Rights – Volume IV – Committee of Experts, Committee of Ministers, Conference of Senior Officials, 30 March – June 1950*, 266.

early in the drafting process, and if such a result had been intended, an amendment to the Statute of the CoE would have been the appropriate way to implement it. Instead the merely optional nature of the jurisdiction of the Court at its inception made it unfeasible to establish the Court as a judicial branch of the CoE. The Court was instead entrusted only with ensuring the observance of the engagements by the contracting States under the ECHR and its protocols, but never intended as a control mechanism for all activities taking place under the umbrella of the CoE.

The qualification of the ECtHR as an organ of the CoE, due to the extensive interactions between the two institutions, is a further potential argument. Although it is true that there are numerous interactions between the Court and the CoM, the PACE, and the institutions of the CoE,[1760] such utilization merely amounts to "organ loan", a concept known from public law describing the service by an organ of a public authority for another public authority.[1761] Such lending of an organ by an international organization, such as the CoE, does not, however, automatically transform the lent organ established by an international treaty (the ECHR) into an organ of the borrowing international organization.[1762] One indication of the fact that the ECtHR is not an organ of the CoE, despite its close connection with it is the way the budget for the ECtHR is determined. Pursuant to Art. 50 ECHR (!) the "expenditure of the Court shall be borne by the CoE". If the Court had been considered an organ of the CoE then this provision would not have been necessary, as such an important organizational question instead would have found its way into the

1760 Examples of the connection between the Court and the organs of the CoE are: the seat of the Court is in Strasbourg where also the CoE has its seat (Rule 19(1) Rules of Court: "The seat of the Court shall be at the seat of the Council of Europe at Strasbourg." Cf. Art. 11 CoE Statute), the judges are elected by the PACE (Art. 22 ECHR), court personnel, i.e. the personel of the Court Registry except for the Registrar and Deputy Registrars are appointed by the Secretary General of the CoE (Rule 18(3) Rules of Court, the Council of Europe Commissioner for Human Rights, who is himself an independent institution within the CoE has the right to submit written comments and take part in hearings (Art. 36(3) ECHR), the CoM supervises the execution of the Court's judgments (Art. 26(2) ECHR), and the Court is financed out of the CoE budget (Art. 50 ECHR).

1761 German: "*Organleihe*".

1762 Ress, 'Der Europäische Gerichtshof für Menschenrechte, seine Reform und die Rolle der nationalen Gerichte', 43.

Statute of the CoE, which reflects the organization's institutional structure and administrative processes.[1763]

c) Conclusions

The legal status of the ECtHR has for long remained an unresolved question which is less than satisfactorily compared to other international courts. One explanation for this may be found in the restricted role the Court played between 1959 and 1998, before becoming permanent and replacing the parallelism of the Court and the ECommHR. With the Court being neither an organ of the CoE nor an autonomous organ equipped with proper legal personality, its legal nature is instead qualified as a treaty organ under the ECHR, i.e. a common organ of the Contracting States.[1764] As one consequence, the Court and the judges are in a direct legal relationship with and dependency on the States. Conversely the Court is closely linked to the CoE and its organs and institutions. For the purpose of the administration of the Court in particular there are significant ties with the CoE. In the interest of providing legal certainty and in some cases ease interactions, it would be useful to determine which organ is authorized to adopt a court statute, like those of the other courts dealt with so far in this work, in which in particular (I) the status of the ECtHR as a judicial person and its structural relationship with the CoE, and (II) the status and condition of service of the judges could be clarified.[1765] Such a statute, which would *inter alia* establish the international legal personality of the Court and provide it with the legal capacity necessary for the

1763 Ress, 'Die Organisationsstruktur internationaler Gerichte, insbesondere des neuen Europäischen Gerichtshofs für Menschenrechte', 562. On the financing of the Court see *infra* Chapter H.IV(7).

1764 *Konventionsorgan* or *Staatengemeinschaftsorgan*. Fribergh, Erik, 'The Authority Over the Court's Registry Within the Council of Europe', in: Caflisch, Lucius *et al.* (eds) *Liber Amicorum Luzius Wildhaber: Human Rights – Strasbourg Views* (N.P. Engel Kehl 2007), 149; Korinek & Holoubek (eds), *Österreichisches Bundesverfassungsrecht: Textsammlung und Kommentar*, Art. 19 para. 19; Boer-Buquicchio, 'Klarstellung zum Status des Europäischen Gerichtshofs für Menschenrechte und seiner Beziehungen zum Europarat', 562; Ress, 'Der Europäische Gerichtshof für Menschenrechte, seine Reform und die Rolle der nationalen Gerichte', 43.

1765 According to G. Ress the reason no statute was adopted is the interest of facilitating fast ratification of the Protocol No. 11; Ress, 'Der Europäische Gerichtshof für Menschenrechte, seine Reform und die Rolle der nationalen Gerichte', 42.

exercise of its functions, would solve not only the above-mentioned larger structural problems, but also a number of auxiliary problems such as the administration of the Court and the status of its judges. Those issues will be dealt with in the following.

2. Administration of the ECtHR

a) Appointment of Registry Staff – Definition of a Problem

Following the new Court's establishment in 1999, an incident occurred that highlighted the incomplete regulation of the administration of the Court and raised the question of appointment procedures for Registry staff. The Court made a proposal for a person to be appointed to the Registry staff, but the CoE Promotions Panel did not accept the appointment and instead proposed a different candidate. When the President of the Court objected and the Secretary General of the CoE chose not to go against the Promotions Panel, no appointment was made.[1766] In another case that occurred in 2003, the Court sought to appoint one of its Section Registrars. The candidate proposed by the Court, however, was not accepted by the Secretary General of the CoE who instead presented his own candidate. When the Court insisted on its nominee as the person better suited for the post, the Secretary General blocked the appointment. As this situation continued for eight months the Court resorted to provisional solutions, before the Court's candidate was ultimately appointed.

These examples show vividly that there are considerable problems in the procedure for the appointment of Registry staff. Since the staff assist the Court in carrying out its judicial business, and in particular because the judicial staff of the Registry carry out an important filter function for the exercise of judicial functions,[1767] these ambiguities may affect the Court's independent performance. The possible influence that Registry staff, including the Registrar himself, may exert on the adjudication of the Court through the processing

1766 See Fribergh, 'The Authority Over the Court's Registry Within the Council of Europe', 157.

1767 Korinek & Holoubek (eds), *Österreichisches Bundesverfassungsrecht: Textsammlung und Kommentar*, Art. 25 para. 10.

and preparing of applications lodged by individuals[1768] is considerable. Indeed their preparatory work forms the very basis for any decision-making by the judges, and in times of the ever increasing workload of the Court, the judges rely heavily, as a matter of fact vitally, on the effective and expedient assistance and work of the administrative staff.[1769] If the appointment of Registry staff is decisively in the hand of a political entity external to the Court, then this creates an ideal avenue for influencing the judicial functioning of the Court.

b) The Normative Framework – The Procedure for the Appointment of Registry Staff

The procedures that *de facto* apply to the selection of Registry staff are the same as those applicable to any other staff appointment in the CoE, namely the Regulations on Appointments, adopted as Appendix II to the Staff Regulations of the CoE.[1770] These rules provide no role for the Court or the Judges to play in the appointment of Registry staff, and the entire process thus appears to rest with the Secretary General, who is the chief administrative officer of the CoE. However, such an arrangement cannot mean that the judges are without influence. As the Court's own rules provide, the President has the right to give or refuse his agreement to any appointment of officials to the Registry.[1771] The Administrative Court of the CoE has acknowledged that this role of the President of the Court amounts to a veto right in matters concerning personnel.[1772] However, this does not remedy the lack of influence

---

1768 In 2009 a record total of 1,625 judgments were handed down, which, given 300 working days a year, means that the ECtHR issued an average of 5.4 judgments every day.

1769 Tomuschat, 'The European Court of Human Rights Overwhelmed by Applications: Problems and Possible Solutions', 10.

1770 Council of Europe, *Staff Regulations – Appendix II: Regulations on appointments* (as amended 12 October 2011) available at <https://wcd.coe.int/ViewDoc.jsp?Ref=COMP/CM/Res(2007)1&Language=lanEnglish&Ver=part10&BackColorInternet=99CCFF&BackColorIntranet=99CCFF&BackColorLogged=99CCCC#P239_37192> (last visited: 21 March 2014).

1771 Rule 18(3).

1772 *Maria Grazia Loria-Albanese c/ Secrétaire Général* (Council of Europe Administrative Tribunal) Recours No. 255/1999 (27 March 2000); cf. Ress, 'Der Europäische Gerichtshof für Menschenrechte, seine Reform und die Rolle der nationalen Gerichte', 51.

of the judges on the selection of Registry staff on the basis of Art. 24 ECHR or, objectively more significantly, binding on the Secretary General; these are merely the rules of the Court. More detailed scrutiny of the legal basis for the Court's role in appointing Registry staff is thus warranted.

Art. 24 ECHR itself provides that the "functions and organization" of the Registry shall be established by the Court. This can be interpreted either broadly, so as to encompass all matters relating to the Registry including the authority to appoint its staff,[1773] or narrowly, where the term "organization" in particular encompasses merely the administration of work, including issues such as working hours. While the narrow interpretation would make the provision empty and ultimately meaningless, the broader interpretation can find some support in teleological reasoning: Whereas issues where the Court cannot do without the support of outside (political) entities, such as the Court's budget, are within the remit of the CoM, the appointment of members of the Registry ought to be reserved for the Court, since such staff serve the Court. In support of this one may refer to Art. 25(e) ECHR, according to which it is the Plenary Court that elects the Registrar and one or more Deputy Registrars. Why should not also other staff of the Registry be appointed by an authority within the Court? It would not be convincing if the senior officials and the staff which they manage were appointed by and thereby ultimately answerable to different authorities.[1774] Put in different words: can it have been the intention of the drafters (especially those of Protocol No. 11) to provide the Court with the authority to choose the Registrar and Deputy Registrars but to leave the same authority regarding all other staff to an outside, and ultimately political, authority?

According to the explanatory report to Protocol No. 11, which introduced the current Art. 24 ECHR, the first sentence of Art. 24 ECHR, which contains the relevant provision on the Registry's functions and organisation, "is derived from Rules 11 and 12 of the former Rules of Court."[1775] For present purposes, this statement provides less guidance than may have been intended,

---

1773 Cf. Art. 16 Statute of the CoE, according to which the CoM has extensive statutory powers, in particular the competence to "decide with binding effect all matters relating to the internal organisation and arrangements of the Council of Europe".

1774 See on this e.g. Fribergh, 'The Authority Over the Court's Registry Within the Council of Europe', 154-156.

1775 Council of Europe, *Protocol No. 11 to the Convention for the Protection of Human Rights and Fundamental Freedoms, restructuring the control machinary established thereby, Explanatory Report*, para. 65.

as these older Rules, now in essence covered by Rules 15 and 16, prescribed the election of the Registrar and Deputy Registrars alone; this is now covered by Art. 26 ECHR establishing the plenary Court's powers in this regard. It is not at all a given that from this one can deduce the Court's equal competence to select Registry staff. A reference to the former Rules 13 and 14 (now Rules 17 and 18), dealing with staff, equipment and facilities of the Court and the duties of the Registrar, would have provided a definitive answer. In a further paragraph the explanatory report to Protocol No. 11 states that "[t]he Court's registry is provided by the Secretary General of the Council of Europe".[1776] This assessment was clearly based on the wording of the old version of Art. 37 ECHR, which provided the same for the secretariat of the ECommHR.[1777] Interestingly, the old version of Art. 37 ECHR was interpreted to mean that the Secretariat works solely for the Commission and under its authority.[1778] The negotiations leading to Protocol No. 11 and the corresponding explanatory report further reveal that it was desired to keep the mention of the Registry in the ECHR rather general and instead to leave the details for the Court to determine in its Rules;[1779] this was also proposed not only by the Court itself[1780] but by the ECommHR, which was of the opinion that matters such as appointment, status and function of the Registry staff ought to be reserved for regulation in the rules of the Court.[1781] Furthermore, when interpreted according to its wording, the phrase "provided by the Secretary General" merely suggests that Registry staff be considered as CoE employees.[1782] It does not set out the procedure for their appointment

---

1776 Ibid, para. 66.

1777 "Le secrétariat de la Commission est assuré par le Secrétaire Général du Conseil de l'Europe."

1778 Cf. Frowein, Jochen Abr. & Peukert, Wolfgang, *Europäische Menschenrechtskonvention: EMRK-Kommentar* (N. P. Engel Kehl 2nd edn. 1996), 647.

1779 See the summary of the drafting history in Fribergh, 'The Authority Over the Court's Registry Within the Council of Europe', 151-154. For a more general overview of the drafting process see Drzemczewski, Andrew, 'A Major Overhaul of the European Human Rights Convention Control Mechanism: Protocol No. 11', in: Academy of European Law (ed) *Collected Courses of the Academy of European Law* (Oxford University Press Oxford 1997), 121-244.

1780 European Court of Human Rights, *Reform Proposal* (31 January 1994) DH-PR (94)4.

1781 European Commission of Human Rights, *Reform Proposal* (17 January 1994) DH-PR (93)2.

1782 Drzemczewski, Andrew, 'The European Human Rights Convention: Protocol No. 11 – Entry into Force and First Year of Application', The Inter-American System

or who the staff are ultimately answerable to. Finally, the explanatory report contains an interesting reference to the influence of judges on the posts of "legal secretaries", a category of staff that was also established through Protocol No. 11.[1783] Here it is stated that those officials "may be appointed upon the proposal of the judges".[1784] This shows that the judges were envisaged to have a decisive say in the appointment of such legal staff, and that the appointment was not to depend just on the Secretary General.[1785] In summary, and against the above elaborations, it is hardly imaginable that anything else was envisaged for the members of staff of the Registry.

c) The Special Case of the Registrar

One possible safeguard of the independence of the Court is that the Registrar and Deputy Registrars of the Court shall be elected by the (Plenary) Court alone.[1786] Thus the individual responsible for the organization and activities of the Registry is not just under the authority of the President of the Court while he is working[1787] but is only put into place if the Plenary Court has agreed to his filling that position. The close relationship between the Registrar and the Court is also expressed in the solemn declaration that the Registrar makes or the oath he takes before the plenary Court or the President of the Court.[1788] Interestingly the oath/declaration speaks of a loyal exercise of the

---

of Human Rights Protection at the Eve of the 21st Century, Conference in San José, Costa Rica (16 November 1999), 233.

1783 The officials of legal secretaries as early as when they were introduced by Protocol No. 11 were difficult to fathom as they did not differ at all from the then already extant legal secretaries in the Secretariat of the Court: see Drzemczewski, 'A Major Overhaul of the European Human Rights Convention Control Mechanism: Protocol No. 11', 188. They were abolished again by Protocol No. 14.

1784 Council of Europe, *Protocol No. 11 to the Convention for the Protection of Human Rights and Fundamental Freedoms, restructuring the control machinary established thereby, Explanatory Report*, para. 66.

1785 Cf. Ress, 'Der Europäische Gerichtshof für Menschenrechte, seine Reform und die Rolle der nationalen Gerichte', 50.

1786 Art. 25(e) ECHR; Rules 15 and 16 Rules of Court.

1787 Cf. Rule 17(1) Rules of Court.

1788 Rule 15(4) Rules of Court. The same applies for Deputy Registrars, cf. Rule 16(2).

functions conferred upon him as Registrar of the ECtHR.[1789] There thus appears to be an expectation of loyalty towards the Court alone.[1790] This gives the Court *de jure* considerable influence over the workings of its administrative arm.

The role of the Registrar is an important one, as he is the one who instructs the Registry staff;[1791] the judges themselves have, as mentioned, no right to issue instructions to the Registry staff. A hierarchy which would allow the judges to exercise control over the staff could thus be established only by allowing the judges to issue instructions to the Registrar, who in turn has the power to instruct its staff by exercising his rights under Rule 17. However, the *de jure* situation under the Rules of Court differs considerably from what the norms binding on the Secretary General prescribe. Here the staff regulations of the CoE in Art. 26(1) demand that the Secretary General is consulted by the President of the Court prior to the election of the Registrar and that the Secretary General shall make the appointments in accordance with the elections.[1792] The discrepancy between staff regulations, ascribing a role to the Secretary General in the election of the Registrar, and the Rules of Court, omitting such participation, arose when the new Court adopted its rules with the entry into force of Protocol No. 11. Consequently, the first Registrar of the new Court was elected without the opinion of the Secretary General being obtained and later elections were preceded by consultations only "as a matter of courtesy on the part of the Court".[1793] The frictions indicated by the

---

1789 "I swear" – or "I solemnly declare" – "that I will exercise loyally, discreetly and conscientiously the functions conferred upon me as Registrar of the European Court of Human Rights."

1790 Other Registry staff are not required by the Rules of Court to take/make a similar oath/declaration, but in its General Instructions No. 3, the President of the Court approved the Registrar's instruction to the Registry staff to take/make a similar oath/declaration. See President of the European Court of Human Rights, *General Instruction No. 3* (10 August 1973) CDH (73) 20.

1791 The recognition of the important function of the Registrar is to be found in Art. 5(1) Sixth Protocol to the General Agreement on Privileges and Immunities of the Council of Europe, which grants the Registrar and the Deputy Registrars (and their families) the same privileges and immunities as the judges. On the powers exercised by the Registrar see Korinek & Holoubek (eds), *Österreichisches Bundesverfassungsrecht: Textsammlung und Kommentar*, Art. 25 para. 7.

1792 Art. 26(1) Staff Regulations of the CoE.

1793 Mahoney, 'Separation of Powers in the Council of Europe: The Status of the European Court of Human Rights vis-à-vis the Authorities of the Council of

normative framework are emphasized by the fact that the Secretary General of the CoE *de facto* considers the Registrar to be subject to the same employment law as ordinary Registry staff.[1794] It goes without saying that this uncertainty could pose serious difficulties for the independent functioning of the Court if it were put to the test. The fact that the relatively smooth functioning of the system is due to the goodwill of those involved should not cause informed observers to shy away from a call for reform.

d) Considerations on Registry Staff Being Answerable to the Secretary General of the CoE

The potential threats to the Court's independence indicated above stem from the political nature of the Secretary General's office. It may certainly be claimed that there are numerous safeguards in place to ensure his autonomy *vis-à-vis* the other political bodies of the CoE: He is for example appointed by the PACE merely on the recommendation of the CoM.[1795] The holder of this position is further not allowed to hold any salaried office from a government, be a member of the Parliamentary Assembly or of any national legislature or engage in any occupation incompatible with his duties.[1796] He is moreover called upon to perform his duties conscientiously, uninfluenced by any national considerations, to stay free from instructions in connection with the performance of his duties from any government or any authority external to the CoE and to refrain from any action which might reflect on his position as an international official responsible only to the Council.[1797] The Member States of the CoE are bound to respect that independence.[1798]

Europe', 157; see also Fribergh, 'The Authority Over the Court's Registry Within the Council of Europe', 155.

1794 Boer-Buquicchio, 'Klarstellung zum Status des Europäischen Gerichtshofs für Menschenrechte und seiner Beziehungen zum Europarat', 562. According to G. Ress the Registrar is *de facto* (and *de jure* according to the Secretary General) subject to instructions of the Secretary General; Ress, 'Der Europäische Gerichtshof für Menschenrechte, seine Reform und die Rolle der nationalen Gerichte', 51.

1795 Art. 36(b) Statute of the CoE.

1796 Art. 36(d) Statute of the CoE. Secretary General W. Schwimmer, e.g., before assuming his new office laid down any party offices that he previously held, see Boer-Buquicchio, 'Klarstellung zum Status des Europäischen Gerichtshofs für Menschenrechte und seiner Beziehungen zum Europarat', 562.

1797 Art. 36(e) Statute of the CoE.

1798 Art. 36(f) Statute of the CoE.

But despite these safeguards the Secretary General remains a political figure within the organizational structure of the CoE. As this position is filled by a member of the PACE, the holder brings with him certain political visions that he will attempt to translate into policies. For that reason it cannot be accepted by the Court that its Registry's staff is answerable to the Secretary General, let alone the CoM. The political nature of these two entities and the influence the Registry has on the judicial activities of the Court have led the former Registrar of the Court, P. Mahoney, to stress the following:

> "The judicial independence of the Court requires that the ultimate hierarchical superior of the staff who assist it in its judicial work be the President of the Court."[1799]

Against the background of the above elaborations, this call remains untouched by the fact that it can be said that the Secretaries General so far have had a good working relationship with the Court, and in particular with the President of the Court.[1800] To make the good relations between the two entities, and in particular the independent functioning of the ECtHR, reliant on the diplomatic skills of two individuals is a less than optimal solution.[1801]

e) Assessment

In view of what has been said above, although the staff members of the Court's Registry are CoE employees in a technical sense as they are appointed by the Secretary General, the Court should have a more decisive influence on their selection. A practical solution, which would be well in line with many of the considerations underlying the independent functioning of the Court, would be to bring the appointment of ordinary staff into line with that used with regard to the Registrar (and Deputy Registrar). Here the function of the Secretary General is a formal one where he only gives effect to the choice of the Court. There is no plausible reason why this order should not also apply to other staff of the Court's Registry. Moreover, this modification could be achieved by relatively easy means, an amendment of the Staff Regulations would be all that was necessary; e.g. the special appointment

1799 Mahoney, 'Separation of Powers in the Council of Europe: The Status of the European Court of Human Rights vis-à-vis the Authorities of the Council of Europe', 158.
1800 Ibid, 152.
1801 Ibid, 152.

procedures in Art. 26 of the Regulations on appointments could be extended to include other staff beside the Registrar and Deputy Registrars. A more permanent solution is, however, indicated by the scheme found in the ECtHR's sister court, the IACtHR. A comparison with the inter-American system[1802] of control over the IACtHR's administrative arm, the Registry and its staff, is therefore instrumental.[1803]

f) Excursus: The Status and Administration of the Inter-American Court of Human Rights

(1) The Inter-American Court of Human Rights and its Status in the Inter-American Human Rights Protection System

Before the regulation of the IACtHR's control over Registry staff is examined, some remarks should be made on the status of the Court and its embedding in the inter-American human rights protection system. In 1948, 21 American States signed the Charter of the Organization of American States.[1804] The OAS, which was conceived as a purely inter-governmental organization without an equivalent to the CoE's parliament, was set up to achieve peace and justice, to promote and strengthen the Contracting States' solidarity and collaboration, and to defend their sovereignty, their territorial integrity, and their independence. As one of its organs the IACommHR[1805] took up its work of promoting the observance and protection of human rights, initially merely as a consultative organ of the Organization.[1806] In 1969 the ACHR was signed,[1807] which envisaged not only the IACommHR as an organ under

1802 See further Fix-Zamudio, Héctor, 'The European and the Inter-American Courts of Human Rights: A Brief Comparison', in: Mahoney, Paul *et al.* (eds) *Protection des droits de l'homme: la perspective européenne – Mélanges à la mémoire de Rolv Ryssdal* (Heymann Köln 2000).

1803 In what follows the focus will be on the IACtHR and no special mention of the IACommHR will be made.

1804 Charter of the Organization of American States (signed 30 April 1948, entered into force 13 December 1951) 119 UNTS 3.

1805 Cf. Art. 53(1)(c) Charter of the Organization of American States and Art. 1 Statute of the Inter-American Court of Human Rights (adopted 31 October 1979, entered into force 1 January 1980) 1144 UNTS 123.

1806 Art. 106 Charter of the Organization of American States.

1807 American Convention on Human Rights (Pact of San José, Costa Rica).

the Convention,[1808] but also provided for the creation of the IACtHR as an organ with competence to oversee the fulfilment of the commitments made by the States Parties to the ACHR.[1809] The IACtHR's legal status is based on the ACHR itself; pursuant to its Art. 33 the Court is only an organ of the ACHR, in other words a common organ of the Contracting States.[1810] Unlike the IACommHR it is not mentioned or recognized as an organ of the OAS in the Charter of the OAS. According to the Statute of the Court, which it drafted itself,[1811] the IACtHR is

> "an autonomous judicial institution whose purpose is the application and interpretation of the American Convention on Human Rights. The Court exercises its functions in accordance with the provisions of the aforementioned Convention and the present Statute."[1812]

The Contracting States of the ACHR acknowledged this status of the Court when they consented to its Statute. The status is further autonomously detailed in the rules of the Court.[1813] Relations with the host country, governments and organizations are governed by agreements concluded by the Court itself.[1814] One such agreement is that between the Secretariat of the OAS and the IACtHR on the Administrative Operation of the Secretariat of the Court, concluded between the Secretary General of the OAS and the President of the Court.[1815] This agreement regulates the administrative functioning of the Court's Secretariat with regard to its relations with the General Secretariat of the OAS, containing provisions on the administration of the budget of the Court and the right for the Court Secretariat to select and hire its staff.

1808 Art. 33 ACHR. While at the same time remaining an organ of the OAS.

1809 Art. 33 ACHR.

1810 Cf. on this the reasoning *supra* with regard to the ECtHR.

1811 Art. 60 ACHR.

1812 Art. 1 Statute of the Inter-American Court of Human Rights.

1813 Art. 60 ACHR.

1814 Art. 27 Statute of the Inter-American Court of Human Rights. See, e.g., Agreement between the Government of the Republic of Costa Rica and the Inter-American Court of Human Rights, which was signed by the Minister for Foreign Affairs of Costa Rica and the President of the IACtHR, representing the court (Agreement between the Government of the Republic of Costa Rica and the Inter-American Court of Human Rights (Headquarters Agreement) (adopted 10 September 1981) 24 HRLJ 302 (2003)).

1815 Agreement between the General Secretariat of The OAS and The Inter-American Court of Human Rights concerning the Administrative Functioning of the Secretariat of the Court (1999) OAS Official Records OEA/Ser.L/V/III.43, doc. 11.

(2) The Responsibility for Court Administration – In Particular Appointment of Administrative Staff

Judges of the IACtHR are elected by an absolute majority vote of the States Parties to the ACHR in the General Assembly of the OAS.[1816] Proposals are made by the Contracting States. The Court draws up its own budget for submission to the General Assembly of the OAS through the General Secretariat (which may not introduce any changes) and administers it itself.[1817] The regulatory framework for the Court's autonomy in personnel matters is Art. 59 ACHR, which provides that

> "[t]he Court shall establish its Secretariat, which shall function under the direction of the Secretary of the Court, in accordance with the administrative standards of the General Secretariat of the Organization in all respects not incompatible with the independence of the Court."

It is laudable, as a matter of principle, that the relationship between the Secretariat's organization and the independence of the Court is recognized. This sharpens appreciation for the work of the judges and acknowledges that the administration of the Secretariat may indeed influence how the judicial function of the Court is exercised, to the extent that it violates the independence of the IACtHR. Moreover, the fact that the provision begins by stating that "[t]he Court shall establish" the Secretariat suggests that it is primarily the Court itself that determines when the Secretariat functions "in accordance with the administrative standards of the General Secretariat of the Organization". The ECtHR has not in the same sense been given the decision-making power as to what administrative standards may violate its independence, and the administrative standards of the CoE are by no means reduced to guidelines.

The Secretary of the IACtHR is appointed by the Court, a rule similar to that for the Registrar of the ECtHR.[1818] All other staff of the Secretariat are

1816 Art. 53 ACHR.

1817 Art. 72 *in fine* ACHR, Art. 26 Statute of the IACtHR and Art. II Agreement between the General Secretariat of The OAS and The Inter-American Court of Human Rights concerning the Administrative Functioning of the Secretariat of the Court.

1818 Art. 14(2) Statute of the IACtHR; Art. 7 Rules of Procedure of the Inter-American Court of Human Rights (adopted 22 November 1969, entered into force 18 July 1978) 1144 UNTS 123. The election of the Secretary follows the same procedure as the election of the President of the Court; Art. 7(2) *in fine* read in conjunction with Art. 3(2) Rules of Procedure of the Inter-American Court of Human Rights.

appointed by the Secretary General of the OAS; however, the appointments are made in consultation with the Secretary of the Court[1819] and only after the personnel have been chosen by the Secretary of the Court.[1820] The precise procedure is laid down in the Agreement between the Secretariat of the OAS and the IACtHR on the Administration of the Secretariat of the Court, which provides that the Secretary of the Court shall select and hire the staff of the Court and that the staff shall be appointed by the Secretary General of the OAS.[1821] On appointment the staff members do not become employees of the General Secretariat of the OAS but employees of the Court.[1822]

In summary, the above procedures evidence a greater respect for the independence of the Court *vis-à-vis* the OAS than can be seen in the case of the ECtHR and the CoE. In particular it must be highlighted that the OAS, by entering into the above-mentioned agreement and thus allowing the IACtHR to select its Secretary, who then has the decisive authority in the appointment of other staff in the Registry, by allowing the administrative standards of the General Secretariat to guide the Secretariat only insofar as it does not violate the independence of the Court, and by making Secretariat staff employees of the Court, the Court's functional independence is well guarded against the political entities of the OAS.

3. The Composition of the ECtHR

a) Legal Framework and Introduction to the Selection Procedure

The judges of the ECtHR are elected by a majority of votes in the PACE with respect to each Contracting Party of the ECHR.[1823] As soon as there is a vacancy in the Court, or one year before the term of office of a judge expires, the affected State is called upon by the Secretary General of the CoE to submit a list of three candidates who meet the criteria in Art. 21 ECHR.

1819 Art. 59 *in fine* ACHR.
1820 Art. 59 *in fine* ACHR; Art. 14(4) Statute of the ACHR.
1821 Art. III(1) Agreement between the General Secretariat of The OAS and The Inter-American Court of Human Rights concerning the Administrative Functioning of the Secretariat of the Court.
1822 Art. III(2) Agreement between the General Secretariat of The OAS and The Inter-American Court of Human Rights concerning the Administrative Functioning of the Secretariat of the Court.
1823 Art. 22 ECHR.

Following this call, the State has four months in which to submit its list of candidates,[1824] which is to be accompanied by completed model *curricula vitae*, which the PACE has drafted.[1825] Whereas the CoE in general and the PACE in particular provide the Contracting Party with information on the criteria for office, very limited guidance is given on the State internal procedure for arriving at the list of nominees. It is only in recent years that the PACE has made proposals for nominating candidates at the national level,[1826] and called upon Contracting States to follow the established procedure for selection,[1827] although the motivation behind many of these efforts is to "improve its own procedure for choosing between the" candidates submitted by the Contracting Party.[1828] Once the list of nominees has been submitted, the CoM is given one and a half months in which to consider the candidates and to send the lists back to the State if they contain obvious flaws, such as unfulfilled criteria according to Art. 21(1) ECHR, or if the lists consist of more or fewer than the prescribed three names.[1829] Several times lists have

---

1824 Parliamentary Assembly of the Council of Europe, *Resolution 1200 – Election of judges to the European Court of Human Rights* (1999) available at <http://assembly.coe.int/Main.asp?link=/Documents/AdoptedText/ta99/ERES1200.htm> (last visited: 21 March 2014).

1825 Parliamentary Assembly of the Council of Europe, *Resolution 1646 – Nomination of candidates and election of judges to the European Court of Human Rights* (2009) available at <http://assembly.coe.int/Main.asp?link=/Documents/AdoptedText/ta09/ERES1646.htm> (last visited: 21 March 2014).

1826 See, e.g., Parliamentary Assembly of the Council of Europe, *Recommendation 1429 – National procedures for nominating candidates for election to the European Court of Human Rights* (1999) available at <http://assembly.coe.int/Mainf.asp?link=/Documents/AdoptedText/ta99/EREC1429.htm> (last visited: 21 March 2014) and Parliamentary Assembly of the Council of Europe, *Resolution 1646 – Nomination of candidates and election of judges to the European Court of Human Rights*.

1827 Parliamentary Assembly of the Council of Europe, *Resolution 1366 – Candidates for the European Court of Human Rights* (2004) available at <http://assembly.coe.int/Main.asp?link=/Documents/AdoptedText/ta04/ERES1366.htm> (last visited: 21 March 2014), Parliamentary Assembly of the Council of Europe, *Recommendation 1649 – Candidates for the European Court of Human Rights* (2004) available at <http://assembly.coe.int//Mainf.asp?link=http://assembly.coe.int/Documents/AdoptedText/ta04/EREC1649.htm> (last visited: 21 March 2014).

1828 Sub-Committee on the election of Judges to the European Court of Human Rights, *Procedure for Electing Judges to the European Court of Human Rights – Information Document Prepared by the Secretariat* (11 October 2010) Doc. AS/Jur (2010)12 rev 3, para. 5.

1829 Korinek & Holoubek (eds), *Österreichisches Bundesverfassungsrecht: Textsammlung und Kommentar*, Art. 22, para. 3.

been sent back to the national authorities for non-compliance with requirements under the ECHR and in resolutions and recommendations of the PACE.[1830] If the list is considered satisfactory, it is then transmitted to the PACE for its assessment of the nominees.

The assessment made by the PACE, besides the evaluation of the standard *curriculum vitae*, includes interviews conducted before the special subcommittee to the Committee on Legal Affairs and Human Rights.[1831] Despite the fact that judges are elected with respect to every Contracting Party, the judges are not to be representatives of their respective home State but instead sit in their individual capacity.[1832] The selection procedure is thus split into first the nomination, which rests with the individual State, and then the election by the PACE. Both the nomination and election procedures are important for the protection of the independence of the Court as these are the processes where the criteria for office, among which are independence and impartiality, can be tested and ensured.

b) The Nomination of Candidates – The Domaine Réservé of States?

The nomination procedure has over the years been characterized by a number of problems that touch upon the independence of the Court, such as a lack of transparency, lack of uniformity and objectivity in the interest of ensuring the maintenance of the criteria for office.[1833] These conditions have contributed to a sometimes rather negative perception of the Court, with news media referring to the judges as "Europe's unelected dictators"[1834] or "unelected

---

1830 See, e.g., Parliamentary Assembly of the Council of Europe, *Nomination of Candidates and Election of Judges to the European Court of Human Rights* (1 December 2008) Doc. 11767, para. 8.

1831 See Rule 48.2 Rules of Procedure of the Assembly (see also Parliamentary Assembly of the Council of Europe, *Resolution 1202 – Rules of Procedure of the Assembly (adopted on 4 November 1999)* (1999) available at <http://assembly.coe.int/Main.asp?link=/RulesofProcedure/PACERuleIndex_E.asp> (last visited: 21 March 2014)).

1832 Cf. Art. 21(2) ECHR.

1833 The criteria for office and their relevance for the independence of the judges and the Court will be dealt with separately: see *infra* Chapter H.V(1).

1834 Editor, 'Do us rights' *The Sun* (11 February 2011).

Strasbourg judges".[1835] An important reason for these circumstances is that the nomination procedure was not discussed in the *travaux préparatoires*,[1836] and that therefore there is no comprehensive procedural framework in the ECHR on national nomination procedures.[1837] In a sense, this is also a compelling consequence of the one-state-one-judge rule that applies to the ECtHR, which has no parallel in the other courts analysed in previous chapters and which in itself raises serious questions regarding the independence of judges, very similar to what has been mentioned in the context of *ad hoc* judges.[1838] If indeed every Contracting Party to the ECHR is to have one judge at the Court[1839] and if thus the perception of the judges as *representatives* of their home States is reinforced, then already a significant concession has been made to the influence of States and the Court has been saddled with a heavy burden in its aim to be (perceived) as independent. The political argument, that the ECtHR must also represent the countries that have signed and ratified the ECHR and thus are directly influenced by the judgments of the Court can provide only a limited explanation.

According to a study conducted in 2003 by a group of eminent European jurists, the absolute discretion of States in the nomination process has resulted in nominations often involving a "tap on the shoulder" by a cabinet member and frequently rewards political loyalty over merit.[1840] It is reported that nominees sometimes lack the necessary experience or even fail to meet the basic criteria of Art. 21 ECHR. It has been attempted to remedy the lack of comprehensive guidelines, able to mitigate the effect of the absolute discretion that the ECHR gives States, with non-binding rules established by the PACE. Thus the PACE as early as in 1977 issued a recommendation that States do not put forward candidates who, by the nature of their functions, are dependent on a government, without an assurance that they will resign from such

---

1835 Chapman, James, 'Day we stood up to Europe: In an unprecedented move, MPs reject European court's ruling that prisoners must get the vote' *Mail Online* (11 February 2011).

1836 Limbach, et al., *Judicial Independence: Law and Practice of Appointments to the European Court of Human Rights*, 7.

1837 Ibid, 17.

1838 On the other hand, the fact that the bench consists of one judge per contracting State makes a geographic representation requirement such as can be found in e.g. the ICJ unnecessary.

1839 Art. 20 ECHR.

1840 Limbach, et al., *Judicial Independence: Law and Practice of Appointments to the European Court of Human Rights*, 9.

functions upon election to the Court. The reason behind this was the fact that some candidates who had been nominated by Contracting States were civil servants and others who, by the very nature of the positions they held, were not independent of their governments.[1841] The PACE was of the opinion that this practice "prejudices the principle of separation of powers and reduces [the PACE's] choice among the three candidates." However, the PACE also referred to the requirement in Rule 4 of the Rules of Court according to which posts or professions that are likely to affect confidence in the independence of the Court prevent a judge from exercising his function of judge. Thus it becomes apparent that in the view of the PACE, certain practices of States in their nomination directly caused problems for the ECtHR's independence.

Furthermore in 1999 the PACE issued a recommendation in which it called upon the CoM to invite Member States to follow a number of criteria when drawing up lists of candidates, including the following:[1842]

> "i. issue a call for candidatures through the specialized press, so as to obtain candidates who are indeed eminent jurists satisfying the criteria laid down in Article 21, paragraph 1, of the Convention;
> ii. ensure that the candidates have experience in the field of human rights, either as practitioners or as activists in non-governmental organisations working in this area;
> iii. select candidates of both sexes in every case;[1843]
> iv. ensure that the candidates are in fact fluent in either French or English and are capable of working in one of these two languages;
> v. put the names of the candidates in alphabetical order."

1841 Parliamentary Assembly of the Council of Europe, *Recommendation 809 – on the qualification of candidates for the European Court of Human Rights* (1977) available at <http://assembly.coe.int/Mainf.asp?link=/Documents/AdoptedText/ta77/EREC809.htm> (last visited: 21 March 2014).

1842 Parliamentary Assembly of the Council of Europe, *Recommendation 1429 – National procedures for nominating candidates for election to the European Court of Human Rights*.

1843 Fundamentally the independence of the judges is not immediately affected by the gender balance on the Court. Gender becomes an issue only if the other criteria for office are not observed, i.e. when for example a judge who is a member of the majority gender of the Court is chosen despite his inferior moral character (etc.) compared to a member of the other gender. Thus, gender as such cannot be said to have an immediate effect on the independence of a judge.

In the interest of the transparency[1844] of the national selection process the PACE also recommended that all Member States consult their national parliaments when drawing up the lists.[1845] These recommendations were based on the shortcomings that had been observed in several of the national nomination procedures,[1846] where the method of selecting candidates varied considerably between the countries and the process was often not governed by rules. Many governments did not include a female contender on their list of candidates,[1847] and the candidates put forward did not always meet the criteria established by the Convention: either they lacked experience in human rights, had never held judicial office, or were not sufficiently fluent in at least one of the CoE's two official languages.[1848]

1844 In its Resolution 1649 the PACE criticized the fact that the CoM has been reluctant to comment on the decision-making process in member states for the nomination of candidates and recalled that the national procedures for selecting candidates are not always satisfactory. As a consequence the PACE again called for more transparency in the national procedures for the selection of candidates. Parliamentary Assembly of the Council of Europe, *Recommendation 1649 – Candidates for the European Court of Human Rights*, para. 17.

1845 Parliamentary Assembly of the Council of Europe, *Recommendation 1429 – National procedures for nominating candidates for election to the European Court of Human Rights*.

1846 These observations resulted, in part, from the "Questionnaire addressed to the national delegations to the Parliamentary Assembly", the response to which was evaluated in the Report by the Committee on Legal Affairs and Human Rights, Parliamentary Assembly of the Council of Europe, *National procedures for nominating candidates for election to the European Court of Human Rights* (8 September 1999) Doc. 8505.

1847 Opinion of the Committee on Equal Opportunities for Women and Men, Parliamentary Assembly of the Council of Europe, *National procedures for nominating candidates for election to the European Court of Human Rights* (17 September 1999) Doc. 8525), formed the basis for the gender equality, as the rapporteur of the Committee on Equal Opportunities for Women and Men here demanded that States set up a list with parity representation (at para. 5).

1848 In 1999 the PACE issued an order in which it referred to recommendation 1429(1999) by instructing the Sub-Committee on the Election of Judges of its Committee on Legal Affairs and Human Rights to ensure that member states apply the criteria, in particular the presence of candidates of both genders. Parliamentary Assembly of the Council of Europe, *Order No. 558 – National procedures for nominating candidates for election to the European Court of Human Rights* (1999) available at <http://assembly.coe.int/Mainf.asp?link=/Documents/AdoptedText/ta99/EDIR558.htm> (last visited: 21 March 2014).

As already touched upon above, one problem inevitably connected to all efforts by the PACE to improve the transparency, fairness and objectivity of the nomination process is that both resolutions and recommendations, the tools at the PACE's disposal, are non-binding instruments which develop their strongest effect by being perceived as "significant guidelines for policy development in the Member States."[1849] This provides the nomination procedure at the State level with considerable protection, turning it into a virtual *domaine réservé* of States. As long as the authority to change the legal framework of the nomination procedure rests with those who clearly benefit from keeping the *status quo*, expectations of change should be modest. The same problem must be said to affect the establishment of the so-called Advisory Panel of Experts on Candidates for Election as Judge to the European Court of Human Rights.[1850] The idea of the Panel of Experts originated from the President of the ECtHR, Judge Jean-Paul Costa,[1851] who saw it as a tool better to ensure the quality of the judges. Whereas the Panel shall intervene before a list was submitted to the PACE by the contracting party, its role is only advisory.[1852] It is authorized only to make recommendations to nominating States and it may forward its views to the PACE. Furthermore, the Panel has no proper authority to collect information on which to assess the suitability of candidates, but is instead dependent "on the basis of the information provided by the High Contracting Party".[1853]

1849 Rule 24.1.a-b Rules of Procedure of the Assembly. See also Kleinsorge, Tanja E.J. (ed) *Council of Europe* (Kluwer Law International 2010), 197.

1850 Committee of Ministers of the CoE, *On the Establishment of an Advisory Panel of Experts on Candidates for Election as Judge to the European Court of Human Rights* (adopted 10 November 2010) Resolution CM/Res(2010)26.

1851 The letter is appended to Parliamentary Assembly of the Council of Europe, *National procedures for the selection of candidates for the European Court of Human Rights* (7 October 2010) Doc. 12391.

1852 Committee of Ministers of the CoE, *On the Establishment of an Advisory Panel of Experts on Candidates for Election as Judge to the European Court of Human Rights*, para. 1.

1853 Ibid, Operating Rules, para. vii. The Panel was established for the first time by a decision of the CoM on 8 December 2010; Committee of Ministers of the CoE, *1101st Meeting, 8 December 2010 – Decisions Adopted* (8 December 2010) CM/Del/Dec(2010)1101.

c) Inadequacies in the Nomination Process and Their Relevance for Independence

The deficiencies of the nomination process just mentioned have different importance for the securing of the independence of ECtHR judges. The question of distribution of seats on the bench between genders is a question of fairness and gender equality which, although it has become an ambition on both the national and international levels, has no direct influence on the susceptibility of the Court to undue influence.[1854] It should be acknowledged that the Assembly in its resolution 1366 of 2004, in which it called for an increase in the proportion of women nominated to the sub-committee, provided the explanation that this would help to "exclude possible gender bias in decision-making processes."[1855] However, the PACE in the same provision reveals that this justification stems from "the parity threshold deemed necessary by the Council of Europe". To apply a rule for the composition of a political body to the administration of a judicial organ is problematic. And thus it must be welcomed that the PACE in its resolution 1627 amended its earlier resolution of 2004 and, while attaching "great importance to both expertise and gender balance in the Court", cites the ECtHR's own justification of gender balance on the bench:[1856]

> "the criterion [developed by the PACE which ensure that lists contain candidates of the sex that is under-represented] derives from a gender-equality policy which reflects the importance of equality between the sexes in contemporary society and the role played by the prohibition of discrimination and by positive discrimination measures in attaining that objective. ... Moreover, there is far-reaching

---

1854 Cf. *Advisory opinion on certain legal questions concerning the lists of candidates submitted with a view to the election of judges to the European Court of Human* (ECtHR [Grand Chamber]) Advisory Opinion No. 1 (12 February 2008), paras. 47-49.

1855 Parliamentary Assembly of the Council of Europe, *Resolution 1366 – Candidates for the European Court of Human Rights*, para. 2. This resolution was later amended by Parliamentary Assembly of the Council of Europe, *Resolution 1426 – Candidates for the European Court of Human Rights* (2005) available at <http://www.assembly.coe.int/ASP/Doc/XrefViewPDF.asp?FileID=17311&Language=EN> (last visited: 21 March 2014).

1856 Parliamentary Assembly of the Council of Europe, *Resolution 1627 – Candidates for the European Court of Human Rights* (2008) available at <http://www.assembly.coe.int/ASP/Doc/XrefViewPDF.asp?FileID=17670&Language=EN> (last visited: 21 March 2014), para. 2.

consensus as to the need to promote gender balance within the State and in the national and international public service, including the judiciary."[1857]

The immediate link between gender balance on the bench and its independence has thus been omitted. Conversely, the lack of required professional qualifications is – like what applies at all other international courts – an important indicator of the identification of judges with their role as purely judicial umpires. The lack of transparency existing in many countries both with regard to the way in which calls for candidatures are made but also concerning the way in which these candidates are selected,[1858] is an obvious threat to an independent bench. According to a report presented to the Committee on Legal Affairs and Human Rights in 2008, a large number of countries still lacked an established national selection procedure,[1859] open calls for candidatures, the involvement of an independent selection body, and language assessments.[1860] The relevance of these steps in the nomination procedure is not to be underestimated, in particular for a court that is the last resort for individuals who often seek the review of burdensome decisions by national authorities. In this context, the close control of national authorities over the nomination procedure is destined to question the independence of the Court.

d) Nomination by Contracting States – A Practical Example

Some of the problems linked to the nomination procedures on the national level can be illustrated by the example of Germany. The procedure for the nomination of new ECtHR judges in Germany until recently lacked transpar-

1857 *Advisory opinion on certain legal questions concerning the lists of candidates submitted with a view to the election of judges to the European Court of Human*, para. 49.

1858 Parliamentary Assembly of the Council of Europe, *Resolution 1646 – Nomination of candidates and election of judges to the European Court of Human Rights*, para. 4 and Sub-Committee on the election of Judges to the European Court of Human Rights, *Procedure for Electing Judges to the European Court of Human Rights – Information Document Prepared by the Secretariat*, para. 9.

1859 According to the report, some *ad hoc* procedures even operated without any formal legal basis, thus contributing further to the secretive nature of decisions on candidates. Parliamentary Assembly of the Council of Europe, *Nomination of Candidates and Election of Judges to the European Court of Human Rights*, para. 17.

1860 Ibid, paras. 17-22.

ency and was without any legal basis. In practice, the list of three nominees was put together by the government, primarily the Ministry of Justice in co-operation with the Federal Foreign Office,[1861] and the procedure often served as a catch-all for partisan concerns.[1862] Some of the criteria applied by the Ministry of Justice in its selection were practical experience in the field of public international law and language skills.[1863] The Ministry of Justice further co-ordinated its selection with those of the Federal Foreign Office and the German Chancellery. A relatively new element in the procedure is that Germany in 2009 for the first time publicized the vacancy and sought applications from a broader public.[1864] But this does not mean that the selection of the three nominees is any less political or even transparent. Which candidates are selected on the basis of the applications that are received is ultimately a decision remaining with the government and taken behind closed doors.[1865] In 2006 the German Federal Council (*Bundesrat*) suggested amending the Law on the Election of Judges (*Richterwahlgesetz*) so as to include in the selection of the nominees the representation of the states, by making the nominations dependent on consultation with the Committee for the Selection of Judges (*Richterwahlausschuss*).[1866] One reason behind this

1861 Meyer-Ladewig, Jens, *Europäische Menschenrechtskonvention: Handkommentar* (Nomos Baden-Baden 2nd edn. 2006), 245-246.

1862 According to F. Wittreck, this is the reason why in 2004 the then German judge of the ECtHR, G. Ress, who was nominated by a conservative government, was replaced by R. Jaeger, who is said to have been close to the social democratic party: Wittreck, *Die Verwaltung der Dritten Gewalt*, 230.

1863 Pieper, Stefan Ulrich, *Verfassungsrichterwahlen: die Besetzung der Richterbank des Bundesverfassungsgerichts und die Besetzung des Europäischen Gerichtshofes sowie des Europäischen Gerichtshofes für Menschenrechte und des Internationalen Gerichtshofes mit deutschen Kandidaten* (Duncker & Humblot Berlin 1998), 74.

1864 Bundesministerium für Justiz und Verbraucherschutz 'Pressemitteilung: Gesucht – Richterin oder Richter für den Europäischen Gerichtshof für Menschenrechte, Stand: 20.11.2009' available at <http://www.bmj.de/SharedDocs/Archiv/DE/Pressemitteilungen/2009/20091120x_Gesucht_Richterin_oder_Richter_fuer_den_Europaeischen_Gerichtshof_fuer_Menschenrechte.html?nn=4795776%22> (last visited: 21 March 2014).

1865 The public perception is still that the selection of nominees is a matter in which political considerations should have a say: "Die Bundesrepublik hat folglich Interessen zu wahren, wenn sie Richter nach Straßburg schickt, auch wenn dies nicht zum förmlichen Anforderungsprofil für den Posten gehört." See Müller-Neuhof, Jost, 'Rechthaber gesucht' *Der Tagesspiegel* (20 Juni 2010).

1866 The legislative proposal was an initiative of the *Land Baden Württemberg*, see Land Baden-Württemberg, *Gesetzesantrag des Landes Baden-Württemberg: En-*

proposal was the perceived increase in the importance of the case law of the ECtHR (as well as other international jurisdictions) for the legal reality in Germany and the executive and opaque procedure for the selection of the nominees, which did not do the standing of these positions any justice.[1867] The proposal was never adopted.[1868]

e) Election of the Judges by the PACE

Although the PACE is bound by Arts. 21-22 ECHR in the election of new judges, it also has a certain latitude in establishing the procedure of the election. The PACE has thus opted to demand that a standard *curriculum vitae* is filled out by the nominees and that interviews with the nominees are conducted by the already mentioned special sub-committee. The practice of the PACE in adopting an increasingly detailed procedure for its own assessment of the nominees has been confirmed by the ECtHR in the advisory opinion of the ECtHR of 12 February 2008 to be part of its task of electing the judges.[1869] According to the ECtHR, in order to choose from among the candidates who are submitted to it, the PACE is first and foremost bound to consider the criteria laid down in Art. 21(1) ECHR. However, in order for it to exercise

> "the freedom of choice conferred on it by Art. 22, which it must exercise in the interests of the proper functioning and the authority of the Court … [i]t is obvious

---

twurf eines Gesetzes zur Änderung des Richterwahlgesetzes (23 December 2005) Drucksache 915/05; Bundesrat, *Gesetzesantrag des Bundesrates: Entwurf eines [...] Gesetzes zur Änderung des Richterwahlgesetzes* (10 February 2006) Drucksache 915/05.

1867 Bundesrat, *Gesetzesantrag des Bundesrates: Entwurf eines [...] Gesetzes zur Änderung des Richterwahlgesetzes*, 3. It was also argued that the participation of the Committee for the Selection of Judges would increase the legitimacy of the selection procedure, as half of its members are appointed by the *Bundestag*, the Parliament of the Federal Republic of Germany (cf. § 5 Abs. 1 Law on the Election of Judges [Richterwahlgesetz]) and that the participation of the ministers of justice of the *Länder* through their participation in the Committee would be appropriate; see id., at 4.

1868 Instead the participation of the Committee for the Selection of Judges became mandatory only with regard to the appointment of judges to the ECJ.

1869 *Advisory opinion on certain legal questions concerning the lists of candidates submitted with a view to the election of judges to the European Court of Human*, para. 43 *in fine*.

> too that the Assembly may take account of additional criteria which it considers relevant for the purposes of choosing between the candidates put forward by a Contracting Party and may, as it has done in a bid to ensure transparency and foreseeability, incorporate those criteria in its resolutions and recommendations."[1870]

The strong wording that it is seemingly "obvious" that the PACE may establish additional criteria and that this has a value for the "proper functioning and the authority of the Court", more than merely suggests that the Court considered it to be in its own interest that one should not just rely on the nominations by Contracting States or the criteria established in Art. 21 ECHR. However, a central problem that has yet to be solved is the fact that the sub-committee too relies on a narrow basis of information, namely still *curricula vitae* submitted by nominating States and rather short interviews held with the nominees directly.

The PACE has also taken the stance that although it has to make a choice on the basis of the list of nominees submitted to it by the contracting States, it is bound primarily to ensure that the criteria of Art. 21(1) are upheld. With respect to ensuring that only independent candidates are being elected, perhaps the most forceful tool at the disposal of the PACE is the power to refuse to consider lists that it does not feel meet the necessary standards. These standards may be those derived directly from Art. 21 ECHR, or even criteria established separately by the Assembly itself. The PACE has in the past not held back in establishing such additional criteria it considered necessary for electing the most suitable candidates (the interest in ensuring the judges' independence was but one driving force, the desire to enable the most efficient court to function another). Hence in the already mentioned resolution 1366 of 2004 the PACE decided not to consider lists of candidates where:[1871]

> i. the areas of competence of the candidates appear to be unduly restricted;
> ii. the list does not include at least one candidate of each sex;
> iii. the candidates:
>   a. do not appear to have sufficient knowledge of at least one of the two official languages, or
>   b. do not appear to be of the stature to meet the criteria in Article 21, paragraph 1, of the European Convention on Human Rights.

1870 Ibid, paras. 44-45.

1871 Parliamentary Assembly of the Council of Europe, *Resolution 1366 – Candidates for the European Court of Human Rights*, para. 3.

In addition the PACE will reject lists where they do not provide it with "a real choice among the candidates submitted by a state party", and where the national selection procedure is deemed not to be fair, transparent and consistent.[1872] While this sounds like a rather strong sanction mechanism that may help to ensure that truly independent judges are voted to the bench, it does suffer from a lack of information on which the PACE may make its decisions.

4. Distribution of Cases

The provisions pertaining to the distribution of cases between the sections of the Court are somewhat worrying from the perspective of ensuring assignment that is not susceptible to bias and e.g. politically motivated allocation of cases. According to Rules 51(1) and 52(1) the President of the Court is vested with the power to assign inter-State applications and individual application to the different sections. For neither of the different kinds of applications do the Rules provide more information on the criteria according to which this assignment is to be made. The President thus alone has the authority to make the distribution and merely in the assignment of individual applications is guided by a traceable criterion, namely the call that decisions "shall endeavour to ensure a fair distribution of cases between the Sections."[1873]

First, it must be asked what a *fair* distribution is and if this criterion is supposed and able to protect against the exertion of influence harming the Court's independence. A distribution can be fair if it is equitable in the sense of distributing the workload of the Court fairly between the sections. *Prima facie* this objective consideration suggests that a practical evaluation of the workload of the sections, the judges and the Court overall be made by the President before he makes his decisions. It becomes even more apparent in the French version of the text, which speaks of "une répartition équitable de la charge de travail". But it may also, in a wider sense, be interpreted to mean assignment free from bias, dishonesty, or injustice, and that applications are assigned in a way that excludes the appearance of bias, i.e. adherence to

1872 Parliamentary Assembly of the Council of Europe, *Resolution 1646 – Nomination of candidates and election of judges to the European Court of Human Rights*, para. 2.

1873 Rule 52(1).

subjective factors.[1874] Since Rule 52(1) uses the notion of fairness in the sense of a principle of proportionality between the different sections of the Court ("fair distribution of cases *between the Sections*"; emphasis added), it appears unlikely that it was intended as a tool to ensure the independent functioning of the Court. This interpretation is slightly questioned by the fact that inter-State applications apparently are not required to be distributed following a fairness standard. If indeed the requirement is only a tool to ensure a balanced workload, then the nature of the application, whether made by a High Contracting Party or by an individual, non-governmental organisation or group of individuals, should be irrelevant, and thus Rule 51(1) should have been put in similar wording to that of Rule 52(1). Even the fact that there are a considerably larger number of individual applications lodged with the Court[1875] does not help, since it is the fairness of the overall workload of the Sections as such that is decisive. The assignment of an application to a Section that would be considered unfair in the sense of a comparatively excessive workload would have to be considered such irrespective of whether it concerned an inter-State or individual application. On the other hand, if the criterion of fairness also entailed considerations that aimed to ensure an unbiased bench, then its absence with regard to inter-State applications, i.e. in Rule 51(1), would be coherent with the same challenging homage to State interests that justifies that "the judges elected in respect of the applicant and respondent Contracting Parties shall sit as ex officio members of the Chamber constituted to consider the case."[1876] Overall, therefore, the criterion of fairness does allow for the consideration of applications in a way that favours independent adjudication. However, irrespective of the interpretation given to this criterion the criticism must remain that there is a lack of randomness in the assignment of applications which would have provided a safeguard against undue influence having directed the distribution of applications. At least if the other judges, or the Bureau, had been able to scrutinize the exercise the discretion under Rules 51(1) and 52(1) it could have been ensured that no undue influence was exerted. However, as the Rules are formulated, only the President makes these decisions.

1874 'Oxford English Dictionary' available at <http://www.oed.com/> (last visited: 21 March 2014): "fair".

1875 See Oeter, Stefan, 'European Commission and Court of Human Rights, Inter-State Applications', in: Bernhardt, Rudolf (ed) *Encyclopedia of Public International Law, Revised Library Edition, Instalment 2* (North-Holland Amsterdam 1995).

1876 Rule 51(2). Cf. Rule 26(1)(a).

The assignment of cases in single-judge formations,[1877] which were introduced by the Court in 2006, is regulated in the Rules of Court in the sense that the President shall draw up in advance the list of Contracting Parties in respect of which each judge shall examine applications.[1878] The President therefore appoints the judges that shall sit in single-judge formations, and before any applications are assigned determines which judge shall be responsible for dealing with these cases. Although this order does not entirely prevent the President allocating a judge to a country in respect of which he has certain prejudices, it does prevent *ad hoc* assignments based on such bias. There is furthermore the limitation following from Art. 26(3) ECHR according to which no judge shall examine an application against the Contracting State in respect of which that judge has been elected.[1879] This must be considered a fair balance of interests, especially as it would be incomprehensible for the applicant if, having gone through all national judicial instances unsuccessfully, he were even in Strasbourg to see his claim being adjudicated upon by a judge from his home State.[1880] The institution of a national judge thus finds its limitation when that judge sits alone.[1881]

Separate from but linked to the question of which judge or formation should deal with a case is the question of the order in which cases are dealt with. Although this merely relates to an administrative issue and does not as such affect the determination of the case on the merits, it is nevertheless important for the applicants to know that their cases cannot be pushed around arbitrarily, but are part of a distribution of work round the Court based on objective criteria. This is ensured in Rule 41 according to which the order of dealing with cases shall be determined by the Court having "regard to the importance and urgency of the issues raised on the basis of criteria fixed by it."[1882] The Chamber, or its President, may, however, derogate from these

1877 See further on the single-judge formation *infra* Chapter H.IV(6).

1878 Rule 27A(1).

1879 Lemmens, Paul, 'Single-Judge Formations, Committees, Chambers and Grand Chamber', in: Lemmens, Paul *et al.* (eds) *Protocol No. 14 and the Reform of the European Court of Human Rights* (Intersentia Antwerpen 2005), 33.

1880 Cf. Böcker, R.A.A., 'Protocol nr. 14 bij het EVRM. Hervorming van de hervorming' (2004) NJB, 1841.

1881 Interestingly despite the fact that every judge must be independent and impartial and despite the ability of a judge to declare himself unable to sit in the case.

1882 So far the Court has not – at least officially – laid down any rules that would apply such *importance* and *urgency* criteria. Instead the cases are dealt with chronologically.

criteria so as to give priority to a particular application. This has e.g. occurred in four cases dealing with the Chechnya conflict.[1883] Since this may occur only in exceptional cases, there is no reason to criticize them for compromising independent decision-making.

5. The Institution of National Judge and Ad Hoc Judge

a) Normative Framework and Rationale

The ECtHR does provide for the use of national judges and the appointment of *ad hoc* judges.[1884] Pursuant to Art. 26(4) ECHR every State involved in a case before the ECtHR has the right to have the judge of its nationality (i.e. the national judge) sit on the bench of a Chamber or Grand Chamber and, if that judge cannot sit, the right to make nominations for an *ad hoc* judge. When considering the parallelism and conditionality of the institutions of national and *ad hoc* judges in Art. 26(4) ECHR and Rule 29 – which rounds off the ECHR provision – it seems that the institution of *ad hoc* judge is used to ensure that every State Party that appears before the Court as a respondent has not just one judge of its own nationality, but indeed one judge that represents that State.[1885] The national judge thus can be said occasionally to serve the same function as the *ad hoc* judge does; the difference is merely the way in which they become judges and the extent of their remit.

1883 *Ibragimov and others v. Russia* (ECtHR) Application No. 34561/03 (29 May 2008); *Betayev and Betayeva v. Russia* (ECtHR) Application No. 37315/03 (29 May 2008); *Sangariyeva and others v. Russia* (ECtHR) Application No. 1839/04 (29 May 2008); *Gekhayeva and others v. Russia* (ECtHR) Application No. 1755/04 (29 May 2008).

1884 Cf. Art. 55(1) ACHR, according to which a judge who is a national of any of the States Parties to a case submitted to the Court, shall retain his right to hear that case. See also Art. 10(1) Statute of the IACtHR. In contrast there is no ability to appoint *ad hoc* judges on the African Court on Human and Peoples' Rights; Art. 22 Protocol to the African Charter on Human and Peoples' Rights on the Establishment of an African Court on Human and Peoples' Rights prevents the judge who is a national of any State which is a party to a case submitted to the Court from hearing that case.

1885 The Report of the Committee on Legal Affairs and Human Rights speaks of "national representativity"; Parliamentary Assembly of the Council of Europe, *Nomination of Candidates and Election of Judges to the European Court of Human Rights*, para. 34.

This representation is ensured by one of three mechanisms to determine a country-specific judge in a particular case: (I) the affected State may have its already elected judge sit on the case, which for practical reasons is likely to be the main rule. (II) If that judge is unable to sit on the case, because the State temporarily does not have its own judge on the Court or that judge was forced to withdraw from the case, the State may appoint one person from among the other (already) elected judges. (III) The State may also, however, opt to appoint as *ad hoc* judge a person who has not at that time already been elected to that office. *Ad hoc* judges at the ECtHR thus serve similar purposes to their counterparts at other courts which have been addressed earlier in this study. According to the rationale that was used with respect to *ad hoc* judges at the ICJ,[1886] the institution is supposed to contribute special legal expertise and experience to the proceedings.[1887] Thus the idea is that the *ad hoc* judge is used as a kind of judge rapporteur, as this task often presupposes the scrutiny of legal documents and materials (e.g. national laws and court judgments) in the language of his home State.[1888] However, already at this point of the analysis it must be pointed out that it can only be a surprise that this institution is also used in a human rights court where the individual, due to the violations of his rights, is supposed to be at the centre of attention. In the context of the ICJ, *ad hoc* judges served the purpose of enabling all the States involved to have one judge who ensures that special expertise with regard to those States is represented on the bench. If this is the main justification for the *ad hoc* judges at the ECtHR as well, and that seems to be the case, then immediately the question must be raised why the individual, who is also a party before the ECtHR, does not have a similar right. The individual is recognized by the ECHR to be a subject of international law, endowed with his own rights and duties. Giving only the States appearing before the ECtHR a right to have their *own* judge on the bench (as opposed to an expert who may assist the Court in gaining knowledge of pertinent national laws, national court judgments etc.) without conceding the same right to the other party, the individual whose rights under the ECHR have allegedly been violated by that State, can be logically sustainable only if the *ad hoc* judge is fully embedded in a dogmatic framework that leaves no doubt as to that judge's independence and impartiality, especially, but not exclusively, *vis-*

1886 Cf. Art. 31 ICJ Statute.

1887 Korinek & Holoubek (eds), *Österreichisches Bundesverfassungsrecht: Textsammlung und Kommentar*, Art. 27 para. 7.

1888 Cf. Rules 48-50; see also ibid, Art. 27 para. 7.

à-vis the State in question. This is especially the case as the criteria for judicial office in Art. 21 ECHR automatically apply only to judges who are being elected in the ordinary procedure. The safeguards that are in place to ensure the independence and impartiality of *ad hoc* judges, and especially those who are appointed specifically for that purpose (i.e. category III above), thus deserve to be examined.

b) Safeguards for the Independence of Ad Hoc Judges

If there is no judge elected in respect of the High Contracting Party concerned or that judge is unable to sit, the Contracting Party must submit the list of potential *ad hoc* judges "in advance".[1889] Although this formulation is rather vague, according to the Explanatory Report to Protocol No. 14, which amended the procedure for appointing *ad hoc* judges to narrow the discretion of States Parties in choosing a person, it ought to be interpreted as meaning that the States must submit their lists before the proceedings have begun.[1890] The new Art. 26(4) ECHR was a response to the earlier Art. 27(2) ECHR,[1891] which merely provided that the State may, if the judge elected in respect of the State party concerned is unable to sit, choose who else should sit as an *ex officio* member of the Chamber or Grand Chamber. This provision effectively enabled the judges to be selected after the proceedings had already commenced, i.e. after the content of the complaint had been made known, and thus increased the risk that *ad hoc* judges were chosen for their particular opinions favourable to the selecting country in the particular case.[1892] In other words, States could ensure for themselves a particular vote on the bench, something which is hardly, if at all, compatible with an independent

1889 Art. 26(4) ECHR and rule 29(1)(b).

1890 See Council of Europe, *Protocol No. 14 to the Convention for the Protection of Human Rights and Fundamental Freedoms, amending the control system of the Convention, Explanatory Report*, para. 64.

1891 Art. 27(2) ECHR old wording: "There shall sit as an ex officio member of the Chamber and the Grand Chamber the judge elected in respect of the State Party concerned or, if there is none or if he is unable to sit, *a person of its choice* who shall sit in the capacity of judge." (Emphasis added.).

1892 Van Leuven, Nathalie, 'The Judges of the European Court and the Commissioner for Human Rights', in: Lemmens, Paul *et al.* (eds) *Protocol No. 14 and the Reform of the European Court of Human Rights* (Intersentia Antwerpen 2005), 25-26.

bench.[1893] The criticism of this system must be extended so as also to encompass the recognition that it violated the principle of the right to a lawful judge, as it did not provide those appearing before the Court with knowledge of which judges and which formation would rule in the case.[1894]

The compiling of the lists in advance nevertheless suggests that the institution of *ad hoc* judge is less open to being instrumentalized for undue purposes with a view to a particular case. However, when it comes to the personal qualifications demanded of *ad hoc* judges, they are not automatically subject to the same safeguards for judicial independence and impartiality as their full-time colleagues. For one reason it is not possible to demand the same kind of forswearing of activities additional to judicial office, as the *ad hoc* judge is not working for the Court on a full-time basis.[1895] Thus the protection of judicial independence must be ensured specifically with reference to this particular situation. *Ad hoc* judges are fundamentally subject to the same requirements for office as are ordinary judges. Pursuant to Rule 29(1)(d) the *ad hoc* judge shall possess the qualifications required by Art. 21(1) ECHR, i.e. be of high moral character and possess either the qualifications required for appointment to high judicial office or be jurisconsults of recognised competence. Rule 29(1)(d) interestingly does not refer to Art. 21(2) ECHR, which contains one of the strongest – if not *the* strongest – protections for ordinary judges' independence and impartiality,[1896] namely the requirement that judges sit in their individual capacity. This provision with respect to ordinary judges is laid down to avoid the conception of judges as representatives of their nominating States and thus to strengthen their independence. Although it is not a necessary conclusion that representation

---

1893 See e.g. Parliamentary Assembly of the Council of Europe, *Nomination of Candidates and Election of Judges to the European Court of Human Rights*, para. 33.

1894 The new system, in the view of a report to the Committee on Legal Affairs and Human Rights in 2011, "strengthens the appearance of independence, since a State Party will no longer play a decisive role in the appointment of an *ad hoc* judge." Parliamentary Assembly of the Council of Europe, *Ad hoc judges at the European Court of Human Rights: an overview, Report, Committee on Legal Affairs and Human Rights, Rapporteur: Mrs Marie-Louise Bemelmans-Videc, the Netherlands, Group of the European People's Party* (19 October 2011) Doc. AS/Jur (2011) 36, para. 13.

1895 Cf. *supra* on more detailed discussion on the requirements that can be posed on *ad hoc* judges.

1896 Frowein, Jochen Abr. & Peukert, Wolfgang, *Europäische Menschenrechtskonvention: EMRK-Kommentar* (N. P. Engel Kehl 3rd edn. 2009), 442.

rules out independence (or impartiality), it nevertheless strengthens the demand for special safeguards for independence if the representative function is not only not ruled out but, in the case of *ad hoc* judges, indeed supported. Rule 29(1)(d) also does not refer to Art. 21(3) ECHR which demands that judges not engage in certain side activities incompatible with their independence, impartiality or with the demands of a full-time office. Whereas, as stated before, *ad hoc* judges *per definitionem* cannot be made subject to the same requirements as their full-time colleagues, it is not convincing not also to demand of them the termination of any activities harmful to their independence and impartiality. As far as side activities are concerned, Rule 29(1)(d) *in fine* instead establishes the rather selective rule that *ad hoc* judges, for the duration of their appointment, "shall not represent any party or third party in any capacity in proceedings before the Court." As welcoming as this provision is, it does not go far enough. Is it for example reasonable that the representation of a party before the Court in different proceedings is the only side activity that may be potentially harmful to the judge's independence? What should reasonably be the view with regard to occupations within a government of the respondent State before the ECtHR? In defence of *ad hoc* judges' independence in this regard, i.e. with regard to affiliations and side activities, one may point to the demand that *ad hoc* judges "must not be unable to sit in the case on any of the grounds referred to in Rule 28". This entails that a person may become an *ad hoc* judge only if he does not have a personal interest in the case, has not previously acted in the case, engages in any political or administrative activity or any professional activity which is incompatible with his independence or impartiality, has not expressed opinions publicly that are objectively capable of adversely affecting his impartiality, or if, for any other reason, his independence or impartiality cannot legitimately be called into doubt. Thus in essence, the fact that Rule 29(1)(d) does not refer to Art. 21(2)-(3) ECHR merely allows the conclusion that *ad hoc* judges are representatives of their States, but not that their side activities are less regulated, or their independence less secured. In support of this one may also refer to the fact that Rule 29(1)(d) does not refer to Rule 4, which details the incompatible activities for full-time judges. Here too, as with to Rule 28, the formulation is chosen "administrative activity or any professional activity which is incompatible with their independence or impartiality", merely adding "or with the demands of a full-time office", which for obvious reasons cannot be applied to *ad hoc* judges. Indeed it can be claimed that Rule 28(2)(c) goes even further, by expressly maintaining that "political" activities which are incompatible with the judge's independence and impartiality disqualify him from sitting on a case.[1897]

c) The Voting Behaviour of Ad Hoc Judges – Evidence of (In-) Dependence?

Although in the past allegations that *ad hoc* judges are partial have been shown to be largely without merit,[1898] there are instances of abusive appointment of *ad hoc* judges. One such example occurred in 2007 when Ukraine announced that it would withdraw its list of candidates for election to the bench of the ECtHR, as the list did not "correspond to the requirements of Article 21 of the Convention and … recommendations of the Council of Europe" because "significant procedural violations [had been] committed", "the transparent voting procedure for the candidates [had] not been ensured" and because the Council of Judges of Ukraine had considered that one of the candidates had "no high moral character".[1899] The list was eventually resubmitted but without the name of a third candidate whom the PACE could have considered. By excluding a nomination for the third judge, Ukraine prevented the PACE from electing a new judge with respect to Ukraine, since the minimum requirement of a list of three candidates nominated by the relevant Contracting Party[1900] had not been met. As a result, Ukraine appointed an *ad hoc* judge for a longer time. The issue was ultimately settled, not at least due to the clarification of the legal issues involved by the advisory opinion of the ECtHR. However, the incident proved that the election procedure, which ensure that judges meet certain requirements in particular with regard to their personal qualifications, could be circumvented.

The overall number of *ad hoc* judges appointed to the ECtHR has been relatively stable since it became a permanent institution. Between 2007 and

---

1897 Although most political activities may already be covered by the formula "any professional activity", reducing the value of that amendment to non-professional political activities, such as consultancy tasks.

1898 Korinek & Holoubek (eds), *Österreichisches Bundesverfassungsrecht: Textsammlung und Kommentar*, Art. 27 para. 7.

1899 *Advisory opinion on certain legal questions concerning the lists of candidates submitted with a view to the election of judges to the European Court of Human Rights (No. 2)* (ECtHR [Grand Chamber]) Advisory Opinion No. 2 (22 January 2010), para. 10.

1900 Art. 22(1) ECHR.

2010 a total of 77 *ad hoc* judges were appointed (19 in 2007; 21 in 2008; 20 in 2009; 17 in 2010), and they took part in a total of 516 judgments of the Court's total 6,170 for that period (79 of 1,503 in 2007; 40 of 1,543 in 2008; 246 of 1,625 in 2009; 151 of 1,499 in 2010). Although the number of cases where *ad hoc* judges are involved is not too high, there is a slight tendency for that number to increase. According to a study of the voting behaviour of ECtHR judges between 1960 and 2006 conducted by E. Voeten,[1901] national judges and *ad hoc* judges showed a certain degree of national bias.[1902] When the majority of the Court was against the government, only 7.7% of the judges that were not nationals of that government voted in favour of the government, but 15.8% of the national judges and 33.1% of *ad hoc* judges did. Where the majority of the Court supported the views taken by the government, only 80.6% of the non-national judges voted in favour of the government, i.e. 19.4% took a position different than that of the government. This compares to 95.3% of national judges and 100% of *ad hoc* judges supporting, together with the majority, the positions represented by the government in the particular case. What these data show is of course not that national or *ad hoc* judges are less independent or impartial than their colleagues who have no particular connection to the government appearing before the Court. This conclusion, although a possible one, is not compelling as a number of other factors have to be taken into account when evaluating the reasons why national and *ad hoc* judges favour the respondent State's position more than other judges. But it does show, as can be expected due to the rationale behind the concepts of national and *ad hoc* judges, that those judges are more likely to support the position of the State that nominated them than their colleagues, even if the majority opinion goes against the government. The reasons for this may vary from the closeness of the legal culture which the national and *ad hoc* judges share with their government, to considerations of career prospects, sensitivity to the legal and/or political issues being raised in a case etc. In particular with regard to instances where the national and *ad hoc* judges vote against the majority of the bench but in support of their own

---

1901 Voeten, Erik, 'The Impartiality of International Judges: Evidence from the European Court of Human Rights' (2008) 102 American Political Science Review 4.

1902 For similar empirical studies see Kuijer, Martin, 'Voting Behaviour and National Bias in the European Court of Human Rights and the International Court of Justice' (1997) 10 Leiden Journal of International Law 1 and Bruinsma, Fred J., 'The Room at the Top: Separate Opinions in the Grand Chambers of the ECHR (1998-2006)' (2008) Ancilla Iuris (anci.ch).

government, which according to the above data is rather likely, the explanation may also be that that particular judge interprets the ECHR more restrictively than the other judges. If the aim of national and *ad hoc* judges is "to ensure the factual knowledge of the law and legal practice of the State concerned",[1903] then some of these motivations cannot be censured as distorting an otherwise independent decision. However, if that is the case, it would still be beneficial to ensure that the Court obtained this expertise through other means, e.g. expert opinions of individuals who do not participate in the decision-making itself, so as to exclude even the appearance and risk of a dependent bench.

What thus remains is the contention that national and *ad hoc* judges do add something to the bench. Since it cannot be ruled out that this something is objectively beneficial, in e.g. the sense of knowledge that only such a judge has, it should be ensured that the national and *ad hoc* judges are subject to strict(er) scrutiny, especially when it comes to their nomination and selection. The current order established with the entry into force of Protocol No. 14, although providing for some improvements on the old legal framework, must be considered imperfect as e.g. not imposing a requirement upon nominating States to reveal the procedure followed by them in compiling a list of *ad hoc* judges and because the PACE is excluded from the process, in that the list is submitted by the States Parties directly to the President of the Court.[1904] The appointment of experts, who do not take part in the decision-making but *merely* ensure that the necessary legal knowledge is available to enable the Court to make decisions based on the law and the applicable factual circumstances, would be one way of avoiding these problems and reducing the risk for an independent judiciary inherent in the use of national and *ad hoc* judges, which is indicated *inter alia* by the above empirical data.

1903 Sub-Committee on the election of Judges to the European Court of Human Rights, *Procedure for Electing Judges to the European Court of Human Rights – Information Document Prepared by the Secretariat*, para. 18.

1904 This point not only touches upon the question of how to verify independence and impartiality, i.e. the suitability of nominees, but also upon the question of the legitimacy of the ECtHR. Cf. Parliamentary Assembly of the Council of Europe, *Opinion No. 251 (2004) – Draft Protocol No. 14 to the Convention for the Protection of Human Rights and Fundamental Freedoms amending the control system of the Convention* (2004) available at <http://www.assembly.coe.int/Main.asp?link=/Documents/AdoptedText/ta04/EOPI251.htm> (last visited: 21 March 2014), para. 10.

d) Conclusions

In essence, *ad hoc* judges are subject to the same standards as ordinary judges, and the protection of their independence and impartiality meets the same standards. However, there are significant differences in that they are not subject to the same election procedure; the PACE has virtually no control function compared to that for ordinary judges. The representative role of the *ad hoc* and national judge is not *per se* a contradiction to the desire to ensure their independence and impartiality, although many of the arguments that have been raised in earlier chapters regarding the risks inherent in the institution of judges being appointed to serve in adjudicating on particular cases apply equally to the ECtHR. This is not at least proven by the empirical data that show a national bias by national and *ad hoc* judges which might also be attributed to a lack of independence and impartiality. The safeguards that are in place subject to the post-Protocol No. 14 ECHR era and the Rules of the Court make this balance to the best possible degree and reduce the remaining risk almost to the integrity of the individual judge. The appeal to the judge's integrity is emphasized by the demand that *ad hoc* judges too take the oath or make the solemn declaration provided for in Rule 3, in which judges commit themselves to exercising their functions honourably, independently and impartially.[1905]

6. The Single-Judge Formation – Increasing the Court's Efficiency at the Expense of Independent Decision-Making?

Protocol No. 14, which entered into force on 1 June 2010, introduced to the control machinery of the ECHR the institution of the single judge, or single-judge formation to use the terminology of the ECHR, a figure already well known from many national legal systems. The function of the single-judge is confined to declaring inadmissible or striking out of the Court's list of cases an individual application where such a decision can be taken without further examination.[1906] The single judge is thus not competent to deliver a judgment on the merits. However, he has a significant influence on the functioning of the Court as he regulates which cases are put forward for final

1905 Rule 29(4).
1906 Art. 27(1) ECHR read in conjunction with Art. 34 ECHR. This is complemented primarily by Rule 27A.

judgment. In other words, and formulated with the interest of the independent functioning of the Court in mind, the institution of the single judge "would be workable only as long as the single judge acts in full impartiality, not being led by considerations of enmity or friendship."[1907] The question is of particular importance because whenever the Court takes decisions in a chamber, or whenever judges sit as a collegiate, they can help to neutralize any bias or possible threats to independence which individual judges may have and which might adversely influence the forthcoming judicial decision. With the individual judge this safety mechanism is not in place, and this thus raises the question what other safeguards, if any, are available to secure the independent functioning of the Court when it is operating in this formation.

The single judge may declare a case inadmissible or strike it out only where such a decision is possible "without further examination".[1908] This means that the judge will take such decisions only in clear-cut cases, i.e. manifestly inadmissible applications.[1909] If the decision on the admissibility of a case goes beyond the use of simple and easily applicable rules, that is if it depends on certain policy issues, the question may no longer be a matter for the single judge.[1910] A further basis for single judges not being expected to deal with more difficult cases alone is the new criterion for admissibility introduced by Protocol No. 14. Pursuant to Art. 35(3)(b) ECHR the ECtHR shall declare inadmissible any individual application if it considers that "the applicant has not suffered a significant disadvantage". This criterion was envisaged to be defined "through the gradual development of the case-law of the Court",[1911] and in particular through the case law of the chambers and the Grand Chamber of the Court, not the single-judge formations. Protocol No. 14 explicitly declared that for the two years following its entry into force this new admissibility criterion would be applicable only by Chambers and

1907 Tomuschat, 'The European Court of Human Rights Overwhelmed by Applications: Problems and Possible Solutions', 14.

1908 Art. 27(1) ECHR.

1909 Council of Europe, *Protocol No. 14 to the Convention for the Protection of Human Rights and Fundamental Freedoms, amending the control system of the Convention, Explanatory Report*, para. 67.

1910 Lemmens, 'Single-Judge Formations, Committees, Chambers and Grand Chamber', 34.

1911 Council of Europe, *Protocol No. 14 to the Convention for the Protection of Human Rights and Fundamental Freedoms, amending the control system of the Convention, Explanatory Report*, para. 80.

the Grand Chamber of the Court.[1912] In other words, when making decisions on the admissibility of cases, the single judge must closely follow the established case law of the Court. His ability to give decisions on a basis that deviates from a predictable application of the applicable law is limited. This is emphasized in the Explanatory Report where it is stated that "[i]n case of doubt as to the admissibility, the judge will refer the application to a committee or a Chamber."[1913]

It should further be remarked as a critique of the single-judge formation, however, that there is no remedy in place with which an applicant who alleges to have been the subject of a false or biased decision by a single judge could have this decision reviewed. Although this is clearly motivated by the aim of increasing the filtering capacity of the Court and thus its efficiency, it is somewhat questionable from the perspective of ensuring that decisions are made on the sole basis of the relevant facts and the applicable law. If this is not the case in a particular situation, then the applicant has no opportunity to have his application referred to the Court for a decision on the merits. In fact, pursuant to Art. 27(3) ECHR, decisions of single judges "shall be final."

One safeguard addresses the issue of potential threats to independent decision-making at a much earlier stage. According to Rule 27A(1) single judges are appointed by the President of the Court after consulting the Bureau.[1914] In the exercise of this appointing authority, the President is free to decide on the number of single judges to be appointed and he must draw up in advance the list of Contracting Parties in respect of which each judge shall examine applications throughout the period for which that judge is appointed. This creates an opportunity for the President to excuse a judge from having to deal with cases in regard to which his independence might be questionable. In addition, if the Bureau, which functions as an advisory organ in this respect, considered the appointments inappropriate, it has the right to report on this matter to the Plenary.[1915] A further safeguard follows from Art. 26(3)

1912 Art. 20(2) Protocol No. 14.

1913 Council of Europe, *Protocol No. 14 to the Convention for the Protection of Human Rights and Fundamental Freedoms, amending the control system of the Convention, Explanatory Report*, para. 67.

1914 Pursuant to Rule 9A the Bureau of the Court is to support and assist the President in carrying out his function in directing the work and administration of the Court, and it is made up of President of the Court, the Vice-Presidents and the Section Presidents and any other members of the Court whose presence the Bureau considers necessary.

1915 Rule 9A(6).

ECHR, and is echoed in Rule 52A(2), according to which a "[single] judge shall not examine any application against the High Contracting Party in respect of which that judge has been elected." I.e. cases have to be assigned to judges other than the national judge. Although not mentioned in the Explanatory Report, this is an important provision in deflecting any appearance of bias and addresses the peril formulated by the former President of the Court, Judge L. Wildhaber, that "[e]ven as a very objective observer you may be more lenient towards your own country."[1916] Any advantage that may flow from a judge having the nationality of a Contracting Party that is a respondent in a case, such as the language and knowledge of the potentially affected national legal system,[1917] is well covered by the institution of non-judicial rapporteurs who are to assist the single judge and who function under the authority of the President of the ECtHR.[1918] It is interesting to note that, apparently, the interest of independent decision-making has led to the explicit rejection of the service of a national judge and the use of non-judicial rapporteurs in the single-judge formation, but not, as mentioned earlier, in the Court as a whole. The fact that single-judge formations have competence only to consider individual applications, and not inter-State cases, is almost certainly the bitter explanation.

In sum, it can be said that there are safeguards in place that help to ensure that the single judges are faced only with cases where there is little or no doubt about their independence. Whereas a more solid safeguard would have been to enable the decisions of single judges to be appealed, this was ruled out for efficiency reasons.

1916 Bruinsma, Fred J. & de Blois, Matthijs, 'Rules of Law from Westport to Wladiwostok. Separate Opinions in the European Court of Human Rights' (1997) 15 Netherlands Quarterly of Human Rights 2, 187.

1917 According to the Explanatory Report to Protocol No. 14, "[i]n principle, the single judge should be assisted by a rapporteur *with knowledge of the language and the legal system of the respondent Party*" (emphasis added; Council of Europe, *Protocol No. 14 to the Convention for the Protection of Human Rights and Fundamental Freedoms, amending the control system of the Convention, Explanatory Report*, para. 58). As has been shown above, these grounds are usually referred to when justifying the institution of national and *ad hoc* judges.

1918 Cf. Art. 24(2) ECHR. Cf. the statements to this effect in ibid, para. 58.

7. Financing the ECtHR

a) The Court's Budget as Part of the Ordinary Budget of the CoE

The financing of the ECtHR is a point of concern for the Court itself and for the entire control mechanism under the ECHR. As regards the level of financing of the Court it is less than satisfactory and part of the efficiency problem of the Court in later years.[1919] The Court's budget covers all costs that occur in the context of the Court's adjudicatory and administrative apparatus, including judges' remuneration, staff salaries and operational expenditure.[1920] Despite recent increases the Court's budget remains low compared to those of other international courts, and especially when considering its workload. Handing down more than 1,100 judgments every year since 2005, the ECtHR is far more active than any of the other international courts subject to this study.[1921] One threat for the budget of the Court is that since it is part of the ordinary budget of the CoE, any increase in the financial resources for the Court would, in times without an increase in contributions by States to the CoE, demand cuts in the funds for other activities within the CoE. It is less than satisfactory that the Court thus stands in direct competition with a wide

---

1919 The current budget for 2012 amounts to 67.207 million EUR (Committee of Ministers of the CoE, *The Ordinary Budget for 2012-2013* (23 November 2011) Resolution CM/Res(2011)28). This is a considerable increase as regards the old Court (e.g. the budget was 7 million EUR in 1989) but also the early days of the new, permanent Court (1998: 23 million EUR; 2005: 41.7 million EUR; 2009: 57.047 million EUR (Committee of Ministers of the CoE, *The Ordinary Budget for 2009* (adopted 25 November 2008) Resolution CM/Res(2008)25). For an overview of the development of the budget between 1989 and 2002 see Committee of Ministers of the CoE, *Report of the Evaluation Group to the Committee of Ministers on the European Court of Human Rights* (adopted 27 September 2001) EG Court(2001)1, paras. 16 et seq.

1920 The budget does not include expenditure on buildings and infrastructure (telephone, cabling, etc.): European Court of Human Rights, *Annual Report 2009* (2010) available at <http://www.echr.coe.int/Documents/Annual_report_2009_ENG.pdf> (last visited: 21 March 2014), paras. 31-32.

1921 As regards staff, the Court is well furnished with a Registry staff of 640 staff members, 270 lawyers and 370 other support staff. 'European Court of Human Rights – The Court – Role of the Registry' available at <http://www.echr.coe.int/Pages/home.aspx?p=court/howitworks> (last visited: 21 March 2014).

array of other activities of the CoE. For this very reason it has been suggested that the Court ought to have its own, separate budget.[1922]

Pursuant to Art. 50 ECHR the costs of the Court are born by the CoE. It could be argued that making an international court rely for its financing on an international parent organization or an assembly of States Parties is not problematic as such, as long as the organization or the assembly in question is able to identify with the purpose of the Court, i.e. does not suffocate the Court for lack of its resources or does not use its budgetary power to influence the adjudicatory function of the Court. As a comparison, the ICJ is, pursuant to Art. 33 UNC, financed by the UN and the ITLOS, pursuant to Art. 19 ITLOS Statute, financed by the States Parties to UNCLOS. But the difference between those cases and the organisational context of the ECtHR is that the ECtHR, as stated above, is not an organ of the CoE and thus not automatically part of the ordinary annual budget of the organization.[1923] Thus it appears legitimate to ask what the basis for the CoE's (perceived) responsibility towards the Court is and how sound it is.

In the past the PACE has proven to be a strong proponent of the independent conception of the ECtHR, seen notably in the already mentioned support it gave to the restructuring of the nomination and election procedure for judges. In light of this it must and has been asked[1924] whether it is not a considerable potential threat to the independence of the Court to delegate the authority to decide on the allocation of the budget to an executive organ, the Secretary General of the CoE.[1925] A better solution might have been to require a parliamentary body with a more direct connection with the electorate and representing the overall organization to decide on the budget for the Court. However, that would necessitate changes in the applicable normative framework.[1926]

1922 Ress, 'Der Europäische Gerichtshof für Menschenrechte, seine Reform und die Rolle der nationalen Gerichte', 50; Engel, 'Status, Ausstattung und Personalhoheit des Inter-Amerikanischen und des Europäischen Gerichtshofs für Menschenrechte: Facetten und Wirkungen des institutionellen Rahmens', 133.

1923 Korinek & Holoubek (eds), *Österreichisches Bundesverfassungsrecht: Textsammlung und Kommentar*, Art. 50 para. 2.

1924 Ress, 'Der Europäische Gerichtshof für Menschenrechte, seine Reform und die Rolle der nationalen Gerichte', 558.

1925 Ress, 'Die Organisationsstruktur internationaler Gerichte, insbesondere des neuen Europäischen Gerichtshofs für Menschenrechte', 558.

1926 Cf. Art. 38 Statute of the CoE.

b) The Lack of the Court's Influence on the Process of Adopting the Budget

The Court's budget is subject to the approval of the CoM in the course of its examination of the overall CoE budget. The process is initiated by the annual budget of the CoE being drafted by the Secretary General of the CoE[1927] and subsequently referred to the CoM for approval. Before the draft is referred to the CoM, the Court is given the opportunity, which it regularly seizes, to submit an opinion on the draft. Neither the Secretary General nor the CoM is, however, bound by the opinions of the judges. The draft budget, when referred to the CoM, is accompanied by the opinion of the Budget Committee,[1928] which is composed of eleven independent experts appointed by the CoM and nominated by the Member States.[1929] The budget is put together by the contributions of the forty-seven Member States, which are fixed according to scales taking into account population and gross national product.[1930] According to Art. 26 Financial Regulations the Secretary General may in the course of a financial year submit supplementary appropriation proposals which are considered and approved in the same way as the initial budget. This ability has been used on several occasions in the past, where the Secretary General has successfully pushed for the appropriation of additional funds for the Court.[1931] However, it remains entirely at the discretion of the Secretary General to determine such additional funds, and he may in this regard be guided by a favourable or less favourable attitude towards the

---

1927 Art. 38 Statute of the CoE.

1928 Art. 23 Financial Regulations and Supplementary Provisions of the Council of Europe (12 July 2006) available at <https://wcd.coe.int/ViewDoc.jsp?id=1021635&BackColorInternet=9999CC&BackColorIntranet=FFBB55&BackColorLogged=FFAC75> (last visited: 21 March 2014).

1929 Five experts shall be appointed upon nomination by the five member states paying the highest contribution to the General Budget of the Organization. Six other experts shall be appointed upon nomination by the governments of the other member states. Eleven alternative members shall be appointed by the CoM, under the same conditions, in respect of each state whose candidate is appointed titular member.

1930 Art. 38(b) Statute of the CoE. Committee of Ministers of the CoE, *The adjustment of the scale of contributions to the Council of Europe Ordinary Budget and Budget of the European Youth Foundation with effect from 1 January 2010* (adopted 25 November 2009) Resolution CM/Res(2009)20.

1931 Committee of Ministers of the CoE, *Budgetary needs of the European Court of Human Rights* (20 December 2000) CM/Del/Dec(2000)734/1.5, 733/1.6 and 731/1.5, GT-BC-2001(2000)1.

Court. There is also no formal procedure enabling the Court to make own proposals to the CoM on additional budgetary resources without the support of the Secretary General. Instead the Court is limited to making informal demands. One such example is the demand made by the President of the ECtHR at the European Ministerial Conference on Human Rights, that considerable extra resources should be made available two years after the major overhaul by Protocol No. 11, and for "arrangements allowing for the separate treatment of the Court's budget."[1932] Further the Court holds regular – but apparently informal – consultations with the Secretary General of the CoE.[1933]

That the ECtHR is not autonomous with regard to budgetary issues is not unlike what applies for other international courts. However, since the Court also does not have a right to make a proposal for its budget, it also has no influence on how the budget is distributed between the different posts. Instead it is the Secretary General who lists how the budget is distributed, e.g. between staff expenditure, information technology, costs of home leave for staff, and other administrative and logistical support. The only way for the Court to influence the budget is by being included in the drafting process upon the invitation of either the Secretary General or the CoM.[1934] The Court, unlike other international courts such as the ICJ, thus does not have its own budget or the ability significantly to influence the budgeting process, e.g. through a right to initiate the drafting of the Court's budget.[1935] The fact that the Court's involvement in the budgetary drafting process is at the discretion of the Secretary General of the CoE must in particular be criticised for being overly custodial and for not allowing the Court to put forward its own interests forcefully.

1932 Steering Committee for Human Rights, *Reforming the European Convention on Human Rights: a work in progress; a compilation of publications and documents relevant to the ongoing reform of the ECHR* (Council of Europe Publishers Strasbourg 2009), 34.

1933 Boer-Buquicchio, 'Klarstellung zum Status des Europäischen Gerichtshofs für Menschenrechte und seiner Beziehungen zum Europarat', 562-563.

1934 See ibid, 562, who speaks of a comprehensive (*umfassend*) inclusion of the Court in the deliberations of the drafting of the parts of the budget referring to the ECtHR.

1935 Korinek & Holoubek (eds), *Österreichisches Bundesverfassungsrecht: Textsammlung und Kommentar*, Art. 50 para. 4.

c) Assessment of the System for Financing of the ECtHR

Whether the bodies that are involved in the process of drafting or adopting the budget, in particular the CoM, actually use their authority to influence the adjudicatory functions of the Court is doubtful. To the degree that the Court is equipped with too little resources, this is likely to be a result of the notorious under-financing that every international court is experiencing and that the judges often criticise. And although the budget is still very low compared to those of the other courts that have been analysed so far, especially when considering the number of cases dealt with by the Court, the budget has increased steadily in recent years and currently amounts to more than 25% of the total general budget of the CoE. Thus it cannot be claimed that the CoE is generally withholding the necessary financial assets from the Court or that the CoE would be generally unwilling to provide the necessary resources. But the argument that can be made is that the normative framework is unsatisfactory in that it does not pay respect to the importance of having the Court actively involved in the budgetary process. This is of course a consequence of the historical context, where the Court grew into the CoE, rather than being conceived, in its current form as a permanent international human rights court, as part of an international organization. It would pay tribute to the important role played by the Court, as well as its self-conception as an independently functioning court, if it were integrated into the budget process.

V. Personal Independence

1. Required Qualifications of Judges

The preconditions for office are laid down in Art. 21 ECHR and provide that judges be of high moral character and either possess the qualifications required for appointment to high judicial office or be jurisconsults of recognized competence. The formulation in Art. 21(1) ECHR is almost identical to the corresponding provision in the ICJ Statute,[1936] whereas the wording of Art. 21(1) ECHR is wider when not limiting the recognised competence of jurisconsults to international law, and when not limiting the qualifications

1936 Art. 2 ICJ Statute.

for appointment to high judicial office to that of their respective countries.[1937] The ECHR does not demand that the judges possess special competence either in international law or in human rights law, the latter of which may come as a surprise in view of the fact that the ECtHR is a human rights court. In comparison, the IACHR mentions recognized competence in the field of human rights as an explicit requirement for any person who aspires to be elected to the IACtHR.[1938]

A provision that must be welcomed as supporting the protection of the independence of the judges is Art. 21(2) ECHR providing that "[t]he judges shall sit on the Court in their individual capacity." Judges of the ECtHR are thus not to be seen as representatives of the country of which they are nationals or of the country that proposes them as candidates. This gains additional importance in the context of the ECtHR where every State Party to the ECHR is entitled to have one judge on the Court,[1939] thus creating an appearance of representation of State interests on the Court through the judges.[1940] The IACHR contains a similar requirement;[1941] however, the importance of this prerequisite in the context of the IACtHR is weakened as not every State Party to the IACHR is entitled to appoint a judge to the bench.[1942] Thus the significance of judges' nationality as a factor which might influence their decision-making is considerably weakened. Nevertheless, Art. 21(2) ECHR serves this important function to mandate that judges be entirely free, when

---

1937 Cf., however, Art. 52(1) IACHR, requiring judges of the IACtHR to "possess the qualifications required for the exercise of the highest judicial functions *in conformity with the law of the state of which they are nationals or of the state that proposes them as candidates.*" (Emphasis added.).

1938 Art. 52(1) IACHR. This provision also demands that judges be "elected in an individual capacity", i.e. are not representatives of their Government, and "possess the qualifications required for the exercise of the highest judicial functions in conformity with the law of the state of which they are nationals or of the state that proposes them as candidates."

1939 Cf. Art. 20 ECHR.

1940 The composition of the IACtHR differs from that of the ECtHR in that only seven judges serve on that court. These judges must be nationals of the member states of the Organization of American States and no two judges may be nationals of the same state (Arts. 52(1)-(2) IACHR).

1941 Judges of the IACtHR are "elected in an individual capacity", Art. 52(1) IACtHR.

1942 And indeed several judges have had nationalities that differed from that of the State making the nomination (cf. Art. 53(2) IACHR).

exercising their judicial function, from any kind of instructions.[1943] From an empirical perspective, however, the evidence shows that judges of the ECtHR are no more likely at least to vote against the majority of the Court when their home State is found to be in violation of the ECHR.[1944] This indicates that the demand that judges sit in their individual capacity only is not merely a theoretical requirement but one that is actually followed in practice.

2. Tenure and Security of Tenure

a) Duration of the Term of Office – The Length of Office and the Need for Re-Election

The original ECHR provided in Art. 40(1) that the tenure of judges should be nine years.[1945] Protocol No. 11 changed the system to renewable six year terms, in order to increase the rotation on the bench,[1946] a fact which was emphasized by leaving the number of possible re-elections unlimited.[1947] However, the PACE voiced its support for the reintroduction of the nine-year term in 2004, referring to the desire to ensure the judges' independence and impartiality.[1948] One of the first suggestions for again introducing the term of nine years for the judges' tenure can be found in the Report of the Evaluation Group to the Committee of Ministers on the European Court of

---

1943 Frowein & Peukert, *Europäische Menschenrechtskonvention: EMRK-Kommentar*, 442.

1944 Ibid, 442. According to the above-mentioned empirical study conducted by E. Voeten, the percentage of judges who voted against the Government was only slightly different between judges who were nationals of the Government (84.2%) and those who did not hold the same nationality (92.3%); Voeten, 'The Impartiality of International Judges: Evidence from the European Court of Human Rights', 425.

1945 Council of Europe, *Collected Edition of the "Travaux Préparatoires" of the European Convention on Human Rights – Volume VII – Standing Committee of the Consultative Assembly, Consultative Assembly, Committee of Experts, Committee of Ministers, Legal Committee, 3 November 1950 – 15 May 1951*, 68.

1946 This term is still used for judges at the IACtHR, cf. Art. 54 IACHR.

1947 Cf. however Art. 54 IACHR.

1948 "The Assembly, being concerned to ensure the independence and impartiality of judges, considers that their appointment should run for nine years non-renewable." Parliamentary Assembly of the Council of Europe, *Resolution 1366 – Candidates for the European Court of Human Rights*, para. 6.

Human Rights of 2001,[1949] where reference was also made to the ECtHR's own case law which, in the interpretation of Art. 6 ECHR, demanded of national courts a high standard of objective independence and impartiality. Furthermore the Committee on Legal Affairs and Human Rights in a report dating from 2003 made the following expressive statement:

> "The Sub-Committee is aware both of anecdotal reports and one specific case concerning judges who have expressed views or ruled contrary to the wishes of their nominating government coming under pressure from that government. The threat of non re-nomination may carry with it substantial adverse consequences for the individual concerned."[1950]

Also in scholarly writing, numerous examples of cases where the absence of re-nomination was identified as a potential form of punishment for judge's participation in certain opinions of the Court were raised.[1951] Building on these comments the PACE set the ball rolling with its recommendation 1649 (2004) wherein it ascertained "that a nine-year term of office would contribute to the greater efficiency and continuity of the Court and would consolidate its independence."[1952] These developments culminated in Protocol No. 14 suggesting a single, non-renewable term of nine years.[1953] In particular, the reform was declared to be motivated by removing the potential weakening

1949 Committee of Ministers of the CoE, *Report of the Evaluation Group to the Committee of Ministers on the European Court of Human Rights*, para. 89.

1950 Parliamentary Assembly of the Council of Europe, *Candidates for the European Court of Human Rights, Report, Committee on Legal Affairs and Human Rights, Rapporteur: Mr Kevin McNamara, United Kingdom, Socialist Group* (7 October 2003) Doc. 9963, para. 68.

1951 See, e.g., Flauss, Jean-François, 'Libres propos sur l'indépendance des juges à la Cour européenne des droits de l'homme', in: Böhmer, Jürgen (ed) *Internationale Gemeinschaft und Menschenrechte – Festschrift für Georg Ress zum 70. Geburtstag am 21. Januar 2005* (Heymann Köln 2005); Schubarth, Martin, 'Der europäische Richter – ein unabhängiger Richter? Mit Hinweisen zum schweizerischen Recht', in: Donatsch, Andreas (ed) *Strafrecht, Strafprozessrecht und Menschenrechte: Festschrift für Stefan Trechsel zum 65. Geburtstag* (Schulthess Zürich 2002), 100 et seq.

1952 Parliamentary Assembly of the Council of Europe, *Recommendation 1649 – Candidates for the European Court of Human Rights*. This was reiterated in Parliamentary Assembly of the Council of Europe, *Resolution 1366 – Candidates for the European Court of Human Rights*, para. 6.

1953 Protocol No. 14 to the Convention for the Protection of Human Rights and Fundamental Freedoms, amending the control system of the Convention (adopted 13 May 2004, entered into force 1 June 2010) CETS No. 194.

of judicial independence that flows from a system of re-appointment.[1954] Extending the term from six to nine years thus was more a necessary consequence of, rather than a decisive reason for, the reform in and of itself, since otherwise the continuity on the Court would have been threatened. Proposals were submitted on an even longer duration of the judges' tenure, e.g. modelled on the tenure of judges of the German constitutional court, which is 12 years.[1955] However, it seems that the drafters of Protocol No. 14 in general and the PACE in particular in their final decision were guided by the recent developments in the international judiciary, most prominently the length of tenure at the ITLOS or the length of tenure and single-term policy at the ICC.[1956] Interestingly, the Institut de Droit International in its sixth resolution of 2011, addressing the position of international judges, made the very same connections that were made in Protocol No. 14. Pursuant to Art. 2 ("Term of Judicial Functions") of the Resolution, the Institute reached the conclusion that "[i]n order to strengthen the independence of judges, it would be desirable that they be appointed for long terms of office, ranging between nine and twelve years" and that such terms "should not be renewable". The earlier provision on a special procedure whereby large groups of judges were replaced at three-year intervals has also been omitted[1957] to ensure that the introduction of a non-renewable term of office does not threaten the continuity of the Court.[1958]

1954 See the Council of Europe, *Protocol No. 14 to the Convention for the Protection of Human Rights and Fundamental Freedoms, amending the control system of the Convention, Explanatory Report*, para. 50. Mahoney, Paul, 'The International Judiciary – Independence and Accountability' (2008) 7 The Law and Practice of International Courts and Tribunals 3, 330.

1955 Grabenwarter suggests a non-renewable tenure of 10-12 years, Grabenwarter, Christoph, 'Zur Zukunft des Europäischen Gerichtshofs für Menschenrechte: Generalbericht zur Tagung' (2003) 30 Europäische Grundrechte-Zeitschrift 4/6, 175. See also Krüger, Hans Christian, 'Die Auswahl der Richter für den neuen Europäischen Gerichtshof für Menschenrechte' (1997) 24 Europäische Grundrechte-Zeitschrift 17/18, 399.

1956 Cf. Institut de Droit International, *The Position of the International Judge – Rapporteur: Gilbert Guillaume – 6th Resolution – Sixth Commission – Session de Rhodes*, para. 36.

1957 Cf. the earlier Art. 23(1)-(4) ECHR.

1958 Council of Europe, *Protocol No. 14 to the Convention for the Protection of Human Rights and Fundamental Freedoms, amending the control system of the Convention, Explanatory Report*, para. 51.

b) A Fixed Retirement Age – Is it Necessary and What are the Advantages?

A controversial and among international courts unique provision is the fixed retirement age at the ECtHR. The obligation for ECtHR judges to step down from the bench upon reaching the age of 70 was included with the entry into force of Protocol No. 11.[1959] The provision sought to bring the Court system into conformity with such rules existing in most domestic legal systems, and because the Court was to function on a permanent basis.[1960] It could be said that a retirement age of this kind addresses a hypothesis flowing from the earlier mentioned question of re-electability: if judges are more likely to decide in a particular way in order to secure their reappointment, then having a mandatory retirement age should make the judges less inclined to present such bias. In other words, the mandatory retirement age may be conceived as a limitation of the adverse effect of re-election. However, the preparatory works do not suggest that this was the case, and moreover especially since the re-electability was omitted with Protocol No. 14, this rationale has lost its basis.

One of the greatest practical threats from this provision would be if candidates who were older than 61 years were to be ruled out, or if States felt reluctant to nominate individuals older than 61 years due to the fear of having to choose a new judge within only a few years. In particular, older judges are by no means physically or even mentally less suited to coping with the work on the ECtHR, although the workload should not be underestimated.[1961] However, Protocol No. 14 provided for this problem, which arose once re-electability had been omitted, and therefore clarified in the Explanatory Report that the relevant provision, Art. 23(1)-(2) ECHR, "may not be understood

---

1959 Art. 23(6) ECHR.

1960 Parliamentary Assembly of the Council of Europe, *70-year age limit for the judges of the European Court of Human Rights, Report, Committee on Legal Affairs and Human Rights, Rapporteur: Lord Kirkhill, United Kingdom, Socialist Group* (6 November 2000) Doc. 8887, para. 2. Council of Europe, *Protocol No. 11 to the Convention for the Protection of Human Rights and Fundamental Freedoms, restructuring the control machinary established thereby, Explanatory Report*, para. 63.

1961 In comparison, as of June 2012, four out of 15 ICJ judges would have had immediately to step down from the bench if a similar set retirement age had been applied to the ICJ. Another three would have had to follow in the next five years. Thet situation is even "worse" at the ITLOS, where at the time of writing 11 of the 21 judges are over 70 years old, with nine judges having served for nine years or longer.

as excluding candidates who, on the date of election, would be older than 61. That would be tantamount to unnecessarily depriving the Court of the possibility of benefiting from experienced persons, if elected."[1962] Instead, it is generally recommended that Member States avoid proposing candidates who, in view of their age, would not be able to hold office for at least half of their nine-year term before reaching the age of 70.[1963] From the perspective of personal independence, i.e. the protection of the judge's individual legal position against external influence, it cannot as a rule be claimed that a fixed retirement age is detrimental, although this is why it was rejected for the ICJ.[1964] As long as it is predetermined and has the legal consequences as defined in the applicable law, then retirement due to age is not an exertion of influence that is detrimental to the independent exercise of a judicial duty. However, it should be cautioned that the rule might influence not only Contracting States in gradually nominating young candidates, but also younger individuals in "seeking" nominations. All fears for the independent character of judges' minds that this could raise would have to remain an assumption as there are no empirical data to suggest that younger individuals chum up to authorities responsible for the nominations, as compared to more senior individuals who would not consider a nomination as another step on their career ladder, but indeed as the culmination of their professional life.

c) Security of Tenure – Removal of Judges

The original ECHR did not provide for the ability to remove a judge, although Art. 18 ICJ Statute was well known to the drafters of the Statute. The lack of such a provision in scholarship was sometimes, surprisingly, interpreted as a further guarantee of the judges' independence.[1965] The new ECHR

1962 Council of Europe, *Protocol No. 14 to the Convention for the Protection of Human Rights and Fundamental Freedoms, amending the control system of the Convention, Explanatory Report*, para. 53; van Leuven, 'The Judges of the European Court and the Commissioner for Human Rights', 25.

1963 The Contracting States seem to have listened to this advice, as the average age of judges serving on the ECtHR as of June 2012 is 56.2 years, with an average of 6.7 years served on the Court.

1964 Cf. *supra* Chapter D.VI(2)(b).

1965 See Weil, *The European Convention on Human Rights: Background, Development and Prospects*, 148 and Eissen, Marc-André, 'La Cour Européenne des Droits de L'Homme – De la Convention au Reglement', in: Association of Attenders and

contains a provision addressing both the procedure and the preconditions for removal of a judge. According to Art. 23(4) ECHR a judge may only be removed from office if a two-thirds majority of his elected colleagues, who must sit in a plenary session,[1966] so decide based on their assessment that the judge in question has "ceased to fulfil the required conditions." The Rule does not mention explicitly what conditions are meant, but this must first and foremost be the criteria for office as laid down in Art. 21 ECHR, i.e. the characteristics of high moral character, judges' exercise of judicial functions in their individual capacity, and the absence of activities incompatible with their independence, impartiality or with the demands of a full-time office.[1967] The rule in Art. 23(4) ECHR is modelled on Art. 18(1) ICJ Statute.[1968] However, unlike the latter text, which requires a unanimous decision of the other members of the Court,[1969] in the present text dismissal from office requires a majority of two-thirds of all the judges of the Court. This higher majority requirement was intended to ensure the independence of the Court.[1970] Yet independence must also be balanced with the desire to keep the Court operational and effective. From a practical viewpoint it may be said that majorities lower than unanimity indeed contribute to a more workable system. Allowing one judge, even excluding the one against whom action for dismissal is contemplated, to block a removal would make the system stiff and less suited to dealing effectively with questions of the loss of required conditions. And this must in particular apply to a court of the size of the ECtHR; it is probably easier for a camel to go through a needle's eye than for 44 judges to agree on a necessarily subjective assessment of a col-

---

Alumni of the Hague Academy of International Law / Groupe Français (ed) *Annuaire français de droit international* (Centre National de la Recherche Scientifique Paris 1959), 625-626.

1966 Rule 7.

1967 It is assumed here that the requirement of possession of the qualifications necessary for appointment to high judicial office or to be jurisconsults of recognised competence cannot fall away once a judge has taken office.

1968 Council of Europe, *Protocol No. 11 to the Convention for the Protection of Human Rights and Fundamental Freedoms, restructuring the control machinary established thereby, Explanatory Report*, para. 64; Drzemczewski, 'The European Human Rights Convention: Protocol No. 11 – Entry into Force and First Year of Application', 231.

1969 See *supra* Chapter D.VI(5).

1970 Council of Europe, *Protocol No. 11 to the Convention for the Protection of Human Rights and Fundamental Freedoms, restructuring the control machinary established thereby, Explanatory Report*, para. 64 *in fine*.

league's fulfilment of the required conditions. However, even a two-thirds majority of the judges requires that 31 judges have to agree on a decision, which is more than the number of judges of any of the other courts addressed in this study. Since it is not so much the percentage of the whole bench that makes the hurdle too high, but rather the actual number of individuals who are required to agree on a particular issue that usually promises to be controversially assessed, it must be concluded that the bar has been raised rather high, and with it the level of protection of independence.

As regards the procedure for dismissal, Rule 7 of the Rules of Court merely provides that any judge may set the procedure in motion, and that the judge in question must be heard before the plenary session makes a decision on the dismissal. If this wording is followed strictly then there is no possibility for the parties to a case to have a judge removed from office. But besides the inconvenience of it, an *e contrario* conclusion to this effect is not compulsory. The mere reason that the Rules of Court do not provide for this does not mean that the Court/the judges would not respond to an application lodged by the parties to a dispute. This is also suggested by the fact that Art. 23(4) ECHR does not mention who the application to remove a judge may or may not come from. It stands to reason that the same procedure would apply for such a situation. The exact time when the judge's seat becomes vacant is also not regulated in detail. In comparison, Art. 18(2)-(3) ICJ Statute provides that the seat becomes vacant as soon as the Registrar of the ICJ has made a formal notification of the removal to the UNSG. In view of the meaning of removal, which is to prevent a judge from sitting on a case for which he is not qualified, the seat must become vacant as soon as is practically possible. This would suggest that Art. 23(3) ECHR, according to which a judge shall hold office until replaced and continue to deal with cases he already has under consideration, is not applicable here.[1971]

d) Assessment of the Tenure System of the ECtHR

The various interests having an impact on the choice between different systems of determining judicial tenure are clearly illustrated by how this question has been resolved throughout the history of the control mechanism of the

---

1971 Korinek & Holoubek (eds), *Österreichisches Bundesverfassungsrecht: Textsammlung und Kommentar*, Art. 24 para. 7 *in fine*.

ECHR. Whereas in the beginning a tenure of nine years, coupled with the possibility of re-election, was chosen for the old court, the merger of the ECommHR with the old court in 1998 also meant the shortening of tenure to six years while maintaining the possibility of re-election, which in 2010 was changed back again by means of Protocol No. 14 to a non-renewable nine years. The current system is the most balanced from the perspective of averting influence from outside on the activities of the judges. Without the possibility of re-election the judges do not even have the incentive to support opinions in favour of their home State with a view to again being nominated for judicial office. At the same time, choosing the longer tenure of nine years over six years provides the judges with a stimulus not to engage in auxiliary activities and strengthens their self-image as part of a full-time court. On the other hand, the rule that judges may only serve one term coupled with a fixed retirement age which must be said to be below the time at which many international law scholars and practitioners stop working creates the risk of attracting to the bench people who enthusiastically aim to get the position and who also will want to keep career options open when they return from Strasbourg.

Another issue that has not been mentioned so far but which is closely linked to the question of tenure and security of tenure, and thereby to the independence of the judges of the ECtHR, is the provision of a pension scheme and social security for the judges. Before 2009, the judges of the Court did not have a pension scheme or social security, a situation which was "anomalous"[1972] and remarkable compared to the situation of other international courts. It was not until the end of 2009 that the CoM, acting under Art. 16 of the Statute of the CoE, i.e. the authority to decide with binding effect all matters relating to the internal organization and arrangements of the CoE, in a resolution approved a pension system and a social insurance scheme for the judges of the ECtHR.[1973] The reason such security of pension

1972 European Court of Human Rights, *Annual Report 2010 – Speech given by Mr Jean-Paul Costa, President of the European Court of Human Rights on the Occasion of the Opening of the Judicial Year, 29 January 2010* (2010) available at <http://www.echr.coe.int/Documents/Annual_report_2010_ENG.pdf> (last visited: 21 March 2014), 34.

1973 Committee of Ministers of the CoE, *On the status and conditions of service of judges of the European Court of Human Rights and of the Commissioner for Human Rights* (adopted 23 September 2009) Resolution CM/Res(2009)5. The Court itself, which had been lobbying for the introduction of both a pension and a social security scheme for the judges, welcomed this step as contributing "to the independence

and social security is significant is apparent. The idea that judges, together with their families, are protected financially and thus are able to perform their judicial assignment conscientiously not only serves the judges individually but more importantly the functioning of the judiciary of which they form a part. If they cannot rely on this protection, they become vulnerable to the exertion of influence by entities which e.g. can hold out the prospect of retirement arrangements. Moreover, since service as an international judge is always a limited occupation, and those who accept that challenge can be expected to return to their countries of origin, it is not unimportant that the service provides them with at least financial protection once this return takes place. According to Art. 10 of Resolution CM/Res(2009)5,

> "[j]udges shall benefit from the Pension Scheme for staff members which is in force at the Council of Europe at the time of their appointment, subject to any modifications rendered necessary by their particular status and conditions of service."

Among these modifications is that judges who have served on the Court for less than five years shall be entitled to a leaving allowance and for service of between five and ten years have a right to choose between a leaving allowance and a limited retirement pension; ordinary staff members of the CoE are entitled to a pension only after the completion of ten or more years' service.[1974] This flexibility should be welcomed. On the other hand, it is not understandable why the more variable rules concerning the scales applicable to the country of the staff member's last posting[1975] do not also apply to judges.

---

of the judges, this being indispensable for the independence of the Court itself." European Court of Human Rights, *Annual Report 2010 – Speech given by Mr Jean-Paul Costa, President of the European Court of Human Rights on the Occasion of the Opening of the Judicial Year, 29 January 2010*, 35.

1974 Art. 7 Council of Europe, *Staff Regulations – Appendix V: Pension Scheme rules* (as amended 9 November 2011) available at <https://wcd.coe.int/ViewDoc.jsp?Ref=COMP/CM/Res%282007%291&Language=lanEnglish&Ver=part13&BackColorInternet=99CCFF&BackColorIntranet=99CCFF&BackColorLogged=99CCCC#P140_13349> (last visited: 21 March 2014).

1975 Art. 33(2)-(7) Council of Europe, *Staff Regulations – Appendix V bis: New Pension Scheme "NPS"* (as amended 27 November 2002) available at <https://wcd.coe.int/ViewDoc.jsp?Ref=COMP/CM/Res%282007%291&Language=lanEnglish&Ver=part14&BackColorInternet=DBDCF2&BackColorIntranet=FDC864&BackColorLogged=FDC864#P333_44875> (last visited: 21 March 2014).

As regards social insurance, Art. 11 of Resolution CM/Res(2009)5 provides that "[j]udges shall be affiliated to the Council of Europe Medical and Social Insurance Scheme". While it must be welcomed, in principle, that the judges thus have been equipped with a social safety net, which considerably contributes to the ability of judges to concentrate on their work, the link to the medical and social insurance scheme which was devised with ordinary staff members of a political organization in mind brings with it occasional problems. It may thus be questioned whether it is appropriate that the "entitlement to the benefits provided by the Organisation's Medical and Social Insurance Scheme shall be suspended throughout periods of unpaid leave".[1976] Such unpaid leave can for example occur when it is granted "following an accident or a serious illness of a child, spouse or partner or ascendant".[1977] The appropriateness of such a provision may be worthy of discussion, but it is unlikely that the outcome of the weighing of interests between the organization and the staff member would have had the same outcome were the rules prepared only for judges of an international court.

3. Incompatible Activities

In the old ECtHR, i.e. before the entry into force of Additional Protocol No. 11, as well as in the ECommHR, the judges were allowed to exercise other occupations beside their judicial office, mainly because the Court was not permanently in session.[1978] This changed when the ECtHR was merged with the ECommHR and when other amendments prescribed by Additional Protocol No. 11 attempted to make the organs more effective and to transform

---

1976 Art. 3(1) Council of Europe, *Staff Regulations – Appendix XII: Regulations on the medical and social insurance scheme* (as amended 16 January 2008) available at <https://wcd.coe.int/ViewDoc.jsp?Ref=COMP/CM/Res%282007%291&Language=lanEnglish&Ver=part21&BackColorInternet=99CCFF&BackColorIntranet=99CCFF&BackColorLogged=99CCCC> (last visited: 21 March 2014).

1977 Art. 3(1) Council of Europe, *Staff Regulations – Appendix VII: Regulations on unpaid leave* (as amended 7 July 2010) available at <https://wcd.coe.int/ViewDoc.jsp?Ref=COMP/CM/Res%282007%291&Language=lanEnglish&Ver=part16&BackColorInternet=99CCFF&BackColorIntranet=99CCFF&BackColorLogged=99CCCC> (last visited: 21 March 2014).

1978 Weil, *The European Convention on Human Rights: Background, Development and Prospects*, 148-151. See also On the history see Robertson, Arthur H., 'The European Court of Human Rights' (1960) 9 American Journal of Comparative Law 1, 15.

the entire control mechanism into a purely judicial mechanism. As the judges switched from sitting on the Court on a part-time basis to full time office, the necessity of providing precise and detailed rules on practices that were incompatible with this (new) role became less.[1979] There is no reason, for example on financial grounds, to feel any obligation to allow ECtHR judges to exercise other activities.

The current Art. 21(3) ECHR provides that "[d]uring their term of office the judges shall not engage in any activity which is incompatible with their independence, impartiality or with the demands of a full-time office". As a control mechanism for this provision, the judges are required to declare to the President of the Court any additional activities they exercise.[1980] The competent organ to make a decision on any questions arising from the application of this provision is the ECtHR itself; which according to Rule 4(1) *in fine* implies the plenary court. It is not explicitly required that the affected judge be excluded from being part of the composition of the Court that makes the decision, but in view of this provision in the case of some other international courts[1981] this may be assumed to apply.[1982] Furthermore, as regards a literal interpretation of Art. 21(3) ECHR, it must be noted that the provision emphasises that only certain activities exercised *during* the judge's term of office are prohibited. Like what comparable clauses in the statutes and founding instruments of other international courts provide, it does not allow any conclusion on consequences of activities a judge has exercised before taking the judicial office. This question must instead be resolved within the context of the preconditions for office laid down in Art. 21(1) ECHR. The consequence is that any previous activities that may have a detrimental effect on the (perceived) independence of a judge may be assessed by the States Parties only in the process of making a nomination, and the PACE only in the framework of the election process.

Art. 21(3) ECHR distinguishes between activities that are incompatible with the judges' independence or impartiality, or with the demands of full-

1979 Cf. Shetreet, Shimon, 'Standards of Conduct of International Judges Outside Activities' (2003) 2 The Law and Practice of International Courts and Tribunals 1, 152.

1980 Rule 4(1) Rules of Court.

1981 Cf. e.g. Art. 40(4) Rome Statute.

1982 Cf., however, *infra* on decisions by a Chamber on the existence of a ground for inability to sit on a case, for withdrawal or exemption (Rule 28(2)), where the affected judge is not allowed to take part in the decision.

time office. This wording suggests that there can be activities that do not violate the postulate of a judge's independence or impartiality, but nevertheless are not compatible with full-time judicial office. The Explanatory Report for Protocol No. 11 defines this prerequisite to mean that "judges must be able fully to assume all the duties inherent in membership of the new permanent Court".[1983] It thus seems that this is in the main a requirement that relates to the efficiency of the Court. The provisions in Art. 21(3) ECHR are further clarified by the Court itself. Pursuant to Rule 4 of the Rules of Court, judges are not allowed to engage in political or administrative activities or any professional activity incompatible with their independence, impartiality and the demands of a full-time judgeship. This means that professional, i.e. reimbursed, activities are not ruled out per se, but that every kind of political and administrative function, be it paid or on a *pro bono* basis, is readily prohibited. Thus the weighing of the conformity of political or administrative activities with the standards of independence and impartiality of judges and the demands of full-time office is not necessary; they are prohibited in any case. In contrast, whether a professional non-political and/or non-administrative activity is compatible with the independence and impartiality of the judges (or the demands of full-time office) is in need of an assessment by the relevant judge, the President, and ultimately the Plenary. This makes the provision relatively generous with regard to judges' professional side activities compared to the rules applicable at other international courts, which regularly ban professional occupations altogether. The explanation for this may be found in the fact that the Court, before the entry into force of Protocol No. 11, used to be a part-time court.[1984] Yet it does nothing to clarify why this was not changed and harmonized using similar rules from other international courts once the Court became permanent. According to J. Frowein, only a very limited lecturing or teaching activity can be considered to be permissible under Art. 21(3) ECHR.[1985] So far, however, there have been no known cases where the application of this provision has led to any diffi-

1983 Council of Europe, *Protocol No. 11 to the Convention for the Protection of Human Rights and Fundamental Freedoms, restructuring the control machinary established thereby, Explanatory Report*, para. 60.

1984 Korinek & Holoubek (eds), *Österreichisches Bundesverfassungsrecht: Textsammlung und Kommentar*, Art. 21, para. 17.

1985 Frowein & Peukert, *Europäische Menschenrechtskonvention: EMRK-Kommentar*, 442. See also Korinek & Holoubek (eds), *Österreichisches Bundesverfassungsrecht: Textsammlung und Kommentar*, Art. 21, para. 18.

culties in practice.[1986] This is certainly attributable to the fact that judges are aware of the impact any such precarious activities may have on the Court's perceived independence and impartiality.

While it is not directly applicable for an assessment of the Court's stance on the incompatible activities of a judge, it is nevertheless interesting to note that the Rule 4 of the Rules was amended on 29 March 2010 by the addition of a second subparagraph providing:

> "A former judge shall not represent a party or third party in any capacity in proceedings before the Court relating to an application lodged before the date on which he or she ceased to hold office. As regards applications lodged subsequently, a former judge may not represent a party or third party in any capacity in proceedings before the Court until a period of two years from the date on which he or she ceased to hold office has elapsed."

It must be seen as a positive development that the Court not only regulates judges' activities off the bench in retrospect and in the present, but also looking forward. This way the Court sends a clear signal that it will not tolerate behaviour which is clearly not compatible with the office of an independent judge. The Institut de Droit International in its 2011 resolution on the position of the international judge took up this same idea but instead provided that a former judge ought to be prohibited from serving as an agent, counsel or advocate before the Court of which he used to be a member for "at least three years following the end of his term."[1987] Rule 4(2) of the Rules of Court appears, in light of this, to differentiate more in order to determine real influences detrimental to judicial independence; it both goes deeper, by including events that occurred while the former judge still held office, and is more generous in the time limit it imposes for a former judge to not represent a party before the Court.

4. Inability to Sit, Withdrawal or Exemption

Rules on when a judge is obliged to withdraw from a particular case or is prohibited from taking part in the deliberations of the Court are not provided for in the ECHR – much in the ECHR's tradition of not establishing an ex-

---

1986 Frowein & Peukert, *Europäische Menschenrechtskonvention: EMRK-Kommentar*, 442.

1987 Art. 3(6) Institut de Droit International, *The Position of the International Judge – 6th Resolution – Sixth Commission – Session de Rhodes.*

tensive organizational framework for the Court – but are instead provided for by the Court's own rules. In Rule 28(2), which has been gradually amended and extended,[1988] elaborate provisions on grounds of disqualification are laid down. They include that a judge

- has a personal interest in the case or a subordinate relationship with any of the parties;
- has previously acted in the case;
- continues to sit in the consideration of the merits of a case but engages in political or administrative activity or any professional activity which is incompatible with his independence or impartiality;
- has publicly expressed opinions that are objectively able adversely to affect his impartiality; or
- for other reasons, has his independence or impartiality legitimately called into doubt.

The original provision in the first Rules of Court of 18 September 1959 was confined to the following grounds for judges to be excluded from the consideration of a bench:[1989] the judge had a personal interest or previously acted either as agent, advocate or adviser to a party or of a person having an interest in the case, or as member of a Tribunal or commission of enquiry, or in any other capacity.[1990] What has changed is thus that the grounds for exemption from proceedings have been equipped with a number of examples in the first two instances (personal interest and previous involvement in the case) and that further grounds have been added: a special rule has been adopted for *ad hoc* judges and judges sitting after the end of their term only to conclude a case,[1991] according to which these judges must be excluded from a case when exercising activities that ordinary (!) judges are not allowed to exercise under

1988 Amended by the Court on 17 June and 8 July 2002, 13 December 2004 and 13 November 2006.

1989 An absolute basis for inability to sit on a case is furthermore established in Art. 27(5) ECHR. Thus a judge from a Chamber which has handed down a judgment that is later referred to the Grand Chamber pursuant to Art. 43 is prohibited from being a member of the Grand Chamber. An exception is made for the President of the Chamber and the judge who sat in respect of the High Contracting Party concerned.

1990 ECtHR, *Rules of Court of the European Court of Human Rights* (adopted 18 September 1959) Reprinted in International Oganisation and Integration, 1968, 945 et seq.

1991 Cf. Rule 26(3).

Rule 4 ("Incompatible Activities")[1992]. In other words, even for *ad hoc* judges and judges sitting after the end of their term only to conclude a case in which the consideration of the merits has already begun, stronger protection of their independence and impartiality is in place. Furthermore, Rule 28 tightens the supervision of independence and impartiality also for ordinary judges by adding the additional ground that a judge has publicly expressed opinions that are objectively capable of adversely affecting his impartiality and by adding a rescue provision that for any other reason for which a judge's independence or impartiality "may legitimately be called into doubt" he or she is prohibited from taking part in the consideration of a case. It must be considered supportive of protecting the Court's independence that in any decision to be taken on the existence of a ground for inability to sit, withdrawal or exemption, the affected judge is to be replaced by the first substitute judge in the Chamber.[1993]

5. Privileges and Immunities

As a result of the above-mentioned administrative integration of the ECtHR in the CoE system, the privileges and immunities of the judges are governed by those rules of the CoE. Pursuant to Art. 51 ECHR, judges shall be entitled, during the exercise of their functions, to the privileges and immunities provided for in Art. 40 of the Statute of the CoE and in the agreements made thereunder. This means, primarily, that judges are exempt from any persecution for the exercise of their duties.[1994] Following from Art. 40 Statute of the CoE[1995] in the territories of the members of the CoE judges enjoy "such privileges and immunities as are reasonably necessary for the fulfilment of their functions" including immunity from arrest and all legal proceedings in the territories of all members. The protection thus goes beyond the mere diplomatic protection that most other international courts provide. The immunities and privileges are further detailed in the General Agreement on

1992 Cf. on incompatible activities *supra* Chapter H.V(3).

1993 Rule 28(4).

1994 Frowein, Jochen Abr. & Peukert, Wolfgang, *Europäische Menschenrechtskonvention: EMRK-Kommentar* (N. P. Engel Kehl 1985), 479. For members of the ECommHR, this has been acknowledged e.g. in the decision Zoernsch v. Waldock and another (1964) 2 All England Law Reports 256.

1995 COE 'Statute of the Council of Europe' (adopted 5 May 1949, entered into force 3 August 1949) CETS No. 1.

Privileges and Immunities of the Council of Europe,[1996] and the Sixth Protocol to the General Agreement on Privileges and Immunities of the Council of Europe.[1997] The Protocol in particular clarifies that "[p]rivileges and immunities are accorded to judges not for the personal benefit of the individuals themselves but in order to safeguard the independent exercise of their functions." Following this persuasion the Protocol extends the immunity from legal process in respect of words spoken or written and acts done by judges in the discharge of their duties until after they have ceased to exercise their duties.[1998] This provision is helpful in clarifying especially to the judges themselves that they do not have to fear any consequences for their actions on the bench even after they have ceased to be judges. No other court analysed in previous chapters has a similar provision. Extending the immunities to the judge's family[1999] protects against indirect influence being exerted on the judge by influencing his family.

VI. Conclusions

> "[T]he success or failure of international instruments, including those like the European Convention, in the end depends on the political will of the States involved. Legal arguments, however cogent they may be, in the final analysis seldom override political considerations when States feel that their vital interests are at stake."[2000]

The independence and impartiality of the judges is a pressing topic at the ECtHR, as is demonstrated by the fact that the ECtHR is the object of continuous reforms seeking to enable it to cope with the overwhelming number of applications, but at the same time not to lose its autonomous function as a judicial organ. Although the effectiveness of the control mechanism under the ECHR is an important concern, especially regarding a human rights

1996 General agreement on privileges and immunities of the Council of Europe.

1997 Sixth Protocol to the General Agreement on Privileges and Immunities of the Council of Europe (adopted 5 March 1996, entered into force 1 November 1998) CETS No. 162.

1998 Art. 3 No. 3 Sixth Protocol to the General Agreement on Privileges and Immunities of the Council of Europe.

1999 Art. 1 No. 3 Sixth Protocol to the General Agreement on Privileges and Immunities of the Council of Europe.

2000 Dijk, Pieter van & Hoof, Godefridus J. H. van, *Theory and Practice of the European Convention on Human Rights* (Kluwer Deventer 2nd edn. 1990), 618.

system which has tremendous symbolic value for a number of national legal systems, ambitious reform attempts must pay due respect to the inherent judicial nature of the mechanism, and with it its independent functioning. By making the Court a full-time court, extending the judges' tenure, removing re-electability and placing constraints on the ability to exercise outside activities, and by making the jurisdiction of the Court compulsory and indefinite for participating States, especially as regards the right of individual petition, has strengthened the judicial character of the Court.

The establishment of the ECtHR has certain particularities which make it questionable whether it is sufficiently autonomous from different political actors. The Court has no autonomous legal personality and is thus, in the lack also of its own statute, relying on the CoE for administrative services e.g. the appointment of Registry staff and its financing, on which it has very limited influence. This has in the past led to complications between the Court and the Secretary General of the CoE, and is a less than optimal regulation if political influences are to be averted. In comparison, the IACtHR itself concludes agreements with the host country, governments and organizations and the Court itself is in charge of its personnel. It is highly unlikely, considering the clear regulation of these questions with regard to e.g. the ICC or the ITLOS, that this limbo would have occurred had the ECtHR been established in the late 20th or early 21st century. As regards the selection of judges to the Court, the nomination process, which is largely at the discretion of Member States, has proven to be intransparent, variable and being used to make politically motivated choices detrimental in the sense that candidates have not fulfilled the required preconditions for office established in the ECHR. It must be affirmed, however, that the PACE has worked tirelessly to ensure that the needs of the ECtHR are being met, as can be seen from the efforts to ensure that the nomination and selection of judges follow objective, verifiable and predictable criteria.

As regards the personal independence of judges serving on the ECtRH, the development of the rules applicable to the tenure of judges reveals how seriously this issue is taken even by the CoE. A renewable term of six years is considered too short and too exposed to political influence being exerted on a judicial body. Both the length of nine years and the omission of the possibility of re-election are in line with what applies to more recently established international courts, and in particular those which immediately affect individuals. It may be discussed whether, from the perspective of the independence of the individual judge the introduction of an age limit is helpful or actually counterproductive in preventing the Court from attracting some of the knowledge, experience and even clarity of mind that comes with age. As there is no indication that the independent character of judges is connected to their age, there is no reason to follow through with this arrangement in the present context. However, compared with the age distribution on the benches of the international courts studied in this thesis, including that of the ECtHR, the age limit does raise legitimate concerns. Furthermore, the extension of tenure from six to nine years raises the question of the financial safeguards there are in place for judges, both during their tenure and upon their retirement. This question is also closely linked to the transformation of the Court into a permanent institution, which caused the Contracting States to reduce the ability to exercise side activities during one's service as a judge. It was long overdue that the judges should be provided with a social security system as well as a pension scheme which eliminates or at least narrows the financial basis for the exertion of influence.

One advantage of the close link between the Court and the CoE may be seen in the extension of the immunities and privileges of officials of the CoE to the judges. Thereby the judges are accorded protection even against their home States, which has been considered insufficient at the other courts analysed in this study.

Chapter I: Summary of Conclusions and Outlook

> "The problem of the impartiality of the international judge is the Cape Horn of international judicial settlement."[2001]

I. The Need for an Independent International Judiciary – Balancing Independence and Courts' Political Nature

The multiplication of international courts and tribunals has in recent decades led to the development of a community of international judicial organs that share certain common characteristics. Almost by definition, international courts have a common function, a mission,[2002] which can be summarized in the aim to help improve international co-operation, by way of dispute resolution or by assisting in implementing the promises of specific areas of law such as the law of the sea, criminal law and human rights. Through this aim international courts have become powerful actors in the international community and have gone beyond their traditional role of merely settling disputes to actively helping to shape the international legal order and support its continued evolution. In so doing, international courts ultimately serve the common purpose of promoting justice and peace in the world community. The benefit of judicial adjudication through courts over other forms of dispute settlement and non-institutionalized judicial adjudication is that they provide a remedy by means of a neutral third and decisions exclusively based on facts and law, committed only to objectivity and impartiality.

In itself, the judicial function is one that must be sharply distinguished from political functions, where the representation and implementation of interests forms a central component. Judicial independence takes on a central role in safeguarding this distinctiveness. But it is not only mandated in opposition to the political role of other actors; as the example of the *ad hoc*

2001 Lauterpacht, *The Function of Law in the International Community*, 203.

2002 Cf. the resolution of the Institut de Droit International on the position of the international judge of 2011, in which the preambular paragraphs refer to the "diversity of … international courts and tribunals as well as of their *common mission*, needs and requirements" (emphasis added); Institut de Droit International, *The Position of the International Judge – 6th Resolution – Sixth Commission – Session de Rhodes.*

Tribunals shows, the commitment of international courts to the principle of judicial independence also stems from the guarantees of the human rights system, which binds not only organs exercising public authority on the national level but also international courts to the degree that they affect the same subjects. The status of judges is closely linked to those functions of the international judiciary since the individual judge is the guarantor of judicial independence; it is in his mind that all the different influences, the facts, the law and political stimuli are gathered and filtered to form (ideally) a neutral decision. But establishing that judicial independence as such is central to the judicial function still leaves unanswered the question what is to be understood by this standard. This study was not able to take its vantage point from the standards developed with respect to national judiciaries, but instead had to fall back on the treaties, statutes, secondary rules and practices of the international courts themselves in order to attempt to define the independence of international judges as it is currently understood. The analysis thus concentrated on selected elements that might qualify as building blocks of judicial independence. Although not all those elements were analysed in detail with regard to every court, in part to keep the analysis within manageable proportions but mainly because they are of different relevance in the different courts, the elements were structured into the two categories of those affecting the structure of the court and those affecting the roles and qualifications of individual judges. In what follows the most significant of the findings of the previous chapters will be highlighted.

II. Contents and Deficits of a Common Core of Judicial Independence

1. Structural Safeguards

International courts usually have international legal personality in order to enter into agreements with host countries, international organizations or States. This is necessary for the courts to make preparations such as the protection of their immunities in the host country or to establish the legal framework for co-operation with international organizations. However, not all courts possess the necessary legal personality but are instead, as in the case of the ECtHR, dependent on an international organization to make the necessary arrangements on their behalf. This is criticised by the affected courts themselves and is, to the degree that it hampers courts in making necessary arrangements for their ordered functioning, a considerable threat to their independence. One salient example is the administration of staff of the ECtHR Registry, where ambiguous and inadequate rules have led to conflicts in the appointment of staff between the Secretary General of the CoE and the ECtHR. The *ad hoc* establishment of the ICTY and ICTR is another structural issue that on several levels threatens the Tribunals' independence. Their character as subsidiary organs to the UNSC authorizes the latter to determine e.g. changes in the composition of the bench, the extension of judicial tenure and the decision on the termination of the Tribunals. However, the Tribunals' judicial character and the fact that they exercise authority over individuals mandate that the UNSC is not allowed to interfere with individual cases, and judges are furthermore not bound by any instructions of the UNSC.

As stated at the outset of this study, irrespective of how judicial independence is defined for the various international jurisdictions, it may not be perceived as an absolute independence. This is apparent from the necessary dependence of international courts on political organs for their funding. International courts are not able to raise funds themselves, with the exception of requiring parties appearing before them to cover their own costs (such as in the ICJ), and thus have to rely on an outside authority to make sufficient funds available. This order is not in itself detrimental to the independence of the court; but all courts analysed in this study through different models have been included in the process of drafting a budget. In the case of the ICJ and the ITLOS the Registrar and the courts' budgetary committees supply the UNGA/Assembly of States Parties with a draft budget as a basis for a decision; the ECtHR is called upon by the CoM to give its opinion on the draft that the political organ presents. As long as the courts are able to submit their opinions in the process of drafting a budget, it is not in any way objectionable to have a political organ decide on the (level of the) budget. However, the level of involvement still provides significant differences in detail. For example, the ECtHR should not be dependent on a political organ in order to give its opinions on a budgetary draft.

With regard to the composition of international courts, the above analysis has proved that States are still largely in charge of the nomination process. This is, as has been emphasised by an increasing body of scholarly literature, one of the most problematic issues for the independence of the courts. It would be inappropriate and potentially counterproductive to demand of Member States of courts such as the ICJ and the ITLOS to give up the right to nominate candidates to the bench, since these courts deal almost exclusively with inter-State disputes, and thus are alternatives to traditional arbitration where almost all aspects of adjudication are at the disposal of States.

Since international courts through their more predictable procedures and consistent case law make a valuable contribution to the development of international law, a shift (back) towards more arbitration is undesirable. But developments in recent years in particular with regard to the ICC and ECtHR have indicated that the influence of States as regards judicial nominations is crumbling. In the ICC the Rome Statute provides for the ability to establish a Committee on Nominations which can verify whether the requirements for access to judicial office are met by the nominated candidates. And with regard to the ECtHR the PACE has for many years had an eye on the national procedures leading to nominations and has adopted numerous proposals for improvement. Although the Committee on Nominations has to be established *ad hoc* by the ASP and furthermore has no right to ignore the States' nominations, and although the PACE's proposals are not binding on Member States, these developments nevertheless indicate progressive tendencies in support of verifying compliance with the requirements for judicial office beyond States. The influence of States on the composition of courts is also illustrated by rules such as that no two judges may be nationals of the same State (e.g. Art. 3 ITLOS Statute) or that every State has the right to one judge on the bench (e.g. Art. 20 ECHR), and the practice of presenting a "clean slate", i.e. that a regional group nominates exactly as many candidates as there are geographical seats available.

The institution of *ad hoc* judge and national judge is another such example where State sovereignty is allowed to translate into equality of representation on the bench, an understanding that cannot readily be justified by maintaining an independent bench that takes decisions based only on the facts of a case and the applicable law. Although these rules can be motivated by the interests of States in disputes with other States before an international court, namely in order to provide each side with the ability to supply the bench with all background knowledge of the respective State's national legal order, the direct representation of State interests on the bench is highly questionable from the perspective of courts giving decisions only on the basis of facts and the law. This applies in an even stronger manner before courts that adjudicate on cases that affect individuals, e.g. the ECtHR. The argument of having judges function as experts on legal conditions relevant for a (State) party appearing before the court is also weakened by the right and ability of every court to seek real expert opinions at any time without allowing such experts also to influence the taking of a decision on the merits of a case. Irrespective of this criticism, which has been long-standing, this study has shown that the use of *ad hoc* judges defies any demand for judicial independence.

2. Personal Independence

As regards the personal independence of judges of different courts, the present thesis has indicated certain similarities amounting to customary rules applicable irrespective of the character of the international court. The legal position of the judges of international courts is firstly circumscribed by general statements in the courts' statutes to the effect that judges are to be independent, impartial and/or to sit on the court in their personal capacity. It thus amounts to a fundamental and unanimous conviction of the international judiciary that its judges ought to decide cases before them fairly on the basis of the relevant facts and the law. The general statements are complemented by the duty of every judge, whether at a human rights court or law of the sea tribunal, to take an oath of office in which the judge *inter alia* declares that he will perform his judicial duties following the highest standards of morality. A new tool in this regard is the Code of Judicial Ethics adopted by the ICC, which is a non-binding instrument which merely reaffirms that the standards thus listed, among them judicial independence and impartiality, ought to be followed.

All governing instruments further demand the fulfilment of certain personal requirements. However, to the degree that these requirements demand mental suitability, such as integrity and high moral character, they can hardly be verified with certainty as such prerequisites are but subjectively determined. Their weakness in safeguarding actual independence on the bench is further emphasised by the above-mentioned practice that States remain in sole control over the nomination procedure and the electoral organs thus have limited leeway in making a decision on the basis of the application of such requirements. Whereas the specific knowledge demanded of judges is different and usually follows the character of the individual court (e.g. recognized competence in the field of the law of the sea in the case of the ITLOS and established competence in criminal law and procedure or in relevant areas of international law), judges must usually hold the qualifications for appointment to the highest judicial office in their respective States. These requirements are objectively verifiable and they must be seen to be a *conditio sine qua non* for the character of a judicial organ and a guarantee of the independence of judges, as independent decision-making implies deciding a case fairly while relying only on the facts and the rule of law without undue influence. The main criticism that must be directed towards these criteria is not so much their substance but the way in which they are enforced. By leaving it up to the States that nominate or propose candidates for the bench, instead of allowing for a centralized verification at the stage of both the nomination and selection, a valuable mechanism for assuring an unbiased and honourable bench is lost.

Judges enjoy important protection of their legal position through the fundamental irremovability from office. This principle is enshrined in every statute analysed in this study, and it amounts to an essential safeguard of their independence, as the lack of such protection contains the danger of making every decision that conflicts with State interests, even if it is made in application of the law on the facts, into a potential ground for removal. The conditions under which a judge may be removed differ in detail but follow certain commonalities, usually permitting exclusion if a judge in the opinion of the other judges no longer fulfils the criteria for office, including being independent. The procedures that have to be complied with prescribe that the judge is heard and that usually a decision on the removal is taken only among the other judges. The majority requirements for such decisions vary; in the ICJ and the ITLOS a unanimous decision of the other judges is necessary, which sets the standard unnecessarily high and makes actual removal unlikely, since every vote against removal amounts to a veto. In the ECtHR and the ICC a two-thirds majority of the judges is required; in the latter an additional two-thirds majority of the members of the ASP has to approve the judges' decision, which further strengthens the presumption that the judge concerned will remain on the bench. Since on both these courts the overall number of judges is relatively high, even a two-thirds majority amounts to a strong vote in favour of protecting against unwarranted allegations of a lack of independence. Removal of judges at the *ad hoc* Tribunals is not regulated; whereas one might see removal through the UNSC as a logical consequence of that organ's control over the Tribunals, this is not compatible with the independent functioning that a judicial organ has to be guaranteed.

Distinct from the removal of judges from office is disqualification from sitting on a particular case or the judge's own recusal. The conditions under which a judge is barred from taking part in a case include bias due to past links with a case or with a party or where a judge has an interest in the outcome of a case or has personal contacts with a party. As the case law of the *ad hoc* Tribunals has proved, assessments of the existence of such grounds for disqualification are frequent and important, to make the court not just actually independent and impartial but also appear as such. It is only in the *ad hoc* Tribunals and the ICC that the parties are themselves expressly enabled to raise questions of recusal before the court. That in the other courts the judges' own initiative to recuse themselves is relied on is unfortunate from the perspective of legal certainty and providing a real safeguard against undue influence on decisions, despite the occasional decision of e.g. ICJ judges not to take part in a decision due to their involvement in a different capacity in a way that may put their independence into question. The ICC provides the additional sanction of disciplinary measures amounting to reprimands or pecuniary injunctions to be decided by the Presidency of the court. Whether this sanction is necessary and what consequences it may have on the decision-making of the judges remains to be seen. That only the judges themselves, through the Presidency, can impose it, instead of external organs or States, must be the minimum requirement in order not to put undue pressure on judges.

The removal procedures are the central building block in the protection of judges' tenure, which according to common wisdom ought to be long in order to enable judges to concentrate fully on their judicial task, without having to worry about the implications their judicial activities may have on their careers (and more) during and after their international service. The standard that has developed for the length of judicial tenure is nine years. An unfortunate exception is constituted by the *ad hoc* Tribunals, motivated by their temporary existence and the resulting difficulty of allowing adequate representation of the principal legal systems of the world and equitable geographical distribution. All courts, except the ICC, provide for renewable tenure, which from the perspective of judicial independence is problematic due to the risk of judges interpreting their function on the court in a way that more than is objectively warranted supports their re-election, e.g. by pleasing States whose support is considered essential for nomination or re-election. In particular in contexts where the subjects appearing before the court or, as in the case of the ICC, the subjects that are significantly affected by the decisions of the court are the same that hold the power in the nomination and/or selection procedure to the bench, eligibility for re-election is hardly reconcilable with the appearance of independence. A mandatory retirement age exists only for judges of the ECtHR, and even there does not bar judges from sitting on the court if they reach that age during their tenure. Overall there is no reason to assume that with increasing age judges become more susceptible to undue influence; on the contrary, age limits may have the effect of excluding the most virtuous individuals of the highest integrity.

The Tenure of International Judges

	ICJ	ITLOS	ICC	ICTY	ICTR	ECtHR
Tenure (years)	9	9	9	4	4	9
Tenure (renewable)	Yes	Yes	No	Yes	Yes	No

Every court the subject of this study takes the problem of outside activities seriously and addresses the issue in its statue or rules of court. Nevertheless, judicial offices that are of only a part-time nature cannot be paid in the same way as regular positions, and thus are unlikely to provide sufficient remuneration to support a judge (and his family). Therefore it is reasonable to allow judges to perform additional activities, e.g. to allow the continuation of certain activities that were exercised when the judgeship began or to allow for the taking up of certain new ones, as in the case of the ITLOS. However, the analysis in this respect has shown that this is indeed hedged about with dangers, and some activities are even incompatible with the (appearance of) the independence of the court. Nevertheless, if the position as judge is of only a temporary nature, which it is for all the courts analysed here, then judges must be allowed to nurture their careers, since it can neither be expected that all judges hold their judicial office as the final step of their careers nor demanded that judges due to their temporary judicial office and perhaps in light of a rather low workload at the court in question are forced to accept a compromise in their careers. What is essential for judges' independence is which organ may make a decision when disagreement occurs on the compatibility between a particular activity and the judicial office. This is always reserved for the relevant court, and thus although reminding one of the authority to decide when a judge is removed, is regulated in a way that to an even greater extent is in support of judges' independence from external interference. The privileges and immunities accorded to judges are usually modelled on diplomatic privileges and immunities; this is not unproblematic as diplomats *per definitionem* are representatives of their home States and thus e.g. have different immunities *vis-à-vis* their home States. In order to guarantee judges their independent function it must be assumed that the immunities thus accorded must also apply *vis-à-vis* their home States.[2003] A

2003 The Institut de Droit International, in its 2011 resolution on the position of the international judge, realized the tense relationship between judges' nationality and

further deficiency that the study has shown is the occasional lack of provisions regarding the right to waive immunities. Uncertainty in this regard creates serious risks for the independent functioning of a court.

III. The Prospects of an Independent International Judiciary

When analysing the independence of international courts it has to be remembered that international adjudication is still largely governed by the principle of consent. More State-centred courts, such as the ICJ and the ITLOS, are substitutes for arbitration and, as a consequence, unless a shift back to the predominance of arbitration is desired, it is inevitable that States must have influence on the activities of the relevant court. Therefore, State sovereignty has, as shown above, often been translated into the conception of international courts e.g. in the composition of the bench. This argument applies to a lesser degree to courts such as the ICC, the *ad hoc* Tribunals and the ECtHR. These courts are detached from States in their operation, although e.g. the jurisdiction as in the case of the ECtHR still has to be accepted by States Parties. They have prosecutors who initiate cases, and their decisions are set to enforce idealistic aims in the interests of a world community. But this does not make them immune from outside influence. On the contrary, the fact that they take decisions which immediately affect individuals makes it necessary for them to comply with international human rights standards, one of which is the right to a fair trial by an independent court. Overall, the functions of international courts, as described above, have shown both the need for independence and the potential dangers to such independence.

Overall, as international courts are gaining power and influence, the need to protect the core judicial function, which is to decide a case fairly, relying only on the facts and the rule of law without any kind of undue pressure, increases simultaneously. As can be observed on the national level, when courts develop and begin to exercise powers, their independence is also eventually strengthened in order to facilitate their *judicial* function. If courts are only the *bouche de la loi*,[2004] without any power to influence the devel-

---

the granting of privileges and immunities and thus stated that the "[t]he main purpose of immunities and privileges is to ensure the independence of judges." Ibid, Art. 6.

2004 Montesquieu, Charles Louis de Secondat, *De l'Esprit des Lois* (Lebigre Frères Paris 1834), Livre XI, Chapitre 4.

opment of the law, then the incentive to establish an extensive principle of an independent judiciary is limited, if not non-existent. But if the decisions of courts, as is the case with international courts, go beyond just settling disputes between parties and punishing criminal acts, if the relevance of judicial decisions is not exhausted by being binding on the parties to a case, but instead develops international law through their consistency and detailed reasoning, then judicial independence takes on a different meaning, namely as a protection of that power exercised by courts. This is also most likely to be the central reason why the aim of gaining or achieving independence is always a struggle, a constant resistance to pressure. And it dissolves the seeming contradiction which this study has had to struggle with, in that almost all courts may objectively subscribe to the aim of being independent and to having independent members, but nonetheless several issues witness to a tribute being paid to the dependent nature of the individual judge, e.g. the practice of not appointing to the bench nationals of the parties to the underlying conflict. This study confirms that the power exercised by courts is genuine and that as a consequence certain common characteristics of the principle of judicial independence have been established. These characteristics not only provide an image of the organizational setup of current international courts but also works as a guide for potential future international courts to be established, which likewise seek to exercise their judicial functions, with the objective of doing so independently.

Annex: Ad Hoc Judges of the ICJ

As of July 2013, 110 individuals have served as *ad hoc* judges in 180 instances at the ICJ.[2005] These judges have been from 51 (original) countries and represented an overall 74 countries according to the following table.

Country of Origin of *Ad Hoc* Judges at the ICJ									
1.	Algeria	12.	Croatia	22.	Guatemala	33.	Nigeria	44.	Sri Lanka
2.	Argentina	13.	Czechoslov-	23.	Guyana	34.	Norway	45.	Sweden
3.	Australia		akia	24.	India	35.	Pakistan	46.	Switzerland
4.	Belgium	14.	Democratic	25.	Iran, Islamic	36.	Peru	47.	United King-
5.	Bosnia and		Republic of		Republic of	37.	Poland		dom of Great
	Herzegovina		the Congo	26.	Israel	38.	Portugal		Britain and
6.	Brazil	15.	Denmark	27.	Italy	39.	Senegal		Northern Ire-
7.	Cameroon	16.	Egypt	28.	Liberia	40.	Serbia and		land
8.	Canada	17.	Federal Re-	29.	Mexico		Montenegro	48.	United Re-
9.	Chile		public of	30.	Morocco	41.	Somalia		public of
10.	Colombia		Germany	31.	Netherlands	42.	South Africa		Tanzania
11.	Cote d'Ivoire	18.	Finland	32.	New Zeal-	43.	Spain	49.	United States
		19.	France		and				of America
		20.	Ghana					50.	Uruguay
		21.	Greece					51.	Yugoslavia

2005 'The Court – All Judges *ad hoc*' available at <http://www.icj-cij.org/court/index.php?p1=1&p2=5&p3=2> (last visited: 21 March 2014).

Countries Represented by *Ad Hoc* Judges before the ICJ

1.	Albania	16.	Colombia	31.	Guinea, Re-	46.	Morocco	61.	Singapore
2.	Argentina	17.	Congo, Re-		public of	47.	Nether-	62.	Slovakia
3.	Australia		public of the	32.	Guinea-Bis-		lands	63.	South Africa
4.	Bahrain	18.	Costa Rica		sau	48.	New Zeal-	64.	Spain
5.	Belgium	19.	Croatia	33.	Honduras		and	65.	Sweden
6.	Benin	20.	Democratic	34.	India	49.	Nicaragua	66.	Switzerland
7.	Bosnia and		Republic of	35.	Indonesia	50.	Niger	67.	Thailand
	Herzegovina		the Congo	36.	Iran, Islamic	51.	Nigeria	68.	The former
8.	Bulgaria	21.	Denmark		Republic of	52.	Pakistan		Yugoslav Re-
9.	Burkina Faso	22.	Djibouti	37.	Israel	53.	Peru		public of
10.	Burundi	23.	Ecuador	38.	Italy	54.	Portugal		Macedonia
11.	Cambodia	24.	El Salvador	39.	Liberia	55.	Qatar	69.	Tunisia
12.	Cameroon	25.	Ethiopia	40.	Libyan Arab	56.	Romania	70.	Uganda
13.	Canada	26.	Federal Re-		Jamahiriya	57.	Rwanda	71.	Ukraine
14.	Chad		public of	41.	Liechten-	58.	Senegal	72.	United King-
15.	Chile		Germany		stein	59.	Serbia		dom of Great
		27.	Finland	42.	Malaysia	60.	Serbia and		Britain and
		28.	France	43.	Mali, Repub-		Montenegro		Northern Ire-
		29.	Greece		lic of				land
		30.	Guatemala	44.	Malta			73.	Uruguay
				45.	Mexico			74.	Yugoslavia

Appendix: International Courts – A Chart

	ICJ	ITLOS	ICC	ICTY	ICTR	ECtHR
General Characteristics						
Permanence	Permanent	Permanent	Permanent	*Ad Hoc*	*Ad Hoc*	Permanent
Seat	The Hague / Netherlands	Hamburg / Germany	The Hague / Netherlands	The Hague / Netherlands	Arusha / Tanzania	Strasbourg / France
Establishment	26 June 1945	1 August 1996	1 July 2002	25 May 1993	8 November 1998	21 January 1959 / 1 November 1998[1]
Staff[2]	114 (2012-2013)	37 (2011-2012)	766 (2012)	990 (2010)[3]	786 (2010)[4]	658 (2011)
Organisation	Court; Registrar	Court; Registrar	Presidency; Appeals-, Trial-, Pre-Trial Division; Office of the Prosecutor; Registry	Chambers (Trial~, Appeals~); Prosecutor; Registry	Chambers (Trial, Appeal); Prosecutor; Registry	Judges; Presidency; Registry
Decisions in the Name of	"The Court … delivers the judgment"	"The Tribunal … delivers the judgment …"	"Pre-Trial Chamber I of the ICC … renders the following decision"	"The Appeals Chamber hereby renders its Judgement"	"This judgment … is rendered by Trial Chamber II of the ICTR" (Followed by reference to the tribunal's establishment by the UN.)	"The European Court of Human Rights … delivers the following judgment"
Functions	Peacekeeping; dispute settlement; development of international law	Settlement of disputes concerning the interpretation or application of UNCLOS	Criminal jurisdiction over persons for the most serious crimes of international concern	Fight against impunity for serious violations of international humanitarian law committed in the territory of the former Yugoslavia since 1991	Fight against impunity for serious violations of international humanitarian law committed in the territory of Rwanda and Rwandan citizens responsible for such violations committed in the territory of neighbouring States	To ensure the observance of the engagements undertaken by the High Contracting Parties in the ECHR and the Protocols thereto

Appendix: International Courts – A Chart

	ICJ	ITLOS	ICC	ICTY	ICTR	ECtHR
Jurisdiction						
Ratione Personae	States	States; International Organizations; Private and Legal Persons	Private Persons	Natural Persons	Natural Persons	States and natural persons
Ratione Materiae	Any legal dispute	Law of the Sea	Genocide; crime against humanity; war crimes and crime of aggression	Grave breaches of the Geneva Conventions; violations of the laws or customs of war; genocide; crime against humanity	Genocide; crimes against humanity; violations of common Art. 3	ECHR
Ratione Temporis	No limitation	No limitation (Attention: advisory jurisdiction)	Crimes committed after 1 July 2002	Crimes committed after 1 January 1991	Crimes committed between 1 January 1994 and 31 December 1994	Presenting of the case within six months of exhaustion of domestic remedies; State violations committed after entry into force of the ECHR
Advisory Jurisdiction	Yes	Yes	No	No	No	Yes
The Bench						
Number of Judges	15	21	18	16	16	47
Quorum	Nine	11	Five (Appeals Chamber); Three (Trial Chamber); 3/1 (Pre-Trial Chamber)	Five (Appeals Chamber); Nine (Max; Trial Chamber; Three permanent + six *ad litem*)	Five (Appeals Chamber); Nine (Max; Trial Chamber; Three permanent + six *ad litem*)	2/3 of the elected judges (for the plenary Court)
Ad Hoc Judges	Yes	Yes	No	Ad litem	Ad litem	Yes
National Judges	Yes	Yes	No	No	No	Yes
One Judge / State Party Only[5]	Yes	Yes	Yes	Yes	Yes	Yes
Requirements for Composition of the Bench	Main forms of civilization and principal legal systems of the world	Principal legal systems of the world and equitable geographical distribution	Principal legal systems of the world; equitable geographical representation; fair gender representation; the need to include judges with special legal expertise (e.g. violence against women or children)	Due account taken of the experience of the judges in criminal law, international law, including international humanitarian law and human rights law	Due account taken of the experience of the judges in criminal law, international law, including international humanitarian law and human rights law	One judge / State party

	ICJ	ITLOS	ICC	ICTY	ICTR	ECtHR
Election of President	Court	Court	Court	Court	Court	Court
Tenure of Presidency	Three years	Three years	Three years	Two years	Two years	Three years
Tenure of Presidency (Renewable)	Yes	Yes	Yes (once)	Yes (once)	Yes (once)	Yes (once)

Requirements/Conditions of Office						
Requirement for National Judicial Offices	Yes	No	Yes	Yes	Yes	Yes
Competence in General International Law	Yes	No	No	No	No	No
Competence in Special Law	No	Yes	Yes	Yes	Yes	No
High Moral Character	Yes	No	Yes	Yes	Yes	Yes
Requirement of Independence	Yes	Yes	Yes	No	No	Yes
Requirement of Impartiality	No	No	Yes	Yes	Yes	Yes
Requirement of Integrity	No	Yes	Yes	Yes	Yes	No
Requirement of Fairness	No	Yes	No	No	No	No
Tenure	Nine years	Nine years	Nine years	Four years	Four years	Nine years
Tenure Renewable	Yes	Yes	No	Yes	Yes	No
Age Limit	No	No	No	No	No	Yes (70 years)
Solemn Declaration	Yes	Yes	Yes	Yes	Yes	Yes
Incompatible Activities	Occupation of a professional nature	Any political or administrative function; associate actively with or be financially interested in any of the operations of any enterprise concerned with the exploration for or exploitation of the resources of the sea or the seabed or other commercial use of the sea or the seabed	Any activity likely to interfere with judicial functions or to affect confidence in independence. Full-time judges shall not engage in any other occupation of a professional nature	Occupation of a professional nature	Occupation of a professional nature	Any activity which is incompatible with their independence, impartiality or with the demands of a full-time office
Decision on Incompatibilities	Court	Court	Court	Court	Court	Court

Appendix: International Courts – A Chart

	ICJ	ITLOS	ICC	ICTY	ICTR	ECtHR
Immunities	Diplomatic privileges and immunities	Diplomatic privileges and immunities	Privileges and immunities as are accorded to heads of diplomatic missions	Privileges and immunities accorded to diplomatic envoys, in accordance with international law	Privileges and immunities accorded to diplomatic envoys, in accordance with international law	Privileges and immunities as are reasonably necessary for the fulfilment of their functions
Salary (per annum, appr.)	186,700 EUR	139,600 EUR	180,000 EUR	170,080 USD	170,080 USD	200,000 EUR
Removal	Unanimous decision of the court	Unanimous opinion of the tribunal	2/3 majority of States Parties + 2/3 majority of the Court	--[6]	--[7]	2/3 majority of the Court

Nomination/Election						
Nominating Body	PCA National Groups	States Parties of UNCLOS	States Parties to the Rome Statute	UN Member States	UN Member States	States Parties
Electing Body	UNGA and UNSC	Meeting of States Parties	ASP	UNGA	UNGA	Parliamentary Assembly of the CoE
Majority Requirement	Absolute majority (UNGA/UNSC)	Largest number of votes; 2/3 majority of the States Parties present and voting; majority of the States Parties	Highest number of votes and a 2/3 majority of the States Parties present and voting	Absolute majority	Absolute majority	Majority
Nomination/Election Administration	UNSG	Registrar (earlier UNSG)	ASP	UNSG	UNSG	Parliamentary Assembly of the CoE

Procedural Issues						
Working Languages	English / French	English / French	English / French	English / French	English / French	English / French
Written Proceedings	Yes	Yes	No	Yes	Yes	Yes
Oral Proceedings	Yes	Yes	Yes	Yes	Yes	Yes
Permanent Chambers	Yes	Yes	Yes	Yes	Yes	Yes
Ad Hoc Chambers	Yes	Yes	No	No	No	No
Public Hearings	Yes	Yes	Yes	Yes	Yes	Yes
Third Party Intervention	Yes (interest of a legal nature)	Yes (interest of a legal nature)	No (but: victim participation)	Yes (limited)	Yes (limited)	Yes
Party Representation	Agents	Agents	Himself; Legal assistance	Himself; Legal assistance	Himself; Legal assistance	Himself; Legal representation

	ICJ	ITLOS	ICC	ICTY	ICTR	ECtHR
Sources	International law; *Ex aequo et bono*	UNCLOS; Other non-incompatible international law; *Ex aequo et bono*	Rome Statute; Elements of Crimes; Rules of Procedure and Evidence; applicable treaties; principles of international law; general principles of (national) law	Statute; Rules of Procedure and Evidence; Geneva Conventions of 12 August 1949	Statute; Rules of Procedure and Evidence; Article 3 common to the Geneva Conventions of 12 August 1949 for the Protection of War Victims and of Additional Protocol II thereto of 8 June 1977	ECHR; Rules of Court

Budget/Financing						
Budget	46,605,800 USD (2010-2011)	20,398,600 EUR (2011-2012)	111,000,000 EUR (2012)	347,566,900 USD (2008-2009)	245,295,800 USD (2010-2011)	65,810,300 EUR (2012)
Drafting of Budget	Registrar; Court	Registrar; Court	Registrar; Court	Management Committee	Management Committee	Secretary General of CoE
Approving of Budget	UNGA	Meeting of States Parties	ASP	UNGA	UNGA	Council of Ministers
Source of Financing	UN	States parties (potentially International Seabed Authority)	States Parties; UN	UN	UN	CoE
Cost of Procedures	Parties	Parties	Court	Court	Court	Parties
Financial Assistance for Parties	Yes	No	Yes	Yes	Yes	Yes

Sources						
Framing of Rules	Court	Court	ASP	Court	Court	Court
Governing Instruments	UNC; Statute, Rules etc.	UNCLOS; Statute; Rules etc.	Rome Statute; Rules etc.	Statute; Rules etc.	Statute; Rules etc.	Statute; Rules etc.
Website	www.icj-cij.org	www.itlos.org	www.icc-cpi.int	www.icty.org	www.ictr.org	www.echr.coe.int

1. The Court was established on 21 January 1959 by virtue of Article 19 ECHR. Effective since 1 November 1998, Protocol No.11 of the ECHR, the Court became full-time and the EcommHR was abolished.
2. Number of staff includes both professional and general service staff.
3. The number of staff serving the ICTY and ICTR has decreased considerably following the reduced workload and the fact that both tribunals will be eventually replaced by the IRMCT. The data shown here is the latest reflecting "normal" operation of the tribunals.
4. *Supra.*
5. The Rule on "*One Judge/State Party Only*" refers to the limitation of one judge per State Party to the constitutive agreement.
6. The statute of the ICTY does not address the issue of dismissal or removal from office.
7. The statute of the ICTR does not address the issue of dismissal or removal from office.

Zusammenfassung: Die Unabhängigkeit internationaler Gerichte – Die Einhaltung eines grundsätzlichen Werts der Rechtspflege durch die internationale Judikative

I. Problemstellung und Aktualität der Fragestellung

Die vorliegende Arbeit setzt sich mit der Frage auseinander, ob die richterliche Unabhängigkeit auch im Völkerrecht, d.h. im Hinblick auf internationale Gerichte, als verfahrensrechtlich relevanter Grundsatz wahrgenommen wird und, wenn ja, wie sie dogmatisch berücksichtigt wird.

Aus der Sicht des nationalen Rechts, und hier insbesondere der Rechtsordnungen kontinentaleuropäischer Prägung, ist der Grundsatz der richterlichen Unabhängigkeit ein wesentlicher Baustein der Verfassungsordnung. Wollte man einen ersten funktional orientierten Ansatzpunkt formulieren, so ist der Zweck dieses Grundsatzes die Sicherung der Neutralität des Richters und der Objektivität der Rechtsprechung. So verstanden, formuliert die richterliche Unabhängigkeit das für den Rechtsstaat wesentliche Leitbild von der durch Interessenwahrnehmung ungebundenen gerichtlichen Rechtskontrolle. Es soll sowohl den einzelnen Richter als auch die rechtsprechende Gewalt insgesamt vor sachfremden Eingriffen schützen und so den sach- und rechtsrichtigen Richterspruch garantieren. Aus dieser Aussage darf freilich nicht gefolgert werden, dass das Unabhängigkeitsprinzip eine absolute Unabhängigkeit des Richters (oder der Gerichte) postuliert. So geht die richterliche Selbständigkeit beispielsweise stets einher mit der strikten Rechts- und Gesetzesbindung. Ferner ist die Unabhängigkeit niemals als Selbstzweck oder gar als Standesprivileg des Richters zu verstehen. Die richterliche Unabhängigkeit dient letztendlich dem Rechtsuchenden und soll diesem auch dann Zugang zu seinem Recht sichern, wenn der Staat ein eigenes Interesse am Ausgang eines Verfahrens hat. Verstanden als praktisches Organisationsprinzip trägt der Grundsatz der richterlichen Unabhängigkeit ferner zur Gewaltenteilung bei, indem er die richterliche Gewalt von den übrigen Gewalten (Legislative und Exekutive) abgrenzt und somit diesen gegenüber als selbständige Kraft etabliert.

Auch auf der Ebene des Völkerrechts wird durch internationale Gerichte zunehmend Rechtsprechungstätigkeit ausgeübt. Seit dem Ende des Zweiten Weltkrieges hat die Zahl der institutionalisierten Gerichte auf internationaler

Ebene stetig zugenommen und zu einer Ausweitung der Gerichtskontrolle auch im internationalen Recht beigetragen. Ausgehend etwa vom Ständigen Internationalen Gerichtshof vor dem Zweiten Weltkrieg, später dem Internationalen Gerichtshof (IGH), etablierten sich alsbald sowohl „global" als auch „regional" eine Vielzahl von Gerichten wie etwa der Internationale Seegerichtshof (ISGH), die beiden Ad-hoc-Strafgerichtshöfe für das ehemalige Jugoslawien (ICTY) und Ruanda (ICTR), der Internationale Strafgerichtshof (IStGH), der Gerichtshof der Europäischen Gemeinschaft sowie Gerichtshöfe der regionalen Menschenrechtskonventionen. Diese Institutionen beschränken sich längst nicht mehr nur auf die gerichtliche Entscheidung zwischenstaatlicher Streitigkeiten, was noch ein Charakteristikum der frühen Beispiele internationaler Gerichtsbarkeit war. Im Einklang mit der Ausweitung des völkerrechtlichen Normgeflechts und der Erschließung neuer Rechtsbereiche durch das Völkerrecht wurden auch zunehmend Klagen von Individuen, unabhängiger Anklagebehörden oder internationaler Organisationen zur Initiierung eines Verfahrens vor internationalen Gerichten anerkannt. Mehren sich so die Anzeichen für eine gleichartige Gestaltung von nationaler und internationaler Gerichtsbarkeit, so steigen gleichzeitig auch die Anforderungen an die verfahrenstechnische Ausgestaltung des völkerrechtlichen Rechtsschutzes. Als zentraler Knotenpunkt, so die Lehre aus dem nationalen Recht, fungiert hier die Rolle des Richters. Auch im Rahmen des Völkerrechts gilt es, die Unabhängigkeit des Richters und der Gerichte umfassend abzusichern, um so den sach- und rechtsrichtigen Richterspruch zu ermöglichen. Denn nur wenn internationale Gerichte in der Lage sind, ihrer Aufgabe als unabhängige Streitschlichtungsorgane gerecht zu werden, können sie eine wahre Alternative zu einseitigen Gegenmaßnahmen darstellen und auch dort einen Fortschritt des Rechtsschutzes ermöglichen, wo Gerichtskontrolle traditionell oder noch nicht vorhanden ist.

Diese theoretischen Erklärungsansätze werden durch Beobachtungen der Praxis bestätigt und ergänzt. So wird deutlich, dass die Frage der Unabhängigkeit von Richtern internationaler Gerichte im Laufe der Etablierung neuer Gerichte zu einem wiederkehrenden Streitpunkt geworden ist. Grund hierfür ist der Anspruch der Urheber dieser Institutionen, ein faires Verfahren zu gewährleisten, wobei die Gerichte selber jedoch nicht immer auf ein ausreichend ausgestaltetes und detailliertes Verfahrensrecht zurückgreifen können. Die frühen Beispiele internationalisierter Gerichtsbarkeit, wie etwa der Ständige Internationale Gerichtshof, waren Organe, die sich ausschließlich mit der Lösung zwischenstaatlicher Streitigkeiten befassten. Auch wenn bereits hier die Gründungsstaaten Wert auf die Unabhängigkeit des jeweiligen

Gerichts legten, so war die Selbstdurchsetzung völkerrechtlicher Ansprüche eine immer noch anerkannte und weit verbreitete Handlungsoption. Dies wiederum schmälerte den Anreiz, ausgewogene und allzu detaillierte Verfahrensregeln festzulegen, die dazu beigetragen hätten, dass die Schlichtung von Streitigkeiten dem unmittelbaren Einfluss der einzelnen Staaten entzogen worden wäre. Spätestens durch die Öffnung des Völkerrechts gegenüber dem Individuum ist die Anforderung, das Verfahren so offen und gerecht wie möglich zu gestalten, zu einem unumgänglichen Kriterium erstarkt.

II. Untersuchungsgegenstand

Der Untersuchungsgegenstand der Arbeit wird, vor allem aus praktischen Erwägungen heraus, auf eine begrenzte Zahl einflussreicher internationaler Gerichte beschränkt. Neben einer Reihe Kriterien, die in der Völkerrechtswissenschaft herkömmlich als Merkmale für internationale Gerichte herangezogen werden, wurde bei der Auswahl der zu untersuchenden Institutionen besonders darauf geachtet, Gerichte auszuwählen, deren Rechtsprechung im Völkerrecht Gewicht zukommt und die gleichzeitig wesentliche Schritte in der Herausbildung der internationalen Judikative darstellen. Nicht berücksichtigt wurden etwa die internationale Schiedsgerichtsbarkeit oder internationale Gerichte, die sich lediglich mit regionalen Rechtsordnungen *sui generis*, etwa dem Europarecht, befassen. Auf dieser Grundlage wurden der IGH, der ISGH, der IStrGH, der ICTY, der ICTR sowie der Europäische Gerichtshof für Menschenrechte (EGMR) in die vorliegende Untersuchung mit aufgenommen.

III. Gang der Untersuchung

Die Arbeit ermittelt zunächst die theoretische Verankerung des Prinzips der richterlichen Unabhängigkeit im Völkerrecht. Aufgrund der besonderen Bedingungen im Völkerrecht spielt hierbei das Verständnis als praktisches Organisationsprinzip oder, in seiner verfassungsrechtlichen Dimension, die richterliche Unabhängigkeit als Teil des Gewaltenteilungsprinzips oder gar die Stellung als selbständiges Rechtsstaatsprinzip, eine untergeordnete Rolle. Stattdessen lässt sich die Geltung der richterlichen Unabhängigkeit im Völkerrecht insbesondere aus dem Recht auf ein faires Gerichtsverfahren sowie, besonders bei zwischenstaatlicher Gerichtsbarkeit, aus der Funktion unabhängiger Rechtsprechung als Garant für die erhöhte Glaubwürdigkeit von Verpflichtungen völkerrechtlicher Akteure ableiten. Daraus folgend ist die Ausweitung der institutionalisierten Gerichtsbarkeit im Völkerrecht (in der englischsprachigen Literatur oft als „proliferation of international courts and tribunals“ bezeichnet) zugleich Indiz für die gestiegene Bedeutung von internationalen Gerichten bei der Einhaltung und Umsetzung zwischen- und überstaatlicher Verpflichtungen sowie eine treibende Kraft bei der Herausbildung eines Kerngehalts richterlicher Unabhängigkeit. Denn die Aufgabe der internationalen Gerichte, für eine an Recht gebundene und von sachfremden Einflüssen unabhängige Rechtsprechung zu sorgen und somit eine Alternative zu weniger verrechtlichten Formen der Konfliktlösung zu bieten, wird erst dann erreicht, wenn die Unabhängigkeit des internationalen Richters geschützt wird.

Die Arbeit orientiert sich bei der Untersuchung der Sicherung richterlicher Unabhängigkeit an einer verzweigten Struktur des Prinzips: Während einerseits untersucht wird, wie externe und ungebührliche Einflussnahmen auf die Institution des Gerichts abgewehrt werden, wird andererseits die Perspektive des individuellen Richters eingenommen, um zu ermitteln, wie dieser in seiner richterlichen Tätigkeit von Weisungen abgeschirmt und in seiner Rechtsstellung gegenüber anderen Akteuren geschützt wird. Im Mittelpunkt der Untersuchung stehen Vorkehrungen zur Sicherung der richterlichen Unabhängigkeit, so wie sie sich insbesondere in gerichtseinsetzenden Verträgen, gerichtlichen Verfahrensordnungen, einschlägigen Sekundärrechtsakten internationaler Organisationen und völkerrechtlichen Menschenrechtsverträgen wiederfinden.

IV. Ergebnis

Die Voraussetzungen für eine Sicherung der richterlichen Unabhängigkeit sind grundsätzlich unterschiedlich bei den untersuchten Gerichten. Während Gerichte wie etwa der IGH und ISGH unabhängig von einer Organisation sind und somit eigene Rechtspersönlichkeit besitzen, sind die Ad-hoc-Strafgerichtshöfe sowie der EGMR stark an eine internationale Organisation, jeweils den UN Sicherheitsrat und den Europarat, gebunden und auf diese angewiesen. Dies führt mitunter zu zweifelhaften Abhängigkeiten, wie beispielsweise in der Frage der Personalhoheit des Gerichtspersonals beim EGMR. Die Einordnung der Ad-hoc-Strafgerichtshöfe als Nebenorgane der UN unterwirft diese *prima facie* einer weitreichenden Kontrolle und

Gestaltungsbefugnis durch den UN Sicherheitsrat. Allerdings konnte dargelegt werden, dass den Ad-hoc-Strafgerichtshöfen aufgrund ihrer Natur als Justizorgane eine besondere Stellung unter den Nebenorganen zukommt und dass diese in der Praxis auch weitestgehend eingehalten wird.

Für wesentliche Bedenken sorgt bei nahezu allen untersuchten Gerichten die Art und Weise der Ernennung, d.h. sowohl die Nominierung als auch die Wahl, der Richter. Dabei ist erkennbar, dass das Nominierungsverfahren häufig vollständig in der Hand einzelner Staaten liegt und der Prozess oftmals weder transparent noch an bindenden Rechtsnormen ausgerichtet ist. Ferner ist die Wahl der Richter von politischen Rücksichtnahmen gekennzeichnet, was z.B. durch die Praxis einiger Staaten oder Staatengruppen, eine genau so große Zahl von Kandidaten zu nominieren, wie es freie Sitze auf der Richterbank gibt, sichtbar wird. Viele dieser Defizite sind angesichts der derzeitigen Struktur im Völkerrecht auf absehbare Zeit nicht änderbar, auch wenn sie für die Unabhängigkeit der Rechtsprechung durchaus problematisch sind. Dennoch sind bei der vergleichenden Betrachtung der Gerichte einzelne Besserungsansätze auszumachen: So arbeitet etwa die Parlamentarische Versammlung des Europarates für ein transparenteres Nominierungsverfahren auf einzelstaatlicher Ebene und eine bessere Einhaltung von für das Richteramt gültige Zugangskriterien. Ferner stellt die Möglichkeit der Vertragsstaaten des Römischen Statuts des IStGH, einen Beratenden Ausschuss für Benennungen einzusetzen, einen wichtigen Schritt in Richtung einer staatenunabhängigen Richterernennung dar. Allerdings zeigen sowohl der beratende Charakter dieses Organs als auch das bisherige Ausbleiben seiner Einsetzung deutlich die Grenzen des bislang Möglichen auf.

Ein wiederkehrender kritischer Punkt bei der Sicherung richterlicher Unabhängigkeit ist die Verwendung von Ad-hoc-Richtern bei internationalen Gerichten. Eine Vielzahl der hier untersuchten Gerichte ermöglicht die Bestellung dieser Richter, obwohl deren Fähigkeit, neutral zu sein und objektiv Recht zu sprechen, mit ihrer angedachten Funktion nahezu und *per definitionem* unvereinbar ist. Auch wenn bei der Beurteilung der Institution des Ad-hoc-Richters gerade bei zwischenstaatlichen Streitigkeiten die freiwillige Unterwerfung unter die jeweilige Gerichtsbarkeit und die Konkurrenz zur wesentlich flexibleren Schiedsgerichtsbarkeit mit berücksichtigt werden müssen, wäre im Interesse einer unabhängigen Rechtsprechung das Ersetzen der Ad-hoc-Richter durch von Staaten ernannte Experten eine ernst zu nehmende Alternative. Die an Ad-hoc-Richtern geübte Kritik gilt insbesondere mit Blick auf Gerichte, deren Rechtsprechung unmittelbare Bedeutung für

Einzelpersonen entfaltet, die keinerlei Einfluss auf die Bestellung von Richtern haben.

Die Finanzausstattung von Gerichten bietet, *prima facie*, einen bedeutenden Indikator für mögliche Einflussnahmen auf die rechtsprechende Tätigkeit des jeweiligen Gerichts. Allerdings zeigt die Untersuchung in dieser Hinsicht, dass – auch wenn die Haushalte der unterschiedlichen Gerichte grundverschieden sind – es doch keinerlei Anzeichen für versuchte Einflussnahmen, etwa durch das Ablehnen von beantragten Haushaltserhöhungen, gibt. Im Gegenteil zeigt die Praxis, dass begründete Nachforderungen der Gerichte akzeptiert werden.

Der Status der Richter ist bei den untersuchten Gerichten prinzipiell sehr ähnlich ausgestaltet, was auf die Entstehung einer gewohnheitsrechtlichen Festigung der Richterstellung schließen lässt. So ist beispielsweise in jedem der untersuchten Gerichtsstatute die grundsätzliche Unabsetzbarkeit der Richter festgeschrieben. Die hohen Mehrheitserfordernisse sowie die Verortung der Entscheidungsgewalt über Entlassung aus dem Richteramt, z.B. aufgrund des Wegfalls eines Zulassungskriteriums – einschließlich der Unabhängigkeit – bei den Gerichten selber, lassen auf eine Allgemeingültigkeit dieses Schutzes bei internationalen Gerichten schließen. Die Abwesenheit einer Regelung dieser Frage bei den Ad-hoc-Strafgerichtshöfen wird zwar in Teilen der Literatur dahingehend interpretiert, dass der UN-Sicherheitsrat hier als zuständig angesehen wird. Angesichts der ansonsten einheitlichen Zuführung der Regelungskompetenz zu den jeweiligen Gerichten selber ist diese Auslegung jedoch nicht überzeugend und widerspräche ferner der Unabhängigkeit der Richter von ungebührlichen Einflussnahmen.

Getrennt von der Möglichkeit eines Ausschlusses vom Richteramt ist die Sanktion, einzelne Richter aufgrund ihrer Befangenheit von einem Verfahren auszuschließen – so etwa in dem Verfahren *Furundžija* aus dem Jahre 2000 vor dem ICTY. Hier wurde der Vorsitzenden Richterin Mumba der Vorwurf der Befangenheit gemacht, da sie vor ihrer Tätigkeit als Richterin in der UN-Kommission für die Rechtsstellung der Frau gearbeitet und dabei systematische Vergewaltigungen in Jugoslawien untersucht und missbilligt hatte. Die Berufungskammer des ICTY wies den Vorwurf mit der Begründung zurück, dass man Richtern durchaus zutrauen müsse, sich von persönlichen Überzeugungen freimachen zu können. Dass ein ähnlicher Sachverhalt auch anders beurteilt werden kann, nämlich dahingehend, dass sogar der Eindruck der Befangenheit vermieden werden muss, zeigt z.B. das Sondervotum von Richter Buergenthal beim IGH zu dem Antrag auf Ausschluss von Richter Elaraby vom Verfahren im Fall des Gutachtens zur umstrittenen Sperranlage in den von Israel besetzten Gebieten. Diese Sichtweise verdient gerade wegen ihres flexibleren auf die Außenbetrachtung der Rechtsprechung und der Gerichte fokussierten Verständnisses der richterlichen Unabhängigkeit Unterstützung. Davon abgesehen verdeutlichen diese beiden Entscheidungen, dass selbst bei scheinbar gleichen Sachverhalten (Äußerungen eines Richters, die dieser vor der Aufnahme der Richtertätigkeit gemacht hat und in denen Verhältnisse angesprochen werden, die später zum Gegenstand eines Verfahrens vor einem internationalen Gericht werden) die Frage der richterlichen Unabhängigkeit diametral unterschiedlich beurteilt werden kann. Dies ist nicht zuletzt ein weiterer Beleg dafür, dass der Inhalt des Grundsatzes der richterlichen Unabhängigkeit für das Völkerrecht nicht einheitlich und klar formuliert ist.

Die Amtszeit der Richter bei internationalen Gerichten ist unterschiedlich geregelt und reicht von vier Jahren bei gleichzeitiger Möglichkeit zur Wiederwahl (ICTY und ICTR), bis neun Jahre (IGH, ISGH) ohne ein Recht auf eine erneute Kandidatur (IStHG, EGMR). Während eine kurze Amtszeit die Gefahr in sich birgt, dass Richter Entscheidungen fällen, die ihre Wiederwahl begünstigen, bietet eine längere Amtszeit ohne Wiederwahlmöglichkeit zwar gewissen Schutz gegen einen Einfluss eines bevorstehenden (Wieder-)Wahlverfahrens auf die Rechtsprechung, ist aber dennoch nicht immer im Interesse einer kontinuierlichen Rechtsprechung und dient nicht dem Erhalt einer geeigneten und berufserfahrenen Richterbank.

Neben der Regelung von Amtszeit und Vergütung von Richtern gehört die Regelung von Nebentätigkeiten zu den Bereichen, in denen aufgezeigt werden konnte, dass mehrere Gerichtsstatute Defizite aufweisen. Auch wenn es zweifelsohne geboten ist, insbesondere Richtern, deren Tätigkeit bei dem jeweiligen Gericht nur zeitlich begrenzt ist, zu ermöglichen, auch bestimmten Nebentätigkeiten nachzugehen (z.B. ISGH), so zeigt die Praxis, dass einige Richter zusätzlichen Tätigkeiten nachgehen, die nur schwer mit einer tatsächlichen Unabhängigkeit oder zumindest dem Anschein der Unabhängigkeit vereinbar sind. In diesem Zusammenhang wäre es wünschenswert, wenn einige Gerichtsstatute striktere Regeln aufweisen oder bestehende Regeln apodiktischer ausgelegt und angewendet würden.

Die Untersuchung von den Richtern gewährten Vorrechten und Immunitäten konnte zeigen, dass nahezu alle Gerichtsstatute auf diplomatische Vorrechte und Immuntäten verweisen, was durchaus als bedeutender Schutz der Unabhängigkeit der Richter gewertet werden kann, jedoch davon absehen, diese selber zu definieren. Dadurch wird einerseits versäumt, den wesentlichen formalen und funktionalen Unterschieden zwischen internationalen

Richtern und Diplomaten und den damit einhergehenden Bedürfnissen auf Schutz ihrer jeweiligen Stellung Rechnung zu tragen. Vor allem wird nicht berücksichtigt, dass Richter einen Schutz gegenüber jeden Staat, einschließlich des jeweiligen Heimatstaates, benötigen, während Diplomaten einer Immunität gegenüber ihrem Entsendestaat *per definitionem* gerade nicht bedürfen. Andererseits wird durch den pauschalen Verweis auf bestehende Immunitätenkataloge beispielsweise vernachlässigt, dass internationale Richter weniger einer funktionalen als vielmehr einer absoluten Immunität bedürfen, um in ihrer Funktionsausübung, die auf verschiedenste Weisen die wirtschaftlichen und politischen Interessen von Staaten beeinflussen können, geschützt zu werden.

In der Gesamtschau machen die Ergebnisse der Arbeit deutlich, dass es einerseits wesentliche Mängel in der Sicherung richterlicher Unabhängigkeit bei internationalen Gerichten gibt. Andererseits tritt hervor, dass gewisse Anforderungen allzeit eingehalten werden, unabhängig von der jeweiligen Gerichtsbarkeit *ratione materiae* (materiell-rechtlich), *ratione personae* (personal) oder gar *ratione temporis* (zeitlich). Dies lässt den Schluss zu, dass dies eine gewohnheitsrechtliche Entwicklung darstellt, die insbesondere für die Errichtung weiterer Gerichte auf internationaler Ebene von Bedeutung ist, sofern auch diese, wie ihre Vorgänger, dem Leitbild der von Interessenwahrnehmung ungebundenen gerichtlichen Rechtskontrolle folgen wollen.

Bibliography

I. Monographs

Adede, Andrónico O., *The System for Settlement of Disputes under the United Nations Convention on the Law of the Sea – A Drafting History and a Commentary* (Nijhoff Dordrecht 1987).

Akkas, Sarkar Ali, *Judicial Independence and Accountability: A Comparative Study of Contemporary Bangladesh Experience* (University of Wollongong Thesis Collections Online 2002).

American Law Institute, *Restatement of the Law (Third), Foreign Relations Law of the United States* (American Law Institute Philadelphia 1987).

Amr, Mohamed Sameh M., *The Role of the International Court of Justice as the Principal Judicial Organ of the United Nations* (Kluwer Law International The Hague 2003).

Aristotle, *Politics* (Dover Publications Inc. Ontario 2000).

Aubert, Vilhelm, *In Search of Law: Sociological Approaches to Law* (Robertson Oxford 1983).

Aust, Anthony, *Handbook of International Law* (Cambridge University Press Cambridge 2nd edn. 2010).

Baker, John H., *An Introduction to English Legal History* (Butterworths London 4th edn. 2002).

Bassiouni, M. Cherif (ed), The Legislative History of the International Criminal Court: Volume 1 – Introduction, Analysis, and Integrated Text of the Statute, Elements of Crimes and Rules of Procedure and Evidence (Transnational Publishers New York 2005).

Bassiouni, M. Cherif (ed), The Legislative History of the International Criminal Court: Volume 2 – Article-by-Article Evolution of the Statute (Transnational Publishers New York 2005).

Bassiouni, M. Cherif and Manikas, Peter, *The Law of the International Criminal Tribunal for the Former Yugoslavia* (Transnational Publ. New York 1996).

Bernhardt, Rudolf, *Die Auslegung völkerrechtlicher Verträge – Insbesondere in der Rechtsprechung internationaler Gerichte* (Karl Heymanns Verlag KG Köln 1963).

Bettermann, Karl August, Neumann, Franz L. and Bachof, Otto (eds), Rechtspflege und Grundrechtsschutz – Die Grundrechte, Handbuch der Theorie und Praxis der Grundrechte (Duncker & Humblot Berlin 1959).

Boczek, Boleslaw Adam, *Historical Dictionary of International Tribunals* (Scarecrow Press Metuchen, New Jersey 1994).

von Bogdandy, Armin, Wolfrum, Rüdiger and von Bernstorff, Jochen (eds), The Exercise of Public Authority by International Institutions: Advancing International Institutional Law (Springer Heidelberg 2010).

Boisson de Chazournes, Laurence, Romano, Cesare P. R. and Mackenzie, Ruth (eds), International Organizations and International Dispute Settlement – Trends and Prospects (Transnational Publishers Ardsley New York 2002).

Bowett, Derek W., *The Law of International Institutions* (Stevens Sons London 4th edn. 1982).

Brown, Chester, *A Common Law of International Adjudication* (Oxford University Press Oxford 2007).

Browning, Andrew (ed), *English Historical Documents: Vol. 8: 1660-1714* (Eyre & Spottiswoode London 1953).

Brütsch, Christian (ed), Law and Legalization in Transnational Relations (Routledge London 2007).

Bustamante y Sirven, Antonio Sánchez de, *La Cour Permanente de Justice Internationale* (Recueil Sirey Paris 1925).

Cassese, Antonio (ed), The Path to the Hague: Selected Documents on the Origins of the ICTY (ICTY The Hague 1997).

Cassese, Antonio (ed), The Rome Statute of the International Criminal Court: A Commentary – Volume I (Oxford University Press Oxford 2002).

Cassese, Antonio, *International Criminal Law* (Oxford University Press Oxford 2nd edn. 2008).

Cassese, Antonio, *International Criminal Law* (Oxford University Press Oxford 2005).

Chandrasekhara Rao, P. and Gautier, Philippe (eds), The Rules of the International Tribunal for the Law of the Sea – A Commentary (Nijhoff Leiden 2006).

Cheng, Bin, *General Principles of Law as Applied by International Courts and Tribunals* (Stevens London 1953).

Coke, Sir Edward, *The reports of Sir Edward Coke, Knt. in Thirteen Parts – A new Edition, with Additional Notes and References, and with Abstracts of the Principal Points, Volume VI, Parts XI-XII-XIII* (Joseph Butterworth and Son London 1826).

Congress of Europe, *Europe Unites: The Story of the Campaign for European Unity, Including a Full Report of the Congress of Europe, held at The Hague, May 1948* (Hollis & Carter London 1949).

Council of Europe, *Collected Edition of the "Travaux Préparatoires" of the European Convention on Human Rights – Volume I – Preparatory Commission of the Council of Europe, Committee of Ministers, Consultative Assembly, 11 May – 8 September 1949* (Martinus Nijhoff The Hague 1975).

Council of Europe, *Collected Edition of the "Travaux Préparatoires" of the European Convention on Human Rights – Volume II – Consultative Assembly, Second Session of the Committee of Ministers, Standing Committee of the Assembly, 10 August – 18 November 1949* (Martinus Nijhoff The Hague 1975).

Council of Europe, *Collected Edition of the "Travaux Préparatoires" of the European Convention on Human Rights – Volume IV – Committee of Experts, Committee of Ministers, Conference of Senior Officials, 30 March – June 1950* (Martinus Nijhoff The Hague 1977).

Council of Europe, *Collected Edition of the "Travaux Préparatoires" of the European Convention on Human Rights – Volume V – Legal committee – Ad hoc joint committee – Committee of ministers – Consultative assembly 23 June – 28 August 1950* (Martinus Nijhoff The Hague 1978).

Council of Europe, *Collected Edition of the "Travaux Préparatoires" of the European Convention on Human Rights – Volume VII – Standing Committee of the Consultative Assembly, Consultative Assembly, Committee of Experts, Committee of Ministers, Legal Committee, 3 November 1950 – 15 May 1951* (Martinus Nijhoff The Hague 1985).

Creifelds, Carl and Weber, Klaus, *Rechtswörterbuch* (Beck München 19th edn. 2007).

Cryer, Robert, *Prosecuting International Crimes – Selectivity and the International Criminal Law Regime* (Cambridge University Press Cambridge 2005).

Dicey, Albert Venn, *Introduction to the Study of the Law of the Constitution* (Macmillan 1885).

Dijk, Pieter van and Hoof, Godefridus J. H. van, *Theory and Practice of the European Convention on Human Rights* (Kluwer Deventer 2nd edn. 1990).

Doehring, Karl, *Völkerrecht – Ein Lehrbuch* (Müller Heidelberg 2nd edn. 2004).

Dudenredaktion, *Duden: das große Wörterbuch der deutschen Sprache in sechs Bänden: Band 6: Sp-Z* (Bibliographisches Institut Mannheim 1981).

Dunn, Frederick Sherwood, *The Practice and Procedure of International Conferences* (Johns Hopkins Press Baltimore 1929).

Dupuy, René-Jean and Recht, Haagse Academie voor Internationaal, *Manuel sur les organisations internationales* (Nijhoff Dordrecht 1988).

Dupuy, René-Jean and Vignes, Daniel (eds), A Handbook on the New Law of the Sea – Volume 1 (Nijhoff Dordrecht 1991).

Dupuy, René-Jean and Vignes, Daniel (eds), A Handbook on the New Law of the Sea – Volume 2 (Nijhoff Dordrecht 1991).

Eichenberger, Kurt, *Die richterliche Unabhängigkeit als staatsrechtliches Problem* (Stämpfli Bern 1960).

Eiriksson, Gudmundur *The International Tribunal for the Law of the Sea* (Nijhoff The Hague 2000).

Eissen, Marc-André, 'La Cour Européenne des Droits de L'Homme – De la Convention au Reglement', in: Association of Attenders and Alumni of the Hague Academy of International Law / Groupe Français (ed), *Annuaire français de droit international* (Centre National de la Recherche Scientifique Paris 1959).

Elias, Taslim Olawale, *New Horizons in International Law* (Sijthoff & Noordhoff Alphen aan den Rijn 1979).

European Commission of Human Rights and European Court of Human Rights, *Yearbook of the European convention on Human Rights – 1958-1959* (Nijhoff The Hague 1960).

European Court of Human Rights, *Annual Report 2011* (Registry of the European Court of Human Rights Strasbourg 2012).

Fachiri, Alexander P., *The Permanent Court of International Justice – Its Constitution, Procedure and Work* (Oxford University Press Oxford 2nd edn. 1932).

Fowler, Henry W. and Thompson, Della (eds), The Concise Oxford Dictionary of Current English (Clarendon Press Oxford 9th edn. 1995).

Franck, Thomas M., *Fairness in International Law and Institutions* (Clarendon Press Oxford 1995).

Franck, Thomas M., *The Structure of Impartiality: Examining the Riddle of one Law in a Fragmented World* (Macmillan New York 1968).

Frank, Veronica, *The European Community and Marine Environmental Protection in the International Law of the Sea – Implementing Global Obligations at the Regional Level* (Nijhoff Leiden 2007).

Frowein, Jochen Abr. and Peukert, Wolfgang, *Europäische Menschenrechtskonvention: EMRK-Kommentar* (N. P. Engel Kehl 1985).

Frowein, Jochen Abr. and Peukert, Wolfgang, *Europäische Menschenrechtskonvention: EMRK-Kommentar* (N. P. Engel Kehl 2nd edn. 1996).

Frowein, Jochen Abr. and Peukert, Wolfgang, *Europäische Menschenrechtskonvention: EMRK-Kommentar* (N. P. Engel Kehl 3rd edn. 2009).

Fuller, Lon L., *Anatomy of the Law* (Praeger New York 1968).

Gardiner, Richard K., *Treaty Interpretation* (Oxford University Press Oxford 2008).

Garner, Bryan A. (ed), Black's Law Dictionary (Thomson Reuters St. Paul 9th edn. 2009).

Goldsmith, Jack L. and Posner, Eric A., *The Limits of International Law* (Oxford University Press Oxford 2005).

Goodrich, Leland M. and Hambro, Edvard, *Charter of the United Nations – Commentary and Documents* (Columbia University Press New York 3rd edn. and rev. 1969).

Gourevitch, Philip, *We wish to inform you that tomorrow we will be killed with our families* (Farrar, Straus and Giroux New York 1998).

Grabenwarter, Christoph, *Europäische Menschenrechtskonvention – Ein Studienbuch* (Beck München 4th edn. 2009).

Greer, Steven, *The European Convention on Human Rights. Achievements, Problems and Prospects* (Cambridge University Press Cambridge 2006).

Guyomar, Geneviève, *Commentaire du règlement de la Cour Internationale de Justice adopté le 14 avril 1978 – interpretation et pratique* (Pedone Paris 1983).

Haesler, Thomas, *The Exhaustion of Local Remedies in the Case Law of International Courts and Tribunals* (Sijthoff Leyden and Bonn 1968).

Hamilton, Alexander, *The Federalist Papers* (Independent Journal 1788).

Hannikainen, Lauri, *Peremptory Norms (Jus Cogens) in International Law – Historical Development, Criteria, Present Status* (Lakimiesliiton Kustannus Helsinki 1988).

Hart, Herbert Lionel Adolphus, *The Concept of Law* (Oxford University Press Oxford 2nd edn. 1994).

Higgins, Rosalyn, *Problems and Process: International Law and How we Use it* (Clarendon Press Oxford 1994).

Hobe, Stephan and Kimminich, Otto, *Einführung in das Völkerrecht* (Francke Tübingen Basel 8th edn. 2004).

Holdsworth, William Searle and Goodhart, Arthur L., *A History of English Law: Vol. 5* (Sweet and Maxwell London 1945).

Holt, James Clark, *Magna Carta* (Cambridge University Press Cambridge 2nd edn. 1992).

Hosler, John D., *Henry II: A Medieval Soldier at War* (Brill Leiden 2007).

Hudson, Manley O., *International Tribunals: Past and Future* (Carnegie Endowment for International Peace Washington 1944).

Hudson, Manley O., *The Permanent Court of International Justice 1920-1942 – A Treatise* (MacMillan New York 1943).

Human Rights Watch, *Genocide, War Crimes and Crimes Against Humanity – A Topical Digest of the Case Law of the International Criminal Tribunal for the Former Yugoslavia* (Human Rights Watch New York 2006).

Institut de Droit International, *Annuaire de l'Institut de Droit International 1954-I* (Verlag für Recht und Gesellschaft A G. Genève 1954).

Institut de Droit International, *Annuaire de l'Institut de Droit International – Session d'Aix-en-Provence Avril/Mai 1954 Tome II* (Verlag für Recht und Gesellschaft A G. Genève 1954).

International Commission of Jurists, *Executive action and the rule of law: a report on the proceedings of the International Congress of Jurists, Rio de Janeiro, Brazil, December 11-15, 1962* (International Commission of Jurists Geneva 1962).

International Law Commission, *Yearbook of the International Law Commission* (United Nations New York 1954).

International Tribunal for the Prosecution of Persons Responsible for Serious Violations of International Humanitarian Law Committed in the Territory of the Former Yugoslavia since 1991, *Yearbook 1997* (United Nations New York 1997).

Ipsen, Knut, *Völkerrecht – ein Studienbuch* (Beck München 3rd edn. 1990).

Janis, Mark Weston (ed), International Courts for the Twenty-First Century (Nijhoff Dordrecht 1992).

Janis, Mark Weston, Kay, Richard S. and Bradley, Anthony W., *European Human Rights Law: Text and Materials* (Clarendon Press Oxford 2nd edn. 1995).

Jenks, Clarence Wilfred, *Law, Freedom, and Welfare* (Stevens & Sons London 1963).

Jennings, Robert Y., 'The Proliferation of Adjudicatory Bodies: Dangers and Possible Answers', in: Boisson de Chazournes, Laurence (ed), *ASIL Bulletin No. 9: Implications of the Proliferation of International Adjuidatory Bodies for Dispute Resolution: Proceedings of a Forum Co-Sponsored by the American Society of International Law and the Graduate Institute of International Studies, Geneva, Switzerland, May 13, 1995* (American Society of International Law Washington 1995).

Kadelbach, Stefan, *Zwingendes Völkerrecht* (Duncker und Humblot Berlin 1992).

Kamardi, Christiane, *Die Ausformung einer Prozessordnung "sui generis" durch das ICTY unter Berücksichtigung des Fair-Trial-Prinzips* (Springer Berlin; Heidelberg 2009).

Kant, Immanuel, *Metaphysische Anfangsgründe der Rechtslehre* (Friedrich Nicolovius Königsberg 1797).

Karg, Moritz, *IGH vs. ISGH – Die Beziehung zwischen zwei völkerrechtlichen Streitbeilegungsorganen* (Nomos Baden-Baden 2005).

Kelsen, Hans, *The Law of the United Nations: A Critical Analysis of its Fundamental Problems* (Stevens London 1950).

Kirkpatrick, Elizabeth M., *The Oxford Paperback Thesaurus* (Oxford University Press Oxford 1994).

Klein, Natalie, *Dispute Settlement in the UN Convention on the Law of the Sea* (Cambridge University Press Cambridge 2005).

Kleinsorge, Tanja E.J. (ed), Council of Europe (Kluwer Law International 2010).

Korinek, Karl and Holoubek, Michael (eds), Österreichisches Bundesverfassungsrecht: Textsammlung und Kommentar (Springer Wien 2007).

Koskenniemi, Martti, *From Apology to Utopia: The Structure of International Legal Argument* (Lakimiesliiton Kustannus Helsinki 1989).

Koster, Martina, *Immunität internationaler Richter – gemessen an derjenigen der Diplomaten und der internationalen Funktionäre* (Verlag Recht und Wirtschaft Heidelberg 2002).

Kreide, Regina and Brunkhorst, Hauke (eds), Transnationale Verrechtlichung: nationale Demokratien im Kontext globaler Politik: Hauke Brunkhorst zum 60. Geburtstag (Campus-Verlag Frankfurt 2008).

La Fontaine, Henri, *Pasicrisie Internationale 1794 – 1900: Histoire documentaire des arbitrages internationaux* (Nijhoff The Hague 1997).

Lauterpacht, Elihu, *Aspects of the Administration of International Justice* (Grotius Cambridge 1991).

Lauterpacht, Hersch, *The Development of International Law by the International Court* (Stevens London 1958).

Lauterpacht, Hersch, *The Function of Law in the International Community* (Clarendon Press Oxford 1933).

League of Nations, *Official Journal – Number 1, February 1920* (Imprimerie 'Sonor', S.A. Genève 1920).

League of Nations, *Official Journal – Number 6, September 1920* (Imprimerie 'Sonor', S.A. Genève 1920).

League of Nations, *Official Journal – Number 8, November-December 1920* (Imprimerie 'Sonor', S.A. Genève 1920).

Lee, Roy S. (ed), The International Criminal Court: The Making of the Rome Statute; Issues, Negotiations, Results (Kluwer Law International The Hague 1999).

Limbach, Jutta, Cruz Villalón, Pedro, Errera, Roger, Lester, Anthony, Morshchakova, Tamara, Sedley, Stephen and Zoll, Andrzej, *Judicial Independence: Law and Practice of Appointments to the European Court of Human Rights* (Interights London 2003).

Locke, John, *The Second Treatise of Government* (Barnes & Noble Publishing New York 2004).

Mackenzie, Ruth, Malleson, Kate, Martin, Penny and Sands, Philippe J., *Selecting International Judges: Principle, Process, and Politics* (Oxford University Press Oxford 2010).

Mackenzie, Ruth, Romano, Cesare P. R., Shany, Yuval and Sands, Philippe J. (eds), The Manual on International Courts and Tribunals (Oxford University Press Oxford 2nd edn. 2009).

Malanczuk, Peter, *Akehurst's Modern Introduction to International Law* (Routledge London 7th edn. 1997).

Martenczuk, Bernd, *Rechtsbindung und Rechtskontrolle des Weltsicherheitsrats – Die Überprüfung nichtmilitärischer Zwangsmaßnahmen durch den Internationalen Gerichtshof* (Duncker & Humblot Berlin 1996).

Masterman, Roger, *The Separation of Powers in the Contemporary Constitution: Judicial Competence and Independence in the United Kingdom* (Cambridge University Press Cambridge 2011).

Merrills, John G., *International Dispute Settlement* (Cambridge University Press Cambridge 3rd edn. 1998).

Merrills, John G., *International Dispute Settlement* (Cambridge University Press Cambridge 5th edn. 2011).

Meyer-Ladewig, Jens, *Europäische Menschenrechtskonvention: Handkommentar* (Nomos Baden-Baden 2nd edn. 2006).

Montesquieu, Charles de Secondat, *The Spirit of the Laws* (Cambridge University Press Cambridge 1989).

Montesquieu, Charles Louis de Secondat, *De l'Esprit des Lois* (Lebigre Frères Paris 1834).

Morris, Virginia and Scharf, Michael P., *An Insider's Duide to the International Criminal Tribunal for the Former Yugoslavia – A Documentary History and Analysis* (Transnational Publishers New York 1996).

Morris, Virginia and Scharf, Michael P., *The International Criminal Tribunal for Rwanda – Volume 1* (Transnational Publishers New York 1996).

Mukagasana, Yolande and Kazinierakis, Alain, *Les blessures du silence* (Actes Sud Arles 2001).

Nitsche, Dennis, *Der Internationale Strafgerichtshof ICC und der Frieden – eine vergleichende Analyse der Befriedungsfunktion internationaler Straftribunale* (Nomos Baden-Baden 2007).

Nordquist, Myron H. (ed), United Nations Convention on the Law of the Sea 1982: A Commentary – Volume V (Nijhoff Dordrecht 1989).

Nordquist, Myron H. and Moore, John Norton (eds), Current marine environmental issues and the International Tribunal for the Law of the Sea – twenty-fifth annual conference of the Center for Oceans Law and Policy, University of Virginia School of Law, held from March 16 – 19, 2001, in Hamburg, Germany (Nijhoff Publishers The Hague 2001).

Nussbaum, Arthur, *A Concise History of the Law of Nations* (Macmillan New York 1954).

Oppenheim, Lassa F. and Lauterpacht, Hersch, *International Law, A Treatise – Disputes, War and Neutrality* (Longmans Green London 7th edn. 1952).

Orakhelashvili, Alexander, *Peremptory Norms in International Law* (Oxford University Press Oxford 2006).

Parry, Clive, *The Sources and Evidences of International Law* (Manchester University Press Manchester 1965).

Permanent Court of International Justice and Advisory Committee of Jurists, *Procès-Verbaux of the Proceedings of the Committee, June 16th-July 24th 1920 with Annexes* (Van Langenhuysen Brothers The Hague 1920).

Permanent Court of International Justice, *Series D. Acts and Documents Concerning the Organization of the Court – Second Addendum to No 2. Modification of the Rules* (A.W. Sijthoff's Leyden 1931).

Pieper, Stefan Ulrich, *Verfassungsrichterwahlen: die Besetzung der Richterbank des Bundesverfassungsgerichts und die Besetzung des Europäischen Gerichtshofes sowie des Europäischen Gerichtshofes für Menschenrechte und des Internationalen Gerichtshofes mit deutschen Kandidaten* (Duncker & Humblot Berlin 1998).

Plucknett, Theodore Frank Thomas, *A Concise History of the Common Law* (Butterworth London 5th edn. 1956).

Pollock, Frederick and Maitland, Frederic William, *The History of English Law Before the Time of Edward I* (The Lawbook Exchange New Jersey 2008).

Prunier, Gérard, *The Rwanda crisis – 1959-1994: History of a Genocide* (Hurst London 1995).

Raz, Joseph, *The Concept of a Legal System: An Introduction to the Theory of Legal System* (Clarendon Press Oxford 2nd edn. 1980).

Reinhardt, Michael, *Konsistente Jurisdiktion* (Mohr Siebeck Tübingen 1997).

Rey-Debove, Josette, Rey, Alain, Chantreau, Sophie and Drivaud, Marie-Hélène, *Le nouveau Petit Robert: dictionnaire alphabétique et analogique de la langue française* (Dictionnaires Le Robert Paris Nouv. éd. du Petit Robert de Paul Robert, 40. éd. 2007).

Rosenne, Shabtai (ed), The Hague Peace Conferences of 1899 and 1907 and International Arbitration: Reports and Documents (T.M.C. Asser The Hague 2001).

Rosenne, Shabtai, *The Court and the United Nations* (Nijhoff Leiden 4th edn. 2006).

Rosenne, Shabtai, *The Law and Practice of the International Court – Vol. 1* (Sijthoff Leyden 1965).

Rosenne, Shabtai, *The Law and Practice of the International Court – Vol. 1 The Court and the United Nations* (Nijhoff Leiden 2006).

Rosenne, Shabtai, *The Law and Practice of the International Court – Vol. 3 Procedure* (Nijhoff Leiden 2006).

Rosenne, Shabtai, *The World Court – What it is and how it Works* (Sythoff Leyden 1962).

Sabel, Robbie, *Procedure at International Conferences: A Study of the Rules of Procedure at the UN and at Inter-Governmental Conferences* (Cambridge University Press Cambridge 2006).

Safferling, Christoph Johannes Maria, *Towards an International Criminal Procedure* (Oxford University Press Oxford 2001).

Sands, Philippe J. (ed), Manual on International Courts and Tribunals (Butterworths London 1999).

Schabas, William A., *An Introduction to the International Criminal Court* (Cambridge University Press Cambridge 3rd edn. 2007).

Schabas, William A., *The International Criminal Court: A Commentary on the Rome Statute* (Oxford University Press Oxford 2010).

Schabas, William A., *The UN International Criminal Tribunals – The Former Yugoslavia, Rwanda and Sierra Leone* (Cambridge University Press Cambridge 2006).

Schenk von Stauffenberg, Berthold, *Statut et Règlement de la Cour Permanente de Justice Internationale – Eléments d'interprétation* (Heymann Berlin 1934).

Schermers, Henry G. and Blokker, Niels, *International Institutional Law: Unity within Diversity* (Nijhoff Boston 4th edn. 2003).

Schmitt, Carl, *Verfassungslehre* (Duncker & Humblot Berlin 1993).

Schücking, Walther and Wehberg, Hans, *Die Satzung des Völkerbundes – Band 1* (Vahlen Berlin 3rd edn. 1931).

Schwarzenberger, Georg, *International Law as Applied by International Courts and Tribunals – Vol. 4 – International Judicial Law* (Stevens & Sons Limited London 1986).

Schwebel, Stephen M., *Justice in International Law: Further Selected Writings* (Cambridge University Press Cambridge 2011).

Scott, James Brown (ed), Instructions to the American Delegates to the Hague Peace Conferences and their Official Reports (Oxford University Press New York 1916).

Scott, James Brown (ed), The Hague Court Reports: Vol. 1 (Oxford University Press New York 1916).

Scott, James Brown, *The Project of a Permanent Court of International Justice and Resolutions of the Advisory Committee of Jurists – Report and Commentary* (Carnegie Endowment for International Peace Washington 1920).

Scott, James Brown, *The Reports to the Hague Conferences of 1899 and 1907* (Clarendon Press Michigan 1917).

Scott, Samuel P. (transl.), *Codex Iustinianus: The Civil Law: Including: The Twelve Tables, The Institutes of Gaius, The Rules of Ulpian, The Opinions of Paulus, The Enactments of Justinian, and The Constitutions of Leo* (Central Trust Company Cincinnati 1932).

Seibert-Fohr, Anja (ed), Judicial Independence in Transition: Strengthening the Rule of Law in the OSCE Region (Springer Heidelberg 2012).

Seibert-Fohr, Anja, *Prosecuting Serious Human Rights Violations* (Oxford University Press Oxford 2009).

Seidl-Hohenveldern, Ignaz and Loibl, Gerhard, *Das Recht der internationalen Organisationen einschließlich der supranationalen Gemeinschaften* (Heymann Köln 4th edn. 1984).

Shany, Yuval, *The Competing Jurisdictions of International Courts and Tribunals* (Oxford University Press Oxford 2003).

Shapiro, Martin M., *Courts: A Comparative and Political Analysis* (University of Chicago Press Chicago 1986).

Shaw, Malcolm N., *International Law* (Cambridge University Press Cambridge 6th edn. 2009).

Shetreet, Shimon (ed), Judicial Independence the Contemporary Debate (Nijhoff Dordrecht 1985).

Shetreet, Shimon, *Judges on Trial – A Study of the Appointment and Accountability of the English Judiciary* (North-Holland Publishers Amsterdam 1976).

Simpson, John Liddle and Fox, Hazel, *International Arbitration: Law and Practice* (Stevens London 1959).

Singh, Nagendra, *The Role and Record of the International Court of Justice: 1946 to 1988; in Celebration of the 40th Anniversary* (Nijhoff Dordrecht 1989).

Soanes, Catherine and Stevenson, Angus (eds), Oxford Dictionary of English (Oxford University Press Oxford 2nd edn. 2007).

Sørensen, Max, *Les sources du droit international: étude sur la jurisprudence de la Cour Permanente de Justice Internationale* (Munksgaard Kopenhagen 1946).

Steering Committee for Human Rights, *Reforming the European Convention on Human Rights: a work in progress; a compilation of publications and documents relevant to the ongoing reform of the ECHR* (Council of Europe Publishers Strasbourg 2009).

Stern, Klaus, *Das Staatsrecht der Bundesrepublik Deutschland, Band 1* (C.H. Beck München 2nd edn. 1984).

Svensson-McCarthy, Anna-Lena, *The International Law of Human Rights and States of Exception. With Special Reference to the Travaux Préparatoires and Case-Law of the International Monitoring Organs* (Nijhoff Den Haag 1998).

Ten Brinke, Daniel and Deml, Hans-Michael (eds), Judges in the Service of the State? Procedures, Criteria and Political Influence on National Selection of Judges for the Highest Judicial Offices and their Possible Influence on the International Criminal Court (Shaker Aachen 2002).

Terris, Daniel, Romano, Cesare P. R. and Swigart, Leigh, *The International Judge – An Introduction to the Men and Women who Decide the World's Cases* (Oxford University Press Oxford 2007).

The European Movement, *European Movement and the Council of Europe* (Hutchinson London 1949).

Triffterer, Otto (ed), Commentary on the Rome Statute of the International Criminal Court – Observers' Notes, Article by Article (Beck München 2nd edn. 2008).

UNCITRAL (ed), UNCITRAL Model Law on International Commercial Arbitration 1985: With Amendments as Adopted in 2006 (United Nations Vienna 2008).

United Nations Information Organizations, *Volume VI – Commission I – General Provisions* (United Nations Information Organizations London New York 1945).

United Nations Information Organizations, *Volume XIII – Commission IV – Judicial Organization* (United Nations Information Organizations London New York 1945).

United Nations Information Organizations, *Volume XIV – United Nations Committee of Jurists* (United Nations Information Organizations London New York 1945).

United Nations, *Repertory of Practice of United Nations Organs – Repertory of Practice (1945-1954), Volume 1 – Extracts relating to Article 7 of the Charter of the United Nations* (United Nations New York 1955).

Van-Hoa, To, *Judicial Independence: A Legal Research on its Theoretical Aspects, Practices from Germany, the United States of America, France, Vietnam, and Recommendations for Vietnam* (Juristförlaget Lund 2006).

Verdross, Alfred and Simma, Bruno, *Universelles Völkerrecht – Theorie und Praxis* (Duncker & Humblot Berlin 3rd edn. 1984).

Villiger, Mark Eugen, *Handbuch der europäischen Menschenrechtskonvention (EMRK): unter besonderer Berücksichtigung der schweizerischen Rechtslage* (Schulthess Zürich 2nd edn. 1999).

Vitzthum, Wolfgang Graf and Bothe, Michael (eds), Völkerrecht (De Gruyter Berlin 3rd edn. 2001).

Weil, Gordon L., *The European Convention on Human Rights: Background, Development and Prospects* (Sythoff Leyden 1963).

Weiss, Claus, *Die Europäische Konvention zum Schutze der Menschenrechte und Grundfreiheiten* (Metzner Frankfurt am Main 1954).

Wense, Wolf von der, *Der UN-Menschenrechtsausschuß und sein Beitrag zum universellen Schutz der Menschenrechte* (Springer Berlin 1999).

Wittreck, Fabian, *Die Verwaltung der Dritten Gewalt* (Mohr Siebeck Tübingen 2006).

Zappalà, Salvatore, *Human Rights in International Criminal Proceedings* (Oxford University Press Oxford 2003).

II. Articles

Abi-Saab, Georges, 'Ensuring the Best Bench: Ways of Selecting Judges', in: Peck, Connie and Lee, Roy (eds), *Increasing the Effectiveness of the International Court of Justice* (Martinus Nijhoff Publishers The Hague 1997), 166-187.

Abi-Saab, Georges, 'Sources of International Law', in: Wolfrum, Rüdiger (ed), *The Max Planck Encyclopedia of Public International Law* (Oxford University Press 2012 Online Edition [available at <http://www.mpepil.com/> last visited: 21 March 2014]).

Adams, George Burton, 'The Origin of the English Courts of Common Law' (1920) 30 Yale Law Journal 8, 798-813.

Adede, Andrónico O., 'Judicial Settlement in Perspective', in: Muller, Sam, Raic, David and Thuranszky, Hanna (eds), *The International Court of Justice: Its Future Role after Fifty Years* (Martinus Nijhoff The Hague 1997), 47-81.

Agmon-Gonnen, Michal, 'Judicial Independence: The Threat from Within' (2005) 38 Israel Law Review 3, 120-153.

Alford, Roger P., 'The Proliferation of International Courts and Tribunals: International Adjudication in Ascendance', in: Hargrove, John Lawrence (ed), *On violence, money, power and culture: reviewing the internationalist legacy, March 24-27, 1999 Washington, D.C.: Proceedings of the Annual Meeting / American Society of International Law* (American Society of International Law Washington D.C. 2000), 160-165.

Alkema, Evert Albert, 'The European Convention as a Constitution and its Court as a Constitutional Court', in: Mahoney, Paul, Matscher, Franz, Petzold, Herbert and Wildhaber, Luzius (eds), *Protection des droits de l'homme: la perspective européenne – Mélanges à la mémoire de Rolv Ryssdal* (Heymann Köln 2000), 507-533.

Allott, Philip, 'The Concept of International Law' (1999) 10 European Journal of International Law 1, 31-50.

Amerasinghe, Chittharanjan Felix, 'Judges of the International Court of Justice – Election and Qualifications' (2001) 14 Leiden Journal of International Law 2, 335-348.

Amerasinghe, Chittharanjan Felix, 'Reflections on the Judicial Function in International Law', in: Ndiaye, Tafsir Malick and Wolfrum, Rüdiger (eds), *Law of the Sea, Environmental Law and Settlement of Disputes: Liber Amicorum Judge Thomas A. Mensah* (Nijhoff Leiden 2007), 121-130.

American Society of International Law, 'The Independence and Impartiality of International Judges', American Society of International Law: proceedings of the 83rd Annual Meeting, Chicago, Illinois, April 5-8, 1989, Conference in Chicago, Illinois (1989).

Anand, 'Role of International Adjudication', in: Gross, Leo (ed), *The Future of the International Court of Justice* (Oceana Publishers Dobbs Ferry, New York 1976), 1-21.

Andenas, Mads, 'A European Perspective on Judicial Independence and Accountability' (2007) 41 International Lawyer 1, 1-19.

Anderson, David H., 'Article 18 ICJ Statute', in: Zimmermann, Andreas, Tomuschat, Christian and Oellers-Frahm, Karin (eds), *The Statute of the International Court of Justice – A Commentary* (Oxford University Press Oxford 2006), 351-357.

Anderson, David H., 'Article 19 ICJ Statute', in: Zimmermann, Andreas, Tomuschat, Christian and Oellers-Frahm, Karin (eds), *The Statute of the International Court of Justice – A Commentary* (Oxford University Press Oxford 2006), 359-367.

Anderson, David H., 'The Internal Judicial Practice of the International Tribunal for the Law of the Sea', in: Chandrasekhara Rao, P. and Khan, Rahmatullah (eds), *The International Tribunal for the Law of the Sea – Law and Practice* (Kluwer Law International The Hague 2001), 197-214.

Ando, Nisuke, 'Permanent Court of Arbitration (PCA)', in: Wolfrum, Rüdiger (ed), *The Max Planck Encyclopedia of Public International Law* (Oxford University Press 2012 Online Edition [available at <http://www.mpepil.com/> last visited: 21 March 2014]).

Aznar-Gómez, Mariano, 'Article 2 ICJ Statute', in: Zimmermann, Andreas, Tomuschat, Christian and Oellers-Frahm, Karin (eds), *The Statute of the International Court of Justice – A Commentary* (Oxford University Press Oxford 2006), 205-218.

Bassiouni, M. Cherif, 'Human Rights in the Context of Criminal Justice. Identifying International Procedural Protections and Equivalent Protections in National Constitutions' (1993) 3 Duke Journal of Comparative and International Law 2, 235-297.

Bassiouni, M. Cherif, 'The United Nations Commission of Experts Established Pursuant to Security Council Resolution 780 (1992)' (1994) 88 American Journal of International Law 4, 784-805.

Bell, John, 'Judicial Cultures and Judicial Independence' (2001) 4 Cambridge Yearbook of European Legal Studies, 47-60.

Benvenisti, Eyal and Downs, George W., 'Prospects for the Increased Independence of International Tribunals' (2011) 12 German Law Journal 5, 1057-1081.

Bergsmo, Morten and Webb, Philippa, 'International Criminal Courts and Tribunals, Complementarity and Jurisdiction', in: Wolfrum, Rüdiger (ed), *The Max Planck Encyclopedia of Public International Law* (Oxford University Press 2012 Online Edition [available at <http://www.mpepil.com/> last visited: 21 March 2014]).

Bernhardt, Rudolf, 'Article 59 ICJ Statute', in: Zimmermann, Andreas, Tomuschat, Christian and Oellers-Frahm, Karin (eds), *The Statute of the International Court of Justice – A Commentary* (Oxford University Press Oxford 2006), 1231-1251.

Bertelman, Hanna, 'International Standards and National Ownership? Judicial Independence in Hybrid Courts: The Extraordinary Chambers in the Courts of Cambodia' (2010) 79 Nordic Journal of International Law 3, 341-382.

Bertodano, Sylvia de, 'Judicial Independence in the International Criminal Court' (2002) 15 Leiden Journal of International Law 2, 409-430.

Blokker, Niels, 'International Organizations or Institutions, Implied Powers', in: Wolfrum, Rüdiger (ed), *The Max Planck Encyclopedia of Public International Law* (Oxford University Press 2012 Online Edition [available at <http://www.mpepil.com/> last visited: 21 March 2014]).

Blokker, Niels, 'Is the Authorization Authorized? Powers and Practice of the UN Security Council to Authorize the Use of Force by "Coalitions of the Able and Willing"' (2000) 11 European Journal of International Law 3, 541-568.

Böcker, R.A.A., 'Protocol nr. 14 bij het EVRM. Hervorming van de hervorming' (2004) NJB, 1840-1844.

Boer-Buquicchio, Maud de, 'Klarstellung zum Status des Europäischen Gerichtshofs für Menschenrechte und seiner Beziehungen zum Europarat' (2003) 30 Europäische Grundrechte-Zeitschrift 17/20, 561-563.

von Bogdandy, Armin and Venzke, Ingo, 'In Whose Name? An Investigation of International Courts' Public Authority and its Democratic Justification' (2012) 23 European Journal of International Law 1, 7-41.

von Bogdandy, Armin and Venzke, Ingo, 'Zur Herrschaft internationaler Gerichte: Eine Untersuchung internationaler öffentlicher Gewalt und ihrer demokratischen Rechtfertigung' (2010) 70 Zeitschrift für ausländisches öffentliches Recht und Völkerrecht 1, 1-49.

Boston, Ana D., 'The Right to a Fair Trial: Balancing Safety and Civil Liberties' (2004) 12 Cardozo Journal of International and Comparative Law 1, 1-40.

Boven, Theodoor C. van, 'Autonomy and Independence of United Nations Judicial Institutions: A Comparative Note', in: Wellens, Karel (ed), *International Law: Theory and Practice: Essays in Honour of Eric Suy* (Nijhoff The Hague 1998), 679-688.

Brower II, Charles H, 'Arbitration', in: Wolfrum, Rüdiger (ed), *The Max Planck Encyclopedia of Public International Law* (Oxford University Press 2012 Online Edition [available at <http://www.mpepil.com/> last visited: 21 March 2014]).

Brown, Chester, 'The Evolution and Application of Rules Concerning Independence of the "International Judiciary"' (2003) 2 The Law and Practice of International Courts and Tribunals 1, 63-96.

Brown, Chester, 'The Proliferation of International Courts and Tribunals: Finding Your Way Through the Maze' (2002) 3 Melbourne Journal of International Law 2, 453-475.

Brownlie, Ian, 'Blaine Sloan Lecture: The Peaceful Settlement of International Disputes in Practice' (1995) 7 Pace International Law Review 2, 257-279.

Brubaker, Joseph R., 'The Judge who Knew too Much: Issue Conflicts in International Adjudication' (2008) 26 Berkeley Journal of International Law 1, 111-152.

Bruinsma, Fred J. and de Blois, Matthijs, 'Rules of Law from Westport to Wladiwostok. Separate Opinions in the European Court of Human Rights' (1997) 15 Netherlands Quarterly of Human Rights 2, 175-186.

Bruinsma, Fred J. and Parmentier, Stephen, 'Interview with Mr Luzius Wildhaber, President of the ECHR' (2003) 21 Netherlands Quarterly of Human Rights 2, 185-201.

Bruinsma, Fred J., 'The Room at the Top: Separate Opinions in the Grand Chambers of the ECHR (1998-2006)' (2008) Ancilla Iuris (anci.ch) 32-43.

Buergenthal, Thomas, 'Human Rights', in: Wolfrum, Rüdiger (ed), *The Max Planck Encyclopedia of Public International Law* (Oxford University Press 2012 Online Edition [available at <http://www.mpepil.com/> last visited: 21 March 2014]).

Buergenthal, Thomas, 'Proliferation of International Courts and Tribunals – Is it Good or Bad?' (2001) 14 Leiden Journal of International Law 2, 267-275.

Bundesministerium für Justiz und Verbraucherschutz 'Pressemitteilung: Gesucht – Richterin oder Richter für den Europäischen Gerichtshof für Menschenrechte, Stand: 20.11.2009' available at <http://www.bmj.de/SharedDocs/Archiv/DE/Pressemitteilungen/2009/20091120x_Gesucht_Richterin_oder_Richter_fuer_den_Europaeischen_Gerichtshof_fuer_Menschenrechte.html?nn=4795776%22> (last visited: 21 March 2014).

Burbank, Stephen B., 'The Architecture of Judicial Independence' (1999) 72 Southern California Law Review 2, 315-351.

Burbank, Stephen B., 'What do we Mean by "Judicial Independence"?' (2003) 64 Ohio State Law Journal 1, 323-339.

Busch, Christoph, 'Fundamental Rights and Private Law in the EU Member States', in: Busch, Christoph and Schulte-Nölke, Hans (eds), *EU Compendium – Fundamental Rights and Private Law* (Walter de Gruyter München 2010), 1-25.

Byers, Michael, 'International Law', in: Reus-Smit, Christian and Snidal, Duncan (eds), *The Oxford Handbook of International Relations* (Oxford University Press Oxford 2008), 612-631.

Byrne, Rosemary, 'Promises of Peace and Reconciliation: Previewing the Legacy of the International Criminal Tribunal for Rwanda' (2006) 14 European Review 4, 485-498.

Cairns, Huntington, 'A Note on Legal Definitions' (1936) 36 Columbia Law Review 7, 1099-1106.

Caron, David D., 'Towards a Political Theory of International Courts and Tribunals' (2006) 24 Berkeley Journal of International Law 2, 401-422.

Caron, David D., 'War and International Adjudication: Reflections on the 1899 Peace Conference' (1999) 94 American Journal of International Law 4, 4-30.

Charney, Jonathan I., 'The Impact on the International Legal System of the Growth of International Courts and Tribunals' (1999) 31 New York University Journal of International Law & Politics 4, 697-708.

Charnovitz, Steve, 'Judicial Independence in the World Trade Organization', in: Boisson de Chazournes, Laurence, Romano, Cesare P. R. and Mackenzie, Ruth (eds), *International Organizations and International Dispute Settlement: Trends and Prospects* (Transnational Publishers Ardsley New York 2002), 219-240.

Chesterman, Simon, 'Rule of Law', in: Wolfrum, Rüdiger (ed), *The Max Planck Encyclopedia of Public International Law* (Oxford University Press 2012 Online Edition [available at <http://www.mpepil.com/> last visited: 21 March 2014]).

'Conversations with Professor Sir Eli Lauterpacht – Fifth Interview (28 March 2008)' available at <http://www.squire.law.cam.ac.uk/eminent_scholars/professor_sir_elihu_lauterpacht_conversations_with_professor_sir_eli_lauterpacht.php> (last visited: 21 March 2014).

Cortado, Rosa Riquelme, 'Central American Court of Justice (1907–18)', in: Wolfrum, Rüdiger (ed), *The Max Planck Encyclopedia of Public International Law* (Oxford University Press 2012 Online Edition [available at <http://www.mpepil.com/> last visited: 21 March 2014]).

Couvreur, Philippe, 'Article 16 ICJ Statute', in: Zimmermann, Andreas, Tomuschat, Christian and Oellers-Frahm, Karin (eds), *The Statute of the International Court of Justice – A Commentary* (Oxford University Press Oxford 2006), 323-336.

Crawford, James, 'The ILC's Draft Statute for an International Criminal Tribunal' (1994) 88 American Journal of International Law 1, 140-152.

De Wet, Erika, 'The Role of Human Rights in Limiting the Enforcement Power of the Security Council: A Principled View', in: Wet, Erika de and Nollkaemper, André (eds), *Review of the Security Council by Member States* (Intersentia Antwerp 2003), 7-29.

de Zayas, Alfred, 'The United Nations and the Guarantee of a Fair Trial in the International Covenant on Civil and Political Rights and the Convention Against Torture and Other Cruela, Inhuman or Degrading Treatment or Punishment', in: Weissbrodt, David and Wolfrum, Rüdiger (eds), *The Right to a Fair Trial* (Springer 1998), 669-696.

Denham, Susan, 'The Diamond in a Democracy: An Iindependent, Accountable Judiciary – Keynote Address to: The Annual Conference of the Australian Institute of Judicial Administration, Darwin, Northern Territory, Australia, 14-16 July 2000' available at <http://www.aija.org.au/2000ac/Papers/Denham.pdf> (last visited: 21 March 2014).

Doehring, Karl, 'Zur Befangenheit internationaler Richter', in: Ando, Nisuke, McWhinney, Edward and Wolfrum, Rüdiger (eds), *Liber Amicorum Judge Shigeru Oda* (Kluwer Law International The Hague 2002), 23-30.

Doehring, Karl, 'Zur Rechtsstellung internationaler Richter', in: Arndt, Hans-Wolfgang and Rudolf, Walter (eds), *Völkerrecht und deutsches Recht: Festschrift für Walter Rudolf zum 70. Geburtstag* (Beck München 2001), 35-41.

Doswald-Beck, Louise, 'Fair Trial, Right to, International Protection ', in: Wolfrum, Rüdiger (ed), *The Max Planck Encyclopedia of Public International Law* (Oxford University Press 2012 Online Edition [available at <http://www.mpepil.com/> last visited: 21 March 2014]).

Downs, George W. and Jones, Michael A., 'Reputation, Compliance, and International Law' (2002) 31 Journal of Legal Studies 1, 95-114.

Downs, George W., Rocke, David M. and Barsoom, Peter N., 'Is the Good News About Compliance Good News About Cooperation?' (1996) 50 International Organization 3, 379-406.

Drzemczewski, Andrew, 'A Major Overhaul of the European Human Rights Convention Control Mechanism: Protocol No. 11', in: Academy of European Law (ed), *Collected Courses of the Academy of European Law* (Oxford University Press Oxford 1997), 121-244.

Drzemczewski, Andrew, 'The European Human Rights Convention: Protocol No. 11 – Entry into Force and First Year of Application', The Inter-American System of Human Rights Protection at the Eve of the 21st Century, Conference in San José, Costa Rica (16 November 1999).

Dugard, John, 'Article 13 ICJ Statute', in: Zimmermann, Andreas, Tomuschat, Christian and Oellers-Frahm, Karin (eds), *The Statute of the International Court of Justice – A Commentary* (Oxford University Press Oxford 2006), 303-313.

Elias, Taslim Olawale, 'Report', in: Mosler, Hermann and Bernhardt, Rudolf (eds), *Judicial Settlement of International Disputes – International Court of Justice, other Courts and Tribunals, Arbitration and Conciliation; an International Symposium* (Springer Berlin 1974), 193-283.

Engel, Norbert Paul, 'Status, Ausstattung und Personalhoheit des Inter-Amerikanischen und des Europäischen Gerichtshofs für Menschenrechte: Facetten und Wirkungen des institutionellen Rahmens' (2003) 30 Europäische Grundrechte-Zeitschrift 4/6, 122-133.

Fassbender, Bardo, 'Article 10 ICJ Statute', in: Zimmermann, Andreas, Tomuschat, Christian and Oellers-Frahm, Karin (eds), *The Statute of the International Court of Justice – A Commentary* (Oxford University Press Oxford 2006), 285-294.

Fassbender, Bardo, 'Article 9 ICJ Statute', in: Zimmermann, Andreas, Tomuschat, Christian and Oellers-Frahm, Karin (eds), *The Statute of the International Court of Justice – A Commentary* (Oxford University Press Oxford 2006), 261-284.

Ferejohn, John, 'Independent Judges, Dependent Judiciary: Explaining Judicial Independence' (1999) 72 Southern California Law Review 2, 353-384.

Fernández De Gurmendi, Silvia A, 'The Role of the Prosecutor', in: Politi, Mauro and Nesi, Giuseppe (eds), *The Rome Statute of the International Criminal Court: A Challenge to Impunity* (Ashgate u.a. Aldershot 2001), 55-59.

Fernández De Gurmendi, Silvia A, 'The Role of the Prosecutor', in: Lee, Roy S. (ed), *The International Criminal Court: The Making of the Rome Statute; Issues, Negotiations, Results* (Kluwer Law International The Hague 1999), 175-188.

Fiss, Owen M., 'The Limits of Judicial Independence' (1993) 25 Inter-American Law Review 1, 57-76.

Fix-Zamudio, Héctor, 'The European and the Inter-American Courts of Human Rights: A Brief Comparison', in: Mahoney, Paul, Matscher, Franz, Petzold, Herbert and Wildhaber, Luzius (eds), *Protection des droits de l'homme: la perspective européenne – Mélanges à la mémoire de Rolv Ryssdal* (Heymann Köln 2000), 507-533.

Flatto, David C, 'The Historical Origins of Judicial Independence and Their Modern Resonances' (2007) 117 Yale Law Journal Pocket Part 8, 8-13.

Flauss, Jean-François, 'Libres propos sur l'indépendance des juges à la Cour européenne des droits de l'homme', in: Böhmer, Jürgen (ed), *Internationale Gemeinschaft und Menschenrechte – Festschrift für Georg Ress zum 70. Geburtstag am 21. Januar 2005* (Heymann Köln 2005), 949-964.

Fleischhauer, Carl-August, 'The Relationship Between the International Court of Justice and the Newly Created International Tribunal for the Law of the Sea in Hamburg', in: von Bogdandy, Armin and Wolfrum, Rüdiger (eds), *Max Planck Yearbook of United Nations Law – Volume 1* (Martinus Nijhoff Publishers Leiden 1997), 327-333.

Franck, Thomas M., 'Legitimacy in the International System' (1988) 82 American Journal of International Law 4, 705-759.

Fribergh, Erik, 'The Authority Over the Court's Registry Within the Council of Europe', in: Caflisch, Lucius, Callewaert, Johan, Liddell, Roderick, Mahoney, Paul and Villiger, Mark E. (eds), *Liber Amicorum Luzius Wildhaber: Human Rights – Strasbourg Views* (N.P. Engel Kehl 2007), 145-158.

Frolich, Ruth, 'Introductory Note to the United Nations Security Council Resolution 1966: International Residual Mechanism for ICTY and ICTR' (2011) 50 ILM 1, 323-326.

Frowein, Jochen Abr. and Krisch, Nico, 'Introduction to Chapter VII UNC', in: Simma, Bruno (ed), *The Charter of the United Nations: A Commentary – Volume I* (Oxford University Press Oxford 2nd edn. 2002), 701-716.

Frowein, Jochen Abr., 'Ius Cogens', in: Wolfrum, Rüdiger (ed), *The Max Planck Encyclopedia of Public International Law* (Oxford University Press 2012 Online Edition [available at <http://www.mpepil.com/> last visited: 21 March 2014]).

Garlickl, Lech, 'Judicial Deliberations: The Strasbourg Perspective', in: Huls, Nick, Adams, Maurice and Bomhoff, Jacco (eds), *The Legitimacy of Highest Courts' Rulings: Judicial Deliberations and Beyond* (Asser The Hague 2009), 389-397.

Gaya, Giorgio, 'Relationship of the ICJ with Other International Courts and Tribunals', in: Zimmermann, Andreas, Tomuschat, Christian and Oellers-Frahm, Karin (eds), *The Statute of the International Court of Justice – A Commentary* (Oxford University Press Oxford 2006), 533-544.

Georget, Patricia, Golitsyn, Vladimir and Zacklin, Ralph, 'Article 6 ICJ Statute', in: Zimmermann, Andreas, Tomuschat, Christian and Oellers-Frahm, Karin (eds), *The Statute of the International Court of Justice – A Commentary* (Oxford University Press Oxford 2006), 249-251.

Goldstone, Richard J., 'International Jurisdiction and Prosecutorial Crimes' (1999) 47 Cleveland State Law Review 4, 473-481.

Golsong, Heribert, 'Implementation of International Protection of Human Rights' (1963) 110 Recueil des Cours / Académie de Droit International de La Haye 3, 7-151.

Göttelmann, Wolfgang and Münch, Wolfgang, 'Article 101 UNC', in: Simma, Bruno (ed), *The Charter of the United Nations: A Commentary – Volume II* (Oxford University Press Oxford 2nd edn. 2002), 1252-1276.

Grabenwarter, Christoph, 'Zur Zukunft des Europäischen Gerichtshofs für Menschenrechte: Generalbericht zur Tagung' (2003) 30 Europäische Grundrechte-Zeitschrift 4/6, 174-179.

Grünhut, Max, 'Die unabhängigkeit der richterlichen Entscheidung' (1930) 1930 Monatszeitschrift für Kriminalpsychologie und Strafrechtsreform 3, 1-17.

Guillaume, Gilbert, 'Editorial Comments on the Proliferation of International Courts – Advantages and Risks of Proliferation: a Blueprint for Action' (2004) 2 Journal of International Criminal Justice 2, 300-312.

Guillaume, Gilbert, 'Some Thoughts on the Independence of International Judges vis-à-vis States' (2003) 2 The Law and Practice of International Courts and Tribunals 1, 163-168.

Guzman, Andrew, 'The Cost of Credibility: Explaining Resistance to Interstate Dispute Resolution Mechanisms' (2002) 31 Journal of Legal Studies 2 (Part 2), 303-326.

Haberland, Stephan, 'Problemfelder für die richterliche Unabhängigkeit' (2002) 80 Deutsche Richterzeitung 8, 301-310.

Hafner, Gerhard, 'Should one Fear the Proliferation of Mechanisms for the Peaceful Settlement of Disputes?', in: Caflisch, Lucius (ed), *The Peaceful Settlement of Disputes between States: Universal and European Perspectives* (Kluwer Law International The Hague 1998), 25-41.

Hall, Christopher Keith, 'The First Proposal for a Permanent International Criminal Court' (1998) 322 International Review of the Red Cross 57-74.

Harris, David, 'The Right to a Fair Trial in Criminal Proceedings as a Human Right' (1967) 16 The International and Comparative Law Quarterly 2, 352-378.

Helfer, Laurence R. and Slaughter, Anne-Marie, 'Why States Create International Tribunals – A Response to Professors Posner and Yoo' (2005) 93 California Law Review 3, 899-956.

Herdegen, Matthias, 'Review of the Security Council by National Courts: A Constitutional Perspective', in: De Wet, Erika and Nollkaemper, André (eds), *Review of the Security Council by Member States* (Intersentia Antwerpen 2003), 77-84.

Heuschling, Luc, 'Why Should Judges Be Independent?', in: Ziegler, Katja S. (ed), *Constitutionalism and the Role of Parliaments* (Hart Publishers Oxford 2007), 239-252.

Higgins, Rosalyn, 'Speech by H.E. Judge Rosalyn Higgins, President of the International Court of Justice, at the Meeting of the Legal Advisers of the Ministry of Foreign Affairs' available at <http://www.icj-cij.org/presscom/files/7/14097.pdf> (last visited: 21 March 2014).

Higgins, Rosalyn, 'Speech by H.E. Judge Rosalyn Higgins, President of the International Court of Justice, to the Sixth Committee of the General Assembly' available at <http://www.icj-cij.org/presscom/files/3/14123.pdf> (last visited: 21 March 2014).

Higgins, Rosalyn, 'Speech by H.E. Judge Rosalyn Higgins, President of the International Court of Justice, to the General Assembly of the United Nations' available at <http://www.icj-cij.org/presscom/files/7/14117.pdf> (last visited: 21 March 2014).

Hilf, Meinhard and Khan, Daniel-Erasmus, 'Article 22 UNC', in: Simma, Bruno (ed), *The Charter of the United Nations: A Commentary – Volume I* (Oxford University Press Oxford 2nd edn. 2002), 420-436.

Jackson, Vicky, 'Judicial Independence: Structure, Context, Attitude', in: Seibert-Fohr, Anja (ed), *Judicial Independence in Transition: Strengthening the Rule of Law in the OSCE Region* (Springer Heidelberg 2012), 19-86.

Jacobs, Francis, 'Seminar on International Law and European Law at the University of Neuchâtel, 14-15 March 1986: Merger of the European Commission and the European Court of Human Rights' (1987) 8 Human Rights Law Journal, 195-196.

Jaenicke, Günther, 'Article 7 UNC', in: Simma, Bruno (ed), *The Charter of the United Nations: A Commentary – Volume I* (Oxford University Press Oxford 2nd edn. 2002), 217-229.

Jennings, Robert Y., 'General Introduction (ICJ Statute)', in: Zimmermann, Andreas, Tomuschat, Christian and Oellers-Frahm, Karin (eds), *The Statute of the International Court of Justice – A Commentary* (Oxford University Press Oxford 2006), 3-37.

Jennings, Robert Y., 'The United Nations at Fifty: The International Court of Justice after Fifty Years' (1995) 89 American Journal of International Law 3, 493-505.

Johnson, D.H.N., 'The Draft Code of Offences Against the Peace and Security of Mankind' (1955) 4 The International and Comparative Law Quarterly 3, 455-468.

Karhilo, Jaana, 'The Establishment of the International Tribunal for Rwanda' (1995) 64 Nordic Journal of International Law 4, 683-713.

Karl, Wolfram, 'Article 69 ICJ Statute', in: Zimmermann, Andreas, Tomuschat, Christian and Oellers-Frahm, Karin (eds), *The Statute of the International Court of Justice – A Commentary* (Oxford University Press Oxford 2006), 1469-1486.

Kaul, Hans-Peter, 'International Criminal Court (ICC)', in: Wolfrum, Rüdiger (ed), *The Max Planck Encyclopedia of Public International Law* (Oxford University Press 2012 Online Edition [available at <http://www.mpepil.com/> last visited: 21 March 2014]).

Keohane, Robert Owen, Moravcsik, Andrew and Slaughter, Anne-Marie, 'Legalized Dispute Resolution: Interstate and Transnational' (2000) 54 International Organization 3, 457-488.

Kilian, Michael, 'Der Einfluss der EMRK auf die deutsche Verfassungsrechtsprechung', in: Höland, Armin (ed), *Wirkungen der Rechtsprechung des Europäischen Gerichtshofs für Menschenrecht im deutschen Recht* (BWV Verlag Berlin 2012), 119-146.

Koh, Harold Hongju, 'Why Do Nations Obey International Law?' (1997) 106 Yale Law Journal 8, 2599-2659.

Kokott, Juliane and Hoffmeister, Frank, 'International Public Order', in: Wolfrum, Rüdiger (ed), *The Max Planck Encyclopedia of Public International Law* (Oxford University Press 2012 Online Edition [available at <http://www.mpepil.com/> last visited: 21 March 2014]).

Kokott, Juliane, 'States, Sovereign Equality', in: Wolfrum, Rüdiger (ed), *The Max Planck Encyclopedia of Public International Law* (Oxford University Press 2012 Online Edition [available at <http://www.mpepil.com/> last visited: 21 March 2014]).

Kooijmans, Pieter H., 'Article 31 ICJ Statute', in: Zimmermann, Andreas, Tomuschat, Christian and Oellers-Frahm, Karin (eds), *The Statute of the International Court of Justice – A Commentary* (Oxford University Press Oxford 2006), 495-506.

Kreß, Claus, 'The Procedural Law of the International Criminal Court in Outline: Anatomy of a Unique Compromise' (2003) 1 Journal of International Criminal Justice 3, 603-617.

Krüger, Hans Christian, 'Die Auswahl der Richter für den neuen Europäischen Gerichtshof für Menschenrechte' (1997) 24 Europäische Grundrechte-Zeitschrift 17/18, 397-401.

Krüger, Hans Christian, 'Selecting Judges for the New European Court of Human Rights' (1996) 17 Human Rights Law Journal 11/12, 401-404.

Kuijer, Martin, 'Voting Behaviour and National Bias in the European Court of Human Rights and the International Court of Justice' (1997) 10 Leiden Journal of International Law 1, 49-67.

Laing, Edward A., 'Automation of International Judicial Bodies: A Preliminary Analysis', in: Chandrasekhara Rao, P. and Khan, Rahmatullah (eds), *The International Tribunal for the Law of the Sea – Law and Practice* (Kluwer Law International The Hague 2001), 217-230.

Larkins, Christopher M., 'Judicial Independence and Democratization. A Theoretical and Conceptual Analysis' (1996) 44 The American Journal of Comparative Law 4, 605-626.

Lemmens, Paul, 'Single-Judge Formations, Committees, Chambers and Grand Chamber', in: Lemmens, Paul and Vandenhole, Wouter (eds), *Protocol No. 14 and the Reform of the European Court of Human Rights* (Intersentia Antwerpen 2005), 31-43.

van Leuven, Nathalie, 'The Judges of the European Court and the Commissioner for Human Rights', in: Lemmens, Paul and Vandenhole, Wouter (eds), *Protocol No. 14 and the Reform of the European Court of Human Rights* (Intersentia Antwerpen 2005), 23-30.

Lord Justice Brooke, 'Judicial Independence – Its History in England and Wales', in: Cunningham, Helen (ed), *Fragile Bastion: Judicial independence in the nineties and beyond* (Judicial Commission of New South Wales Sydney 2000), 89-112.

M Blokker, Niels, 'International Organizations or Institutions, Implied Powers', in: Wolfrum, Rüdiger (ed), *The Max Planck Encyclopedia of Public International Law* (Oxford University Press 2012 Online Edition [available at <http://www.mpepil.c om/> last visited: 21 March 2014]).

MacDonald, Gabrielle Kirk, 'Crimes of Sexual Violence: The Experience of the International Criminal Tribunal' (2000) 39 Columbia Journal of Transnational Law 1, 1-17.

Mackenzie, Ruth and Sands, Philippe J., 'International Courts and Tribunals and the Independence of the International Judge' (2003) 44 Harvard International Law Journal 1, 271-285.

Mackenzie, Ruth and Sands, Philippe J., 'Judicial Selection for International Courts: Towards Common Principles and Practices', in: Malleson, Kate (ed), *Appointing Judges in an Age of Judicial Power – Critical Perspectives from Around the World* (University of Toronto Press Toronto 2006), 213-237.

Mahoney, Paul and Prebensen, Sørensen, 'The European Court of Human Rights', in: Macdonald, Ronald St. J. (ed), *The European System for the Protection of Human Rights* (Nijhoff Dordrecht 1993), 621-643.

Mahoney, Paul, 'Separation of Powers in the Council of Europe: The Status of the European Court of Human Rights vis-à-vis the Authorities of the Council of Europe' (2003) 24 Human Rights Law Journal 5/8, 152-161.

Mahoney, Paul, 'The International Judiciary – Independence and Accountability' (2008) 7 The Law and Practice of International Courts and Tribunals 3, 313-349.

Majone, Giandomenico, 'Two Logics of Delegation: Agency and Fiduciary Relations in EU Governance' (2001) 2 European Union Politics 1, 103-122.

Malanczuk, Peter, 'Reconsidering the Relationship between the ICJ and the Security Council', in: Heere, Wypo P. (ed), *International Law and The Hague's 750th Anniversary* (T.M.C. Asser Press 1999), 87-99.

Maogoto, Jackson Nyamuya, 'Early Efforts to Establish an International Criminal Court', in: Doria, José, Gasser, Hans-Peter and Bassiouni, M. Cherif (eds), *The Legal Regime of the International Criminal Court – Essays in Honour of Professor Igor Blishchenko* (Martinus Nijhoff Publishers Leiden 2009), 3-22.

Marston, Geoffrey, 'The London Committee and the Statute of the International Court of Justice', in: Lowe, Vaughan and Fitzmaurice, Malgosia (eds), *Fifty Years of the International Court of Justice: Essays in Honour of Sir Robert Jennings* (Cambridge University Press Cambridge 1996), 40-60.

McGoldrick, Dominic, 'The Interface between Public Emergency Powers and International Law' (2004) 2 International Journal of Constitutional Law 2, 380-429.

McWhinney, Edward, 'Law, Politics and "Regionalism" in the Nomination and Election of World Court Judges' (1986-1987) 13 Syracuse Journal of International Law and Commerce 1, 1-28.

McWhinney, Edward, 'The International Court as Constitutional Court and the Blurring of the Arbitral/Judicial Processes', in: Muller, Sam (ed), *The Flame Rekindled – New Hopes for International Arbitration* (Nijhoff Dordrecht 1994), 81-90.

Meron, Theodor, 'Budget Approval by the General Assembly of the United Nations: Duty or Discretion' (1967) 42 The British Yearbook of International Law, 91-122.

Meron, Theodor, 'Judicial Independence and Impartiality in International Criminal Tribunals' (2005) 99 American Journal of International Law 2, 359-369.

Meron, Theodor, 'On a Hierarchy of International Human Rights' (1986) 80 American Journal of International Law 1, 1-23.

Miller, Nathan J., 'Independence in the International Judiciary: General Overview of the Issues', Meeting of the Study Group of the International Law Association, Conference in Burgh House, Hampstead, London (2002).

Miller, Vaughne, 'Protocol 11 and the New European Court of Human Rights' (4 December 1998) House of Commons Library Research Papers.

Morris, Virginia and Bourloyannis-Vrailas, M.-Christiane, 'The Work of the Sixth Committee at the Fifty-First Session of the UN General Assembly' (1997) 91 American Journal of International Law 3, 542-554.

Mosler, Hermann and Oellers-Frahm, Karin, 'Article 92 UNC', in: Simma, Bruno (ed), *The Charter of the United Nations: A Commentary – Volume II* (Oxford University Press Oxford 2nd edn. 2002), 1139-1171.

Mosler, Hermann, 'The International Judiciary from the Point of View of an International Judge', in: *Thesaurus Acroasium of the Institute of Public International Law and International Relations of Thessaloniki* (Institute of Public International Law and International Relations of Thessaloniki 1998), 135-186.

Nergelius, Joakim and Zimmermann, Dominik, 'Judicial Independence in Sweden', in: Seibert-Fohr, Anja (ed), *Judicial Independence in Transition: Strengthening the Rule of Law in the OSCE Region* (Springer Heidelberg 2012), 185-229.

Oberto, Giacomo, 'Richterliche Unabhängigkeit: Rechtsvergleichende Betrachtung ihrer Institutionellen Ausgestaltung in den Ländern Europas' (2004) 37 Zeitschrift für Rechtspolitik 6, 207-210.

O'Brien, James, 'The International Tribunal for Violations of International Humanitarian Law in the Former Yugoslavia' (1993) 87 American Journal of International Law 4, 639-659.

Oellers-Frahm, Karin, 'Article 41 ICJ Statute', in: Zimmermann, Andreas, Tomuschat, Christian and Oellers-Frahm, Karin (eds), *The Statute of the International Court of Justice – A Commentary* (Oxford University Press Oxford 2006), 923-966.

Oellers-Frahm, Karin, 'Der institutionelle Rahmen: Status, Ausstattung und Personalhoheit internationaler Gerichte – Der IGH, der Internationale Strafgerichtshof und das Jugoslawien-Tribunal im Vergleich' (2003) 30 Europäische Grundrechte-Zeitschrift 4/6, 107-117.

Oellers-Frahm, Karin, 'International Courts and Tribunals, Judges and Arbitrators', in: Wolfrum, Rüdiger (ed), *The Max Planck Encyclopedia of Public International Law* (Oxford University Press 2012 Online Edition [available at <http://www.mpepil.com/> last visited: 21 March 2014]).

Oeter, Stefan, 'European Commission and Court of Human Rights, Inter-State Applications', in: Bernhardt, Rudolf (ed), *Encyclopedia of Public International Law, Revised Library Edition, Instalment 2* (North-Holland Amsterdam 1995), 144-154.

Oeter, Stefan, 'Ius cogens und der Schutz der Menschenrechte', in: Ehrenzeller, Bernhard, Breitenmoser, Stephan, Sassòli, Marco, Stoffel, Walter and Wagner Pfeifer, Beatrice (eds), *Menschenrechte, Demokratie und Rechtsstaat – Liber Amicorum Luzius Wildhaber* (Dike/Nomos Zürich/Baden-Baden 2007), 499-521.

Oeter, Stefan, 'Vielfalt der Gerichte – Einheit des Prozessrechts?', in: Hofmann, Rainer, Reinisch, August, Pfeiffer, Thomas, Oeter, Stefan and Stadler, Astrid (eds), *Die Rechtskontrolle von Organen der Staatengemeinschaft: Vielfalt der Gerichte – Einheit des Prozessrechts?* (C.F. Müller Heidelberg 2007), 149-175.

Olivier, Clémentine, 'Revisiting General Comment No. 29 of the United Nations Human Rights Committee about Fair Trial Rights and Derogations in Times of Public Emergency' (2004) 17 Leiden Journal of International Law 2, 405-419.

Orakhelashvili, Alexander, 'The Impact of Peremptory Norms on the Interpretation and Application of United Nations Security Council Resolutions' (2005) 16 European Journal of International Law 1, 59-88.

Ouguergouz, Fatsah, 'African Charter on Human and Peoples' Rights (1981)', in: Wolfrum, Rüdiger (ed), *The Max Planck Encyclopedia of Public International Law* (Oxford University Press 2012 Online Edition [available at <http://www.mpepil.com/> last visited: 21 March 2014]).

Partsch, Karl Josef, 'Die Entstehung der Europäischen Menschenrechtskonvention' (1953) 1953/54 Zeitschrift für ausländisches öffentliches Recht und Völkerrecht 15, 631-660.

Pasquino, Pasquale, 'Prolegomena to a Theory of Judicial Power: The Concept of Judicial Independence in Theory and History' (2003) 2 The Law and Practice of International Courts and Tribunals 1, 11-25.

Paulus, Andreas, 'Article 29 UNC', in: Simma, Bruno (ed), *The Charter of the United Nations: A Commentary – Volume I* (Oxford University Press Oxford 2nd edn. 2002), 539-563.

Pauwelyn, Joost, 'Fragmentation of International Law', in: Wolfrum, Rüdiger (ed), *The Max Planck Encyclopedia of Public International Law* (Oxford University Press 2012 Online Edition [available at <http://www.mpepil.com/> last visited: 21 March 2014]).

Pellet, Alain, 'Article 38 ICJ Statute', in: Zimmermann, Andreas, Tomuschat, Christian and Oellers-Frahm, Karin (eds), *The Statute of the International Court of Justice – A Commentary* (Oxford University Press Oxford 2006), 677-792.

Pellet, Alain, 'Peaceful Settlement of International Disputes', in: Wolfrum, Rüdiger (ed), *The Max Planck Encyclopedia of Public International Law* (Oxford University Press 2012 Online Edition [available at <http://www.mpepil.com/> last visited: 21 March 2014]).

Perkins, John A., 'The Changing Foundations of International Law: From State Consent to State Responsibility' (1997) 15 Boston University International Law Journal 2, 433-509.

Pinto, Moragodage Christopher Walter, 'The Court and other International Tribunals', in: Peck, Connie (ed), *Increasing the effectiveness of the International Court of Justice – Proceedings of the ICJ/UNITAR Colloquium to celebrate the 50th anniversary of the Court* (Nijhoff The Hague 1997), 281-308.

Pocar, Fausto, 'The Proliferation of International Criminal Courts and Tribunals – A Necessity in the Current International Community' (2004) 2 Journal of International Criminal Justice 2, 304-308.

Posner, Eric A. and Yoo, John C., 'Judicial Independence in International Tribunals' (2005) 93 California Law Review 1, 1-74.

Prott, Lyndel V., 'The Role of the Judge of the International Court of Justice' (1974) 10 Revue Belge de Droit International 473-507.

Rädler, Peter, 'Independence and Impartiality of Judges', in: Weissbrodt, David and Wolfrum, Rüdiger (eds), *The Right to a Fair Trial* (Springer Berlin 1998), 727-746.

Rah, Sicco and Wallrabenstein, Tilo, 'The International Tribunal for the Law of the Sea and its Future' (2007) Ocean Yearbook, 41-67.

Randelzhofer, Albrecht, 'Article 2(4) UNC', in: Simma, Bruno (ed), *The Charter of the United Nations: A Commentary – Volume I* (Oxford University Press Oxford 2nd edn. 2002), 112-136.

Ress, Georg, 'Der Europäische Gerichtshof für Menschenrechte, seine Reform und die Rolle der nationalen Gerichte', in: Karl, Wolfram (ed), *Internationale Gerichtshöfe und nationale Rechtsordnung – Internationales Symposium am Österreichischen Institut für Menschenrechte am 28. und 29. November 2003 in Salzburg zu Ehren von em.o.Univ.-Prof. DDr. Dr. h.c. Franz Matscher* (N. P. Engel Kehl 2005), 39-76.

Ress, Georg, 'Die Organisationsstruktur internationaler Gerichte, insbesondere des neuen Europäischen Gerichtshofs für Menschenrechte', in: Hafner, Gerhard (ed), *Liber amicorum: Professor Ignaz Seidl-Hohenveldern in honour of his 80th birthday* (Kluwer The Hague 1998), 541-574.

Ress, Georg, 'Rechtsstellung, Aufgabenbereich und Legitimation des Europäischen Gerichtshofs für Menschenrechte', in: Holoubek, Michael and Korinek, Karl (eds), *Dimensionen des modernen Verfassungsstaates: Symposion zum 60. Geburtstag von Karl Korinek* (Springer Wien 2002), 129-149.

Reus-Smit, Christian, 'The Politics of International Law', in: Reus-Smit, Christian (ed), *The Politics of International Law* (Cambridge University Press Cambridge 2004), 14-44.

Reut-Nicolussi, Eduard, 'The Reform of the Permanent Court of International Justice', in: Grotius Society (ed), *Transactions of the Grotius Society* (Longmans, Green & Co. London 1939), 135-149.

Riedel, Eibe, 'Article 55 (c) UNC', in: Simma, Bruno (ed), *The Charter of the United Nations: A Commentary – Volume II* (Oxford University Press Oxford 2nd edn. 2002), 917-941.

Robertson, Arthur H., 'The European Court of Human Rights' (1960) 9 American Journal of Comparative Law 1, 1-28.

Romano, Cesare P. R., 'Mixed Criminal Tribunals (Sierra Leone, East Timor, Kosovo, Cambodia)', in: Wolfrum, Rüdiger (ed), *The Max Planck Encyclopedia of Public International Law* (Oxford University Press 2012 Online Edition [available at <http://www.mpepil.com/> last visited: 21 March 2014]).

Romano, Cesare P. R., 'The Proliferation of International Judicial Bodies: the Pieces of the Puzzle' (1999) 31 New York University Journal of International Law & Politics 4, 709-751.

Romano, Cesare P. R., 'The Shift from the Consensual to the Compulsory Paradigm in International Adjudication: Elements for a Theory of Consent' (2007) 39 New York University Journal of International Law & Politics 4, 791-872.

Rosenne, Shabtai and Gebhard, Julia, 'Conferences on the Law of the Sea', in: Wolfrum, Rüdiger (ed), *The Max Planck Encyclopedia of Public International Law* (Oxford University Press 2012 Online Edition [available at <http://www.mpepil.com/> last visited: 21 March 2014]).

Rosenne, Shabtai, 'International Courts and Tribunals, Jurisdiction and Admissibility of Inter-State Applications', in: Wolfrum, Rüdiger (ed), *The Max Planck Encyclopedia of Public International Law* (Oxford University Press 2012 Online Edition [available at <http://www.mpepil.com/> last visited: 21 March 2014]).

Rosenne, Shabtai, 'Permanent Court of International Justice (PCIJ)', in: Wolfrum, Rüdiger (ed), *The Max Planck Encyclopedia of Public International Law* (Oxford University Press 2012 Online Edition [available at <http://www.mpepil.com/> last visited: 21 March 2014]).

Rothwell, Donald, 'Building on the Strengths and Addressing the Challenges: The Role of Law of the Sea Institutions' (2004) 35 Ocean Development and International Law 2, 131-156.

Rothwell, Donald, 'The International Tribunal for the Law of the Sea and Marine Environmental Protection – Expanding the Horizons of International Oceans Governance' (2003) 17 Ocean Yearbook, 26-55.

Rudolf, Beate, 'United Nations Committees and Subsidiary Bodies, System of', in: Wolfrum, Rüdiger (ed), *The Max Planck Encyclopedia of Public International Law* (Oxford University Press 2012 Online Edition [available at <http://www.mpepil.com/> last visited: 21 March 2014]).

Russell, Peter H., 'Toward a General Theory of Judicial Independence', in: Russell, Peter H. and O'Brien, David M. (eds), *Judicial Independence in the Age of Democracy – Critical Perspectives from around the World* (University Press of Virginia Charlottesville 2001), 1-24.

Sabel, Robbie, 'Conferences and Congresses, International', in: Wolfrum, Rüdiger (ed), *The Max Planck Encyclopedia of Public International Law* (Oxford University Press 2012 Online Edition [available at <http://www.mpepil.com/> last visited: 21 March 2014]).

Sands, Philippe J., 'Enhancing Participation in International Litigation' (1998) 24 Commonwealth Law Bulletin 1, 540-562.

Sands, Philippe J., 'Litigating Environmental Disputes – Courts, Tribunals and the Progressive Development of International Environmental Law', in: Ndiaye, Tafsir Malick and Wolfrum, Rüdiger (eds), *Law of the Sea, Environmental Law and Settlement of Disputes: Liber Amicorum Judge Thomas A. Mensah* (Nijhoff Leiden 2007), 313-325.

Sands, Philippe J., 'The Independence of the International Judiciary: Some Introductory Thoughts', in: Charnovitz, Steve, Steger, Debra P. and Van den Bossche, Peter (eds), *Law in the Service of Human Dignity – Essays in Honour of Florentino Feliciano* (Cambridge University Press Cambridge 2005), 313-322.

Sarooshi, Dan, 'The Legal Framework Governing United Nations Subsidiary Organs' (1996) 67 The British Yearbook of International Law, 413-478.

Schabas, William A., 'Independence and Impartiality of the International Criminal Judiciary', in: Decaux, Emmanuel (ed), *From Human Rights to International Criminal Law: Studies in Honour of an African Jurist, the Late Judge Laïty Kama* (Brill Leiden 2007), 571-591.

Schermers, Henry G., 'A European Supreme Court', in: Mahoney, Paul, Matscher, Franz, Petzold, Herbert and Wildhaber, Luzius (eds), *Protection des droits de l'homme: la perspective européenne – Mélanges à la mémoire de Rolv Ryssdal* (Heymann Köln 2000), 507-533.

Schlochauer, Hans-Jürgen, 'Internationale Gerichtsbarkeit', in: Strupp, Karl and Schlochauer, Hans-Jürgen (eds), *Wörterbuch des Völkerrechts: Zweiter Band* (de Gruyter Berlin 1961), 56-64.

Schmalenbach, Kirsten, 'International Organizations or Institutions, General Aspects', in: Wolfrum, Rüdiger (ed), *The Max Planck Encyclopedia of Public International Law* (Oxford University Press 2012 Online Edition [available at <http://www.mpepi l.com/> last visited: 21 March 2014]).

Schomburg, Wolfgang and Nemitz, Jan Christoph, 'International Criminal Courts and Tribunals, Procedure', in: Wolfrum, Rüdiger (ed), *The Max Planck Encyclopedia of Public International Law* (Oxford University Press 2012 Online Edition [available at <http://www.mpepil.com/> last visited: 21 March 2014]).

Schreuer, Christoph and Ebner, Christian, 'Article 100 UNC', in: Simma, Bruno (ed), *The Charter of the United Nations: A Commentary – Volume II* (Oxford University Press Oxford 2nd edn. 2002), 1230-1251.

Schubarth, Martin, 'Der europäische Richter – ein unabhängiger Richter? Mit Hinweisen zum schweizerischen Recht', in: Donatsch, Andreas (ed), *Strafrecht, Strafprozessrecht und Menschenrechte: Festschrift für Stefan Trechsel zum 65. Geburtstag* (Schulthess Zürich 2002), 93-106.

Schwebel, Stephen M., 'National Judges and Judges Ad Hoc of the International Court of Justice' (1999) 48 The International and Comparative Law Quarterly 4, 889-900.

Scobbie, Iain, '"Une hérésie en matière judiciaire"? The role of the judge ad hoc in the International Court' (2005) 4 The Law and Practice of International Courts and Tribunals 3, 421-464.

Seibert-Fohr, Anja, 'Constitutional Guarantees of Judicial Independence in Germany', in: Riedel, Eibe and Wolfrum, Rüdiger (eds), *Recent Trends in German and European Constitutional Law* (Springer Heidelberg 2006), 267-287.

Shany, Yuval, 'No Longer a Weak Department of Power? Reflections on the Emergence of a New International Judiciary' (2009) 20 European Journal of International Law 1, 73-91.

Shelton, Dinah, 'Form, Function, and the Powers of International Courts' (2009) 9 Chicago Journal of International Law 2, 537-571.

Shelton, Dinah, 'The Independence of International Tribunals', in: Trindade, Antônio Augusto Cançado (ed), *The Modern World of Human Rights: Essays in Honour of Thomas Buergenthal* (Instituto Interamericano de Derechos Humanos San José 1996), 299-334.

Shetreet, Shimon, 'Standards of Conduct of International Judges Outside Activities' (2003) 2 The Law and Practice of International Courts and Tribunals 1, 127-161.

Shraga, Daphna and Zacklin, Ralph, 'The International Criminal Tribunal for Rwanda' (1996) 7 European Journal of International Law 4, 501-518.

Skinnider, Eileen, 'Ensuring the Independence of the International Criminal Court' (2006) 7 Global International Courts Review 2, 25-38.

Smith, Roger, 'Constitutional Reform, the Lord Chancellor, and Human Rights: The Battle of Form and Substance' (2005) 32 Journal of Law and Society 1, 187-201.

Sohn, L, 'A Tribunal for the Sea-Bed or the Ocean' (1972) 32 Zeitschrift für ausländisches öffentliches Recht und Völkerrecht, 253-264.

Song, Sang-Hyun, 'The Independence of the ICC and Safeguards against Political Influence', Symposium on the International Criminal Court, Conference in Beijing, China (3-4 February 2007).

Sorel, Jean-Marc, 'International Courts and Tribunals, Procedure', in: Wolfrum, Rüdiger (ed), *The Max Planck Encyclopedia of Public International Law* (Oxford University Press 2012 Online Edition [available at <http://www.mpepil.com/> last visited: 21 March 2014]).

Spelliscy, Shane, 'The Proliferation of International Tribunals – A Chink in the Armor' (2001) 40 Columbia Journal of Transnational Law 1, 143-175.

Spiermann, Ole, 'Historical Introduction (ICJ Statute)', in: Zimmermann, Andreas, Tomuschat, Christian and Oellers-Frahm, Karin (eds), *The Statute of the International Court of Justice – A Commentary* (Oxford University Press Oxford 2006), 39-62.

Steinberger, Helmut, 'The International Court of Justice', in: Mosler, Hermann and Bernhardt, Rudolf (eds), *Judicial Settlement of International Disputes – International Court of Justice, other Courts and Tribunals, Arbitration and Conciliation; an International Symposium* (Springer Berlin 1974), 193-283.

Swart, Mia, 'To Recuse or not to Recuse? How Independent are the Judges of International Criminal Tribunals?' (2003) 28 South African Yearbook of International Law, 182-199.

The Project on International Courts and Tribunals, 'The International Judiciary in Context' available at <http://www.pict-pcti.org/publications/synoptic_chart/synop_c4.pdf> (last visited: 21 March 2014).

Thirlway, Hugh, 'Advisory Opinions', in: Wolfrum, Rüdiger (ed), *The Max Planck Encyclopedia of Public International Law* (Oxford University Press 2012 Online Edition [available at <http://www.mpepil.com/> last visited: 21 March 2014]).

Thirlway, Hugh, 'The International Court of Justice', in: Evans, Malcolm D. (ed), *International Law* (Oxford University Press Oxford 2nd edn 2006), 582-585.

Tomuschat, Christian, 'Artikel 33 UNC', in: Simma, Bruno (ed), *Charta der Vereinten Nationen: Kommentar* (Beck München 1991), 472-481.

Tomuschat, Christian, 'International Courts and Tribunals', in: Bernhardt, Rudolf (ed), *Encyclopedia of Public International Law: Instalment 1 Settlement of Disputes* (North-Holland Publishing Company Amsterdam 1981), 92-99.

Tomuschat, Christian, 'International Courts and Tribunals', in: Wolfrum, Rüdiger (ed), *The Max Planck Encyclopedia of Public International Law* (Oxford University Press 2012 Online Edition [available at <http://www.mpepil.com/> last visited: 21 March 2014]).

Tomuschat, Christian, 'International Courts and Tribunals with Regionally Restricted and/or Specialized Jurisdiction', in: Mosler, Hermann and Bernhardt, Rudolf (eds), *Judicial Settlement of International Disputes, International Court of Justice, Other Courts and Tribunals, Arbitration and Conciliation; An International Symposium* (Springer Berlin 1974), 285-416.

Tomuschat, Christian, 'National Representation of Judges and Legitimacy of International Jurisdictions: Lessons from ICJ to ECJ', in: Pernice, Ingolf, Kokott, Juliane and Saunders, Cheryl (eds), *The Future of the European Judicial System in a Comparative Perspective* (Nomos Berlin 2006), 183-190.

Tomuschat, Christian, 'The European Court of Human Rights Overwhelmed by Applications: Problems and Possible Solutions', in: Wolfrum, Rüdiger and Deutsch, Ulrike (eds), *The European Court of Human Rights overwhelmed by applications: problems and possible solutions – international workshop, Heidelberg, December 17 – 18, 2007* (Springer Berlin 2009), 1-18.

Trechsel, Stefan, 'Gericht und Richter nach der EMRK', in: Hauser, Peter (ed), *Gedächtnisschrift für Peter Noll* (Schulthess Polygraphischer Verlag Zürich 1984), 385-401.

Treves, Tullio, 'The Law of the Sea "System" of Institutions', in: von Bogdandy, Armin and Wolfrum, Rüdiger (eds), *Max Planck Yearbook of United Nations Law – Volume 2* (Martinus Nijhoff Publishers Leiden 1998), 325-340.

Triffterer, Otto, 'Der Ständige Internationale Strafgerichtshof – Anspruch und Wirklichkeit', in: Gössel, Karl Heinz and Zipf, Heinz (eds), *Gedächtnisschrift für Heinz Zipf* (Müller Heidelberg 1999), 493-558.

Udombana, Nsongurua J., 'The African Commission on Human and Peoples' Rights and the Development of Fair Trial Norms in Africa' (2006) 6 African Human Rights Law Journal 1, 299-332.

United Nations, 'Report of the Inter-Allied Committee on the Future of the Permanent Court of International Justice, February 10, 1944' (1945) 39 American Journal of International Law 1, Supplement: Official Documents, 1-56.

Vagts, Detlev F., 'The International Legal Profession: A Need for More Governance?' (1996) 90 American Journal of International Law 2, 250-261.

Valencia-Ospina, Eduardo, 'International Courts and Tribunals, Agents, Counsel and Advocates', in: Wolfrum, Rüdiger (ed), *The Max Planck Encyclopedia of Public International Law* (Oxford University Press 2012 Online Edition [available at <http://www.mpepil.com/> last visited: 21 March 2014]).

Van Dijk, Pieter, 'Article 6 § 1 of the Convention and the Concept of "Objective Impartiality"', in: Mahoney, Paul, Matscher, Franz, Petzold, Herbert and Wildhaber, Luzius (eds), *Protection des droits de l'homme: la perspective européenne – Mélanges à la mémoire de Rolv Ryssdal* (Heymann Köln 2000), 1495-1510.

Vitzthum, Wolfgang Graf, 'International Seabed Area', in: Wolfrum, Rüdiger (ed), *The Max Planck Encyclopedia of Public International Law* (Oxford University Press 2012 Online Edition [available at <http://www.mpepil.com/> last visited: 21 March 2014]).

Voeten, Erik, 'The Impartiality of International Judges: Evidence from the European Court of Human Rights' (2008) 102 American Political Science Review 4, 417-433.

Vukas, Budislav, 'Treaties, Third-Party Effect', in: Wolfrum, Rüdiger (ed), *The Max Planck Encyclopedia of Public International Law* (Oxford University Press 2012 Online Edition [available at <http://www.mpepil.com/> last visited: 21 March 2014]).

Wald, Patricia M., 'Judging War Crimes' (2000) 1 Chicago Journal of International Law 1, 189-196.

Walter, Christian, 'Subjects of International Law', in: Wolfrum, Rüdiger (ed), *The Max Planck Encyclopedia of Public International Law* (Oxford University Press 2012 Online Edition [available at <http://www.mpepil.com/> last visited: 21 March 2014]).

Watts QC, Sir Arthur, 'Codification and Progressive Development of International Law', in: Wolfrum, Rüdiger (ed), *The Max Planck Encyclopedia of Public International Law* (Oxford University Press 2012 Online Edition [available at <http://www.mpepil.com/> last visited: 21 March 2014]).

Weeramantry, Christopher G., 'Expanding the Potential of the World Court', in: Jasentuliyana, Nandasiri (ed), *Perspectives on International Law* (Kluwer Law 1995), 309-346.

White, Robin C.A. and Boussiakou, Iris, 'Separate Opinions in the European Court of Human Rights' (2009) 9 Human Rights Law Review 1, 37-60.

Wildhaber, Luzius, 'A Constitutional Future for the European Court of Human Rights' (2002) 23 Human Rights Law Journal 5-7, 161-165.

Wolfrum, Rüdiger, 'Article 1 UNC', in: Simma, Bruno (ed), *The Charter of the United Nations: A Commentary – Volume I* (Oxford University Press Oxford 2nd edn. 2002), 39-47.

Wolfrum, Rüdiger, 'Artikel 1 UNC', in: Simma, Bruno (ed), *Charta der Vereinten Nationen: Kommentar* (Beck München 1991), 1-11.

Wolfrum, Rüdiger, 'Interim (Provisional) Measures of Protection', in: Wolfrum, Rüdiger (ed), *The Max Planck Encyclopedia of Public International Law* (Oxford University Press 2012 Online Edition [available at <http://www.mpepil.com/> last visited: 21 March 2014]).

Wolfrum, Rüdiger, 'International Courts and Tribunals, Evidence', in: Wolfrum, Rüdiger (ed), *The Max Planck Encyclopedia of Public International Law* (Oxford University Press 2012 Online Edition [available at <http://www.mpepil.com/> last visited: 21 March 2014]).

Wolfrum, Rüdiger, 'Provisional Measures of the International Tribunal for the Law of the Sea', in: Chandrasekhara Rao, P. and Khan, Rahmatullah (eds), *The International Tribunal for the Law of the Sea – Law and Practice* (Kluwer Law International The Hague 2001), 172-186.

Wood, Michael, 'International Seabed Authority (ISA)', in: Wolfrum, Rüdiger (ed), *The Max Planck Encyclopedia of Public International Law* (Oxford University Press 2012 Online Edition [available at <http://www.mpepil.com/> last visited: 21 March 2014]).

Wood, Michael, 'The International Seabed Authority – Fifth to Twelfth Sessions (1999-2006)', in: von Bogdandy, Armin and Wolfrum, Rüdiger (eds), *Max Planck Yearbook of United Nations Law – Volume 11* (Martinus Nijhoff Publishers Leiden 2007), 47-98.

Wood, Michael, 'The International Tribunal for the Law of the Sea and General International Law' (2007) 22 International Journal of Marine and Coastal Law 3, 351-367.

Woodhouse, Diana, 'Judges and the Lord Chancellor in the Changing United Kingdom Constitution: Independence and Accountability' (2005) 16 Public Law Review 3, 227-244.

Wouters, Jan, Verhoeven, Sten and Demeyere, Bruno, 'The International Courts's Office of the Prosecutor – Navigating between Independence and Accountability', in: Doria, José, Gasser, Hans-Peter and Bassiouni, M. Cherif (eds), *The Legal Regime of the International Criminal Court – Essays in Honour of Professor Igor Blishchenko* (Martinus Nijhoff Publishers Leiden 2009), 345-386.

Yankov, Alexander, 'The International Tribunal for the Law of the Sea and the Comprehensive Dispute Settlement System of the Law of the Sea', in: Chandrasekhara Rao, P. and Khan, Rahmatullah (eds), *The International Tribunal for the Law of the Sea – Law and Practice* (Kluwer Law International The Hague 2001), 59-72.

Ziegler, Katja S., 'Jay Treaty (1794)', in: Wolfrum, Rüdiger (ed), *The Max Planck Encyclopedia of Public International Law* (Oxford University Press 2012 Online Edition [available at <http://www.mpepil.com/> last visited: 21 March 2014]).

III. Treaties, Conventions and Other Legal Instruments

Ad Hoc Committee on the Establishment of an International Criminal Court, *Report of the Ad Hoc Committee on the Establishment of an International Criminal Court* (6 September 1995) UN Doc. A/50/22.

Advisory Committee on Administrative and Budgetary Questions, *Conditions of service and compensation for officials other than Secretariat officials: members of the International Court of Justice and judges and ad litem judges of the International Tribunal for the Former Yugoslavia and the International Criminal Tribunal for Rwanda – Thirty-seventh report of the Advisory Committee on Administrative and Budgetary Questions on the programme budget for the biennium 2008-2009* (12 March 2008) UN Doc. A/62/7/Add.36.

Advisory Committee on Administrative and Budgetary Questions, *Twelfth report of the Advisory Committee on Administrative and Budgetary Questions – Programme Budget for the Biennium 1994-1995 – Conditions of service and compensation for officials other than Secretariat officials, Pension scheme for the members of the International Court of Justice* (8 March 1995) UN Doc. A/49/7/Add.11.

African Charter on Human and Peoples' Rights (Banjul Charter) (adopted 27 June1981, entered into force 21 October 1986) 1520 UNTS 217.

Agreement between the General Secretariat of The OAS and The Inter-American Court of Human Rights concerning the Administrative Functioning of the Secretariat of the Court (1999) OAS Official Records OEA/Ser.L/V/III.43, doc. 11.

Agreement between the Government of the Republic of Costa Rica and the Inter-American Court of Human Rights (Headquarters Agreement) (adopted 10 September 1981) 24 HRLJ 302 (2003).

Agreement between the United Nations and the Government of Sierra Leone on the Establishment of a Special Court for Sierra Leone (adopted 16 January 2002, entered into force 12 April 2002) 2178 UNTS 138.

Agreement for the Implementation of the Provisions of the United Nations Convention on the Law of the Sea of 10 December 1982 Relating to the Conservation and Management of Straddling Fish Stocks and Highly Migratory Fish Stocks (adopted 4 August 1995, entered into force 11 December 2001) 2167 UNTS 3.

Agreement on Cooperation and Relationship between the United Nations and the International Tribunal for the Law of the Sea (adopted 18 December 1997, entered into force 12 March 1998) 2000 UNTS 467.

Agreement on the Privileges and Immunities of the International Criminal Court (adopted 9 September 2002, entered into force 22 July 2004) Official Records ICC-ASP/1/3 (Part II-E).

Agreement relating to the Implementation of Part XI of the United Nations Convention on the Law of the Sea of 10 December 1982 (adopted 28 July 1994, entered into force 28 July 1996) 1836 UNTS 41.

American Convention on Human Rights (Pact of San José, Costa Rica) (adopted 22 November 1969, entered into force 18 July 1978) 1144 UNTS 123.

An Act for the further Limitation of the Crown and better securing the Rights and Liberties of the Subject (1700 & 1701) Statutes of the Realm: Volume 7: 1695-1701 (1820), 636-638.

Arab Charter on Human Rights (revised) (adopted 22 May 2004, entered into force 15 March 2008) (2005) 12 IHRR 893.

Assembly of States Parties – Report of the Bureau on the establishment of an Advisory Committee on nominations of judges of the International Criminal Court (adopted 30 November 2011) Official Records Resolution ICC-ASP/10/36.

Assembly of States Parties to the Rome Statute of the International Criminal Court – First session, New York, 3-10 September 2002 (adopted 9 September 2002, entered into force 22 July 2004) Official Records ICC-ASP/1/3.

Assembly of States Parties to the Rome Statute of the International Criminal Court – Second Session, Official Records, Part III – Conditions of Service and Compensation and Staff Regulations (8-12 September 2003) Official Records Resolution ICC-ASP/2/10.

Australia, Belgium, Bolivia, Colombia, El Salvador, Luxembourg, Netherlands, Singapore and United States of America,, *Working paper on the settlement of law of the sea disputes* (27 August 1974) UN Doc. A/CONF.62/L.7.

Budget appropriations for the first financial period and financing of appropriations for the first financial period (adopted 3 September 2002) Official Records ICC-ASP/1/Res.12.

Bundesrat, *Gesetzesantrag des Bundesrates: Entwurf eines [...] Gesetzes zur Änderung des Richterwahlgesetzes* (10 February 2006) Drucksache 915/05.

Centre for International Courts and Tribunals and University College London, *Selecting International Judges: Principle, Process and Politics – Discussion Paper* (2008) available at <http://www.ucl.ac.uk/laws/cict/docs/Selecting_Int_Judges.pdf> (last visited: 21 March 2014).

Charter of the Organization of American States (signed 30 April 1948, entered into force 13 December 1951) 119 UNTS 3.

Code of Judicial Ethics (adopted 9 March 2005, entered into force 9 March 2005) Official Records ICC-BD/02-01-05.

COE 'Statute of the Council of Europe' (adopted 5 May 1949, entered into force 3 August 1949) CETS No. 1.

Commission on Human Rights, *The Administration of Justice and the Human Rights of Detainees – The right to a fair trial: Current recognition and measures necessary for its strengthening, Final report prepared by Mr. Stanislav Chernichenko and Mr. William Treat* (3 June 1994) UN Doc. E/CN.4/Sub.2/1994/24.

Commission on the Status of Women, *Commission on the Status of Women, Report on the 37th Session, 17-26 March 1993* (28 May 1993) UN Doc. E/1993/27.

Commission on the Status of Women, *Commission on the Status of Women, Report on the 38th Session, 7-18 March 1994* (1 January 1994) UN Doc. E/1994/27.

Commission on the Status of Women, *Commission on the Status of Women, Report on the 39th Session, 15 March-7 April 1995* (1 January 1995) UN Doc. E/1995/26.

Committee of Experts, *Draft Principles on the Independence of the Judiciary ("Siracusa Principles")* (1981) available at <http://www.mpil.de/shared/data/pdf/pdfjudind/syracusa_principles.pdf> (last visited: 21 March 2014).

Committee of Ministers of the CoE, *1101st Meeting, 8 December 2010 – Decisions Adopted* (8 December 2010) CM/Del/Dec(2010)1101.

Committee of Ministers of the CoE, *Budgetary needs of the European Court of Human Rights* (20 December 2000) CM/Del/Dec(2000)734/1.5, 733/1.6 and 731/1.5, GT-BC-2001(2000)1.

Committee of Ministers of the CoE, *On the Establishment of an Advisory Panel of Experts on Candidates for Election as Judge to the European Court of Human Rights* (adopted 10 November 2010) Resolution CM/Res(2010)26.

Committee of Ministers of the CoE, *On the status and conditions of service of judges of the European Court of Human Rights and of the Commissioner for Human Rights* (adopted 23 September 2009) Resolution CM/Res(2009)5.

Committee of Ministers of the CoE, *Recommendation No. R (94) 12 of the Committee of Ministers to Member States on Independence, Efficiency and Role of Judges* (adopted 13 October 1994) available at <https://wcd.coe.int/ViewDoc.jsp?id=524871&Site=CM> (last visited: 21 March 2014).

Committee of Ministers of the CoE, *Report of the Evaluation Group to the Committee of Ministers on the European Court of Human Rights* (adopted 27 September 2001) EG Court(2001)1.

Committee of Ministers of the CoE, *States' obligation to co-operate with the European Court of Human Rights* (adopted 26 June 2001) Resolution ResDH(2001)66.

Committee of Ministers of the CoE, *States' obligation to co-operate with the European Court of Human Rights* (adopted 4 July 2006) Resolution ResDH(2006)45.

Committee of Ministers of the CoE, *The adjustment of the scale of contributions to the Council of Europe Ordinary Budget and Budget of the European Youth Foundation with effect from 1 January 2010* (adopted 25 November 2009) Resolution CM/Res(2009)20.

Committee of Ministers of the CoE, *The Ordinary Budget for 2009* (adopted 25 November 2008) Resolution CM/Res(2008)25.

Committee of Ministers of the CoE, *The Ordinary Budget for 2012-2013* (23 November 2011) Resolution CM/Res(2011)28.

Committee on International Criminal Jurisdiction, *Report of the 1951 Committee on International Criminal Jurisdiction* (1 – 31 August 1951) UN Doc. A/2136.

Committee on the Peaceful Uses of the Sea-Bed and the Ocean Floor Beyond the Limits of National jurisdiction, *Report of the Committee on the Peaceful Uses of the Sea-Bed and the Ocean Floor Beyond the Limits of National jurisdiction* (1971) UN Doc. A/8421.

Conference of the Chief Justices of Asia and the Pacific, *Beijing Statement of Principles of the Independence of the Judiciary in the LAWASIA Region* (19 August 1995) available at <http://lawasia.asn.au/beijing-statement.htm> (last visited: 21 March 2014).

Consolidated Version of the Treaty establishing the European Community (adopted 25 March 1957, entered into force 1 January 1958) OJ C 321E.

Consolidated Version of the Treaty on the Functioning of the European Union (signed 13 December 2007, entered into force 1 December 2009) OJ C83/47.

Convention for the Pacific Settlement of International Disputes (adopted 18 October 1907, entered into force 26 January 1910) 205 CTS 233.

Convention for the Protection of Human Rights and Fundamental Freedoms (adopted 4 November 1950, entered into force 3 September 1953) 213 UNTS 221.

Convention on Conciliation and Arbitration within the CSCE (adopted 15 December 1992, entered into force 5 December 1994) 32 ILM 557.

Convention on Fishing and Conservation of the Living Resources of the High Seas (adopted 29 April 1958, entered into force 20 March 1966) 559 UNTS 285.

Convention on the Continental Shelf (adopted 29 April 1958, entered into force 10 June 1964) 499 UNTS 311.

Convention on the Elimination of All Forms of Discrimination against Women (adopted 18 December 1979, entered into force 3 September 1981) 1249 UNTS 13.

Convention on the High Seas (adopted 29 April 1958, entered into force 30 September 1962) 450 UNTS 11.

Convention on the Prevention and Punishment of Crimes against Internationally Protected Persons, Including Diplomatic Agents (adopted 14 December 1973, entered into force 20 February 1977) 1035 UNTS 167.

Convention on the Privileges and Immunities of the United Nations (adopted 13 February 1946, entered into force 17 September 1946) 1 UNTS 15.

Convention on the Settlement of Investment Disputes between States and Nationals of Other States (adopted 18 March 1965, entered into force 14 October 1966) 575 UNTS 159.

Convention on the Territorial Sea and the Contiguous Zone (adopted 29 April 1958, entered into force on 10 September 1964) 516 UNTS 205.

Corell, Hans, Türk, Helmut and Thune, Gro Hillestad, *Proposal for an International War Crimes Tribunal for the Former Yugoslavia by Rapporteurs (Corell – Türk – Thune) under the CSCE Moscow Human Rights Dimension to Bosnia-Hergegovina and Croatia* (9 February 1993) UN Doc. S/25307.

Council of Europe, *Protocol No. 8 to the Convention for the Protection of Human Rights and Fundamental Freedoms, Explanatory Report* (19 March 1985) available at <http://conventions.coe.int/Treaty/en/Reports/Html/118.htm> (last visited: 21 March 2014).

Council of Europe, *Protocol No. 11 to the Convention for the Protection of Human Rights and Fundamental Freedoms, restructuring the control machinary established thereby, Explanatory Report* (11 May 1994) available at <http://conventions.coe.int/treaty/en/Reports/Html/155.htm> (last visited: 21 March 2014).

Council of Europe, *Protocol No. 14 to the Convention for the Protection of Human Rights and Fundamental Freedoms, amending the control system of the Convention, Explanatory Report* (13 June 2004) available at <http://conventions.coe.int/Treaty/EN/Reports/Html/194.htm> (last visited: 21 March 2014).

Council of Europe, *Staff Regulations – Appendix II: Regulations on appointments* (as amended 12 October 2011) available at <https://wcd.coe.int/ViewDoc.jsp?Ref=COMP/CM/Res(2007)1&Language=lanEnglish&Ver=part10&BackColorInternet=99CCFF&BackColorIntranet=99CCFF&BackColorLogged=99CCCC#P239_37192> (last visited: 21 March 2014).

Council of Europe, *Staff Regulations – Appendix V bis: New Pension Scheme "NPS"* (as amended 27 November 2002) available at <https://wcd.coe.int/ViewDoc.jsp?Ref=COMP/CM/Res%282007%291&Language=lanEnglish&Ver=part14&BackColorInternet=DBDCF2&BackColorIntranet=FDC864&BackColorLogged=FDC864#P333_44875> (last visited: 21 March 2014).

Council of Europe, *Staff Regulations – Appendix V: Pension Scheme rules* (as amended 9 November 2011) available at <https://wcd.coe.int/ViewDoc.jsp?Ref=COMP/CM/Res%282007%291&Language=lanEnglish&Ver=part13&BackColorInternet=99CCFF&BackColorIntranet=99CCFF&BackColorLogged=99CCCC#P140_13349> (last visited: 21 March 2014).

Council of Europe, *Staff Regulations – Appendix VII: Regulations on unpaid leave* (as amended 7 July 2010) available at <https://wcd.coe.int/ViewDoc.jsp?Ref=COMP/CM/Res%282007%291&Language=lanEnglish&Ver=part16&BackColorInternet=99CCFF&BackColorIntranet=99CCFF&BackColorLogged=99CCCC> (last visited: 21 March 2014).

Council of Europe, *Staff Regulations – Appendix XII: Regulations on the medical and social insurance scheme* (as amended 16 January 2008) available at <https://wcd.coe.int/ViewDoc.jsp?Ref=COMP/CM/Res%282007%291&Language=lanEnglish&Ver=part21&BackColorInternet=99CCFF&BackColorIntranet=99CCFF&BackColorLogged=99CCCC> (last visited: 21 March 2014).

Covenant of the League of Nations (adopted 28 June 1919, entered into force 10 January 1920) (1919) 225 CTS 195.

Draft Decision by the Fifth Committee, *Conditions of service and compensation for officials other than Secretariat officials: members of the International Court of Justice and judges and ad litem judges of the International Tribunal for the Former Yugoslavia and the International Criminal Tribunal for Rwanda* (27 March 2008) UN Doc. A/C.5/62/L.31.

ECtHR, *Rules of Court of the European Court of Human Rights* (adopted 18 September 1959) Reprinted in International Oganisation and Integration, 1968, 945 et seq.

ECtHR, *Rules of the European Court of Human Rights* (adopted 18 September 1959, last amended 6 May 2013, entered into force 1 January 2014) available at <http://www.echr.coe.int/Documents/Rules_Court_ENG.pdf> (last visited: 21 March 2014).

Elements of Crimes (adopted 9 September 2002, entered into force 9 September 2002) Official Records ICC-ASP/1/3 (Part II-B).

European Commission of Human Rights, *Reform Proposal* (17 January 1994) DH-PR (93)2.

European Court of Human Rights, *Annual Report 2009* (2010) available at <http://www.echr.coe.int/Documents/Annual_report_2009_ENG.pdf> (last visited: 21 March 2014).

European Court of Human Rights, *Annual Report 2010 – Speech given by Mr Jean-Paul Costa, President of the European Court of Human Rights on the Occasion of the Opening of the Judicial Year, 29 January 2010* (2010) available at <http://www.echr.coe.int/Documents/Annual_report_2010_ENG.pdf> (last visited: 21 March 2014).

European Court of Human Rights, *Reform Proposal* (31 January 1994) DH-PR (94)4.

Fifth Committee, *Conditions of service and compensation for officials other than Secretariat officials: members of the International Court of Justice and judges and ad litem judges of the International Tribunal for the Former Yugoslavia and the International Criminal Tribunal for Rwanda* (29 March 2007) UN Doc. A/C.5/61/L.40.

Financial Regulations and Rules (latest amendment adopted on 22 November 2008) (adopted 9 September 2002) Official Records ICC-ASP/7/5 (Part. II-D).

Financial Regulations and Rules of the International Tribunal for the Law of the Sea – Prepared by the Tribunal (1 January 2005) available at <http://www.itlos.org/fileadmin/itlos/documents/basic_texts/Financial.Regs.Rules.E.pdf> (last visited: 21 March 2014).

Financial Regulations and Supplementary Provisions of the Council of Europe (12 July 2006) available at <https://wcd.coe.int/ViewDoc.jsp?id=1021635&BackColorInternet=9999CC&BackColorIntranet=FFBB55&BackColorLogged=FFAC75> (last visited: 21 March 2014).

First World Conference on the Independence of Justice, *Universal Declaration on the Independence of Justice* (1983) available at <http://www.mpil.de/shared/data/pdf/pdfjudind/montreal_declaration.pdf> (last visited: 21 March 2014).

General agreement on privileges and immunities of the Council of Europe (adopted 2 September 1949, entered into force 10 September 1952) CETS No. 2.

Headquarters Agreement between the International Criminal Court and the Host State (adopted 7 June 2007, entered into force 1 March 2008) Official Records ICC-BD/04-01-08.

Human Rights Committee, *General Comment 29, States of Emergency (Article 4)* (31 August 2001) UN Doc. CCPR/C/21/Rev. 1/Add.11.

Human Rights Committee, *González del Río v. Peru, Communication No. 263/1987* (2 November 1992) UN Doc. CCPR/C/46/D/263/1987.

Human Rights Committee, *Report of the Human Rights Committee (Volume II)* (21 September 1994) UN Doc. A/49/40.

ICJ, *Press Release 2002/27 – United Nations General Assembly and Security Council proceed to the election of five Members of the Court* (22 October 2002) available at <http://www.icj-cij.org/presscom/index.php?pr=105&pt=&p1=6&p2=1> (last visited: 21 March 2014).

ICJ, *Press Release 2005/23 – United Nations General Assembly and Security Council proceed to the election of five Members of the Court* (8 November 2005) available at <http://www.icj-cij.org/presscom/index.php?pr=638&pt=&p1=6&p2=1> (last visited: 21 March 2014).

ICJ, *Staff Regulations for the Registry of the International Court of Justice* (approved 7 March 1979, last amended 20 March 2012) available at <http://www.icj-cij.org/registry/en/regulations.pdf> (last visited: 21 March 2014).

ICTR, *ICTR Press Release* (12 December 1995) available at <http://www.unictr.org/tabid/155/Default.aspx?id=617> (last visited: 21 March 2014).

ICTY, *Report of the International Criminal Tribunal for the Prosecution of Persons Responsible for Genocide and Other Serious Violations of International Humanitarian Law Committed in the Territory of Rwanda and Rwandan Citizens Responsible for Genocide and Other Such Violations Committed in the Territory of Neighbouring States Between 1 January and 31 December 1994* (24 September 1996) UN Doc. A/51/399-S/1996/778.

ILC, *Report of the International Law Commission Covering the Work of its Fifth Session* (1 June-14 August 1953) UN Doc. A/CN.4/76.

Institut de Droit International, *The Position of the International Judge – 6th Resolution – Sixth Commission – Session de Rhodes* (2011) available at <http://www.idi-iil.org/> (last visited: 21 March 2014).

Institut de Droit International, *The Position of the International Judge – Rapporteur: Gilbert Guillaume – 6th Resolution – Sixth Commission – Session de Rhodes* (2011) available at <http://www.idi-iil.org/> (last visited: 21 March 2014).

Inter-American Commission on Human Rights, *Report on Terrorism and Human Rights* (22 October 2002) OAS Official Records OEA/Ser.L/V/II.116, Doc. 5 rev. 1 corr.

International Bar Association, *Minimum Standards of Judicial Independence* (1982) available at <http://www.ibanet.org/Document/Default.aspx?DocumentUid=BB019013-52B1-427C-AD25-A6409B49FE29> (last visited: 21 March 2014).

International Bar Association, *Rule of Law Resolution* (September 2005) available at <http://www.ibanet.org/> (last visited: 21 March 2014).

International Convention for the Pacific Settlement of International Disputes (adopted 29 July 1899, entered into force 4 September 1900) 187 CTS 410.

International Cour of Justice, *Instructions for the Registry* (October 1946) available at <http://www.icj-cij.org/registry/index.php?p1=2&p2=3&p3=2&PHPSESSID=5c40 7&PHPSESSID=5c407> (last visited: 21 March 2014).

International Court of Justice, *Report of the International Court of Justice, 1 August 1995-31 July 1996* (1 January 1996) UN Doc. A/51/4.

International Court of Justice, *Report of the International Court of Justice, 1 August 2006-31 July 2007* (1 January 2007) UN Doc. A/62/4(SUPP).

International Court of Justice, *Report of the International Court of Justice, 1 August 2007-31 July 2008* (1 January 2008) UN Doc. A/63/4(SUPP).

International Court of Justice, *Report of the International Court of Justice, 1 August 2008-31 July 2009* (1 August 2009) UN Doc. A/64/4(SUPP).

International Court of Justice, *Report of the International Court of Justice, 1 August 2009-31 July 2010* (1 January 2010) UN Doc. A/65/4(SUPP).

International Court of Justice, *Report of the International Court of Justice, 1 August 2010-31 July 2011* (1 August 2011) UN Doc. A/66/4(SUPP).

International Covenant on Civil and Political Rights (adopted 19 December 1966, entered into force 23 March 1976) 999 UNTS 171.

International Covenant on Economic, Social and Cultural Rights (adopted 16 December 1966, entered into force 3 January 1976) 993 UNTS 3.

International Law Commission, *Report of the International Law Commission on its Second Session, 5 June to 29 July 1950, Official Records of the General Assembly, Fifth session, Supplement No.12 (A/1316)* (July 1950) UN Doc. A/CN.4/34.

International Law Commission, *Report of the International Law Commission on the work of its forty-sixth session* (22 July 1994) UN Doc. A/49/10.

International Law Commission, *Report of the International Law Commission on the work of its forty-third session* (29 April – 19 July 1991) UN Doc. A/46/10.

International Law Commission, *Revised Report of the Working Group on the Draft Statute for an International Criminal Court* (19 July 1993) UN Doc. A/CN.4/L.490.

ITLOS, *Resolution on the Internal Judicial Practice of the International Tribunal for the Law of the Sea* (31 October 1997) ITLOS/10.

Land Baden-Württemberg, *Gesetzesantrag des Landes Baden-Württemberg: Entwurf eines Gesetzes zur Änderung des Richterwahlgesetzes* (23 December 2005) Drucksache 915/05.

Multilateral Meeting on the Statute for Judges in Europe, *European Charter on the Statute for Judges* (10 July 1998) available at <http://www.coe.int/t/dghl/monitoring/greco/e valuations/round 4/European-Charter-on-Statute-of-Judges_EN.pdf> (last visited: 21 March 2014).

Negotiated Relationship Agreement between the International Criminal Court and the United Nations (adopted 4 October 2004, entered into force 22 July 2004) Official Records ICC-ASP/3/Res.1.

Optional Protocol of Signature Concerning the Compulsory Settlement of Disputes (adopted 29 April 1958, entered into force 30 September 1962) 450 UNTS 169.

Parliamentary Assembly of the Council of Europe, *70-year age limit for the judges of the European Court of Human Rights, Report, Committee on Legal Affairs and Human Rights, Rapporteur: Lord Kirkhill, United Kingdom, Socialist Group* (6 November 2000) Doc. 8887.

Parliamentary Assembly of the Council of Europe, *Ad hoc judges at the European Court of Human Rights: an overview, Report, Committee on Legal Affairs and Human Rights, Rapporteur: Mrs Marie-Louise Bemelmans-Videc, the Netherlands, Group of the European People's Party* (19 October 2011) Doc. AS/Jur (2011) 36.

Parliamentary Assembly of the Council of Europe, *Candidates for the European Court of Human Rights, Report, Committee on Legal Affairs and Human Rights, Rapporteur: Mr Kevin McNamara, United Kingdom, Socialist Group* (7 October 2003) Doc. 9963.

Parliamentary Assembly of the Council of Europe, *National procedures for nominating candidates for election to the European Court of Human Rights* (8 September 1999) Doc. 8505.

Parliamentary Assembly of the Council of Europe, *National procedures for nominating candidates for election to the European Court of Human Rights* (17 September 1999) Doc. 8525.

Parliamentary Assembly of the Council of Europe, *National procedures for the selection of candidates for the European Court of Human Rights* (7 October 2010) Doc. 12391.

Parliamentary Assembly of the Council of Europe, *Nomination of Candidates and Election of Judges to the European Court of Human Rights* (1 December 2008) Doc. 11767.

Parliamentary Assembly of the Council of Europe, *Opinion No. 251 (2004) – Draft Protocol No. 14 to the Convention for the Protection of Human Rights and Fundamental Freedoms amending the control system of the Convention* (2004) available at <http://www.assembly.coe.int/Main.asp?link=/Documents/AdoptedText/ta04/EOPI251.htm> (last visited: 21 March 2014).

Parliamentary Assembly of the Council of Europe, *Order No. 558 – National procedures for nominating candidates for election to the European Court of Human Rights* (1999) available at <http://assembly.coe.int/Mainf.asp?link=/Documents/AdoptedText/ta99/EDIR558.htm> (last visited: 21 March 2014).

Parliamentary Assembly of the Council of Europe, *Recommendation 1087 – on the improvement of the procedures of the European Convention on Human Rights* (1988) available at <http://assembly.coe.int/main.asp?Link=/documents/adoptedtext/ta88/erec1087.htm> (last visited: 21 March 2014).

Parliamentary Assembly of the Council of Europe, *Recommendation 1194 – on the reform of the control mechanism of the European Convention on Human Rights* (1992) available at <http://assembly.coe.int/Mainf.asp?link=/Documents/AdoptedText/ta92/EREC1194.htm> (last visited: 21 March 2014).

Parliamentary Assembly of the Council of Europe, *Recommendation 1429 – National procedures for nominating candidates for election to the European Court of Human Rights* (1999) available at <http://assembly.coe.int/Mainf.asp?link=/Documents/AdoptedText/ta99/EREC1429.htm> (last visited: 21 March 2014).

Parliamentary Assembly of the Council of Europe, *Recommendation 1649 – Candidates for the European Court of Human Rights* (2004) available at <http://assembly.coe.int//Mainf.asp?link=http://assembly.coe.int/Documents/AdoptedText/ta04/EREC1649.htm> (last visited: 21 March 2014).

Parliamentary Assembly of the Council of Europe, *Recommendation 809 – on the qualification of candidates for the European Court of Human Rights* (1977) available at <http://assembly.coe.int/Mainf.asp?link=/Documents/AdoptedText/ta77/EREC809.htm> (last visited: 21 March 2014).

Parliamentary Assembly of the Council of Europe, *Resolution 1200 – Election of judges to the European Court of Human Rights* (1999) available at <http://assembly.coe.int/Main.asp?link=/Documents/AdoptedText/ta99/ERES1200.htm> (last visited: 21 March 2014).

Parliamentary Assembly of the Council of Europe, *Resolution 1202 – Rules of Procedure of the Assembly (adopted on 4 November 1999)* (1999) available at <http://assembly.coe.int/Main.asp?link=/RulesofProcedure/PACERuleIndex_E.asp> (last visited: 21 March 2014).

Parliamentary Assembly of the Council of Europe, *Resolution 1366 – Candidates for the European Court of Human Rights* (2004) available at <http://assembly.coe.int/Main.asp?link=/Documents/AdoptedText/ta04/ERES1366.htm> (last visited: 21 March 2014).

Parliamentary Assembly of the Council of Europe, *Resolution 1426 – Candidates for the European Court of Human Rights* (2005) available at <http://www.assembly.coe.int/ASP/Doc/XrefViewPDF.asp?FileID=17311&Language=EN> (last visited: 21 March 2014).

Parliamentary Assembly of the Council of Europe, *Resolution 1627 – Candidates for the European Court of Human Rights* (2008) available at <http://www.assembly.coe.int/ASP/Doc/XrefViewPDF.asp?FileID=17670&Language=EN> (last visited: 21 March 2014).

Parliamentary Assembly of the Council of Europe, *Resolution 1646 – Nomination of candidates and election of judges to the European Court of Human Rights* (2009) available at <http://assembly.coe.int/Main.asp?link=/Documents/AdoptedText/ta09/ERES1646.htm> (last visited: 21 March 2014).

Parliamentary Assembly of the Council of Europe, *The reform of the control mechanism of the European Convention on Human Rights, Report, Rapporteur: Mr Vogel, Germany* (15 September 1992) Doc. 6659.

PCIJ, *Acts and Documents concerning the Organisation of the Court: No. 2 Preparation of the Rules of Court* (30 January-24 March 1922) Ser. D, No. 2.

PCIJ, *Rules of Court* (adopted 24 March 1922) available at <http://www.icj-cij.org/pcij/serie_D/D_01.pdf> (last visited: 21 March 2014).

Preparatory Commission of the United Nations, *Report of the Preparatory Commission of the United Nations* (23 December 1945) UN Doc. PC/20.

Preparatory Committee on the Establishment of an International Criminal Court, *Report of the Preparatory Committee on the Establishment of an International Criminal Court* (14 April 1998) UN Doc. A/CONF.183/2/Add.1.

Preparatory Committee on the Establishment of an International Criminal Court, *Report of the Preparatory Committee on the Establishment of an International Criminal Court, Volume I (Proceedings of the Preparatory Committee during March-April and August 1996)* (13 September 1996) UN Doc. A/51/22.

President of the European Court of Human Rights, *General Instruction No. 3* (10 August 1973) CDH (73) 20.

President of the International Court of Justice, *Document transmitted by the President of the International Court of Justice to the Secretary-General on the implications of General Assembly resolution 61/262 in regard to certain provisions of the Statute of the Court* (2007) UN Doc. A/62/538 Annex II.

President of the International Court of Justice, *Letter dated 3 April 2007 from the President of the International Court of Justice to the President of the General Assembly* (3 April 2007) UN Doc. A/61/837.

President of the International Court of Justice, *Letter from the President of the International Court of Justice to the Minister for Foreign Affairs of the Netherlands* (26 June 1946) available <http://www.icj-cij.org/documents/index.php?p1=4&p2=5&p3=3> (last visited: 21 March 2014).

Procedure for the Nomination and Election of Judges of the International Criminal Court (adopted 10 September 2004) Official Records Resolution ICC-ASP/3/Res.6.

Programme budget for 2009, the Working Capital Fund for 2009, scale of assessments for the apportionment of expenses of the International Criminal Court, financing appropriations for the year 2009 and the Contingency Fund (adopted 21 November 2008) Official Records Resolution ICC-ASP/7/Res.4.

Programme budget for 2010, the Working Capital Fund for 2010, scale of assessments for the apportionment of expenses of the International Criminal Court, financing appropriations for the year 2010, the Contingency Fund, conversion of a GTA psychologist post to an established one, Legal aid (defence) and the Addis Ababa Liaison Office (adopted 26 November 2009) Official Records Resolution ICC-ASP/8/Res.7.

Programme budget for 2011, the Working Capital Fund for 2011, scale of assessments for the apportionment of expenses of the International Criminal Court, financing appropriations for 2011 and the Contingency Fund (adopted 10 December 2010) Official Records Resolution ICC-ASP/9/Res.4.

Programme budget for 2012, the Working Capital Fund for 2012, scale of assessments for the apportionment of expenses of the International Criminal Court, financing appropriations for 2012 and the Contingency Fund (adopted 21 December 2011) Official Records Resolution ICC-ASP/10/Res.4.

Protocol No. 2 to the Convention for the Protection of Human Rights and Fundamental Freedoms, conferring upon the European Court of Human Rights competence to give advisory opinions (adopted 6 May 1963, entered into force 21 September 1970) CETS No. 044.

Protocol No. 5 to the Convention for the Protection of Human Rights and Fundamental Freedoms, amending Articles 22 and 40 of the Convention (adopted 20 January, entered into force 20 December 1971) CETS No. 055.

Protocol No. 8 to the Convention for the Protection of Human Rights and Fundamental Freedoms (adopted 19 March 1985, entered into force 1 January 1990) CETS No. 118.

Protocol No. 11 to the Convention for the Protection of Human Rights and Fundamental Freedoms Restructuring the Control Machinery Established Thereby (adopted 11 May 1994, entered into force 1 November 1998) 2061 UNTS 12.

Protocol No. 14 to the Convention for the Protection of Human Rights and Fundamental Freedoms, amending the control system of the Convention (adopted 13 May 2004, entered into force 1 June 2010) CETS No. 194.

Regulations of the Court (as amended on 14 June and 14 November 2007) (adopted 26 Mai 2004, entered into force 26 Mai 2004, date of entry into force of amendments 18 December 2007) Official Records ICC-BD/01-02-07.

Regulations of the Trust Fund for Victims (adopted 3 December 2005) Official Records ICC-ASP/4/Res.3.

Relevant criteria for voluntary contributions to the International Criminal Court (adopted 3 September 2002) Official Records ICC-ASP/1/Res.11.

Report of the Advisory Committee on Administrative and Budgetary Questions, *Conditions of service and compensation for officials other than Secretariat officials* (6 December 2006) UN Doc. A/61/612.

Report of the Advisory Committee on Administrative and Budgetary Questions, *Financing of the International Tribunal for the Prosecution of Persons Responsible for Serious Violations of International Humanitarian Law Committed in the Territory of the Former Yugoslavia since 1991* (29 March 1994) UN Doc. A/48/915.

Report of the Advisory Committee on Administrative and Budgetary Questions, *Programme Budget for the Biennium 1994-1995 – Financing of the International Tribunal for the Prosecution of Persons Responsible for Serious Violations of International Humanitarian Law Committed in the Territory of the Former Yugoslavia since 1991* (10 March 1995) UN Doc. A/49/7/Add.12.

Report of the Advisory Committee on Administrative and Budgetary Questions, *Seventh report: conditions of service and compensation for officials other than Secretariat officials: members of the International Court of Justice* (10 November 1998) UN Doc. A/53/7/Add.6.

Report of the Advisory Committee on Nominations of Judges on the work of its first meeting (adopted 31 May 2013) Official Records Resolution ICC-ASP/12/23.

Report of the Committee on the Peaceful uses of the Sea-Bed and the Ocean Floor Beyond the Limits of National Jurisdiction, *Draft Articles for a Chapter on the Settlement of Disputes: submitted by the United States of America* (21 August 1973) UN Doc. A/AC.138/97.

Report of the Committee on the Peaceful uses of the Sea-Bed and the Ocean Floor Beyond the Limits of National Jurisdiction, *Draft Ocean Space Treaty – Working Paper Submitted by Malta* (16 July 1971) UN Doc. A/AC.138/53.

Report of the Committee on the Peaceful uses of the Sea-Bed and the Ocean Floor Beyond the Limits of National Jurisdiction, *International Sea-Bed Régime and Machinery Working Paper, submitted by the Delegation of Canada* (24 August 1971) UN Doc. A/AC.138/59.

Report of the Committee on the Peaceful uses of the Sea-Bed and the Ocean Floor Beyond the Limits of National Jurisdiction, *International Sea-Bed Régime: United Kingdom Proposals for Elements of a Convention* (30 July 1971) UN Doc. A/AC.138/46.

Report of the Fifth Committee, *Programme budget for the biennium 2004-2005* (6 April 2005) UN Doc. A/59/448/Add.3.

Report of the Fifth Committee, *Programme budget for the biennium 2006-2007* (10 April 2007) UN Doc. A/61/592/Add.4.

Report of the Study Group of the International Law Commission, *Fragmentation of International Law: Difficulties Arising from the Diversification and Expansion of International Law: Finalized by Martti Koskenniemi* (13 April 2006) UN Doc. A/CN.4/L.682.

Ricardo J. Alfaro, *Report on the Question of International Criminal Jurisdiction by Ricardo J. Alfaro, Special Rapporteur* (3 March 1950) UN Doc. A/CN.4/15 (1950).

Rome Statute of the International Criminal Court (adopted 17 July 1998, entered into force 1 July 2002) 2187 UNTS 90.

Rules of Procedure and Evidence (adopted 9 September 2002, entered into force 9 September 2002) Official Records ICC-ASP/1/3 (Part II-A).

Rules of Procedure of the Assembly of States Parties (adopted 8-12 September 2002) Official Records ICC-ASP/1/3/Part.II-A.

Rules of Procedure of the Inter-American Court of Human Rights (adopted 22 November 1969, entered into force 18 July 1978) 1144 UNTS 123.

Seventh United Nations Congress on the Prevention of Crime and the Treatment of Offenders, *United Nations Basic Principles on the Independence of the Judiciary* (1985) available at <http://www.ohchr.org/EN/ProfessionalInterest/Pages/IndependenceJudiciary.aspx> (last visited: 21 March 2014).

Sixth Protocol to the General Agreement on Privileges and Immunities of the Council of Europe (adopted 5 March 1996, entered into force 1 November 1998) CETS No. 162.

Special Agreement relating to the Seat of the Council of Europe (adopted 2 September 1949, entered into force 28 November 1949) CETS No. 3.

Special Court for Sierra Leone, *Rules of Procedure and Evidence* (adopted 16 June 2002, last amended 16 November 2011) available at <http://www.sc-sl.org/DOCUMENTS/tabid/176/Default.aspx> (last visited: 21 March 2014).

Special Court for Sierra Leone, *Transcript: Case No. SCSL-2003-01-T The Prosecutor of the Special Court v. Charles Ghankay Taylor, Wednesday, 16 May 2012, 09.30 a.m, Sentencing Hearing, Trial Chamber II* (16 May 2012) available at <http://www.sc-sl.org/CASES/ProsecutorvsCharlesTaylor/Transcripts/tabid/160/Default.aspx> (last visited: 21 March 2014).

Special Rapporteur on the Independence of Judges and Lawyers, *Independence and Impartiality of the Judiciary, Jurors and Assessors and the Independence of Lawyers: Report of the Special Rapporteur, Param Cumaraswamy, Submitted in Accordance with Commission on Human Rights Resolution 1994/41* (6 February 1995) UN Doc. E/CN.4/1995/39.

Staff Regulations (adopted 12 September 2003, entered into force 12 September 2003) Official Records ICC-ASP/2/Res.2.

Statute of the Central American Court of Justice (1995) 34 ILM 921.

Statute of the Inter-American Court of Human Rights (adopted 31 October 1979, entered into force 1 January 1980) 1144 UNTS 123.

Statute of the International Atomic Energy Agency (adopted 26 October 1956, entered into force 29 July 1957) 276 UNTS 3.

Statute of the International Court of Justice (adopted 26 June 1945, entered into force 24 October 1945) 145 BSP 832.

Statute of the International Tribunal for the Law of the Sea (Annex VI of the United Nations Convention on the Law of the Sea) (adopted 10 December 1982, entered into force 16 November 1994) 1833 UNTS 561.

Statute of the Permanent Court of International Justice (adopted 16 December 1920, entered into force 20 August 1921) 6 LNTS 389.

Statute of the Special Court for Sierra Leone (adopted 16 January 2002) 2178 UNTS 145.

Strengthening the International Criminal Court and the Assembly of States Parties (adopted 10 September 2004) Official Records Resolution ICC-ASP/3/Res.3.

Strengthening the International Criminal Court and the Assembly of States Parties (adopted 10 December 2010) Official Records Resolution ICC-ASP/9/Res.3.

Study Group of the International Law Association on the Practice and Procedure of International Courts and Tribunals and Project on International Courts and Tribunals, *Burgh House Principles on the Independence of the International Judiciary* (2004) available at <http://www.ucl.ac.uk/laws/cict/docs/burgh_final_21204.pdf> (last visited: 21 March 2014).

Sub-Committee on the election of Judges to the European Court of Human Rights, *Procedure for Electing Judges to the European Court of Human Rights – Information Document Prepared by the Secretariat* (11 October 2010) Doc. AS/Jur (2010)12 rev 3.

Third United Nations Conference on the Law of the Sea, *1st Plenary meeting* (3 December 1973) UN Doc. A/CONF.62/SR.1.

Third United Nations Conference on the Law of the Sea, *5th Plenary meeting* (11 December 1973) UN Doc. A/CONF.62/SR.5.

Third United Nations Conference on the Law of the Sea, *51st Plenary meeting* (29 August 1974) UN Doc. A/CONF.62/SR.51.

Third United Nations Conference on the Law of the Sea, *58th Plenary meeting* (5 April 1976) UN Doc. A/CONF.62/SR.58.

Third United Nations Conference on the Law of the Sea, *59th Plenary meeting* (5 April 1976) UN Doc. A/CONF.62/SR.59.

Third United Nations Conference on the Law of the Sea, *60th Plenary meeting* (6 April 1976) UN Doc. A/CONF.62/SR.60.

Third United Nations Conference on the Law of the Sea, *61th Plenary meeting* (6 April 1976) UN Doc. A/CONF.62/SR.61.

Third United Nations Conference on the Law of the Sea, *62nd Plenary meeting* (7 April 1976) UN Doc. A/CONF.62/SR.62.

Third United Nations Conference on the Law of the Sea, *63rd Plenary meeting* (8 April 1976) UN Doc. A/CONF.62/SR.63.

Third United Nations Conference on the Law of the Sea, *64th Plenary meeting* (9 April 1976) UN Doc. A/CONF.62/SR.64.

Third United Nations Conference on the Law of the Sea, *65th Plenary meeting* (12 April 1976) UN Doc. A/CONF.62/SR.65.

Third United Nations Conference on the Law of the Sea, *Informal single negotiating text (part IV)* (21 July 1975) UN Doc. A/CONF.62/WP.9.

Third United Nations Conference on the Law of the Sea, *Informal single negotiating text (part IV)* (6 May 1976) UN Doc. A/CONF.62/WP.9/Rev. 1.

Third United Nations Conference on the Law of the Sea, *Informal single negotiating text, part I* (7 May 1975) UN Doc. A/CONF.62/WP.8/Part I.

Third United Nations Conference on the Law of the Sea, *Revised single negotiating text (part I)* (6 May 1976) UN Doc. A/CONF.62/WP.8/REV.1/Part I.

Third United Nations Conference on the Law of the Sea, *Revised single negotiating text (part IV)* (3 November 1976) UN Doc. A/CONF.62/WP.9/REV.2.

Treaty between Her Majesty and the United States of America, for the Amicable Settlement of all Causes of Differences between the two Countries (adopted 8 May 1871, entered into force 17 June 1871) 61 BSP 40.

Treaty concerning the establishment and the statute of a Benelux Court of Justice (adopted 31 March 1965, entered into force 1 January 1974) 924 UNTS 41.

Treaty Creating the Court of Justice of the Cartagena Agreement (adopted 28 May 1979, entered into force 19 May 1983) 18 ILM 1203.

Treaty of Amity, Commerce and Navigation, between His Britannick Majesty; and The United States of America, by Their President, with the advice and consent of Their Senate (adopted 19 November 1794, entered into force 28 October 1795) 1 BSP 784.

Treaty of Peace and Amity, between His Britannic Majesty and The United States of America (adopted 24 December 1814) 2 BSP 357.

Treaty of Peace between the Allied and Associated Powers and Germany (Versailles Peace Treaty) (signed 28 June 1919, entered into force 10 January 1920) 225 CTS 188.

UN Special Rapporteur on the Study on the Independence of the Judiciary, *Draft Universal Declaration on the Independence of Justice ("Singhvi Declaration")* (1989) E/CN.4/Sub.2/1985/18/Add.5/Rev. 1.

UNGA and UNSC, *Election of five members of the International Court of Justice – Memorandum by the Secretary-General* (26 July 2011) A/66/182–S/2011/452.

UNGA, *"Ethnic Cleansing" and Racial Hatred* (15 March 1993) UN Doc. A/RES/47/80.

UNGA, *91st plenary meeting Official Records* (3 April 2008) UN Doc. A/62/PV.91.

UNGA, *93rd plenary meeting Official Records* (4 April 2007) UN Doc. A/61/PV.93.

UNGA, *Appointment and terms of reference of a United Nations Mediator in Palestine* (14 May 1948) UN Doc. A/RES/186 (S-2).

UNGA, *Conditions of service and compensation for officials other than Secretariat officials: members of the International Court of Justice and judges and ad litem judges of the International Tribunal for the Former Yugoslavia and the International Criminal Tribunal for Rwanda* (3 May 2007) UN Doc. A/RES/61/262.

UNGA, *Conditions of service and compensation for officials other than Secretariat officials: members of the International Court of Justice and judges and ad litem judges of the International Tribunal for the Former Yugoslavia and the International Criminal Tribunal for Rwanda* (3 April 2008) UN Doc. 62/547.

UNGA, *Conditions of service and compensation for officials other than Secretariat officials: members of the International Court of Justice, judges of the International Tribunal for the Former Yugoslavia, judges of the International Tribunal for Rwanda and ad litem judges of the International Tribunal for the Former Yugoslavia* (27 June 2002) UN Doc. A/RES/56/285.

UNGA, *Convening of a second international conference of plenipotentiaries: letter dated 24 April 1958 from the Chairman of the Delegation of Cuba to the President of the Conference* (14 April 1958) UN Doc. A/CONF.13/L.25.

UNGA, *Convening of a Second UN Conference on the Law of the Sea* (10 December 1958) UN Doc. A/RES/1307 (XIII).

UNGA, *Declaration on the Occasion of the Twenty-Fifth Anniversary of the United Nations* (24 October 1970) UN Doc. A/RES/2627 (XXV).

UNGA, *Definition of Aggression* (14 December 1974) UN Doc. A/RES/3314 (XXIX).

UNGA, *Draft Code of Offences against the Peace and Security of Mankind* (10 December 1981) UN Doc. A/RES/36/106.

UNGA, *Establishment of an Interim Committee of the General Assembly* (13 November 1947) UN Doc. A/RES/111 (II).

UNGA, *Establishment of an International Criminal Court* (9 December 1994) UN Doc. A/RES/49/53.

UNGA, *Establishment of an International Criminal Court* (11 December 1995) UN Doc. A/RES/50/46.

UNGA, *Establishment of an International Criminal Court* (15 December 1997) UN Doc. A/RES/52/160.

UNGA, *Establishment of the International Criminal Court* (12 December 2001) UN Doc. A/RES/56/85.

UNGA, *Formulation of the Principles Recognized in the Charter of the Nurnberg Tribunal and in the Judgment of the Tribunal* (21 November 1947) UN Doc. A/RES/177 (II).

UNGA, *International Conference of Plenipotentiaries to Examine the Law of the Sea* (21 February 1957) UN Doc. A/RES/1105 (XI).

UNGA, *International Criminal Jurisdiction* (12 December 1950) UN Doc. A/RES/489 (V).

UNGA, *International Criminal Jurisdiction* (5 December 1952) UN Doc. A/RES/687 (VII).

UNGA, *International criminal responsibility of individuals and entities engaged in illicit trafficking in narcotic drugs across national frontiers and other transnational criminal activities* (4 December 1989) UN Doc. A/RES/44/39.

UNGA, *Letter dated 19 May 1993 from the Chargé dàffaires a.i. of the Permanent Mission of Yugoslavia to the United Nations addressed to the Secretary-General* (21 May 1993) UN Doc. A/48/170 S/25801.

UNGA, *Letter Dated 94/09/28 From the Permanent Representative of Rwanda to the United Nations Addressed to the President of the Security Council* (29 September 1994) UN Doc. S/1994/1115.

UNGA, *Need for Greater use by the United Nations and its Organs of the International Court of Justice* (14 November 1947) UN Doc. A/RES/171 (II).

UNGA, *Observer status for the International Tribunal for the Law of the Sea in the General Assembly* (17 December 1996) UN Doc. A/RES/51/204.

UNGA, *Peaceful Settlement of International Disputes* (12 December 1974) UN Doc. A/RES/3283 (XXIX).

UNGA, *Privileges and Immunities of Members of the International Court of Justice, the Registrar, Officials of the Registry, Assessors, the Agents and Counsel of the Parties and of the Witnesses and Experts* (11 December 1946) UN Doc. A/RES/90 (I).

UNGA, *Proposed programme budget for the biennium 2010-2011 – Part III International justice and law – Section 7 International Court of Justice* (1 April 2009) UN Doc. A/64/6 (Sect. 7).

UNGA, *Proposed programme budget for the biennium 2012-2013 – Part III International justice and law – Section 7 International Court of Justice* (17 March 2011) UN Doc. A/66/6 (Sect. 7).

UNGA, *Provisional Verbatim Record of the 8th Meeting, Held at Headquarters, New York, on Wednesday, 23 September 1992* (23 September 1992) UN Doc. A/47/PV.8.

UNGA, *Questions relating to the programme budget for the biennium 1998–1999* (18 December 1998) UN Doc. A/RES/53/214.

UNGA, *Rape and abuse of women in the areas of armed conflict in the former Yugoslavia* (20 December 1993) UN Doc. A/RES/48/143.

UNGA, *Rape and abuse of women in the areas of armed conflict in the former Yugoslavia* (6 March 1995) UN Doc. A/RES/49/205.

UNGA, *Re-establishment of the Interim Committee of the General Assembly* (3 December 1948) UN Doc. A/RES/196 (III).

UNGA, *Re-establishment of the Interim Committee of the General Assembly* (21 November 1949) UN Doc. A/RES/295 (IV).

UNGA, *Report of the Committee of the Whole* (14 April 1960) UN Doc. A/CONF.19/L.4.

UNGA, *Report of the International Law Commission* (16 December 1970) UN Doc. A/RES/2734 (XXV).

UNGA, *Reservation Exclusively for Peaceful Purposes of the Sea-Bed and the Ocean Floor, and the Subsoil Thereof, Underlying the High Seas beyond the Limits of Present National Jurisdiction and use of their Resources in the Interests of Mankind, and Convening of the Third United Nations Conference on the Law of the Sea* (16 November 1973) UN Doc. A/RES/3067 (XXVIII).

UNGA, *Reservation Exclusively for Peaceful Purposes of the Sea-Bed and the Ocean Floor, and the Subsoil Thereof, Underlying the High Seas beyond the Limits of Present National Jurisdiction and Use of their Resources in the Interests of Mankind, and Convening of a Conference on the Law of the Sea* (17 December 1970) UN Doc. A/RES/2750 (XXV).

UNGA, *Resolution on the Privileges and Immunities of the International Court of Justice* (13 February 1946) UN Doc. A/RES/22(I)C.

UNGA, *Special subjects relating to the programme budget for the biennium 2004–2005* (13 April 2005) UN Doc. A/RES/59/282.

UNGA, *Staff Regulations of the United Nations and provisional Staff Rules* (21 October 2009) UN Doc. ST/SGB/2009/7.

UNGA, *Statute of the Administrative Tribunal of the United Nations (as amended by resolution 782 B (VIII) on 9 December 1953, 957 (X) on 8 November 1955, 50/54 on 11 December 1995, 52/166 on 15 December 1997, 55/159 on 12 December 2000, 58/87 on 9 December 2003, 59/283 of 13 April 2005)* (24 November 1949) UN Doc. A/RES/351 A (IV).

UNGA, *Study by the International Law Commission of the Question of an International Criminal Jurisdiction* (9 December 1948) UN Doc. A/RES/260 (III) B.

UNGA, *Summary of internal Secretariat studies of constitutional questions relating to agencies within the framework of the United Nations* (15 November 1954) UN Doc. A/C.1/758.

UNGA, *The situation in Bosnia and Herzegovina* (18 December 1992) UN Doc. A/RES/47/121.

UNGA, *The situation in Bosnia and Herzegovina* (20 December 1993) UN Doc. A/RES/48/88.

UNGA, *The situation in Bosnia and Herzegovina* (8 November 1994) UN Doc. A/RES/49/10.

UNGA, *United Nations Press Release* (17 September 1993) UN Doc. GA/8500.

United Nations Commission on the Status of Women, *Fourth World Conference on Women, Platform for Action* (17 October 1995) UN Doc. A/CONF.177/20.

United Nations Convention on the Law of the Sea – Meeting of States Parties, *Annual report of the International Tribunal for the Law of the Sea for 2010* (4 April 2011) SPLOS/222.

United Nations Convention on the Law of the Sea – Meeting of States Parties, *Arrangement for the allocation of seats on the International Tribunal for the Law of the Sea and the Commission on the Limits of the Continental Shelf* (26 June 2009) SPLOS/201.

United Nations Convention on the Law of the Sea – Meeting of States Parties, *Decision on adjustment of the remuneration of members of the International Tribunal for the Law of the Sea* (21 June 2005) SPLOS/132.

United Nations Convention on the Law of the Sea – Meeting of States Parties, *Decision on budgetary matters of the International Tribunal for the Law of the Sea for 2005-2006* (23 June 2004) SPLOS/117.

United Nations Convention on the Law of the Sea – Meeting of States Parties, *Decision on budgetary matters of the International Tribunal for the Law of the Sea for 2007-2008* (23 June 2006) SPLOS/145.

United Nations Convention on the Law of the Sea – Meeting of States Parties, *Decision on budgetary matters of the International Tribunal for the Law of the Sea for 2009-2010* (20 June 2008) SPLOS/180.

United Nations Convention on the Law of the Sea – Meeting of States Parties, *Decision on Pension Scheme Regulations for Members of the International Tribunal for the Law of the Sea* (7 June 1999) SPLOS/47.

United Nations Convention on the Law of the Sea – Meeting of States Parties, *Decisions on Budgetary Matters of the International Tribunal for the Law of the Sea for 2011-2012* (9 July 2010) SPLOS/217.

United Nations Convention on the Law of the Sea – Meeting of States Parties, *Election of seven members of the International Tribunal for the Law of the Sea – List of candidates nominated by States Parties* (15 March 2011) SPLOS/219.

United Nations Convention on the Law of the Sea – Meeting of States Parties, *Election of seven members of the International Tribunal for the Law of the Sea – List of candidates nominated by States Parties* (11 March 2008) SPLOS/171.

United Nations Convention on the Law of the Sea – Meeting of States Parties, *Election of seven members of the International Tribunal for the Law of the Sea – List of candidates nominated by States Parties: withdrawal of a candidate* (2 April 2008) SPLOS/171/Add.1.

United Nations Convention on the Law of the Sea – Meeting of States Parties, *First Elections of the Members of the International Tribunal for the Law of the Sea* (31 July 1996) SPLOS/L.3/REV.1.

United Nations Convention on the Law of the Sea – Meeting of States Parties, *Meeting of States Parties to Law of Sea Convention 136th-137th Meetings (AM & PM) – States Parties to Convention on Law of the Sea Hear Briefing by International Tribunal President, on Draft Budget Proposals, Other Financial Matters* (15 June 2010) SEA/1941.

United Nations Convention on the Law of the Sea – Meeting of States Parties, *Report of the twenty-first Meeting of States Parties* (29 June 2011) SPLOS/231.

United Nations Convention on the Law of the Sea – Meeting of States Parties, *Revised Budget Estimates for the International Tribunal for the Law of the Sea Covering the Period 1996-1997* (10 April 1996) SPLOS/WP.3/Rev. 1.

United Nations Convention on the Law of the Sea – Meeting of States Parties, *Rules of Procedure for Meetings of States Parties* (24 January 2005) SPLOS/2/Rev. 4.

United Nations Diplomatic Conference of Plenipotentiaries on the Establishment of an International Criminal Court, *Final Act of the United Nations Diplomatic Conference of Plenipotentiaries on the Establishment of an International Criminal Court* (17 July 1998) UN Doc. A/CONF.183/10.

United Nations Diplomatic Conference of Plenipotentiaries on the Establishment of an International Criminal Court, *Summary Record of the 9th Plenary Meeting* (17 July 1998) UN Doc. A/CONF.183/SR.9.

Universal Declaration of Human Rights 10 December 1948 GA Res. 217A (III), UN Doc. A/810 at 71 (1948).

UNSC, (22 December 2010) UN Doc. S/RES/1966 (2010).

UNSC, *Additional deployment to Sarajevo airport* (13 July 1992) UN Doc. S/RES/764 (1992).

UNSC, *Adjustment of the mandate of the UN Assistance Mission for Rwanda due to the current situation in Rwanda and settlement of the Rwandan conflict* (21 April 1994) UN Doc. S/RES/912 (1994).

UNSC, *Establishment of an international tribunal for the prosecution of persons responsible for serious violations of international humanitarian law committed in the territory of the former Yugoslavia* (27 August 1997) UN Doc. S/RES/1126 (1997).

UNSC, *Extension of the mandate and deployment of the 2 additional battalions of the UN Assistance Mission for Rwanda and settlement of the conflict in Rwanda* (8 June 1994) UN Doc. S/RES/925 (1994).

UNSC, *Former Yugoslavia* (13 August 1992) UN Doc. S/RES/771 (1992).

UNSC, *Former Yugoslavia* (6 October 1992) UN Doc. S/RES/780 (1992).

UNSC, *International Criminal Tribunal for Rwanda* (19 May 2003) UN Doc. S/RES/1482 (2003).

UNSC, *International Criminal Tribunal for the Prosecution of Persons Responsible for Genocide and Other Serious Violations of International Humanitarian Law Committed in the Territory of Rwanda and Rwandan Citizens Responsible for Genocide and Other Such Violations Committed in the Territory of Neighbouring States between 1 January and 31 December 1994* (13 June 2006) UN Doc. S/RES/1684 (2006).

UNSC, *International Criminal Tribunal for the Prosecution of Persons Responsible for Genocide and Other Serious Violations of International Humanitarian Law Committed in the Territory of Rwanda and Rwandan Citizens Responsible for Genocide and Other Such Violations Committed in the Territory of Neighbouring States between 1 January and 31 December 1994* (18 July 2008) UN Doc. S/RES/1824 (2008).

UNSC, *International Criminal Tribunal for the Prosecution of Persons Responsible for Genocide and Other Serious Violations of International Humanitarian Law Committed in the Territory of Rwanda and Rwandan Citizens Responsible for Genocide and Other Such Violations Committed in the Territory of Neighbouring States between 1 January and 31 December 1994* (7 July 2009) UN Doc. S/RES/1878 (2009).

UNSC, *International Criminal Tribunal for the Prosecution of Persons Responsible for Genocide and Other Serious Violations of International Humanitarian Law Committed in the Territory of Rwanda and Rwandan Citizens Responsible for Genocide and Other Such Violations Committed in the Territory of Neighbouring States between 1 January and 31 December 1994* (29 June 2010) UN Doc. S/RES/1932 (2010).

UNSC, *International Criminal Tribunal for the Prosecution of Persons Responsible for Genocide and Other Serious Violations of International Humanitarian Law Committed in the Territory of Rwanda and Rwandan Citizens Responsible for Genocide and Other Such Violations Committed in the Territory of Neighbouring States between 1 January and 31 December 1994* (21 December 2011) UN Doc. S/RES/2029 (2011).

UNSC, *International Tribunal for the Prosecution of Persons Responsible for Serious Violations of International Humanitarian Law Committed in the Territory of the Former Yugoslavia since 1991* (29 September 2008) UN Doc. S/RES/1837 (2008).

UNSC, *International Tribunal for the Prosecution of Persons Responsible for Serious Violations of International Humanitarian Law Committed in the Territory of the Former Yugoslavia since 1991* (7 July 2009) UN Doc. S/RES/1877 (2009).

UNSC, *International Tribunal for the Prosecution of Persons Responsible for Serious Violations of International Humanitarian Law Committed in the Territory of the Former Yugoslavia since 1991* (16 December 2009) UN Doc. S/RES/1900 (2009).

UNSC, *International Tribunal for the Prosecution of Persons Responsible for Serious Violations of International Humanitarian Law Committed in the Territory of the Former Yugoslavia since 1991* (29 June 2010) UN Doc. S/RES/1931 (2010).

UNSC, *International Tribunal for the Prosecution of Persons Responsible for Serious Violations of International Humanitarian Law Committed in the Territory of the Former Yugoslavia since 1991* (29 June 2011) UN Doc. S/RES/1993 (2011).

UNSC, *On the appointment of the Prosecutor of the International Tribunal for the Prosecution of Persons Responsible for Serious Violations of International Humanitarian Law Committed in the Territory of the Former Yugoslavia since 1991* (8 July 1994) UN Doc. S/RES/936 (1994).

UNSC, *On the decision to designate Arusha as the seat of the International Tribunal for Rwanda* (22 February 1995) UN Doc. S/RES/977 (1995).

UNSC, *Provisional Verbatim Record of the 3175th Meeting, Held at Headquarters, New York, on Monday, 22 February 1993* (22 February 1993) UN Doc. S/PV.3175.

UNSC, *Reports of the Secretary-General on the Sudan* (31 March 2005) UN Doc. S/RES/1593 (2005).

UNSC, *Requesting the Secretary-General to establish a Commission of Experts to examine violations of international humanitarian law committed in Rwanda* (1 July 1994) UN Doc. S/RES/935 (1994).

UNSC, *Security Council 3453rd Meeting, Tuesday, 8 November 1994* (8 November 1994) UN Doc. S/PV.3453.

UNSC, *Statute of the International Tribunal for Rwanda* (8 November 1994) UN Doc. S/RES/955 (1994).

UNSC, *Statute of the International Tribunal for the Former Yugoslavia* (25 May 1993) UN Doc. S/RES/827 (1993).

UNSC, *The expansion of the mandate of the UN Assistance Mission for Rwanda and imposition of an arms embargo on Rwanda* (17 May 1994) UN Doc. S/RES/918 (1994).

UNSC, *The International Tribunal for the former Yugoslavia (ICTY)* (13 May 1998) UN Doc. S/RES/1166.

UNSC, *Tribunal (Former Yugoslavia)* (20 August 1993) UN Doc. S/RES/857 (1993).

UNSC, *Tribunal (Former Yugoslavia)* (21 October 1993) UN Doc. S/RES/877 (1993).

UNSC, *Tribunal (Former Yugoslavia)* (22 February 1993) UN Doc. S/RES/808 (1993).

UNSC, *Tribunal (Former Yugoslavia)* (25 May 1993) UN Doc. S/RES/827 (1993).

UNSC, *Tribunal (Rwanda)* (8 November 1994) UN Doc. S/RES/955 (1994).

UNSG, *Conditions of service and compensation for officials other than Secretariat officials* (2 November 2006) UN Doc. A/61/554.

UNSG, *Conditions of service and compensation for officials other than Secretariat officials: members of the International Court of Justice and judges and ad litem judges of the International Tribunal for the Former Yugoslavia and the International Criminal Tribunal for Rwanda: Report of the Secretary General* (8 November 2007) UN Doc. A/62/538.

UNSG, *Conditions of service and compensation for officials other than Secretariat officials: members of the International Court of Justice and judges and ad litem judges of the International Tribunal for the Former Yugoslavia and the International Criminal Tribunal for Rwanda: Report of the Secretary General* (15 July 2010) UN Doc. A/65/134.

UNSG, *Election of judges of the International Criminal Tribunal for the Prosecution of Persons Responsible for Genocide and Other Serious Violations of International Humanitarian Law Committed in the Territory of Rwanda and Rwandan Citizens Responsible for Genocide and Other Such Violations Committed in the Territory of Neighbouring States between 1 January and 31 December 1994 – Memorandum by the Secretary-General* (13 December 2002) UN Doc. A/57/492.

UNSG, *Election of judges of the International Criminal Tribunal for the Prosecution of Persons Responsible for Genocide and Other Serious Violations of International Humanitarian Law Committed in the Territory of Rwanda and Rwandan Citizens Responsible for Genocide and Other Such Violations Committed in the Territory of Neighbouring States between 1 January and 31 December 1994 – Memorandum by the Secretary-General* (3 April 2001) UN Doc. A/55/872.

UNSG, *Election of judges of the International Criminal Tribunal for the Prosecution of Persons Responsible for Genocide and Other Serious Violations of International Humanitarian Law Committed inthe Territory of Rwanda and Rwandan Citizens Responsible for Genocide and Other Such Violations Committed inthe Territory of Neighbouring States between 1 January and 31 December 1994 – Memorandum by the Secretary-General* (2 May 1995) UN Doc. A/49/893.

UNSG, *Election of judges of the International Tribunal for the Prosecution of Persons Responsible for Serious Violations of International Humanitarian Law Committed in the Territory of the Former Yugoslavia since 1991 – Memorandum by the Secretary-General* (21 October 2004) UN Doc. A/59/438.

UNSG, *Election of judges of the International Criminal Tribunal for the Prosecutionof Persons Responsible for Genocide and Other Serious Violations of International Humanitarian Law Committed inthe Territory of Rwanda and Rwandan Citizens Responsible for Genocide and Other Such Violations Committed inthe Territory of Neighbouring States between 1 January and 31 December 1994 – Memorandum by the Secretary-General* (1 October 1998) UN Doc. A/53/443.

UNSG, *Election of judges of the International Tribunal for the Prosecution of Persons Responsible for Serious Violations of International Humanitarian Law Committed in the Territory of the Former Yugoslavia since 1991 – Memorandum by the Secretary-General* (16 September 1998) UN Doc. A/53/351.

UNSG, *Election of judges of the International Tribunal for the Prosecution of Persons Responsible for Serious Violations of International Humanitarian Law Committed in the Territory of the Former Yugoslavia since 1991 – Memorandum by the Secretary-General* (18 April 1997) UN Doc. A/51/877.

UNSG, *Election of judges of the International Tribunal for the Prosecution of Persons Responsible for Serious Violations of International Humanitarian Law Committed in the Territory of the Former Yugoslavia since 1991 – Memorandum by the Secretary-General* (26 August 1996) UN Doc. A/47/1005.

UNSG, *Financial Regulations and Rules of the United Nations* (9 May 2003) UN Doc. ST/SGB/2003/7.

UNSG, *Identical letters dated 5 May 1998 from the Secretary-General addressed to the President of the General Assembly and the President of the Security Council* (6 May 1998) UN Doc. S/1998/376.

UNSG, *Report of the International Tribunal for the Prosecution of Persons Responsible for Serious Violations of International Humanitarian Law Committed in the Territory of the Former Yugoslavia since 1991 – Note by the Secretary-General* (29 August 1994) UN Doc. A/49/342.

UNSG, *Report of the Secretary-General – Conditions of service for the judges of the International Criminal Tribunal for the Former Yugoslavia and the International Criminal Tribunal for Rwanda* (22 October 1997) UN Doc. A/52/520.

UNSG, *Report of the Secretary-General – Proposed Programme Budget for the Biennium 1996-1997 – Conditions of service and compensation for officials other than Secretariat officials, Members of the International Court of Justice* (2 November 1995) UN Doc. A/C.5/50/18.

UNSG, *Report of the Secretary-General – The rule of law and transitional justice in conflict and post-conflict societies* (23 August 2004) UN Doc. S/2004/616.

UNSG, *Report of the Secretary-General Pursuant to Paragraph 2 of Security Council Resolution 808 (1993)* (3 May 1993) UN Doc. S/25704.

UNSG, *Report of the Secretary-General Pursuant to Paragraph 5 of Security Council Resolution 955 (1994)* (13 February 1995) UN Doc. S/1995/134.

UNSG, *Statement by the President of the Security Council Condemning Slaughter of Civilians in Kigali and Other Parts of Rwanda* (30 April 1994) UN Doc. S/PRST/1994/21.

Vienna Convention on the Law of Treaties (adopted 23 May 1969, entered into force 27 January 1980) 1155 UNTS 331.

IV. Table of Cases

1. International Courts and Human Rights Bodies

Advisory opinion on certain legal questions concerning the lists of candidates submitted with a view to the election of judges to the European Court of Human (ECtHR [Grand Chamber]) Advisory Opinion No. 1 (12 February 2008).

Aerial Incident of 10 August 1999 (Pakistan v India) (Jurisdiction of the Court) ICJ Rep. 12 (2000).

Ahmet Sadik v. Greece (ECtHR) Application No. 18877/91 (15 November 1996).

Al-Nashif v. Bulgaria (ECtHR) Application No. 50963/99 (20 June 2002).

Anglo-Iranian Oil Co. (United Kingdom v. Iran) ICJ Rep. 93 (1952).

Anglo-Iranian Oil Co. Case (Jurisdiction), Judgment of July 22nd, 1952 (Dissenting Opinion of Judge Levi Carneiro) ICJ Rep. 93 (1952).

Anni Äärelä and Jouni Näkkäläjärvi v. Finland (Human Rights Committee) Communication No. 779/1997 (4 February 1997).

Application for Review of Judgement No. 158 of the United Nations Administrative Tribunal (Advisory Opinion) ICJ Rep. 166 (1973).

Application for Review of Judgement No. 273 of the United Nations Administrative Tribunal (Advisory Opinion) (Separate Opinion of Judge Mosler) ICJ Rep. 325 (1982).

Application of the Convention on the Prevention and Punishment of the Crime of Genocide (Bosnia and Herzegovina v Serbia and Montenegro) (Order of 13 September 1993) (Separate Opinion of Judge Lauterpacht) ICJ Rep. 407 (1993).

Arbitral Award of 31 July 1989 (Guinea-Bissau v Senegal) ICJ Rep. 53 (1991).

Avocats Sans Frontières (on behalf of Bwampamye) v. Burundi (African Commission on Human and Peoples' Rights) Communication No. 231/99 (6 November 2000).

Barcelona Traction, Light and Power Co Ltd (New Application: 1962) (Belgium v Spain) (Preliminary Objections) (Judge Tanaka Separate Opinion) ICJ Rep. 65 (1964).

Barcelona Traction, Light and Power Co Ltd (New Application: 1962) (Belgium v Spain) (Second Phase) (Separate Opinion of Judge Tanaka) ICJ Rep. 114 (1970).

Barcelona Traction, Light and Power Company, Limited (Belgium v. Spain) (Preliminary Objections) ICJ Rep. 6 (1964).

Betayev and Betayeva v. Russia (ECtHR) Application No. 37315/03 (29 May 2008).

Bramelid and Malmström v. Sweden (ECommHR) Applications No. 8588/79; 8589/79 (12 December 1983).

C.G. and Others v. Bulgaria (ECtHR) Application No. 1365/07 (24 April 2008).

Case 26/62 NV Algemene Transport- en Expeditie Onderneming van Gend & Loos v Netherlands Inland Revenue Administration ECR 1 (1963).

Case concerning Land Reclamation by Singapore in and around the Straits of Johor (Malaysia v Singapore) Request for provisional measures (Order) ITLOS Case No. 12 (8 October 2003).

Case concerning the Aerial Incident of July 27th, 1955 (Israel v. Bulgaria) (Preliminary Objections) ICJ Rep. 127 (1959).

Case concerning the Conservation and Sustainable Exploitation of Swordfish Stocks in the South-Eastern Pacific Ocean (Chile/European Union) Order 2009/1 ITLOS Case No. 7 (16 December 2009).

Case of Liu v. Russia (ECtHR) Application No. 42086/05 (6 December 2007).

Case of Loizidou v. Turkey (Preliminary Objections) (ECtHR) Application No. 15318/89 (23 March 1995).

Certain Phosphate Lands in Nauru (Nauru v. Australia) ICJ Rep. 240 (1992).

Certain Property (Liechtenstein v Germany) (Preliminary Objections) ICJ Rep. 6 (2005).

Civil Liberties Organisation, Legal Defence Centre, Legal Defence and Assistance Project v. Nigeria (African Commission on Human and Peoples' Rights) Comm. No. 218/98 (1998).

Conditions of Admission of a State to Membership in the United Nations (Article 4 of the Charter) (Advisory Opinion) ICJ Rep. 57 (1948).

Conditions of Admission of a State to Membership in the United Nations (Article 4 of the Charter) (Order) (Dissenting Opinion by M. Zoričič (translation)) ICJ Rep. 94 (1948).

De Cubber v. Belgium (ECtHR) Application No. 9186/80 (26 October 1984).

Delcourt v. Belgium (ECtHR) Application No. 2689/65 (17 January 1970).

Demicoli v. Malta (ECommHR) Application No. 13057/87 (15 March 1990).

Demicoli v. Malta (ECtHR) Application No. 13057/87 (27 August 1991).

Effect of Awards of Compensation Made by the United Nations Administrative Tribunal (Advisory Opinion) ICJ Rep. 47 (1954).

Fischer v. Austria (ECtHR) Application No. 16922/90 (26 April 1995).

Frontier Dispute (Benin/Niger) ICJ Rep. 90 (2005).

Gabčíkovo-Nagymaros Project (Hungary/Slovakia) ICJ Rep. 7 (1997).

Gekhayeva and others v. Russia (ECtHR) Application No. 1755/04 (29 May 2008).

Habeas Corpus in Emergency Situations (Arts. 27(2), 25(1) and 7(6) American Convention on Human Rights), Advisory Opinion (IACtHR) OC-8/87 (30 January 1987).

Ibragimov and others v. Russia (ECtHR) Application No. 34561/03 (29 May 2008).

Interpretation of Peace Treaties with Bulgaria, Hungary and Romania (Advisory Opinion) ICJ Rep. 65 (1950).

Interpretation of the Agreement of 25 March 1951 between the WHO and Egypt (Advisory Opinion) ICJ Rep. 73 (1980).

Ireland v. The United Kingdom (ECtHR) Application No. 5310/71 (18 January 1978).

James and others v. The United Kingdom (ECtHR) Application No. 8793/79 (21 February 1986).

Judgments of the Administrative Tribunal of the ILO upon Complaints Made against UNESCO (Advisory Opinion) (Separate Opinion of Judge Winiarski (translation)) ICJ Rep. 104 (1956).

Judgments of the Administrative Tribunal of the ILO upon Complaints Made against UNESCO (Advisory Opinion) (Separate Opinion of Judge Winiarski) ICJ Rep. 104 (1956).

Judicial Guarantees in States of Emergency (Arts. 27(2), 25 and 8 of the American Convention on Human Rights), Advisory Opinion (IACtHR) OC-9/87 (6 October 1987).

LaGrand Case (Germany v United States of America) (Judgment) ICJ Rep. 466 (2001).

Land and Maritime Boundury between Cameroon and Nigeria (Cameroon v. Nigeria: Equatorial Guineu intervening) ICJ Rep. 303 (2002).

Land, Island and Maritime Frontier Dispute (El Salvador/Honduras: Nicaragua intervening) ICJ Rep. 351 (1992).

Land, Island and Maritime Frontier Dispute (El Salvador/Honduras: Nicaragua intervening) (Order) (Dissenting Opinion of Judge Shahabuddeen) ICJ Rep. 18 (1990).

Land, Island and Maritime Frontier Dispute (El Salvador/Honduras: Nicaragua intervening) (Order) (Dissenting Opinion of Judge Tarassov) ICJ Rep. 11 (1990).

Langborger v. Sweden (ECtHR) Application No. 11179/84 (22 June 1989).

Lawless v. Ireland (ECtHR) Application No. 332/57 (14 November 1960).

Legal Consequences for States of the Continued Presence of South Africa in Namibia (South West Africa) notwithstanding Security Council Resolution 276 (1970) (Advisory Opinion) ICJ Rep. 16 (1971).

Legal Consequences of the Construction of a Wall in the Occupied Palestinian Territory (Advisory Opinion) ICJ Rep. 136 (2004).

Legal Consequences of the Construction of a Wall in the Occupied Palestinian Territory (Order) ICJ Rep. 3 (2004).

Legal Consequences of the Construction of a Wall in the Occupied Palestinian Territory (Order) (Dissenting Opinion of Judge Buergenthal) ICJ Rep. 7 (2004).

Legality of the Threat or Use of Nuclear Weapons (Advisory Opinion) ICJ Rep. 226 (1996).

Legality of the Use by a State of Nuclear Weapons in Armed Conflict (Advisory Opinion) ICJ Rep. 66 (1996).

Legality of Use of Force (Serbia and Montenegro v. Belgium) Joint declaration of Vice-President Ranjeva, Judges Guillaume, Higgins, Kooijmans, Al Khasawneh, Buergenthal and Elaraby ICJ Rep. 330 (2004).

Marckx v. Belgium (ECtHR) Application No. 6833/74 (13 June 1979).

Maria Grazia Loria-Albanese c/ Secrétaire Général (Council of Europe Administrative Tribunal) Recours No. 255/1999 (27 March 2000).

Military and Paramilitary Activities in and against Nicaragua (Nicaragua v United States of America) (Merits) ICJ Rep. 14 (1986).

Military and Paramilitary Activities in and against Nicaragua (Nicaragua v United States of America) (Merits) (Separate opinion of Judge Lachs) ICJ Rep. 14 (1986).

Military and Paramilitary Activities in and against Nicaragua (Nicaragua v. United States of America) (Jurisdiction and Admissibility) (Judgment) ICJ Rep. 392 (1984).

Neumeister v. Austria (ECtHR) Application No. 1936/63 (27 June 1968).

Norris v. Ireland (ECtHR) Application No. 10581/83 (26 October 1988).

Pétur Thór Sigurðsson v. Iceland (ECtHR) Application No. 39731/98 (10 July 2003).

Piersack v. Belgium (ECtHR) Application No. 8692/79 (1 October 1982).

Prosecutor v. Dario Kordić & Mario Čerkez, Bureau Decision "Prosecution's Motion regarding the Trial Chamber's Decision of 12 June 2003" (ICTY) IT-95-14/2-PT (4 May 1998).

Prosecutor v. Dario Kordić & Mario Čerkez, Judgement (ICTY) Case No. IT-95-14/2-A (17 December 2004).

Prosecutor v. Dragan Nikolić, Judgement on Sentencing Appeal (ICTY) Case No. IT-94-2-I (4 February 2005).

Prosecutor v. Dragan Nikolić, Sentencing Judgement (ICTY) Case No. IT-94-2-S (18 December 2003).

Prosecutor v. Duško Tadić, Appeals Chamber, Decision on the defence motion for interlocutory appeal on jurisdiction (ICTY) Case No. IT-94-1-AR72 (2 October 1995).

Prosecutor v. Duško Tadić, Appeals Chamber, Judgement (ICTY) Case No. IT-94-1-A (15 July 1999).

Prosecutor v. Duško Tadić, Decision on Defence Motion of Jurisdiction (ICTY) Case No. IT-94-1 (10 August 1995).

Prosecutor v. Furundžija, Appeals Chamber, Judgement (ICTY) Case No. IT-95-17/1-A (21 July 2000).

Prosecutor v. Furundžija, Appellant's Reply Brief (Public Version) (ICTY) Case No. IT-95-17/1-A (23 June 2000).

Prosecutor v. Furundžija, Defendant's Amended Appellate Brief (Public Version) (ICTY) Case No. IT-95-17/1-A (23 June 2000).

Prosecutor v. Furundžija, Respondent's Brief of the Prosecution (Public Version) (ICTY) Case No. IT-95-17/1-A (30 September 1999 (public version on 28 June 2000)).

Prosecutor v. Furundžija, Trial Chamber, Judgement (ICTY) Case No. IT-95-17/1-T (10 December 1998).

Prosecutor v. Milorad Krnojelac, Judgement (ICTY) Case No. IT-97-25-A (17 September 2003).

Prosecutor v. Momir Nikolić, Sentencing Judgement (ICTY) Case No. IT-02-60/1-S (2 December 2003).

Prosecutor v. Radoslav Brdjanin, Decision on Application for Disqualification (ICTY) Case No. IT-99-36-R77 (11 June 2003).

Prosecutor v. Sesay, Decision on Defence Motion Seeking the Disqualification of Justice Robertson from the Appeals Chamber (ICTR) Case No. SCSL-2004-15-AR15, A.Ch. (12 March 2004).

Prosecutor v. Zejnil Delalic, Zdravko Mucic (aka "Pavo"), Hazim Delic and Esad Landžo (aka "Zenga") ("Čelebići Case"), Judgement (ICTY) Case No. IT-96-21-A (20 February 2001).

Prosecutor v. Zejnil Delalić, Zdravko Mucić (aka "Pavo"), Hazim Delić and Esad Landžo (aka "Zenga") (ICTY) Case No. IT-96-21-A (20 February 2001).

Prosecutor v. Zejnil Delalić, Zdravko Mucić (aka "Pavo"), Hazim Delić and Esad Landžo (aka "Zenga"), Decision of the Bureau on Motion to disqualify Judges pursuant to Rule 15 or in the Alternative that certain Judges recuse themselves (ICTY) Case No. IT-96-21-A (25 October 1999).

Prosecutor v. Zejnil Delalić, Zdravko Mucić (aka "Pavo"), Hazim Delić and Esad Landžo (aka "Zenga"), Decision of the Bureau on Motion to disqualify Judges pursuant to Rule 15 or in the Alternative that certain Judges recuse themselves, Declaration of Judge Shahabuddeen (ICTY) Case No. IT-96-21-A (25 October 1999).

Reparation for injuries suffered in the service of the United Nations (Advisory Opinion) ICJ Rep. 174 (1949).

Ringeisen v. Austria (ECtHR) Application No. 2614/65 (16 July 1971).

Sangariyeva and others v. Russia (ECtHR) Application No. 1839/04 (29 May 2008).

South West Africa (Ethiopia v. South Africa; Liberia v. South Africa) (Order of 18 March 1965) ICJ Rep. 3 (1965).

South West Africa (Ethiopia v. South Africa; Liberia v. South Africa) (Second Phase) ICJ Rep. 6 (1966).

Southern Bluefin Tuna Cases (New Zealand v. Japan; Australia v. Japan) Requests for provisional measures (Order) ITLOS Cases Nos 3 and 4 (27 August 1999).

Swedish Engine Drivers' Union v. Sweden (ECtHR) Application No. 5614/72 (6 February 1976).

The 'Wimbledon' (Government of His Britannic Majesty v German Empire) PCIJ Series A No. 1 (1922).

The M/V 'SAIGA' (No 2) Case (Saint Vincent and the Grenadines v Guinea) Request for provisional measures (Order) ITLOS Case No. 2 (11 March 1998).

The Prosecutor of the Tribunal against Dragan Nikolić (ICTY) Case No. IT-94-2-I (4 November 1994).

The Prosecutor v. Jean-Paul Akayesu (ICTR) Case No. ICTR-96-4-T (2 September 1998).

The Prosecutor versus Joseph Kanyabashi (ICTR) Case No. ICTR-96-15-T (18 June 1997).

UN Sub-Commission on Prevention of Discrimination and Protection of Minorities, Report of the Sub-Commission on Prevention of Discrimination and Protections of Minorities on its 46th Session, The Administration of Justice and the Human Rights of Detainees (UNCHR) UN Doc. E/CN.4/Sub.2/1994/24 (3 June 1994).

Zand v. Austria (ECommHR) Application No. 7360/76 (12 October 1978).

2. Arbitration Awards

Bering Sea (Fur Seal) Arbitration (United Kingdom v United States of America) (Arbitration Tribunal) International Environmental Law Reports, Vol. I, 43 (1893).

Lake Lancoux Arbitration (Spain v France) (Arbitral Tribunal) 12 RIAA 281 (1957).

Pious Fund (United States of America v Mexico) 9 RIAA 11 (1902).

3. National Courts

Board of Com'rs of White County v Gwin 36 N.E. 237 (1894).

Bundesgerichtshof (BGH) RiZ(R) 5/09 (21 October 2010).

Bundesverfassungsgericht (BVerfG) BVerfGE 27, 211 (14 November 1969).

Colt and Glover v. Bishop of Coventry ("Case of Commendams") (King's Bench) Hobart's Reports 140:6 (1616).

Decision by the Appellate Committee of the House of Lords, Lead Opinion of Lord Browne-Wilkinson (House of Lords) 2 W.L.R. 272 (15 January 1999).

Judges 46 Am.Jur. 2d (1994).

President of the Republic of South Africa and Others v. South African Rugby Football Union and Others, Judgement on Recusal Application (Constitutional Court of South Africa) (7) BCLR 725 (CC) (3 June 1999).

Prohibitions Del Roy (King's Bench Division) 77 E.R. 1342 (1616).

R v. Bow Street Metropolitan Stipendiary Magistrate and others, ex parte Pinochet Ugarte (No 2) (House of Lords (England and Wales)) 1 All ER 577 (1999).

R v. Gough (House of Lords) A.C. 646 (1993).

R. v. Sussex Justices, ex p. McCarthy (King's Bench Division) (King's Bench Division) 1 K.B. 256 (1924).

R.D.S. v. The Queen (Supreme Court of Canada) 3 S.C.R. 484 (27 September 1997).

Re JRL; Ex parte CJL (Supreme Court of Canada) CLR 343, 352 (1986).

Re Polities; Ex parte Hoyts Corporation Pty Ltd (High Court of Australia) 173 CLR 78 (1991).

Trail Smelter Case (United States of America v Canada) (Arbitral Tribunal) 3 RIAA 1907 (1941).

U.S. v. Bremers et al. (US Supreme Court) 195 F. 3d 221, 226 [5th Cir.] (1999).

Valente v. The Queen 2 SCR 673 (1985).

Webb v. The Queen (High Court of Australia) 181 CLR 41 (30 June 1994).

V. Press

Chapman, James, 'Day we stood up to Europe: In an unprecedented move, MPs reject European court's ruling that prisoners must get the vote' *Mail Online* (11 February 2011).

Editor, 'Do us rights' *The Sun* (11 February 2011).

Flügge, Christoph, 'UN Tribunal Judge on the Karadžić Trial: 'A Victory for Justice'' *Der Spiegel* (7 September 2009).

Getz, Arlene, 'Rocking The Courtroom – The ICC Prosecutor on His Work, Human Rights and Sudan' *Newsweek* (21 March 2009).

Greenhouse, Steven, 'US, Having Won Changes, Is Set to Sign Law of the Sea' *New York Times* (1 July 1994).

Lyle, Tara, 'Is the European Court of Human Rights the Villain it is Being Presented as?' *The Independent* (19 April 2012).

Morris, Harvey, 'Britain vs. the European Court of Human Rights' *International Herald Tribune* (19 April 2012).

Müller-Neuhof, Jost, 'Rechthaber gesucht' *Der Tagesspiegel* (20 Juni 2010).

Musoke, Cyprian, 'ICC boss launches war victims office' *The New Vision* (4 June 2010).

Online edition, 'Lavrov warns UN court against tackling Georgia's lawsuit' *The Voice of Russia* (16 September 2010).

Patrick, Angela, 'Don't believe the myth: Strasbourg is doing a good job' *The Guardian* (17 April 2012).

Ratnesar, Romesh, 'The Don Quixote of Darfur' *Time* (2 November 2007).

Scharf, Michael, 'Indicted for War Crimes, the What?' *Washington Post* (3 October 1999).

Simons, Marlise, 'Argentine Prosecutor Turns Focus to New War Crimes Court' *The New York Times* (29 September 2003).

Slack, James, 'UK judge who went native in Strasbourg' *Daily Mail* (25 January 2012).

Stone, Norman, 'Dubrovnik: the case for a war crime trial – why not restore the Nuremberg Tribunal?' *Guardian* (13 November 1991).

Vermin, J, 'Crossing the line' *Russia Law Online* (26 May 2010).

VI. Other Sources

'Assembly of States Parties to the Rome Statute of the International Criminal Court – Election of the Judges of the International Criminal Court – Election to Fill Three Judicial Vacancies (Sixth Session of the Assembly of States Parties, held from 30 November to 14 December 2007) – Results' available at <http://www.icc-cpi.int/NR/rdonlyres/1A306C85-5B10-486C-8644-9F16E7476C56/277120/Election_of_Judgesbasic30Nov 2100.pdf> (last visited: 21 March 2014).

'Cambridge Advanced Learner's Dictionary' available at <http://dictionary.cambridge.org/> (last visited: 21 March 2014).

'Commission on the Status of Women – Follow-up to Beijing and Beijing +5' available at <http://www.un.org/womenwatch/daw/csw/index.html#terms> (last visited: 21 March 2014).

Congress of North American Bosniaks, 'CNAB Demands Removal of ICTY Judge Christoph Flügge (10 July 2009)' available at <http://www.bosniak.org/cnab-demands-removal-of-icty-judge-christoph-flugge/> (last visited: 21 March 2014).

'Contractors – International Seabed Authority' available at <http://www.isa.org.jm/en/scientific/exploration/contractors> (last visited: 21 March 2014).

'Convention for the Protection of Human Rights and Fundamental Freedoms – State of Ratification' available at <http://conventions.coe.int/Treaty/Commun/ChercheSig.asp?NT=005&CM=1&DF=11/07/2010&CL=ENG> (last visited: 21 March 2014).

'Council of Europe – Human Rights (Convention and Protocols only)' available at <http://conventions.coe.int/Treaty/Commun/ListeTraites.asp?MA=3&CM=7&CL=ENG> (last visited: 21 March 2014).

'Court of Conciliation and Arbitration' available at <http://www.osce.org/cca/43295> (last visited: 21 March 2014).

'Documents of the Meeting of States Parties to the United Nations Convention on the Law of the Sea (SPLOS)' available at <http://www.un.org/depts/los/meeting_states_parties/SPLOS_documents.htm> (last visited: 21 March 2014).

'European Court of Human Rights – Pending Applications Allocated to a Judicial Formation – 30/09/2010' available at <http://www.echr.coe.int/NR/rdonlyres/99F89D38-902E-4725-9D3D-4A8BB74A7401/0/Pending_applications_chart.pdf> (last visited: 21 March 2014).

'European Court of Human Rights – Statistics 1/1-30/9/2010' available at <http://www.echr.coe.int/NR/rdonlyres/8699082A-A7B9-47E2-893F-5685A72B78FB/0/Statistics_2010.pdf> (last visited: 21 March 2014).

'European Court of Human Rights – The Court – Role of the Registry' available at <http://www.echr.coe.int/Pages/home.aspx?p=court/howitworks> (last visited: 21 March 2014).

'European Court of Human Rights – The European Court of Human Rights in Facts and Figures 2011' available at <http://www.echr.coe.int/Documents/Facts_Figures_2011_ENG.pdf> (last visited: 21 March 2014).

Human Rights Watch, 'ICC: Recommendations for Nominating and Electing Candidates to Serve as Judges – Letter to Foreign Ministers of ICC States Parties (18 May 2011)' available at <http://www.hrw.org/news/2011/05/18/icc-recommendations-nominating-and-electing-candidates-serve-judges> (last visited: 21 March 2014).

'ICC – Structure of the Court' available at <http://www.icc-cpi.int/en_menus/icc/structure%20of%20the%20court/Pages/structure%20of%20the%20court.aspx> (last visited: 21 March 2014).

'ICC – The States Parties to the Rome Statute' available at <http://www.icc-cpi.int/en_menus/asp/states%20parties/Pages/the%20states%20parties%20to%20the%20rome%20statute.aspx> (last visited: 21 March 2014).

'ICTR Budget and Staff' available at <http://www.unictr.org/AboutICTR/GeneralInformation/tabid/101/Default.aspx> (last visited: 21 March 2014).

'ICTY – The Cost of Justice' available at <http://www.icty.org/sid/325> (last visited: 21 March 2014).

'Independent Panel on International Criminal Court Judicial Elections – Terms of Reference, adopted 12 May 2011' <http://www.iccindependentpanel.org/content/terms-reference-independent-panel> (last visited: 21 March 2014).

'International Covenant on Civil and Political Rights – Statuts as at 21 March 2014' available at <http://treaties.un.org/Pages/ViewDetails.aspx?src=TREATY&mtdsg_no=IV-4&chapter=4&lang=en> (last visited: 21 March 2014).

'International Seabed Authority' available at <http://www.isa.org.jm/en/home> (last visited: 21 March 2014).

'International Tribunal for the Law of the Sea – Cases' available at <http://www.itlos.org/index.php?id=10> (last visited: 21 March 2014).

'International Tribunal for the Law of the Sea – Experts under article 289 of the Convention' available at <http://www.itlos.org/index.php?id=20> (last visited: 21 March 2014).

'International Tribunal for the Law of the Sea – Members' available at <http://www.itlos.org/index.php?id=96> (last visited: 21 March 2014).

'ITLOS General Information – Sessions' available at <http://www.itlos.org/index.php?id=22> (last visited: 21 March 2014).

'Judicial Independence: Colombia should leave the International Criminal Court' available at <http://colombiareports.com/opinion/131-gustavo-silva-cano/6673-judicial-independence-colombia-should-leave-the-international-criminal-court.html> (last visited: 21 March 2014).

'Law on Nomination of Judges from the Republic of Slovenia to International Tribunals/Courts (17 July 2001)' available at <http://www.iccnow.org/documents/SlovenialLaw.pdf> (last visited: 21 March 2014).

'Meeting of States Parties to the Convention' available at <http://www.un.org/Depts/los/meeting_states_parties/meeting_states_parties.htm> (last visited: 21 March 2014).

'Oxford English Dictionary' available at <http://www.oed.com/> (last visited: 21 March 2014).

'Permanent Court of Arbitration – Members of the Permanent Court of Arbitration' available at <http://www.pca-cpa.org/showpage.asp?pag_id=1041> (last visited: 21 March 2014).

'Permanent Court of Arbitration – Past Cases' available at <http://www.pca-cpa.org/showpage.asp?pag_id=1146> (last visited: 21 March 2014).

'Permanent Court of Arbitration – Rules of Procedure' available at <http://www.pca-cpa.org/showpage.asp?pag_id=1188> (last visited: 21 March 2014).

'Permanent Court of Arbitration – Structure' available at <http://www.pca-cpa.org/showpage.asp?pag_id=1039> (last visited: 21 March 2014).

'Permanent Court of Arbitration' available at <http://www.pca-cpa.org/> (last visited: 21 March 2014).

'Second Election of Judges of the International Criminal Court – Resumed Fourth Session of the Assembly of States Parties, held from 26 to 27 January 2006 at United Nations Headquarters' available at <http://www.icc-cpi.int/NR/rdonlyres/9F5E7613-DF43-4DE6-BD97-D32BFB4E645E/277233/E_totalelectionresults_26jan1630.pdf> (last visited: 21 March 2014).

'States Parties to the Convention on Law of the Sea Elect Seven Members of International Tribunal as They Begin Eighteenth Meeting' <http://www.un.org/News/Press/docs/2008/sea1901.doc.htm> (last visited: 21 March 2014).

'Statute of the Council of Europe – State of Ratification' available at <http://conventions.coe.int/Treaty/Commun/ChercheSig.asp?NT=001&CM=8&DF=11/07/2010&CL=ENG> (last visited: 21 March 2014).

'The Avalon Project: Nuremberg Trial Proceedings Vol. 2 – Second Day, Wednesday, 21 November 1945, Morning Session' available at <http://avalon.law.yale.edu/imt/11-21-45.asp> (last visited: 21 March 2014).

'The Court – All Judges *ad hoc*' available at <http://www.icj-cij.org/court/index.php?p1=1&p2=5&p3=2> (last visited: 21 March 2014).

'The Division for Ocean Affairs and the Law of the Sea' available at <http://www.un.org/Depts/los/doalos_activities/about_doalos.htm> (last visited: 21 March 2014).

'The Public Relations Office of HRH Crown Prince Alexander II: Crown Prince Alexander's Statement Regarding Decision by International Court of Justice on Kosovo' <http://www.royalfamily.org/statements/state-det/state-2274.html> (last visited: 21 March 2014).

'United Nations Convention on the Law of the Sea – Status' available at <http://treaties.un.org/Pages/ViewDetailsIII.aspx?&src=TREATY&mtdsg_no=XXI~6&chapter=21&Temp=mtdsg3&lang=en#1> (last visited: 21 March 2014).

'United Nations Member States – Growth in United Nations Membership, 1945-Present' available at <http://www.un.org/en/members/growth.shtml> (last visited: 21 March 2014).

'United Nations Regional Groups of Member States' available at <http://www.un.org/depts/DGACM/RegionalGroups.shtml> (last visited: 21 March 2014).

'United Nations Treaty Collection' available at <http://treaties.un.org/> (last visited: 21 March 2014).